Blackstone's Statutes on
MEDICAL LAW

Blackstone's Statutes on

MEDICAL LAW

Edited by

M. A. Jones

Senior Lecturer in Law and Dean of the Faculty of Law
at the University of Liverpool

and

Anne E. Morris

Lecturer in Law at the University of Liverpool

BLACKSTONE
PRESS LIMITED

First published in Great Britain 1992 by Blackstone Press Limited,
9-15 Aldine Street, London W12 8AW. Telephone 081-740 1173

© Michael A. Jones and Anne E. Morris, 1992

ISBN: 1 85431 142 5

British Library Cataloguing in Publication Data
A CIP catalogue record for this book is available from the British Library

Typeset by Style Photosetting Ltd, Mayfield, East Sussex
Printed by Redwood Press Ltd, Melksham

CONTENTS

EDITORS' PREFACE

The emergence of Medical Law as a distinct subject at both undergraduate and postgraduate level has created a need for a collection of statutes specifically designed for students taking such courses. This collection includes both statutory and non-statutory materials with the objective of making the sources more accessible to students, and in a form acceptable for use in examinations.

In selecting the materials we were conscious of the fact that courses in Medical Law, or Health Services Law, or Law and Medicine, tend to be diverse in their content, and we have attempted to cover a broad spectrum of interests. Inevitably, the choice of material for inclusion in this collection has been influenced by considerations of space. We have concentrated on the medical profession, and have not generally included provisions on allied professions such as Dentists, Opticians, Pharmacists, or Nurses, though there are occasional references to these groups. We have also had to exclude some legislation of more general application, such as the Medicines Act 1968, on the grounds of space, though we have included part of the Medicinal Products: Prescription by Nurses etc. Act 1992, which amends the Medicines Act, for information. In other instances we have resorted to editing down lengthy statutes or statutory instruments, without, we trust, removing the substantive core.

We wish to thank the General Medical Council for permission to reprint the Council's 'Blue Book', *Professional Conduct and Discipline: Fitness to Practise*, and Butterworth & Co (Publishers) Ltd for the assistance of Lexis in preparing the amended text of the National Health Service Act 1977, the National Health Service (General Medical and Pharmaceutical Services) Regulations 1974 and the National Health Service (Service Committees and Tribunal) Regulations 1974.

The legislation, which states the law of England and Wales, is arranged in chronological order, and is printed (as amended) as at the end of March 1992.

Michael A. Jones
Anne E. Morris
April 1992

OFFENCES AGAINST THE PERSON ACT 1861
(1861, c. 100)

18.   Shooting or attempting to shoot, or wounding with intent to do grievous bodily harm
Whosoever shall unlawfully and maliciously by any means whatsoever wound or cause any grevious bodily harm to any person, with intent to do some grievous bodily harm to any person, or with intent to resist or prevent the lawful apprehension or detainer of any person, shall be guilty of felony, and being convicted thereof shall be liable to be kept in penal servitude for life.

20.   Inflicting bodily injury, with or without weapon
Whosoever shall unlawfully and maliciously wound or inflict any grievous bodily harm upon any other person, either with or without any weapon or instrument, shall be guilty of a misdemeanor, and being convicted thereof shall be liable to be kept in penal servitude.

23.   Maliciously administering poison, &c. so as to endanger life or inflict grievous bodily harm
Whosoever shall unlawfully and maliciously administer to or cause to be administered to or taken by any other person any poison or other destructive or noxious thing, so as thereby to endanger the life of such person, or so as thereby to inflict upon such person any grievous bodily harm, shall be guilty of felony, and being convicted thereof shall be liable to be kept in penal servitude for any term not exceeding ten years.

24.   Maliciously administering poison, &c. with intent to injure, aggrieve, or annoy any other person
Whosoever shall unlawfully and maliciously administer to or cause to be administered to or taken by any other person any poison or other destructive or noxious thing, with intent to injure, aggrieve, or annoy such person, shall be guilty of a misdemeanor, and being convicted thereof shall be liable to be kept in penal servitude.

47.   Assault occasioning bodily harm. Common assault
Whosoever shall be convicted upon an indictment of any assault occasioning actual bodily harm shall be liable to be kept in penal servitude; and whosoever shall be convicted upon an indictment for a common assault shall be liable, at the discretion of the court, to be imprisoned for any term not exceeding one year.

Attempts to procure Abortion

58.   Administering drugs or using instruments to procure abortion
Every woman, being with child, who, with intent to procure her own miscarriage, shall unlawfully administer to herself any poison or other noxious thing, or shall unlawfully use any instrument or other means whatsoever with the like intent, and whosoever, with intent to procure the miscarriage of any woman, whether she be or be not with child, shall unlawfully administer to her or cause to be taken by her any poison or other noxious thing, or shall unlawfully use any instrument or other means whatsoever with

the like intent, shall be guilty of felony, and being convicted thereof shall be liable to be kept in penal servitude for life.

59. Procuring drugs, &c. to cause abortion

Whosoever shall unlawfully supply or procure any poison or other noxious thing, or any instrument or thing whatsoever, knowing that the same is intended to be unlawfully used or employed with intent to procure the miscarriage of any woman, whether she be or be not with child, shall be guilty of a misdemeanor, and being convicted thereof shall be liable to be kept in penal servitude.

PERJURY ACT 1911
(1911, c. 6)

4. False statements, &c. as to births or deaths

(1) If any person—

(a) wilfully makes any false answer to any question put to him by any registrar of births or deaths relating to the particulars required to be registered concerning any birth or death, or, wilfully gives to any such registrar any false information concerning any birth or death or the cause of any death; or

(b) wilfully makes any false certificate or declaration under or for the purposes of any Act relating to the registration of births or deaths, or, knowing any such certificate or declaration to be false, uses the same as true or gives or sends the same as true to any person; or

(c) wilfully makes, gives or uses any false statement or declaration as to a child born alive as having been still-born, or as to the body of a deceased person or a still-born child in any coffin, or falsely pretends that any child born alive was still-born; or

(d) makes any false statement with intent to have the same inserted in any register of births or deaths:

he shall be guilty of a misdemeanour and shall be liable—

(i) on conviction thereof on indictment, to penal servitude for a term not exceeding seven years, or to imprisonment for a term not exceeding two years, or to a fine instead of either of the said punishments; and

(ii) on summary conviction thereof, to a penalty not exceeding the prescribed sum.

(2) A prosecution on indictment for an offence against this section shall not be commenced more than three years after the commission of the offence.

VENEREAL DISEASE ACT 1917
(1917, c. 21)

1. Prevention of the treatment of venereal disease otherwise than by duly qualified persons

(1) In any area in which this section is in operation a person shall not, unless he is a duly qualified medical practitioner, for reward either direct or indirect, treat any person for venereal disease or prescribe any remedy therefor, or give any advice in connection with the treatment thereof, whether the advice is given to the person to be treated or to any other person.

3. Penalties

If any person acts in contravention of any of the provisions of this Act, he shall be liable on conviction on indictment to imprisonment, with or without hard labour, for a term not exceeding two years, or on summary conviction to a fine not exceeding the prescribed sum, or to imprisonment, with or without hard labour, for a term not exceeding six months.

4. Definition

In this Act the expression "venereal disease" means syphilis, gonorrhœa, or soft chancre.

INFANT LIFE (PRESERVATION) ACT 1929
(1929, c. 34)

1. Punishment for child destruction

(1)   Subject as hereinafter in this subsection provided, any person who, with intent to destroy the life of a child capable of being born alive, by any wilful act causes a child to die before it has an existence independent of its mother, shall be guilty of felony, to wit, of child destruction, and shall be liable on conviction thereof on indictment to penal servitude for life:

> Provided that no person shall be found guilty of an offence under this section unless it is proved that the act which caused the death of the child was not done in good faith for the purpose only of preserving the life of the mother.

(2)   For the purposes of this Act, evidence that a woman had at any material time been pregnant for a period of twenty-eight weeks or more shall be primâ facie proof that she was at that time pregnant of a child capable of being born alive.

2. Prosecution of offences

(2)   Where upon the trial of any person for the murder or manslaughter of any child, or for infanticide, or for an offence under section fifty-eight of the Offences against the Person Act 1861 (which relates to administering drugs or using instruments to procure abortion), the jury are of opinion that the person charged is not guilty of murder, manslaughter or infanticide, or of an offence under the said section fifty-eight, as the case may be, but that he is shown by the evidence to be guilty of the felony of child destruction, the jury may find him guilty of that felony, and thereupon the person convicted shall be liable to be punished as if he had been convicted upon an indictment for child destruction.

(3)   Where upon the trial of any person for the felony of child destruction the jury are of opinion that the person charged is not guilty of that felony, but that he is shown by the evidence to be guilty of an offence under the said section fifty-eight of the Offences against the Person Act 1861, the jury may find him guilty of that offence, and thereupon the person convicted shall be liable to be punished as if he had been convicted upon an indictment under that section.

CHILDREN AND YOUNG PERSONS ACT 1933
(1933, c. 12)

1. Cruelty to persons under sixteen

(1)   If any person who has attained the age of sixteen years and has responsibility for any child or young person under that age, wilfully assaults, ill-treats, neglects, abandons, or exposes him, or causes or procures him to be assaulted, ill-treated, neglected, abandoned, or exposed, in a manner likely to cause him unnecessary suffering or injury to health (including injury to or loss of sight, or hearing, or limb, or organ of the body, and any mental derangement), that person shall be guilty of a misdemeanor, and shall be liable—

(a)   on conviction on indictment, to a fine or alternatively, or in addition thereto, to imprisonment for any term not exceeding ten years;

(b)   on summary conviction, to a fine not exceeding the prescribed sum, or alternatively, or in addition thereto, to imprisonment for any term not exceeding six months.

(2)   For the purposes of this section—

(a)   a parent or other person legally liable to maintain a child or young person, or the legal guardian of a child or young person, shall be deemed to have negelected him in a manner likely to cause injury to his health if he has failed to provide adequate food, clothing, medical aid or lodging for him, or if, having been unable otherwise to provide such food, clothing, medical aid or lodging, he has failed to take steps to procure it to be provided under the enactments applicable in that behalf;

(3)   A person may be convicted of an offence under this section—

(a)   notwithstanding that actual suffering or injury to health, or the likelihood of actual suffering or injury to health, was obviated by the action of another person;

(b)   notwithstanding the death of the child or young person in question.

NATIONAL ASSISTANCE ACT 1948
(1948, c. 29)

47.   Removal to suitable premises of persons in need of care and attention

(1)   The following provisions of this section shall have effect for the purposes of securing the necessary care and attention for persons who—

(a)   are suffering from grave chronic disease or, being aged, infirm or physically incapacitated, are living in insanitary conditions, and

(b)   are unable to devote to themselves, and are not receiving from other persons, proper care and attention.

(2)   If the medical officer of health certifies in writing to the appropriate authority that he is satisfied after thorough inquiry and consideration that in the interests of any such person as aforesaid residing in the area of the authority, or for preventing injury to the health of, or serious nuisance to, other persons, it is necessary to remove any such person as aforesaid from the premises in which he is residing, the appropriate authority may apply to a court of summary jurisdiction having jurisdiction in the place where the premises are situated for an order under the next following subsection.

(3)   On any such application the court may, if satisfied on oral evidence of the allegations in the certificate, and that it is expedient so to do, order the removal of the person to whom the application relates, by such officer of the appropriate authority as may be specified in the order, to a suitable hospital or other place in, or within convenient distance of, the area of the appropriate authority, and his detention and maintenance therein:

Provided that the court shall not order the removal of a person to any premises, unless either the person managing the premises has been heard in the proceedings or seven clear days' notice has been given to him of the intended application and of the time and place at which it is proposed to be made.

(4)   An order under the last foregoing subsection may be made so as to authorise a person's detention for any period not exceeding three months, and the court may from time to time by order extend that period for such further period, not exceeding three months, as the court may determine.

(5)   An order under subsection (3) of this section may be varied by an order of the court so as to substitute for the place referred to in that subsection such other suitable place in, or within convenient distance of, the area of the appropriate authority as the court may determine, so however that the proviso to the said subsection (3) shall with the necessary modification apply to any proceedings under this subsection.

(6)   At any time after the expiration of six clear weeks from the making of an order under subsection (3) or (4) of this section an application may be made to the court by or on behalf of the person in respect of whom the order was made, and on any such application the court may, if in the circumstances it appears expedient so to do, revoke the order.

(7) No application under this section shall be entertained by the court unless, seven clear days before the making of the application, notice has been given of the intended application and of the time and place at which it is proposed to be made—

(a) where the application is for an order under subsection (3) or (4) of this section, to the person in respect of whom the application is made or to some person in charge of him;

(b) where the application is for the revocation of such an order, to the medical officer of health.

(8) Where in pursuance of an order under this section a person is maintained neither in hospital accommodation provided by the Minister of Health under the National Health Service Act 1977 or by the Secretary of State under the National Health Service (Scotland) Act 1978, nor in premises where accommodation is provided by, or by arrangement with, a local authority under Part III of this Act, the cost of his maintenance shall be borne by the appropriate authority.

(11) Any person who wilfully disobeys, or obstructs the execution of, an order under this section shall be guilty of an offence and liable on summary conviction to a fine not exceeding level 1 on the standard scale.

SEXUAL OFFENCES ACT 1956
(1956, c. 69)

Intercourse with girls under sixteen

5. Intercourse with girl under thirteen
It is a felony for a man to have unlawful sexual intercourse with a girl under the age of thirteen.

6. Intercourse with girl between thirteen and sixteen
(1) It is an offence, subject to the exceptions mentioned in this section, for a man to have unlawful sexual intercourse with a girl under the age of sixteen.

(3) A man is not guilty of an offence under this section because he has unlawful sexual intercourse with a girl under the age of sixteen, if he is under the age of twenty-four and has not previously been charged with a like offence, and he believes her to be of the age of sixteen or over and has reasonable cause for the belief.

In this subsection, "a like offence" means an offence under this section or an attempt to commit one, or an offence under paragraph (1) of section five of the Criminal Law Amendment Act 1885 (the provision replaced for England and Wales by this section).

Intercourse with defectives

7. Intercourse with defective
(1) It is an offence, subject to the exception mentioned in this section for a man to have unlawful sexual intercourse with a woman who is a defective.

(2) A man is not guilty of an offence under this section because he has unlawful sexual intercourse with a woman if he does not know and has no reason to suspect her to be a defective.

Assaults

14. Indecent assault on a woman
(1) It is an offence, subject to the exception mentioned in subsection (3) of this section, for a person to make an indecent assault on a woman.

(2) A girl under the age of sixteen cannot in law give any consent which would prevent an act being an assault for the purposes of this section.

(4) A woman who is a defective cannot in law give any consent which would prevent an act being an assault for the purposes of this section, but a person is only to be treated

as guilty of an indecent assault on a defective by reason of that incapacity to consent, if that person knew or had reason to suspect her to be a defective.

15. Indecent assault on a man
(1) It is an offence for a person to make an indecent assault on a man.

(2) A boy under the age of sixteen cannot in law give any consent which would prevent an act being an assault for the purposes of this section.

(3) A man who is a defective cannot in law give any consent which would prevent an act being an assault for the purposes of this section, but a person is only to be treated as guilty of an indecent assault on a defective by reason of that incapacity to consent, if that person knew or had reason to suspect him to be a defective.

MENTAL HEALTH ACT 1959
(1959, c. 72)

128. Sexual intercourse with patients
(1) Without prejudice to section seven of the Sexual Offences Act 1956, it shall be an offence, subject to the exception mentioned in this section,—

(a) for a man who is an officer on the staff of or is otherwise employed in, or is one of the managers of, a hospital or mental nursing home to have unlawful sexual intercourse with a woman who is for the time being receiving treatment for mental disorder in that hospital or home, or to have such intercourse on the premises of which the hospital or home forms part with a woman who is for the time being receiving such treatment there as an out-patient;

(b) for a man to have unlawful sexual intercourse with a woman who is a mentally disordered patient and who is subject to his guardianship under the Mental Health Act 1983 or is otherwise in his custody or care under the Mental Health Act 1983 or in pursuance of arrangements under Part III of the National Assistance Act 1948, or the National Health Service Act 1977 or as a resident in a residential care home within the meaning of Part I of the Registered Homes Act 1984.

(2) It shall not be an offence under this section for a man to have sexual intercourse with a woman if he does not know and has no reason to suspect her to be a mentally disordered patient.

(3) Any person guilty of an offence under this section shall be liable on conviction on indictment to imprisonment for a term not exceeding two years.

(4) No proceedings shall be instituted for an offence under this section except by or with the consent of the Director of Public Prosecutions.

(5) This section shall be construed as one with the Sexual Offences Act 1956; and section forty-seven of that Act (which relates to the proof of exceptions) shall apply to the exception mentioned in this section.

HUMAN TISSUE ACT 1961
(1961, c. 54)

1. Removal of parts of bodies for medical purposes
(1) If any person, either in writing at any time or orally in the presence of two or more witnesses during his last illness, has expressed a request that his body or any specified part of his body be used after his death for therapeutic purposes or for purposes of medical education or research, the person lawfully in possession of his body after his death may, unless he has reason to believe that the request was subsequently withdrawn, authorise the removal from the body of any part or, as the case may be, the specified part, for use in accordance with the request.

(2) Without prejudice to the foregoing subsection, the person lawfully in possession of the body of a deceased person may authorise the removal of any part from the body for use for the said purposes if, having made such reasonable enquiry as may be practicable, he has no reason to believe—

(a) that the deceased had expressed an objection to his body being so dealt with after his death, and had not withdrawn it; or

(b) that the surviving spouse or any surviving relative of the deceased objects to the body being so dealt with.

(3) Subject to subsections (4), (4A) and (5) of this section, the removal and use of any part of a body in accordance with an authority given in pursuance of this section shall be lawful.

(4) No such removal, except of eyes or parts of eyes, shall be effected except by a registered medical practitioner, who must have satisfied himself by personal examination of the body that life is extinct.

(4A) No such removal of an eye or part of an eye shall be effected except by—

(a) a registered medical practitioner, who must have satisfied himself by personal examination of the body that life is extinct; or

(b) a person in the employment of a health authority or NHS trust acting on the instructions of a registered medical practitioner who must, before giving those instructions, be satisfied that the person in question is sufficiently qualified and trained to perform the removal competently and must also either—

(i) have satisfied himself by personal examination of the body that life is extinct, or

(ii) be satisfied that life is extinct on the basis of a statement to that effect by a registered medical practitioner who has satisfied himself by personal examination of the body that life is extinct.

(5) Where a person has reason to believe that an inquest may be required to be held on any body or that a post-mortem examination of any body may be required by the coroner, he shall not, except with the consent of the coroner,—

(a) give an authority under this section in respect of the body; or

(b) act on such an authority given by any other person.

(6) No authority shall be given under this section in respect of any body by a person entrusted with the body for the purpose only of its interment or cremation.

(7) In the case of a body lying in a hospital, nursing home or other institution, any authority under this section may be given on behalf of the person having the control and management thereof by any officer or person designated for that purpose by the first-mentioned person.

(8) Nothing in this section shall be construed as rendering unlawful any dealing with, or with any part of, the body of a deceased person which is lawful apart from this Act.

2.   (2) No post-mortem examination shall be carried out otherwise than by or in accordance with the instructions of a fully registered medical practitioner, and no post-mortem examination which is not directed or requested by the coroner or any other competent legal authority shall be carried out without the authority of the person lawfully in possession of the body; and subsections (2), (5), (6) and (7) of section one of this Act shall, with the necessary modifications, apply with respect to the giving of that authority.

SUICIDE ACT 1961
(1961, c. 60)

1. Suicide to cease to be a crime
The rule of law whereby it is a crime for a person to commit suicide is hereby abrogated.

2. Criminal liability for complicity in another's suicide

(1) A person who aids, abets, counsels or procures the suicide of another, or an attempt by another to commit suicide, shall be liable on conviction on indictment to imprisonment for a term not exceeding fourteen years.

(2) If on the trial of an indictment for murder or manslaughter it is proved that the accused aided, abetted, counselled or procured the suicide of the person in question, the jury may find him guilty of that offence.

(4) No proceedings shall be instituted for an offence under this section except by or with the consent of the Director of Public Prosecutions.

ABORTION ACT 1967
(1967, c. 87)

1. Medical termination of pregnancy

(1) Subject to the provisions of this section, a person shall not be guilty of an offence under the law relating to abortion when a pregnancy is terminated by a registered medical practitioner if two registered medical practitioners are of the opinion, formed in good faith—

(a) that the pregnancy has not exceeded its twenty-fourth week and that the continuance of the pregnancy would involve risk, greater than if the pregnancy were terminated, of injury to the physical or mental health of the pregnant woman or any existing children of her family; or

(b) that the termination is necessary to prevent grave permanent injury to the physical or mental health of the pregnant woman; or

(c) that the continuance of the pregnancy would involve risk to the life of the pregnant woman, greater than if the pregnancy were terminated; or

(d) that there is a substantial risk that if the child were born it would suffer from such physical or mental abnormalities as to be seriously handicapped.

(2) In determining whether the continuance of a pregnancy would involve such risk of injury to health as is mentioned in paragraph (a) or (b) of subsection (1) of this section, account may be taken of the pregnant woman's actual or reasonably foreseeable environment.

(3) Except as provided by subsection (4) of this section, any treatment for the termination of pregnancy must be carried out in a hospital vested in the Secretary of State for the purposes of his functions under the National Health Service Act 1977 or the National Health Service (Scotland) Act 1978 or in a hospital vested in a National Health Service trust or in a place approved for the purposes of this section by the Secretary of State.

(3A) The power under subsection (3) of this section to approve a place includes power, in relation to treatment consisting primarily in the use of such medicines as may be specified in the approval and carried out in such manner as may be so specified, to approve a class of places.

(4) Subsection (3) of this section, and so much of subsection (1) as relates to the opinion of two registered medical practitioners, shall not apply to the termination of a pregnancy by a registered medical practitioner in a case where he is of the opinion, formed in good faith, that the termination is immediately necessary to save the life or to prevent grave permanent injury to the physical or mental health of the pregnant woman.

2. Notification

(1) The Secretary of State in respect of England and Wales, and the Secretary of State in respect of Scotland, shall by statutory instrument make regulations to provide—

(a)   for requiring any such opinion as is referred to in section 1 of this Act to be certified by the practitioners or practitioner concerned in such form and at such time as may be prescribed by the regulations, and for requiring the preservation and disposal of certificates made for the purposes of the regulations;

(b)   for requiring any registered medical practitioner who terminates a pregnancy to give notice of the termination and such other information relating to the termination as may be so prescribed;

(c)   for prohibiting the disclosure, except to such persons or for such purposes as may be so prescribed, of notices given or information furnished pursuant to the regulations.

(2)   The information furnished in pursuance of regulations made by virtue of paragraph (b) of subsection (1) of this section shall be notified solely to the Chief Medical Officers of the Department of Health, or of the Welsh Office, or of the Scottish Home and Health Department.

(3)   Any person who wilfully contravenes or wilfully fails to comply with the requirements of regulations under subsection (1) of this section shall be liable on summary conviction to a fine not exceeding level 5 on the standard scale.

(4)   Any statutory instrument made by virtue of this section shall be subject to annulment in pursuance of a resolution of either House of Parliament.

4.   Conscientious objection to participation in treatment

(1)   Subject to subsection (2) of this section, no person shall be under any duty, whether by contract or by any statutory or other legal requirement, to participate in any treatment authorised by this Act to which he has a conscientious objection:

Provided that in any legal proceedings the burden of proof of conscientious objection shall rest on the person claiming to rely on it.

(2)   Nothing in subsection (1) of this section shall affect any duty to participate in treatment which is necessary to save the life or to prevent grave permanent injury to the physical or mental health of a pregnant woman.

(3)   In any proceedings before a court in Scotland, a statement on oath by any person to the effect that he has a conscientious objection to participating in any treatment authorised by this Act shall be sufficient evidence for the purpose of discharging the burden of proof imposed upon him by subsection (1) of this section.

5.   Supplementary Provisions

(1)   No offence under the Infant Life (Preservation) Act 1929 shall be committed by a registered medical practitioner who terminates a pregnancy in accordance with the provisions of this Act.

(2)   For the purposes of the law relating to abortion, anything done with intent to procure a woman's miscarriage (or, in the case of a woman carrying more than one foetus, her miscarriage of any foetus) is unlawfully done unless authorised by section 1 of this Act and, in the case of a woman carrying more than one foetus, anything done with intent to procure her miscarriage of any foetus is authorised by that section if—

(a)   the ground for termination of the pregnancy specified in subsection (1)(d) of that section applies in relation to any foetus and the thing is done for the purpose of procuring the miscarriage of that foetus, or

(b)   any of the other grounds for termination of the pregnancy specified in that section applies.

6.   Interpretation

In this Act, the following expressions have meanings hereby assigned to them:—

"the law relating to abortion" means sections 58 and 59 of the Offences against the Person Act 1861, and any rule of law relating to the procurement of abortion.

FAMILY LAW REFORM ACT 1969
(1969, c. 46)

1. Reduction of age of majority from 21 to 18

(1) As from the date on which this section comes into force a person shall attain full age on attaining the age of eighteen instead of on attaining the age of twenty-one; and a person shall attain full age on that date if he has then already attained the age of eighteen but not the age of twenty-one.

(2) The foregoing subsection applies for the purposes of any rule of law, and, in the absence of a definition or of any indication of a contrary intention, for the construction of "full age", "infant", "infancy", "minor", "minority" and similar expressions in—

(a) any statutory provision, whether passed or made before, on or after the date on which this section comes into force; and

(b) any deed, will or other instrument of whatever nature (not being a statutory provision) made on or after that date.

8. Consent by persons over 16 to surgical, medical and dental treatment

(1) The consent of a minor who has attained the age of sixteen years to any surgical, medical or dental treatment which, in the absence of consent, would constitute a trespass to his person, shall be as effective as it would be if he were of full age; and where a minor has by virtue of this section given an effective consent to any treatment it shall not be necessary to obtain any consent for it from his parent or guardian.

(2) In this section "surgical, medical or dental treatment" includes any procedure undertaken for the purposes of diagnosis, and this section applies to any procedure (including, in particular, the administration of an anaesthetic) which is ancillary to any treatment as it applies to that treatment.

(3) Nothing in this section shall be construed as making ineffective any consent which would have been effective if this section had not been enacted.

MISUSE OF DRUGS ACT 1971
(1971, c. 38)

17. Power to obtain information from doctors, pharmacists etc. in certain circumstances

(1) If it appears to the Secretary of State that there exists in any area in Great Britain a social problem caused by the extensive misuse of dangerous or otherwise harmful drugs in that area, he may by notice in writing served on any doctor or pharmacist practising in or in the vicinity of that area, or on any person carrying on a retail pharmacy business within the meaning of the Medicines Act 1968 at any premises situated in or in the vicinity of that area, require him to furnish to the Secretary of State, with respect to any such drugs specified in the notice and as regards any period so specified, such particulars as may be so specified relating to the quantities in which and the number and frequency of the occasions on which those drugs—

(a) in the case of a doctor, were prescribed, administered or supplied by him;

(b) in the case of a pharmacist, were supplied by him; or

(c) in the case of a person carrying on a retail pharmacy business, were supplied in the course of that business at any premises so situated which may be specified in the notice.

(2) A notice under this section may require any such particulars to be furnished in such manner and within such time as may be specified in the notice and, if served on a pharmacist or person carrying on a retail pharmacy business, may require him to

furnish the names and addresses of doctors on whose prescriptions any dangerous or otherwise harmful drugs to which the notice relates were supplied, but shall not require any person to furnish any particulars relating to the identity of any person for or to whom any such drug has been prescribed, administered or supplied.

(3) A person commits an offence if without reasonable excuse (proof of which shall lie on him) he fails to comply with any requirement to which he is subject by virtue of subsection (1) above.

(4) A person commits an offence if in purported compliance with a requirement imposed under this section he gives any information which he knows to be false in a material particular or recklessly gives any information which is so false.

Law enforcement and punishment of offences

23. Powers to search and obtain evidence

(1) A constable or other person authorised in that behalf by a general or special order of the Secretary of State (or in Northern Ireland either of the Secretary of State or the Ministry of Home Affairs for Northern Ireland) shall, for the purposes of the execution of this Act, have power to enter the premises of a person carrying on business as a producer or supplier of any controlled drugs and to demand the production of, and to inspect, any books or documents relating to dealings in any such drugs and to inspect any stocks of any such drugs.

(4) A person commits an offence if he—

(a) intentionally obstructs a person in the exercise of his powers under this section; or

(b) conceals from a person acting in the exercise of his powers under subsection (1) above any such books, documents, stocks or drugs as are mentioned in that subsection; or

(c) without reasonable excuse (proof of which shall lie on him) fails to produce any such books or documents as are so mentioned where their production is demanded by a person in the exercise of his powers under that subsection.

CONGENITAL DISABILITIES (CIVIL LIABILITY) ACT 1976
(1976, c. 28)

1. Civil liability to child born disabled

(1) If a child is born disabled as the result of such an occurrence before its birth as is mentioned in subsection (2) below, and a person (other than the child's own mother) is under this section answerable to the child in respect of the occurrence, the child's disabilities are to be regarded as damage resulting from the wrongful act of that person and actionable accordingly at the suit of the child.

(2) An occurrence to which this section applies is one which—

(a) affected either parent of the child in his or her ability to have a normal, healthy child; or

(b) affected the mother during her pregnancy, or affected her or the child in the course of its birth, so that the child is born with disabilities which would not otherwise have been present.

(3) Subject to the following subsections, a person (here referred to as "the defendant") is answerable to the child if he was liable in tort to the parent or would, if sued in due time have been so; and it is no answer that there could not have been such liability because the parent suffered no actionable injury, if there was a breach of legal duty which, accompanied by injury, would have given rise to the liability.

(4) In the case of an occurrence preceding the time of conception, the defendant is not answerable to the child if at that time either or both of the parents knew the risk of

their child being born disabled (that it to say, the particular risk created by the occurrence); but should it be the child's father who is the defendant, this subsection does not apply if he knew of the risk and the mother did not.

(5)   The defendant is not answerable to the child, for anything he did or omitted to do when responsible in a professional capacity for treating or advising the parent, if he took reasonable care having due regard to then received professional opinion applicable to the particular class of case; but this does not mean that he is answerable only because he departed from received opinion.

(6)   Liability to the child under this section may be treated as having been excluded or limited by contract made with the parent affected, to the same extent and subject to the same restrictions as liability in the parent's own case; and a contract term which could have been set up by the defendant in an action by the parent, so as to exclude or limit his liability to him or her, operates in the defendant's favour to the same, but no greater, extent in an action under this section by the child.

(7)   If in the child's action under this section it is shown that the parent affected shared the responsibility for the child being born disabled, the damages are to be reduced to such extent as the court thinks just and equitable having regard to the extent of the parent's responsibility.

1A. Extension of section 1 to cover infertility treatments

(1)   In any case where—

(a)   a child carried by a woman as the result of the placing in her of an embryo or of sperm and eggs or her artificial insemination is born disabled,

(b)   the disability results from an act or omission in the course of the selection, or the keeping or use outside the body, of the embryo carried by her or of the gametes used to bring about the creation of the embryo, and

(c)   a person is under this section answerable to the child in respect of the act or omission,

the child's disabilities are to be regarded as damage resulting from the wrongful act of that person and actionable accordingly at the suit of the child.

(2)   Subject to subsection (3) below and the applied provisions of section 1 of this Act, a person (here referred to as "the defendant") is answerable to the child if he was liable in tort to one or both of the parents (here referred to as "the parent or parents concerned") or would, if sued in due time, have been so; and it is no answer that there could not have been such liability because the parent or parents concerned suffered no actionable injury, if there was a breach of legal duty which, accompanied by injury, would have given rise to the liability.

(3)   The defendant is not under this section answerable to the child if at the time the embryo, or the sperm and eggs, are placed in the woman or the time of her insemination (as the case may be) either or both of the parents knew the risk of their child being born disabled (that is to say, the particular risk created by the act or omission).

(4)   Subsections (5) to (7) of section 1 of this Act apply for the purposes of this section as they apply for the purposes of that but as if references to the parent or the parent affected were references to the parent or parents concerned.

2.   Liability of woman driving when pregnant

A woman driving a motor vehicle when she knows (or ought reasonably to know) herself to be pregnant is to be regarded as being under the same duty to take care for the safety of her unborn child as the law imposes on her with respect to the safety of other people; and if in consequence of her breach of that duty her child is born with disabilities which would not otherwise have been present, those disabilities are to be regarded as damage resulting from her wrongful act and actionable accordingly at the suit of the child.

3.　Disabled birth due to radiation

(1)　Section 1 of this Act does not affect the operation of the Nuclear Installations Act 1965 as to liability for, and compensation in respect of, injury or damage caused by occurrences involving nuclear matter or the emission of ionising radiations.

(2)　For the avoidance of doubt anything which—
　　(a)　affects a man in his ability to have a normal, healthy child; or
　　(b)　affects a woman in that ability, or so affects her when she is pregnant that her child is born with disabilities which would not otherwise have been present,
is an injury for the purposes of that Act.

(3)　If a child is born disabled as the result of an injury to either of its parents caused in breach of a duty imposed by any of sections 7 to 11 of that Act (nuclear site licensees and others to secure that nuclear incidents do not cause injury to persons, etc.), the child's disabilities are to be regarded under the subsequent provisions of that Act (compensation and other matters) as injuries caused on the same occasion, and by the same breach of duty, as was the injury to the parent.

(4)　As respects compensation to the child, section 13(6) of that Act (contributory fault of person injured by radiation) is to be applied as if the reference there to fault were to the fault of the parent.

(5)　Compensation is not payable in the child's case if the injury to the parent preceded the time of the child's conception and at that time either or both of the parents knew the risk of their child being born disabled (that is to say, the particular risk created by the injury).

4.　Interpretation and other supplementary provisions

(1)　References in this Act to a child being born disabled or with disabilities are to its being born with any deformity, disease or abnormality, including predisposition (whether or not susceptible of immediate prognosis) to physical or mental defect in the future.

(2)　In this Act—
　　(a)　"born" means born alive (the moment of a child's birth being when it first has a life separate from its mother), and "birth" has a corresponding meaning; and
　　(b)　"motor vehicle" means a mechanically propelled vehicle intended or adapted for use on roads.
and reference to embyros shall be construed in accordance with section 1 of the Human Fertilisation and Embryology Act 1990.

(3)　Liability to a child under section 1, 1A or 2 of this Act is to be regarded—
　　(a)　as respects all its incidents and any matters arising or to arise out of it; and
　　(b)　subject to any contrary context or intention, for the purpose of construing references in enactments and documents to personal or bodily injuries and cognate matters,
as liability for personal injuries sustained by the child immediately after its birth.

(4)　No damages shall be recoverable under any of those sections in respect of any loss of expectation of life, nor shall any such loss be taken into account in the compensation payable in respect of a child under the Nuclear Installations Act 1965 as extended by section 3, unless (in either case) the child lives for at least 48 hours.

(4A)　In any case where a child carried by a woman as the result of the placing in her of an embryo or of sperm and eggs or her artificial insemination is born disabled, any reference in section 1 of this Act to a parent includes a reference to a person who would be a parent but for sections 27 to 29 of the Human Fertilisation and Embryology Act 1990.

(5)　This Act applies in respect of births after (but not before) its passing, and in respect of any such birth it replaces any law in force before its passing, whereby a person could be liable to a child in respect of disabilities with which it might be born;

but in section 1(3) of this Act the expression "liable in tort" does not include any reference to liability by virtue of this Act, or to liability by virtue of any such law.

(6) References to the Nuclear Installations Act 1965 are to that Act as amended; and for the purposes of section 28 of that Act (power by Order in Council to extend the Act to territories outside the United Kingdom) section 3 of this Act is to be treated as if it were a provision of that Act.

5. Crown application
This Act binds the Crown.

NATIONAL HEALTH SERVICE ACT 1977
(1977, c. 49)

[Note: "Family Practitioner Committee": to be construed as a reference to a "Family Health Services Authority" by virtue of the National Health Service and Community Care Act 1990, s. 2(1), (2)]

PART I

1. Secretary of State's duty as to health service
(1) It is the Secretary of State's duty to continue the promotion in England and Wales of a comprehensive health service designed to secure improvement —
  (a) in the physical and mental health of the people of those countries, and
  (b) in the prevention, diagnosis and treatment of illness,
and for that purpose to provide or secure the effective provision of services in accordance with this Act.

(2) The services so provided shall be free of charge except in so far as the making and recovery of charges is expressly provided for by or under any enactment, whenever passed.

2. Secretary of State's general power as to services
Without prejudice to the Secretary of State's powers apart from this section, he has power —
  (a) to provide such services as he considers appropriate for the purpose of discharging any duty imposed on him by this Act; and
  (b) to do any other thing whatsoever which is calculated to facilitate, or is conducive or incidental to, the discharge of such a duty.
This section is subject to section 3(3) below.

3. Services generally
(1) It is the Secretary of State's duty to provide throughout England and Wales, to such extent as he considers necessary to meet all reasonable requirements —
  (a) hospital accommodation;
  (b) other accommodation for the purpose of any service provided under this Act;
  (c) medical, dental, nursing and ambulance services;
  (d) such other facilities for the care of expectant and nursing mothers and young children as he considers are appropriate as part of the health service;
  (e) such facilities for the prevention of illness, the care of persons suffering from illness and the after-care of persons who have suffered from illness as he considers are appropriate as part of the health service;
  (f) such other services as are required for the diagnosis and treatment of illness.

(2) Where any hospital provided by the Secretary of State in accordance with this Act was a voluntary hospital transferred by virtue of the National Health Service Act 1946, and —

(a)   the character and associations of that hospital before its transfer were such as to link it with a particular religious denomination, then

(b)   regard shall be had in the general administration of the hospital to the preservation of that character and those associations.

(3)   Nothing in section 2 above or in this section affects the provisions of Part II of this Act (which relates to arrangements with practitioners for the provision of medical, dental, ophthalmic and pharmaceutical services).

4. Special hospitals

The duty imposed on the Secretary of State by section 1 above to provide services for the purposes of the health service includes a duty to provide and maintain establishments (in this Act referred to as "special hospitals") for persons subject to detention under the Mental Health Act 1983 who in his opinion require treatment under conditions of special security on account of their dangerous, violent or criminal propensities.

5. Other services

(1)   It is the Secretary of State's duty —

(a)   to provide for the medical inspection at appropriate intervals of pupils in attendance at schools maintained by local education authorities or at grant-maintained schools and for the medical treatment of such pupils;

(b)   to arrange, to such extent as he considers necessary to meet all reasonable requirements in England and Wales, for the giving of advice on contraception, the medical examination of persons seeking advice on contraception, the treatment of such persons and the supply of contraceptive substances and appliances.

(1A)   It is also the Secretary of State's duty to provide, to such extent as he considers necessary to meet all reasonable requirements —

(a)   for the dental inspection of pupils in attendance at schools maintained by local education authorities or at grant-maintained schools;

(b)   for the dental treatment of such pupils; and

(c)   for the education of such pupils in dental health.

(2)   The Secretary of State may —

(a)   provide invalid carriages for persons appearing to him to be suffering from severe physical defect or disability and, at the request of such a person, may provide for him a vehicle other than an invalid carriage (and the additional provisions set out in Schedule 2 to this Act have effect in relation to this paragraph);

(b)   arrange to provide accommodation and treatment outside Great Britain for persons suffering from respiratory tuberculosis;

(c)   provide a microbiological service, which may include the provision of laboratories, for the control of the spread of infectious diseases and carry on such other activities as in his opinion can conveniently be carried on in conjunction with that service;

(d)   conduct, or assist by grants or otherwise (without prejudice to the general powers and duties conferred on him under the Ministry of Health Act 1919) any person to conduct, research into any matters relating to the causation, prevention, diagnosis or treatment of illness, and into any such other matters connected with any service provided under this Act as he considers appropriate.

(2A)   Charges may be made for services or materials supplied by virtue of paragraph (c) of subsection (2) above; and the powers conferred by that paragraph may be exercised both for the purposes of the health service and for other purposes.

(2B)   The Secretary of State's functions may be performed outside England and Wales, in so far as they relate —

(a)   to holidays for patients;

(b)   to the transfer of patients to or from Scotland, Northern Ireland, the Isle of Man or the Channel Islands;

(c)   to the return of patients who have received treatment in England and Wales to countries or territories outside the British Islands;

(d)   to taking a patient outside the tunnel system (which expression has the meaning given in section 1(7) of the Channel Tunnel Act 1987) for the purposes of medical treatment.

6.   Central Health Services Council, and standing advisory committees

(3)   The Secretary of State may by order constitute standing advisory committees for the purpose of advising him on such of the services provided under this Act as may be specified in the order and the provisions of Schedule 4 to this Act shall have effect in relation to such committees.

(4)   Any committee so constituted shall consist of persons appointed by the Secretary of State after consultation with such representative organisations as he recognises for the purpose.

(5)   It shall be the duty of a committee so constituted to advise the Secretary of State —

(a)   upon such matters relating to the services with which the committee are concerned as they think fit, and

(b)   upon any questions referred to them by the Secretary of State relating to those services.

7.   Medical Practices Committee

(1)   Subject to subsection (1A) below the Medical Practices Committee —

(a)   shall consist of a chairman and eight other members appointed by the Secretary of State after consultation with such organisations as he may recognise as representative of the medical profession; and

(b)   the chairman and six of the other members shall be medical practitioners, and five at least of those six shall be actively engaged in medical practice.

8.   Regional Health Authorities

(1)   It is the Secretary of State's duty to establish by order in accordance with Part I of Schedule 1 to the National Health Service and Community Care Act 1990 —

(a)   authorities for such regions in England as he may by order determine; and

(b)   authorities for such districts in Wales or those regions in England as he may by order determine,

and orders determining regions, or districts in pursuance of this subsection shall be separate from orders establishing authorities for the regions, or districts.

(1A)   The authorities established by order under subsection (1) above shall be named as follows —

(a)   an authority established for a region shall be called a Regional Health Authority;

(c)   an authority for a district shall be called either a District Health Authority or by a special name indicating the authority's connection with the district or a place in the district,

(2)   The Secretary of State may by order vary the region of a Regional Health Authority or the district of a District Health Authority whether or not the variation entails the determination of a new or the abolition of an existing region or district.

(3)   It is the Secretary of State's duty to exercise the powers conferred on him by the preceding provisions of this section so as to secure —

(a)   that the regions determined in pursuance of those provisions together comprise the whole of England, that the districts so determined together comprise the whole of Wales and those regions and that no region includes part only of any district; and

(b)   that the provision of health services in each region can conveniently be associated with a university which has a school of medicine or with two or more such universities.

10.   Family Practitioner Committees

(1)   It is the duty of the Secretary of State by order to establish, in accordance with Part II of Schedule 1 to the National Health Service and Community Care Act 1990, authorities to be called Family Practitioner Committees.

(2)   Family Practitioner Committees shall be known by such names, in addition to that title, as the order may specify.

(3)   When the Secretary of State makes an order under subsection (1) above establishing a Family Practitioner Committee, he shall also (either in the same or another instrument) make an order in relation to that Committee specifying a locality for which the Committee is to act.

(4)   The Secretary of State may by order —
   (a)   vary a Committee's locality;
   (b)   abolish a Committee;
   (c)   establish a new one.

(5)   The Secretary of State shall so exercise his powers under subsections (3) and (4) above as to secure —
   (a)   that the localities for which Family Practitioner Committees are at any time acting together comprise the whole of England and Wales; but
   (b)   that none of them extends both into England and into Wales.

11.   Special health authorities

(1)   If the Secretary of State considers that a special body should be established for the purpose of performing any functions which he may direct the body to perform on his behalf, or on behalf of a District Health Authority or a Family Practitioner Committee, he may by order establish a body for that purpose.

(2)   The Secretary of State may, subject to the provisions of Part III of Schedule 5 to this Act, make such further provision relating to that body as he thinks fit.

(3)   A body established in pursuance of this section shall (without prejudice to the power conferred by subsection (4) below to allocate a particular name to the body) be called a special health authority.

(4)   Without prejudice to the generality of the power conferred by this section to make an order, that order may in particular contain provisions as to —
   (a)   the membership of the body established by the order;
   (b)   the transfer to the body of officers, property, rights and liabilities; and
   (c)   the name by which the body is to be known.

(5)   It is the Secretary of State's duty before he makes such an order to consult with respect to the order such bodies as he may recognise as representing officers who in his opinion are likely to be transferred or affected by transfers in pursuance of the order.

12.   Supplementary provisions for ss 8 to 11

The provisions of Part III of Schedule 5 to this Act have effect, so far as applicable, in relation to —
   (a)   Regional Health Authorities and District Health Authorities established under section 8 above;
   (b)   Family Practitioner Committees established under section 10 above;
   (c)   any special health authority established under section 11 above.

13.   Secretary of State's directions

(1)   The Secretary of State may direct a Regional Health Authority, a District Health Authority of which the district is in Wales or a special health authority to exercise on his behalf such of his functions relating to the health service as are specified

in the directions, and (subject to section 14 below) it shall be the duty of the body in question to comply with the directions.

(2)   The Secretary of State's functions under subsection (1) above —

(a)   include any of his functions under enactments relating to mental health and nursing homes, but

(b)   exclude the duty imposed on him by section 1(1) above to secure the effective provision of the services mentioned in section 15 below.

14.   Regional Health Authority's directions

(1)   A Regional Health Authority may direct any District Health Authority of which the district is included in its region to exercise such of the functions exercisable by the Regional Health Authority by virtue of section 13 above as are specified in the directions, and it is the District Health Authority's duty to comply with the directions.

(2)   If the Secretary of State directs a Regional Health Authority to secure that any of its functions specified in his directions are or are not exercisable by a District Health Authority it is the Regional Health Authority's duty to comply with his directions.

15.   Duty of Family Practitioner Committee

(1)   It is the duty of each Family Practitioner Committee, in accordance with regulations and subject to any directions from the relevant Regional Health Authority —

(a)   to administer the arrangements made in pursuance of this Act for the provision of general medical services, general dental services, general ophthalmic services and pharmaceutical services for their locality;

(b)   to perform such management and other functions relating to those services as may be prescribed.

(1A)   In relation to a Family Health Services Authority for a locality in England, any reference in this Act or the National Health Service and Community Care Act 1990 to the relevant Regional Health Authority is a reference to that Authority in whose region lies the whole or the greater part of the Authority's locality.

(1B)   In relation to a medical practitioner, any reference in this Act or the National Health Service and Community Care Act 1990 to the relevant Family Health Services Authority shall be construed as follows —

(a)   if he practices in partnership with other medical practitioners, the relevant Authority is that Authority on whose medical list the members of the practice are included and, if some are included on one Authority's medical list and some on another's or if any of the members is included in the medical lists of two or more Authorities, the relevant Authority is that Authority in whose locality resides the largest number of individuals who are on the lists of patients of the members of the practice; and

(b)   in any other case, the relevant Authority is that Authority on whose medical list he is included and, if there is more than one, that one of them in whose locality resides the largest number of individuals who are on his list of patients.

17.   Directions as to exercise of functions

(1)   The Secretary of State may give directions with respect to the exercise of any functions exercisable by virtue of sections 13 to 16 above and may also give directions with respect to the exercise by health authorities or Family Health Services Authorities of functions under the National Health Service and Community Care Act 1990; and, subject to any section, a Regional Health Authority may give directions with respect to the exercise —

(a)   by a District Health Authority of which the district is included in its region, of any functions exercisable by the District Health Authority by virtue of section 14 above; and

(b)   by a Family Health Services Authority in relation to which it is the relevant Regional Health Authority, of any functions exercisable by the Family Health Services Authority by virtue of section 15 above or the National Health Service and Community Care Act 1990.

(2)   It shall be the duty of a body to whom directions are given under subsection (1) above to comply with the directions.

19. Local advisory committees

(1)   Where the Secretary of State is satisfied that a committee formed for Wales, or for the region of a Regional Health Authority, is representative of persons of any of the following categories —

(a)   the medical practitioners, or

(b)   the dental practitioners, or

(c)   the nurses and midwives, or

(d)   the registered pharmacists, or

(e)   the ophthalmic and dispensing opticians,

of Wales or of the region, then it shall be his duty to recognise the committee.

(2)   A committee recognised in pursuance of subsection (1) above shall be called —

(a)   the Welsh Medical, Dental, Nursing and Midwifery, Pharmaceutical or Optical Committee, as the case may be;

(b)   the Regional Medical, Dental, Nursing and Midwifery, Pharmaceutical or Optical Committee, as the case may be, for the region in question.

(3)   Where the Secretary of State is satisfied that a committee formed for the area of an Area Health Authority or for the district of a District Health Authority is representative of persons of any of the categories mentioned in paragraphs (a) to (e) in subsection (1) it shall be his duty to recognise the committee.

A committee recognised in pursuance of this subsection shall be called the Area or the District Medical, Dental, Nursing and Midwifery, Pharmaceutical or Optical Committee, as the case may be, for the area or district in question.

(4)   The Secretary of State's duty under subsections (1) and (3) above is subject to paragraph 1 of Schedule 6 to this Act, and that Schedule has effect in relation to a committee recognised in pursuance of this section.

20. Community Health Councils

(1)   It is the Secretary of State's duty to establish in accordance with this section a council for the area of each Area Health Authority and a council for the district of each District Health Authority, or separate councils for such separate parts of the areas or districts of those Authorities as he thinks fit, and such a council shall be called a Community Health Council.

(2)   The Secretary of State —

(a)   may if he thinks fit discharge this duty by establishing a Community Health Council for a district which includes the areas or parts of the areas of two or more Area Health Authorities or for a district which includes the districts or parts of the districts of two or more District Health Authorities, but

(b)   shall be treated as not having discharged that duty unless he secures that there is no part of the area of an Area Health Authority or of the district of a District Health Authority which is not included in some Community Health Council's district.

(3)   The additional provisions of Schedule 7 to this Act have effect in relation to Community Health Councils.

22. Co-operation between health authorities and local authorities

(1)   In exercising their respective functions health authorities, Family Practitioner Committees and local authorities shall co-operate with one another in order to secure and advance the health and welfare of the people of England and Wales.

(2)   There shall be committees, to be called joint consultative committees, who shall advise bodies represented on them on the performance of their duties under subsection (1) above, and on the planning and operation of services of common concern to those authorities.

23.   Voluntary organisations and other bodies
(1)   The Secretary of State may, where he considers it appropriate, arrange with any person or body (including a voluntary organisation) for that person or body to provide, or assist in providing, any service under this Act.

(2)   The Secretary of State may make available —

(a)   to any person or body (including a voluntary organisation) carrying out any arrangements under subsection (1) above, or

(b)   to any voluntary organisation eligible for assistance under section 64 or section 65 of the Health Services and Public Health Act 1968 (assistance made available by the Secretary of State or local authorities),

any facilities (including goods or materials, or the use of any premises and the use of any vehicle, plant or apparatus) provided by him for any service under this Act; and, where anything is so made available, the services of persons employed by the Secretary of State or by a health authority in connection with it.

(3)   The powers conferred by this section may be exercised on such terms as may be agreed, including terms as to the making of payments by or to the Secretary of State, and any goods or materials may be made available either temporarily or permanently.

25.   Supplies not readily obtainable
Where the Secretary of State has acquired —

(a)   supplies of human blood for the purposes of any service under this Act, or

(b)   any part of a human body for the purpose of, or in the course of providing, any such service, or

(c)   supplies of any other substances or preparations not readily obtainable,

he may arrange to make such supplies or that part available (on such terms, including terms as to charges, as he thinks fit) to any person.

This section is subject to section 62 below (restriction of powers under section 25).

PART II

29.   Arrangements and regulations for general medical services
(1)   It is the duty of every Family Practitioner Committee, in accordance with regulations, to arrange as respects their locality with medical practitioners to provide personal medical services for all persons in the locality who wish to take advantage of the arrangements.

(1A)   The services so provided are referred to in this Act as "general medical services".

(2)   Regulations may provide for the definition of the personal medical services to be provided and for securing that the arrangements will be such that all persons availing themselves of those services will receive adequate personal care and attendance, and the regulations shall include provision —

(a)   for the preparation and publication of lists of medical practitioners who undertake to provide general medical services;

(b)   for conferring a right on any person to choose, in accordance with the prescribed procedure, the medical practitioner by whom he is to be attended, subject to the consent of the practitioner so chosen and to any prescribed limit on the number of patients to be accepted by any practitioner;

(c)   for the distribution among medical practitioners whose names are on the lists of any persons who have indicated a wish to obtain general medical services but who have not made any choice of medical practitioner or have been refused by the practitioner chosen;

(d)   for the issue to patients or their personal representatives by medical practitioners providing those services of such certificates as may be prescribed being certificates reasonably required by them under or for the purposes of any enactment;

(e)   for the removal from the list of medical practitioners undertaking to provide general medical services for persons in any locality of the name of any one in whose case it has been determined in such manner as may be prescribed that he has never provided, or has ceased to provide, such general medical services for persons in that locality;

(f)   for the making of arrangements for the temporary provision of general medical services in the locality of a Family Practitioner Committee;

(g)   for the circumstances in which a name added to the list by virtue of subsection (6) below may be removed from it.

(3)   Regulations under subsection (2) above may provide for the personal medical services there mentioned to include the provision of, and services connected with, any such advice, examination and treatment as are mentioned in paragraph (b) of section 5(1) above.

(4)   The remuneration to be paid under the arrangements mentioned in subsection (1) above to a practitioner who provides general medical services shall not, except in special circumstances, consist wholly or mainly of a fixed salary which has no reference to the number of patients for whom he has undertaken to provide such services.

(5)   Regulations shall —

(a)   include provision for the making to a medical practitioner providing general medical services of payments in respect of qualifying services provided by a spouse or other relative of his; and

(b)   provide that the rates and conditions of payment and the qualifying services in respect of which the payments may be made shall be such as may be determined by the Secretary of State after consultation with such bodies as he may recognise as representing such medical practitioners.

(6)   The persons with whom arrangements for the temporary provision of general medical services in a locality may be made by virtue of regulations under subsection (2) above include medical practitioners who are not on the list of medical practitioners providing such services in the locality, and the power to prepare and publish lists of medical practitioners conferred by paragraph (a) of that subsection accordingly includes power to add the names of medical practitioners with whom such arrangements are made to the list.

(7)   Regulations may provide that this Act and any regulations made under it shall apply in relation —

(a)   to the making of arrangements for the temporary provision of general medical services; and

(b)   to the provision of general medical services in pursuance of any such arrangements,

subject to such modifications as may be specified in the regulations.

(8)   Where the registration of a medical practitioner in the register of medical practitioners is suspended —

(a)   by a direction of the Health Committee of the General Medical Council under section 37(1) or (2) of the Medical Act 1983 (unfitness to practise by reason of physical or mental condition);

(b)   by an order of that Committee under section 38(1) of that Act (order for immediate suspension); or

(c)   by an interim order of the Preliminary Proceedings Committee of the Council under section 42(3)(b) of that Act,

the suspension shall not terminate any arrangements made with him for the provision of general medical services, but he shall not provide such services in person during the suspension.

30. Applications to provide general medical services

(1) Subject to subsection (1A) below, all applications made by medical practitioners in the prescribed manner to a Family Practitioner Committee for inclusion in a list kept by that Committee of the names of medical practitioners undertaking to provide general medical services for persons in the Committee's locality shall be referred by the Committee to the Medical Practices Committee and . . . any medical practitioner whose application is granted by that Committee shall subject to the provisions of this Part of this Act relating to the disqualification of practitioners be entitled to the inclusion of his name in the list.

(1A) No medical practitioner who is a national of a member State and is registered by virtue of a qualification granted in a member State shall be entitled to have his application for the inclusion of his name in the list kept by any Family Practitioner Committee unless he satisfies the Family Practitioner Committee that he has that knowledge of English which, in the interests of himself and his patients, is necessary for the provision of general medical services in the Committee's locality; and where a Family Practitioner Committee is not so satisfied with respect to any applicant the Family Practitioner Committee shall not refer his application to the Medical Practices Committee.

31. Requirement of suitable experience

(1) Where the Secretary of State so prescribes, and after a day so prescribed —

(a) the Medical Practices Committee shall refuse any application under section 30 above if the medical practitioner is not suitably experienced, and

(b) a Family Practitioner Committee shall not arrange under section 29 above with a medical practitioner for him to provide general medical services for persons in the Committee's locality unless the Medical Practices Committee have granted an application by him for the inclusion of his name in the list kept by the Family Practitioner Committee of medical practitioners undertaking to provide general medical services for persons in their locality.

(2) For the purposes of this section a medical practitioner is "suitably experienced" if, but only if, he either —

(a) has acquired the prescribed medical experience, or

(b) is by virtue of regulations made under section 32 below exempt from the need to have acquired that experience,

and "medical experience" includes hospital experience in any speciality.

33. Distribution of general medical services

(1) The Medical Practices Committee may refuse any application under section 30 above on the grounds that the number of medical practitioners undertaking to provide general medical services in the locality of the Family Practitioner Committee concerned or in the relevant part of that locality is already adequate.

(1A) The Secretary of State may by order specify —

(a) the maximum number of medical practitioners with whom, in any year, all the Family Health Services Authorities for localities in England, taken as a whole, may enter into arrangements under section 29 above for the provision of general medical services; and

(b) the maximum number of medical practitioners with whom, in any year, all the Family Health Services Authorities for localities in Wales, taken as a whole, may enter into such arrangements.

43. Persons authorised to provide pharmaceutical services

(1) No arrangements shall be made by a Family Practitioner Committee (except as may be provided by or under regulations) with a medical practitioner or dental

practitioner under which he is required or agrees to provide pharmaceutical services to any person to whom he is rendering general medical services or general dental services.

(2) No arrangements for the dispensing of medicines shall be made (except as may be provided by or under regulations) with persons other than persons who are registered pharmacists, or are persons lawfully conducting a retail pharmacy business in accordance with section 69 of the Medicines Act 1968 and who undertake that all medicines supplied by them under the arrangements made under this Part of this Act shall be dispensed either by or under the direct supervision of a registered pharmacist.

44. Recognition of local representative committees

(1) Where a Family Health Services Authority is satisfied that a committee formed for its locality is representative —

(a) of the medical practitioners providing general medical services or general ophthalmic services in that locality, or

(b) of the dental practitioners providing general dental services in that locality, or

(c) of the ophthalmic opticians providing general ophthalmic services in that locality, or

(d) of the persons providing pharmaceutical services in that locality, the Family Health Services Authority may recognise that committee; and any committee so recognised shall be called the Local Medical Committee, the Local Dental Committee, the Local Optical Committee or the Local Pharmaceutical Committee, as the case may be, for the locality concerned.

45. Functions of local representative committees

(1) The Family Practitioner Committee for a locality in respect of which committees are recognised under section 44 above shall, in exercising their functions under this Part of this Act, consult with those committees on such occasions and to such extent as may be prescribed; and those committees shall exercise such other functions as may be prescribed.

46. Disqualification of practitioners

(1) There shall be a tribunal (in this section and sections 47 to 49 below referred to as "the Tribunal") which shall be constituted in accordance with Schedule 9 to this Act to inquire into cases where representations are made in the prescribed manner to the Tribunal by a Family Practitioner Committee or any other person that the continued inclusion of a person's name in a list prepared under this Part of this Act —

(a) of medical practitioners undertaking to provide general medical services;

(b) of medical practitioners undertaking to provide general ophthalmic services,

(c) of dental practitioners undertaking to provide general dental services,

(d) of ophthalmic opticians undertaking to provide general ophthalmic services,

(f) of persons undertaking to provide pharmaceutical services, would be prejudicial to the efficiency of the services in question.

The supplementary provisions contained in Schedule 9 apply in relation to the Tribunal.

(2) The Tribunal, on receiving representations from a Family Practitioner Committee shall, and in any other case may, inquire into the case, and, if they are of opinion that the continued inclusion of that person's name in any list to which the representations relate would be prejudicial to the efficiency of those services —

(a) shall direct that his name be removed from that list; and

(b) may also, if they think fit, direct that his name be removed from, or not be included in, any corresponding list kept by any other Family Practitioner Committee under this Part.

(3) An appeal shall lie to the Secretary of State from any direction of the Tribunal under subsection (2) above, and the Secretary of State may confirm or revoke that direction.

(4)   Where the Tribunal direct that the name of any person be removed from or not included in any list or lists the Family Practitioner Committee or Committees concerned shall —

    (a)   if no appeal is brought, at the end of the period for bringing an appeal, or

    (b)   if an appeal is brought and the decision of the Tribunal is confirmed by the Secretary of State, on receiving notice of the Secretary of State's decision,

remove the name of the person concerned from the list or lists in question.

47. Removal of disqualification

(1)   Any person whose name has been removed by a direction under section 46 above from any list or lists shall be disqualified for inclusion in any list to which that direction relates until the Tribunal or the Secretary of State direct under this section to the contrary.

(2)   For the purpose of deciding whether or not to issue a direction under this section (or under paragraph 8 of Schedule 14 to this Act), the Tribunal or the Secretary of State, as the case may be, may hold an inquiry.

51. University clinical teaching and research

It is the Secretary of State's duty to make available, in premises provided by him by virtue of this Act, such facilities as he considers are reasonably required by any university which has a medical or dental school, in connection with clinical teaching and with research connected with clinical medicine or, as the case may be, clinical dentistry.

53. Immunisation

Where the Secretary of State arranges with medical practitioners for the vaccination or immunisation of persons against disease, he shall so far as reasonably practicable give every medical practitioner providing general medical services an opportunity to participate in the arrangements.

54. Prohibition of sale of medical practices

(1)   Where the name of any medical practitioner is or has been at any time entered on any list of medical practitioners undertaking to provide general medical services, it shall be unlawful subsequently to sell the goodwill or any part of the goodwill of the medical practice of that medical practitioner.

This subsection is subject to subsections (2) and (3) below; and the additional provisions contained in Schedule 10 to this Act have effect for the purposes of this section.

(2)   Where a medical practitioner whose name has ceased to be entered on any list of medical practitioners undertaking to provide general medical services practises in the locality of a Family Practitioner Committee without his name ever having been entered on a list of medical practitioners undertaking to provide general medical services there, subsection (1) above does not render unlawful the sale of the goodwill or any part of the goodwill of his practice in that locality.

(3)   Subsection (1) above does not prevent the sale of the goodwill or any part of the goodwill of a medical practice carried on in any such locality, being a sale by a medical practitioner whose name has never been entered on a list of medical practitioners undertaking to provide general medical services there, notwithstanding that any part of the goodwill to be sold is attributable to such a practice previously carried on by a person whose name was entered on such a list.

56. Inadequate services

If the Secretary of State is satisfied, after such inquiry as he may think fit, as respects the locality of a Family Practitioner Committee or part of the locality of such a

Committee that the persons whose names are included in any list prepared under this Part of this Act —

    (a)   of medical practitioners undertaking to provide general medical services,

    (b)   of dental practitioners undertaking to provide general dental services,

    (c)   of persons undertaking to provide general ophthalmic services, or

    (d)   of persons undertaking to provide pharmaceutical services,

are not such as to secure the adequate provision of the services in question in that locality or part, or that for any other reason any considerable number of persons in any such locality or part are not receiving satisfactory services under the arrangements in force under this Part, then —

    (i)   he may authorise the Family Practitioner Committee to make such other arrangements as he may approve, or may himself make such other arrangements, and

    (ii)   he may dispense with any of the requirements of regulations made under this Part so far as appears to him necessary to meet exceptional circumstances and enable such arrangements to be made.

62.   Restriction of powers under s. 25

The Secretary of State shall exercise the powers conferred on him by the provisions of section 25 above (supplies not readily obtainable) only if and to the extent that he is satisfied that anything which he proposes to do or allow under those powers —

    (a)   will not to a significant extent interfere with the performance by him of any duty imposed on him by this Act to provide accommodation or services of any kind; and

    (b)   will not to a significant extent operate to the disadvantage of persons seeking or afforded admission or access to accommodation or services at health service hospitals (whether as resident or non-resident patients) otherwise than as private patients.

63.   Hospital accommodation on part payment

(1)   The Secretary of State may authorise the accommodation described in this section to be made available for patients to such extent as he may determine, and may recover such charges as he may determine in respect of such accommodation and calculate them on any basis that he considers to be the appropriate commercial basis. The accommodation mentioned above is —

    (a)   in single rooms or small wards which is not for the time being needed by any patient on medical grounds;

    (b)   at any health service hospital or group of hospitals, or a hospital in which patients are treated under arrangements made by virtue of section 23 above, or at the health service hospitals in a particular area of a hospital in which patients are so treated.

(1C)   References in subsection (1) above to a health service hospital do not include references to a hospital vested in an NHS trust.

64.   Expenses payable by remuneratively employed resident patients

The Secretary of State may require any person —

    (a)   who is a resident patient for whom the Secretary of State provides services under this Act; and

    (b)   who is absent during the day for the purpose of engaging in remunerative employment from the hospital where he is a patient,

to pay such part of the cost of his maintenance in the hospital and any incidental cost as may seem reasonable to the Secretary of State having regard to the amount of that person's remuneration, and the Secretary of State may recover the amount so required.

65.   Accommodation and services for private patients

(1)   Subject to the provisions of this section, to such extent as they may determine, a District or Special Health Authority may make available at a hospital or hospitals for which they have responsibility accommodation and services, for patients who give

undertakings (or for whom undertakings are given) to pay, in respect of the accommodation and services made available, such charges as the Authority may determine and may make and recover such charges as the Authority may determine in respect of such accommodation and services and calculate them on any basis that the Authority considers to be the appropriate commercial basis; but the Authority shall do so only if and to the extent that the Authority is satisfied that to do so —

(a) will not to a significant extent interfere with the performance by the Authority of any function conferred on the Authority under this Act to provide accommodation or services of any kind; and

(b) will not to a significant extent operate to the disadvantage of persons seeking or afforded admission or access to accommodation or services at health service hospitals (whether as resident or non-resident patients) otherwise than under this section.

(1A) Before determining to make any accommodation or services available as mentioned in subsection (1) above, a District or Special Health Authority shall consult organisations representative of the interests of persons likely to be affected by the determination.

(2) A District or Special Health Authority may allow accommodation and services which are made available under subsection (1) above to be so made available in connection with treatment, in pursuance of arrangements made by a medical practitioner or dental practitioner serving (whether in an honorary or paid capacity) on the staff of a health service hospital for the treatment of private patients of that practitioner.

(3) The Secretary of State may give directions to a District or Special Health Authority in relation to the exercise of its functions under this section; and it shall be the duty of an authority to whom directions are so given to comply with them.

(4) References in the preceding provisions of this section to a health service hospital do not include references to a hospital vested in an NHS trust.

72. Permission for use of facilities in private practice

(1) A person to whom this section applies who wishes to use any relevant health service accommodation or facilities for the purpose of providing medical, dental, pharmaceutical, ophthalmic or chiropody services to non-resident private patients may apply in writing to the Secretary of State for permission under this section.

(2) Any application for permission under this section must specify —

(a) which of the relevant health service accommodation or facilities the applicant wishes to use for the purpose of providing services to such patients; and

(b) which of the kinds of services mentioned in subsection (1) above he wishes the permission to cover.

(3) On receiving an application under this section the Secretary of State —

(a) shall consider whether anything for which permission is sought would interfere with the giving of full and proper attention to persons seeking or afforded access otherwise than as private patients to any services provided under this Act; and

(b) shall grant the permission applied for unless in his opinion anything for which permission is sought would so interfere.

(4) Any grant of permission under this section shall be on such terms (including terms as to the payment of charges for the use of the relevant health service accommodation or facilities pursuant to the permission) as the Secretary of State may from time to time determine.

(5) The persons to whom this section applies are —

(a) persons of any of the following descriptions who provide services under Part II of this Act, namely, medical practitioners, dental practitioners, registered pharmacists, and ophthalmic opticians; and

(b) other persons who provide pharmaceutical or ophthalmic services under Part II; and

(c) chiropodists who provide services under this Act at premises where services are provided under Part II.

(6) In this section —

(a) "relevant health service accommodation or facilities", in relation to a person to whom this section applies, means any accommodation or facilities available at premises provided by the Secretary of State by virtue of this Act, being accommodation or facilities which that person is for the time being authorised to use for purposes of Part II; or

(b) in the case of a person to whom this section applies by virtue of paragraph (c) of subsection (5) above, accommodation or facilities which that person is for the time being authorised to use for purposes of this Act at premises where services are provided under Part II.

77. Charges for drugs, medicines or appliances, or pharmaceutical services

(1) Regulations may provide for the making and recovery in such manner as may be prescribed of such charges as may be prescribed in respect of —

(a) the supply under this Act (otherwise than under Part II) of drugs, medicines or appliances (including the replacement and repair of those appliances),

(b) such of the pharmaceutical services referred to in Part II as may be prescribed,

and paragraphs (a) and (b) of this subsection may include the supply of substances and appliances mentioned in paragraph (b) of section 5(1) above.

(2) Regulations under subsection (1) above may provide for the grant, on payment of such sums as may be prescribed by those regulations, of certificates conferring on the persons to whom the certificates are granted exemption from charges otherwise exigible under the regulations in respect of drugs, medicines and appliances supplied during such period as may be prescribed, and different sums may be so prescribed in relation to different periods.

(3) The additional provisions of paragraphs 1 and 4 of Schedule 12 to this Act have effect in relation to this section.

84. Inquiries

(1) The Secretary of State may cause an inquiry to be held in any case where he deems it advisable to do so in connection with any matter arising under this Act or Part I of the National Health Service and Community Care Act 1990.

(2) For the purpose of any such inquiry (but subject to subsection (3) below) the person appointed to hold the inquiry —

(a) may by summons require any person to attend, at a time and place stated in the summons, to give evidence or to produce any documents in his custody or under his control which relate to any matter in question at the inquiry; and

(b) may take evidence on oath, and for that purpose administer oaths, or may, instead of administering an oath, require the person examined to make a solemn affirmation.

(3) Nothing in this section —

(a) requires a person, in obedience to a summons under the section, to attend to give evidence or to produce any documents unless the necessary expenses of his attendance are paid or tendered to him; or

(b) empowers the person holding the inquiry to require the production of the title, or of any instrument relating to the title, or any land not being the property of a local authority.

(4) Any person who refuses or deliberately fails to attend in obedience to a summons under this section, or to give evidence, or who deliberately alters, suppresses, conceals, destroys, or refuses to produce any book or other document which he is required or is liable to be required to produce for the purposes of this section, shall be

liable on summary conviction to a fine not exceeding level 3 on the standard scale or to imprisonment for a term not exceeding 6 months, or to both.

(5) Where the Secretary of State causes an inquiry to be held under this section —

(a) the costs incurred by him in relation to the inquiry (including such reasonable sum not exceeding £30 a day as he may determine for the services of any officer engaged in the inquiry) shall be paid by such local authority or party to the inquiry as he may direct, and

(b) he may cause the amount of the costs so incurred to be certified, and any amount so certified and directed to be paid by any authority or person shall be recoverable from that authority or person by the Secretary of State summarily as a civil debt.

No local authority shall be ordered to pay costs under this subsection in the case of any inquiry unless it is a party to that inquiry.

(6) Where the Secretary of State causes an inquiry to be held under this section he may make orders —

(a) as to the costs of the parties at the inquiry, and

(b) as to the parties by whom the costs are to be paid,

and every such order may be made a rule of the High Court on the application of any party named in the order.

85. Default powers

(1) Where the Secretary of State is of opinion, on complaint or otherwise, that —

(a) any Regional Health Authority;
(b) any Area Health Authority;
(bb) any District Health Authority;
(c) any special health authority;
(d) any Family Practitioner Committee;
(e) an NHS trust
(f) the Medical Practices Committee; or
(g) Dental Practice Board;

have failed to carry out any functions conferred or imposed on them by or under this Act or Part I of the National Health Service and Community Care Act 1990, or have in carrying out those functions failed to comply with any regulations or directions relating to those functions, he may after such inquiry as he may think fit make an order declaring them to be in default.

(2) The members of the body in default shall forthwith vacate their office, and the order —

(a) shall provide for the appointment, in accordance with the provisions of this Act, of new members of the body; and

(b) may contain such provisions as seem to the Secretary of State expedient for authorising any person to act in the place of the body in question pending the appointment of new members.

(5) An order made under this section may contain such supplementary and incidental provisions as appear to the Secretary of State to be necessary or expedient, including —

(a) provision for the transfer to the Secretary of State of property and liabilities of the body in default; and

(b) where any such order is varied or revoked by a subsequent order, provision in the revoking order or a subsequent order for the transfer to the body in default of any property or liabilities acquired or incurred by the Secretary of State in discharging any of the functions transferred to him.

86. Emergency powers

If the Secretary of State —

(a)   considers that by reason of an emergency it is necessary, in order to ensure that a service falling to be provided in pursuance of this Act or Part I of the National Health Service and Community Care Act 1990 is provided, to direct that during the period specified by the directions a function conferred on any body or person by virtue of this Act or that Part shall to the exclusion of or concurrently with that body or person be performed by another body or person, then

(b)   he may give directions accordingly and it shall be the duty of the bodies or persons in question to comply with the directions.

The powers conferred on the Secretary of State by this section are in addition to any other powers exercisable by him.

PART V

HEALTH SERVICE COMMISSIONER FOR ENGLAND AND HEALTH SERVICE COMMISSIONER FOR WALES

106.   Appointment and tenure of office of Commissioners

(1)   For the purpose of conducting investigations in accordance with this Part of this Act, there shall be appointed —

(a)   a Commissioner to be known as the Health Service Commissioner for England; and

(b)   a Commissioner to be known as the Health Service Commissioner for Wales.

(2)   Her Majesty may by Letters Patent from time to time appoint a person to be a Commissioner; and a person so appointed shall, subject to subsections (3) and (3A) below, hold office during good behaviour.

(3)   A person appointed to be a Commissioner may be relieved of office by Her Majesty at his own request, or may be removed from office by Her Majesty in consequence of Addresses from both Houses of Parliament, and shall in any case vacate office on completing the year of service in which he attains the age of sixty-five.

(3A)   Her Majesty may declare the office of Health Service Commissioner for England or Health Service Commissioner for Wales to have been vacated if satisfied that the person appointed to be the Commissioner is incapable for medical reasons —

(a)   of performing the duties of his office; and

(b)   of requesting to be relieved of it.

(4)   A person who is a member of a relevant body (within the meaning of section 109 below) shall not be appointed to be a Commissioner; and a Commissioner shall not become a member of a relevant body.

109.   Bodies subject to investigation

In this Part of this Act "relevant body" means any of the following bodies —

(a)   Regional Health Authorities;

(b)   Area Health Authorities;

(bb)   District Health Authorities;

(c)   any special health authority established on or before 1st April 1974;

(d)   any special health authority established after that 1st April and designated by Order in Council as an authority to which this section applies;

(da)   NHS trusts;

(dd)   the Dental Practice Board;

(e)   Family Practitioner Committees; and

(f)   the Public Health Laboratory Service Board;

Except where the context otherwise requires, any reference in this Part of this Act to a relevant body includes a reference to an officer of the body.

110.   Investigations for England, and for Wales

The Health Service Commissioner for England shall not conduct an investigation under this Part of this Act in respect of —

(a)   an Area Health Authority of which the area is in Wales,
(aa) a District Health Authority of which the district is in Wales,
(b)   a Family Practitioner Committee whose locality is in Wales, or
(ba) an NHS trust which is managing a hospital or other establishment or facility
which is in Wales,
(c)   a special health authority exercising functions only or mainly in Wales,
and the Health Service Commissioner for Wales shall not conduct such an investigation
in respect of a relevant body other than one of those bodies.

111.   Who may complain

(1)   A complaint under this Part of this Act may be made by any individual, or by
any body of persons whether incorporated or not, not being —
(a)   a local authority or other authority or body constituted for purposes of the
public service or of local government, or for the purposes of carrying on under national
ownership any industry or undertaking or part of an industry or undertaking;
(b)   any other authority or body whose members are appointed by Her Majesty or
any Minister of the Crown or government department, or whose revenues consist
wholly or mainly of money provided by Parliament.

(2)   Where the person by whom a complaint might have been made under the
preceding provisions of this Part has died, or is for any reason unable to act for himself,
the complaint may be made —
(a)   by his personal representative, or
(b)   by a member of his family, or
(c)   by some body or individual suitable to represent him,
but, except as aforesaid and as provided by section 117 below, a complaint shall not be
entertained under this Part unless made by the person aggrieved himself.

112.   Reply

Before proceeding to investigate a complaint —
(a)   a Commissioner shall satisfy himself that the complaint has been brought by
or on behalf of the person aggrieved to the notice of the relevant body in question, and
that that body had been afforded a reasonable opportunity to investigate and reply to
the complaint, but
(b)   a Commissioner shall disregard the provisions of paragraph (a) in relation to
a complaint made by an officer of the relevant body in question on behalf of the person
aggrieved if the officer is authorised by virtue of section 111(2) above to make the
complaint and the Commissioner is satisfied that in the particular circumstances those
provisions ought to be disregarded.

113.   Commissioner's discretion

(1)   In determining whether to initiate, continue or discontinue an investigation
under this Part of this Act, a Commissioner shall, subject to section 110 above and
sections 115 and 116 below, act in accordance with his own discretion.

(2)   Any question whether a complaint is duly made to a Commissioner under this
Part shall be determined by the Commissioner.

114.   Procedure, and additional procedural provisions

(1)   A Commissioner —
(a)   shall not entertain a complaint under this Part of this Act unless it is made in
writing to him by or on behalf of the person aggrieved not later than one year from the
day on which the person aggrieved first had notice of the matters alleged in the
complaint, but
(b)   may conduct an investigation pursuant to a complaint not made within that
period if he considers it reasonable to do so.

(2)   The additional provisions contained in Part I of Schedule 13 to this Act, which relate to procedure and other matters, have effect for the purposes of this Part.

115.   Matters subject to investigation

A Commissioner may investigate —
  (a)   an alleged failure in a service provided by a relevant body, or
  (b)   an alleged failure of such a body to provide a service which it was a function of the body to provide, or
  (c)   any other action taken by or on behalf of such a body,
in a case where a complaint is duly made by or on behalf of any person that he has sustained injustice or hardship in consequence of the failure or in consequence of maladministration connected with the other action.

This section is subject to sections 110 and 113 above and section 116 below.

116.   Matters not subject to investigation

(1)   Except as hereafter provided, a Commissioner shall not conduct an investigation under this Part of this Act in respect of any of the following matters —
  (a)   any action in respect of which the person aggrieved has or had a right of appeal, reference or review to or before a tribunal constituted by or under any enactment or by virtue of Her Majesty's prerogative, or
  (b)   any action in respect of which the person aggrieved has or had a remedy by way of proceedings in any court of law,
but a Commissioner may conduct an investigation notwithstanding that the person aggrieved has or had such a right or remedy, if satisfied that in the particular circumstances it is not reasonable to expect him to resort or have resorted to it.

(2)   Without prejudice to subsection (1) above —
  (a)   a Commissioner shall not conduct an investigation under this Part in respect of any such action as is described in Part II of Schedule 13 of this Act; and
  (b)   nothing in sections 110, 113 and 115 above shall be construed as authorising such an investigation in respect of action taken in connection with any general medical services, general dental services, general ophthalmic services or pharmaceutical services by a person providing the services.

(3)   Her Majesty may by Order in Council amend Part II of Schedule 13 so as to exclude from it action described in sub-paragraph (3) or (4) of paragraph 19 of that Schedule.

117.   Reference to Commissioner by relevant body

Notwithstanding anything in sections 111 and 112 and section 114(1) above, a relevant body —
  (a)   may itself (excluding its officers) refer to a Commissioner a complaint that a person has, in consequence of a failure or maladministration for which the body is responsible, sustained such injustice or hardship as is mentioned in section 115 above if the complaint —
    (i)   is made in writing to the relevant body by that person, or by a person authorised by virtue of section 111(2) above to make the complaint to the Commissioner on his behalf, and
    (ii)   is so made not later than one year from the day mentioned in section 114(1) above, or within such other period as the Commissioner considers appropriate in any particular case, but
  (b)   shall not be entitled to refer a complaint in pursuance of paragraph (a) after the expiry of twelve months beginning with the day on which the body received the complaint.

A complaint referred to a Commissioner in pursuance of this section shall, subject to section 113 above, be deemed to be duly made to him under this Part of this Act.

118. Consultations between Commissioners and Local Commissioners

(1) Where, at any stage in the course of conducting an investigation under this Part of this Act, the Commissioner conducting the investigation —

(a) forms the opinion that the complaint relates partly to a matter which could be the subject of an investigation under Part III of the Local Government Act 1974, then

(b) he shall consult about the complaint with the appropriate Local Commissioner within the meaning of Part III of that Act of 1974, and

(c) if he considers it necessary, inform the person initiating the complaint under this Part of the steps necessary to initiate a complaint under Part III of that Act of 1974.

(1A) Where, at any stage in the course of conducting an investigation under this Part of this Act, the Commissioner conducting the investigation forms the opinion that the complaint relates partly to a matter which could be the subject of an investigation under the Parliamentary Commissioner Act 1967, he shall —

(a) unless he also holds office as the Parliamentary Commissioner, consult about the complaint with the Parliamentary Commissioner; and

(b) if he consider it necessary, inform the person initiating the complaint under this Part of this Act of the steps necessary to initiate a complaint under the Parliamentary Commissioner Act 1967.

(1B) Where, at any stage in the course of conducting an investigation under this Part of this Act, the Commissioner conducting the investigation forms the opinion that the complaint relates partly to a matter within the jurisdiction of another Health Service Commissioner (whether under this Part of this Act or under Part VI of the National Health Service (Scotland) Act 1978), he shall —

(a) unless he also holds office as that other Health Service Commissioner, consult about the complaint with him; and

(b) if he considers it necessary, inform the person initiating the complaint under this Part of this Act of the steps necessary to initiate a complaint to the other Health Service Commissioner.

(2) Where a Commissioner consults with another Commissioner in accordance with this section, the consultations may extend to any matter relating to the complaint, including —

(a) the conduct of any investigation into the complaint; and

(b) the form, content and publication of any report of the results of such an investigation.

(3) Nothing in paragraph 16 of Schedule 13 to this Act applies in relation to the disclosure of information by a Commissioner or his officers in the course of consultations held in accordance with this section.

119. Reports by Commissioners

(1) In any case where a Commissioner conducts an investigation under this Part of this Act, he shall send a report of the results of his investigation —

(a) to the person who made the complaint,

(aa) to any member of the House of Commons who, to the Commissioner's knowledge, assisted in the making of the complaint (or if he is no longer a member to such other member as the Commissioner thinks appropriate),

(b) to the relevant body in question,

(c) to any person who is alleged in the complaint to have taken or authorised the action complained of,

(d) if the relevant body in question is not an Area or District Health Authority for an area or district in England, to the Secretary of State,

(e) if that body is an Area or District Health Authority for an area or district in England, to the Regional Health Authority of which the region includes that area or district.

(2)   In any case where a Commissioner decides not to conduct an investigation under this Part, he shall send a statement of his reasons for doing so to the person who made the complaint and to any such member of the House of Commons as is mentioned in subsection (1)(aa) above and to the relevant body in question.

(3)   If, after conducting an investigation under this Part, it appears to a Commissioner that the person aggrieved has sustained such injustice or hardship as is mentioned in section 115 above, and that the injustice or hardship has not been and will not be remedied, he may if he thinks fit —

(b)   make a special report to the Secretary of State who shall, as soon as is reasonably practicable, lay a copy of the report before each House of Parliament.

(4)   Each of the Commissioners shall —

(b)   annually make the Secretary of State a report on the performance of his other functions under this Part, and may from time to time make to the Secretary of State such reports with respect to those functions as the Commissioner thinks fit, and the Secretary of State shall lay a copy of every such report before each House of Parliament.

(5)   For the purposes of the law of defamation, the publication of any matter by a Commissioner in sending or making a report in pursuance of subsection (1), (3) or (4) above, or in sending a statement in pursuance of subsection (2) above, shall be absolutely privileged.

120.   Interpretation of Part V

(1)   In this Part of this Act and in Schedule 13 to this Act —
   "action" includes failure to act, and other expressions connoting action shall be construed accordingly;
   "Commissioner" means the Health Service Commissioner for England or the Health Service Commissioner for Wales, and "Commissioners" means both those persons;
   "person aggrieved" means the person who claims or is alleged to have sustained such injustice or hardship as is mentioned in section 115 above; and
   "relevant body" has the meaning given by section 109 above, and (except where the context otherwise requires) includes a reference to an officer of the body.

(2)   Nothing in this Part of this Act authorises or requires a Commissioner to question the merits of a decision taken without maladministration by a relevant body in the exercise of a discretion vested in that body.

PART VI

Miscellaneous and Supplementary

124.   Special notices of births and deaths

(1)   The requirements of this section with respect to the notification of births and deaths are in addition to, and not in substitution for, the requirements of any Act relating to the registration of births and deaths.

(2)   It is the duty of each registrar of births and deaths to furnish, to the prescribed medical officer of the Area or District Health Authority, of which the area or district includes the whole or part of the registrar's sub-district, such particulars of each birth and death which occurred in the Authority's area or district as are entered (on and after 1st April 1974) in a register of births or deaths kept for that sub-district.

(3)   Regulations may provide as to the manner in which and the times at which particulars are to be furnished in pursuance of subsection (2) above.

(4)   In the case of every child born, it is the duty —

(a)   of the child's father, if at the time of the birth he is actually residing on the premises where the birth takes place, and

(b)   of any person in attendance upon the mother at the time of, or within six hours after, the birth, to give notice of the birth (as provided in subsection (5) below) to the prescribed medical officer of the Area or District Health Authority for the area or district in which the birth takes place.

This subsection applies to any child which has issued forth from its mother after the expiry of the twenty-eighth week of pregnancy whether alive or dead.

(5)   Notice under subsection (4) above shall be given either —

(a)   by posting within 36 hours after the birth a prepaid letter or postcard addressed to the prescribed medical officer of the Area or District Health Authority at his office and containing the required information, or

(b)   by delivering within that period at that officer's office a written notice containing the required information,

and an Area or District Health Authority shall, upon application to them, supply without charge to any medical practitioner or midwife residing or practising within their area or district prepaid addressed envelopes together with the forms of notice.

(6)   Any person who fails to give notice of a birth in accordance with subsection (4) above is liable on summary conviction to a fine not exceeding level 1 on the standard scale, unless he satisfies the court that he believed, and had reasonable grounds for believing, that notice had been duly given by some other person.

Proceedings in respect of this offence shall not, without the Attorney-General's written consent, be taken by any person other than a party aggrieved or the Area or District Health Authority concerned.

(7)   A registrar of births and deaths shall, for the purpose of obtaining information concerning births which have occurred in his sub-district, have access at all reasonable times to notices of births received by a medical officer under this section, or to any book in which those notices may be recorded.

128.   Interpretation and construction

(1)   In this Act and Part I of the National Health Service and Community Care Act 1990, unless the contrary intention appears —

"District Health Authority" means the authority for a district whether or not its name incorporates the word "District";

"dental practitioner" means a person registered in the dentists register under the Dentists Act 1984;

"disabled persons" means persons who are blind, deaf or dumb or who suffer from mental disorder of any description and other persons who are substantially and permanently handicapped by illness, injury or congenital deformity or such other disability as may be prescribed;

"equipment" includes any machinery, apparatus or appliance, whether fixed or not, and any vehicle;

"functions" includes powers and duties;

"health authority" means a Regional or District Health Authority or a special health authority but does not include a Family Practitioner Committee;

"the health service" means the health service established in pursuance of section 1 of the National Health Service Act 1946 and continued under section 1(1) above;

"health service hospital" means a hospital vested in the Secretary of State for the purposes of his functions under this Act or vested in an NHS trust;

"hospital" means —

(a)   any institution for the reception and treatment of persons suffering from illness,

(b)   any maternity home, and

(c)   any institution for the reception and treatment of persons during convalescence or persons requiring medical rehabilitation,

and includes clinics, dispensaries and out-patient departments maintained in connection with any such home or institution, and "hospital accommodation" shall be construed accordingly;

"illness" includes mental disorder within the meaning of the Mental Health Act 1983 and any injury or disability requiring medical or dental treatment or nursing;

"local authority" means a county council, a district council, a London borough council, and the Common Council of the City of London; and includes the King Edward VII Welsh National Memorial Association;

"local education authority" has the same meaning as in the Education Act 1944;

"local social services authority" means the council of a non-metropolitan county, or of a metropolitan district or London borough, or the Common Council of the City of London;

"medical" includes surgical;

"medical practitioner" means a registered medical practitioner within the meaning of Schedule 1 to the Interpretation Act 1978;

"medicine" includes such chemical re-agents as are included in a list for the time being approved by the Secretary of State for the purposes of section 41 above;

"modifications" includes additions, omissions and amendments;

"NHS contract" has the meaning assigned by section 4(1) of the National Health Service and Community Care Act 1990;

"National Health Service trust" has the meaning assigned by section 5 of the National Health Service and Community Care Act 1990 and "NHS trust" shall be construed accordingly;

"officer" includes servant;

"operational date", in relation to an NHS trust, shall be construed in accordance with paragraph 3(1)(e) of Schedule 2 to the National Health Service and Community Care Act 1990;

"patient" includes an expectant or nursing mother and a lying-in woman;

"prescribed" means prescribed by regulations made by the Secretary of State under this Act or Part I of the National Health Service and Community Care Act 1990;

"primary functions" shall be construed in accordance with section 3 of the National Health Service and Community Care Act 1990;

"property" includes rights;

"registered pharmacist" means a pharmacist registered in the register of pharmaceutical chemists;

"regulations" means regulations made by the Secretary of State under this Act or Part I of the National Health Service and Community Care Act 1990;

"special hospital" has the meaning given by section 4 above;

"voluntary organisation" means a body the activities of which are carried on otherwise than for profit, but does not include any public or local authority;

(2) References in this Act to the purposes of a hospital shall be construed as referring both to the general purposes of the hospital and to any specific purpose of the hospital.

(3) Any reference in this Act to any enactment is a reference to it as amended or applied by or under any other enactment including this Act.

SCHEDULES
SCHEDULE 5
PART III

8. Each Regional Health Authority, District Health Authority, special health authority and Family Practitioner Committee (hereinafter in this Schedule referred to severally as "an authority") shall be a body corporate.

15. (1)   An authority shall, notwithstanding that it is exercising any function on behalf of the Secretary of State or another authority, be entitled to enforce any rights acquired in the exercise of that function, and be liable in respect of any liabilities incurred (including liabilities in tort) in the exercise of that function, in all respects as if it were acting as a principal.

Proceedings for the enforcement of such rights and liabilities shall be brought, and brought only, by or, as the case may be, against the authority in question in its own name.

SCHEDULE 7

1.   It is the duty of a Community Health Council (in this Schedule referred to as a "Council") —

    (a)   to represent the interests in the health service of the public in its district; and

    (b)   to perform such other functions as may be conferred on it by virtue of paragraph 2 below.

2.   Regulations may provide as to

    (a)   the membership of Councils (including the election by members of a Council of a chairman of the Council);

    (b)   the proceedings of Councils;

    (c)   the staff, premises and expenses of Councils;

    (d)   the consultation of Councils by Regional Health Authorities, NHS trusts, District Health Authorities or relevant Family Practitioner Committees with respect to such matters, and on such occasions, as may be prescribed;

    (e)   the furnishing of information to Councils by Regional and District Health Authorities, NHS trusts or relevant Family Health Services Authorities, and the right of members of Councils to enter and inspect premises controlled by such health authorities or NHS trusts;

    (f)   the consideration by Councils of matters relating to the operation of the health service within their districts, and the giving of advice by Councils to such Authorities and Committees on such matters;

    (g)   the preparation and publication of reports by Councils on such matters, and the furnishing and publication by such Authorities or Committees of comments on the reports; and

    (h)   the functions to be exercised by Councils in addition to the functions exercisable by them by virtue of paragraph 1(a) above and the preceding provisions of this paragraph.

SCHEDULE 13

ADDITIONAL PROVISIONS AS TO THE HEALTH SERVICE COMMISSIONER FOR ENGLAND AND THE HEALTH SERVICE COMMISSIONER FOR WALES (ss. 114(2), 116(2))

Procedure in respect of investigations

1.   Where the Commissioner proposes to conduct an investigation pursuant to a complaint under Part V of this Act, he shall afford to the relevant body concerned, and to any other person who is alleged in the complaint to have taken or authorised the action complained of, an opportunity to comment on any allegations contained in the complaint.

2.   Every such investigation shall be conducted in private, but except for that the procedure for conducting an investigation shall be such as the Commissioner considers appropriate in the circumstances of the case.

3.   Without prejudice to the generality of paragraph 2 above, the Commissioner may obtain information from such persons and in such manner, and make such inquiries, as he thinks fit, and may determine whether any person may be represented, by counsel or solicitor or otherwise, in the investigation.

4.   The Commissioner may, if he thinks fit, pay to the person by whom the complaint was made and to any other person who attends or furnishes information for the purposes of an investigation under Part V of this Act —
    (a)   sums in respect of expenses properly incurred by them,
    (b)   allowances by way of compensation for the loss of their time,
in accordance with such scales and subject to such conditions as may be determined by the Minister for the Civil Service.

5.   The conduct of an investigation under Part V of this Act shall not affect any action taken by the relevant body concerned, or any power or duty of that body to take further action with respect to any matters subject to the investigation.

6.   Where the person aggrieved has been removed from the United Kingdom under any Order in force under the Immigration Act 1971 he shall, if the Commissioner so directs, be permitted to re-enter and remain in the United Kingdom, subject to such conditions as the Secretary of State may direct, for the purposes of the investigation.

Evidence

7.   For the purposes of an investigation under Part V of this Act the Commissioner may require any employee officer or member of the relevant body concerned or any other person who in his opinion is able to furnish information or produce documents relevant to the investigation to furnish any such information or produce any such document.

8.   For the purposes of any such investigation the Commissioner shall have the same powers as the Court (which in this Schedule means, in relation to England and Wales, the High Court, in relation to Scotland, the Court of Session, and in relation to Northern Ireland, the High Court of Northern Ireland) in respect of the attendance and examination of witnesses (including the administration of oaths or affirmations and the examination of witnesses abroad) and in respect of the production of documents.

9.   No obligation to maintain secrecy or other restriction upon the disclosure of information obtained by or furnished to persons in Her Majesty's service, whether imposed by any enactment or by any rule of law, shall apply to the disclosure of information for the purposes of an investigation under Part V of this Act.
The Crown shall not be entitled in relation to any such investigation to any such privilege in respect of the production of documents or the giving or evidence as is allowed by law in legal proceedings.

10.   No person shall be required or authorised by Part V of this Act and this Schedule to furnish any information or answer any question relating to proceedings of the Cabinet or of any committee of the Cabinet or to produce so much of any document as relates to such proceedings.
For the purposes of this paragraph a certificate issued by the Secretary of the Cabinet with the approval of the Prime Minister and certifying that any information, question, document, or part of a document so relates shall be conclusive.

11.   Subject to paragraph 9 above, no person shall be compelled for the purposes of an investigation under Part V of this Act to give any evidence or produce any document which he could not be compelled to give or produce in civil proceedings before the Court.

Obstruction and contempt

12.   If any person without lawful excuse obstructs the Commissioner or any officer of the Commissioner in the performance of his functions under Part V of this Act and this Schedule, or is guilty of any act or omission in relation to an investigation under that Part which, if that investigation were a proceeding in the Court, would constitute contempt of court, the Commissioner may certify the offence to the Court.

13.   Where an offence is certified under paragraph 12 above, the Court may inquire into the matter and, after hearing any witnesses who may be produced against or on behalf of the person charged with the offence, and after hearing any statement that may be offered in defence, deal with him in any manner in which the Court could deal with him if he had committed the like offence in relation to the Court.

14.   Nothing in paragraphs 12 and 13 above shall be construed as applying to the taking of any such action as is mentioned in paragraphs 5 and 6 above.

Secrecy of information

16.   Information obtained by the Commissioner or his officers in the course of or for the purposes of an investigation under Part V of this Act shall not be disclosed except —

(a)   for the purposes of the investigation and of any report to be made in respect of the investigation under that Part,

(b)   for the purposes of any proceedings for an offence under the Official Secrets Acts 1911 to 1989 alleged to have been committed in respect of information obtained by the Commissioner or any of his officers by virtue of that Part or for an offence of perjury alleged to have been committed in the course of an investigation under that Part or for the purposes of an inquiry with a view to the taking of such proceedings, or

(c)   for the purposes of any proceedings under paragraphs 12 and 13 above,

and the Commissioner and his officers shall not be called upon to give evidence in any proceedings (other than those mentioned in this paragraph) of matters coming to his or their knowledge in the course of an investigation under that Part.

16A.   (1)   Where the Commissioner also holds office as a relevant commissioner and a person initiates a complaint to him in his capacity as such a commissioner which relates partly to a matter with respect to which that person has previously initiated a complaint to him in his capacity as the Commissioner, or subsequently initiates such a complaint, information obtained by the Commissioner or his officers in the course of or for the purposes of the investigation under Part V of this Act may be disclosed for the purposes of his carrying out his functions in relation to the other complaint.

(2)   In this paragraph "relevant commissioner" —

(a)   in relation to the Health Service Commissioner for England, means the Parliamentary Commissioner, the Health Service Commissioner for Wales and the Health Service Commissioner for Scotland; and

(b)   in relation to the Health Service Commissioner for Wales, means the Parliamentary Commissioner, the Health Service Commissioner for England and the Health Service Commissioner for Scotland.

17.   A Minister of the Crown may give notice in writing to the Commissioner, with respect to any document or information specified in the notice, or any class of documents or information so specified, that in the Minister's opinion the disclosure of that document or information, or of documents or information of that class, would be prejudicial to the safety of the State or otherwise contrary to the public interest.

18.   Where a notice under paragraph 17 above is given nothing in this Schedule shall be construed as authorising or requiring the Commissioner or any officer of the Commissioner to communicate to any person or for any purpose any document or

information specified in the notice, or any document or information of a class so specified.

Matters not Subject to Investigation by the Health Service Commissioner for England or the Health Service Commissioner for Wales

19.　The following matters are not subject to investigation by the Health Service Commissioner for England or the Health Service Commissioner for Wales —

(1)　Action taken in connection with the diagnosis of illness or the care or treatment of a patient, being action which, in the opinion of the Commissioner in question, was taken solely in consequence of the exercise of clinical judgment, whether formed by the person taking the action or any other person.

(2)　Action taken by a Family Practitioner Committee in the exercise of its functions under the National Health Service (Service Committees and Tribunal) Regulations 1974, or any instrument amending or replacing those regulations.

(3)　Action taken in respect of appointments or removals, pay, discipline, superannuation or other personnel matters in relation to service under this Act.

(4)　Action taken in matters relating to contractual or other commercial transactions, other than in matters arising from arrangements between a relevant body and another body which is not a relevant body for the provison of services for patients by that other body; and in determining what matters arise from such arrangements there shall be disregarded any arrangements for the provision of services at an establishment maintained by a Minister of the Crown for patients who are mainly members of the armed forces of the Crown.

(5)　Action which has been, or is, the subject of an inquiry under section 84 above.

UNFAIR CONTRACT TERMS ACT 1977
(1977, c. 50)

1.　Scope of Part I

(1)　For the purposes of this Part of this Act, "negligence" means the breach—

(a)　of any obligation, arising from the express or implied terms of a contract, to take reasonable care or exercise reasonable skill in the performance of the contract;

(b)　of any common law duty to take reasonable care or exercise reasonable skill (but not any stricter duty);

(c)　of the common duty of care imposed by the Occupiers' Liability Act 1957 or the Occupiers' Liability Act (Northern Ireland) 1957.

(2)　This Part of this Act is subject to Part III; and in relation to contracts, the operation of sections 2 to 4 and 7 is subject to the exceptions made by Schedule 1.

(3)　In the case of both contract and tort, sections 2 to 7 apply (except where the contrary is stated in section 6(4)) only to business liability, that is liability for breach of obligations or duties arising—

(a)　from things done or to be done by a person in the course of a business (whether his own business or another's); or

(b)　from the occupation of premises used for business purposes of the occupier; and references to liability are to be read accordingly but liability of an occupier of premises for breach of an obligation or duty towards a person obtaining access to the premises for recreational or educational purposes, being liability for loss or damage suffered by reason of the dangerous state of the premises, is not a business liability of the occupier unless granting that person such access for the purposes concerned falls within the business purposes of the occupier.

(4)　In relation to any breach of duty or obligation, it is immaterial for any purpose of this Part of this Act whether the breach was inadvertent or intentional, or whether liability for it arises directly or vicariously.

2. Negligence liability

(1)   A person cannot by reference to any contract term or to a notice given to persons generally or to particular persons exclude or restrict his liability for death or personal injury resulting from negligence.

(2)   In the case of other loss or damage, a person cannot so exclude or restrict his liability for negligence except in so far as the term or notice satisfies the requirement of reasonableness.

(3)   Where a contract term or notice purports to exclude or restrict liability for negligence a person's agreement to or awareness of it is not of itself to be taken as indicating his voluntary acceptance of any risk.

3. Liability arising in contract

(1)   This section applies as between contracting parties where one of them deals as consumer or on the other's written standard terms of business.

(2)   As against that party, the other cannot by reference to any contract term—

(a)   when himself in breach of contract, exclude or restrict any liability of his in respect of the breach; or

(b)   claim to be entitled—

(i)   to render a contractual performance substantially different from that which was reasonably expected of him, or

(ii)   in respect of the whole or any part of his contractual obligation, to render no performance at all,

except in so far as (in any of the cases mentioned above in this subsection) the contract term satisfies the requirement of reasonableness.

6. Sale and hire-purchase

(2)   As against a person dealing as consumer, liability for breach of the obligations arising from—

(a)   section 13, 14 or 15 of the 1979 Act (seller's implied undertakings as to conformity of goods with description or sample, or as to their quality or fitness for a particular purpose);

(b)   section 9, 10 or 11 of the 1973 Act (the corresponding things in relation to hire-purchase),

cannot be excluded or restricted by reference to any contract term.

(4)   The liabilities referred to in this section are not only the business liabilities defined by section 1(3), but include those arising under any contract of sale of goods or hire-purchase agreement.

11. The "reasonableness" test

(1)   In relation to a contract term, the requirement of reasonableness for the purposes of this Part of this Act, section 3 of the Misrepresentation Act 1967 and section 3 of the Misrepresentation Act (Northern Ireland) 1967 is that the term shall have been a fair and reasonable one to be included having regard to the circumstances which were, or ought reasonably to have been, known to or in the contemplation of the parties when the contract was made.

(2)   In determining for the purposes of section 6 or 7 above whether a contract term satisfies the requirement of reasonableness, regard shall be had in particular to the matters specified in Schedule 2 to this Act; but this subsection does not prevent the court or arbitrator from holding, in accordance with any rule of law, that a term which purports to exclude or restrict any relevant liability is not a term of the contract.

(3)   In relation to a notice (not being a notice having contractual effect), the requirement of reasonableness under this Act is that is should be fair and reasonable to allow reliance on it, having regard to all the circumstances obtaining when the liability arose or (but for the notice) would have arisen.

(4)   Where by reference to a contract term or notice a person seeks to restrict liability to a specified sum of money, and the question arises (under this or any other Act) whether the term or notice satisfies the requirement of reasonableness, regard shall be had in particular (but without prejudice to subsection (2) above in the case of contract terms) to—

(a)   the resources which he could expect to be available to him for the purpose of meeting the liability should it arise; and

(b)   how far it was open to him to cover himself by insurance.

(5)   It is for those claiming that a contract term or notice satisfies the requirement of reasonableness to show that it does.

12.   "Dealing as consumer"

(1)   A party to a contract "deals as consumer" in relation to another party if—

(a)   he neither makes the contract in the course of a business nor holds himself out as doing so; and

(b)   the other party does make the contract in the course of a business; and

(c)   in the case of a contract governed by the law of sale of goods or hire-purchase, or by section 7 of this Act, the goods passing under or in pursuance of the contract are of a type ordinarily supplied for private use or consumption.

(2)   But on a sale by auction or by competitive tender the buyer is not in any circumstances to be regarded as dealing as consumer.

(3)   Subject to this, it is for those claiming that a party does not deal as consumer to show that he does not.

13.   Varieties of exemption clause

(1)   To the extent that this Part of this Act prevents the exclusion or restriction of any liability it also prevents—

(a)   making the liability or its enforcement subject to restrictive or onerous conditions;

(b)   excluding or restricting any right or remedy in respect of the liability, or subjecting a person to any prejudice in consequence of his pursuing any such right or remedy;

(c)   excluding or restricting rules of evidence or procedure;

and (to that extent) sections 2 and 5 to 7 also prevent excluding or restricting liability by reference to terms and notices which exclude or restrict the relevant obligation or duty.

(2)   But an agreement in writing to submit present or future differences to arbitration is not to be treated under this Part of this Act as excluding or restricting any liability.

14.   Interpretation of Part I

In this Part of this Act—

"business" includes a profession and the activities of any government department or local or public authority;

"goods" has the same meaning as in the Sale of Goods Act 1979;

"hire-purchase agreement" has the same meaning as in the Consumer Credit Act 1974;

"negligence" has the meaning given by section 1(1);

"notice" includes an announcement, whether or not in writing, and any other communication or pretended communication; and

"personal injury" includes any disease and any impairment of physical or mental condition.

VACCINE DAMAGE PAYMENTS ACT 1979
(1979, c. 17)

1.   Payments to persons severely disabled by vaccination

(1)   If, on consideration of a claim, the Secretary of State is satisfied—

(a)   that a person is, or was immediately before his death, severely disabled as a result of vaccination against any of the diseases to which this Act applies; and

(b)   that the conditions of entitlement which are applicable in accordance with section 2 below are fulfilled,

he shall in accordance with this Act make a payment of the relevant statutory sum to or for the benefit of that person or to his personal representatives.

(1A)   In subsection (1) above "statutory sum" means £30,000 or such other sum as is specified by the Secretary of State for the purposes of this Act by order made by statutory instrument with the consent of the Treasury; and the relevant statutory sum for the purposes of that subsection is the statutory sum at the time when a claim for payment is first made.

(2)   The diseases to which this Act applies are—

   (a)   diphtheria,

   (b)   tetanus,

   (c)   whooping cough,

   (d)   poliomyelitis,

   (e)   measles,

   (f)   mumps,

   (g)   rubella,

   (h)   tuberculosis,

   (i)   smallpox, and

   (j)   any other disease which is specified by the Secretary of State for the purposes of this Act by order made by statutory instrument.

(3)   Subject to section 2(3) below, this Act has effect with respect to a person who is severely disabled as a result of a vaccination given to his mother before he was born as if the vaccination had been given directly to him and, in such circumstances as may be prescribed by regulations under this Act, this Act has effect with respect to a person who is severely disabled as a result of contracting a disease through contact with a third person who was vaccinated against it as if the vaccination had been given to him and the disablement resulted from it.

(4)   For the purposes of this Act, a person is severely disabled if he suffers disablement to the extent of 80 per cent. or more, assessed as for the purposes of section 57 of the Social Security Act 1975 or the Social Security (Northern Ireland) Act 1975 (disablement gratuity and pension).

(4A)   No order shall be made by virtue of subsection (1A) above unless a draft of the order has been laid before Parliament and been approved by a resolution of each House.

(5)   A statutory instrument under subsection (2)(i) above shall be subject to annulment in pursuance of a resolution of either House of Parliament.

2.   Conditions of entitlement

(1)   Subject to the provisions of this section, the conditions of entitlement referred to in section 1(1)(b) above are—

   (a)   that the vaccination in question was carried out—

     (i)   in the United Kingdom or the Isle of Man, and

     (ii)   on or after 5th July 1948, and

     (iii)   in the case of vaccination against smallpox, before 1st August 1971;

   (b)   except in the case of vaccination against poliomyelitis or rubella, that the vaccination was carried out either at a time when the person to whom it was given was under the age of eighteen or at the time of an outbreak within the United Kingdom or the Isle of Man of the disease against which the vaccination was given; and

(c) that the disabled person was over the age of two on the date when the claim was made or, if he died before that date, that he died after 9th May 1978 and was over the age of two when he died.

(2) An order under section 1(2)(i) above specifying a disease for the purposes of this Act may provide that, in relation to vaccination against that disease, the conditions of entitlement specified in subsection (1) above shall have effect subject to such modifications as may be specified in the order.

(3) In a case where this Act has effect by virtue of section 1(3) above, the reference in subsection (1)(b) above to the person to whom a vaccination was given is a reference to the person to whom it was actually given and not to the disabled person.

(4) With respect to claims made after such date as may be specified in the order and relating to vaccination against such disease as may be so specified, the Secretary of State may by order made by statutory instrument—

(a) provide that, in such circumstances as may be specified in the order, one or more of the conditions of entitlement appropriate to vaccination against that disease need not be fulfilled; or

(b) add to the conditions of entitlement which are appropriate to vaccination against that disease, either generally or in such circumstances as may be specified in the order.

(5) Regulations under this Act shall specify the cases in which vaccinations given outside the United Kingdom and the Isle of Man to persons defined in the regulations as serving members of Her Majesty's forces or members of their families are to be treated for the purposes of this Act as carried out in England.

(6) The Secretary of State shall not make an order containing any provision made by virtue of paragraph (b) of subsection (4) above unless a draft of the order has been laid before Parliament and approved by a resolution of each House; and a statutory instrument by which any other order is made under that subsection shall be subject to annulment in pursuance of a resolution of either House of Parliament.

3. Determination of claims

(1) Any reference in this Act, other than section 7, to a claim is a reference to a claim for a payment under section 1(1) above which is made—

(a) by or on behalf of the disabled person concerned or, as the case may be, by his personal representatives; and

(b) in the manner prescribed by regulations under this Act; and

(c) within the period of six years beginning on the latest of the following dates, namely, the date of the vaccination to which the claim relates, the date on which the disabled person attained the age of two and 9th May 1978;

and, in relation to a claim, any reference to the claimant is a reference to the person by whom the claim was made and any reference to the disabled person is a reference to the person in respect of whose disablement a payment under subsection (1) above is claimed to be payable.

(2) As soon as practicable after he has received a claim, the Secretary of State shall give notice in writing to the claimant of his determination whether he is satisfied that a payment is due under section 1(1) above to or for the benefit of the disabled person or to his personal representatives.

(3) If the Secretary of State is not satisfied that a payment is due as mentioned in subsection (2) above, the notice in writing under that subsection shall state the grounds on which he is not so satisfied.

(4) If, in the case of any claim, the Secretary of State—

(a) is satisfied that the conditions of entitlement which are applicable in accordance with section 2 above are fulfilled, but

(b) is not satisfied that the disabled person is or, where he has died, was immediately before his death severely disabled as a result of vaccination against any of the diseases to which this Act applies,

the notice in writing under subsection (2) above shall inform the claimant that, if an application for review is made to the Secretary of State, the matters referred to in paragraph (b) above will be reviewed by an independent medical tribunal in accordance with section 4 below.

(5) If in any case a person is severely disabled, the question whether his severe disablement results from vaccination against any of the diseases to which this Act applies shall be determined for the purposes of this Act on the balance of probability.

4. Review of extent of disablement and causation by independent tribunals

(1) Regulations under this Act shall make provision for independent medical tribunals to determine matters referred to them under this section, and such regulations may make provision with respect to—

(a) the terms of appointment of the persons who are to serve on the tribunals;

(b) the procedure to be followed for the determination of matters referred to the tribunals;

(c) the summoning of persons to attend to give evidence or produce documents before the tribunals and the administration of oaths to such persons.

(2) Where an application for review is made to the Secretary of State as mentioned in section 3(4) above, then, subject to subsection (3) below, the Secretary of State shall refer to a tribunal under this section—

(a) the question of the extent of the disablement suffered by the disabled person;

(b) the question whether he is or, as the case may be, was immediately before his death disabled as a result of the vaccination to which the claim relates; and

(c) the question whether, if he is or was so disabled, the extent of his disability is or was such as to amount to severe disablement.

(3) The Secretary of State may refer to differently constituted tribunals the questions in paragraphs (a) to (c) of subsection (2) above, and the Secretary of State need not refer to a tribunal any of those questions if—

(a) he and the claimant are not in dispute with respect to it; or

(b) the decision of a tribunal on another of those questions is such that the disabled person cannot be or, as the case may be, could not immediately before his death have been severely disabled as a result of the vaccination to which the claim relates.

(4) For the purposes of this Act, the decision of a tribunal on a question referred to them under this section shall be conclusive except in so far as it falls to be reconsidered by virtue of section 5 below.

5. Reconsideration of determinations and recovery of payments in certain cases

(1) Subject to subsection (2) below, the Secretary of State may reconsider a determination that a payment should not be made under section 1(1) above on the ground—

(a) that there has been a material change of circumstances since the determination was made, or

(b) that the determination was made in ignorance of, or was based on a mistake as to, some material fact,

and the Secretary of State may, on the ground set out in paragraph (b) above, reconsider a determination that such a payment should be made.

(2) Regulations under this Act shall prescribe the manner and the period in which—

(a) an application may be made to the Secretary of State for his reconsideration of a determination; and

(b) the Secretary of State may of his own motion institute such a reconsideration.

(3) The Secretary of State shall give notice in writing of his decision on a reconsideration under this section to the person who was the claimant in relation to the claim which gave rise to the determination which has been reconsidered and also, where the disabled person is alive and was not the claimant, to him; and the provisions of subsections (3) to (5) of section 3 and section 4 above shall apply as if—

(a) the notice under this subsection were a notice under section 3(2) above; and

(b) any reference in those provisions to the claimant were a reference to the person who was the claimant in relation to the claim which gave rise to the determination which has been reconsidered.

(4) If, whether fraudulently or otherwise, any person misrepresents or fails to disclose any material fact and in consequence of the misrepresentation or failure a payment is made under section 1(1) above, the person to whom the payment was made shall be liable to repay the amount of that payment to the Secretary of State unless he can show that the misrepresentation or failure occurred without his connivance or consent.

(5) Except as provided by subsection (4) above, no payment under section 1(1) above shall be recoverable by virtue of a reconsideration of a determination under this section.

6. Payments to or for the benefit of disabled persons

(1) Where a payment under section 1(1) above falls to be made in respect of a disabled person who is over eighteen and capable of managing his own affairs, the payment shall be made to him.

(2) Where such a payment falls to be made in respect of a disabled person who has died, the payment shall be made to his personal representatives.

(3) Where such a payment falls to be made in respect of any other disabled person, the payment shall be made for his benefit by paying it to such trustees as the Secretary of State may appoint to be held by them upon such trusts or, in Scotland, for such purposes and upon such conditions as may be declared by the Secretary of State.

(4) The making of a claim for, or the receipt of, a payment under section 1(1) above does not prejudice the right of any person to institute or carry on proceedings in respect of disablement suffered as a result of vaccination against any disease to which this Act applies; but in any civil proceedings brought in respect of disablement resulting from vaccination against such a disease, the court shall treat a payment made to or in respect of the disabled person concerned under section 1(1) above as paid on account of any damages which the court awards in respect of such disablement.

7. Payments, claims, etc. made prior to the Act

(1) Any reference in this section to an extra-statutory payment is a reference to a payment of £10,000 made by the Secretary of State to or in respect of a disabled person after 9th May 1978 and before the passing of this Act pursuant to a non-statutory scheme of payments for severe vaccine damage.

(2) No such claim as is referred to in section 3(1) above shall be entertained if an extra-statutory payment has been made to or for the benefit of the disabled person or his personal representatives.

8. Regulations

(1) Any reference in the preceding provisions of this Act to regulations under this Act is a reference to regulations made by the Secretary of State.

(2) Any power of the Secretary of State under this Act to make regulations—

(a) shall be exercisable by statutory instrument which shall be subject to annulment in pursuance of a resolution of either House of Parliament; and

(b) includes power to make such incidental or supplementary provision as appears to the Secretary of State to be appropriate.

(3) Regulations made by the Secretary of State may contain provision—

(a) with respect to the information and other evidence to be furnished in connection with a claim;

(b) requiring disabled persons to undergo medical examination before their claims are determined or for the purpose of a reconsideration under section 5 above;

(c) restricting the disclosure of medical evidence and advice tendered in connection with a claim or a reconsideration under section 5 above; and

(d) conferring functions on the tribunals constituted under section 4 above with respect to the matters referred to in paragraphs (a) to (c) above.

9. Fraudulent statements etc.

(1) Any person who, for the purpose of obtaining any payment under this Act, whether for himself or some other person,—

(a) knowingly makes any false statement or representation, or

(b) produces or furnishes or causes or knowingly allows to be produced or furnished any document or information which he knows to be false in a material particular,

shall be liable on summary conviction to a fine not exceeding £1,000.

NURSES, MIDWIVES AND HEALTH VISITORS ACT 1979
(1979, c. 36)

17. Attendance by unqualified persons at childbirth

(1) A person other than a registered midwife or a registered medical practitioner shall not attend a woman in childbirth.

(3) Subsection (1) does not apply—

(a) where the attention is given in a case of sudden or urgent necessity; or

(b) in the case of a person who, while undergoing training with a view to becoming a medical practitioner or to becoming a midwife, attends a woman in childbirth as part of a course of practical instruction in midwifery recognised by the General Medical Council or one of the National Boards.

(4) A person who contravenes subsection (1) shall be liable on summary conviction to a fine of not more than level 4 on the standard scale.

SALE OF GOODS ACT 1979
(1979, c. 54)

14. Implied terms about quality or fitness

(1) Except as provided by this section and section 15 below and subject to any other enactment, there is no implied condition or warranty about the quality or fitness for any particular purpose of goods supplied under a contract of sale.

(2) Where the seller sells goods in the course of a business, there is an implied condition that the goods supplied under the contract are of merchantable quality, except that there is no such condition—

(a) as regards defects specifically drawn to the buyer's attention before the contract is made; or

(b) if the buyer examines the goods before the contract is made, as regards defects which that examination ought to reveal.

(3) Where the seller sells goods in the course of a business and the buyer, expressly or by implication, makes known—

(a)   to the seller, or

(b)   where the purchase price or part of it is payable by instalments and the goods were previously sold by a credit-broker to the seller, to that credit-broker,

any particular purpose for which the goods are being bought, there is an implied condition that the goods supplied under the contract are reasonably fit for that purpose, whether or not that is a purpose for which such goods are commonly supplied, except where the circumstances show that the buyer does not rely, or that it is unreasonable for him to rely, on the skill or judgment of the seller or credit-broker.

(4)   An implied condition or warranty about quality or fitness for a particular purpose may be annexed to a contract of sale by usage.

(5)   The preceding provisions of this section apply to a sale by a person who in the course of a business is acting as agent for another as they apply to a sale by a principal in the course of a business and either the buyer knows that fact or reasonable steps are taken to bring it to the notice of the buyer before the contract is made.

(6)   Goods of any kind are of merchantable quality within the meaning of subsection (2) above if they are as fit for the purpose or purposes for which goods of that kind are commonly bought as it is reasonable to expect having regard to any description applied to them, the price (if relevant) and all the other relevant circumstances.

HEALTH SERVICES ACT 1980
(1980, c. 53)

1. Power to make changes in the local administration of the health service in England and Wales

(1)   For the purposes of the administration of the health service in England and Wales after the passing of this Act—

(a)   regions in England need not consist wholly of areas having Area Health Authorities; and

(b)   Wales need not consist wholly of areas having such authorities,

and the Secretary of State may, by order under section 8(1) of the National Health Service Act 1977 (in this Act referred to as "the Act of 1977"), establish authorities for districts in English regions or in Wales in accordance with that section and may, by order under subsection (2) of that section, vary a district whether or not the variation entails the determination of a new or the abolition of an existing district.

(2)   The power to determine districts under that section may be exercised so that a district corresponds with an existing area and the power under that section to establish authorities for districts may be exercised by constituting the existing authority for an area the authority for a district (and re-naming it accordingly) without otherwise affecting its corporate status.

(3)   The authority for a district shall, according as is provided in the order establishing the authority, be called either—

(a)   a District Health Authority, or

(c)   by a special name indicating its connection with the district or any place in the district,

(5)   In this Act and the Act of 1977, except where the context requires otherwise, "District Health Authority" and "Area Health Authority" mean respectively the authority for a district and the authority for an area whether or not the name of the authority incorporates in the case of the authority for a district, the word "District".

(6)   A District Health Authority shall have in relation to its district the same functions as an Area Health Authority has in relation to its area and may perform functions outside its district on behalf of the Secretary of State to the same extent as an Area Health Authority can do so.

(8)   The Secretary of State may by order under this subsection make such repeals in or other modifications of the Act of 1977, this Act or any other enactment or instrument referring to Area Health Authorities as appear to him to be necessary having regard to the replacement of Area Health Authorities by District Health Authorities by virtue of this section.

(9)   The power to make an order under subsection (8) above shall be exercisable by statutory instrument which shall be subject to annulment in pursuance of a resolution of either House of Parliament.

(10)   Expressions used in this section and the Act of 1977 have the same meaning in this section as they have in that Act.

SUPREME COURT ACT 1981
(1981, c. 54)

33.   Powers of High Court exercisable before commencement of action

(1)   On the application of any person in accordance with rules of court, the High Court shall, in such circumstances as may be specified in the rules, have power to make an order providing for any one or more of the following matters, that is to say—

(a)   the inspection, photographing, preservation, custody and detention of property which appears to the court to be property which may become the subject-matter of subsequent proceedings in the High Court, or as to which any question may arise in any such proceedings; and

(b)   the taking of samples of any such property as is mentioned in paragraph (a), and the carrying out of any experiment on or with any such property.

(2)   On the application, in accordance with rules of court, of a person who appears to the High Court to be likely to be a party to subsequent proceedings in that court in which a claim in respect of personal injuries to a person, or in respect of a person's death, is likely to be made, the High Court shall, in such circumstances as may be specified in the rules, have power to order a person who appears to the court to be likely to be a party to the proceedings and to be likely to have or to have had in his possession, custody or power any documents which are relevant to an issue arising or likely to arise out of that claim—

(a)   to disclose whether those documents are in his possession, custody or power; and

(b)   to produce such of those documents as are in his possession, custody or power to the applicant or, on such conditions as may be specified in the order—

(i)   to the applicant's legal advisers; or

(ii)   to the applicant's legal advisers and any medical or other professional adviser of the applicant; or

(iii)   if the applicant has no legal adviser, to any medical or other professional adviser of the applicant.

34.   Power of High Court to order disclosure of documents, inspection of property etc. in proceedings for personal injuries or death

(1)   This section applies to any proceedings in the High Court in which a claim is made in respect of personal injuries to a person, or in respect of a person's death.

(2)   On the application, in accordance with rules of court, of a party to any proceedings to which this section applies, the High Court shall, in such circumstances as may be specified in the rules, have power to order a person who is not a party to the proceedings and who appears to the court to be likely to have in his possession, custody or power any documents which are relevant to an issue arising out of the said claim—

(a)   to disclose whether those documents are in his possession, custody or power; and

(b)   to produce such of those documents as are in his possession, custody or power to the applicant or, on such conditions as may be specified in the order—
(i)   to the applicant's legal advisers; or
(ii)   to the applicant's legal advisers and any medical or other professional adviser of the applicant; or
(iii)   if the applicant has no legal adviser, to any medical or other professional adviser of the applicant.
(3)   On the application, in accordance with rules of court, of a party to any proceedings to which this section applies, the High Court shall, in such circumstances as may be specified in the rules, have power to make an order providing for any one or more of the following matters, that is to say—
(a)   the inspection, photographing, preservation, custody and detention of property which is not the property of, or in the possession of, any party to the proceedings but which is the subject-matter of the proceedings or as to which any question arises in the proceedings;
(b)   the taking of samples of any such property as is mentioned in paragraph (a) and the carrying out of any experiment on or with any such property.
(4)   The preceding provisions of this section are without prejudice to the exercise by the High Court of any power to make orders which is exercisable apart from those provisions.

35.   Provisions supplementary to ss. 33 and 34

(1)   The High Court shall not make an order under section 33 or 34 if it considers that compliance with the order, if made, woud be likely to be injurious to the public interest.
(5)   In sections 32A, 33 and 34 and this section—
"property" includes any land, chattel or other corporeal property of any description;
"personal injuries" includes any disease and any impairment of a person's physical or mental condition.

41.   Wards of court

(1)   Subject to the provisions of this section, no minor shall be made a ward of court except by virtue of an order to that effect made by the High Court.
(2)   Where an application is made for such an order in respect of a minor, the minor shall become a ward of court on the making of the application, but shall cease to be a ward of court at the end of such period as may be prescribed unless within that period an order has been made in accordance with the application.
(2A)   Subsection (2) does not apply with respect to a child who is the subject of a care order (as defined by section 105 of the Children Act 1989).
(3)   The High Court may, either upon an application in that behalf or without such an application, order that any minor who is for the time being a ward of court shall cease to be a ward of court.

SUPPLY OF GOODS AND SERVICES ACT 1982
(1982, c. 29)

12.   The contracts concerned

(1)   In this Act a "contract for the supply of a service" means, subject to subsection (2) below, a contract under which a person ("the supplier") agrees to carry out a service.
(2)   For the purposes of this Act, a contract of service or apprenticeship is not a contract for the supply of a service.

(3)   Subject to subsection (2) above, a contract is a contract for the supply of a service for the purposes of this Act whether or not goods are also—

(a)   transferred or to be transferred, or

(b)   bailed or to be bailed by way of hire,

under the contract, and whatever is the nature of the consideration for which the service is to be carried out.

(4)   The Secretary of State may by order provide that one or more of sections 13 to 15 below shall not apply to services of a description specified in the order, and such an order may make different provision for different circumstances.

(5)   The power to make an order under subsection (4) above shall be exercisable by statutory instrument subject to annulment in pursuance of a resolution of either House of Parliament.

13.   Implied term about care and skill

In a contract for the supply of a service where the supplier is acting in the course of a business, there is an implied term that the supplier will carry out the service with reasonable care and skill.

16.   Exclusion of implied terms, etc.

(1)   Where a right, duty or liability would arise under a contract for the supply of a service by virtue of this Part of this Act, it may (subject to subsection (2) below and the 1977 Act) be negatived or varied by express agreement, or by the course of dealing between the parties, or by such usage as binds both parties to the contract.

(2)   An express term does not negative a term implied by this Part of this Act unless inconsistent with it.

(3)   Nothing in this Part of this Act prejudices—

(a)   any rule of law which imposes on the supplier a duty stricter than that imposed by section 13 or 14 above; or

(b)   subject to paragraph (a) above, any rule of law whereby any term not inconsistent with this Part of this Act is to be implied in a contract for the supply of a service.

(4)   This Part of this Act has effect subject to any other enactment which defines or restricts the rights, duties or liabilities arising in connection with a service of any description.

MENTAL HEALTH ACT 1983
(1983, c. 20)

PART I
APPLICATION OF ACT

1.   Application of Act: "mental disorder"

(1)   The provisions of this Act shall have effect with respect to the reception, care and treatment of mentally disordered patients, the management of their property and other related matters.

(2)   In this Act—

"mental disorder" means mental illness, arrested or incomplete development of mind, psychopathic disorder and any other disorder or disability of mind and "mentally disordered" shall be construed accordingly;

"severe mental impairment" means a state of arrested or incomplete development of mind which includes severe impairment of intelligence and social functioning and is associated with abnormally aggressive or seriously irresponsible conduct on the part of the person concerned and "severely mentally impaired" shall be construed accordingly;

"mental impairment" means a state of arrested or incomplete development of mind (not amounting to severe mental impairment) which includes significant impairment of intelligence and social functioning and is associated with abnormally aggressive or seriously irresponsible conduct on the part of the person concerned and "mentally impaired" shall be construed accordingly;

"psychopathic disorder" means a persistent disorder or diasability of mind (whether or not including significant impairment of intelligence) which results in abnormally aggressive or seriously irresponsible conduct on the part of the person concerned;

and other expressions shall have the meanings assigned to them in section 145 below.

(3)   Nothing in subsection (2) above shall be construed as implying that a person may be dealt with under this Act as suffering from mental disorder, or from any form of mental disorder described in this section, by reason only of promiscuity or other immoral conduct, sexual deviancy or dependence on alcohol or drugs.

PART II
COMPULSORY ADMISSION TO HOSPITAL AND GUARDIANSHIP
Procedure for hospital admission

2.   Admission for assessment

(1)   A patient may be admitted to a hospital and detained there for the period allowed by subsection (4) below in pursuance of an application (in this Act referred to as "an application for admission for assessment") made in accordance with subsections (2) and (3) below.

(2)   An application for admission for assessment may be made in respect of a patient on the grounds that—

(a)   he is suffering from mental disorder of a nature or degree which warrants the detention of the patient in a hospital for assessment (or for assessment followed by medical treatment) for at least a limited period; and

(b)   he ought to be so detained in the interests of his own health or safety or with a view to the protection of other persons.

(3)   An application for admission for assessment shall be founded on the written recommendations in the prescribed form of two registered medical practitioners, including in each case a statement that in the opinion of the practitioner the conditions set out in subsection (2) above are complied with.

(4)   Subject to the provisions of section 29(4) below, a patient admitted to hospital in pursuance of an application for admission for assessment may be detained for a period not exceeding 28 days beginning with the day on which he is admitted, but shall not be detained after the expiration of that period unless before it has expired he has become liable to be detained by virtue of a subsequent application, order or direction under the following provisions of this Act.

3.   Admission for treatment

(1)   A patient may be admitted to a hospital and detained there for the period allowed by the following provisions of this Act in pursuance of an application (in this Act referred to as "an application for admission for treatment") made in accordance with this section.

(2)   An application for admission for treatment may be made in respect of a patient on the grounds that—

(a)   he is suffering from mental illness, severe mental impairment, psychopathic disorder or mental impairment and his mental disorder is of a nature or degree which makes it appropriate for him to receive medical treatment in a hospital; and

(b)   in the case of psychopathic disorder or mental impairment, such treatment is likely to alleviate or prevent a deterioration of his condition; and

(c)   it is necessary for the health or safety of the patient or for the protection of other persons that he should receive such treatment and it cannot be provided unless he is detained under this section.

(3)   An application for admission for treatment shall be founded on the written recommendations in the prescribed form of two registered medical practitioners, including in each case a statement that in the opinion of the practitioner the conditions set out in subsection (2) above are complied with; and each such recommendation shall include—

(a)   such particulars as may be prescribed of the grounds for that opinion so far as it relates to the conditions set out in paragraphs (a) and (b) of that subsection; and

(b)   a statement of the reasons for that opinion so far as it relates to the conditions set out in paragraph (c) of that subsection, specifying whether other methods of dealing with the patient are available and, if so, why they are not appropriate.

4.   Admission for assessment in cases of emergency

(1)   In any case of urgent necessity, an application for admission for assessment may be made in respect of a patient in accordance with the following provisions of this section, and any application so made is in this Act referred to as "an emergency application".

(2)   An emergency application may be made either by an approved social worker or by the nearest relative of the patient; and every such application shall include a statement that it is of urgent necessity for the patient to be admitted and detained under section 2 above, and that compliance with the provisions of this Part of this Act relating to applications under that section would involve undesirable delay.

(3)   An emergency application shall be sufficient in the first instance if founded on one of the medical recommendations required by section 2 above, given, if practicable, by a practitioner who has previous acquaintance with the patient and otherwise complying with the requirements of section 12 below so far as applicable to a single recommendation, and verifying the statement referred to in subsection (2) above.

(4)   An emergency application shall cease to have effect on the expiration of a period of 72 hours from the time when the patient is admitted to the hospital unless—

(a)   the second medical recommendation required by section 2 above is given and received by the managers within that period; and

(b)   that recommendation and the recommendation referred to in subsection (3) above together comply with all the requirements of section 12 below (other than the requirement as to the time of signature of the second recommendation).

(5)   In relation to an emergency application, section 11 below shall have effect as if in subsection (5) of that section for the words "the period of 14 days ending with the date of the application" there were substituted the words "the previous 24 hours".

5.   Application in respect of patient already in hospital

(1)   An application for the admission of a patient to a hospital may be made under this Part of this Act notwithstanding that the patient is already an in-patient in that hospital or, in the case of an application for admission for treatment that the patient is for the time being liable to be detained in the hospital in pursuance of an application for admission for assessment; and where an application is so made the patient shall be treated for the purposes of this Part of this Act as if he had been admitted to the hospital at the time when that application was received by the managers.

(2)   If, in the case of a patient who is an in-patient in a hospital, it appears to the registered medical practitioner in charge of the treatment of the patient that an application ought to be made under this Part of this Act for the admission of the patient to hospital, he may furnish to the managers a report in writing to that effect; and in any such case the patient may be detained in the hospital for a period of 72 hours from the time when the report is so furnished.

(3)   The registered medical practitioner in charge of the treatment of a patient in a hospital may nominate one (but not more than one) other registered medical practitioner on the staff of that hospital to act for him under subsection (2) above in his absence.

(4)   If, in the case of a patient who is receiving treatment for mental disorder as an in-patient in a hospital, it appears to a nurse of the prescribed class—

(a)   that the patient is suffering from mental disorder to such a degree that it is necessary for his health or safety or for the protection of others for him to be immediately restrained from leaving the hospital; and

(b)   that it is not practicable to secure the immediate attendance of a practitioner for the purpose of furnishing a report under subsection (2) above,

the nurse may record that fact in writing; and in that event the patient may be detained in the hospital for a period of six hours from the time when that fact is so recorded or until the earlier arrival at the place where the patient is detained of a practitioner having power to furnish a report under that subsection.

(5)   A record made under subsection (4) above shall be delivered by the nurse (or by a person authorised by the nurse in that behalf) to the managers of the hospital as soon as possible after it is made; and where a record is made under that subsection the period mentioned in subsection (2) above shall begin at the time when it is made.

(6)   The reference in subsection (1) above to an in-patient does not include an in-patient who is liable to be detained in pursuance of an application under this Part of this Act and the references in subsections (2) and (4) above do not include an in-patient who is liable to be detained in a hospital under this Part of this Act.

(7)   In subsection (4) above "prescribed" means prescribed by an order made by the Secretary of State.

6.   Effect of application for admission

(1)   An application for the admission of a patient to a hospital under this Part of this Act, duly completed in accordance with the provisions of this Part of this Act, shall be sufficient authority for the applicant, or any person authorised by the applicant, to take the patient and convey him to the hospital at any time within the following period, that is to say—

(a)   in the case of an application other than an emergency application, the period of 14 days beginning with the date on which the patient was last examined by a registered medical practitioner before giving a medical recommendation for the purposes of the application;

(b)   in the case of an emergency application, the period of 24 hours beginning at the time when the patient was examined by the practitioner giving the medical recommendation which is referred to in section 4(3) above, or at the time when the application is made, whichever is the earlier.

(2)   Where a patient is admitted within the said period to the hospital specified in such an application as is mentioned in subsection (1) above, or, being within that hospital, is treated by virtue of section 5 above as if he had been so admitted, the application shall be sufficient authority for the managers to detain the patient in the hospital in accorance with the provisions of this Act.

(3)   Any application for the admission of a patient under this Part of this Act which appears to be duly made and to be founded on the necessary medical recommendations may be acted upon without further proof of the signature or qualification of the person by whom the application or any such medical recommendation is made or given or of any matter of fact or opinion stated in it.

(4)   Where a patient is admitted to a hospital in pursuance of an application for admission for treatment, any previous application under this Part of this Act by virtue of which he was liable to be detained in a hospital or subject to guardianship shall cease to have effect.

Guardianship

7. Application for guardianship

(1) A patient who has attained the age of 16 years may be received into guardianship, for the period allowed by the following provisions of this Act, in pursuance of an application (in this Act referred to as "a guardianship application") made in accordance with this section.

(2) A guardianship application may be made in respect of a patient on the grounds that—

(a) he is suffering from mental disorder, being mental illness, severe mental impairment, psychopathic disorder or mental impairment and his mental disorder is of a nature or degree which warrants his reception into guardianship under this section; and

(b) it is necessary in the interests of the welfare of the patient or for the protection of other persons that the patient should be so received.

(3) A guardianship application shall be founded on the written recommendations in the prescribed form of two registered medical practitioners, including in each case a statement that in the opinion of the practitioner the conditions set out in subsection (2) above are complied with; and each such recommendation shall include—

(a) such particulars as may be prescribed of the grounds for that opinion so far as it relates to the conditions set out in paragraph (a) of that subsection; and

(b) a statement of the reasons for that opinion so far as it relates to the conditions set out in paragraph (b) of that subsection.

(4) A guardianship application shall state the age of the patient or, if his exact age is not known to the applicant, shall state (if it be the fact) that the patient is believed to have attained the age of 16 years.

(5) The person named as guardian in a guardianship application may be either a local social services authority or any other person (including the applicant himself); but a guardianship application in which a person other than a local social services authority is named as guardian shall be of no effect unless it is accepted on behalf of that person by the local social services authority for the area in which he resides, and shall be accompanied by a statement in writing by that person that he is willing to act as guardian.

8. Effect of guardianship application, etc.

(1) Where a guardianship application, duly made under the provisions of this Part of this Act and forwarded to the local social services authority within the period allowed by subsection (2) below is accepted by that authority, the application shall, subject to regulations made by the Secretary of State, confer on the authority or person named in the application as guardian, to the exclusion of any other person—

(a) the power to require the patient to reside at a place specified by the authority or person named as guardian;

(b) the power to require the patient to attend at places and times so specified for the purpose of medical treatment, occupation, education or training;

(c) the power to require access to the patient to be given, at any place where the patient is residing, to any registered medical practitioner, approved social worker or other person so specified.

(2) The period within which a guardianship application is required for the purposes of this section to be forwarded to the local social services authority is the period of 14 days beginning with the date on which the patient was last examined by a registered medical practitioner before giving a medical recommendation for the purposes of the application.

(3) A guardianship application which appears to be duly made and to be founded on the necessary medical recommendations may be acted upon without further proof of

the signature or qualification of the person by whom the application or any such medical recommendation is made or given, or of any matter of fact or opinion stated in the application.

(4)   If within the period of 14 days beginning with the day on which a guardianship application has been accepted by the local social services authority the application, or any medical recommendation given for the purposes of the application, is found to be in any respect incorrect or defective, the application or recommendation may, within that period and with the consent of that authority, be amended by the person by whom it was signed; and upon such amendment being made the application or recommendation shall have effect and shall be deemed to have had effect as if it had been originally made as so amended.

(5)   Where a patient is received into gurdianship in pursuance of a guardianship application, any previous application under this Part of this Act by virtue of which he was subject to guardianship or liable to be detained in a hospital shall cease to have effect.

9.   Regulations as to guardianship

(1)   Subject to the provisions of this Part of this Act, the Secretary of State may make regulations—

(a)   for regulating the exercise by the guardians of patients received into guardianship under this Part of this Act of their powers as such; and

(b)   for imposing on such guardians, and upon local social services authorities in the case of patients under the guardianship of persons other than local social services authorities, such duties as he considers necessary or expedient in the interests of the patients.

(2)   Regulations under this section may in particular make provision for requiring the patients to be visited, on such occasions or at such intervals as may be prescribed by the regulations, on behalf of such local social services authorities as may be so prescribed, and shall provide for the appointment, in the case of every patient subject to the guardianship of a person other than a local social services authority, of a registered medical practitioner to act as the nominated medical attendant of the patient.

10.   Transfer of guardianship in case of death, incapacity, etc., of guardian

(1)   If any person (other than a local social services authority) who is the guardian of a patient received into guardianship under this Part of this Act—

(a)   dies; or

(b)   gives notice in writing to the local social services authority that he desires to relinquish the functions of guardian,

the guardianship of the patient shall thereupon vest in the local social services authority, but without prejudice to any power to transfer the patient into the guardianship of another person in pursuance of regulations under section 19 below.

(2)   If any such person, not having given notice under subsection (1)(b) above, is incapacitated by illness or any other cause from performing the functions of guardian of the patient, those functions may, during his incapacity, be performed on his behalf by the local social services authority or by any other person approved for the purposes by that authority.

(3)   If it appears to the county court, upon application made by an approved social worker, that any person other than a local social services authority having the guardianship of a patient received into guardianship under this Part of this Act has performed his functions negligently or in a manner contrary to the interests of the welfare of the patient, the court may order that the guardianship of the patient be transferred to the local social services authority or to any other person approved for the purpose by that authority.

(4)   Where the guardianship of a patient is transferred to a local social services authority or other person by or under this section, subsection (2)(c) of section 19 below shall apply as if the patient had been transferred into the guardianship of that authority or person in pursuance of regulations under that section.

General provisions as to applications and recommendations

11.   General provisions as to applications

(1)   Subject to the provisions of this section, an application for admission for assessment, an application for admission for treatment and a guardianship application may be made either by the nearest relative of the patient or by an approved social worker; and every such application shall specify the qualification of the applicant to make the application.

(2)   Every application for admission shall be addressed to the managers of the hospital to which admission is sought and every guardianship application shall be forwarded to the local social services authority named in the application as guardian, or, as the case may be, to the local social services authority for the area in which the person so named resides.

(3)   Before or within a reasonable time after an application for the admission of a patient for assessment is made by an approved social worker, that social worker shall take such steps as are practicable to inform the person (if any) appearing to be the nearest relative of the patient that the application is to be or has been made and of the power of the nearest relative under section 23(2)(a) below.

(4)   Neither an application for admission for treatment nor a guardianship application shall be made by an approved social worker if the nearest relative of the patient has notified that social worker, or the local social services authority by whom that social worker is appointed, that he objects to the application being made and, without prejudice to the foregoing provision, no such application shall be made by such a social worker except after consultation with the person (if any) appearing to be the nearest relative of the patient unless it appears to that social worker that in the circumstances such consultation is not reasonably practicable or would involve unreasonable delay.

(5)   None of the applications mentioned in subsection (1) above shall be made by any person in respect of a patient unless that person has personally seen the patient within the period of 14 days ending with the date of the application.

(6)   An application for admission for treatment or a guardianship application, and any recommendation given for the purposes of such an application, may describe the patient as suffering from more than one of the following forms of mental disorder, namely mental illness, severe mental impairment, psychopathic disorder or mental impairment; but the application shall be of no effect unless the patient is described in each of the recommendations as suffering from the same form of mental disorder, whether or not he is also described in either of those recommendations as suffering from another form.

(7)   Each of the applications mentioned in subsection (1) above shall be sufficient if the recommendations on which it is founded are given either as separate recommendations, each signed by a registered medical practitioner, or as a joint recommendation signed by two such practitioners.

12.   General provisions as to medical recommendations

(1)   The recommendations required for the purposes of an application for the admission of a patient under this Part of this Act (in this Act referred to as "medical recommendations") shall be signed on or before the date of the application, and shall be given by practitioners who have personally examined the patient either together or separately, but where they have examined the patient separately not more than five days must have elapsed between the days on which the separate examination took place.

(2) Of the medical recommendations given for the purposes of any such application, one shall be given by a practitioner approved for the purposes of this section by the Secretary of State as having special experience in the diagnosis or treatment of mental disorder; and unless that practitioner has previous acquaintance with the patient, the other such recommendation shall, if practicable, be given by a registered medical practitioner who has such previous acquaintance.

(3) Subject to subsection (4) below, where the application is for the admission of the patient to a hospital which is not a mental nursing home, one (but not more than one) of the medical recommendations may be given by a practitioner on the staff of that hospital, except where the patient is proposed to be accommodated under section 65 or 66 of the National Health Service Act 1977 or paragraph 14 of Schedule 2 to the National Health Service and Community Care Act 1990 (which relate to accommodation for private patients).

(4) Subsection (3) above shall not preclude both the medical recommendations being given by practitioners on the staff of the hospital in question if—

(a) compliance with that subsection would result in delay involving serious risk to the health or safety of the patient; and

(b) one of the practitioners giving the recommendations works at the hospital for less than half of the time which he is bound by contract to devote to work in the health service; and

(c) where one of those practitioners is a consultant, the other does not work (whether at the hospital or elsewhere) in a grade in which he is under that consultant's directions.

(5) A medical recommendation for the purposes of an application for the admission of a patient under this Part of this Act shall not be given by—

(a) the applicant;

(b) a partner of the applicant or of a practitioner by whom another medical recommendation is given for the purposes of the same application;

(c) a person employed as an assistant by the applicant or by any such practitioner;

(d) a person who receives or has an interest in the receipt of any payments made on account of the maintenance of the patient; or

(e) except as provided by subsection (3) or (4) above, a practitioner on the staff of the hospital to which the patient is to be admitted,

or by the husband, wife, father, father-in-law, mother, mother-in-law, son, son-in-law, daughter, daughter-in-law, brother, brother-in-law, sister or sister-in-law of the patient, or of any person mentioned in paragraphs (a) to (e) above, or of a practitioner by whom another medical recommendation is given for the purposes of the same application.

(6) A general practitioner who is employed part-time in a hospital shall not for the purposes of this section be regarded as a practitioner on its staff.

(7) Subsections (1), (2) and (5) above shall apply to applications for guardianship as they apply to applications for admission but with the substitution for paragraph (e) of subsection (5) above of the following paragraph—

"(e) the person named as guardian in the application ".

13. Duty of approved social workers to make applications for admission or guardianship

(1) It shall be the duty of an approved social worker to make an application for admission to hospital or a guardianship application in respect of a patient within the area of the local social services authority by which that officer is appointed in any case where he is satisfied that such an application ought to be made and is of the opinion, having regard to any wishes expressed by relatives of the patient or any other relevant circumstances, that it is necessary or proper for the application to be made by him.

(2) Before making an application for the admission of a patient to hospital an approved social worker shall interview the patient in a suitable manner and satisfy himself that detention in a hospital is in all the circumstances of the case the most appropriate way of providing the care and medical treatment of which the patient stands in need.

(3) An application under this section by an approved social worker may be made outside the area of the local social services authority by which he is appointed.

(4) It shall be the duty of a local social services authority, if so required by the nearest relative of a patient residing in their area, to direct an approved social worker as soon as practicable to take the patient's case into consideration under subsection (1) above with a view to making an application for his admission to hospital; and if in any such case that approved social worker decides not to make an application he shall inform the nearest relative of his reasons in writing.

(5) Nothing in this section shall be construed as authorising or requiring an application to be made by an approved social worker in contravention of the provisions of section 11(4) above, or as restricting the power of an approved social worker to make any application under this Act.

14. Social reports
Where a patient is admitted to a hospital in pursuance of an application (other than an emergency application) made under this Part of this Act by his nearest relative, the managers of the hospital shall as soon as practicable give notice of that fact to the local social services authority for the area in which the patient resided immediately before his admission; and that authority shall as soon as practicable arrange for a social worker of their social services department to interview the patient and provide the managers with a report of his social circumstances.

15. Rectification of applications and recommendations
(1) If within the period of 14 days beginning with the day on which a patient has been admitted to a hospital in pursuance of an application for admission for assessment or for treatment the application, or any medical recommendation given for the purpose of the application, is found to be in any respect incorrect or defective, the application or recommendation may, within that period and with the consent of the managers of the hospital, be amended by the person by whom it was signed; and upon such amendment being made the application or recommendation shall have effect and shall be deemed to have had effect as if it had been originally made as so amended.

(2) Without prejudice to subsection (1) above, if within the period mentioned in that subsection it appears to the managers of the hospital that one of the two medical recommendations on which an application for the admission of a patient is founded is insufficient to warrant the detention of the patient in pursuance of the application, they may, within that period, give notice in writing to that effect to the applicant; and where any such notice is given in respect of a medical recommendation, that recommendation shall be disregarded, but the application shall be, and shall be deemed always to have been, sufficient if—

(a) a fresh medical recommendation complying with the relevant provisions of this Part of this Act (other than the provisions relating to the time of signature and the interval between examinations) is furnished to the managers within that period; and

(b) that recommendation, and the other recommendation on which the application is founded, together comply with those provisions.

(3) Where the medical recommendations upon which an application for admission is founded are, taken together, insufficient to warrant the detention of the patient in pursuance of the application, a notice under subsection (2) above may be given in respect of either of those recommendations; but this subsection shall not apply in a case where the application is of no effect by virtue of section 11(6) above.

(4)   Nothing in this section shall be construed as authorising the giving of notice in respect of an application made as an emergency application, or the detention of a patient admitted in pursuance of such an application, after the period of 72 hours referred to in section 4(4) above, unless the conditions set out in paragraphs (a) and (b) of that section are complied with or would be complied with apart from any error or defect to which this section applies.

Position of patients subject to detention or guardianship

16.   Reclassification of patients
(1)   If in the case of a patient who is for the time being detained in a hospital in pursuance of an application for admission for treatment, or subject to guardianship in pursuance of a guardianship application, it appears to the appropriate medical officer that the patient is suffering from a form of mental disorder other than the form or forms specified in the application, he may furnish to the managers of the hospital, or to the guardian, as the case may be, a report to that effect; and where a report is so furnished, the application shall have effect as if that other form of mental disorder were specified in it.

(2)   Where a report under subsection (1) above in respect of a patient detained in a hospital is to the effect that he is suffering from psychopathic disorder or mental impairment but not from mental illness or severe mental impairment the appropriate medical officer shall include in the report a statement of his opinion whether further medical treatment in hospital is likely to alleviate or prevent a deterioration of the patient's condition; and if he states that in his opinion such treatment is not likely to have that effect the authority of the managers to detain the patient shall cease.

(3)   Before furnishing a report under subsection (1) above the appropriate medical officer shall consult one or more other persons who have been professionally concerned with the patient's medical treatment.

(4)   Where a report is furnished under this section in respect of a patient, the managers or guardian shall cause the patient and the nearest relative to be informed.

(5)   In this section "appropriate medical officer" means—
   (a)   in the case of a patient who is subject to the guardianship of a person other than a local social services authority, the nominated medical attendant of the patient; and
   (b)   in any other case, the responsible medical officer.

17.   Leave of absence from hospital
(1)   The responsible medical officer may grant to any patient who is for the time being liable to be detained in a hospital under this Part of this Act leave to be absent from the hospital subject to such conditions (if any) as that officer considers necessary in the interests of the patient or for the protection of other persons.

(2)   Leave of absence may be granted to a patient under this section either indefinitely or on specified occasions or for any specified period; and where leave is so granted for a specified period, that period may be extended by further leave granted in the absence of the patient.

(3)   Where it appears to the responsible medical officer that it is necessary so to do in the interests of the patient or for the protection of other persons, he may, upon granting leave of absence under this section, direct that the patient remain in custody during his absence; and where leave of absence is so granted the patient may be kept in the custody of any officer on the staff of the hospital, or of any other person authorised in writing by the managers of the hospital or, if the patient is required in accordance with conditions imposed on the grant of leave of absence to reside in another hospital, of any officer on the staff of that other hospital.

(4)   In any case where a patient is absent from a hospital in pursuance of leave of absence granted under this section, and it appears to the responsible medical officer that it is necessary so to do in the interests of the patient's health or safety or for the protection of other persons, that officer may, subject to subsection (5) below, by notice in writing given to the patient or to the person for the time being in charge of the patient, revoke the leave of absence and recall the patient to the hospital.

(5)   A patient to whom leave of absence is granted under this section shall not be recalled under subsection (4) above after he has ceased to be liable to be detained under this Part of this Act; and without prejudice to any other provision of this Part of this Act any such patient shall cease to be so liable at the expiration of the period of six months beginning with the first day of his absence on leave unless either—

(a)   he has returned to the hospital, or has been transferred to another hospital under the following provisions of this Act, before the expiration of that period; or

(b)   he is absent without leave at the expiration of that period.

18.   Return and readmission of patients absent without leave

(1)   Where a patient who is for the time being liable to be detained under this Part of this Act in a hospital—

(a)   absents himself from the hospital without leave granted under section 17 above; or

(b)   fails to return to the hospital on any occasion on which, or at the expiration of any period for which, leave of absence was granted to him under that section, or upon being recalled under that section; or

(c)   absents himself without permission from any place where he is required to reside in accordance with conditions imposed on the grant of leave of absence under that section,

he may, subject to the provisions of this section, be taken into custody and returned to the hospital or place by any approved social worker, by any officer on the staff of the hospital, by any constable, or by any person authorised in writing by the managers of the hospital.

(2)   Where the place referred to in paragraph (c) of subsection (1) above is a hospital other than the one in which the patient is for the time being liable to be detained, the references in that subsection to an officer on the staff of the hospital and the managers of the hospital shall respectively include references to an officer on the staff of the first-mentioned hospital and the managers of that hospital.

(3)   Where a patient who is for the time being subject to guardianship under this Part of this Act absents himself without the leave of the guardian from the place at which he is required by the guardian to reside, he may, subject to the provisions of this section, be taken into custody and returned to that place by any officer on the staff of a local social services authority, by any constable, or by any person authorised in writing by the guardian or a local social services authority.

(4)   A patient shall not be taken into custody under this section after the expiration of the period of 28 days beginning with the first day of his absence without leave; and a patient who has not returned or been taken into custody under this section within the said period shall cease to be liable to be detained or subject to guardianship, as the case may be, at the expiration of that period.

(5)   A patient shall not be taken into custody under this section if the period for which he is liable to be detained is that specified in section 2(4), 4(4) or 5(2) or (4) above and that period has expired.

(6)   In this Act "absent without leave" means absent from any hospital or other place and liable to be taken into custody and returned under this section, and related expressions shall be construed accordingly.

19. Regulations as to transfer of patients

(1)   In such circumstances and subject to such conditions as may be prescribed by regulations made by the Secretary of State—

(a)   a patient who is for the time being liable to be detained in a hospital by virtue of an application under this Part of this Act may be transferred to another hospital or into the guardianship of a local social services authority or of any person approved by such an authority;

(b)   a patient who is for the time being subject to the guardianship of a local social services authority or other person by virtue of an application under this Part of this Act may be transferred into the guardianship of another local social services authority or person, or be transferred to a hospital.

(2)   Where a patient is transferred in pursuance of regulations under this section, the provisions of this Part of this Act (including this subsection) shall apply to him as follows, that is to say—

(a)   in the case of a patient who is liable to be detained in a hospital by virtue of an application for admission for assessment or for treatment and is transferred to another hospital, as if the application were an application for admission to that other hospital and as if the patient had been admitted to that other hospital at the time when he was originally admitted in pursuance of the application;

(b)   in the case of a patient who is liable to be detained in a hospital by virtue of such an application and is transferred into guardianship, as if the application were a guardianship application duly accepted at the said time;

(c)   in the case of a patient who is subject to guardianship by virtue of a guardianship application and is transferred into the guardianship of another authority or person, as if the application were for his reception into the guardianship of that authority or person and had been accepted at the time when it was originally accepted;

(d)   in the case of a patient who is subject to guardianship by virtue of a guardianship application and is transferred to a hospital, as if the guardianship application were an application for admission to that hospital for treatment and as if the patient had been admitted to the hospital at the time when the application was originally accepted.

(3)   Without prejudice to subsections (1) and (2) above, any patient, who is for the time being liable to be detained under this Part of this Act in a hospital vested in the Secretary of State for the purposes of his functions under the National Health Service Act 1977 or any accommodation used under Part I of that Act by the managers of such a hospital, or in a hospital vested in a National Health Service trust may at any time be removed to any other such hospital or accommodation which is managed by the managers of, or is vested in the National Health Service trust for, the first mentioned hospital; and paragraph (a) of subsection (2) above shall apply in relation to a patient so removed as it applies in relation to a patient transferred in pursuance of regulations made under this section.

(4)   Regulations made under this section may make provision for regulating the conveyance to their destination of patients authorised to be transferred or removed in pursuance of the regulations or under subsection (3) above.

Duration of detention or guardianship and discharge

20. Duration of authority

(1)   Subject to the following provisions of this Part of this Act, a patient admitted to hospital in pursuance of an application for admission for treatment, and a patient placed under guardianship in pursuance of a guardianship application, may be detained in a hospital or kept under guardianship for a period not exceeding six months beginning with the day on which he was so admitted, or the day on which the guardianship application was accepted, as the case may be, but shall not be so detained or kept for

any longer period unless the authority for his detention or guardianship is renewed under this section.

(2)   Authority for the detention or guardianship of a patient may, unless the patient has previously been discharged, be renewed—

    (a)   from the expiration of the period referred to in subsection (1) above, for a further period of six months;

    (b)   from the expiration of any period of renewal under paragraph (a) above, for a further period of one year,

and so on for periods of one year at a time.

(3)   Within the period of two months ending on the day on which a patient who is liable to be detained in pursuance of an application for admission for treatment would cease under this section to be so liable in default of the renewal of the authority for his detention, it shall be the duty of the responsible medical officer—

    (a)   to examine the patient; and

    (b)   if it appears to him that the conditions set out in subsection (4) below are satisfied, to furnish to the managers of the hospital where the patient is detained a report to that effect in the prescribed form;

and where such a report is furnished in respect of a patient the managers shall, unless they discharge the patient, cause him to be informed.

(4)   The conditions referred to in subsection (3) above are that—

    (a)   the patient is suffering from mental illness, severe mental impairment, psychopathic disorder or mental impairment, and his mental disorder is of a nature or degree which makes it appropriate for him to receive medical treatment in a hospital; and

    (b)   such treatment is likely to alleviate or prevent a deterioration of his condition; and

    (c)   it is necessary for the health or safety of the patient or for the protection of other persons that he should receive such treatment and that it cannot be provided unless he continues to be detained;

but, in the case of mental illness or severe mental impairment, it shall be an alternative to the condition specified in paragraph (b) above that the patient, if discharged, is unlikely to be able to care for himself, to obtain the care which he needs or to guard himself against serious exploitation.

(5)   Before furnishing a report under subsection (3) above the responsible medical officer shall consult one or more other persons who have been professionally concerned with the patient's medical treatment.

(6)   Within the period of two months ending with the day on which a patient who is subject to guardianship under this Part of this Act would cease under this section to be so liable in default of the renewal of the authority for his guardianship, it shall be the duty of the appropriate medical officer—

    (a)   to examine the patient; and

    (b)   if it appears to him that the conditions set out in subsection (7) below are satisfied, to furnish to the guardian and, where the guardian is a person other than a local social services authority, to the responsible local social services authority a report to that effect in the prescribed form;

and where such a report is furnished in respect of a patient, the local social services authority shall, unless they discharge the patient, cause him to be informed.

(7)   The conditions referred to in subsection (6) above are that—

    (a)   the patient is suffering from mental illness, severe mental impairment, psychopathic disorder or mental impairment and his mental disorder is of a nature or degree which warrants his reception into guardianship; and

    (b)   it is necessary in the interests of the welfare of the patient or for the protection of other persons that the patient should remain under guardianship.

(8) Where a report is duly furnished under subsection (3) or (6) above, the authority for the detention or guardianship of the patient shall be thereby renewed for the period prescribed in that case by subsection (2) above.

(9) Where the form of mental disorder specified in a report furnished under subsection (3) or (6) above is a form of disorder other than that specified in the application for admission for treatment or, as the case may be, in the guardianship application, that application shall have effect as if that other form of mental disorder were specified in it; and where on any occasion a report specifying such a form of mental disorder is furnished under either of those subsections the appropriate medical officer need not on that occasion furnish a report under section 16 above.

(10) In this section "appropriate medical officer" has the same meaning as in section 16(5) above.

21. Special provisions as to patients absent without leave

(1) If on the day on which, apart from this section, a patient would cease to be liable to be detained or subject to guardianship under this Part of this Act or, within the period of one week ending with that day, the patient is absent without leave, he shall not cease to be so liable or subject—

(a) in any case, until the expiration of the period during which he can be taken into custody under section 18 above or the day on which he is returned or returns himself to the hospital or place where he ought to be, whichever is the earlier; and

(b) if he is so returned or so returns himself within the period first mentioned in paragraph (a) above, until the expiration of the period of one week beginning with the day on which he is so returned or so returns.

(2) Where the period for which a patient is liable to be detained or subject to guardianship is extended by virtue of this section, any examination and report to be made and furnished under section 20(3) or (6) above may be made and furnished within that period as so extended.

(3) Where the authority for the detention or guardianship of a patient is renewed by virtue of this section after the day on which, apart from this section, the authority would have expired under section 20 above, the renewal shall take effect as from that day.

22. Special provisions as to patients sentenced to imprisonment, etc.

(1) Where a patient who is liable to be detained by virtue of an application for admission for treatment or is subject to guardianship by virtue of a guardianship application is detained in custody in pursuance of any sentence or order passed or made by a court in the United Kingdom (including an order committing or remanding him in custody), and is so detained for a period exceeding, or for successive periods exceeding in the aggregate, six months, the application shall cease to have effect at the expiration of that period.

(2) Where any such patient is so detained in custody but the application does not cease to have effect under subsection (1) above, then—

(a) if apart from this subsection the patient would have ceased to be liable to be so detained or subject to guardianship on or before the day on which he is discharged from custody, he shall not cease and shall be deemed not to have ceased to be so liable or subject until the end of that day; and

(b) in any case, sections 18 and 21 above shall apply in relation to the patient as if he had absented himself without leave on that day.

23. Discharge of patients

(1) Subject to the provisions of this section and section 25 below, a patient who is for the time being liable to be detained or subject to guardianship under this Part of this Act shall cease to be so liable or subject if an order in writing discharging him from

detention or guardianship (in this Act referred to as "an order for discharge") is made in accordance with this section.

(2)   An order for discharge may be made in respect of a patient—

(a)   where the patient is liable to be detained in a hospital in pursuance of an application for admission for assessment or for treatment by the responsible medical officer, by the managers or by the nearest relative of the patient;

(b)   where the patient is subject to guardianship, by the responsible medical officer, by the responsible local social services authority or by the nearest relative of the patient.

(3)   Where the patient is liable to be detained in a mental nursing home in pursuance of an application for admission for assessment or for treatment, an order for his discharge may, without prejudice to subsection (2) above, be made by the Secretary of State and, if the patient is maintained under a contract with a National Health Service trust, Regional Health Authority, District Health Authority or Special Health Authority, by that trust or authority.

(4)   The powers conferred by this section on any authority, trust or body of persons may be exercised subject to subsection (5) below by any three or more members of that authority, trust or body authorised by them in that behalf or by three or more members of a committee or sub-committee of that authority, trust or body which has been authorised by them in that behalf.

(5)   The reference in subsection (4) above to the members of an authority, trust or body or the members of a committee or sub-committee of an authority, trust or body,—

(a)   in the case of a District or Special Health Authority or a committee or sub-committee of such an authority, is a reference only to the chairman of the authority and such members (of the authority, committee or sub-committee, as the case may be) as are not also officers of the authority, within the meaning of the National Health Service Act 1977; and

(b)   in the case of a National Health Service trust or a committee or sub-committee of such a trust, is a reference only to the chairman of the trust and such directors or (in the case of a committee or sub-committee) members as are not also employees of the trust.

24.   Visiting and examination of patients

(1)   For the purpose of advising as to the exercise by the nearest relative of a patient who is liable to be detained or subject to guardianship under this Part of this Act of any power to order his discharge, any registered medical practitioner authorised by or on behalf of the nearest relative of the patient may, at any reasonable time, visit the patient and examine him in private.

(2)   Any registered medical practitioner authorised for the purposes of subsection (1) above to visit and examine a patient may require the production of and inspect any records relating to the detention or treatment of the patient in any hospital.

(3)   Where application is made by the Secretary of State or a Regional Health Authority, District Health Authority, National Health Service trust or special health authority to exercise, in respect of a patient liable to be detained in a mental nursing home, any power to make an order for his discharge, the following persons, that is to say—

(a)   any registered medical practitioner authorised by the Secretary of State or, as the case may be, that authority or trust; and

(b)   any other person (whether a registered medical practitioner or not) authorised under Part II of the Registered Homes Act 1984 to inspect the home, may at any reasonable time visit the patient and interview him in private.

(4)   Any person authorised for the purposes of subsection (3) above to visit a patient may require the production of and inspect any documents constituting or alleged to

constitute the authority for the detention of the patient under this Part of this Act; and any person so authorised, who is a registered medical practitioner, may examine the patient in private, and may require the production of and inspect any other records relating to the treatment of the patient in the home.

25. Restrictions on discharge by nearest relative

(1) An order for the discharge of a patient who is liable to be detained in a hospital shall not be made by his nearest relative except after giving not less than 72 hours' notice in writing to the managers of the hospital; and if, within 72 hours after such notice has been given, the responsible medical officer furnishes to the managers a report certifying that in the opinion of that officer the patient, if discharged, would be likely to act in a manner dangerous to other persons or to himself—

(a) any order for the discharge of the patient made by that relative in pursuance of the notice shall be of no effect; and

(b) no further order for the discharge of the patient shall be made by that relative during the period of six months beginning with the date of the report.

(2) In any case where a report under subsection (1) above is furnished in respect of a patient who is liable to be detained in pursuance of an application for admission for treatment the managers shall cause the nearest relative of the patient to be informed.

Functions of relatives of patients

26. Definition of "relative" and "nearest relative"

(1) In this Part of this Act "relative" means any of the following persons:—

(a) husband or wife;
(b) son or daughter;
(c) father or mother;
(d) brother or sister;
(e) grandparent;
(f) grandchild;
(g) uncle or aunt;
(h) nephew or niece.

(2) In deducing relationships for the purposes of this section, any relationship of the half-blood shall be treated as a relationship of the whole blood, and an illegitimate person shall be treated as the legitimate child of his mother.

(3) In this Part of this Act, subject to the provisions of this section and to the following provisions of this Part of this Act, the "nearest relative" means the person first described in subsection (1) above who is for the time being surviving, relatives of the whole blood being preferred to relatives of the same description of the half-blood and the elder or eldest of two or more relatives described in any paragraph of that subsection being preferred to the other or others of those relatives, regardless of sex.

(4) Subject to the provisions of this section and to the following provisions of this Part of this Act, where the patient ordinarily resides with or is cared for by one or more of his relatives (or, if he is for the time being an in-patient in a hospital, he last ordinarily resided with or was cared for by one or more of his relatives) his nearest relative shall be determined—

(a) by giving preference to that relative or those relatives over the other or others; and

(b) as between two or more such relatives, in accordance with subsection (3) above.

(5) Where the person who, under subsection (3) or (4) above, would be the nearest relative of a patient—

(a) in the case of a patient ordinarily resident in the United Kingdom, the Channel Islands or the Isle of Man, is not so resident; or

(b)   is the husband or wife of the patient, but is permanently separated from the patient, either by agreement or under an order of a court, or has deserted or has been deserted by the patient for a period which has not come to an end; or

(c)   is a person other than the husband, wife, father or mother of the patient, and is for the time being under 18 years of age;
the nearest relative of the patient shall be ascertained as if that person were dead.

(6)   In this section "husband" and "wife" include a person who is living with the patient as the patient's husband or wife, as the case may be (or, if the patient is for the time being an in-patient in a hospital, was so living until the patient was admitted), and has been or had been so living for a period of not less than six months; but a person shall not be treated by virtue of this subsection as the nearest relative of a married patient unless the husband or wife of the patient is disregarded by virtue of paragraph (b) of subsection (5) above.

(7)   A person, other than a relative, with whom the patient ordinarily resides (or, if the patient is for the time being an in-patient in a hospital, last ordinarily resided before he was admitted), and with whom he has or had been ordinarily residing for a period of not less than five years, shall be treated for the purposes of this Part of this Act as if he were a relative but—

(a)   shall be treated for the purposes of subsection (3) above as if mentioned last in subsection (1) above; and

(b)   shall not be treated by virtue of this subsection as the nearest relative of a married patient unless the husband or wife of the patient is disregarded by virtue of paragraph (b) of subsection (5) above.

27.   Children and young persons in care
Where—

(a)   a patient who is a child or young person is in the care of a local authority by virtue of a care order within the meaning of the Children Act 1989; or

(b)   the rights and powers of a parent of a patient who is a child or young person are vested in a local authority by virtue of section 16 of the Social Work (Scotland) Act 1968,
the authority shall be deemed to be the nearest relative of the patient in preference to any person except the patient's husband or wife (if any).

28.   Nearest relative of minor under guardianship etc.
(1)   Where—

(a)   a guardian has been appointed for a person who has not attained the age of eighteen years; or

(b)   a residence order (as defined by section 8 of the Children Act 1989) is in force with respect to such a person,
the guardian (or guardians, where there is more than one) or the person named in the residence order shall, to the exclusion of any other person, be deemed to be his nearest relative.

(2)   Subsection (5) of section 26 above shall apply in relation to a person who is, or who is one of the persons, deemed to be the nearest relative of a patient by virtue of this section as it applies in relation to a person who would be the nearest relative under subsection (3) of that section.

(3)   In this section "guardian" does not include a guardian under this Part of this Act.

(4)   In this section "court" includes a court in Scotland or Northern Ireland, and "enactment" includes an enactment of the Parliament of Northern Ireland, a Measure of the Northern Ireland Assembly and an Order in Council under Schedule 1 of the Northern Ireland Act 1974.

29. Appointment by court of acting nearest relative

(1) The county court may, upon application made in accordance with the provisions of this section in respect of a patient, by order direct that the functions of the nearest relative of the patient under this Part of this Act and sections 66 and 69 below shall, during the continuance in force of the order, be exercisable by the applicant, or by any other person specified in the application, being a person who, in the opinion of the court, is a proper person to act as the patient's nearest relative and is willing to do so.

(2) An order under this section may be made on the application of—

(a) any relative of the patient;

(b) any other person with whom the patient is residing (or, if the patient is then an in-patient in a hospital, was last residing before he was admitted); or

(c) an approved social worker;

but in relation to an application made by such a social worker, subsection (1) above shall have effect as if for the words "the applicant" there were substituted the words "the local social services authority".

(3) An application for an order under this section may be made upon any of the following grounds, that is to say—

(a) that the patient has no nearest relative within the meaning of this Act, or that it is not reasonably practicable to ascertain whether he has such a relative, or who that relative is;

(b) that the nearest relative of the patient is incapable of acting as such by reason of mental disorder or other illness;

(c) that the nearest relative of the patient unreasonably objects to the making of an application for admission for treatment or a guardianship application in respect of the patient; or

(d) that the nearest relative of the patient has exercised without due regard to the welfare of the patient or the interests of the public his power to discharge the patient from hospital or guardianship under this Part of this Act, or is likely to do so.

(4) If, immediately before the expiration of the period for which a patient is liable to be detained by virtue of an application for admission for assessment, an application under this section, which is an application made on the ground specified in subsection (3)(c) or (d) above, is pending in respect of the patient, that period shall be extended—

(a) in any case, until the application under this section has been finally disposed of; and

(b) if an order is made in pursuance of the application under this section, for a further period of seven days;

and for the purposes of this subsection an application under this section shall be deemed to have been finally disposed of at the expiration of the time allowed for appealing from the decision of the court or, if notice of appeal has been given within that time, when the appeal has been heard or withdrawn, and "pending" shall be construed accordingly.

(5) An order made on the ground specified in subsection (3)(a) or (b) above may specify a period for which it is to continue in force unless previously discharged under section 30 below.

(6) While an order made under this section is in force, the provisions of this Part of this Act (other than this section and section 30 below) and sections 66, 69, 132(4) and 133 below shall apply in relation to the patient as if for any reference to the nearest relative of the patient there were substituted a reference to the person having the functions of that relative and (without prejudice to section 30 below) shall so apply notwithstanding that the person who was the patient's nearest relative when the order was made is no longer his nearest relative; but this subsection shall not apply to section 66 below in the case mentioned in paragraph (h) of subsection (1) of that section.

30.   Discharge and variation of orders under s. 29

(1)   An order made under section 29 above in respect of a patient may be discharged by the county court upon application made—

(a)   in any case, by the person having the functions of the nearest relative of the patient by virtue of the order;

(b)   where the order was made on the ground specified in paragraph (a) or paragraph (b) of section 29(3) above, or where the person who was the nearest relative of the patient when the order was made has ceased to be his nearest relative, on the application of the nearest relative of the patient.

(2)   An order made under section 29 above in respect of a patient may be varied by the county court, on the application of the person having the functions of the nearest relative by virtue of the order or on the application of an approved social worker, by substituting for the first-mentioned person a local social services authority or any other person who in the opinion of the court is a proper person to exercise those functions, being an authority or person who is willing to do so.

(3)   If the person having the functions of the nearest relative of a patient by virtue of an order under section 29 above dies—

(a)   subsections (1) and (2) above shall apply as if for any reference to that person there were substituted a reference to any relative of the patient, and

(b)   until the order is discharged or varied under those provisions the functions of the nearest relative under this Part of this Act and sections 66 and 69 below shall not be exercisable by any person.

(4)   An order under section 29 above shall, unless previously discharged under subsection (1) above, cease to have effect at the expiration of the period, if any, specified under subsection (5) of that section or, where no such period is specified—

(a)   if the patient was on the date of the order liable to be detained in pursuance of an application for admission for treatment or by virtue of an order or direction under Part III of this Act (otherwise than under section 35, 36 or 38) or was subject to guardianship under this Part of this Act or by virtue of such an order or direction, or becomes so liable or subject within the period of three months beginning with that date, when he ceases to be so liable or subject (otherwise than on being transferred in pursuance of regulations under section 19 above);

(b)   if the patient was not on the date of the order, and has not within the said period become, so liable or subject, at the expiration of that period.

(5)   The discharge or variation under this section of an order made under section 29 above shall not affect the validity of anything previously done in pursuance of the order.

Supplemental

31.   Procedure on applications to county court

County court rules which relate to applications authorised by this Part of this Act to be made to a county court may make provision—

(a)   for the hearing and determination of such applications otherwise than in open court;

(b)   for the admission on the hearing of such applications of evidence of such descriptions as may be specified in the rules notwithstanding anything to the contrary in any enactment or rule of law relating to the admissibility of evidence;

(c)   for the visiting and interviewing of patients in private by or under the directions of the court.

32.   Regulations for purposes of Part II

(1)   The Secretary of State may make regulations for prescribing anything which, under this Part of this Act, is required or authorised to be prescribed, and otherwise for carrying this Part of this Act into full effect.

(2)   Regulations under this section may in particular make provision—
    (a)   for prescribing the form of any application, recommendation, report, order, notice or other document to be made or given under this Part of this Act;
    (b)   for prescribing the manner in which any such application, recommendation, report, order, notice or other document may be proved, and for regulating the service of any such application, report, order or notice;
    (c)   for requiring the managers of hospitals and local social services authorities to keep such registers or other records as may be prescribed by the regulations in respect of patients liable to be detained or subject to guardianship under this Part of this Act, and to furnish or make available to those patients, and their relatives, such written statements of their rights and powers under this Act as may be so prescribed;
    (d)   for the determination in accordance with the regulations of the age of any person whose exact age cannot be ascertained by reference to the registers kept under the Births and Deaths Registration Act 1953; and
    (e)   for enabling the functions under this Part of this Act of the nearest relative of a patient to be performed, in such circumstances and subject to such conditions (if any) as may be prescribed by the regulations, by any person authorised in that behalf by that relative;
and for the purposes of this Part of this Act any application, report or notice the service of which is regulated under paragraph (b) above shall be deemed to have been received by or furnished to the authority or person to whom it is authorised or required to be furnished, addressed or given if it is duly served in accordance with the regulations.

(3)   Without prejudice to subsections (1) and (2) above, but subject to section 23(4) above, regulations under this section may determine the manner in which functions under this Part of this Act of the managers of hospitals, local social services authorities, Regional Health Authorities, District Health Authorities, National Health Service trusts or special health authorities are to be exercised, and such regulations may in particular specify the circumstances in which, and the conditions subject to which, any such functions may be performed by officers of or other persons acting on behalf of those managers, authorities and trusts.

33.   Special provisions as to wards of court

(1)   An application for the admission to hospital of a minor who is a ward of court may be made under this Part of this Act with the leave of the court; and section 11(4) above shall not apply in relation to an application so made.

(2)   Where a minor who is a ward of court is liable to be detained in a hospital by virtue of an application for admission under this Part of this Act, any power exercisable under this Part of this Act or under section 66 below in relation to the patient by his nearest relative shall be exercisable by or with the leave of the court.

(3)   Nothing in this Part of this Act shall be construed as authorising the making of a guardianship application in respect of a minor who is a ward of court, or the transfer into guardianship of any such minor.

34.   Interpretation of Part II

(1)   In this Part of this Act—
"the nominated medical attendant", in relation to a patient who is subject to the guardianship of a person other than a local social services authority, means the person appointed in pursuance of regulations made under section 9(2) above to act as the medical attendant of the patient;
"the responsible medical officer" means—
    (a)   in relation to a patient liable to be detained by virtue of an application for admission for assessment or an application for admission for treatment, the registered medical practitioner in charge of the treatment of the patient;

(b)   in relation to a patient subject to guardianship, the medical officer authorised by the local social services authority to act (either generally or in any particular case or for any particular purpose) as the responsible medical officer.

(2)   Except where otherwise expressly provided, this Part of this Act applies in relation to a mental nursing home, being a home in respect of which the particulars of registration are for the time being entered in the separate part of the register kept for the purposes of section 23(5)(b) of the Registered Homes Act 1984, as it applies in relation to a hospital, and references in this Part of this Act to a hospital, and any reference in this Act to a hospital to which this Part of this Act applies, shall be construed accordingly.

(3)   In relation to a patient who is subject to guardianship in pursuance of a guardianship application, any reference in this Part of this Act to the responsible local social services authority is a reference—

(a)   where the patient is subject to the guardianship of a local social services authority, to that authority;

(b)   where the patient is subject to the guardianship of a person other than a local social services authority, to the local social services authority for the area in which that person resides.

PART III
PATIENTS CONCERNED IN CRIMINAL PROCEEDINGS OR UNDER SENTENCE
Remands to hospital

35.   Remand to hospital for report on accused's mental condition

(1)   Subject to the provisions of this section, the Crown Court or a magistrates' court may remand an accused person to a hospital specified by the court for a report on his mental condition.

(2)   For the purposes of this section an accused person is—

(a)   in relation to the Crown Court, any person who is awaiting trial before the court for an offence punishable with imprisonment or who has been arraigned before the court for such an offence and has not yet been sentenced or otherwise dealt with for the offence on which he has been arraigned;

(b)   in relation to a magistrates' court, any person who has been convicted by the court of an offence punishable on summary conviction with imprisonment and any person charged with such an offence if the court is satisfied that he did the act or made the omission charged or he has consented to the exercise by the court of the powers conferred by this section.

(3)   Subject to subsection (4) below, the powers conferred by this section may be exercised if—

(a)   the court is satisfied, on the written or oral evidence of a registered medical practitioner, that there is reason to suspect that the accused person is suffering from mental illness, psychopathic disorder, severe mental impairment or mental impairment; and

(b)   the court is of the opinion that it would be impracticable for a report on his mental condition to be made if he were remanded on bail;
but those powers shall not be exercised by the Crown Court in respect of a person who has been convicted before the court if the sentence for the offence of which he has been convicted is fixed by law.

(4)   The court shall not remand an accused person to a hospital under this section unless satisfied, on the written or oral evidence of the registered medical practitioner who would be responsible for making the report or of some other person representing the managers of the hospital, that arrangements have been made for his admission to that hospital and for his admission to it within the period of seven days beginning with

the date of the remand; and if the court is so satisfied it may, pending his admission, give directions for his conveyance to and detention in a place of safety.

(5)   Where a court has remanded an accused person under this section it may further remand him if it appears to the court, on the written or oral evidence of the registered medical practitioner responsible for making the report, that a further remand is necessary for completing the assessment of the accused person's mental condition.

(6)   The power of further remanding an accused person under this section may be exercised by the court without his being brought before the court if he is represented by counsel or a solicitor and his counsel or solicitor is given an opportunity of being heard.

(7)   An accused person shall not be remanded or further remanded under this section for more than 28 days at a time or for more than 12 weeks in all; and the court may at any time terminate the remand if it appears to the court that it is appropriate to do so.

(8)   An accused person remanded to hospital under this section shall be entitled to obtain at his own expense an independent report on his mental condition from a registered medical practitioner chosen by him and to apply to the court on the basis of it for his remand to be terminated under subsection (7) above.

(9)   Where an accused person is remanded under this section—

(a)   a constable or any other person directed to do so by the court shall convey the accused person to the hospital specified by the court within the period mentioned in subsection (4) above; and

(b)   the managers of the hospital shall admit him within that period and thereafter detain him in accordance with the provisions of this section.

(10)   If an accused person absconds from a hospital to which he has been remanded under this section, or while being conveyed to or from that hospital, he may be arrested without warrant by any constable and shall, after being arrested, be brought as soon as practicable before the court that remanded him; and the court may thereupon terminate the remand and deal with him in any way in which it could have dealt with him if he had not been remanded under this section.

36.   Remand of accused person to hospital for treatment

(1)   Subject to the provisions of this section, the Crown Court may, instead of remanding an accused person in custody, remand him to a hospital specified by the court if satisfied, on the written or oral evidence of two registered medical practitioners, that he is suffering from mental illness or severe mental impairment of a nature or degree which makes it appropriate for him to be detained in a hospital for medical treatment.

(2)   For the purposes of this section an accused person is any person who is in custody awaiting trial before the Crown Court for an offence punishable with imprisonment (other than an offence the sentence for which is fixed by law) or who at any time before sentence is in custody in the course of a trial before that court for such an offence.

(3)   The court shall not remand an accused person under this section to a hospital unless it is satisfied, on the written or oral evidence of the registered medical practitioner who would be in charge of his treatment or of some other person representing the managers of the hospital, that arrangements have been made for his admission to that hospital and for his admission to it within the period of seven days beginning with the date of the remand; and if the court is so satisfied it may, pending his admission, give directions for his conveyance to and detention in a place of safety.

(4)   Where a court has remanded an accused person under this section it may further remand him if it appears to the court, on the written or oral evidence of the responsible medical officer, that a further remand is warranted.

(5)   The power of further remanding an accused person under this section may be exercised by the court without his being brought before the court if he is represented by counsel or a solicitor and his counsel or solicitor is given an opportunity of being heard.

(6)   An accused person shall not be remanded or further remanded under this section for more than 28 days at a time or for more than 12 weeks in all; and the court may at any time terminate the remand if it appears to the court that it is appropriate to do so.

(7)   An accused person remanded to hospital under this section shall be entitled to obtain at his own expense an independent report on his mental condition from a registered medical practitioner chosen by him and to apply to the court on the basis of it for his remand to be terminated under subsection (6) above.

(8)   Subsections (9) and (10) of section 35 above shall have effect in relation to a remand under this section as they have effect in relation to a remand under that section.

Hospital and guardianship orders

37.   Powers of courts to order hospital admission or guardianship

(1)   Where a person is convicted before the Crown Court of an offence punishable with imprisonment other than an offence the sentence for which is fixed by law, or is convicted by a magistrates' court of an offence punishable on summary conviction with imprisonment, and the conditions mentioned in subsection (2) below are satisfied, the court may by order authorise his admission to and detention in such hospital as may be specified in the order or, as the case may be, place him under the guardianship of a local social services authority or of such other person approved by a local social services authority as may be so specified.

(2)   The conditions referred to in subsection (1) above are that—

   (a)   the court is satisfied, on the written or oral evidence of two registered medical practitioners, that the offender is suffering from mental illness, psychopathic disorder, severe mental impairment or mental impairment and that either—

      (i)   the mental disorder from which the offender is suffering is of a nature or degree which makes it appropriate for him to be detained in a hospital for medical treatment and, in the case of psychopathic disorder or mental impairment, that such treatment is likely to alleviate or prevent a deterioration of his condition; or

      (ii)   in the case of an offender who has attained the age of 16 years, the mental disorder is of a nature or degree which warrants his reception into guardianship under this Act; and

   (b)   the court is of the opinion, having regard to all the circumstances including that nature of the offence and the character and antecedents of the offender, and to the other available methods of dealing with him, that the most suitable method of disposing of the case is by means of an order under this section.

(3)   Where a person is charged before a magistrates' court with any act or omission as an offence and the court would have power, on convicting him of that offence, to make an order under subsection (1) above in his case as being a person suffering from mental illness or severe mental impairment, then, if the court is satisfied that the accused did the act or made the omission charged, the court may, if it thinks fit, make such an order without convicting him.

(4)   An order for the admission of an offender to a hospital (in this Act referred to as "a hospital order") shall not be made under this section unless the court is satisfied on the written or oral evidence of the registered medical practitioner who would be in charge of his treatment or of some other person representing the managers of the hospital that arrangements have been made for his admission to that hospital in the event of such an order being made by the court, and for his admission to it within the period of 28 days beginning with the date of the making of such an order; and the court

may, pending his admission within that period, give such directions as it thinks fit for his conveyance to and detention in a place of safety.

(5)   If within the said period of 28 days it appears to the Secretary of State that by reason of an emergency or other special circumstances it is not practicable for the patient to be received into the hospital specified in the order, he may give directions for the admission of the patient to such other hospital as appears to be appropriate instead of the hospital so specified; and where such directions are given—

(a)   the Secretary of State shall cause the person having the custody of the patient to be informed, and

(b)   the hospital order shall have effect as if the hospital specified in the directions were substituted for the hospital specified in the order.

(6)   An order placing an offender under the guardianship of a local social services authority or of any other person (in this Act referred to as "a guardianship order") shall not be made under this section unless the court is satisfied that that authority or person is willing to receive the offender into guardianship.

(7)   A hospital order or guardianship order shall specify the form or forms of mental disorder referred to in subsection (2)(a) above from which, upon the evidence taken into account under that subsection, the offender is found by the court to be suffering; and no such order shall be made unless the offender is described by each of the practitioners whose evidence is taken into account under that subsection as suffering from the same one of those forms of mental disorder, whether or not he is also described by either of them as suffering from another of them.

(8)   Where an order is made under this section, the court shall not pass sentence of imprisonment or impose a fine or make a probation order in respect of the offence or make any such order as is mentioned in paragraph (b) or (c) of section 7(7) of the Children and Young Persons Act 1969 in respect of the offender, but may make any other order which the court has power to make apart from this section; and for the purposes of this subsection "sentence of imprisonment" includes any sentence or order for detention.

38.   Interim hospital orders

(1)   Where a person is convicted before the Crown Court of an offence punishable with imprisonment (other than an offence the sentence for which is fixed by law) or is convicted by a magistrates' court of an offence punishable on summary conviction with imprisonment and the court before or by which he is convicted is satisfied, on the written or oral evidence of two registered medical practitioners—

(a)   that the offender is suffering from mental illness, psychopathic disorder, severe mental impairment or mental impairment; and

(b)   that there is reason to suppose that the mental disorder from which the offender is suffering is such that it may be appropriate for a hospital order to made in his case,

the court may, before making a hosital order or dealing with him in some other way, make an order (in this Act referred to as "an interim hospital order") authorising his admission to such hospital as may be specified in the order and his detention there in accordance with this section.

(2)   In the case of an offender who is subject to an interim hospital order the court may make a hospital order without his being brought before the court if he is represented by counsel or a solicitor and his counsel or solicitor is given an opportunity of being heard.

(3)   At least one of the registered medical practitioners whose evidence is taken into account under subsection (1) above shall be employed at the hospital which is to be specified in the order.

(4)   An interim hospital order shall not be made for the admission of an offender to a hospital unless the court is satisfied, on the written or oral evidence of the registered

medical practitioner who would be in charge of his treatment or of some other person representing the managers of the hospital, that arrangements have been made for his admission to that hospital and for his admission to it within the period of 28 days beginning with the date of the order; and if the court is so satisfied the court may, pending his admission, give directions for his conveyance to and detention in a place of safety.

(5)   An interim hospital order—

(a)   shall be in force for such period, not exceeding 12 weeks, as the court may specify when making the order; but

(b)   may be renewed for furt'ier periods of not more than 28 days at a time if it appears to the court, on the writter or oral evidence of the responsible medical officer, that the continuation of the order i warranted;

but no such order shall continue ir force for more than six months in all and the court shall terminate the order if it makes a hospital order in respect of the offender or decides after considering the written or oral evidence of the responsible medical officer to deal with the offender in some other way.

(6)   The power of renewing an interim hospital order may be exercised without the offender being brought before the court if he is represented by counsel or a solicitor and his counsel or solicitor is given an opportunity of being heard.

(7)   If an offender absconds from a hospital in which he is detained in pursuance of an interim hospital order, or while being conveyed to or from such a hospital, he may be arrested without warrant by a constable and shall, after being arrested, be brought as soon as practicable before the court that made the order; and the court may thereupon terminate the order and deal with him in any way in which it could have dealt with him if no such order had been made.

39.   Information as to hospitals

(1)   Where a court is minded to make a hospital order or interim hospital order in respect of any person it may request—

(a)   the Regional Health Authority for the region in which that person resides or last resided; or

(b)   any other Regional Health Authority that appears to the court to be appropriate,

to furnish the court with such information as that Authority has or can reasonably obtain with respect to the hospital or hospitals (if any) in its region or elsewhere at which arrangements could be made for the admission of that person in pursuance of the order, and that Authority shall comply with any such request.

(2)   In its application to Wales subsection (1) above shall have effect as if for any reference to any such Authority as is mentioned in paragraph (a) or (b) of that subsection there were substituted a reference to the Secretary of State, and as if for the words "in its region or elsewhere" there were substituted the words "in Wales".

40.   Effect of hospital orders, guardianship orders and interim hospital orders

(1)   A hospital order shall be sufficient authority—

(a)   for a constable, an approved social worker or any other person directed to do so by the court to convey the patient to the hospital specified in the order within a period of 28 days; and

(b)   for the managers of the hospital to admit him at any time within that period and thereafter detain him in accordance with the provisions of this Act.

(2)   A guardianship order shall confer on the authority or person named in the order as guardian the same powers as a guardianship application made and accepted under Part II of this Act.

(3)   Where an interim hospital order is made in respect of an offender—

(a) a constable or any other person directed to do so by the court shall convey the offender to the hospital specified in the order within the period mentioned in section 38(4) above; and

(b) the managers of the hospital shall admit him within that period and thereafter detain him in accordance with the provisions of section 38 above.

(4) A patient who is admitted to a hospital in pursuance of a hospital order, or placed under guardianship by a guardianship order, shall, subject to the provisions of this subsection, be treated for the purposes of the provisions of this Act mentioned in Part I of Schedule 1 to this Act as if he had been so admitted or placed on the date of the order in pursuance of an application for admission for treatment or a guardianship application, as the case may be, duly made under Part II of this Act, but subject to any modifications of those provisions specified in that Part of that Schedule.

(5) Where a patient is admitted to a hospital in pursuance of a hospital order, or placed under guardianship by a guardianship order, any previous application, hospital order or guardianship order by virtue of which he was liable to be detained in a hospital or subject to guardianship shall cease to have effect; but if the first-mentioned order, or the conviction on which it was made, is quashed on appeal, this subection shall not apply and section 22 above shall have effect as if during any period for which the patient was liable to be detained or subject to guardianship under the order, he had been detained in custody as mentioned in that section.

Restriction orders

41. Power of higher courts to restrict discharge from hospital

(1) Where a hospital order is made in respect of an offender by the Crown Court, and it appears to the court, having regard to the nature of the offence, the antecedents of the offender and the risk of his committing further offences if set at large, that it is necessary for the protection of the public from serious harm so to do, the court may, subject to the provisions of this section, further order that the offender shall be subject to the special restrictions set out in this section, either without limit of time or during such period as may be specified in the order; and an order under this section shall be known as "a restriction order".

(2) A restriction order shall not be made in the case of any person unless at least one of the registered medical practitioners whose evidence is taken into account by the court under section 37(2)(a) above has given evidence orally before the court.

(3) The special restrictions applicable to a patient in respect of whom a restriction order is in force are as follows—

(a) none of the provisions of Part II of this Act relating to the duration, renewal and expiration of authority for the detention of patients shall apply, and the patient shall continue to be liable to be detained by virtue of the relevant hospital order until he is duly discharged under the said Part II or absolutely discharged under section 42, 73, 74 or 75 below;

(b) no application shall be made to a Mental Health Review Tribunal in respect of a patient under section 66 or 69(1) below;

(c) the following powers shall be exercisable only with the consent of the Secretary of State, namely—

(i) power to grant leave of absence to the patient under section 17 above;

(ii) power to transfer the patient in pursuance of regulations under section 19 above; and

(iii) power to order the discharge of the patient under section 23 above;

and if leave of absence is granted under the said section 17 power to recall the patient under that section shall vest in the Secretary of State as well as the responsible medical officer; and

(d)   the power of the Secretary of State to recall the patient under the said section 17 and power to take the patient into custody and return him under section 18 above may be exercised at any time;

and in relation to any such patient section 40(4) above shall have effect as if it referred to Part II of Schedule 1 to this Act instead of Part I of that Schedule.

(4)   A hospital order shall not cease to have effect under section 40(5) above if a restriction order in respect of the patient is in force at the material time.

(5)   Where a restriction order in respect of a patient ceases to have effect while the relevant hospital order continues in force, the provisions of section 40 above and Part I of Schedule 1 to this Act shall apply to the patient as if he had been admitted to the hospital in pursuance of a hospital order (without a restriction order) made on the date on which the restriction order ceased to have effect.

(6)   While a person is subject to a restriction order the responsible medical officer shall at such intervals (not exceeding one year) as the Secretary of State may direct examine and report to the Secretary of State on that person; and every report shall contain such particulars as the Secretary of State may require.

42.   Powers of Secretary of State in respect of patients subject to restriction orders

(1)   If the Secretary of State is satisfied that in the case of any patient a restriction order is no longer required for the protection of the public from serious harm, he may direct that the patient shall cease to be subject to the special restrictions set out in section 41(3) above; and where the Secretary of State so directs, the restriction order shall cease to have effect, and section 41(5) above shall apply accordingly.

(2)   At any time while a restriction order is in force in respect of a patient, the Secretary of State may, if he thinks fit, by warrant discharge the patient from hospital, either absolutely or subject to conditions; and where a person is absolutely discharged under this subsection, he shall thereupon cease to be liable to be detained by virtue of the relevant hospital order, and the restriction order shall cease to have effect accordingly.

(3)   The Secretary of State may at any time during the continuance in force of a restriction order in respect of a patient who has been conditionally discharged under subsection (2) above by warrant recall the patient to such hospital as may be specified in the warrant.

(4)   Where a patient is recalled as mentioned in subsection (3) above—

(a)   if the hospital specified in the warrant is not the hospital from which the patient was conditionally discharged, the hospital order and the restriction order shall have effect as if the hospital specified in the warrant were substituted for the hospital specified in the hospital order;

(b)   in any case, the patient shall be treated for the purposes of section 18 above as if he had absented himself without leave from the hospital specified in the warrant, and, if the restriction order was made for a specified period, that period shall not in any event expire until the patient returns to the hospital or is returned to the hospital under that section.

(5)   If a restriction order in respect of a patient ceases to have effect after the patient has been conditionally discharged under this section, the patient shall, unless previously recalled under subsection (3) above, be deemed to be absolutely discharged on the date when the order ceases to have effect, and shall cease to be liable to be detained by virtue of the relevant hospital order accordingly.

(6)   The Secretary of State may, if satisfied that the attendance at any place in Great Britain of a patient who is subject to a restriction order is desirable in the interests of justice or for the purposes of any public inquiry, direct him to be taken to that place; and where a patient is directed under this subsection to be taken to any place he shall,

unless the Secretary of State otherwise directs, be kept in custody while being so taken, while at that place and while being taken back to the hospital in which he is liable to be detained.

43. Power of magistrates' courts to commit for restriction order

(1) If in the case of a person of or over the age of 14 years who is convicted by a magistrates' court of an offence punishable on summary conviction with imprisonment—

(a) the conditions which under section 37(1) above are required to be satisfied for the making of a hospital order are satisfied in respect of the offender; but

(b) it appears to the court, having regard to the nature of the offence, the antecedents of the offender and the risk of his committing further offences if set at large, that if a hospital order is made a restriction order should also be made,
the court may, instead of making a hospital order or dealing with him in any other manner, commit him in custody to the Crown Court to be dealt with in respect of the offence.

(2) Where an offender is committed to the Crown Court under this section, the Crown Court shall inquire into the circumstances of the case and may—

(a) if that court would have power so to do under the foregoing provisions of this Part of this Act upon the conviction of the offender before that court of such an offence as is described in section 37(1) above, make a hospital order in his case, with or without a restriction order;

(b) if the court does not make such an order, deal with the offender in any other manner in which the magistrates' court might have dealt with him.

(3) The Crown Court shall have the same power to make orders under sections 35, 36 and 38 above in the case of a person committed to the court under this section as the Crown Court has under those sections in the case of an accused person within the meaning of section 35 or 36 above or of a person convicted before that court as mentioned in section 38 above.

(4) The power of a magistrates' court under section 38 of the Magistrates' Courts Act 1980 (which enables such a court to commit an offender to the Crown Court where the court is of the opinion that greater punishment should be inflicted for the offence than the court has power to inflict) shall also be exercisable by a magistrates' court where it is of the opinion that greater punishment should be inflicted as aforesaid on the offender unless a hospital order is made in his case with a restriction order.

(5) The power of the Crown Court to make a hospital order, with or without a restriction order, in the case of a person convicted before that court of an offence may, in the same circumstances and subject to the same conditions, be exercised by such a court in the case of a person committed to the court under section 5 of the Vagrancy Act 1824 (which provides for the committal to the Crown Court of persons who are incorrigible rogues within the meaning of that section).

44. Committal to hospital under s. 43

(1) Where an offender is committed under section 43(1) above and the magistrates' court by which he is committed is satisfied on written or oral evidence that arrangements have been made for the admission of the offender to a hospital in the event of an order being made under this section, the court may, instead of committing him in custody, by order direct him to be admitted to that hospital, specifying it, and to be detained there until the case is disposed of by the Crown Court, and may give such directions as it thinks fit for his production from the hospital to attend the Crown Court by which his case is to be dealt with.

(2) The evidence required by subsection (1) above shall be given by the registered medical practitioner who would be in charge of the offender's treatment or by some other person representing the managers of the hospital in question.

(3)   The power to give directions under section 37(4) above, section 37(5) above and section 40(1) above shall apply in relation to an order under this section as they apply in relation to a hospital order, but as if references to the period of 28 days mentioned in section 40(1) above were omitted; and subject as aforesaid an order under this section shall, until the offender's case is disposed of by the Crown Court, have the same effect as a hospital order together with a restriction order, made without limitation of time.

45.   Appeals from magistrates' courts

(1)   Where on the trial of an information charging a person with an offence a magistrates' court makes a hospital order or guardianship order in respect of him without convicting him, he shall have the same right of appeal against the order as if it had been made on his conviction; and on any such appeal the Crown Court shall have the same powers as if the appeal had been against both conviction and sentence.

(2)   An appeal by a child or young person with respect to whom any such order has been made, whether the appeal is against the order or against the finding upon which the order was made, may be brought by him or by his parent or guardian on his behalf.

Detention during Her Majesty's pleasure

46.   Persons ordered to be kept in custody during Her Majesty's pleasure

(1)   The Secretary of State may by warrant direct that any person who, by virtue of any enactment to which this subsection applies, is required to be kept in custody during Her Majesty's pleasure or until the directions of Her Majesty are known shall be detained in such hospital (not being a mental nursing home) as may be specified in the warrant and, where that person is not already detained in the hospital, give directions for his removal there.

(2)   The enactments to which subsection (1) above applies are section 16 of the Courts-Martial (Appeals) Act 1968, section 116 of the Army Act 1955, section 116 of the Air Force Act 1955 and section 63 of the Naval Discipline Act 1957.

(3)   A direction under this section in respect of any person shall have the same effect as a hospital order together with a restriction order, made without limitation of time; and where such a direction is given in respect of a person while he is in the hospital, he shall be deemed to be admitted in pursuance of, and on the date of, the direction.

Transfer to hospital of prisoners, etc.

47.   Removal to hospital of persons serving sentences of imprisonment, etc.

(1)   If in the case of a person serving a sentence of imprisonment the Secretary of State is satisfied, by reports from at least two registered medical practitioners—

(a)   that the said person is suffering from mental illness, psychopathic disorder, severe mental impairment or mental impairment; and

(b)   that the mental disorder from which that person is suffering is of a nature or degree which makes it appropriate for him to be detained in a hospital for medical treatment and, in the case of psychopathic disorder or mental impairment, that such treatment is likely to alleviate or prevent a deterioration of his condition;

the Secretary of State may, if he is of the opinion having regard to the public interest and all the circumstances that it is expedient so to do, by warrant direct that that person be removed to and detained in such hospital (not being a mental nursing home) as may be specified in the direction; and a direction under this section shall be known as "a transfer direction".

(2)   A transfer direction shall cease to have effect at the expiration of the period of 14 days beginning with the date on which it is given unless within that period the person with respect to whom it was given has been received into the hospital specified in the direction.

(3)   A transfer direction with respect to any person shall have the same effect as a hospital order made in his case.

(4)   A transfer direction shall specify the form or forms of mental disorder referred to in paragraph (a) of subsection (1) above from which, upon the reports taken into account under that subsection, the patient is found by the Secretary of State to be suffering; and no such direction shall be given unless the patient is described in each of those reports as suffering from the same form of disorder, whether or not he is also described in either of them as suffering from another form.

(5)   References in this Part of this Act to a person serving a sentence of imprisonment include references—

(a)   to a person detained in pursuance of any sentence or order for detention made by a court in criminal proceedings (other than an order under any enactment to which section 46 above applies);

(b)   to a person committed to custody under section 115(3) of the Magistrates' Courts Act 1980 (which relates to persons who fail to comply with an order to enter into recognisances to keep the peace or be of good behaviour); and

(c)   to a person committed by a court to a prison or other institution to which the Prison Act 1952 applies in default of payment of any sum adjudged to be paid on his conviction.

48.   Removal to hospital of other prisoners

(1)   If in the case of a person to whom this section applies the Secretary of State is satisfied by the same reports as are required for the purposes of section 47 above that that person is suffering from mental impairment of a nature or degree which makes it appropriate for him to be detained in a hospital for medical treatment and that he is in urgent need of such treatment, the Secretary of State shall have the same power of giving a transfer direction in respect of him under that section as if he were serving a sentence of imprisonment.

(2)   This section applies to the following persons, that is to say—

(a)   persons detained in a prison or remand centre, not being persons serving a sentence of imprisonment or persons falling within the following paragraphs of this subsection;

(b)   persons remanded in custody by a magistrates' court;

(c)   civil prisoners, that is to say, persons committed by a court to prison for a limited term (including persons committed to prison in pursuance of a writ of attachment), who are not persons falling to be dealt with under section 47 above;

(d)   persons detained under the Immigration Act 1971.

(3)   Subsections (2) to (4) of section 47 above shall apply for the purposes of this section and of any transfer direction given by virtue of this section as they apply for the purposes of that section and of any transfer direction under that section.

49.   Restriction on discharge of prisoners removed to hospital

(1)   Where a transfer direction is given in respect of any person, the Secretary of State, if he thinks fit, may by warrant further direct that that person shall be subject to the special restrictions set out in section 41 above; and where the Secretary of State gives a transfer direction in respect of any such person as is described in paragraph (a) or (b) of section 48(2) above, he shall also give a direction under this section applying those restrictions to him.

(2)   A direction under this section shall have the same effect as a restriction order made under section 41 above and shall be known as "a restriction direction".

(3)   While a person is subject to a restriction direction the responsible medical officer shall at such intervals (not exceeding one year) as the Secretary of State may direct examine and report to the Secretary of State on that person; and every report shall contain such particulars as the Secretary of State may require.

50.   Further provisions as to prisoners under sentence

(1)   Where a transfer direction and a restriction direction have been given in respect of a person serving a sentence of imprisonment and before the expiration of that person's sentence the Secretary of State is notified by the responsible medical officer, any other registered medical practitioner or a Mental Health Review Tribunal that that person no longer requires treatment in hospital for mental disorder or that no effective treatment for his disorder can be given in the hospital to which he has been removed, the Secretary of State may—

(a)   by warrant direct that he be remitted to any prison or other institution in which he might have been detained if he had not been removed to hospital, there to be dealt with as if he had not been so removed; or

(b)   exercise any power of releasing him on licence or discharging him under supervision which would have been exercisable if he had been remitted to such a prison or institution as aforesaid,

and on his arrival in the prison or other institution or, as the case may be, his release or discharge as aforesaid, the transfer direction and the restriction direction shall cease to have effect.

(2)   A restriction direction in the case of a person serving a sentence of imprisonment shall cease to have effect on the expiration of the sentence.

(3)   Subject to subsection (4) below, references in this section to the expiration of a person's sentence are references to the expiration of the period during which he would have been liable to be detained in a prison or other institution if the transfer direction had not been given.

(4)   For the purposes of section 49(2) of the Prison Act 1952 (which provides for discounting from the sentences of certain prisoners periods while they are unlawfully at large) a patient who, having been transferred in pursuance of a transfer direction from any such institution as is referred to in that section, is at large in circumstances in which he is liable to be taken into custody under any provision of this Act, shall be treated as unlawfully at large and absent from that institution.

51.   Further provisions as to detained persons

(1)   This section has effect where a transfer direction has been given in respect of any such person as is described in paragraph (a) of section 48(2) above and that person is in this section referred to as "the detainee".

(2)   The transfer direction shall cease to have effect when the detainee's case is disposed of by the court having jurisdiction to try or otherwise deal with him, but without prejudice to any power of that court to make a hospital order or other order under this Part of this Act in his case.

(3)   If the Secretary of State is notified by the responsible medical officer, any other registered medical practitioner or a Mental Health Review Tribunal at any time before the detainee's case is disposed of by that court—

(a)   that the detainee no longer requires treatment in hospital for mental disorder; or

(b)   that no effective treatment for his disorder can be given at the hospital to which he has been removed,

the Secretary of State may by warrant direct that he be remitted to any place where he might have been detained if he had not been removed to hospital, there to be dealt with as if he had not been so removed, and on his arrival at the place to which he is so remitted the transfer direction shall cease to have effect.

(4)   If (no direction having been given under subsection (3) above) the court having jurisdiction to try or otherwise deal with the detainee is satisfied on the written or oral evidence of the responsible medical officer—

(a)   that the detainee no longer requires treatment in hospital for mental disorder; or

(b)   that no effective treatment for his disorder can be given at the hospital to which he has been removed,
the court may order him to be remitted to any such place as is mentioned in subsection (3) above or released on bail and on his arrival at that place or, as the case may be, his release on bail the transfer direction shall cease to have effect.

(5)   If (no direction or order having been given or made under subsection (3) or (4) above) it appears to the court having jurisdiction to try or otherwise deal with the detainee—

(a)   that it is impracticable or inappropriate to bring the detainee before the court; and

(b)   that the conditions set out in subsection (6) below are satisfied,
the court may make a hospital order (with or without a restriction order) in his case in his absence and, in the case of a person awaiting trial, without convicting him.

(6)   A hospital order may be made in respect of a person under subsection (5) above if the court—

(a)   is satisfied, on the written or oral evidence of at least two registered medical practitioners, that the detainee is suffering from mental illness or severe mental impairment of a nature or degree which makes it appropriate for the patient to be detained in a hospital for medical treatment; and

(b)   is of the opinion, after considering any depositions or other documents required to be sent to the proper officer of the court, that it is proper to make such an order.

(7)   Where a person committed to the Crown Court to be dealt with under section 43 above is admitted to a hospital in pursuance of an order under section 44 above, subsections (5) and (6) above shall apply as if he were a person subject to a transfer direction.

52.   Further provisions as to persons remanded by magistrates' courts

(1)   This section has effect where a transfer direction has been given in respect of any such person as is described in paragraph (b) of section 48(2) above; and that person is in this section referred to as "the accused".

(2)   Subject to subsection (5) below, the transfer direction shall cease to have effect on the expiration of the period of remand unless the accused is committed in custody to the Crown Court for trial or to be otherwise dealt with.

(3)   Subject to subsection (4) below, the power of further remanding the accused under section 128 of the Magistrates' Courts Act 1980 may be exercised by the court without his being brought before the court; and if the court further remands the accused in custody (whether or not he is brought before the court) the period of remand shall, for the purposes of this section, be deemed not to have expired.

(4)   The court shall not under subsection (3) above further remand the accused in his absence unless he has appeared before the court within the previous six months.

(5)   If the magistrates' court is satisfied, on the written or oral evidence of the responsible medical officer—

(a)   that the accused no longer requires treatment in hospital for mental disorder; or

(b)   that no effective treatment for his disorder can be given in the hospital to which he has been removed,
the court may direct that the transfer direction shall cease to have effect notwithstanding that the period of remand has not expired or that the accused is committed to the Crown Court as mentioned in subsection (2) above.

(6)   If the accused is committed to the Crown Court as mentioned in subsection (2) above and the transfer direction has not ceased to have effect under subsection (5) above, section 51 above shall apply as if the transfer direction given in his case were a direction given in respect of a person falling within that section.

(7)   The magistrates' court may, in the absence of the accused, inquire as examining justices into an offence alleged to have been committed by him and commit him for trial in accordance with section 6 of the Magistrates' Court Act 1980 if—

(a)   the court is satisfied, on the written or oral evidence of the responsible medical officer, that the accused is unfit to take part in the proceedings; and

(b)   where the court proceeds under subsection (1) of that section, the accused is represented by counsel or a solicitor.

53.   Further provisions as to civil prisoners and persons detained under the Immigration Act 1971

(1)   Subject to subsection (2) below, a transfer direction given in respect of any such person as is described in paragraph (c) or (d) of section 48(2) above shall cease to have effect on the expiration of the period during which he would, but for his removal to hospital, be liable to be detained in the place from which he was removed.

(2)   Where a transfer direction and a restriction direction have been given in respect of any such person as is mentioned in subsection (1) above, then, if the Secretary of State is notified by the responsible medical officer, any other registered medical practitioner or a Mental Health Review Tribunal at any time before the expiration of the period there mentioned—

(a)   that that person no longer requires treatment in hospital for mental disorder; or

(b)   that no effective treatment for his disorder can be given in the hospital to which he has been removed,

the Secretary of State may by warrant direct that he be remitted to any place where he might have been detained if he had not been removed to hospital, and on his arrival at the place to which he is so remitted the transfer direction and the restriction direction shall cease to have effect.

Supplemental

54.   Requirements as to medical evidence

(1)   The registered medical practitioner whose evidence is taken into account under section 35(3)(a) above and at least one of the registered medical practitioners whose evidence is taken into account under sections 36(1), 37(2)(a), 38(1) and 51(6)(a) above and whose reports are taken into account under sections 47(1) and 48(1) above shall be a practitioner approved for the purposes of section 12 above by the Secretary of State as having special experience in the diagnosis or treatment of mental disorder.

(2)   For the purposes of any provision of this Part of this Act under which a court may act on the written evidence of—

(a)   a registered medical practitioner or a registered medical practitioner of any description; or

(b)   a person representing the managers of a hospital,

a report in writing purporting to be signed by a registered medical practitioner or a registered medical practitioner of such a description or by a person representing the managers of a hospital may, subject to the provisions of this section, be received in evidence without proof of the signature of the practitioner or that person and without proof that he has the requisite qualifications or authority or is of the requisite description; but the court may require the signatory of any such report to be called to give oral evidence.

(3)   Where, in pursuance of a direction of the court, any such report is tendered in evidence otherwise than by or on behalf of the person who is the subject of the report, then—

(a)   if that person is represented by counsel or a solicitor, a copy of the report shall be given to his counsel or solicitor;

(b) if that person is not so represented, the substance of the report shall be disclosed to him or, where he is a child or young person, to his parent or guardian if present in court; and

(c) except where the report relates only to arrangements for his admission to a hospital, that person may require the signatory of the report to be called to give oral evidence, and evidence to rebut the evidence contained in the report may be called by or on behalf of that person.

55. Interpretation of Part III

(1) In this Part of this Act—

"child" and "young person" have the same meaning as in the Children and Young Persons Act 1933;

"civil prisoner" has the meaning given to it by section 48(2)(c) above;

"guardian", in relation to a child or young person, has the same meaning as in the Children and Young Persons Act 1933;

"place of safety", in relation to a person who is not a child or young person, means any police station, prison or remand centre, or any hospital the managers of which are willing temporarily to receive him, and in relation to a child or young person has the same meaning as in the Children and Young Persons Act 1933;

"responsible medical officer", in relation to a person liable to be detained in a hospital within the meaning of Part II of this Act, means the registered medical practitioner in charge of the treatment of the patient.

(2) Any reference in this Part of this Act to an offence punishable on summary conviction with imprisonment shall be construed without regard to any prohibition or restriction imposed by or under any enactment relating to the imprisonment of young offenders.

(3) Where a patient who is liable to be detained in a hospital in pursuance of an order or direction under this Part of this Act is treated by virtue of any provision of this Part of this Act as if he had been admitted to the hospital in pursuance of a subsequent order or direction under this Part of this Act or a subsequent application for admission for treatment under Part II of this Act, he shall be treated as if the subsequent order, direction or application had described him as suffering from the form or forms of mental disorder specified in the earlier order or direction or, where he is treated as if he had been so admitted by virtue of a direction under section 42(1) above, such form of mental disorder as may be specified in the direction under that section.

(4) Any reference to a hospital order, a guardianship order or a restriction order in section 40(2), (4) or (5), section 41(3) to (5), or section 42 above or section 69(1) below shall be construed as including a reference to any order or direction under this Part of this Act having the same effect as the first-mentioned order; and the exceptions and modifications set out in Schedule 1 to this Act in respect of the provisions of this Act described in that Schedule accordingly include those which are consequential on the provisions of this subsection.

(5) Section 34(2) above shall apply for the purposes of this Part of this Act as it applies for the purposes of Part II of this Act.

(6) References in this Part of this Act to persons serving a sentence of imprisonment shall be construed in accordance with section 47(5) above.

(7) Section 99 of the Children and Young Persons Act 1933 (which relates to the presumption and determination of age) shall apply for the purposes of this Part of this Act as it applies for the purposes of that Act.

PART IV
CONSENT TO TREATMENT

56. Patients to whom Part IV applies

(1)   This Part of this Act applies to any patient liable to be detained under this Act except—

(a)   a patient who is liable to be detained by virtue of an emergency application and in respect of whom the second medical recommendation referred to in section 4(4)(a) above has not been given and received;

(b)   a patient who is liable to be detained by virtue of section 5(2) or (4) or 35 above or section 135 or 136 below or by virtue of a direction under section 37(4) above; and

(c)   a patient who has been conditionally discharged under section 42(2) above or section 73 or 74 below and has not been recalled to hospital.

(2)   Section 57 and, so far as relevant to that section, sections 59, 60 and 62 below, apply also to any patient who is not liable to be detained under this Act.

57. Treatment requiring consent and a second opinion

(1)   This section applies to the following forms of medical treatment for mental disorder—

(a)   any surgical operation for destroying brain tissue or for destroying the functioning of brain tissue; and

(b)   such other forms of treatment as may be specified for the purposes of this section by regulations made by the Secretary of State.

(2)   Subject to section 62 below, a patient shall not be given any form of treatment to which this section applies unless he has consented to it and—

(a)   a registered medical practitioner appointed for the purposes of this Part of this Act by the Secretary of State (not being the responsible medical officer) and two other persons appointed for the purposes of this paragraph by the Secretary of State (not being registered medical practitioners) have certified in writing that the patient is capable of understanding the nature, purpose and likely effects of the treatment in question and has consented to it; and

(b)   the registered medical practitioner referred to in paragraph (a) above has certified in writing that, having regard to the likelihood of the treatment alleviating or preventing a deterioration of the patient's condition, the treatment should be given.

(3)   Before giving a certificate under subsection (2)(b) above the registered medical practitioner concerned shall consult two other persons who have been professionally concerned with the patient's medical treatment, and of those persons one shall be a nurse and the other shall be neither a nurse nor a registered medical practitioner.

(4)   Before making any regulations for the purpose of this section the Secretary of State shall consult such bodies as appear to him to be concerned.

58. Treatment requiring consent or a second opinion

(1)   This section applies to the following forms of medical treatment for mental disorder—

(a)   such forms of treatment as may be specified for the purposes of this section by regulations made by the Secretary of State;

(b)   the administration of medicine to a patient by any means (not being a form of treatment specified under paragraph (a) above or section 57 above) at any time during a period for which he is liable to be detained as a patient to whom this Part of this Act applies if three months or more have elapsed since the first occasion in that period when medicine was administered to him by any means for his mental disorder.

(2)   The Secretary of State may by order vary the length of the period mentioned in subsection (1)(b) above.

(3)   Subject to section 62 below, a patient shall not be given any form of treatment to which this section applies unless—

(a)   he has consented to that treatment and either the responsible medical officer or a registered medical practitioner appointed for the purposes of this Part of this Act by the Secretary of State has certified in writing that the patient is capable of understanding its nature, purpose and likely effects and has consented to it; or

(b)   a registered medical practitioner appointed as aforesaid (not being the responsible medical officer) has certified in writing that the patient is not capable of understanding the nature, purpose and likely effects of that treatment or has not consented to it but that, having regard to the likelihood of its alleviating or preventing a deterioration of his condition, the treatment should be given.

(4)   Before giving a certificate under subsection (3)(b) above the registered medical practitioner concerned shall consult two other persons who have been professionally concerned with the patient's medical treatment, and of those persons one shall be a nurse and the other shall be neither a nurse nor a registered medical practitioner.

(5)   Before making any regulations for the purposes of this section the Secretary of State shall consult such bodies as appear to him to be concerned.

59.   Plans of treatment

Any consent or certificate under section 57 or 58 above may relate to a plan of treatment under which the patient is to be given (whether within a specified period or otherwise) one or more of the forms of treatment to which that section applies.

60.   Withdrawal of consent

(1)   Where the consent of a patient to any treatment has been given for the purposes of section 57 or 58 above, the patient may, subject to section 62 below, at any time before the completion of the treatment withdraw his consent, and those sections shall then apply as if the remainder of the treatment were a separate form of treatment.

(2)   Without prejudice to the application of subsection (1) above to any treatment given under the plan of treatment to which a patient has consented, a patient who has consented to such a plan may, subject to section 62 below, at any time withdraw his consent to further treatment, or to further treatment of any description, under the plan.

61.   Review of treatment

(1)   Where a patient is given treatment in accordance with section 57(2) or 58(3)(b) above a report on the treatment and the patient's condition shall be given by the responsible medical officer to the Secretary of State—

(a)   on the next occasion on which the responsible medical officer furnishes a report in respect of the patient under section 20(3) above; and

(b)   at any other time if so required by the Secretary of State.

(2)   In relation to a patient who is subject to a restriction order or restriction direction subsection (1) above shall have effect as if paragraph (a) required the report to be made—

(a)   in the case of treatment in the period of six months beginning with the date of the order or direction, at the end of that period;

(b)   in the case of treatment at any subsequent time, on the next occasion on which the responsible medical officer makes a report in respect of the patient under section 41(6) or 49(3) above.

(3)   The Secretary of State may at any time give notice to the responsible medical officer directing that, subject to section 62 below, a certificate given in respect of a patient under section 57(2) or 58(3)(b) above shall not apply to treatment given to him after a date specified in the notice and sections 57 and 58 above shall then apply to any such treatment as if that certificate had not been given.

62. Urgent treatment

(1)   Sections 57 and 58 above shall not apply to any treatment—

(a)   which is immediately necessary to save the patient's life; or

(b)   which (not being irreversible) is immediately necessary to prevent a serious deterioration of his condition; or

(c)   which (not being irreversible or hazardous) is immediately necessary to alleviate serious suffering by the patient; or

(d)   which (not being irreversible or hazardous) is immediately necessary and represents the minimum interference necessary to prevent the patient from behaving violently or being a danger to himself or to others.

(2)   Sections 60 and 61(3) above shall not preclude the continuation of any treatment or of treatment under any plan pending compliance with section 57 or 58 above if the responsible medical officer considers that the discontinuance of the treatment or of treatment under the plan would cause serious suffering to the patient.

(3)   For the purposes of this section treatment is irreversible if it has unfavourable irreversible physical or psychological consequences and hazardous if it entails significant physical hazard.

63. Treatment not requiring consent

The consent of a patient shall not be required for any medical treatment given to him for the mental disorder from which he is suffering, not being treatment falling within section 57 or 58 above, if the treatment is given by or under the direction of the responsible medical officer.

64. Supplementary provisions for Part IV

(1)   In this Part of this Act "the responsible medical officer" means the registered medical practitioner in charge of the treatment of the patient in question and "hospital" includes a mental nursing home.

(2)   Any certificate for the purposes of this Part of this Act shall be in such form as may be prescribed by regulations made by the Secretary of State.

PART V
MENTAL HEALTH REVIEW TRIBUNALS

Constitution etc.

65. Mental Health Review Tribunals

(1)   There shall continue to be a tribunal known as a Mental Health Review Tribunal for every region for which a Regional Health Authority is established in pursuance of the National Health Service Act 1977 and for Wales, for the purpose of dealing with applications and references by and in respect of patients under the provisions of this Act.

(2)   The provisions of Schedule 2 to this Act shall have effect with respect to the constitution of Mental Health Review Tribunals.

(3)   Subject to the provisions of Schedule 2 to this Act, and to rules made by the Lord Chancellor under this Act, the jurisdiction of a Mental Health Review Tribunal may be exercised by any three or more of its members, and references in this Act to a Mental Health Review Tribunal shall be construed accordingly.

(4)   The Secretary of State may pay to the members of Mental Health Review Tribunals such remuneration and allowances as he may with the consent of the Treasury determine, and defray the expenses of such tribunals to such amount as he may with the consent of the Treasury determine, and may provide for each such tribunal such officers and servants, and such accommodation, as the tribunal may require.

Applications and references concerning Part II patients

66. Applications to tribunals

(1) Where—

(a) a patient is admitted to a hospital in pursuance of an application for admission for assessment; or

(b) a patient is admitted to a hospital in pursuance of an application for admission for treatment; or

(c) a patient is received into guardianship in pursuance of a guardianship application; or

(d) a report is furnished under section 16 above in respect of a patient; or

(e) a patient is transferred from guardianship to a hospital in pursuance of regulations made under section 19 above; or

(f) a report is furnished under section 20 above in respect of a patient and the patient is not discharged; or

(g) a report is furnished under section 25 above in respect of a patient who is detained in pursuance of an application for admission for treatment; or

(h) an order is made under section 29 above in respect of a patient who is or subsequently becomes liable to be detained or subject to guardianship under Part II of this Act,

an application may be made to a Mental Health Review Tribunal within the relevant period—

(i) by the patient (except in the cases mentioned in paragraphs (g) and (h) above) or, in the case mentioned in paragraph (d) above, by his nearest relative, and

(ii) in the cases mentioned in paragraphs (g) and (h) above, by his nearest relative.

(2) In subsection (1) above "the relevant period" means—

(a) in the case mentioned in paragraph (a) of that subsection, 14 days beginning with the day on which the patient is admitted as so mentioned;

(b) in the case mentioned in paragraph (b) of that subsection, six months beginning with the day on which the patient is admitted as so mentioned;

(c) in the case mentioned in paragraph (c) of that subsection, six months beginning with the day on which the application is accepted;

(d) in the cases mentioned in paragraphs (d) and (g) of that subsection, 28 days beginning with the day on which the applicant is informed that the report has been furnished;

(e) in the case mentioned in paragraph (e) of that subsection, six months beginning with the day on which the patient is transferred;

(f) in the case mentioned in paragraph (f) of that subsection, the period for which authority for the patient's detention or guardianship is renewed by virtue of the report;

(g) in the case mentioned in paragraph (h) of that subsection, 12 months beginning with the date of the order, and in any subsequent period of 12 months during which the order continues in force.

(3) Section 32 above shall apply for the purposes of this section as it applies for the purposes of Part II of this Act.

67. References to tribunals by Secretary of State concerning Part II patients

(1) The Secretary of State may, if he thinks fit, at any time refer to a Mental Health Review Tribunal the case of any patient who is liable to be detained or subject to guardianship under Part II of this Act.

(2) For the purpose of furnishing information for the purposes of a reference under subsection (1) above any registered medical practitioner authorised by or on behalf of the patient may, at any reasonable time, visit the patient and examine him in private and require the production of and inspect any records relating to the detention or treatment of the patient in any hospital.

(3)   Section 32 above shall apply for the purposes of this section as it applies for the purposes of Part II of this Act.

68.   Duty of managers of hospitals to refer cases to tribunal

(1)   Where a patient who is admitted to a hospital in pursuance of an application for admission for treatment or a patient who is transferred from guardianship to hospital does not exercise his right to apply to a Mental Health Review Tribunal under section 66(1) above by virtue of his case falling within paragraph (b) or, as the case may be, paragraph (e) of that section, the managers of the hospital shall at the expiration of the period for making such an application refer the patient's case to such a tribunal unless an application or reference in respect of the patient has then been made under section 66(1) above by virtue of his case falling within paragraph (d), (g) or (h) of that section or under section 67(1) above.

(2)   If the authority for the detention of a patient in a hospital is renewed under section 20 above and a period of three years (or, if the patient has not attained the age of sixteen years, one year) has elapsed since his case was last considered by a Mental Health Review Tribunal, whether on his own application or otherwise, the managers of the hospital shall refer his case to such a tribunal.

(3)   For the purpose of furnishing information for the purposes of any reference under this section, any registered medical practitioner authorised by or on behalf of the patient may at any reasonable time visit and examine the patient in private and require the production of and inspect any records relating to the detention or treatment of the patient in any hospital.

(4)   The Secretary of State may by order vary the length of the periods mentioned in subsection (2) above.

(5)   For the purposes of subsection (1) above a person who applies to a tribunal but subsequently withdraws his application shall be treated as not having exercised his right to apply, and where a person withdraws his application on a date after the expiration of the period mentioned in that subsection, the managers shall refer the patient's case as soon as possible after that date.

Applications and references concerning Part III patients

69.   Applications to tribunals concerning patients subject to hospital and guardianship orders

(1)   Without prejudice to any provision of section 66(1) above as applied by section 40(4) above, an application to a Mental Health Review Tribunal may also be made—

(a)   in respect of a patient admitted to a hospital in pursuance of a hospital order, by the nearest relative of the patient in the period between the expiration of six months and the expiration of 12 months beginning with the date of the order and in any subsequent period of 12 months; and

(b)   in respect of a patient placed under guardianship by a guardianship order—

(i)   by the patient, within the period of six months beginning with the date of the order;

(ii)   by the nearest relative of the patient, within the period of 12 months beginning with the date of the order and in any subsequent period of 12 months.

(2)   Where a person detained in a hospital—

(a)   is treated as subject to a hospital order or transfer direction by virtue of section 41(5) above, 82(2) or 85(2) below, section 77(2) of the Mental Health (Scotland) Act 1984 or section 5(1) of the Criminal Procedure (Insanity) Act 1964; or

(b)   is subject to a direction having the same effect as a hospital order by virtue of section 46(3), 47(3) or 48(3) above,

then, without prejudice to any provision of Part II of this Act as applied by section 40 above, that person may make an application to a Mental Health Review Tribunal in the period of six months beginning with the date of the order or direction mentioned in paragraph (a) above or, as the case may be, the date of the direction mentioned in paragraph (b) above.

70. Applications to tribunals concerning restricted patients
A patient who is a restricted patient within the meaning of section 79 below and is detained in a hospital may apply to a Mental Health Review Tribunal—
    (a)   in the period between the expiration of six months and the expiration of 12 months beginning with the date of the relevant hospital order or transfer direction; and
    (b)   in any subsequent period of 12 months.

71. References by Secretary of State concerning restricted patients
    (1)   The Secretary of State may at any time refer the case of a restricted patient to a Mental Health Review Tribunal.
    (2)   The Secretary of State shall refer to a Mental Health Review Tribunal the case of any restricted patient detained in a hospital whose case has not been considered by such a tribunal, whether on his own application or otherwise, within the last three years.
    (3)   The Secretary of State may by order vary the length of the period mentioned in subsection (2) above.
    (4)   Any reference under subsection (1) above in respect of a patient who has been conditionally discharged and not recalled to hospital shall be made to the tribunal for the area in which the patient resides.
    (5)   Where a person who is treated as subject to a hospital order and a restriction order by virtue of an order under section 5(1) of the Criminal Procedure (Insanity) Act 1964 does not exercise his right to apply to a Mental Health Review Tribunal in the period of six months beginning with the date of that order, the Secretary of State shall at the expiration of that period refer his case to a tribunal.
    (6)   For the purposes of subsection (5) above a person who applies to a tribunal but subsequently withdraws his application shall be treated as not having exercised his right to apply, and where a patient withdraws his application on a date after the expiration of the period there mentioned the Secretary of State shall refer his case as soon as possible after that date.

Discharge of patients

72. Powers of tribunals
    (1)   Where application is made to a Mental Health Review Tribunal by or in respect of a patient who is liable to be detained under this Act, the tribunal may in any case direct that the patient be discharged, and—
    (a)   the tribunal shall direct the discharge of a patient liable to be detained under section 2 above if they are satisfied—
        (i)   that he is not then suffering from mental disorder or from mental disorder of a nature or degree which warrants his detention in a hospital for assessment (or for assessment followed by medical treatment) for at least a limited period; or
        (ii)   that his detention as aforesaid is not justified in the interests of his own health or safety or with a view to the protection of other persons;
    (b)   the tribunal shall direct the discharge of a patient liable to be detained otherwise than under section 2 above if they are satisfied—
        (i)   that he is not then suffering from mental illness, psychopathic disorder, severe mental impairment or mental impairment or from any of those forms of disorder of a nature or degree which makes it appropriate for him to be liable to be detained in a hospital for medical treatment; or
        (ii)   that it is not necessary for the health or safety of the patient or for the protection of other persons that he should receive such treatment; or

(iii)   in the case of an application by virtue of paragraph (g) of section 66(1) above, that the patient, if released, would not be likely to act in a manner dangerous to other persons or to himself.

(2)   In determining whether to direct the discharge of a patient detained otherwise than under section 2 above in a case not falling within pararaph (b) of subsection (1) above, the tribunal shall have regard—

(a)   to the likelihood of medical treatment alleviating or preventing a deterioration of the patient's condition; and

(b)   in the case of a patient suffering from mental illness or severe mental impairment, to the likelihood of the patient, if discharged, being able to care for himself, to obtain the care he needs or to guard himself against serious exploitation.

(3)   A tribunal may under subsection (1) above direct the discharge of a patient on a future date specified in the direction; and where a tribunal do not direct the discharge of a patient under that subsection the tribunal may—

(a)   with a view to facilitating his discharge on a future date, recommend that he be granted leave of absence or transferred to another hospital or into guardianship; and

(b)   further consider his case in the event of any such recommendation not being complied with.

(4)   Where application is made to a Mental Health Review Tribunal by or in respect of a patient who is subject to guardianship under this Act, the tribunal may in any case direct that the patient be discharged, and shall so direct if they are satisfied—

(a)   that he is not then suffering from mental illness, psychopathic disorder, severe mental impairment or mental impairment; or

(b)   that it is not necessary in the interests of the welfare of the patient, or for the protection of other persons, that the patient should remain under such guardianship.

(5)   Where application is made to a Mental Health Review Tribunal under any provision of this Act by or in respect of a patient and the tribunal do not direct that the patient be discharged, the tribunal may, if satisfied that the patient is suffering from a form of mental disorder other than the form specified in the application, order or direction relating to him, direct that that application, order or direction be amended by substituting for the form of mental disorder specified in it such other form of mental disorder as appears to the tribunal to be appropriate.

(6)   Subsections (1) to (5) above apply in relation to references to a Mental Health Review Tribunal as they apply in relation to applications made to such a tribunal by or in respect of a patient.

(7)   Subsection (1) above shall not apply in the case of a restricted patient except as provided in sections 73 and 74 below.

73.   Power to discharge restricted patients

(1)   Where an application to a Mental Health Review Tribunal is made by a restricted patient who is subject to a restriction order, or where the case of such a patient is referred to such a tribunal, the tribunal shall direct the absolute discharge of the patient if satisfied—

(a)   as to the matters mentioned in paragraph (b)(i) or (ii) of section 72(1) above; and

(b)   that it is not appropriate for the patient to remain liable to be recalled to hospital for further treatment.

(2)   Where in the case of any such patient as is mentioned in subsection (1) above the tribunal are satisfied as to the matters referred to in paragraph (a) of that subsection but not as to the matter referred to in paragraph (b) of that subsection the tribunal shall direct the conditional discharge of the patient.

(3)   Where a patient is absolutely discharged under this section he shall thereupon cease to be liable to be detained by virtue of the relevant hospital order, and the restriction order shall cease to have effect accordingly.

(4) Where a patient is conditionally discharged under this section—

(a) he may be recalled by the Secretary of State under subsection (3) of section 42 above as if he had been conditionally discharged under subsection (2) of that section; and

(b) the patient shall comply with such conditions (if any) as may be imposed at the time of discharge by the tribunal or at any subsequent time by the Secretary of State.

(5) The Secretary of State may from time to time vary any condition imposed (whether by the tribunal or by him) under subsection (4) above.

(6) Where a restriction order in respect of a patient ceases to have effect after he has been conditionally discharged under his section the patient shall, unless previously recalled, be deemed to be absolutely discharged on the date when the order ceases to have effect and shall cease to be liable to be detained by virtue of the relevant hospital order.

(7) A tribunal may defer a direction for the conditional discharge of a patient until such arrangements as appear to the tribunal to be necessary for that purpose have been made to their satisfaction; and where by virtue of any such deferment no direction has been given on an application or reference before the time when the patient's case comes before the tribunal on a subsequent application or reference, the previous application or reference shall be treated as one on which no direction under this section can be given.

(8) This section is without prejudice to section 42 above.

74. Restricted patients subject to restriction directions

(1) Where an application to a Mental Health Review Tribunal is made by a restricted patient who is subject to a restriction direction, or where the case of such a patient is referred to such a tribunal, the tribunal—

(a) shall notify the Secretary of State whether, in their opinion, the patient would, if subject to a restriction order, be entitled to be absolutely or conditionally discharged under section 73 above; and

(b) if they notify him that the patient would be entitled to be conditionally discharged, may recommend that in the event of his not being discharged under his section he should continue to be detained in hospital.

(2) If in the case of a patient not falling within subsection (4) below—

(a) the tribunal notify the Secretary of State that the patient would be entitled to be absolutely or conditionally discharged; and

(b) within the period of 90 days beginning with the date of that notification the Secretary of State gives notice to the tribunal that the patient may be so discharged, the tribunal shall direct the absolute or, as the case may be, the conditional discharge of the patient.

(3) Where a patient continues to be liable to be detained in a hospital at the end of the period referred to in subsection (2)(b) above because the Secretary of State has not given the notice there mentioned, the managers of the hospital shall, unless the tribunal have made a recommendation under subsection (1)(b) above, transfer the patient to a prison or other institution in which he might have been detained if he had not been removed to hospital, there to be dealt with as if he had not been so removed.

(4) If, in the case of a patient who is subject to a transfer direction under section 48 above, the tribunal notify the Secretary of State that the patient would be entitled to be absolutely or conditionally discharged, the Secretary of State shall, unless the tribunal have made a recommendation under subsection (1)(b) above, by warrant direct that the patient be remitted to a prison or other institution in which he might have been detained if he had not been removed to hospital, there to be dealt with as if he had not been so removed.

(5)   Where a patient is transferred or remitted under subsection (3) or (4) above the relevant transfer direction and the restriction direction shall cease to have effect on his arrival in the prison or other institution.

(6)   Subsections (3) to (8) of section 73 above shall have effect in relation to this section as they have effect in relation to that section, taking references to the relevant hospital order and the restriction order as references to the transfer direction and the restriction direction.

(7)   This section is without prejudice to sections 50 to 53 above in their application to patients who are not discharged under this section.

75.   Applications and references concerning conditionally discharged restricted patients

(1)   Where a restricted patient has been conditionally discharged under section 42(2), 73 or 74 above and is subsequently recalled to hospital—

(a)   the Secretary of State shall, within one month of the day on which the patient returns or is returned to hospital, refer his case to a Mental Health Review Tribunal; and

(b)   section 70 above shall apply to the patient as if the relevant hospital order or transfer direction had been made on that day.

(2)   Where a restricted patient has been conditionally discharged as aforesaid but has not been recalled to hospital he may apply to a Mental Health Review Tribunal—

(a)   in the period between the expiration of 12 months and the expiration of two years beginning with the date on which he was conditionally discharged; and

(b)   in any subsequent period of two years.

(3)   Sections 73 and 74 above shall not apply to an application under subsection (2) above but on any such application the tribunal may—

(a)   vary any condition to which the patient is subject in connection with his discharge or impose any condition which might have been imposed in connection therewith; or

(b)   direct that the restriction order or restriction direction to which he is subject shall cease to have effect;

and if the tribunal give a direction under paragraph (b) above the patient shall cease to be liable to be detained by virtue of the relevant hospital order or transfer direction.

General

76.   Visiting and examination of patients

(1)   For the purpose of advising whether an application to a Mental Health Review Tribunal should be made by or in respect of a patient who is liable to be detained or subject to guardianship under Part II of this Act or of furnishing information as to the condition of a patient for the purposes of such an application, any registered medical practitioner authorised by or on behalf of the patient or other person who is entitled to make or has made the application—

(a)   may at any reasonable time visit the patient and examine him in private, and

(b)   may require the production of and inspect any records relating to the detention or treatment of the patient in any hospital.

(2)   Section 32 above shall apply for the purposes of this section as it applies for the purposes of Part II of this Act.

77.   General provisions concerning tribunal applications

(1)   No application shall be made to a Mental Health Review Tribunal by or in respect of a patient except in such cases and at such times as are expressly provided by this Act.

(2)   Where under this Act any person is authorised to make an application to a Mental Health Review Tribunal within a specified period, not more than one such

application shall be made by that person within that period but for that purpose there shall be disregarded any application which is withdrawn in accordance with rules made under section 78 below.

(3) Subject to subsection (4) below an application to a Mental Health Review Tribunal authorised to be made by or in respect of a patient under this Act shall be made by notice in writing addressed to the tribunal for the area in which the hospital in which the patient is detained is situated or in which the patient is residing under guardianship as the case may be.

(4) Any application under section 75(2) above shall be made to the tribunal for the area in which the patient resides.

78. Procedure of tribunals

(1) The Lord Chancellor may make rules with respect to the making of applications to Mental Health Review Tribunals and with respect to the proceedings of such tribunals and matters incidental to or consequential on such proceedings.

(2) Rules made under this section may in particular make provision—

(a) for enabling a tribunal, or the chairman of a tribunal, to postpone the consideration of any application by or in respect of a patient, or of any such application of any specified class, until the expiration of such period (not exceeding 12 months) as may be specified in the rules from the date on which an application by or in respect of the same patient was last considered and determined by that or any other tribunal under this Act;

(b) for the transfer of proceedings from one tribunal to another in any case where, after the making of the application, the patient is removed out of the area of the tribunal to which it was made;

(c) for restricting the persons qualified to serve as members of a tribunal for the consideration of any application, or of an application of any specified class;

(d) for enabling a tribunal to dispose of an application without a formal hearing where such a hearing is not requested by the applicant or it appears to the tribunal that such a hearing would be detrimental to the health of the patient;

(e) for enabling a tribunal to exclude members of the public, or any specified class of members of the public, from any proceedings of the tribunal, or to prohibit the publication of reports of any such proceedings or the names of any persons concerned in such proceedings;

(f) for regulating the circumstances in which, and the persons by whom, applicants and patients in respect of whom applications are made to a tribunal may, if not desiring to conduct their own case, be represented for the purposes of those applications;

(g) for regulating the methods by which information relevant to an application may be obtained by or furnished to the tribunal, and in particular for authorising the members of a tribunal, or any one or more of them, to visit and interview in private any patient by or in respect of whom an application has been made;

(h) for making available to any applicant, and to any patient in respect of whom an application is made to a tribunal, copies of any documents obtained by or furnished to the tribunal in connection with the application, and a statement of the substance of any oral information so obtained or furnished except where the tribunal considers it undesirable in the interests of the patient or for other special reasons;

(i) for requiring a tribunal, if so requested in accordance with the rules, to furnish such statements of the reasons for any decision given by the tribunal as may be prescribed by the rules, subject to any provision made by the rules for withholding such a statement from a patient or any other person in cases where the tribunal considers that furnishing it would be undesirable in the interests of the patient or for other special reasons;

(j)   for conferring on the tribunals such ancillary powers as the Lord Chancellor thinks necessary for the purposes of the exercise of their functions under this Act;

(k)   for enabling any functions of a tribunal which relate to matters preliminary or incidental to an application to be performed by the chairman of the tribunal.

(3)   Subsections (1) and (2) above apply in relation to references to Mental Health Review Tribunals as they apply in relation to applications to such tribunals by or in respect of patients.

(4)   Rules under this section may make provision as to the procedure to be adopted in cases concerning restricted patients and, in particular—

(a)   for restricting the persons qualified to serve as president of a tribunal for the consideration of an application or reference relating to a restricted patient;

(b)   for the transfer of proceedings from one tribunal to another in any case where, after the making of a reference or application in accordance with section 71(4) or 77(4) above, the patient ceases to reside in the area of the tribunal to which the reference or application was made.

(5)   Rules under this section may be so framed as to apply to all applications or references or to applications or references of any specified class and may make different provision in relation to different cases.

(6)   Any functions conferred on the chairman of a Mental Health Review Tribunal by rules under this section may, if for any reason he is unable to act, be exercised by another member of that tribunal appointed by him for the purpose.

(7)   A Mental Health Review Tribunal may pay allowances in respect of travelling expenses, subsistence and loss of earnings to any person attending the tribunal as an applicant or witness, to the patient who is the subject of the proceedings if he attends otherwise than as the applicant or a witness and to any person (other than counsel or a solicitor) who attends as the representative of an applicant.

(8)   A Mental Health Review Tribunal may, and if so required by the High Court shall, state in the form of a special case for determination by the High Court any question of law which may arise before them.

(9)   The Arbitration Act 1950 shall not apply to any proceedings before a Mental Health Review Tribunal except so far as any provisions of that Act may be applied, with or without modifications, by rules made under this section.

79.   Interpretation of Part V

(1)   In this Part of this Act "restricted patient" means a patient who is subject to a restriction order or restriction direction and this Part of this Act shall, subject to the provisions of this section, have effect in relation to any person who—

(a)   is subject to a direction which by virtue of section 46(3) above has the same effect as a hospital order and a restriction order; or

(b)   is treated as subject to a hospital order and a restriction order by virtue of an order under section 5(1) of the Criminal Procedure (Insanity) Act 1964 or section 6 or 14(1) of the Criminal Appeal Act 1968; or

(c)   is treated as subject to a hospital order and a restriction order or to a transfer direction and a restriction direction by virtue of section 82(2) or 85(2) below or section 77(2) of the Mental Health (Scotland) Act 1984,
as it has effect in relation to a restricted patient.

(2)   Subject to the following provisions of this section, in this Part of this Act "the relevant hospital order" and "the relevant transfer direction", in relation to a restricted patient, mean the hospital order or transfer direction by virtue of which he is liable to be detained in a hospital.

(3)   In the case of a person within paragraph (a) of subsection (1) above, references in this Part of this Act to the relevant hospital order or restriction order shall be construed as references to the direction referred to in that paragraph.

(4)   In the case of a person within paragraph (b) of subsection (1) above, references in this Part of this Act to the relevant hospital order or restriction order shall be construed as references to the order under the provisions mentioned in that paragraph.

(5)   In the case of a person within paragraph (c) of subsection (1) above, references in this Part of this Act to the relevant hospital order, the relevant transfer direction, the restriction order or the restriction direction or to a transfer direction under section 48 above shall be construed as references to the hospital order, transfer direction, restriction order, restriction direction or transfer direction under that section to which that person is treated as subject by virtue of the provisions mentioned in that paragraph.

(6)   In this Part of this Act, unless the context otherwise requires, "hospital" means a hospital within the meaning of Part II of this Act.

PART VII
MANAGEMENT OF PROPERTY AND AFFAIRS OF PATIENTS

93.   Judicial authorities and Court of Protection

(1)   The Lord Chancellor shall from time to time nominate one or more judges of the Supreme Court (in this Act referred to as "nominated judges") to act for the purposes of this Part of this Act.

(2)   There shall continue to be an office of the Supreme Court, called the Court of Protection, for the protection and management, as provided by this Part of this Act, of the property and affairs of persons under disability; and there shall continue to be a Master of the Court of Protection appointed by the Lord Chancellor under section 89 of the Supreme Court Act 1981.

(4)   The Lord Chancellor may nominate other officers of the Court of Protection (in this Part of this Act referred to as "nominated officers") to act for the purposes of this Part of this Act.

94.   Exercise of the judge's functions: "the patient"

(1)   Subject to subsection (1A) below the functions expressed to be conferred by this Part of this Act on the judge shall be exercisable by the Lord Chancellor or by any nominated judge, and shall also be exercisable by the Master of the Court of Protection, by the Public Trustee, or by any nominated officer, but—

(a)   in the case of the Master, the Public Trustee or any nominated officer, subject to any express provision to the contrary in this Part of this Act or any rules made under this Part of this Act,

(aa)   in the case of the Public Trustee, subject to any directions of the Master and so far only as may be provided by any rules made under this Part of this Act or (subject to any such rules) by directions of the Master;

(b)   in the case of any nominated officer, subject to any directions of the Master and so far only as may be provided by the instrument by which he is nominated;
and references in this Part of this Act to the judge shall be construed accordingly.

(1A)   In such cases or circumstances as may be prescribed by any rules under this Part of this Act or (subject to any such rules) by directions of the Master, the functions of the judge under this Part of this Act shall be exercised by the Public Trustee (but subject to any directions of the Master as to their exercise).

(2)   The functions of the judge under this Part of this Act shall be exercisable where, after considering medical evidence, he is satisfied that a person is incapable, by reason of mental disorder, of managing and administering his property and affairs; and a person as to whom the judge is so satisfied is referred to in this Part of this Act as a patient.

95.   General functions of the judge with respect to property and affairs of patient

(1)   The judge may, with respect to the property and affairs of a patient, do or secure the doing of all such things as appear necessary or expedient—

(a)   for the maintenance or other benefit of the patient,

(b)   for the maintenance or other benefit of members of the patient's family,

(c)   for making provision for other persons or purposes for whom or which the patient might be expected to provide if he were not mentally disordered, or

(d)   otherwise for administering the patient's affairs.

(2)   In the exercise of the powers conferred by this section regard shall be had first of all to the requirements of the patient, and the rules of law which restricted the enforcement by a creditor of rights against property under the control of the judge in lunacy shall apply to property under the control of the judge; but, subject to the foregoing provisions of this subsection, the judge shall, in administering a patient's affairs, have regard to the interests of creditors and also to the desirability of making provision for obligations of the patient notwithstanding that they may not be legally enforceable.

96.   Powers of the judge as to patient's property and affairs

(1)   Without prejudice to the generality of section 95 above, the judge shall have power to make such orders and give such directions and authorities as he thinks fit for the purposes of that section and in particular may for those purposes make orders or give directions or authorities for—

(a)   the control (with or without the transfer or vesting of property or the payment into or lodgment in the Supreme Court of money or securities) and management of any property of the patient;

(b)   the sale, exchange, charging or other disposition of or dealing with any property of the patient;

(c)   the acquisition of any property in the name or on behalf of the patient;

(d)   the settlement of any property of the patient, or the gift of any property of the patient to any such persons or for any such purposes as are mentioned in paragraphs (b) and (c) of section 95(1) above;

(e)   the execution for the patient of a will making any provision (whether by way of disposing of property or exercising a power or otherwise) which could be made by a will executed by the patient if he were not mentally disordered;

(f)   the carrying on by a suitable person of any profession, trade or business of the patient;

(g)   the dissolution of a partnership of which the patient is a member;

(h)   the carrying out of any contract entered into by the patient;

(i)   the conduct of legal proceedings in the name of the patient or on his behalf;

(j)   the reimbursement out of the property of the patient, with or without interest, of money applied by any person either in payment of the patient's debts (whether legally enforceable or not) or for the maintenance or other benefit of the patient or members of his family or in making provision for other persons or purposes for whom or which he might be expected to provide if he were not mentally disordered;

(k)   the exercise of any power (including a power to consent) vested in the patient, whether beneficially, or as guardian or trustee, or otherwise.

(2)   If under subsection (1) above provision is made for the settlement of any property of a patient, or the exercise of a power vested in a patient of appointing trustees or retiring from a trust, the judge may also make as respects the property settled or trust property such consequential vesting or other orders as the case may require, including (in the case of the exercise of such a power) any order which could have been made in such a case under Part IV of the Trustee Act 1925.

(3)   Where under this section a settlement has been made of any property of a patient, and the Lord Chancellor or a nominated judge is satisfied, at any time before the death of the patient, that any material fact was not disclosed when the settlement was made, or that there has been any substantial change in circumstances, he may by

order vary the settlement in such manner as he thinks fit, and give any consequential directions.

(4) The power of the judge to make or give an order, direction or authority for the execution of a will for a patient—

(a) shall not be exercisable at any time when the patient is a minor, and

(b) shall not be exercised unless the judge has reason to believe that the patient is incapable of making a valid will for himself.

(5) The powers of a patient as patron of a benefice shall be exercisable by the Lord Chancellor only.

98. Judge's powers in cases of emergency

Where it is represented to the judge, and he has reason to believe, that a person may be incapable, by reason of mental disorder, of managing and administering his property and affairs, and the judge is of the opinion that it is necessary to make immediate provision for any of the matters referred to in section 95 above, then pending the determination of the question whether that person is so incapable the judge may exercise in relation to the property and affairs of that person any of the powers conferred on him in relation to the property and affairs of a patient by this Part of this Act so far as is requisite for enabling that provision to be made.

99. Power to appoint receiver

(1) The judge may by order appoint as receiver for a patient a person specified in the order or the holder for the time being of an office so specified.

(2) A person appointed as receiver for a patient shall do all such things in relation to the property and affairs of the patient as the judge, in the exercise of the powers conferred on him by sections 95 and 96 above, orders or directs him to do and may do any such thing in relation to the property and affairs of the patient as the judge, in the exercise of those powers, authorises him to do.

(3) A receiver appointed for any person shall be discharged by order of the judge on the judge being satisfied that that person has become capable of managing and administering his property and affairs, and may be discharged by order of the judge at any time if the judge considers it expedient to do so; and a receiver shall be discharged (without any order) on the death of the patient.

102. Lord Chancellor's Visitors

(1) There shall continue to be the following panels of Lord Chancellor's Visitors of patients constituted in accordance with this section, namely—

(a) a panel of Medical Visitors;

(b) a panel of Legal Visitors; and

(c) a panel of General Visitors (being Visitors who are not required by this section to possess either a medical or legal qualification for appointment).

(2) Each panel shall consist of persons appointed to it by the Lord Chancellor, the appointment of each person being for such term and subject to such conditions as the Lord Chancellor may determine.

(3) A person shall not be qualified to be appointed—

(a) to the panel of Medical Visitors unless he is a registered medical practitioner who appears to the Lord Chancellor to have special knowledge and experience of cases of mental disorder;

(b) to the panel of Legal Visitors unless he has a 10 year general qualification within the meaning of section 71 of the Courts and Legal Services Act 1990.

(4) If the Lord Chancellor so determines in the case of any Visitor appointed under this section, he shall be paid out of money provided by Parliament such remuneration and allowances as the Lord Chancellor may, with the concurrence of the Treasury, determine.

103. Functions of Visitors

(1)   Patients shall be visited by Lord Chancellor's Visitors in such circumstances, and in such manner, as may be prescribed by directions of a standing nature given by the Master of the Court of Protection with the concurrence of the Lord Chancellor.

(2)   Where it appears to the judge in the case of any patient that a visit by a Lord Chancellor's Visitor is necessary for the purpose of investigating any particular matter or matters relating to the capacity of the patient to manage and administer his property and affairs, or otherwise relating to the exercise in relation to him of the functions of the judge under this Part of this Act, the judge may order that the patient shall be visited for that purpose.

(3)   Every visit falling to be made under subsection (1) or (2) above shall be made by a General Visitor unless, in a case where it appears to the judge that it is in the circumstances essential for the visit to be made by a Visitor with medical or legal qualifications, the judge directs that the visit shall be made by a Medical or a Legal Visitor.

(4)   A Visitor making a visit under this section shall make such report on the visit as the judge may direct.

(5)   A Visitor making a visit under this section may interview the patient in private.

(6)   A Medical Visitor making a visit under this section may carry out in private a medical examination of the patient and may require the production of and inspect any medical records relating to the patient.

(7)   The Master of the Court of Protection may visit any patient for the purpose mentioned in subsection (2) above and may interview the patient in private.

(8)   A report made by a Visitor under this section, and information contained in such a report, shall not be disclosed except to the judge and any person authorised by the judge to receive the disclosure.

(9)   If any person discloses any report or information in contravention of subsection (8) above, he shall be guilty of an offence and liable on summary conviction to imprisonment for a term not exceeding three months or to a fine not exceeding level 3 on the standard scale or both.

(10)   In this section references to patients include references to persons alleged to be incapable, by reason of mental disorder, of managing and administering their property and affairs.

105. Appeals

(1)   Subject to and in accordance with rules under this Part of this Act, an appeal shall lie to a nominated judge from any decision of the Master of the Court of Protection or any nominated officer.

112. Interpretation of Part VII

In this Part of this Act, unless the context otherwise requires—

"nominated judge" means a judge nominated in pursuance of subsection (1) of section 93 above;

"nominated officer" means an officer nominated in pursuance of subsection (4) of that section;

"patient" has the meaning assigned to it by section 94 above;

"property" includes any thing in action, and any interest in real or personal property;

"the judge" shall be construed in accordance with section 94 above;

"will" includes a codicil.

PART VIII
MISCELLANEOUS FUNCTIONS OF LOCAL AUTHORITIES AND THE SECRETARY OF STATE

Approved social workers

114. Appointment of approved social workers

(1)   A local social services authority shall appoint a sufficient number of approved social workers for the purpose of discharging the functions conferred on them by this Act.

(2)   No person shall be appointed by a local social services authority as an approved social worker unless he is approved by the authority as having appropriate competence in dealing with persons who are suffering from mental disorder.

(3)   In approving a person for appointment as an approved social worker a local social services authority shall have regard to such matters as the Secretary of State may direct.

115. Powers of entry and inspection

An approved social worker of a local social services authority may at all reasonable times after producing, if asked to do so, some duly authenticated document showing that he is such a social worker, enter and inspect any premises (not being a hospital) in the area of that authority in which a mentally disordered patient is living, if he has reasonable cause to believe that the patient is not under proper care.

Visiting patients

116. Welfare of certain hospital patients

(1)   Where a patient to whom this section applies is admitted to a hospital or nursing home in England and Wales (whether for treatment for mental disorder or for any other reason) then, without prejudice to their duties in relation to the patient apart from the provisions of this section, the authority shall arrange for visits to be made to him on behalf of the authority, and shall take such other steps in relation to the patient while in the hospital or nursing home as would be expected to be taken by his parents.

(2)   This section applies to—

   (a)   a child or young person—

      (i)   who is in the care of a local authority by virtue of a care order within the meaning of the Children Act 1989, or

      (ii)   in respect of whom the rights and powers of a parent are vested in a local authority by virtue of section 16 of the Social Work (Scotland) Act 1968;

   (b)   a person who is subject to the guardianship of a local social services authority under the provisions of this Act or the Mental Health (Scotland) Act 1984; or

   (c)   a person the functions of whose nearest relative under this Act or under the Mental Health (Scotland) Act 1984 are for the time being transferred to a local social services authority.

After-care

117. After-care

(1)   This section applies to persons who are detained under section 3 above, or admitted to a hospital in pursuance of a hospital order made under section 37 above, or transferred to a hospital in pursuance of a transfer direction made under section 47 or 48 above, and then cease to be detained and leave hospital.

(2)   It shall be the duty of the District Health Authority and of the local social services authority to provide, in co-operation with relevant voluntary agencies, after-care services for any person to whom this section applies until such time as the District Health Authority and the local social services authority are satisfied that the person concerned is no longer in need of such services.

(3) In this section "the District Health Authority" means such District Health Authority as may be determined in accordance with regulations made by the Secretary of State, and "the local social services authority" means the local social services authority for the area in which the person concerned is resident or to which he is sent on discharge by the hospital in which he was detained.

Functions of the Secretary of State

118. Code of practice

(1) The Secretary of State shall prepare, and from time to time revise, a code of practice—

(a) for the guidance of registered medical practitioners, managers and staff of hospitals and mental nursing homes and approved social workers in relation to the admission of patients to hospitals and mental nursing homes under this Act; and

(b) for the guidance of registered medical practitioners and members of other professions in relation to the medical treatment of patients suffering from mental disorder.

(2) The code shall, in particular, specify forms of medical treatment in addition to any specified by regulations made for the purposes of section 57 above which in the opinion of the Secretary of State give rise to special concern and which should accordingly not be given by a registered medical practitioner unless the patient has consented to the treatment (or to a plan of treatment including that treatment) and a certificate in writing as to the matters mentioned in subsection (2)(a) and (b) of that section has been given by another registered medical practitioner, being a practitioner appointed for the purposes of this section by the Secretary of State.

(3) Before preparing the code or making any alteration in it the Secretary of State shall consult such bodies as appear to him to be concerned.

(4) The Secretary of State shall lay copies of the code and of any alteration in the code before Parliament; and if either House of Parliament passes a resolution requiring the code or any alteration in it to be withdrawn the Secretary of State shall withdraw the code or alteration and, where he withdraws the code, shall prepare a code in substitution for the one which is withdrawn.

(5) No resolution shall be passed by either House of Parliament under subsection (4) above in respect of a code or alteration after the expiration of the period of 40 days beginning with the day on which a copy of the code or alteration was laid before that House; but for the purposes of this subsection no account shall be taken of any time during which Parliament is dissolved or prorogued or during which both Houses are adjourned for more than four days.

(6) The Secretary of State shall publish the code as for the time being in force.

119. Practitioners approved for Part IV and s. 118

(1) The Secretary of State may make such provision as he may with the approval of the Treasury determine for the payment of remuneration, allowances, pensions or gratuities to or in respect of registered medical practitioners appointed by him for the purposes of Part IV of this Act and section 118 above and to or in respect of other persons appointed for the purposes of section 57(2)(a) above.

(2) A registered medical practitioner or other person appointed by the Secretary of State for the purposes of the provisions mentioned in subsection (1) above may, for the purpose of exercising his functions under those provisions, at any reasonable time—

(a) visit and interview and, in the case of a registered medical practitioner, examine in private any patient detained in a mental nursing home; and

(b) require the production of and inspect any records relating to the treatment of the patient in that home.

120. General protection of detained patients

(1) The Secretary of State shall keep under review the exercise of the powers and the discharge of the duties conferred or imposed by this Act so far as relating to the detention of patients or to patients liable to be detained under this Act and shall make arrangements for persons authorised by him in that behalf—

(a) to visit and interview in private patients detained under this Act in hospitals and mental nursing homes; and

(b) to investigate—

(i) any complaint made by a person in respect of a matter that occurred while he was detained under this Act in a hospital or mental nursing home and which he considers has not been satisfactorily dealt with by the managers of that hospital or mental nursing home; and

(ii) any other complaint as to the exercise of the powers or the discharge of the duties conferred or imposed by this Act in respect of a person who is or has been so detained.

(2) The arrangements made under this section in respect of the investigation of complaints may exclude matters from investigation in specified circumstances and shall not require any person exercising functions under the arrangements to undertake or continue with any investigation where he does not consider it appropriate to do so.

(3) Where any such complaint as is mentioned in subsection (1)(b)(ii) above is made by a Member of Parliament and investigated under the arrangements made under this section the results of the investigation shall be reported to him.

(4) For the purpose of any such review as is mentioned in subsection (1) above or of carrying out his functions under arrangements made under this section any person authorised in that behalf by the Secretary of State may at any reasonable time—

(a) visit and interview and, if he is a registered medical practitioner, examine in private any patient in a mental nursing home; and

(7) The powers and duties referred to in subsection (1) above do not include any power or duty conferred or imposed by Part VII of this Act.

121. Mental Health Act Commission

(1) Without prejudice to section 126(3) of the National Health Service Act 1977 (power to vary or revoke orders or directions) there shall continue to be a special health authority known as the Mental Health Act Commission established under section 11 of that Act.

(2) Without prejudice to the generality of his powers under section 13 of that Act, the Secretary of State shall direct the Commission to perform on his behalf—

(a) the function of appointing registered medical practitioners for the purposes of Part IV of this Act and section 118 above and of appointing other persons for the purposes of section 57(2)(a) above; and

(b) the functions of the Secretary of State under sections 61 and 120(1) and (4) above.

(3) The registered medical practitioners and other persons appointed for the purposes mentioned in subsection (2)(a) above may include members of the Commission.

(4) The Secretary of State may, at the request of or after consultation with the Commission and after consulting such other bodies as appear to him to be concerned, direct the Commission to keep under review the care and treatment, or any aspect of the care and treatment, in hospitals and mental nursing homes of patients who are not liable to be detained under this Act.

(5) For the purpose of any such review as is mentioned in subsection (4) above any person authorised in that behalf by the Commission may at any reasonable time—

(a) visit and interview and, if he is a registered medical practitioner, examine in private any patient in a mental nursing home; and

(b)   require the production of and inspect any records relating to the treatment of any person who is or has been a patient in a mental nursing home.

(6)   The Secretary of State may make such provision as he may with the approval of the Treasury determine for the payment of remuneration, allowances, pensions or gratuities to or in respect of persons exercising functions in relation to any such review as is mentioned in subsection (4) above.

(7)   The Commission shall review any decision to withhold a postal packet (or anything contained in it) under subsection (1)(b) or (2) of section 134 below if an application in that behalf is made—

(a)   in a case under subsection (1)(b), by the patient; or

(b)   in a case under subsection (2), either by the patient or by the person by whom the postal packet was sent;

and any such application shall be made within six months of the receipt by the applicant of the notice referred to in subsection (6) of that section.

(8)   On an application under subsection (7) above the Commission may direct that the postal packet which is the subject of the application (or anything contained in it) shall not be withheld and the managers in question shall comply with any such direction.

(9)   The Secretary of State may by regulations make provision with respect to the making and determination of applications under subsection (7) above, including provision for the production to the Commission of any postal packet which is the subject of such an application.

(10)   The Commission shall in the second year after its establishment and subsequently in every second year publish a report on its activities; and copies of every such report shall be sent by the Commission to the Secretary of State who shall lay a copy before each House of Parliament.

122.   Provision of pocket-money for in-patients in hospital

(1)   The Secretary of State may pay to persons who are receiving treatment as in-patients (whether liable to be detained or not) in special hospitals or other hospitals, being hospitals wholly or mainly used for the treatment of persons suffering from mental disorder, such amounts as he thinks fit in respect of their occasional personal expenses where it appears to him that they would otherwise be without resources to meet those expenses.

(2)   For the purposes of the National Health Service Act 1977, the making of payments under this section to persons for whom hospital services are provided under that Act shall be treated as included among those services.

123.   Transfers to and from special hospitals

(1)   Without prejudice to any other provisions of this Act with respect to the transfer of patients, any patient who is for the time being liable to be detained in a special hospital under this Act (other than under section 35, 36 or 38 above) may, upon the directions of the Secretary of State, at any time be removed into any other special hospital.

(2)   Without prejudice to any such provision, the Secretary of State may give directions for the transfer of any patient who is for the time being liable to be so detained into a hospital which is not a special hospital.

(3)   Subsections (2) and (4) of section 19 above shall apply in relation to the transfer or removal of a patient under this section as they apply in relation to the transfer or removal of a patient from one hospital to another under that section.

125.   Inquiries

(1)   The Secretary of State may cause an inquiry to be held in any case where he thinks it advisable to do so in connection with any matter arising under this Act.

(2)   Subsections (2) to (5) of section 250 of the Local Government Act 1972 shall apply to any inquiry held under this Act, except that no local authority shall be ordered to pay costs under subsection (4) of that section in the case of any inquiry unless the authority is a party to the inquiry.

PART IX
OFFENCES

126.   Forgery, false statements, etc.

(1)   Any person who without lawful authority or excuse has in his custody or under his control any document to which this subsection applies, which is, and which he knows or believes to be, false within the meaning of Part I of the Forgery and Counterfeiting Act 1981, shall be guilty of an offence.

(2)   Any person who without lawful authority or excuse makes or has in his custody or under his control, any document so closely resembling a document to which subsection (1) above applies as to be calculated to deceive shall be guilty of an offence.

(3)   The documents to which subsection (1) above applies are any documents purporting to be—

(a)   an application under Part II of this Act;

(b)   a medical recommendation or report under this Act; and

(c)   any other document required or authorised to be made for any of the purposes of this Act.

(4)   Any person who—

(a)   wilfully makes a false entry or statement in any application, recommendation, report, record or other document required or authorised to be made for any of the purposes of this Act; or

(b)   with intent to deceive, makes use of any such entry or statement which he knows to be false,

shall be guilty of an offence.

(5)   Any person guilty of an offence under this section shall be liable—

(a)   on summary conviction, to imprisonment for a term not exceeding six months or to a fine not exceeding the statutory maximum, or to both;

(b)   on conviction on indictment, to imprisonment for a term not exceeding two years or to a fine of any amount, or to both.

127.   Ill-treatment of patients

(1)   It shall be an offence for any person who is an officer on the staff of or otherwise employed in, or who is one of the managers of, a hospital or mental nursing home—

(a)   to ill-treat or wilfully to neglect a patient for the time being receiving treatment for mental disorder as an in-patient in that hospital or home; or

(b)   to ill-treat or wilfully to neglect, on the premises of which the hospital or home forms part, a patient for the time being receiving such treatment there as an out-patient.

(2)   It shall be an offence for any individual to ill-treat or wilfully to neglect a mentally disordered patient who is for the time being subject to his guardianship under this Act or otherwise in his custody or care (whether by virtue of any legal or moral obligation or otherwise).

(3)   Any person guilty of an offence under this section shall be liable—

(a)   on summary conviction, to imprisonment for a term not exceeding six months or to a fine not exceeding the statutory maximum, or to both;

(b)   on conviction on indictment, to imprisonment for a term not exceeding two years or to a fine of any amount, or to both.

(4)   No proceedings shall be instituted for an offence under this section except by or with the consent of the Director of Public Prosecutions.

128. Assisting patients to absent themselves without leave, etc.

(1)   Where any person induces or knowingly assists another person who is liable to be detained in a hospital within the meaning of Part II of this Act or is subject to guardianship under this Act to absent himself without leave he shall be guilty of an offence.

(2)   Where any person induces or knowingly assists another person who is in legal custody by virtue of section 137 below to escape from such custody he shall be guilty of an offence.

(3)   Where any person knowingly harbours a patient who is absent without leave or is otherwise at large and liable to be retaken under this Act or gives him any assistance with intent to prevent, hinder or interfere with his being taken into custody or returned to the hospital or other place where he ought to be he shall be guilty of an offence.

(4)   Any person guilty of an offence under this section shall be liable—

  (a)   on summary conviction, to imprisonment for a term not exceeding six months or to a fine not exceeding the statutory maximum, or to both;

  (b)   on conviction on indictment, to imprisonment for a term not exceeding two years or to a fine of any amount, or to both.

129. Obstruction

(1)   Any person who without reasonable cause—

  (a)   refuses to allow the inspection of any premises; or

  (b)   refuses to allow the visiting, interviewing or examination of any person by a person authorised in that behalf by or under this Act; or

  (c)   refuses to produce for the inspection of any person so authorised any document or record the production of which is duly required by him; or

  (d)   otherwise obstructs any such person in the exercise of his functions,
shall be guilty of an offence.

(2)   Without prejudice to the generality of subsection (1) above, any person who insists on being present when required to withdraw by a person authorised by or under this Act to interview or examine a person in private shall be guilty of an offence.

(3)   Any person guilty of an offence under this section shall be liable on summary conviction to imprisonment for a term not exceeding three months or to a fine not exceeding level 4 on the standard scale or to both.

130. Prosecutions by local authorities

A local social services authority may institute proceedings for any offence under this Part of this Act, but without prejudice to any provision of this Part of this Act requiring the consent of the Director of Public Prosecutions for the institution of such proceedings.

PART X
MISCELLANEOUS AND SUPPLEMENTARY

131. Informal admission of patients

(1)   Nothing in this Act shall be construed as preventing a patient who requires treatment for mental disorder from being admitted to any hospital or mental nursing home in pursuance of arrangements made in that behalf and without any application, order or direction rendering him liable to be detained under this Act, or from remaining in any hospital or mental nursing home in pursuance of such arrangements after he has ceased to be so liable to be detained.

(2)   In the case of a minor who has attained the age of 16 years and is capable of expressing his own wishes, any such arrangements as are mentioned in subsection (1) above may be made, carried out and determined even though there are one or more persons who have parental responsibility for him (within the meaning of the Children Act 1989).

132. Duty of managers of hospitals to give information to detained patients

(1) The managers of a hospital or mental nursing home in which a patient is detained under this Act shall take such steps as are practicable to ensure that the patient understands—

(a) under which of the provisions of this Act he is for the time being detained and the effect of that provision; and

(b) what rights of applying to a Mental Health Review Tribunal are available to him in respect of his detention under that provision;

and those steps shall be taken as soon as practicable after the commencement of the patient's detention under the provision in question.

(2) The managers of a hospital or mental nursing home in which a patient is detained as aforesaid shall also take such steps as are practicable to ensure that the patient understands the effect, so far as relevant in his case, of sections 23, 25, 56 to 64, 66(1)(g), 118 and 120 above and section 134 below; and those steps shall be taken as soon as practicable after the commencement of the patient's detention in the hospital or nursing home.

(3) The steps to be taken under subsections (1) and (2) above shall include giving the requisite information both orally and in writing.

(4) The managers of a hospital or mental nursing home in which a patient is detained as aforesaid shall, except where the patient otherwise requests, take such steps as are practicable to furnish the person (if any) appearing to them to be his nearest relative with a copy of any information given to him in writing under subsections (1) and (2) above; and those steps shall be taken when the information is given to the patient or within a reasonable time thereafter.

133. Duty of managers of hospitals to inform nearest relatives of discharge

(1) Where a patient liable to be detained under this Act in a hospital or mental nursing home is to be discharged otherwise than by virtue of an order for discharge made by his nearest relative, the managers of the hospital or mental nursing home shall, subject to subsection (2) below, take such steps as are practicable to inform the person (if any) appearing to them to be the nearest relative of the patient; and that information shall, if practicable, be given at least seven days before the date of discharge.

(2) Subsection (1) above shall not apply if the patient or his nearest relative has requested that information about the patient's discharge should not be given under this section.

134. Correspondence of patients

(1) A postal packet addressed to any person by a patient detained in a hospital under this Act and delivered by the patient for dispatch may be withheld from the Post Office—

(a) if that person has requested that communications addressed to him by the patient should be withheld; or

(b) subject to subsection (3) below, if the hospital is a special hospital and the managers of the hospital consider that the postal packet is likely—

(i) to cause distress to the person to whom it is addressed or to any other person (not being a person on the staff of the hospital); or

(ii) to cause danger to any person;

and any request for the purposes of paragraph (a) above shall be made by a notice in writing given to the managers of the hospital, the registered medical practitioner in charge of the treatment of the patient or the Secretary of State.

(2) Subject to subsection (3) below, a postal packet addressed to a patient detained in a special hospital under this Act may be withheld from the patient if, in the opinion of the managers of the hospital, it is necessary to do so in the interests of the safety of the patient or for the protection of other persons.

(3)   Subsections (1)(b) and (2) above do not apply to any postal packet addressed by a patient to, or sent to a patient by or on behalf of—

(a)   any Minister of the Crown or Member of either House of Parliament;

(b)   the Master or any other officer of the Court of Protection or any of the Lord Chancellor's Visitors;

(c)   the Parliamentary Commissioner for Administration, the Health Service Commissioner for England, the Health Service Commissioner for Wales or a Local Commissioner within the meaning of Part III of the Local Government Act 1974;

(d)   a Mental Health Review Tribunal;

(e)   a health authority within the meaning of the National Health Service Act 1977, a local social services authority, a Community Health Council or a probation and after-care committee appointed under paragraph 2 of Schedule 3 to the Powers of Criminal Courts Act 1973;

(f)   the managers of the hospital in which the patient is detained;

(g)   any legally qualified person instructed by the patient to act as his legal adviser; or

(h)   the European Commission of Human Rights or the European Court of Human Rights.

(4)   The managers of a hospital may inspect and open any postal packet for the purposes of determining—

(a)   whether it is one to which subsection (1) or (2) applies, and

(b)   in the case of a postal packet to which subsection (1) or (2) above applies, whether or not if should be withheld under that subsection;

and the power to withhold a postal packet under either of those subsections includes power to withhold anything contained in it.

(5)   Where a postal packet or anything contained in it is withheld under subsection (1) or (2) above the managers of the hospital shall record that fact in writing.

(6)   Where a postal packet or anything contained in it is withheld under subsection (1)(b) or (2) above the managers of the hospital shall within seven days give notice of that fact to the patient and, in the case of a packet withheld under subsection (2) above, to the person (if known) by whom the postal packet was sent; and any such notice shall be given in writing and shall contain a statement of the effect of section 121(7) and (8) above.

(7)   The functions of the managers of a hospital under this section shall be discharged on their behalf by a person on the staff of the hospital appointed by them for that purpose and different persons may be appointed to discharge different functions.

(8)   The Secretary of State may make regulations with respect to the exercise of the powers conferred by this section.

(9)   In this section "hospital" has the same meaning as in Part II of this Act, "postal packet" has the same meaning as in the Post Office Act 1953 and the provisions of this section shall have effect notwithstanding anything in section 56 of that Act.

135.   Warrant to search for and remove patients

(1)   If it appears to a justice of the peace, on information on oath laid by an approved social worker, that there is reasonable cause to suspect that a person believed to be suffering from mental disorder—

(a)   has been, or is being, ill-treated, neglected or kept otherwise than under proper control, in any place within the jurisdiction of the justice, or

(b)   being unable to care for himself, is living alone in any such place,

the justice may issue a warrant authorising any constable to enter, if need be by force, any premises specified in the warrant in which that person is believed to be, and, if thought fit, to remove him to a place of safety with a view to the making of an application in respect of him under Part II of this Act, or of other arrangements for his treatment or care.

(2) If it appears to a justice of the peace, on information on oath laid by any constable or other person who is authorised by or under this Act or under section 83 of the Mental Health (Scotland) Act 1984 to take a patient to any place, or to take into custody or retake a patient who is liable under this Act or under the said section 83 to be so taken or retaken—

(a) that there is reasonable cause to believe that the patient is to be found on premises within the jurisdiction of the justice; and

(b) that admission to the premises has been refused or that a refusal of such admission is apprehended,

the justice may issue a warrant authorising any constable to enter the premises, if need be by force, and remove the patient.

(3) A patient who is removed to a place of safety in the execution of a warrant issued under this section may be detained there for a period not exceeding 72 hours.

(4) In the execution of a warrant issued under subsection (1) above, a constable shall be accompanied by an approved social worker and by a registered medical practitioner, and in the execution of a warrant issued under subsection (2) above a constable may be accompanied—

(a) by a registered medical practitioner;

(b) by any person authorised by or under this Act or under section 83 of the Mental Health (Scotland) Act 1984 to take or retake the patient.

(5) It shall not be necessary in any information or warrant under subsection (1) above to name the patient concerned.

(6) In this section "place of safety" means residential accommodation provided by a local social services authority under Part III of the National Assistance Act 1948, a hospital as defined by this Act, a police station, a mental nursing home or residential home for mentally disordered persons or any other suitable place the occupier of which is willing temporarily to receive the patient.

136. Mentally disordered persons found in public places

(1) If a constable finds in a place to which the public have access a person who appears to him to be suffering from mental disorder and to be in immediate need of care or control, the constable may, if he thinks it necessary to do so in the interests of that person or for the protection of other persons, remove that person to a place of safety within the meaning of section 135 above.

(2) A person removed to a place of safety under this section may be detained there for a period not exceeding 72 hours for the purpose of enabling him to be examined by a registered medical practitioner and to be interviewed by an approved social worker and of making any necessary arrangements for his treatment or care.

137. Provisions as to custody, conveyance and detention

(1) Any person required or authorised by or by virtue of this Act to be conveyed to any place or to be kept in custody or detained in a place of safety or at any place to which he is taken under section 42(6) above shall, while being so conveyed, detained or kept, as the case may be, be deemed to be in legal custody.

(2) A constable or any other person required or authorised by or by virtue of this Act to take any person into custody, or to convey or detain any person shall, for the purposes of taking him into custody or conveying or detaining him, have all the powers, authorities, protection and privileges which a constable has within the area for which he acts as constable.

(3) In this section "convey" includes any other expression denoting removal from one place to another.

138. Retaking of patients escaping from custody

(1) If any person who is in legal custody by virtue of section 137 above escapes, he may, subject to the provisions of this section, be retaken—

(a) in any case, by the person who had his custody immediately before the escape, or by any constable or approved social worker;

(b) if at the time of the escape he was liable to be detained in a hospital within the meaning of Part II of this Act, or subject to guardianship under this Act, by any other person who could take him into custody under section 18 above if he had absented himself without leave.

(2) A person to whom paragraph (b) of subsection (1) above applies shall not be retaken under this section after the expiration of the period within which he could be retaken under section 18 above if he had absented himself without leave on the day of the escape unless he is subject to a restriction order under Part III of this Act or an order or direction having the same effect as such an order; and subsection (4) of the said section 18 shall apply with the necessary modifications accordingly.

(3) A person who escapes while being taken to or detained in a place of safety under section 135 or 136 above shall not be retaken under this section after the expiration of the period of 72 hours beginning with the time when he escapes or the period during which he is liable to be so detained, whichever expires first.

(4) This section, so far as it relates to the escape of a person liable to be detained in a hospital within the meaning of Part II of this Act, shall apply in relation to a person who escapes—

(a) while being taken to or from such a hospital in pursuance of regulations under section 19 above, or of any order, direction or authorisation under Part III or VI of this Act (other than under section 35, 36, 38, 53, 83 or 85) or under section 123 above; or

(b) while being taken to or detained in a place of safety in pursuance of an order under Part III of this Act (other than under section 35, 36 or 38 above) pending his admission to such a hospital,

as if he were liable to be detained in that hospital and, if he had not previously been received in that hospital, as if he had been so received.

(5) In computing for the purposes of the power to give directions under section 37(4) above and for the purposes of sections 37(5) and 40(1) above the period of 28 days mentioned in those sections, no account shall be taken of any time during which the patient is at large and liable to be retaken by virtue of this section.

(6) Section 21 above shall, with any necessary modifications, apply in relation to a patient who is at large and liable to be retaken by virtue of this section as it applies in relation to a patient who is absent without leave and references in that section to section 18 above shall be construed accordingly.

139. Protection for acts done in pursuance of this Act

(1) No person shall be liable, whether on the ground of want of jurisdiction or on any other ground, to any civil or criminal proceedings to which he would have been liable apart from this section in respect of any act purporting to be done in pursuance of this Act or any regulations or rules made under this Act, or in, or in pursuance of anything done in, the discharge of functions conferred by any other enactment on the authority having jurisdiction under Part VII of this Act, unless the act was done in bad faith or without reasonable care.

(2) No civil proceedings shall be brought against any person in any court in respect of any such act without the leave of the High Court; and no criminal proceedings shall be brought against any person in any court in respect of any such act except by or with the consent of the Director of Public Prosecutions.

(3) This section does not apply to proceedings for an offence under this Act, being proceedings which, under any other provision of this Act, can be instituted only by or

with the consent of the Director of Public Prosecutions.

(4) This section does not apply to proceedings against the Secretary of State or against a health authority within the meaning of the National Health Service Act 1977 or against a National Health Service trust established under the National Health Service and Community Care Act 1990.

(5) In relation to Northern Ireland the reference in this section to the Director of Public Prosecutions shall be construed as a reference to the Director of Public Prosecutions for Northern Ireland.

140. Notification of hospitals having arrangements for reception of urgent cases

It shall be the duty of every Regional Health Authority and in Wales every District Health Authority to give notice to every local social services authority for an area wholly or partly comprised within the region or district, as the case may be, of the Authority specifying the hospital or hospitals administered by or otherwise available to the Authority in which arrangements are from time to time in force for the reception, in case of special urgency, of patients requiring treatment for mental disorder.

142. Pay, pensions, etc., of mentally disordered persons

(1) Where a periodic payment falls to be made to any person by way of pay or pension or otherwise in connection with the service or employment of that or any other person, and the payment falls to be made directly out of moneys provided by Parliament or the Consolidated Fund, or other moneys administered by or under the control or supervision of a government department, the authority by whom the sum in question is payable, if satisfied after considering medical evidence that the person to whom it is payable (referred to in this section as "the patient") is incapable by reason of mental disorder of managing and administering his property and affairs, may, instead of paying the sum to the patient, apply it in accordance with subsection (2) below.

(2) The authority may pay the sum or such part of it as they think fit to the institution or person having the care of the patient, to be applied for his benefit and may pay the remainder (if any) or such part of the remainder as they think fit—

(a) to or for the benefit of persons who appear to the authority to be members of the patient's family or other persons for whom the patient might be expected to provide if he were not mentally disordered, or

(b) in reimbursement, with or without interest, of money applied by any person either in payment of the patient's debts (whether legally enforceable or not) or for the maintenance or other benefit of the patient or such persons as are mentioned in paragraph (a) above.

(3) In this section "government department" does not include a Northern Ireland department.

145. Interpretation

(1) In this Act, unless the context otherwise requires—

"absent without leave" has the meaning given to it by section 18 above and related expressions shall be construed accordingly;

"application for admission for assessment" has the meaning given in section 2 above;

"application for admission for treatment" has the meaning given in section 3 above;

"approved social worker" means an officer of a local social services authority appointed to act as an approved social worker for the purposes of this Act;

"hospital" means—

(a) any health service hospital within the meaning of the National Health Service Act 1977; and

(b)   any accommodation provided by a local authority and used as a hospital by or on behalf of the Secretary of State under that Act;
and "hospital within the meaning of Part II of this Act" has the meaning given in section 34 above;
"hospital order" and "guardianship order" have the meanings respectively given in section 37 above;
"interim hospital order" has the meaning given in section 38 above;
"local social services authority" means a council which is a local authority for the purpose of the Local Authority Social Services Act 1970;
"the managers" means—

(a)   in relation to a hospital vested in the Secretary of State for the purposes of his functions under the National Health Service Act 1977, and in relation to any accommodation provided by a local authority and used as a hospital by or on behalf of the Secretary of State under that Act, the District Health Authority or special health authority responsible for the administration of the hospital;

(b)   in relation to a special hospital, the Secretary of State;

(bb)   in relation to a hospital vested in a National Health Service Trust, the directors of the trust;

(c)   in relation to a mental nursing home registered in pursuance of the Registered Homes Act 1984, the person or persons registered in respect of the home; and in this definition "hospital" means a hospital within the meaning of Part II of this Act;
"medical treatment" includes nursing, and also includes care, habilitation and rehabilitation under medical supervision;
"mental disorder", "severe mental impairment", "mental impairment" and "psychopathic disorder" have the meanings given in section 1 above;
"mental nursing home" has the same meaning as in the Registered Homes Act 1984;
"nearest relative", in relation to a patient, has the meaning given in Part II of this Act;
"patient" (except in Part VII of this Act) means a person suffering or appearing to be suffering from mental disorder;
"restriction direction" has the meaning given to it by section 49 above;
"restriction order" has the meaning given to it by section 41 above;
"special hospital" has the same meaning as in the National Health Service Act 1977;
"standard scale" has the meaning given in section 75 of the Criminal Justice Act 1982;
"transfer direction" has the meaning given to it by section 47 above.

(2)   "Statutory maximum" has the meaning given in section 74 of the Criminal Justice Act 1982.

(3)   In relation to a person who is liable to be detained or subject to guardianship by virtue of an order or direction under Part III of this Act (other than under section 35, 36 or 38), any reference in this Act to any enactment contained in Part II of this Act or in section 66 or 67 above shall be construed as a reference to that enactment as it applies to that person by virtue of Part III of this Act.

SCHEDULE

SCHEDULE 1
APPLICATION OF CERTAIN PROVISIONS TO PATIENTS SUBJECT TO HOSPITAL AND GUARDIANSHIP ORDERS

PART I
PATIENTS NOT SUBJECT TO SPECIAL RESTRICTIONS

1.   Sections 9, 10, 17, 21, 24(3) and (4), 26 to 28, 31, 32, 34, 67 and 76 shall apply in relation to the patient without modification.

2.   Sections 16, 18, 19, 20, 22, 23 and 66 shall apply in relation to the patient with the modifications specified in paragraphs 3 to 9 below.

3.   In section 16(1) for references to an application for admission or a guardianship application there shall be substituted references to the order or direction under Part III of this Act by virtue of which the patient is liable to be detained or subject to guardianship.

4.   In section 18 subsection (5) shall be omitted.

5.   In section 19(2) for the words from "as follows" to the end of the subsection there shall be substituted the words "as if the order or direction under Part III of this Act by virtue of which he was liable to be detained or subject to guardianship before being transferred were an order or direction for his admission or removal to the hospital to which he is transferred, or placing him under the guardianship of the authority or person into whose guardianship he is transferred, as the case may be".

6.   In section 20—

   (a)   in subsection (1) for the words from "day on which he was" to "as the case may be" there shall be substituted the words "date of the relevant order or direction under Part III of this Act"; and

   (b)   in subsection (9) for the words "the application for admission for treatment or, as the case may be, in the guardianship application, that application" there shall be substituted the words "the relevant order or direction under Part III of this Act, that order or direction".

7.   In section 22 for references to an application for admission or a guardianship application there shall be substituted references to the order or direction under Part III of this Act by virtue of which the patient is liable to be detained or subject to guardianship.

8.   In section 23(2)—

   (a)   in paragraph (a) the words "for assessment or" shall be omitted; and

   (b)   in paragraphs (a) and (b) the references to the nearest relative shall be omitted.

9.   In section 66—

   (a)   in subsection (1), paragraphs (a), (b), (c), (g) and (h), the words in parenthesis in paragraph (i) and paragraph (ii) shall be omitted; and

   (b)   in subsection (2), paragraphs (a), (b), (c) and (g) shall be omitted and in paragraph (d) for the words "cases mentioned in paragraphs (d) and (g)" there shall be substituted the words "case mentioned in paragraph (d)".

PART II
PATIENTS SUBJECT TO SPECIAL RESTRICTIONS

1.   Sections 24(3) and (4), 32 and 76 shall apply in relation to the patient without modification.

2.   Sections 17 to 19, 22, 23 and 34 shall apply in relation to the patient with the modifications specified in paragraphs 3 to 8 below.

3. In section 17—

(a) in subsection (1) after the word "may" there shall be inserted the words "with the consent of the Secretary of State";

(b) in subsection (4) after the words "the responsible medical officer" and after the words "that officer" there shall be inserted the words "or the Secretary of State"; and

(c) in subsection (5) after the word "recalled" there shall be inserted the words "by the responsible medical officer", and for the words from "he has ceased" to the end of the subsection there shall be substituted the words "the expiration of the period of six months beginning with the first day of his absence on leave".

4. In section 18 there shall be omitted—

(a) in subsection (1) the words "subject to the provisions of this section"; and

(b) subsections (3), (4) and (5).

5. In section 19—

(a) in subsection (1) after the word "may" in paragraph (a) there shall be inserted the words "with the consent of the Secretary of State", and the words from "or into" to the end of the subsection shall be omitted; and

(b) in subsection(2) for the words from "as follows" to the end of the subsection there shall be substituted the words "as if the order or direction under Part III of this Act by virtue of which he was liable to be detained before being transferred were an order or direction for his admission or removal to the hospital to which he is transferred".

6. In section 22 subsection (1) and paragraph (a) of subsection (2) shall not apply.

7. In section 23—

(a) in subsection (1) references to guardianship shall be omitted and after the word "made" there shall be inserted the words "with the consent of the Secretary of State and" and

(b) in subsection (2)—

(i) in paragraph (a) the words "for assessment or" and "or by the nearest relative of the patient" shall be omitted; and

(ii) paragraph (b) shall be omitted.

8. In section 34, in subsection (1) the definition of "the nominated medical attendant" and subsection (3) shall be omitted.

MEDICAL ACT 1983
(1983, c. 54)

PART I
PRELIMINARY

The General Medical Council

1. The General Medical Council

(1) There shall continue to be a body corporate known as the General Medical Council (in this Act referred to as "the General Council") having the functions assigned to them by this Act.

(2) The General Council shall be constituted as provided by Her Majesty by Order in Council under this section subject to the provisions of Part I of Schedule 1 to this Act.

(3) There shall continue to be four committees of the General Council known as the Education Committee, the Preliminary Proceedings Committee, the Professional Conduct Committee and the Health Committee (in this Act referred to as "the statutory committees") constituted in accordance with Part III of Schedule 1 to this Act and having the functions assigned to them by this Act.

(4)   Schedule 1 to this Act shall have effect with respect to the General Council, its branch councils and committees, its proceedings, its officers and its accounts.

2.   Registration of medical practitioners

(1)   There shall continue to be kept by the registrar of the General Council (in this Act referred to as "the Registrar") two registers of medical practitioners registered under this Act containing the names of those registered and the qualifications they are entitled to have registered under this Act.

(2)   The two registers referred to are "the register of medical practitioners" consisting of four lists, namely —
  (a)   the principal list,
  (b)   the overseas list,
  (c)   the visiting overseas doctors list, and
  (d)   the visiting EEC practitioners list,
and "the register of medical practitioners with limited registration".

(3)   Medical practitioners shall be registered as fully registered medical practitioners or provisionally or with limited registration as provided in Parts II and III of this Act and in the appropriate list of the register of medical practitioners or in the register of medical practitioners with limited registration as provided in Part IV of this Act.

PART V
PROFESSIONAL CONDUCT AND FITNESS TO PRACTISE

35.   General Council's power to advise on conduct or ethics

The powers of the General Council shall include the power to provide, in such manner as the Council think fit, advice for members of the medical profession on standards of professional conduct or on medical ethics.

36.   Professional misconduct and criminal offences

(1)   Where a fully registered person —
  (a)   is found by the Professional Conduct Committee to have been convicted in the British Islands of a criminal offence, whether while so registered or not; or
  (b)   is judged by the Professional Conduct Committee to have been guilty of serious professional misconduct, whether while so registered or not;
the Committee may, if they think fit, direct —
  (i)   that his name shall be erased from the register;
  (ii)   that his registration in the register shall be suspended (that is to say, shall not have effect) during such period not exceeding twelve months as may be specified in the direction; or
  (iii)   that his registration shall be conditional on his compliance, during such period not exceeding three years as may be specified in the direction, with such requirements so specified as the Committee think fit to impose for the protection of members of the public or in his interests.

(2)   Where a fully registered person whose registration is subject to conditions imposed under subsection (1) above by the Professional Conduct Committee or under section 42(3)(c) below by the Preliminary Proceedings Committee is judged by the Professional Conduct Committee to have failed to comply with any of the requirements imposed on him as conditions of his registration the Committee may, if they think fit, direct —
  (a)   that his name shall be erased from the register; or
  (b)   that his registration in the register shall be suspended (that is to say, shall not have effect) during such period not exceeding twelve months as may be specified in the direction.

(3) Where the Professional Conduct Committee have given a direction for suspension under subsection (1) or (2) above, the Committee may —

(a) direct that the current period of suspension shall be extended for such further period from the time when it would otherwise expire as may be specified in the direction;

(b) direct that the name of the person whose registration is suspended shall be erased from the register; or

(c) direct that the registration of the person whose registration is suspended shall, as from the expiry of the current period of suspension, be conditional on his compliance, during such period not exceeding three years as may be specified in the direction, with such requirements so specified as the Committee think fit to impose for the protection of members of the public or in his interests;

but the Committee shall not extend any period of suspension under this section for more than twelve months at a time.

(4) Where the Professional Conduct Committee have given a direction for conditional registration, the Committee may —

(a) direct that the current period of conditional registration shall be extended for such further period from the time when it would otherwise expire as may be specified in the direction; or

(b) revoke the direction or revoke or vary any of the conditions imposed by the direction;

but the Committee shall not extend any period of conditional registration under this section for more than twelve months at a time.

(5) Subsection (2) above shall apply to a fully registered person whose registration is subject to conditions imposed under subsection (3)(c) above as it applies to a fully registered person whose registration is subject to conditions imposed under subsection (1) above, and subsection (3) above shall apply accordingly.

(6) Where the Professional Conduct Committee give a direction under this section for erasure, for suspension or for conditional registration or vary the conditions imposed by a direction for conditional registration the Registrar shall forthwith serve on the person to whom the direction applies a notification of the direction or of the variation and of his right to appeal against the decision in accordance with section 40 below.

(7) In subsection (6) above the references to a direction for suspension and a direction for conditional registration include references to a direction extending a period of suspension or a period of conditional registration.

(8) While a person's registration in the register is suspended by virtue of this section he shall be treated as not being registered in the register notwithstanding that his name still appears in it.

(9) This section applies to a provisionally registered person and to a person registered with limited registration whether or not the circumstances are such that he falls within the meaning in this Act of the expression "fully registered person".

37. Unfitness to practise through illness, etc.

(1) Where the fitness to practise of a fully registered person is judged by the Health Committee to be seriously impaired by reason of his physical or mental condition the Committee may, if they think fit, direct —

(a) that his registration in the register shall be suspended (that is to say, shall not have effect) during such period not exceeding twelve months as may be specified in the direction; or

(b) that his registration shall be conditional on his compliance, during such period not exceeding three years as may be specified in the direction, with such requirements so specified as the Committee think fit to impose for the protection of members of the public or in his interests.

(2)   Where a fully registered person whose registration is subject to conditions imposed under subsection (1) above by the Health Committee or under section 42(3)(c) below by the Preliminary Proceedings Committee is judged by the Health Committee to have failed to comply with any of the requirements imposed on him as conditions of his registration the Committee may, if they think fit, direct that his registration in the register shall be suspended (that is to say, shall not have effect) during such period not exceeding twelve months as may be specified in the direction.

(3)   Where the Health Committee have given a direction for suspension under subsection (1) or (2) above, the Committee may —

(a)   direct that the current period of suspension shall be extended for such further period from the time when it would otherwise expire as may be specified in the direction; or

(b)   direct that the registration of the person whose registration is suspended shall, as from the expiry of the current period of suspension, be conditional on his compliance, during such period not exceeding three years as may be specified in the direction, with such requirements so specified as the Committee think fit to impose for the protection of members of the public or in his interests;

but the Committee shall not extend any period of suspension under this section for more than twelve months at a time.

(4)   Where the Health Committee have given a direction for conditional registration, the Committee may —

(a)   direct that the current period of conditional registration shall be extended for such further period from the time when it would otherwise expire as may be specified in the direction; or

(b)   revoke the direction or revoke or vary any of the conditions imposed by the direction;

but the Committee shall not extend any period of conditional registration under this section for more than twelve months at a time.

(5)   Subsection (2) above shall apply to a fully registered person whose registration is subject to conditions imposed under subsection (3)(b) above as it applies to a fully registered person whose registration is subject to conditions imposed under subsection (1) above, and subsection (3) above shall apply accordingly.

(6)   Where the Health Committee give a direction under this section for suspension or for conditional registration or vary the conditions imposed by a direction for conditional registration the Registrar shall forthwith serve on the person to whom the direction applies a notification of the direction or of the variation and of his right to appeal against the decision in accordance with section 40 below.

(7)   In subsection (6) above the references to a direction for suspension and a direction for conditional registration include references to a direction extending a period of suspension or a period of conditional registration.

(8)   While a person's registration in the register is suspended by virtue of this section he shall be treated as not being registered in the register notwithstanding that his name still appears in it.

(9)   This section applies to a provisionally registered person and to a person registered with limited registration whether or not the circumstances are such that he falls within the meaning in this Act of the expression "fully registered person".

38. Power to order immediate suspension after a finding of professional misconduct or unfitness to practise

(1)   On giving a direction for erasure or a direction for suspension under section 36(1) or (2) or 37(1) or (2) above in respect of any person the Professional Conduct Committee or the Health Committee, if satisfied that to do so is necessary for the protection of members of the public or would be in the best interests of that person,

may order that his registration in the register shall be suspended forthwith in accordance with this section; and in this subsection the reference to section 36(2) includes a reference to that provision as applied by section 36(5) and the reference to section 37(2) includes a reference to that provision as applied by section 37(5).

(2)   Where, on the giving of a direction an order under subsection (1) above is made in respect of a person, his registration in the register shall, subject to subsection (4) below, be suspended (that is to say, shall not have effect) from the time when the order is made until the time when the direction takes effect in accordance with paragraph 10 of Schedule 4 to this Act or an appeal against it under section 40 below is (otherwise than by the dismissal of the appeal) determined.

(3)   Where the Professional Conduct Committee or the Health Committee make an order under subsection (1) above the Registrar shall forthwith serve a notification of the order on the person to whom it applies.

(4)   If, when an order under subsection (1) above is made, the person to whom it applies is neither present nor represented at the proceedings, subsection (2) above shall have effect as if, for the reference to the time when the order is made, there were substituted a reference to the time of service of a notification of the order as determined for the purposes of paragraph 8 of Schedule 4 to this Act.

(5)   While a person's registration in the register is suspended by virtue of subsection (1) above he shall be treated as not being registered in the register notwithstanding that his name still apears in it.

(6)   The court may terminate any suspension of a person's registration in the register imposed under subsection (1) above, and the decision of the court on any application under this subsection shall be final.

(7)   In this section "the court" —

(a)   in the case of a person whose address in the register is in Scotland, means the Court of Session;

(b)   in the case of a person whose address in the register is in Northern Ireland, means the High Court of Justice in Northern Ireland; and

(c)   in the case of any other person, means the High Court of Justice in England and Wales.

39.   Fraud or error in relation to registration

(1)   If the General Council are satisfied that any entry in the register has been fraudulently procured or incorrectly made they may direct that the entry shall be erased from the register.

(2)   Where the General Council give a direction for the erasure of a person's name under this section the Registrar shall forthwith serve on that person a notification of the direction and of his right to appeal against the decision in accordance with section 40 below.

40.   Appeals

(1)   The following decisions are appealable decisions for the purposes of this section, that is to say —

(a)   a decision of the Professional Conduct Committee under section 36 above giving a direction for erasure, for suspension or for conditional registration or varying the conditions imposed by a direction for conditional registration;

(b)   a decision of the Health Committee under section 37 above giving a direction for suspension or for conditional registration or varying the conditions imposed by a direction for conditional registration; or

(c)   a decision of the General Council under section 39 above giving a direction for erasure.

(2)   In subsection (1) above the references to a direction for suspension and a direction for conditional registration include references to a direction extending a period of suspension or a period of conditional registration.

(3)   Any person in respect of whom an appealable decision has been taken may, within twenty-eight days of the service of the notification of the decision under section 36(6), 37(6) or 39(2) above appeal against the decision in accordance with this section.

(4)   In the case of an appealable decision —

    (a)   of the Professional Conduct Committee under section 36 above;

    (b)   of the Health Committee under section 37 above; or

    (c)   of the General Council under section 39 above directing that an entry be erased because it has been fraudulently procured,

an appeal under this section shall lie to Her Majesty in Council subject, however, to subsection (5) below and to such rules as Her Majesty in Council may by Order provide for the purpose of regulating appeals under this section.

(5)   No appeal under this section shall lie from a decision of the Health Committee except on a question of law.

(6)   The Judicial Committee Act 1833 shall apply in relation to the Professional Conduct Committee, the Health Committee and the General Council as it applies in relation to any court from which an appeal lies to Her Majesty in Council.

(7)   Without prejudice to the application of that Act, on an appeal under this section to Her Majesty in Council from the Professional Conduct Committee or the Health Committee the Judicial Committee may, in their report, recommend to Her Majesty in Council —

    (a)   that the appeal be dismissed;

    (b)   that the appeal be allowed and the direction or variation questioned by the appeal quashed;

    (c)   that such other direction or variation as the Professional Conduct Committee or, as the case may be, the Health Committee could have given or made be substituted for the direction or variation questioned by the appeal; or

    (d)   that the case be remitted to the Professional Conduct Committee or, as the case may be, the Health Committee for that Committee to dispose of the case under section 36 or 37 above in accordance with the directions of the Judicial Committee.

(8)   On an appeal under this section to Her Majesty in Council from the General Council the Judicial Committee may, in their report, recommend —

    (a)   that the appeal be dismissed;

    (b)   that the appeal be allowed and the direction questioned by the appeal quashed; or

    (c)   that the case be remitted to the General Council for that Council to dispose of the case under section 39 above in accordance with the directions of the Judicial Committee.

(9)   In the case of an appealable decision of the General Council under section 39 above other than a decision falling within subsection (4)(c) above an appeal under this section shall lie to the Privy Council.

(10)   On an appeal under this section to the Privy Council the Privy Council may —

    (a)   dismiss the appeal; or

    (b)   allow the appeal and quash the direction questioned by the appeal.

(11)   On an appeal under this section from the Professional Conduct Committee or the Health Committee the General Council may appear as respondent; and for the purpose of enabling directions to be given as to the costs of any such appeal the Council shall be deemed to be a party thereto, whether they appear on the hearing of the appeal or not.

41.   Restoration of names to the register

(1)   Subject to subsection (2) below, where the name of a person has been erased from the register under section 36 above the Professional Conduct Committee may, if they think fit, direct his name to be restored to the register.

(2)   No application for the restoration of a name to the register under this section shall be made to the Professional Conduct Committee —

(a)   before the expiration of ten months from the date of erasure; or

(b)   in any period of ten months in which an application for the restoration of his name has already been made by or on behalf of the person whose name has been erased.

(3)   In the case of a person who was provisionally registered under section 15 or 21 above before his name was erased a direction under subsection (1) above shall be a direction that his name be restored by way of provisional registration under section 15 or 21 above, as the case requires.

(4)   The requirements of Part II or Part III of this Act as to the experience required for registration as a fully registered medical practitioner shall not apply to registration in pursuance of a direction under subsection (1) above.

42.   Preliminary proceedings as to professional misconduct and unfitness to practise

(1)   The Preliminary Proceedings Committee shall have the functions assigned to them by this section.

(2)   It shall be the duty of the Committee to decide whether any case referred to them for consideration in which a practitioner is alleged to be liable to have his name erased under section 36 above or his registration suspended or made subject to conditions under section 36 or 37 above ought to be referred for inquiry by the Professional Conduct Committee or the Health Committee.

(3)   If the Committee decide that a case ought to be referred for inquiry by the Professional Conduct Committee or the Health Committee —

(a)   they shall give a direction designating the Committee which is to inquire into the case; and

(b)   they may, subject to subsection (4) below, if satisfied that to do so is necessary for the protection of members of the public, make an order for interim suspension in respect of the person whose case they have decided to refer for inquiry; or

(c)   they may, subject to subsection (4) below, if satisfied that to do so is necessary for the protection of members of the public or is in his interests, make an order for interim conditional registration in respect of that person, that is to say, an order that his registration shall be conditional on his compliance, during such period not exceeding two months as is specified in the order, with such requirements so specified as the Committee think fit to impose for the protection of members of the public or in his interests.

(4)   No order for interim suspension or for interim conditional registration shall be made by the Preliminary Proceedings Committee in respect of any person unless he has been afforded an opportunity of appearing before the Committee and being heard on the question whether such an order should be made in his case; and for the purposes of this subsection a person may be represented before the Committee by counsel or a solicitor, or (if rules under paragraph 5 of Schedule 4 to this Act so provide and he so elects) by a person of such other description as may be specified in the rules.

(5)   If the Committee decide that a case ought to be referred for inquiry by the Professional Conduct Committee or the Health Committee the Registrar shall serve a notification of the decision on the person whose case has been so referred and if the Committee also make an order for interim suspension or for interim conditional registration the Registrar shall include in the notification of the decision a notification of the order and shall serve the notification forthwith.

(6)   Where an order for interim suspension is made in respect of a person, his registration in the register shall be suspended (that is to say, shall not have effect) from the time of service of a notification of the order as determined for the purposes of paragraph 8 of Schedule 4 to this Act until the expiration of such period, not exceeding two months, as is specified in the order.

(7) The Professional Conduct Committee or the Health Committee may revoke any order for interim suspension or for interim conditional registration made by the Preliminary Proceedings Committee under this section.

(8) While a person's registration in the register is suspended by virtue of an order for interim suspension under this section he shall be treated as not being registered in the register notwithstanding that his name still appears in the register.

43. Proceedings before Professional Conduct, Health and Preliminary Proceedings Committees

Schedule 4 to this Act (which contains supplementary provisions about proceedings before the Professional Conduct Committee, the Health Committee and the Preliminary Proceedings Committee) shall have effect.

44. Effect of disqualification in another member State on registration in the United Kingdom

(1) A person who is subject to a disqualifying decision in a member State of the Communities in which he is or has been established in medical practice shall not be entitled to be registered by virtue of section 3(b) above for so long as the decision remains in force in relation to him.

(2) A disqualifying decision in respect of a person is a decision, made by responsible authorities of the member State of the Communities in which he was established in medical practice or in which he acquired a primary United Kingdom or primary European qualification, and —

(a) expressed to be made on the grounds that he has committed a criminal offence or on grounds related to his professional conduct, and

(b) having in that State the effect either that he is no longer registered or otherwise officially recognised as a medical practitioner, or that he is prohibited from practising medicine there.

(3) If a person has been registered by virtue of section 3(b) above and it is subsequently shown to the satisfaction of the Registrar that he was subject to a disqualifying decision in force at the time of registration, and that the decision remains in force, the Registrar shall remove the person's name from the register.

(4) If registration is refused or a person's name is removed from the register in accordance with subsection (3) above —

(a) the Registrar shall, on request, state in writing the reasons for the refusal, or the removal, as the case may be;

(b) the person may appeal by giving notice in writing to the General Council; and

(c) any such appeal shall be determined by the General Council or, if the Council have delegated their functions under this subsection to a committee, by that committee.

(5) If a person has been registered as a fully registered medical practitioner by virtue of section 3(b) above at a time when a disqualifying decision was in force in respect of him, and he has been so registered for a period of not less than one month throughout which the decision had effect —

(a) the Professional Conduct Committee may direct that his registration be suspended for such period, not exceeding the length of the first-mentioned period, as the Committee think fit, and the period of suspension shall begin on a date to be specified in the Committee's direction; and

(b) sections 36(6) and 40 of and paragraphs 1, 2, 8, 9, 10 and 13 of Schedule 4 to this Act shall have effect, with any necessary modifications, in relation to suspension under this subsection.

(6) Where on or after the date on which a person was registered by virtue of section 3(b) above a disqualifying decision relating to him comes into force, this Part of this Act shall apply, with any necessary modifications, as if it had been found that he had been convicted of the criminal offence referred to in the disqualifying decision, or that his

professional conduct had been such as is imputed to him by that decision, as the case may be.

(7) Subsection (1) of section 18 above shall not apply to a person and that person shall not be registered as a visiting EEC practitioner at any time when he is subject to a disqualifying decision imposed by a member State or its competent authority (within the meaning of that section).

45. Disciplinary provisions affecting practitioners who render services while visiting the United Kingdom

(1) If a national of a member State of the Communities who has medical qualifications entitling him to registration under section 3 above but is not so registered and who renders medical services while visiting the United Kingdom (whether or not registered as a visiting EEC practitioner) —

(a) is found by the Professional Conduct Committee to have been convicted of a criminal offence in any member State where he was practising medicine; or

(b) is judged by the Professional Conduct Committee to have been guilty of serious professional misconduct, the Committee may, if they think fit, impose on him a prohibition in respect of the rendering of medical services in the United Kingdom in the future.

(2) A prohibition imposed under this section shall either relate to a period specified by the Professional Conduct Committee or be expressed to continue for an indefinite period.

(3) A person may apply to the General Council for termination of a prohibition imposed on him under this section and the Council may, on any such application, terminate the prohibition or reduce the period of it; but no application may be made under this subsection —

(a) earlier than ten months from the date on which the prohibition was imposed; or

(b) in the period of ten months following a decision made on an earlier application.

(4) Section 18(1) above does not apply to a person and that person shall not be registered as a visiting EEC practitioner at a time when he is subject to a prohibition imposed by the Professional Conduct Committee under this section.

PART VI
PRIVILEGES OF REGISTERED PRACTITIONERS

46. Recovery of fees

(1) Except as provided in subsection (2) below, no person shall be entitled to recover any charge in any court of law for any medical advice or attendance, or for the performance of any operation, or for any medicine which he has both prescribed and supplied unless he proves that he is fully registered.

(2) Subsection (1) above shall not apply to fees in respect of medical services lawfully rendered in the United Kingdom by a person who is a national of any member State of the Communities without first being registered under this Act if he has previously complied with the requirements of subsection (2) of section 18 above or subsequently complies with those requirements as modified in respect of urgent cases by subsection (3) of that section.

(3) Where a practitioner is a fellow of a college of physicians, fellows of which are prohibited by byelaw from recovering by law their expenses, charges or fees, then, notwithstanding that he is fully registered, the prohibitory byelaw, so long as it is in force, may be pleaded in bar of any legal proceedings instituted by him for the recovery of expenses, charges or fees.

47. Appointments not to be held except by fully registered practitioners

(1)   Subject to subsection (2) below, no person who is not fully registered shall hold any appointment as physician, surgeon or other medical officer —

(a)   in the naval, military or air service,

(b)   in any hospital or other place for the reception of persons suffering from mental disorder, or in any other hospital, infirmary or dispensary not supported wholly by voluntary contributions,

(c)   in any prison, or

(d)   in any other public establishment, body or institution, or to any friendly or other society for providing mutual relief in sickness, infirmity or old age.

(2)   Nothing in this section shall prevent any person who is not a Commonwealth citizen from being and acting as the resident physician or medical officer of any hospital established exclusively for the relief of foreigners in sickness, so long as he —

(a)   has obtained from a foreign university a degree or diploma of doctor in medicine and has passed the regular examinations entitling him to practise medicine in his own country, and

(b)   is engaged in no medical practice except as such a resident physician or medical officer.

(3)   Suspension of the registration of a fully registered person by a direction of the Health Committee under section 37(1) or (2) above, an order of that Committee under section 38(1) above or an interim order of the Preliminary Proceedings Committee under section 42(3)(b) above shall not terminate any appointment such as is mentioned in subsection (1) above, but the person suspended shall not perform the duties of such an appointment during the suspension.

48. Certificates invalid if not signed by fully registered practitioner

A certificate required by any enactment, whether passed before or after the commencement of this Act, from any physician, surgeon, licentiate in medicine and surgery or other medical practitioner shall not be valid unless the person signing it is fully registered.

49. Penalty for pretending to be registered

(1)   Subject to subsection (2) below, any person who wilfully and falsely pretends to be or takes or uses the name or title of physician, doctor of medicine, licentiate in medicine and surgery, bachelor of medicine, surgeon, general practitioner or apothecary, or any name, title, addition or description implying that he is registered under any provision of this Act, or that he is recognised by law as a physician or surgeon or licentiate in medicine and surgery or a practitioner in medicine or an apothecary, shall be liable on summary conviction to a fine not exceeding level 5 on the standard scale (as defined in section 75 of the Criminal Justice Act 1982); and for the purposes of this subsection —

(a)   section 37 of that Act; and

(b)   an order under section 143 of the Magistrates' Courts Act 1980 which alters the sums specified in subsection (2) of the said section 37,

shall extend to Northern Ireland and the said section 75 shall have effect as if after the words "England and Wales" there were inserted the words "or Northern Ireland".

(2)   Subsection (1) above shall not apply to anything done by a person who is a national of any member State of the Communities for the purposes of or in connection with the lawful rendering of medical services by him without first being registered under this Act if he has previously complied with the requirements of subsection (2) of section 18 above or subsequently complies with its requirements as modified in respect of urgent cases by subsection (3) of that section.

PUBLIC HEALTH (CONTROL OF DISEASE) ACT 1984
(1984, c. 22)

10. Notifiable diseases
In this Act, "notifiable disease" means any of the following diseases —
  (a)   cholera;
  (b)   plague;
  (c)   relapsing fever;
  (d)   smallpox; and
  (e)   typhus.

11. Cases of notifiable disease and food poisoning to be reported
  (1)   If a registered medical practitioner becomes aware, or suspects, that a patient whom he is attending within the district of a local authority is suffering from a notifiable disease or from food poisoning, he shall, unless he believes, and has reasonable grounds for believing, that some other registered medical practitioner has complied with this subsection with respect to the patient, forthwith send to the proper officer of the local authority for that district a certificate stating —
  (a)   the name, age and sex of the patient and the address of the premises where the patient is,
  (b)   the disease or, as the case may be, particulars of the poisoning from which the patient is, or is suspected to be, suffering and the date, or approximate date, of its onset, and
  (c)   if the premises are a hospital, the day on which the patient was admitted, the address of the premises from which he came there and whether or not, in the opinion of the person giving the certificate, the disease or poisoning from which the patient is, or is suspected to be, suffering was contracted in the hospital.
  (2)   A local authority shall, upon application, supply forms of certificate for use under this section free of charge to any registered medical practitioner practising in their district.
  (3)   The officer who receives the certificate shall, on the day of its receipt (if possible) and in any case within 48 hours after is receipt, send a copy —
  (a)   to the District Health Authority within whose district are situated the premises whose address is specified in the certificate in accordance with subsection (1)(a) above, and
  (b)   if the certificate is given with respect to a patient in a hospital who came there from premises outside the district of the local authority within whose district the hospital is situated and the certificate states that the patient did not contract the disease or the poisoning in the hospital —
  (i)   to the proper officer of the local authority for the district within which the premises from which the patient came are situated, and
  (ii)   to the District Health Authority for the district in which those premises are situated, if that Authority is not responsible for the administration of the hospital, and
  (iii)   to the proper officer of the relevant port health authority, if those premises were a ship or hovercraft situated within the port health district for which that authority is constituted.
  (4)   A person who fails to comply with an obligation imposed on him by subsection (1) above shall be liable on summary conviction to a fine not exceeding level 1 on the standard scale.
  (5)   In this section, "hospital" means any institution for the reception and treatment of persons suffering from illness, any maternity home and any institution for the reception and treatment of persons during convalescence or persons requiring medical rehabilitation, and "illness" includes mental disorder within the meaning of the Mental

Health Act 1983 and any injury or disability requiring medical, surgical or dental treatment or nursing.

13. Regulations for control of certain diseases

(1) Subject to the provisions of this section, the Secretary of State may, as respects the whole or any part of England and Wales, including coastal waters, make regulations—

(a) with a view to the treatment of persons affected with any epidemic, endemic or infectious disease and for preventing the spread of such diseases,

(b) for preventing danger to public health from vessels or aircraft arriving at any place, and

(c) for preventing the spread of infection by means of any vessel or aircraft leaving any place, so far as may be necessary or expedient for the purpose of carrying out any treaty, convention, arrangement or engagement with any other country.

(2) Without prejudice to the generality of subsection (1) above, the Secretary of State may by any such regulations apply, with or without modifications, to any disease to which the regulations relate any enactment (including any enactment in this Act) relating to the notification of disease or to notifiable diseases.

15. Contravention of regulations under s. 13

Any person who wilfully neglects or refuses to obey or carry out, or obstructs the execution of, any regulations made under section 13 above shall, in a case where no provision is made in the regulations for his punishment, be liable on summary conviction —

(a) to a fine not exceeding level 5 on the standard scale, and

(b) in the case of a continuing offence, to a further fine not exceeding £50 for every day on which the offence continues after conviction.

17. Exposure of persons and articles liable to convey notifiable disease

(1) A person who —

(a) knowing that he is suffering from a notifiable disease, exposes other persons to the risk of infection by his presence or conduct in any street, public place, place of entertainment or assembly, club, hotel, inn or shop,

(b) having the care of a person whom he knows to be suffering from a notifiable disease, causes or permits that person to expose other persons to the risk of infection by his presence or conduct in any such place as aforesaid, or

(c) gives, lends, sells, transmits or exposes, without previous disinfection, any clothing, bedding or rags which he knows to have been exposed to infection from any such disease, or any other article which he knows to have been so exposed and which is liable to carry such infection,

shall be liable on summary conviction to a fine not exceeding level 1 on the standard scale.

(2) A person shall not incur any liability under this section by transmitting with proper precautions any article for the purpose of having it disinfected.

18. Information to be furnished by occupier in case of notifiable disease or food poisoning

(1) On the application of the proper officer of the local authority for any district, the occupier of any premises in the district in which there is or has been any person suffering from a notifiable disease or food poisoning shall furnish such information within his knowledge as that officer may reasonably require for the purpose of enabling measures to be taken to prevent the spread of the disease or, as the case may be, to trace the source of food poisoning.

(2) If any person required to furnish information under this section fails to furnish it, or knowingly furnishes false information, he shall be liable on summary conviction to a fine not exceeding level 1 on the standard scale.

(3)   In this section, "occupier", in relation to any premises, includes —

(a)   a person having the charge, management or control of the premises, or of a building of which the premises form part, and

(b)   in the case of premises consisting of a building the whole of which is ordinarily let out in separate tenements, or of a lodging house the whole of which is ordinarily let to lodgers, the person receiving the rent payable by the tenants or by the lodgers, as the case may be, either on his own account or as the agent of another person.

19.   Trading etc. by person with notifiable disease

A person who, knowing that he is suffering from a notifiable disease, engages in or carries on any trade, business or occupation which he cannot engage in or carry on without risk of spreading the disease shall be liable on summary conviction to a fine not exceeding level 1 on the standard scale.

Infectious persons

35.   Medical examination

(1)   If a justice of the peace (acting, if he deems it necessary, ex parte) is satisfied, on a written certificate issued by a registered medical practitioner nominated by the local authority for a district —

(a)   that there is reason to believe that some person in the district —

(i)   is or has been suffering from a notifiable disease, or

(ii)   though not suffering from such a disease, is carrying an organism that is capable of causing it, and

(b)   that in his own interest, or in the interest of his family, or in the public interest, it is expedient that he should be medically examined, and

(c)   that he is not under the treatment of a registered medical practitioner or that the registered medical practitioner who is treating him consents to the making of an order under this section,

the justice may order him to be medically examined by a registered medical practitioner so nominated.

(2)   An order under this section may be combined with a warrant under subsection (3) or section 61 below authorising a registered medical practitioner nominated by the local authority to enter any premises, and for the purposes of that subsection that practitioner shall, if not an officer of the local authority, be treated as one.

(3)   In this section, references to a person's being medically examined shall be construed as including references to his being submitted to bacteriological and radiological tests and similar investigations.

36.   Medical examination of group of persons believed to comprise carrier of notifiable disease

(1)   If a justice of the peace (acting, if he deems it necessary, ex parte) is satisfied, on a written certificate issued by the proper officer of the local authority for a district —

(a)   that there is reason to believe that one of a group of persons, though not suffering from a notifiable disease, is carrying an organism that is capable of causing it, and

(b)   that in the interest of those persons or their families, or in the public interest, it is expedient that those persons should be medically examined,

the justice may order them to be medically examined by a registered medical practitioner nominated by the local authority for that district.

(2)   Subsections (2) and (3) of section 35 above apply in relation to subsection (1) above as they apply in relation to subsection (1) of that section.

37.   Removal to hospital of person with notifiable disease

(1)   Where a justice of the peace (acting, if he deems it necessary, ex parte) is satisfied, on the application of the local authority, that a person is suffering from a notifiable disease and —

(a)   that his circumstances are such that proper precautions to prevent the spread of infection cannot be taken, or that such precautions are not being taken, and

(b)   that serious risk of infection is thereby caused to other persons, and

(c)   that accommodation for him is available in a suitable hospital vested in the Secretary of State, or, pursuant to arrangements made by a District Health Authority (whether under an NHS contract or otherwise) in a suitable hospital vested in a NHS trust or other person the justice may, with the consent of the District Health Authority in whose district lies the area, or the greater part of the area, of the local authority, order him to be removed to it.

(2)   An order under this section may be addressed to such officer of the local authority as the justice may think expedient, and that officer and any officer of the hospital may do all acts necessary for giving effect to the order.

38.   Detention in hospital of person with notifiable disease

(1)   Where a justice of the peace (acting, if he deems it necessary, ex parte) in and for the place in which a hospital for infectious diseases is situated is satisfied, on the application of any local authority, that an inmate of the hospital who is suffering from a notifiable disease would not on leaving the hospital be provided with lodging or accommodation in which proper precautions could be taken to prevent the spread of the disease by him, the justice may order him to be detained in the hospital.

(2)   An order made under subsection (1) above may direct detention for a period specified in the order, but any justice of the peace acting in and for the same place may extend a period so specified as often as it appears to him to be necessary to do so.

(3)   Any person who leaves a hospital contrary to an order made under this section for his detention there shall be liable on summary conviction to a fine not exceeding level 1 on the standard scale, and the court may order him to be taken back to the hospital.

(4)   An order under this section may be addressed —

(a)   in the case of an order for a person's detention, to such officer of the hospital, and

(b)   in the case of an order made under subsection (3) above, to such officer of the local authority on whose application the order for detention was made,

as the justice may think expedient, and that officer and any officer of the hospital may do all acts necessary for giving effect to the order.

DATA PROTECTION ACT 1984
(1984, c. 35)

PART I
PRELIMINARY

1.   Definition of "data" and related expressions

(1)   The following provisions shall have effect for the interpretation of this Act.

(2)   "Data" means information recorded in a form in which it can be processed by equipment operating automatically in response to instructions given for that purpose.

(3)   "Personal data" means data consisting of information which relates to a living individual who can be identified from that information (or from that and other information in the possession of the data user), including any expression of opinion about the individual but not any indication of the intentions of the data user in respect of that individual.

(4)   "Data subject" means an individual who is the subject of personal data.

(5) "Data user" means a person who holds data, and a person "holds" data if —

    (a) the data form part of a collection of data processed or intended to be processed by or on behalf of that person as mentioned in subsection (2) above; and

    (b) that person (either alone or jointly or in common with other persons) controls the contents and use of the data comprised in the collection; and

    (c) the data are in the form in which they have been or are intended to be processed as mentioned in paragraph (a) above or (though not for the time being in that form) in a form into which they have been converted after being so processed and with a view to being further so processed on a subsequent occasion.

(6) A person carries on a "computer bureau" if he provides other persons with services in respect of data, and a person provides such services if —

    (a) as agent for other persons he causes data held by them to be processed as mentioned in subsection (2) above; or

    (b) he allows other persons the use of equipment in his possession for the processing as mentioned in that subsection of data held by them.

(7) "Processing", in relation to data, means amending, augmenting, deleting or re-arranging the data or extracting the information constituting the data and, in the case of personal data, means performing any of these operations by reference to the data subject.

(8) Subsection (7) above shall not be construed as applying to any operation performed only for the purpose of preparing the text of documents.

(9) "Disclosing", in relation to data, includes disclosing information extracted from the data; and where the identification of the individual who is the subject of personal data depends partly on the information constituting the data and partly on other information in the possession of the data user, the data shall not be regarded as disclosed or transferred unless the other information is also disclosed or transferred.

2. The data protection principles

(1) Subject to subsection (3) below, references in this Act to the data protection principles are to the principles set out in Part I of Schedule 1 to this Act; and those principles shall be interpreted in accordance with Part II of that Schedule.

(2) The first seven principles apply to personal data held by data users and the eighth applies both to such data and to personal data in respect of which services are provided by persons carrying on computer bureaux.

(3) The Secretary of State may by order modify or supplement those principles for the purpose of providing additional safeguards in relation to personal data consisting of information as to —

    (a) the racial origin of the data subject;

    (b) his political opinions or religious or other beliefs;

    (c) his physical or mental health or his sexual life; or

    (d) his criminal convictions;

and references in this Act to the data protection principles include, except where the context otherwise requires, references to any modified or additional principle having effect by virtue of an order under this subsection.

(4) An order under subsection (3) above may modify a principle either by modifying the principle itself or by modifying its interpretation; and where an order under that subsection modifies a principle or provides for an additional principle it may contain provisions for the interpretation of the modified or additional principle.

(5) An order under subsection (3) above modifying the third data protection principle may, to such extent as the Secretary of State thinks appropriate, exclude or modify in relation to that principle any exemption from the non-disclosure provisions which is contained in Part IV of this Act; and the exemptions from those provisions contained in that Part shall accordingly have effect subject to any order made by virtue of this subsection.

(6)   An order under subsection (3) above may make different provisions in relation to data consisting of information of different descriptions.

3.   The Registrar and the Tribunal

(1)   For the purposes of this Act there shall be —

(a)   an officer known as the Data Protection Registrar (in this Act referred to as "the Registrar"); and

(b)   a tribunal known as the Data Protection Tribunal (in this Act referred to as "the Tribunal").

(2)   The Registrar shall be appointed by Her Majesty by Letters Patent.

(3)   The Tribunal shall consist of —

(a)   a chairman appointed by the Lord Chancellor after consultation with the Lord Advocate;

(b)   such number of deputy chairmen appointed as aforesaid as the Lord Chancellor may determine; and

(c)   such number of other members appointed by the Secretary of State as he may determine.

(4)   The members of the Tribunal appointed under subsection (3)(a) and (b) above shall be —

(a)   persons who have a 7 year general qualification within the meaning of section 71 of the Courts and Legal Services Act 1990;

(b)   advocates or solicitors of Scotland of at least 7 years standing; or

(c)   members of the Bar of Northern Ireland or solicitors of the Supreme Court of Northern Ireland of at least 7 years standing.

(5)   The members of the Tribunal appointed under subsection (3)(c) above shall be —

(a)   persons to represent the interests of data users; and

(b)   persons to represent the interests of data subjects.

(6)   Schedule 2 to this Act shall have effect in relation to the Registrar and the Tribunal.

PART II
REGISTRATION AND SUPERVISION OF DATA USERS AND COMPUTER BUREAUX

Registration

4.   Registration of data users and computer bureaux

(1)   The Registrar shall maintain a register of data users who hold, and of persons carrying on computer bureaux who provide services in respect of, personal data and shall make an entry in the register in pursuance of each application for registration accepted by him under this Part of this Act.

(2)   Each entry shall state whether it is in respect of a data user, of a person carrying on a computer bureau or of a data user who also carries on such a bureau.

(3)   Subject to the provisions of this section, an entry in respect of a data user shall consist of the following particulars —

(a)   the name and address of the data user;

(b)   a description of the personal data to be held by him and of the purpose or purposes for which the data are to be held or used;

(c)   description of the source or sources from which he intends or may wish to obtain the data or the information to be contained in the data;

(d)   description of any person or persons to whom he intends or may wish to disclose the data;

(e)   the names or a description of any countries or territories outside the United Kingdom to which he intends or may wish directly or indirectly to transfer the data; and

(f)   one or more addresses for the receipt of requests from data subjects for access to the data.

(4)   Subject to the provisions of this section, an entry in respect of a person carrying on a computer bureau shall consist of that person's name and address.

(5)   Subject to the provisions of this section, an entry in respect of a data user who also carries on a computer bureau shall consist of his name and address and, as respects the personal data to be held by him, the particulars specified in subsection (3)(b) to (f) above.

(6)   In the case of a registered company the address referred to in subsections (3)(a), (4) and (5) above is that of its registered office, and the particulars to be included in the entry shall include the company's number in the register of companies.

(7)   In the case of a person (other than a registered company) carrying on a business the address referred to in subsections (3)(a), (4) and (5) above is that of his principal place of business.

(8)   The Secretary of State may by order vary the particulars to be included in entries made in the register.

5.   Prohibition of unregistered holding etc. of personal data

(1)   A person shall not hold personal data unless an entry in respect of that person as a data user, or as a data user who also carries on a computer bureau, is for the time being contained in the register.

(2)   A person in respect of whom such an entry is contained in the register shall not —

(a)   hold personal data of any description other than that specified in the entry;

(b)   hold any such data, or use any such data held by him, for any purpose other than the purpose or purposes described in the entry;

(c)   obtain such data, or information to be contained in such data, to be held by him from any source which is not described in the entry;

(d)   disclose such data held by him to any person who is not described in the entry; or

(e)   directly or indirectly transfer such data held by him to any country or territory outside the United Kingdom other than one named or described in the entry.

(3)   A servant or agent of a person to whom subsection (2) above applies shall, as respects personal data held by that person, be subject to the same restrictions on the use, disclosure or transfer of the data as those to which that person is subject under paragraphs (b), (d) and (e) of that subsection and, as respects personal data to be held by that person, to the same restrictions as those to which he is subject under paragraph (c) of that subsection.

(4)   A person shall not, in carrying on a computer bureau, provide services in respect of personal data unless an entry in respect of that person as a person carrying on such a bureau, or as a data user who also carries on such a bureau, is for the time being contained in the register.

(5)   Any person who contravenes subsection (1) above or knowingly or recklessly contravenes any of the other provisions of this section shall be guilty of an offence.

Supervision

10.   Enforcement notices

(1)   If the Registrar is satisfied that a registered person has contravened or is contravening any of the data protection principles he may serve him with a notice ("an enforcement notice") requiring him to take, within such time as is specified in the notice, such steps as are so specified for complying with the principle or principles in question.

(2)   In deciding whether to serve an enforcement notice the Registrar shall consider whether the contravention has caused or is likely to cause any person damage or distress.

(3)   An enforcement notice in respect of a contravention of the fifth data protection principle may require the data user —

(a)   to rectify or erase the data and any other data held by him and containing an expression of opinion which appears to the Registrar to be based on the inaccurate data; or

(b)   in the case of such data as are mentioned in subsection (2) of section 22 below, either to take the steps mentioned in paragraph (a) above or to take such steps as are specified in the notice for securing compliance with the requirements specified in that subsection and, if the Registrar thinks fit, for supplementing the data with such statement of the true facts relating to the matters dealt with by the data as the Registrar may approve.

(4)   The Registrar shall not serve an enforcement notice requiring the person served with the notice to take steps for complying with paragraph (a) of the seventh data protection principle in respect of any data subject unless satisfied that the person has contravened section 21 below by failing to supply information to which the data subject is entitled and which has been duly requested in accordance with that section.

(5)   An enforcement notice shall contain —

(a)   a statement of the principle or principles which the Registrar is satisfied have been or are being contravened and his reasons for reaching that conclusion; and

(b)   particulars of the rights of appeal conferred by section 13 below.

(6)   Subject to subsection (7) below, the time specified in an enforcement notice for taking the steps which it requires shall not expire before the end of the period within which an appeal can be brought against the notice and, if such an appeal is brought, those steps need not be taken pending the determination or withdrawal of the appeal.

(7)   If by reason of special circumstances the Registrar considers that the steps required by an enforcement notice should be taken as a matter of urgency he may include a statement to that effect in the notice; and in that event subsection (6) above shall not apply but the notice shall not require the steps to be taken before the end of the period of seven days beginning with the date on which the notice is served.

(8)   The Registrar may cancel an enforcement notice by written notification to the person on whom it was served.

(9)   Any person who fails to comply with an enforcement notice shall be guilty of an offence; but it shall be a defence for a person charged with an offence under this subsection to prove that he exercised all due diligence to comply with the notice in question.

11.   De-registration notices

(1)   If the Registrar is satisfied that a registered person has contravened or is contravening any of the data protection principles he may —

(a)   serve him with a notice ("a de-registration notice") stating that he proposes, at the expiration of such period as is specified in the notice, to remove from the register all or any of the particulars constituting the entry or any of the entries contained in the register in respect of that person; and

(b)   subject to the provisions of this section, remove those particulars from the register at the expiration of that period.

(2)   In deciding whether to serve a de-registration notice the Registrar shall consider whether the contravention has caused or is likely to cause any person damage or distress, and the Registrar shall not serve such a notice unless he is satisfied that compliance with the principle or principles in question cannot be adequately secured by the service of an enforcement notice.

(3)   A de-registration notice shall contain —

(a)   a statement of the principle or principles which the Registrar is satisfied have been or are being contravened and his reasons for reaching that conclusion and deciding that compliance cannot be adequately secured by the service of an enforcement notice; and

(b)   particulars of the rights of appeal conferred by section 13 below.

(4)   Subject to subsection (5) below, the period specified in a de-registration notice pursuant to subsection (1)(a) above shall not expire before the end of the period within which an appeal can be brought against the notice and, if such an appeal is brought, the particulars shall not be removed pending the determination or withdrawal of the appeal.

(5)   If by reason of special circumstances the Registrar considers that any particulars should be removed from the register as a matter of urgency he may include a statement to that effect in the de-registration notice; and in that event subsection (4) above shall not apply but the particulars shall not be removed before the end of the period of seven days beginning with the date on which the notice is served.

(6)   The Registrar may cancel a de-registration notice by written notification to the person on whom it was served.

(7)   References in this section to removing any particulars include references to restricting any description which forms part of any particulars.

Miscellaneous and supplementary

15.   Unauthorised disclosure by computer bureau

(1)   Personal data in respect of which services are provided by a person carrying on a computer bureau shall not be disclosed by him without the prior authority of the person for whom those services are provided.

(2)   Subsection (1) above applies also to any servant or agent of a person carrying on a computer bureau.

(3)   Any person who knowingly or recklessly contravenes this section shall be guilty of an offence.

PART III
RIGHTS OF DATA SUBJECTS

21.   Right of access to personal data

(1)   Subject to the provisions of this section, an individual shall be entitled—

(a)   to be informed by any data user whether the data held by him include personal data of which that individual is the data subject; and

(b)   to be supplied by any data user with a copy of the information constituting any such personal data held by him;

and where any of the information referred to in paragraph (b) above is expressed in terms which are not intelligible without explanation the information shall be accompanied by an explanation of those terms.

(2)   A data user shall not be obliged to supply any information under subsection (1) above except in response to a request in writing and on payment of such fee (not exceeding the prescribed maximum) as he may require; but a request for information under both paragraphs of that subsection shall be treated as a single request and a request for information under paragraph (a) shall, in the absence of any indication to the contrary, be treated as extending also to information under paragraph (b).

(3)   In the case of a data user having separate entries in the register in respect of data held for different purposes a separate request must be made and a separate fee paid under this section in respect of the data to which each entry relates.

(4)   A data user shall not be obliged to comply with a request under this section—

(a)   unless he is supplied with such information as he may reasonably require in order to satisfy himself as to the identity of the person making the request and to locate the information which he seeks; and

(b)   if he cannot comply with the request without disclosing information relating to another individual who can be identified from that information, unless he is satisfied that the other individual has consented to the disclosure of the information to the person making the request.

(5)   In paragraph (b) of subsection (4) above the reference to information relating to another individual includes a reference to information identifying that individual as the source of the information sought by the request; and that paragraph shall not be construed as excusing a data user from supplying so much of the information sought by the request as can be supplied without disclosing the identity of the other individual concerned, whether by the omission of names or other identifying particulars or otherwise.

(6)   A data user shall comply with a request under this section within forty days of receiving the request or, if later, receiving the information referred to in paragraph (a) of subsection (4) above and, in a case where it is required, the consent referred to in paragraph (b) of that subsection.

(7)   The information to be supplied pursuant to a request under this section shall be supplied by reference to the data in question at the time when the request is received except that it may take account of any amendment or deletion made between that time and the time when the information is supplied, being an amendment or deletion that would have been made regardless of the receipt of the request.

(8)   If a court is satisfied on the application of any person who has made a request under the foregoing provisions of this section that the data user in question has failed to comply with the request in contravention of those provisions, the court may order him to comply with the request; but a court shall not make an order under this subsection if it considers that it would in all the circumstances be unreasonable to do so, whether because of the frequency with which the applicant has made requests to the data user under those provisions or for any other reason.

(9)   The Secretary of State may by order provide for enabling a request under this section to be made on behalf of any individual who is incapable by reason of mental disorder of managing his own affairs.

22.   Compensation for inaccuracy

(1)   An individual who is the subject of personal data held by a data user and who suffers damage by reason of the inaccuracy of the data shall be entitled to compensation from the data user for that damage and for any distress which the individual has suffered by reason of the inaccuracy.

(2)   In the case of data which accurately record information received or obtained by the data user from the data subject or a third party, subsection (1) above does not apply if the following requirements have been complied with—

(a)   the data indicate that the information was received or obtained as aforesaid or the information has not been extracted from the data except in a form which includes an indication to that effect; and

(b)   if the data subject has notified the data user that he regards the information as incorrect or misleading, an indication to that effect has been included in the data or the information has not been extracted from the data except in a form which includes an indication to that effect.

(3)   In proceedings brought against any person by virtue of this section it shall be a defence to prove that he had taken such care as in all the circumstances was reasonably required to ensure the accuracy of the data at the material time.

(4)   Data are inaccurate for the purposes of this section if incorrect or misleading as to any matter of fact.

23. Compensation for loss or unauthorised disclosure

(1)   An individual who is the subject of personal data held by a data user or in respect of which services are provided by a person carrying on a computer bureau and who suffers damage by reason of—

(a)   the loss of the data;

(b)   the destruction of the data without the authority of the data user or, as the case may be, of the person carrying on the bureau; or

(c)   subject to subsection (2) below, the disclosure of the data, or access having been obtained to the data, without such authority as aforesaid,

shall be entitled to compensation from the data user or, as the case may be, the person carrying on the bureau for that damage and for any distress which the individual has suffered by reason of the loss, destruction, disclosure or access.

(2)   In the case of a registered data user, subsection (1)(c) above does not apply to disclosure to, or access by, any person falling within a description specified pursuant to section 4(3)(d) above in an entry in the register relating to that data user.

(3)   In proceedings brought against any person by virtue of this section it shall be a defence to prove that he had taken such care as in all the circumstances was reasonably required to prevent the loss, destruction, disclosure or access in question.

24. Rectification and erasure

(1)   If a court is satisfied on the application of a data subject that personal data held by a data user of which the applicant is the subject are inaccurate within the meaning of section 22 above, the court may order the rectification or erasure of the data and of any data held by the data user and containing an expression of opinion which appears to the court to be based on the inaccurate data.

(2)   Subsection (1) above applies whether or not the data accurately record information recieved or obtained by the data user from the data subject or a third party but where the data accurately record such information, then—

(a)   if the requirements mentioned in section 22(2) above have been complied with, the court may, instead of making an order under subsection (1) above, make an order requiring the data to be supplemented by such statement of the true facts relating to the matters dealt with by the data as the court may approve; and

(b)   if all or any of those requirements have not been complied with, the court may, instead of making an order under that subsection, make such order as it thinks fit for securing compliance with those requirements with or without a further order requiring the data to be supplemented by such a statement as is mentioned in paragraph (a) above.

(3)   If a court is satisfied on the application of a data subject—

(a)   that he has suffered damage by reason of the disclosure of personal data, or of access having been obtained to personal data, in circumstances entitling him to compensation under section 23 above; and

(b)   that there is a substantial risk of further disclosure of or access to the data without such authority as is mentioned in that section,

the court may order the erasure of the data; but, in the case of data in respect of which services were being provided by a person carrying on a computer bureau, the court shall not make such an order unless such steps as are reasonably practicable have been taken for notifying the person for whom those services were provided and giving him an opportunity to be heard.

25. Jurisdiction and procedure

(1)   The jurisdiction conferred by sections 21 and 24 above shall be exercisable by the High Court or a county court or, in Scotland, by the Court of Session or the sheriff.

(2)   For the purpose of determining any question whether an applicant under subsection (8) of section 21 above is entitled to the information which he seeks

(including any question whether any relevant data are exempt from that section by virtue of Part IV of this Act) a court may require the information constituting any data held by the data user to be made available for its own inspection but shall not, pending the determination of that question in the applicant's favour, require the information sought by the applicant to be disclosed to him or his representatives whether by discovery (or, in Scotland, recovery) or otherwise.

PART IV
EXEMPTIONS

26. Preliminary

(1)   References in any provision of Part II or III of this Act to personal data do not include references to data which by virtue of this Part of this Act are exempt from that provision.

(2)   In this Part of this Act "the subject access provisions" means—

(a)   section 21 above; and

(b)   any provision of Part II of this Act conferring a power on the Registrar to the extent to which it is exercisable by reference to paragraph (a) of the seventh data protection principle.

(3)   In this Part of this Act "the non-disclosure provisions" means—

(a)   sections 5(2)(d) and 15 above; and

(b)   any provision of Part II of this Act conferring a power on the Registrar to the extent to which it is exercisable by reference to any data protection principle inconsistent with the disclosure in question.

(4)   Except as provided by this Part of this Act the subject access provisions shall apply notwithstanding any enactment or rule of law prohibiting or restricting the disclosure, or authorising the withholding, of information.

29.   Health and social work

(1)   The Secretary of State may by order exempt from the subject access provisions, or modify those provisions in relation to, personal data consisting of information as to the physical or mental health of the data subject.

(2)   The Secretary of State may by order exempt from the subject access provisions, or modify those provisions in relation to, personal data of such other descriptions as may be specified in the order, being information —

(a)   held by government departments or local authorities or by voluntary organisations or other bodies designated by or under the order; and

(b)   appearing to him to be held for, or acquired in the course of, carrying out social work in relation to the data subject or other individuals;

but the Secretary of State shall not under this subsection confer any exemption or make any modification except so far as he considers that the application to the data of those provisions (or of those provisions without modification) would be likely to prejudice the carrying out of social work.

(3)   An order under this section may make different provision in relation to data consisting of information of different descriptions.

33.   Domestic or other limited purposes

(6)   Personal data held only for —

(a)   preparing statistics; or

(b)   carrying out research,

are exempt from the subject access provisions; but it shall be a condition of that exemption that the data are not used or disclosed for any other purpose and that the resulting statistics or the results of the research are not made available in a form which identifies the data subjects of any of them.

34. Other exemptions

(5) Personal data are exempt from the non-disclosure provisions in any case in which the disclosure is —

(a) required by or under any enactment, by any rule of law or by the order of a court; or

(b) made for the purpose of obtaining legal advice or for the purposes of, or in the course of, legal proceedings in which the person making the disclosure is a party or a witness.

(6) Personal data are exempt from the non-disclosure provisions in any case in which —

(a) the disclosure is to the data subject or a person acting on his behalf; or

(b) the data subject or any such person has requested or consented to the particular disclosure in question; or

(c) the disclosure is by a data user or a person carrying on a computer bureau to his servant or agent for the purpose of enabling the servant or agent to perform his functions as such; or

(d) the person making the disclosure has reasonable grounds for believing that the disclosure falls within any of the foregoing paragraphs of this subsection.

(8) Personal data are exempt from the non-disclosure provisions in any case in which the disclosure is urgently required for preventing injury or other damage to the health of any person or persons; and in proceedings against any person for contravening a provision mentioned in section 26(3)(a) above it shall be a defence to prove that he had reasonable grounds for believing that the disclosure in question was urgently required for that purpose.

35A. Information about human embryos, etc.

Personal data consisting of information showing that an identifiable individual was, or may have been, born in consequence of treatment services (within the meaning of the Human Fertilisation and Embryology Act 1990) are exempt from the subject access provisions except so far as their disclosure under those provisions is made in accordance with section 31 of that Act (the Authority's register of information).

38. Application to government departments and police

(1) Except as provided in subsection (2) below, a government department shall be subject to the same obligations and liabilities under this Act as a private person; and for the purposes of this Act each government department shall be treated as a person separate from any other government department and a person in the public service of the Crown shall be treated as a servant of the government department to which his responsibilities or duties relate.

(2) A government department shall not be liable to prosecution under this Act but —

(a) sections 5(3) and 15(2) above (and, so far as relating to those provisions, sections 5(5) and 15(3) above) shall apply to any person who by virtue of this section falls to be treated as a servant of the government department in question; and

(b) section 6(6) above and paragraph 12 of Schedule 4 to this Act shall apply to a person in the public service of the Crown as they apply to any other person.

41. General interpretation

In addition to the provisions of sections 1 and 2 above, the following provisions shall have effect for the interpretation of this Act —

"business" includes any trade or profession;

"data equipment" means equipment for the automatic processing of data or for recording information so that it can be automatically processed;

"data material" means any document or other material used in connection with data equipment;

"a de-registration notice" means a notice under section 11 above;

"enactment" includes an enactment passed after this Act;

"an enforcement notice" means a notice under section 10 above;

"the European Convention" means the Convention for the Protection of Individuals with regard to Automatic Processing of Personal Data which was opened for signature on 28th January 1981;

"government department" includes a Northern Ireland department and any body or authority exercising statutory functions on behalf of the Crown;

"prescribed" means prescribed by regulations made by the Secretary of State;

"the Registrar" means the Data Protection Registrar;

"the register", except where the reference is to the register of companies, means the register maintained under section 4 above and (except where the reference is to a registered company, to the registered office of a company or to registered post) references to registration shall be construed accordingly;

"registered company" means a company registered under the enactments relating to companies for the time being in force in any part of the United Kingdom;

"a transfer prohibition notice" means a notice under section 12 above;

"the Tribunal" means the Data Protection Tribunal.

SCHEDULE

SCHEDULE 1
THE DATA PROTECTION PRINCIPLES
PART I
THE PRINCIPLES

Personal data held by data users

1.   The information to be contained in personal data shall be obtained, and personal data shall be processed, fairly and lawfully.

2.   Personal data shall be held only for one or more specified and lawful purposes.

3.   Personal data held for any purpose or purposes shall not be used or disclosed in any manner incompatible with that purpose or those purposes.

4.   Personal data held for any purpose or purposes shall be adequate, relevant and not excessive in relation to that purpose or those purposes.

5.   Personal data shall be accurate and, where necessary, kept up to date.

6.   Personal data held for any purpose or purposes shall not be kept for longer than is necessary for that purpose or those purposes.

7.   An individual shall be entitled —

   (a)   at reasonable intervals and without undue delay or expense —

     (i)   to be informed by any data user whether he holds personal data of which that individual is the subject; and

     (ii)   to access to any such data held by a data user; and

   (b)   where appropriate, to have such data corrected or erased.

Personal data held by data users or in respect of which services are provided by persons carrying on computer bureaux

8.   Appropriate security measures shall be taken against unauthorised access to, or alteration, disclosure or destruction of, personal data and against accidental loss or destruction of personal data.

PART II
INTERPRETATION

The first principle

1.—(1) Subject to sub-paragraph (2) below, in determining whether information was obtained fairly regard shall be had to the method by which it was obtained, including in particular whether any person from whom it was obtained was deceived or misled as to the purpose or purposes for which it is to be held, used or disclosed.

(2) Information shall in any event be treated as obtained fairly if it is obtained from a person who —

(a) is authorised by or under any enactment to supply it; or

(b) is required to supply it by or under any enactment or by any convention or other instrument imposing an international obligation on the United Kingdom;

and in determining whether information was obtained fairly there shall be disregarded any disclosure of the information which is authorised or required by or under any enactment or required by any such convention or other instrument as aforesaid.

The second principle

2. Personal data shall not be treated as held for a specified purpose unless that purpose is described in particulars registered under this Act in relation to the data.

The third principle

3. Personal data shall not be treated as used or disclosed in contravention of this principle unless —

(a) used otherwise than for a purpose of a description registered under this Act in relation to the data; or

(b) disclosed otherwise than to a person of a description so registered.

The fifth principle

4. Any question whether or not personal data are accurate shall be determined as for the purposes of section 22 of this Act but, in the case of such data as are mentioned in subsection (2) of that section, this principle shall not be regarded as having been contravened by reason of any inaccuracy in the information there mentioned if the requirements specified in that subsection have been complied with.

The seventh principle

5.—(1) Paragraph (a) of this principle shall not be construed as conferring any rights inconsistent with section 21 of this Act.

(2) In determining whether access to personal data is sought at reasonable intervals regard shall be had to the nature of the data, the purpose for which the data are held and the frequency with which the data are altered.

(3) The correction or erasure of personal data is appropriate only where necessary for ensuring compliance with the other data protection principles.

The eighth principle

6. Regard shall be had —

(a) to the nature of the personal data and the harm that would result from such access, alteration, disclosure, loss or destruction as are mentioned in this principle; and

(b) to the place where the personal data are stored, to security measures programmed into the relevant equipment and to measures taken for ensuring the reliability of staff having access to the data.

Use for historical, statistical or research purposes

7. Where personal data are held for historical, statistical or research purposes and not used in such a way that damage or distress is, or is likely to be, caused to any data subject —

(a) the information contained in the data shall not be regarded for the purposes of the first principle as obtained unfairly by reason only that its use for any such purpose was not disclosed when it was obtained; and

(b) the data may, notwithstanding the sixth principle, be kept indefinitely.

POLICE AND CRIMINAL EVIDENCE ACT 1984
(1984, c. 60)

9. Special provisions as to access

(1) A constable may obtain access to excluded material or special procedure material for the purposes of a criminal investigation by making an application under Schedule 1 below and in accordance with that Schedule.

(2) Any Act (including a local Act) passed before this Act under which a search of premises for the purposes of a criminal investigation could be authorised by the issue of a warrant to a constable shall cease to have effect so far as it relates to the authorisation of searches —

(a) for items subject to legal privilege; or

(b) for excluded material; or

(c) for special procedure material consisting of documents or records other than documents.

11. Meaning of "excluded material"

(1) Subject to the following provisions of this section, in this Act "excluded material" means —

(a) personal records which a person has acquired or created in the course of any trade, business, profession or other occupation or for the purposes of any paid or unpaid office and which he holds in confidence;

(b) human tissue or tissue fluid which has been taken for the purposes of diagnosis or medical treatment and which a person holds in confidence;

(c) journalistic material which a person holds in confidence and which consists —

(i) of documents; or

(ii) of records other than documents.

(2) A person holds material other than journalistic material in confidence for the purposes of this section if he holds it subject —

(a) to an express or implied undertaking to hold it in confidence; or

(b) to a restriction on disclosure or an obligation of secrecy contained in any enactment, including an enactment contained in an Act passed after this Act.

12. Meaning of "personal records"

In this Part of this Act "personal records" means documentary and other records concerning an individual (whether living or dead) who can be identified from them and relating —

(a) to his physical or mental health;

(b) to spiritual counselling or assistance given or to be given to him; or

(c) counselling or assistance given or to be given to him, for the purposes of his personal welfare, by any voluntary organisation or by any individual who —

(i) by reason of his office or occupation has responsibilities for his personal welfare; or

(ii) by reason of an order of a court has responsibilities for his supervision.

ENDURING POWERS OF ATTORNEY ACT 1985
(1985, c. 29)

Enduring powers of attorney

1. Enduring power of attorney to survive mental incapacity of donor

(1) Where an individual creates a power of attorney which is an enduring power within the meaning of this Act then —

(a) the power shall not be revoked by any subsequent mental incapacity of his; but

(b) upon such incapacity supervening the donee of the power may not do anything under the authority of the power except as provided by subsection (2) below or as directed or authorised by the court under section 5 unless or, as the case may be, until the instrument creating the power is registered by the court under section 6; and

(c) section 5 of the Powers of Attorney Act 1971 (protection of donee and third persons) so far as applicable shall apply if and so long as paragraph (b) above operates to suspend the donee's authority to act under the power as if the power had been revoked by the donor's mental incapacity.

(2) Notwithstanding subsection (1)(b) above, where the attorney has made an application for registration of the instrument then, until the application has been initially determined, the attorney may take action under the power —

(a) to maintain the donor or prevent loss to his estate; or

(b) to maintain himself or other persons in so far as section 3(4) permits him to do so.

(3) Where the attorney purports to act as provided by subsection (2) above then, in favour of a person who deals with him without knowledge that the attorney is acting otherwise than in accordance with paragraph (a) or (b) of that subsection, the transaction between them shall be as valid as if the attorney were acting in accordance with paragraph (a) or (b).

3. Scope of authority etc. of attorney under enduring power

(1) An enduring power may confer general authority (as defined in subsection (2) below) on the attorney to act on the donor's behalf in relation to all or a specified part of the property and affairs of the donor or may confer on him authority to do specified things on the donor's behalf and the authority may, in either case, be conferred subject to conditions and restrictions.

(2) Where an instrument is expressed to confer general authority on the attorney it operates to confer, subject to the restriction imposed by subsection (5) below and to any conditions or restrictions contained in the instrument, authority to do on behalf of the donor anything which the donor can lawfully do by an attorney.

(3) Subject to any conditions or restrictions contained in the instrument, an attorney under an enduring power, whether general or limited, may (without obtaining any consent) execute or exercise all or any of the trusts, powers or discretions vested in the donor as trustee and may (without the concurrence of any other person) give a valid receipt for capital or other money paid.

(4) Subject to any conditions or restrictions contained in the instrument, an attorney under an enduring power, whether general or limited, may (without obtaining any consent) act under the power so as to benefit himself or other persons than the donor to the following extent but no further, that is to say —

(a) he may so act in relation to himself or in relation to any other person if the donor might be expected to provide for his or that person's needs respectively; and

(b) he may do whatever the donor might be expected to do to meet those needs.

(5) Without prejudice to subsection (4) above but subject to any conditions or restrictions contained in the instrument, an attorney under an enduring power,

whether general or limited, may (without obtaining any consent) dispose of the property of the donor by way of gift to the following extent but no further, that is to say —

(a)   he may make gifts of a seasonal nature or at a time, or on an anniversary, of a birth or marriage, to persons (including himself) who are related to or connected with the donor, and

(b)   he may make gifts to any charity to whom the donor made or might be expected to make gifts,

provided that the value of each such gift is not unreasonable having regard to all the circumstances and in particular the size of the donor's estate.

10.   Application of Mental Health Act provisions relating to the court

(1)   The provisions of Part VII of the Mental Health Act 1983 (relating to the Court of Protection) specified below shall apply to persons within and proceedings under this Act in accordance with the following paragraphs of this subsection and subsection (2) below, that is to say —

(a)   section 103 (functions of Visitors) shall apply to persons within this Act as it applies to the persons mentioned in that section;

(b)   section 104 (powers of judge) shall apply to proceedings under this Act with respect to persons within this Act as it applies to the proceedings mentioned in subsection (1) of that section;

(c)   section 105(1) (appeals to nominated judge) shall apply to any decision of the Master of the Court of Protection or any nominated officer in proceedings under this Act as it applies to any decision to which that subsection applies and an appeal shall lie to the Court of Appeal from any decision of a nominated judge whether given in the exercise of his original jurisdiction or on the hearing of an appeal under section 105(1) as extended by this paragraph;

(d)   section 106 except subsection (4) (rules of procedure) shall apply to proceedings under this Act and persons within this Act as it applies to the proceedings and persons mentioned in that section.

(2)   Any functions conferred or imposed by the provisions of the said Part VII applied by subsection (1) above shall be exercisable also for the purposes of this Act and the persons who are "within this Act" are the donors of and attorneys under enduring powers of attorney whether or not they would be patients for the purposes of the said Part VII.

(3)   In this section "nominated judge" and "nominated officer" have the same meanings as in Part VII of the Mental Health Act 1983.

13.   Interpretation

"mentally incapable" or "mental incapacity", except where it refers to revocation at common law, means, in relation to any person, that he is incapable by reason of mental disorder of managing and administering his property and affairs and "mentally capable" and "mental capacity" shall be construed accordingly;

"mental disorder" has the same meaning as it has in the Mental Health Act 1983;

(2)   Any question arising under or for the purposes of this Act as to what the donor of the power might at any time be expected to do shall be determined by assuming that he had full mental capacity at the time but otherwise by reference to the circumstances existing at that time.

PROHIBITION OF FEMALE CIRCUMCISION ACT 1985
(1985, c. 38)

1.   Prohibition of female circumcision

Subject to section 2 below, it shall be an offence for any person —

(a)   to excise, infibulate or otherwise mutilate the whole or any part of the labia majora or labia minora or clitoris of another person; or

(b)   to aid, abet, counsel or procure the performance by another person of any of those acts on that other person's own body.

(2)   A person guilty of an offence under this section shall be liable —

(a)   on conviction on indictment, to a fine or to imprisonment for a term not exceeding five years or to both; or

(b)   on summary conviction, to a fine not exceeding the statutory maximum (as defined in section 74 of the Criminal Justice Act 1982) or to imprisonment for a term not exceeding six months, or to both.

2. Saving for necessary surgical operations

(1)   Subsection (1)(a) of section 1 shall not render unlawful the performance of a surgical operation if that operation —

(a)   is necessary for the physical or mental health of the person on whom it is performed and is performed by a registered medical practitioner; or

(b)   is performed on a person who is in any stage of labour or has just given birth and is so performed for purposes connected with that labour or birth by —

(i)   a registered medical practitioner or a registered midwife; or

(ii)   a person undergoing a course of training with a view to becoming a registered medical practitioner or a registered midwife.

(2)   In determining for the purposes of this section whether an operation is necessary for the mental health of a person, no account shall be taken of the effect on that person of any belief on the part of that or any other person that the operation is required as a matter of custom or ritual.

HOSPITAL COMPLAINTS PROCEDURE ACT 1985
(1985, c. 42)

1. Hospital complaints procedure

(1)   It shall be the duty of the Secretary of State to give to each health authority in England and Wales and to each Health Board in Scotland such directions under section 17 of the National Health Service Act 1977 or section 2(5) of the National Health Service (Scotland) Act 1978 (directions as to exercise of functions) as appear to him necessary for the purpose of securing that, as respects each hospital for the management of which that authority or Board is responsible —

(a)   such arrangements are made for dealing with complaints made by or on behalf of persons who are or have been patients at that hospital; and

(b)   such steps are taken for publicising the arrangements so made, as (in each case) are specified or described in the directions.

(2)   No right of appeal, reference or review conferred under this section shall preclude an investigation under Part V of the said Act of 1977 or Part VI of the said Act of 1978 (investigations by Health Service Commissioners) in respect of any matter.

(3)   In this section —

(a)   in its application to England and Wales, expressions which are also used in the said Act of 1977 have the same meanings as in that Act;

(b)   in its application to Scotland, expressions which are also used in the said Act of 1978 have the same meanings as in that Act.

1A.   It shall also be the duty of the Secretary of State to give directions under paragraph 6(2)(e) of Schedule 2 to the National Health Service and Community Care Act 1990 and paragraph 6(2)(e) of Schedule 7A to the National Health Service (Scotland) Act 1978, to any NHS trust which is responsible for the management of a hospital, to comply with directions under section 1 above.

SURROGACY ARRANGEMENTS ACT 1985
(1985, c. 49)

1. Meaning of "surrogate mother", "surrogacy arrangement" and other terms

(1) The following provisions shall have effect for the interpretation of this Act.

(2) "Surrogate mother" means a woman who carries a child in pursuance of an arrangement —

  (a) made before she began to carry the child, and

  (b) made with a view to any child carried in pursuance of it being handed over to, and parental responsibility being met (so far as practicable) by, another person or other persons.

(3) An arrangement is a surrogacy arrangement if, were a woman to whom the arrangement relates to carry a child in pursuance of it, she would be a surrogate mother.

(4) In determining whether an arrangement is made with such a view as is mentioned in subsection (2) above regard may be had to the circumstances as a whole (and, in particular, where there is a promise or understanding that any payment will or may be made to the woman or for her benefit in respect of the carrying of any child in pursuance of the arrangement, to that promise or understanding).

(5) An arrangement may be regarded as made with such a view though subject to conditions relating to the handing over of any child.

(6) A woman who carries a child is to be treated for the purposes of subsection (2)(a) above as beginning to carry it at the time of the insemination or of the placing in her of an embryo, of an egg in the process of fertilisation or of sperm and eggs, as the case may be, that results in her carrying the child.

(7) "Body of persons" means a body of persons corporate or unincorporate.

(8) "Payment" means payment in money or money's worth.

(9) This Act applies to arrangements whether or not they are lawful.

1A. Surrogacy arrangements unenforceable

No surrogacy arrangement is enforceable by or against any of the persons making it.

2. Negotiating surrogacy arrangements on a commercial basis, etc.

(1) No person shall on a commercial basis do any of the following acts in the United Kingdom, that is —

  (a) initiate or take part in any negotiations with a view to the making of a surrogacy arrangement,

  (b) offer or agree to negotiate the making of a surrogacy arrangement, or

  (c) compile any information with a view to its use in making, or negotiating the making of, surrogacy arrangements;

and no person shall in the United Kingdom knowingly cause another to do any of those acts on a commercial basis.

(2) A person who contravenes subsection (1) above is guilty of an offence; but it is not a contravention of that subsection —

  (a) for a woman, with a view to becoming a surrogate mother herself, to do any act mentioned in that subsection or to cause such an act to he done, or

  (b) for any person, with a view to a surrogate mother carrying a child for him, to do such an act or to cause such an act to be done.

(3) For the purposes of this section, a person does an act on a commercial basis (subject to subsection (4) below) if —

  (a) any payment is at any time received by himself or another in respect of it, or

  (b) he does it with a view to any payment being received by himself or another in respect of making, or negotiating or facilitating the making of, any surrogacy arrangement.

In this subsection "payment" does not include payment to or for the benefit of a surrogate mother or prospective surrogate mother.

(4)   In proceedings against a person for an offence under subsection (1) above, he is not to be treated as doing an act on a commercial basis by reason of any payment received by another in respect of the act if it is proved that —

(a)   in a case where the payment was received before he did the act, he did not do the act knowing or having reasonable cause to suspect that any payment had been received in respect of the act; and

(b)   in any other case, he did not do the act with a view to any payment being received in respect of it.

(5)   Where —

(a)   a person acting on behalf of a body of persons takes any part in negotiating or facilitating the making of a surrogacy arrangement in the United Kingdom, and

(b)   negotiating or facilitating the making of surrogacy arrangements is an activity of the body,

then, if the body at any time receives any payment made by or on behalf of —

(i)   a woman who carries a child in pursuance of the arrangement,

(ii)   the person or persons for whom she carries it, or

(iii)   any person connected with the woman or with that person or those persons, the body is guilty of an offence.

For the purposes of this subsection, a payment received by a person connected with a body is to be treated as received by the body.

(6)   In proceedings against a body for an offence under subsection (5) above, it is a defence to prove that the payment concerned was not made in respect of the arrangement mentioned in paragraph (a) of that subsection.

(7)   A person who in the United Kingdom takes part in the management or control —

(a)   of any body of persons, or

(b)   of any of the activities of any body of persons,

is guilty of an offence if the activity described in subsection (8) below is an activity of the body concerned.

(8)   The activity referred to in subsection (7) above is negotiating or facilitating the making of surrogacy arrangements in the United Kingdom, being —

(a)   arrangements the making of which is negotiated or facilitated on a commercial basis, or

(b)   arrangements in the case of which payments are received (or treated for the purposes of subsection (5) above as received) by the body concerned in contravention of subsection (5) above.

(9)   In proceedings against a person for an offence under subsection (7) above, it is a defence to prove that he neither knew nor had reasonable cause to suspect that the activity described in subsection (8) above was an activity of the body concerned; and for the purposes of such proceedings any arrangement falling within subsection (8)(b) above shall be disregarded if it is proved that the payment concerned was not made in respect of the arrangement.

3.   Advertisements about surrogacy

(1)   This section applies to any advertisement containing an indication (however expressed) —

(a)   that any person is or may be willing to enter into a surrogacy arrangement or to negotiate or facilitate the making of a surrogacy arrangement, or

(b)   that any person is looking for a woman willing to become a surrogate mother or for persons wanting a woman to carry a child as a surrogate mother.

(2)   Where a newspaper or periodical containing an advertisement to which this section applies is published in the United Kingdom, any proprietor, editor or publisher

of the newspaper or periodical is guilty of an offence.

(3)　Where an advertisement to which this section applies is conveyed by means of a telecommunication system so as to be seen or heard (or both) in the United Kingdom, any person who in the United Kingdom causes it to be so conveyed knowing it to contain such an indication as is mentioned in subsection (1) above is guilty of an offence.

(4)　A person who publishes or causes to be published in the United Kingdom an advertisement to which this section applies (not being an advertisement contained in a newspaper or periodical or conveyed by means of a telecommunication system) is guilty of an offence.

(5)　A person who distributes or causes to be distributed in the United Kingdom an advertisement to which this section applies (not being an advertisement contained in a newspaper or periodical published outside the United Kingdom or an advertisement conveyed by means of a telecommunication system) knowing it to contain such an indication as is mentioned in subsection (1) above is guilty of an offence.

(6)　In this section "telecommunication system" has the same meaning as in the Telecommunications Act 1984.

4. Offences

(1)　A person guilty of an offence under this Act shall be liable on summary conviction —

(a)　in the case of an offence under section 2 to a fine not exceeding level 5 on the standard scale or to imprisonment for a term not exceeding 3 months or both,

(b)　in the case of an offence under section 3 to a fine not exceeding level 5 on the standard scale.

In this subsection "the standard scale" has the meaning given by section 75 of the Criminal Justice Act 1982.

(2)　No proceedings for an offence under this Act shall be instituted —

(a)　in England and Wales, except by or with the consent of the Director of Public Prosecutions; and

(b)　in Northern Ireland, except by or with the consent of the Director of Public Prosecutions for Northern Ireland.

(3)　Where an offence under this Act committed by a body corporate is proved to have been committed with the consent or connivance of, or to be attributable to any neglect on the part of, any director, manager, secretary or other similar officer of the body corporate or any person who was purporting to act in any such capacity, he as well as the body corporate is guilty of the offence and is liable to be proceeded against and punished accordingly.

(4)　Where the affairs of a body corporate are managed by its members, subsection (3) above shall apply in relation to the acts and defaults of a member in connection with his functions of management as if he were a director of the body corporate.

(5)　In any proceedings for an offence under section 2 of this Act, proof of things done or of words written, spoken or published (whether or not in the presence of any party to the proceedings) by any person taking part in the management or control of a body of persons or of any of the activities of the body, or by any person doing any of the acts mentioned in subsection (1)(a) to (c) of that section on behalf of the body, shall be admissible as evidence of the activities of the body.

(6)　In relation to an offence under this Act, section 127(1) of the Magistrates' Courts Act 1980 (information must be laid within six months of commission of offence), section 331(1) of the Criminal Procedure (Scotland) Act 1975 (proceedings must be commenced within that time) and Article 19(1) of the Magistrates' Courts (Northern Ireland) Order 1981 (complaint must be made within that time) shall have effect as if for the reference to six months there were substituted a reference to two years.

AIDS (CONTROL) ACT 1987
(1987, c. 33)

1.   Periodical reports on matters relating to AIDS and HIV

(1)   Reports shall be made in accordance with this section —

(a)   to each Regional Health Authority by the District Health Authority for each district in the region; and

(b)   to the Secretary of State by —
   (i)   each Regional Health Authority;
   (ii)   each District Health Authority in Wales;
   (iii)   each Health Board in Scotland, and
   (iv)   each NHS trust.

(2)   The reports made by a District Health Authority, an NHS trust and a Health Board shall contain the information specified in the Schedule to this Act and such other relevant information as the Secretary of State may direct; and the reports made by a Regional Health Authority shall contain the information supplied to it in the reports of the District Health Authorities in the region.

(3)   The reports made by a Regional Health Authority, District Health Authority, NHS trust or Health Board shall be published by the Authority trust or Board by which they are made and the information contained in the reports made by District Health Authorities in Wales shall be published by the Secretary of State.

(4)   The reports shall be in such form and shall be made at such times or intervals and relate to such periods as the Secretary of State may direct but those periods shall not be more than twelve months and the first reports shall be made and published not later than the end of 1988.

(5)   The Secretary of State may by order made by statutory instrument —

(a)   make provision for requiring any special health authority specified in the order to make reports to him under this section and for that purpose modify the Schedule to this Act in its application to that authority;

(b)   amend the Schedule to this Act.

(6)   The Schedule to this Act may be modified or amended under subsection (5) above either by altering or deleting any of the matters for the time being specified in it or by specifying additional relevant information.

(7)   An order under subsection (5) above shall be subject to annulment in pursuance of a resolution of either House of Parliament.

(8)   Directions and orders under this section may make different provision for different cases and directions under subsection (4) above may require reports in respect of periods falling wholly or partly before the coming into force of this Act.

(9)   In this section "Regional Health Authority", "District Health Authority" and "special health authority" have the same meaning as in the National Health Service Act 1977, "Health Board" has the same meaning as in the National Health Service (Scotland) Act 1978 and "relevant information" means information relating to, or to any matter connected with, AIDS or HIV.

(10)   In this section "NHS trust" means a National Health Service trust established under Part I of the National Health Service and Community Care Act 1990 or, as the case may be, under the National Health Service (Scotland) Act 1978.

SCHEDULE

CONTENTS OF REPORTS

1.   The number of persons known to the Authority, NHS trust or Board to be persons with AIDS at the end of the period to which the report relates ("the reporting period") having been diagnosed as such —

  (a) in that period; and

  (b) up to the end of that period,

by facilities or services provided by the Authority, NHS trust or Board.

  2. The number of persons known to the Authority, NHS trust or Board to have been diagnosed as persons with AIDS by such facilities or services in the reporting period or a previous reporting period and to have died —

  (a) in the reporting period; and

  (b) up to the end of the reporting period.

  2A. The number of positive results known to the Authority or Board to have been obtained in the reporting period from blood samples taken for the purposes of HIV antibody tests by facilities or services provided by the Authority or Board.

  3. Where the number to be reported under any of the foregoing provisions is between one and nine (inclusive) the report shall state only that the number is less than ten.

  4. Particulars of the facilities and services provided by the Authority, NHS trust or Board, or known to it to have been provided in its district or area by others, in the reporting period for testing for, and preventing the spread of, AIDS and HIV and for treating, counselling and caring for persons with AIDS or infected with HIV.

  5. The number of persons employed by the Authority, NHS trust or Board wholly or mainly in providing in the reporting period such facilities and services as are mentioned in paragraph 4 above.

  6. An estimate of the facilities and services which the Authority, NHS trust or Board will provide in the twelve months following the reporting period for the purposes mentioned in paragraph 4 above.

  7. Particulars of action taken by the Authority, NHS trust or Board, or known to it to have been taken in its district or area by others, in the reporting period to educate the public in relation to AIDS and HIV and to provide training for testing for AIDS and HIV and for the treatment, counselling and care of persons with AIDS or infected with HIV.

FAMILY LAW REFORM ACT 1987
(1987, c. 42)

27. Artificial insemination

  (1) Where after the coming into force of this section a child is born in England and Wales as the result of the artificial insemination of a woman who —

  (a) was at the time of the insemination a party to a marriage (being a marriage which had not at that time been dissolved or annulled); and

  (b) was artificially inseminated with the semen of some person other than the other party to that marriage,

then, unless it is proved to the satisfaction of any court by which the matter has to be determined that the other party to that marriage did not consent to the insemination, the child shall be treated in law as the child of the parties to that marriage and shall not be treated as the child of any person other than the parties to that marriage.

  (2) Any reference in this section to a marriage includes a reference to a void marriage if at the time of the insemination resulting in the birth of the child both or either of the parties reasonably believed that the marriage was valid; and for the purposes of this section it shall be presumed, unless the contrary is shown, that one of the parties so believed at that time that the marriage was valid.

  (3) Nothing in this section shall affect the succession to any dignity or title of honour or render any person capable of succeeding to or transmitting a right to succeed to any such dignity or title.

[Note: see the Human Fertilisation and Embryology Act 1990 ss. 28 and 49(3)(4)]

CONSUMER PROTECTION ACT 1987
(1987, c. 43)

PART I
PRODUCT LIABILITY

1. Purpose and construction of Part I

(1) This Part shall have effect for the purpose of making such provision as is necessary in order to comply with the product liability Directive and shall be construed accordingly.

(2) In this Part, except in so far as the context otherwise requires —

"agricultural produce" means any produce of the soil, of stockfarming or of fisheries;

"dependant" and "relative" have the same meaning as they have in, respectively, the Fatal Accidents Act 1976 and the Damages (Scotland) Act 1976;

"producer", in relation to a product, means —

(a)   the person who manufactured it;

(b)   in the case of a substance which has not been manufactured but has been won or abstracted, the person who won or abstracted it;

(c)   in the case of a product which has not been manufactured, won or abstracted but essential characteristics of which are attributable to an industrial or other process having been carried out (for example, in relation to agricultural produce), the person who carried out that process;

"product" means any goods or electricity and (subject to subsection (3) below) includes a product which is comprised in another product, whether by virtue of being a component part or raw material or otherwise; and

"the product liability Directive" means the Directive of the Council of the European Communities, dated 25th July 1985, (No. 85/374/EEC) on the approximation of the laws, regulations and administrative provisions of the member States concerning liability for defective products.

(3) For the purposes of this Part a person who supplies any product in which products are comprised, whether by virtue of being component parts or raw materials or otherwise, shall not be treated by reason only of his supply of that product as supplying any of the products so comprised.

2. Liability for defective products

(1) Subject to the following provisions of this Part, where any damage is caused wholly or partly by a defect in a product, every person to whom subsection (2) below applies shall be liable for the damage.

(2) This subsection applies to —

(a)   the producer of the product;

(b)   any person who, by putting his name on the product or using a trade mark or other distinguishing mark in relation to the product, has held himself out to be the producer of the product;

(c)   any person who has imported the product into a member State from a place outside the member States in order, in the course of any business of his, to supply it to another.

(3) Subject as aforesaid, where any damage is caused wholly or partly by a defect in a product, any person who supplied the product (whether to the person who suffered the damage, to the producer of any product in which the product in question is comprised or to any other person) shall be liable for the damage if —

(a)   the person who suffered the damage requests the supplier to identify one or more of the persons (whether still in existence or not) to whom subsection (2) above applies in relation to the product;

(b)   that request is made within a reasonable period after the damage occurs and at a time when it is not reasonably practicable for the person making the request to identify all those persons; and

(c)   the supplier fails, within a reasonable period after receiving the request, either to comply with the request or to identify the person who supplied the product to him.

(4)   Neither subsection (2) nor subsection (3) above shall apply to a person in respect of any defect in any game or agricultural produce if the only supply of the game or produce by that person to another was at a time when it had not undergone an industrial process.

(5)   Where two or more persons are liable by virtue of this Part for the same damage, their liability shall be joint and several.

(6)   This section shall be without prejudice to any liability arising otherwise than by virtue of this Part.

3.   Meaning of "defect"

(1)   Subject to the following provisions of this section, there is a defect in a product for the purposes of this Part if the safety of the product is not such as persons generally are entitled to expect; and for those purposes "safety", in relation to a product, shall include safety with respect to products comprised in that product and safety in the context of risks of damage to property, as well as in the context of risks of death or personal injury.

(2)   In determining for the purposes of subsection (1) above what persons generally are entitled to expect in relation to a product all the circumstances shall be taken into account, including —

(a)   the manner in which, and purposes for which, the product has been marketed, its get-up, the use of any mark in relation to the product and any instructions for, or warnings with respect to, doing or refraining from doing anything with or in relation to the product;

(b)   what might reasonably be expected to be done with or in relation to the product; and

(c)   the time when the product was supplied by its producer to another;
and nothing in this section shall require a defect to be inferred from the fact alone that the safety of a product which is supplied after that time is greater than the safety of the product in question.

4.   Defences

(1)   In any civil proceedings by virtue of this Part against any person ("the person proceeded against") in respect of a defect in a product it shall be a defence for him to show —

(a)   that the defect is attributable to compliance with any requirement imposed by or under any enactment or with any Community obligation; or

(b)   that the person proceeded against did not at any time supply the product to another; or

(c)   that the following conditions are satisfied, that is to say —

(i)   that the only supply of the product to another by the person proceeded against was otherwise than in the course of a business of that person's; and

(ii)   that section 2(2) above does not apply to that person or applies to him by virtue only of things done otherwise than with a view to profit; or

(d)   that the defect did not exist in the product at the relevant time; or

(e)   that the state of scientific and technical knowledge at the relevant time was not such that a producer of products of the same description as the product in question might be expected to have discovered the defect if it had existed in his products while they were under his control; or

(f)   that the defect —

(i)   constituted a defect in a product ("the subsequent product") in which the product in question had been comprised; and

(ii)   was wholly attributable to the design of the subsequent product or to compliance by the producer of the product in question with instructions given by the producer of the subsequent product.

(2)   In this section "the relevant time", in relation to electricity, means the time at which it was generated, being a time before it was transmitted or distributed, and in relation to any other product, means —

(a)   if the person proceeded against is a person to whom subsection (2) of section 2 above applies in relation to the product, the time when he supplied the product to another;

(b)   if that subsection does not apply to that person in relation to the product, the time when the product was last supplied by a person to whom that subsection does apply in relation to the product.

5.   Damage giving rise to liability

(1)   Subject to the following provisions of this section, in this Part "damage" means death or personal injury or any loss of or damage to any property (including land).

(2)   A person shall not be liable under section 2 above in respect of any defect in a product for the loss of or any damage to the product itself or for the loss of or any damage to the whole or any part of any product which has been supplied with the product in question comprised in it.

(3)   A person shall not be liable under section 2 above for any loss of or damage to any property which, at the time it is lost or damaged, is not —

(a)   of a description of property ordinarily intended for private use, occupation or consumption; and

(b)   intended by the person suffering the loss or damage mainly for his own private use, occupation or consumption.

(4)   No damages shall be awarded to any person by virtue of this Part in respect of any loss of or damage to any property if the amount which would fall to be so awarded to that person, apart from this subsection and any liability for interest, does not exceed £275.

(5)   In determining for the purposes of this Part who has suffered any loss of or damage to property and when any such loss or damage occurred, the loss or damage shall be regarded as having occurred at the earliest time at which a person with an interest in the property had knowledge of the material facts about the loss or damage.

(6)   For the purposes of subsection (5) above the material facts about any loss of or damage to any property are such facts about the loss or damage as would lead a reasonable person with an interest in the property to consider the loss or damage sufficiently serious to justify his instituting proceedings for damages against a defendant who did not dispute liability and was able to satisfy a judgment.

(7)   For the purposes of subsection (5) above a person's knowledge includes knowledge which he might reasonably have been expected to acquire —

(a)   from facts observable or ascertainable by him; or

(b)   from facts ascertainable by him with the help of appropriate expert advice which it is reasonable for him to seek;

but a person shall not be taken by virtue of this subsection to have knowledge of a fact ascertainable by him only with the help of expert advice unless he has failed to take all reasonable steps to obtain (and, where appropriate, to act on) that advice.

(8)   Subsections (5) to (7) above shall not extend to Scotland.

6.   Application of certain enactments etc.

(1)   Any damage for which a person is liable under section 2 above shall be deemed to have been caused —

(a)   for the purposes of the Fatal Accidents Act 1976, by that person's wrongful act, neglect or default;

(2)   Where —

(a)   a person's death is caused wholly or partly by a defect in a product, or a person dies after suffering damage which has been so caused;

(b)   a request such as mentioned in paragraph (a) of subsection (3) of section 2 above is made to a supplier of the product by that person's personal representatives or, in the case of a person whose death is caused wholly or partly by the defect, by any dependant or relative of that person; and

(c)   the conditions specified in paragraphs (b) and (c) of that subsection are satisfied in relation to that request,

this Part shall have effect for the purposes of the Law Reform (Miscellaneous Provisions) Act 1934, the Fatal Accidents Act 1976 and the Damages (Scotland) Act 1976 as if liability of the supplier to that person under that subsection did not depend on that person having requested the supplier to identify certain persons or on the said conditions having been satisfied in relation to a request made by that person.

(3)   Section 1 of the Congenital Disabilities (Civil Liability) Act 1976 shall have effect for the purposes of this Part as if —

(a)   a person were answerable to a child in respect of an occurrence caused wholly or partly by a defect in a product if he is or has been liable under section 2 above in respect of any effect of the occurrence on a parent of the child, or would be so liable if the occurrence caused a parent of the child to suffer damage;

(b)   the provisions of this Part relating to liability under section 2 above applied in relation to liability by virtue of paragraph (a) above under the said section 1; and

(c)   subsection (6) of the said section 1 (exclusion of liability) were omitted.

(4)   Where any damage is caused partly by a defect in a product and partly by the fault of the person suffering the damage, the Law Reform (Contributory Negligence) Act 1945 and section 5 of the Fatal Accidents Act 1976 (contributory negligence) shall have effect as if the defect were the fault of every person liable by virtue of this Part for the damage caused by the defect.

(5)   In subsection (4) above "fault" has the same meaning as in the said Act of 1945.

(7)   It is hereby declared that liability by virtue of this Part is to be treated as liability in tort for the purposes of any enactment conferring jurisdiction on any court with respect to any matter.

(8)   Nothing in this Part shall prejudice the operation of section 12 of the Nuclear Installations Act 1965 (rights to compensation for certain breaches of duties confined to rights under that Act).

7.   Prohibition on exclusions from liability

The liability of a person by virtue of this Part to a person who has suffered damage caused wholly or partly by a defect in a product, or to a dependant or relative of such a person, shall not be limited or excluded by any contract term, by any notice or by any other provision.

8.   Power to modify Part I

(1)   Her Majesty may by Order in Council make such modifications of this Part and of any other enactment (including an enactment contained in the following Parts of this Act, or in an Act passed after this Act) as appear to Her Majesty in Council to be necessary or expedient in consequence of any modification of the product liability Directive which is made at any time after the passing of this Act.

9.   Application of Part I to Crown

(1)   Subject to subsection (2) below, this Part shall bind the Crown.

(2)   The Crown shall not, as regards the Crown's liability by virtue of this Part, be bound by this Part further than the Crown is made liable in tort or in reparation under the Crown Proceedings Act 1947, as that Act has effect from time to time.

46.   Meaning of "supply"
(1)   Subject to the following provisions of this section, references in this Act to supplying goods shall be construed as references to doing any of the following, whether as principal or agent, that is to say —
   (a)   selling, hiring out or lending the goods;
   (b)   entering into a hire-purchase agreement to furnish the goods;
   (c)   the performance of any contract for work and materials to furnish the goods;
   (d)   providing the goods in exchange for any consideration (including trading stamps) other than money;
   (e)   providing the goods in or in connection with the performance of any statutory function; or
   (f)   giving the goods as a prize or otherwise making a gift of the goods;
and, in relation to gas or water, those references shall be construed as including references to providing the service by which the gas or water is made available for use.
(2)   For the purposes of any reference in this Act to supplying goods, where a person ("the ostensible supplier") supplies goods to another person ("the customer") under a hire-purchase agreement, conditional sale agreement or credit-sale agreement or under an agreement for the hiring of goods (other than a hire-purchase agreement) and the ostensible supplier —
   (a)   carries on the business of financing the provision of goods for others by means of such agreement; and
   (b)   in the course of that business acquired his interest in the goods supplied to the customer as a means of financing the provision of them for the customer by a further person ("the effective supplier"),
the effective supplier and not the ostensible supplier shall be treated as supplying the goods to the customer.

ACCESS TO MEDICAL REPORTS ACT 1988
(1988, c. 28)

1.   Right of access
It shall be the right of an individual to have access, in accordance with the provisions of this Act, to any medical report relating to the individual which is to be, or has been, supplied by a medical practitioner for employment purposes or insurance purposes.

2.   Interpretation
   (1)   In this Act —
      "the applicant" means the person referred to in section 3(1) below;
      "care" includes examination, investigation or diagnosis for the purposes of, or in connection with, any form of medical treatment;
      "employment purposes", in the case of any individual, means the purposes in relation to the individual of any person by whom he is or has been, or is seeking to be, employed (whether under a contract of service or otherwise);
      "health professional" has the same meaning as in the Data Protection (Subject Access Modification) (Health) Order 1987;
      "insurance purposes", in the case of any individual, means the purposes in relation to the individual of any person carrying on an insurance business with whom the individual has entered into, or is seeking to enter into, a contract of insurance, and "insurance business" and "contract of insurance" have the same meaning as in the Insurance Companies Act 1982;

"medical practitioner" means a person registered under the Medical Act 1983;

"medical report", in the case of an individual, means a report relating to the physical or mental health of the individual prepared by a medical practitioner who is or has been responsible for the clinical care of the individual.

(2)   Any reference in this Act to the supply of a medical report for employment or insurance purposes shall be construed —

(a)   as a reference to the supply of such a report for employment or insurance purposes which are purposes of the person who is seeking to be supplied with it; or

(b)   (in the case of a report that has already been supplied) as a reference to the supply of such a report for employment or insurance purposes which, at the time of its being supplied, were purposes of the person to whom it was supplied.

3. Consent to applications for medical reports for employment or insurance purposes

(1)   A person shall not apply to a medical practitioner for a medical report relating to any individual to be supplied to him for employment or insurance purposes unless —

(a)   that person ("the applicant") has notified the individual that he proposes to make the application; and

(b)   the individual has notified the applicant that he consents to the making of the application.

(2)   Any notification given under subsection (1)(a) above must inform the individual of his right to withhold his consent to the making of the application, and of the following rights under this Act, namely —

(a)   the rights arising under sections 4(1) to (3) and 6(2) below with respect to access to the report before or after it is supplied,

(b)   the right to withhold consent under subsection (1) of section 5 below, and

(c)   the right to request the amendment of the report under subsection (2) of that section,

as well as of the effect of section 7 below.

4. Access to reports before they are supplied

(1)   An individual who gives his consent under section 3 above to the making of an application shall be entitled, when giving his consent, to state that he wishes to have access to the report to be supplied in response to the application before it is so supplied; and, if he does so, the applicant shall —

(a)   notify the medical practitioner of that fact at the time when the application is made, and

(b)   at the same time notify the individual of the making of the application;

and each such notification shall contain a statement of the effect of subsection (2) below.

(2)   Where a medical practitioner is notified by the applicant under subsection (1) above that the individual in question wishes to have access to the report before it is supplied, the practitioner shall not supply the report unless —

(a)   he has given the individual access to it and any requirements of section 5 below have been complied with, or

(b)   the period of 21 days beginning with the date of the making of the application has elapsed without his having received any communication from the individual concerning arrangements for the individual to have access to it.

(3)   Where a medical practitioner —

(a)   receives an application for a medical report to be supplied for employment or insurance purposes without being notified by the applicant as mentioned in subsection (1) above, but

(b)   before supplying the report receives a notification from the individual that he wishes to have access to the report before it is supplied,

the practitioner shall not supply the report unless —

(i)   he has given the individual access to it and any requirements of section 5 below have been complied with, or

(ii)   the period of 21 days beginning with the date of that notification has elapsed without his having received (either with that notification or otherwise) any communication from the individual concerning arrangements for the individual to have access to it.

(4)   References in this section and section 5 below to giving an individual access to a medical report are references to —

(a)   making the report or a copy of it available for his inspection; or

(b)   supplying him with a copy of it;

and where a copy is supplied at the request, or otherwise with the consent, of the individual the practitioner may charge a reasonable fee to cover the costs of supplying it.

5. Consent to supplying of report and correction of errors

(1)   Where an individual has been given access to a report under section 4 above the report shall not be supplied in response to the application in question unless the individual has notified the medical practitioner that he consents to its being so supplied.

(2)   The individual shall be entitled, before giving his consent under subsection (1) above, to request the medical practitioner to amend any part of the report which the individual considers to be incorrect or misleading; and, if the individual does so, the practitioner —

(a)   if he is to any extent prepared to accede to the individual's request, shall amend the report accordingly;

(b)   if he is to any extent not prepared to accede to it but the individual requests him to attach to the report a statement of the individual's views in respect of any part of the report which he is declining to amend, shall attach such a statement to the report.

(3)   Any request made by an individual under subsection (2) above shall be made in writing.

6. Retention of reports

(1)   A copy of any medical report which a medical practitioner has supplied for employment or insurance purposes shall be retained by him for at least six months from the date on which it was supplied.

(2)   A medical practitioner shall, if so requested by an individual, give the individual access to any medical report relating to him which the practitioner has supplied for employment or insurance purposes in the previous six months.

(3)   The reference in subsection (2) above to giving an individual access to a medical report is a reference to —

(a)   making a copy of the report available for his inspection; or

(b)   supplying him with a copy of it;

and where a copy is supplied at the request, or otherwise with the consent, of the individual the practitioner may charge a reasonable fee to cover the costs of supplying it.

7. Exemptions

(1)   A medical practitioner shall not be obliged to give an individual access, in accordance with the provisions of section 4(4) or 6(3) above, to any part of a medical report whose disclosure would in the opinion of the practitioner be likely to cause serious harm to the physical or mental health of the individual or others or would indicate the intentions of the practitioner in respect of the individual.

(2)   A medical practitioner shall not be obliged to give an individual access, in accordance with those provisions, to any part of a medical report whose disclosure would be likely to reveal information about another person, or to reveal the identity of

another person who has supplied information to the practitioner about the individual, unless —

    (a)   that person has consented; or

    (b)   that person is a health professional who has been involved in the care of the individual and the information relates to or has been provided by the professional in that capacity.

    (3)   Where it appears to a medical practitioner that subsection (1) or (2) above is applicable to any part (but not the whole) of a medical report —

    (a)   he shall notify the individual of that fact; and

    (b)   references in the preceding sections of this Act to the individual being given access to the report shall be construed as references to his being given access to the remainder of it;

and other references to the report in sections 4(4), 5(2) and 6(3) above shall similarly be construed as references to the remainder of the report.

    (4)   Where it appears to a medical practitioner that subsection (1) or (2) above is applicable to the whole of a medical report —

    (a)   he shall notify the individual of that fact; but

    (b)   he shall not supply the report unless he is notified by the individual that the individual consents to its being supplied;

and accordingly, if he is so notified by the individual, the restrictions imposed by section 4(2) and (3) above on the supply of the report shall not have effect in relation to it.

8. Application to the court

    (1)   If a court is satisfied on the application of an individual that any person, in connection with a medical report relating to that individual, has failed or is likely to fail to comply with any requirement of this Act, the court may order that person to comply with that requirement.

    (2)   The jurisdiction conferred by this section shall be exercisable by a county court or, in Scotland, by the sheriff.

9. Notifications under this Act

Any notification required or authorised to be given under this Act —

    (a)   shall be given in writing; and

    (b)   may be given by post.

10. Short title, commencement and extent

    (2)   This Act shall come into force on 1st January 1989.

    (3)   Nothing in this Act applies to a medical report prepared before the coming into force of this Act.

HEALTH AND MEDICINES ACT 1988
(1988, c. 49)

HIV testing kits and services

23. HIV testing kits and services

    (1)   The Secretary of State may provide by regulations that a person—

    (a)   who sells or supplies to another an HIV testing kit or any component part of such a kit;

    (b)   who provides another with HIV testing services; or

    (c)   who advertises such kits or component parts or such services,

shall be guilty of an offence.

    (4)   If any person contravenes regulations under this section, he shall be liable—

    (a)   on summary conviction to a fine not exceeding the statutory maximum; and

(b)   on conviction on indictment to a fine or to imprisonment for a term of not more than two years, or to both.

(5)   Where an offence under this section which is committed by a body corporate is proved to have been committed with the consent or connivance of, or to be attributable to any neglect on the part of, any director, manager, secretary or other similar officer of the body corporate, or any person who was purporting to act in any such capacity, he as well as the body corporate shall be guilty of that offence and shall be liable to be proceeded against and punished accordingly.

(6)   In this section—

"HIV" means Human Immunodeficiency Virus of any type;

"HIV testing kit" means a diagnostic kit the purpose of which is to detect the presence of HIV or HIV antibodies; and

"HIV testing services" means diagnostic services the purpose of which is to detect the presence of HIV or HIV antibodies in identifiable individuals.

<h1 style="text-align:center">ROAD TRAFFIC ACT 1988
(1988, c. 52)</h1>

Other duties to give information or documents

172.   Duty to give information as to identity of driver, etc., in certain cases

(1)   This section applies —

(a)   to any offence under the preceding provisions of this Act except—

(i)   an offence under Part V, or

(ii)   an offence under section 13, 16, 51(2), 61(4), 67(9), 68(4), 96 or 120,

and to an offence under section 178 of this Act,

(b)   to any offence under sections 25, 26 and 27 of the Road Traffic Offenders Act 1988, and

(c)   to any offence against any other enactment relating to the use of vehicles on roads, except an offence under paragraph 8 of Schedule 1 to the Road Traffic (Driver Licensing and Information Systems) Act 1989.

(2)   Where the driver of a vehicle is alleged to be guilty of an offence to which this section applies—

(a)   the person keeping the vehicle shall give such information as to the identity of the driver as he may be required to give by or on behalf of a chief officer of police, and

(b)   any other person shall if required as stated above give any information which it is in his power to give and may lead to identification of the driver.

In this subsection references to the driver of a vehicle include references to the person riding a cycle.

(3)   A person who fails to comply with the requirement of subsection (2)(a) above is guilty of an offence unless he shows to the satisfaction of the court that he did not know and could not with reasonable diligence have ascertained who the driver of the vehicle or, as the case may be, the rider of the cycle was.

(4)   A person who fails to comply with the requirement of subsection (2)(b) above is guilty of an offence.

<h1 style="text-align:center">HUMAN ORGAN TRANSPLANTS ACT 1989
(1989, c. 31)</h1>

1.   Prohibition of commercial dealings in human organs

(1)   A person is guilty of an offence if in Great Britain he—

(a)   makes or receives any payment for the supply of, or for an offer to supply, an organ which has been or is to be removed from a dead or living person and is intended to be transplanted into another person whether in Great Britain or elsewhere;

(b)   seeks to find a person willing to supply for payment such an organ as is mentioned in paragraph (a) above or offers to supply such an organ for payment;

(c)   initiates or negotiates any arrangement involving the making of any payment for the supply of, or for an offer to supply, such an organ; or

(d)   takes part in the management or control of a body of persons corporate or unincorporate whose activities consist of or include the initiation or negotiation of such arrangements.

(2)   Without prejudice to paragraph (b) of subsection (1) above, a person is guilty of an offence if he causes to be published or distributed, or knowingly publishes or distributes, in Great Britain an advertisement—

(a)   inviting persons to supply for payment any such organs as are mentioned in paragraph (a) of that subsection or offering to supply any such organs for payment; or

(b)   indicating that the advertiser is willing to initiate or negotiate any such arrangement as is mentioned in paragraph (c) of that subsection.

(3)   In this section "payment" means payment in money or money's worth but does not include any payment for defraying or reimbursing—

(a)   the cost of removing, transporting or preserving the organ to be supplied; or

(b)   any expenses or loss of earnings incurred by a person so far as reasonably and directly attributable to his supplying an organ from his body.

(4)   In this section "advertisement" includes any form of advertising whether to the public generally, to any section of the public or individually to selected persons.

(5)   A person guilty of an offence under subsection (1) above is liable on summary conviction to imprisonment for a term not exceeding three months or a fine not exceeding level 5 on the standard scale or both; and a person guilty of an offence under subsection (2) above is liable on summary conviction to a fine not exceeding level 5 on that scale.

2.   Restriction on transplants between persons not genetically related

(1)   Subject to subsection (3) below, a person is guilty of an offence if in Great Britain he—

(a)   removes from a living person an organ intended to be transplanted into another person; or

(b)   transplants an organ removed from a living person into another person, unless the person into whom the organ is to be or, as the case may be, is transplanted is genetically related to the person from whom the organ is removed.

(2)   For the purposes of this section a person is genetically related to—

(a)   his natural parents and children;

(b)   his brothers and sisters of the whole or half blood;

(c)   the brothers and sisters of the whole or half blood of either of his natural parents; and

(d)   the natural children of his brothers and sisters of the whole or half blood or of the brothers and sisters of the whole or half blood of either of his natural parents; but persons shall not in any particular case be treated as related in any of those ways unless the fact of the relationship has been established by such means as are specified by regulations made by the Secretary of State.

(3)   The Secretary of State may by regulations provide that the prohibition in subsection (1) above shall not apply in cases where—

(a)   such authority as is specified in or constituted by the regulations is satisfied—

(i)   that no payment has been or is to be made in contravention of section 1 above; and

(ii)   that such other conditions as are specified in the regulations are satisfied; and

(b)   such other requirements as may be specified in the regulations are complied with.

(4) The expenses of any such authority shall be defrayed by the Secretary of State out of money provided by Parliament.

(5) A person guilty of an offence under this section is liable on summary conviction to imprisonment for a term not exceeding three months or a fine not exceeding level 5 on the standard scale or both.

(6) The power to make regulations under this section shall be exercisable by statutory instrument.

3. Information about transplant operations

(1) The Secretary of State may make regulations requiring such persons as are specified in the regulations to supply to such authority as is so specified such information as may be so specified with respect to transplants that have been or are proposed to be carried out in Great Britain using organs removed from dead or living persons.

(2) Any such authority shall keep a record of information supplied to it in pursuance of the regulations made under this section.

(3) Any person who without reasonable excuse fails to comply with those regulations is guilty of an offence and liable on summary conviction to a fine not exceeding level 3 on the standard scale; and any person who, in purported compliance with those regulations, knowingly or recklessly supplies information which is false or misleading in a material respect is guilty of an offence and liable on summary conviction to a fine not exceeding level 5 on the standard scale.

4. Offences by bodies corporate

(1) Where an offence under this Act committed by a body corporate is proved to have been committed with the consent or connivance of, or to be attributable to any neglect on the part of, any director, manager, secretary or other similar officer of the body corporate or any person who was purporting to act in any such capacity, he as well as the body corporate is guilty of the offence and is liable to be proceeded against and punished accordingly.

(2) Where the affairs of a body corporate are managed by its members, subsection (1) above shall apply to the acts and defaults of a member in connection with his functions of management as if he were a director of the body corporate.

5. Prosecutions

No proceedings for an offence under section 1 or 2 above shall be instituted in England and Wales except by or with the consent of the Director of Public Prosecutions.

7. Short title, interpretation, commencement and extent

(2) In this Act "organ" means any part of a human body consisting of a structured arrangement of tissues which, if wholly removed, cannot be replicated by the body.

CHILDREN ACT 1989
(1989, c. 41)

PART I
INTRODUCTORY

1. Welfare of the child

(1) When a court determines any question with respect to—

    (a) the upbringing of a child; or

    (b) the administration of a child's property or the application of any income arising from it,

the child's welfare shall be the court's paramount consideration.

(2) In any proceedings in which any question with respect to the upbringing of a child arises, the court shall have regard to the general principle that any delay in determining the question is likely to prejudice the welfare of the child.

(3)   In the circumstances mentioned in subsection (4), a court shall have regard in particular to—

(a)   the ascertainable wishes and feelings of the child concerned (considered in the light of his age and understanding);

(b)   his physical, emotional and educational needs;

(c)   the likely effect on him of any change in his circumstances;

(d)   his age, sex, background and any characteristics of his which the court considers relevant;

(e)   any harm which he has suffered or is at risk of suffering;

(f)   how capable each of his parents, and any other person in relation to whom the court considers the question to be relevant, is of meeting his needs;

(g)   the range of powers available to the court under this Act in the proceedings in question.

(4)   The circumstances are that—

(a)   the court is considering whether to make, vary or discharge a section 8 order, and the making, variation or discharge of the order is opposed by any party to the proceedings; or

(b)   the court is considering whether to make, vary or discharge an order under Part IV.

(5)   Where a court is considering whether or not to make one or more orders under this Act with respect to a child, it shall not make the order or any of the orders unless it considers that doing so would be better for the child than making no order at all.

2. Parental responsibility for children

(1)   Where a child's father and mother were married to each other at the time of his birth, they shall each have parental responsibility for the child.

(2)   Where a child's father and mother were not married to each other at the time of his birth—

(a)   the mother shall have parental responsibility for the child;

(b)   the father shall not have parental responsibility for the child, unless he acquires it in accordance with the provisions of this Act.

(3)   References in this Act to a child whose father and mother were, or (as the case may be) were not, married to each other at the time of his birth must be read with section 1 of the Family Law Reform Act 1987 (which extends their meaning).

(4)   The rule of law that a father is the natural guardian of his legitimate child is abolished.

(5)   More than one person may have parental responsibility for the same child at the same time.

(6)   A person who has parental responsibility for a child at any time shall not cease to have that responsibility solely because some other person subsequently acquires parental responsibility for the child.

(7)   Where more than one person has parental responsibility for a child, each of them may act alone and without the other (or others) in meeting that responsibility; but nothing in this Part shall be taken to affect the operation of any enactment which requires the consent of more than one person in a matter affecting the child.

(8)   The fact that a person has parental responsibility for a child shall not entitle him to act in any way which would be incompatible with any order made with respect to the child under this Act.

(9)   A person who has parental responsibility for a child may not surrender or transfer any part of that responsibility to another but may arrange for some or all of it to be met by one or more persons acting on his behalf.

(10)   The person with whom any such arrangement is made may himself be a person who already has parental responsibility for the child concerned.

(11) The making of any such arrangement shall not affect any liability of the person making it which may arise from any failure to meet any part of his parental responsibility for the child concerned.

3. Meaning of "parental responsibility"

(1) In this Act "parental responsibility" means all the rights, duties, powers, responsibilities and authority which by law a parent of a child has in relation to the child and his property.

(2) It also includes the rights, powers and duties which a guardian of the child's estate (appointed, before the commencement of section 5, to act generally) would have had in relation to the child and his property.

(3) The rights referred to in subsection (2) include, in particular, the right of the guardian to receive or recover in his own name, for the benefit of the child, property of whatever description and wherever situated which the child is entitled to receive or recover.

(4) The fact that a person has, or does not have, parental responsibility for a child shall not affect—

(a) any obligation which he may have in relation to the child (such as a statutory duty to maintain the child); or

(b) any rights which, in the event of the child's death, he (or any other person) may have in relation to the child's property.

(5) A person who—

(a) does not have parental responsibility for a particulr child; but

(b) has care of the child,

may (subject to the provisions of this Act) do what is reasonable in all the circumstances of the case for the purpose of safeguarding or promoting the child's welfare.

4. Acquisition of parental responsibility by father

(1) Where a child's father and mother were not married to each other at the time of his birth—

(a) the court may, on the application of the father, order that he shall have parental responsibility for the child; or

(b) the father and mother may by agreement ("a parental responsibility agreement") provide for the father to have parental responsibility for the child.

(2) No parental responsibility agreement shall have effect for the purposes of this Act unless—

(a) it is made in the form prescribed by regulations made by the Lord Chancellor; and

(b) where regulations are made by the Lord Chancellor prescribing the manner in which such agreements must be recorded, it is recorded in the prescribed manner.

(3) Subject to section 12(4), an order under subsection (1)(a), or a parental responsibility agreement, may only be brought to an end by an order of the court made on the application—

(a) of any person who has parental responsibility for the child; or

(b) with leave of the court, of the child himself.

(4) The court may only grant leave under subsection (3)(b) if it is satisfied that the child has sufficient understanding to make the proposed application.

5. Appointment of guardians

(1) Where an application with respect to a child is made to the court by any individual, the court may by order appoint that individual to be the child's guardian if—

(a) the child has no parent with parental responsibility for him; or

(b) a residence order has been made with respect to the child in favour of a parent or guardian of his who has died while the order was in force.

(2) The power conferred by subsection (1) may also be exercised in any family proceedings if the court considers that the order should be made even though no application has been made for it.

(3) A parent who has parental responsibility for his child may appoint another individual to be the child's guardian in the event of his death.

(4) A guardian of a child may appoint another individual to take his place as the child's guardian in the event of his death.

(5) An appointment under subsection (3) or (4) shall not have effect unless it is made in writing, is dated and is signed by the person making the appointment or—

(a) in the case of an appointment made by a will which is not signed by the testator, is signed at the direction of the testator in accordance with the requirements of section 9 of the Wills Act 1837; or

(b) in any other case, is signed at the direction of the person making the appointment, in his presence and in the presence of two witnesses who each attest the signature.

(6) A person appointed as a child's guardian under this section shall have parental responsibility for the child concerned.

(7) Where—

(a) on the death of any person making an appointment under subsection (3) or (4), the child concerned has no parent with parental responsibility for him; or

(b) immediately before the death of any person making such an appointment, a residence order in his favour was in force with respect to the child,
the appointment shall take effect on the death of that person.

(8) Where, on the death of any person making an appointment under subsection (3) or (4)—

(a) the child concerned has a parent with parental responsibility for him; and

(b) subsection (7)(b) does not apply,
the appointment shall take effect when the child no longer has a parent who has parental responsibility for him.

(9) Subsections (1) and (7) do not apply if the residence order referred to in paragraph (b) of those subsections was also made in favour of a surviving parent of the child.

(10) Nothing in this section shall be taken to prevent an appointment under subsection (3) or (4) being made by two or more persons acting jointly.

(11) Subject to any provision made by rules of court, no court shall exercise the High Court's inherent jurisdiction to appoint a guardian of the estate of any child.

(12) Where rules of court are made under subsection (11) they may prescribe the circumstances in which, and conditions subject to which, an appointment of such a guardian may be made.

(13) A guardian of a child may only be appointed in accordance with the provisions of this section.

6. Guardians: revocation and disclaimer

(1) An appointment under section 5(3) or (4) revokes an earlier such appointment (including one made in an unrevoked will or codicil) made by the same person in respect of the same child, unless it is clear (whether as the result of an express provision in the later appointment or by any necessary implication) that the purpose of the later appointment is to appoint an additional guardian.

(2) An appointment under section 5(3) or (4) (including one made in an unrevoked will or codicil) is revoked if the person who made the appointment revokes it by a written and dated instrument which is signed—

(a) by him; or

(b) at his direction, in his presence and in the presence of two witnesses who each attest the signature.

(3) An appointment under section 5(3) or (4) (other than one made in a will or codicil) is revoked if, with the intention of revoking the appointment, the person who made it—
  (a) destroys the instrument by which it was made; or
  (b) has some other person destroy that instrument in his presence.

(4) For the avoidance of doubt, an appointment under section 5(3) or (4) made in a will or codicil is revoked if the will or codicil is revoked.

(5) A person who is appointed as a guardian under section 5(3) or (4) may disclaim his appointment by an instrument in writing signed by him and made within a reasonable time of his first knowing that the appointment has taken effect.

(6) Where regulations are made by the Lord Chancellor prescribing the manner in which such disclaimers must be recorded, no such disclaimer shall have effect unless it is recorded in the prescribed manner.

(7) Any appointment of a guardian under section 5 may be brought to an end at any time by order of the court—
  (a) on the application of any person who has parental responsibility for the child;
  (b) on the application of the child concerned, with leave of the court; or
  (c) in any family proceedings, if the court considers that it should be brought to an end even though no application has been made.

7. Welfare reports

(1) A court considering any question with respect to a child under this Act may—
  (a) ask a probation officer; or
  (b) ask a local authority to arrange for—
    (i) an officer of the authority; or
    (ii) such other person (other than a probation officer) as the authority considers appropriate,
to report to the court on such matters relating to the welfare of that child as are required to be dealt with in the report.

(2) The Lord Chancellor may make regulations specifying matters which, unless the court orders otherwise, must be dealt with in any report under this section.

(3) The report may be made in writing, or orally, as the court requires.

(4) Regardless of any enactment or rule of law which would otherwise prevent it from doing so, the court may take account of—
  (a) any statement contained in the report; and
  (b) any evidence given in respect of the matters referred to in the report,
in so far as the statement or evidence is, in the opinion of the court, relevant to the question which it is considering.

(5) It shall be the duty of the authority or probation officer to comply with any request for a report under this section.

PART II
ORDERS WITH RESPECT TO CHILDREN IN FAMILY PROCEEDINGS

General

8. Residence, contact and other orders with respect to children

(1) In this Act—
  "a contact order" means an order requiring the person with whom a child lives, or is to live, to allow the child to visit or stay with the person named in the order, or for that person and the child otherwise to have contact with each other;
  "a prohibited steps order" means an order that no step which could be taken by a parent in meeting his parental responsibility for a child, and which is of a kind specified in the order, shall be taken by any person without the consent of the court;

"a residence order" means an order settling the arrangements to be made as to the person with whom a child is to live; and

"a specific issue order" means an order giving directions for the purpose of determining a specific question which has arisen, or which may arise, in connection with any aspect of parental responsibility for a child.

(2)   In this Act "a section 8 order" means any of the orders mentioned in subsection (1) and any order varying or discharging such an order.

(3)   For the purposes of this Act "family proceedings" means any proceedings—

(a)   under the inherent jurisdiction of the High Court in relation to children; and

(b)   under the enactments mentioned in subsection (4),

but does not include proceedings on an application for leave under section 100(3).

(4)   The enactments are—

(a)   Parts I, II and IV of this Act;

(b)   the Matrimonial Causes Act 1973;

(c)   the Domestic Violence and Matrimonial Proceedings Act 1976;

(d)   the Adoption Act 1976;

(e)   the Domestic Proceedings and Magistrates' Courts Act 1978;

(f)   sections 1 and 9 of the Matrimonial Homes Act 1983;

(g)   Part III of the Matrimonial and Family Proceedings Act 1984.

9.   Restrictions on making section 8 orders

(1)   No court shall make any section 8 order, other than a residence order, with respect to a child who is in the care of a local authority.

(2)   No application may be made by a local authority for a residence order or contact order and no court shall make such an order in favour of a local authority.

(3)   A person who is, or was at any time within the last six months, a local authority foster parent of a child may not apply for leave to apply for a section 8 order with respect to the child unless—

(a)   he has the consent of the authority;

(b)   he is a relative of the child; or

(c)   the child has lived with him for at least three years preceding the application.

(4)   The period of three years mentioned in subsection (3)(c) need not be continuous but must have begun not more than five years before the making of the application.

(5)   No court shall exercise its powers to make a specific issue order or prohibited steps order—

(a)   with a view to achieving a result which could be achieved by making a residence or contact order; or

(b)   in any way which is denied to the High Court (by section 100(2)) in the exercise of its inherent jurisdiction with respect to children.

(6)   No court shall make any section 8 order which is to have effect for a period which will end after the child has reached the age of sixteen unless it is satisfied that the circumstances of the case are exceptional.

(7)   No court shall make any section 8 order, other than one varying or discharging such an order, with respect to a child who has reached the age of sixteen unless it is satisfied that the circumstances of the case are exceptional.

10.   Power of court to make section 8 orders

(1)   In any family proceedings in which a question arises with respect to the welfare of any child, the court may make a section 8 order with respect to the child if—

(a)   an application for the order has been made by a person who—

(i)   is entitled to apply for a section 8 order with respect to the child; or

(ii)   has obtained the leave of the court to make the application; or

(b)   the court considers that the order should be made even though no such application has been made.

(2) The court may also make a section 8 order with respect to any child on the application of a person who—

(a) is entitled to apply for a section 8 order with respect to the child; or

(b) has obtained the leave of the court to make the application.

(3) This section is subject to the restrictions imposed by section 9.

(4) The following persons are entitled to apply to the court for any section 8 order with respect to a child—

(a) any parent or guardian of the child;

(b) any person in whose favour a residence order is in force with respect to the child.

(5) The following persons are entitled to apply for a residence or contact order with respect to a child—

(a) any party to a marriage (whether or not subsisting) in relation to whom the child is a child of the family;

(b) any person with whom the child has lived for a period of at least three years;

(c) any person who—

(i) in any case where a residence order is in force with respect to the child, has the consent of each of the persons in whose favour the order was made;

(ii) in any case where the child is in the care of a local authority, has the consent of that authority; or

(iii) in any other case, has the consent of each of those (if any) who have parental responsibility for the child.

(6) A person who would not otherwise be entitled (under the previous provisions of this section) to apply for the variation or discharge of a section 8 order shall be entitled to do so if—

(a) the order was made on his application; or

(b) in the case of a contact order, he is named in the order.

(7) Any person who falls within a category of person prescribed by rules of court is entitled to apply for any such section 8 order as may be prescribed in relation to that category of person.

(8) Where the person applying for leave to make an application for a section 8 order is the child concerned, the court may only grant leave if it is satisfied that he has sufficient understanding to make the proposed application for the section 8 order.

(9) Where the person applying for leave to make an application for a section 8 order is not the child concerned, the court shall, in deciding whether or not to grant leave, have particular regard to—

(a) the nature of the proposed application for the section 8 order;

(b) the applicant's connection with the child;

(c) any risk there might be of that proposed application disrupting the child's life to such an extent that he would be harmed by it; and

(d) where the child is being looked after by a local authority—

(i) the authority's plans for the child's future; and

(ii) the wishes and feelings of the child's parents.

(10) The period of three years mentioned in subsection (5)(b) need not be continuous but must not have begun more than five years before, or ended more than three months before, the making of the application.

PART IV
CARE AND SUPERVISION

General

31. Care and supervision orders

(1) On the application of any local authority or authorised person, the court may make an order—

    (a)   placing the child with respect to whom the application is made in the care of a designated local authority; or

    (b)   putting him under the supervision of a designated local authority or of a probation officer.

    (2)   A court may only make a care order or supervision order if it is satisfied—

    (a)   that the child concerned is suffering, or is likely to suffer, significant harm; and

    (b)   that the harm, or likelihood of harm, is attributable to—

        (i)   the care given to the child, or likely to be given to him if the order were not made, not being what it would be reasonable to expect a parent to give to him; or

        (ii)   the child's being beyond parental control.

    (3)   No care order or supervision order may be made with respect to a child who has reached the age of seventeen (or sixteen, in the case of a child who is married).

    (4)   An application under this section may be made on its own or in any other family proceedings.

    (5)   The court may—

    (a)   on an application for a care order, make a supervision order;

    (b)   on an application for a supervision order, make a care order.

    (6)   Where an authorised person proposes to make an application under this section he shall—

    (a)   if it is reasonably practicable to do so; and

    (b)   before making the application,

consult the local authority appearing to him to be the authority in whose area the child concerned is ordinarily resident.

    (7)   An application made by an authorised person shall not be entertained by the court if, at the time when it is made, the child concerned is—

    (a)   the subject of an earlier application for a care order, or supervision order, which has not been disposed of; or

    (b)   subject to—

        (i)   a care order or supervision order;

        (ii)   an order under section 7(7)(b) of the Children and Young Persons Act 1969; or

        (iii)   a supervision requirement within the meaning of the Social Work (Scotland) Act 1968.

    (8)   The local authority designated in a care order must be—

    (a)   the authority within whose area the child is ordinarily resident; or

    (b)   where the child does not reside in the area of a local authority, the authority within whose area any circumstances arose in consequence of which the order is being made.

    (9)   In this section—

"authorised person" means—

    (a)   the National Society for the Prevention of Cruelty to Children and any of its officers; and

    (b)   any person authorised by order of the Secretary of State to bring proceedings under this section and any officer of a body which is so authorised;

"harm" means ill-treatment or the impairment of health or development;

"development" means physical, intellectual, emotional, social or behavioural development;

"health" means physical or mental health; and

"ill-treatment" includes sexual abuse and forms of ill-treatment which are not physical.

    (10)   Where the question of whether harm suffered by a child is significant turns on the child's health or development, his health or development shall be compared with that which could reasonably be expected of a similar child.

(11)   In this Act—

"a care order" means (subject to section 105(1)) an order under subsection (1)(a) and (except where express provision to the contrary is made) includes an interim care order made under section 38; and

"a supervision order" means an order under subsection (1)(b) and (except where express provision to the contrary is made) includes an interim supervision order made under section 38.

32.   Period within which application for order under this Part must be disposed of

(1)   A court hearing an application for an order under this Part shall (in the light of any rules made by virtue of subsection (2))—

(a)   draw up a timetable with a view to disposing of the application without delay; and

(b)   give such directions as it considers appropriate for the purpose of ensuring, so far as is reasonably practicable, that that timetable is adhered to.

(2)   Rules of court may—

(a)   specify periods within which specified steps must be taken in relation to such proceedings; and

(b)   make other provision with respect to such proceedings for the purpose of ensuring, so far as is reasonably practicable, that they are disposed of without delay.

Care orders

33.   Effect of care order

(1)   Where a care order is made with respect to a child it shall be the duty of the local authority designated by the order to receive the child into their care and to keep him in their care while the order remains in force.

(2)   Where—

(a)   a care order has been made with respect to a child on the application of an authorised person; but

(b)   the local authority designated by the order was not informed that that person proposed to make the application,

the child may be kept in the care of that person until received into the care of the authority.

(3)   While a care order is in force with respect to a child, the local authority designated by the order shall—

(a)   have parental responsibility for the child; and

(b)   have the power (subject to the following provisions of this section) to determine the extent to which a parent or guardian of the child may meet his parental responsibility for him.

(4)   The authority may not exercise the power in subsection (3)(b) unless they are satisfied that it is necessary to do so in order to safeguard or promote the child's welfare.

(5)   Nothing in subsection (3)(b) shall prevent a parent or guardian of the child who has care of him from doing what is reasonable in all the circumstances of the case for the purpose of safeguarding or promoting his welfare.

(6)   While a care order is in force with respect to a child, the local authority designated by the order shall not—

(a)   cause the child to be brought up in any religious persuasion other than that in which he would have been brought up if the order had not been made; or

(b)   have the right—

(i)   to consent or refuse to consent to the making of an application with respect to the child under section 18 of the Adoption Act 1976;

(ii)   to agree or refuse to agree to the making of an adoption order, or an order under section 55 of the Act of 1976, with respect to the child; or

(iii)   to appoint a guardian for the child.

(7)   While a care order is in force with respect to a child, no person may—

(a)   cause the child to be known by a new surname; or

(b)   remove him from the United Kingdom,

without either the written consent of every person who has parental responsibility for the child or the leave of the court.

(8)   Subsection (7)(b) does not—

(a)   prevent the removal of such a child, for a period of less than one month, by the authority in whose care he is; or

(b)   apply to arrangements for such a child to live outside England and Wales (which are governed by paragraph 19 of Schedule 2).

(9)   The power in subsection (3)(b) is subject (in addition to being subject to the provisions of this section) to any right, duty, power, responsibility or authority which a parent or guardian of the child has in relation to the child and his property by virtue of any other enactment.

PART V
PROTECTION OF CHILDREN

43.   Child assessment orders

(1)   On the application of a local authority or authorised person for an order to be made under this section with respect to a child, the court may make the order if, but only if, it is satisfied that—

(a)   the applicant has reasonable cause to suspect that the child is suffering, or is likely to suffer, significant harm;

(b)   an assessment of the state of the child's health or development, or of the way in which he has been treated, is required to enable the applicant to determine whether or not the child is suffering, or is likely to suffer, significant harm; and

(c)   it is unlikely that such an assessment will be made, or be satisfactory, in the absence of an order under this section.

(2)   In this Act "a child assessment order" means an order under this section.

(3)   A court may treat an application under this section as an application for an emergency protection order.

(4)   No court shall make a child assessment order if it is satisfied—

(a)   that there are grounds for making an emergency protection order with respect to the child; and

(b)   that it ought to make such an order rather than a child assessment order.

(5)   A child assessment order shall—

(a)   specify the date by which the assessment is to begin; and

(b)   have effect for such period, not exceeding 7 days beginning with that date, as may be specified in the order.

(6)   Where a child assessment order is in force with respect to a child it shall be the duty of any person who is in a position to produce the child—

(a)   to produce him to such person as may be named in the order; and

(b)   to comply with such directions relating to the assessment of the child as the court thinks fit to specify in the order.

(7)   A child assessment order authorises any person carrying out the assessment, or any part of the assessment, to do so in accordance with the terms of the order.

(8)   Regardless of subsection (7), if the child is of sufficient understanding to make an informed decision he may refuse to submit to a medical or psychiatric examination or other assessment.

(9)   The child may only be kept away from home—
  (a)   in accordance with directions specified in the order;
  (b)   if it is necessary for the purposes of the assessment; and
  (c)   for such period or periods as may be specified in the order.
(10)   Where the child is to be kept away from home, the order shall contain such directions as the court thinks fit with regard to the contact that he must be allowed to have with other persons while away from home.
(11)   Any person making an application for a child assessment order shall take such steps as are reasonably practicable to ensure that notice of the application is given to—
  (a)   the child's parents;
  (b)   any person who is not a parent of his but who has parental responsibility for him;
  (c)   any other person caring for the child;
  (d)   any person in whose favour a contact order is in force with respect to the child;
  (e)   any person who is allowed to have contact with the child by virtue of an order under section 34; and
  (f)   the child,
before the hearing of the application.
(12)   Rules of court may make provision as to the circumstances in which—
  (a)   any of the persons mentioned in subsection (11); or
  (b)   such other person as may be specified in the rules,
may apply to the court for a child assessment order to be varied or discharged.
(13)   In this section "authorised person" means a person who is an authorised person for the purposes of section 31.

44.   Orders for emergency protection of children

(1)   Where any person ("the applicant") applies to the court for an order to be made under this section with respect to a child, the court may make the order if, but only if, it is satisfied that—
  (a)   there is reasonable cause to believe that the child is likely to suffer significant harm if—
    (i)   he is not removed to accommodation provided by or on behalf of the applicant; or
    (ii)   he does not remain in the place in which he is then being accommodated;
  (b)   in the case of an application made by a local authority—
    (i)   enquiries are being made with respect to the child under section 47(1)(b); and
    (ii)   those enquiries are being frustrated by access to the child being unreasonably refused to a person authorised to seek access and that the applicant has reasonable cause to believe that access to the child is required as a matter of urgency; or
  (c)   in the case of an application made by an authorised person—
    (i)   the applicant has reasonable cause to suspect that a child is suffering, or is likely to suffer, significant harm;
    (ii)   the applicant is making enquiries with respect to the child's welfare; and
    (iii)   those enquiries are being frustrated by access to the child being unreasonably refused to a person authorised to seek access and the applicant has reasonable cause to believe that access to the child is required as a matter of urgency.
(2)   In this section—
  (a)   "authorised person" means a person who is an authorised person for the purposes of section 31; and
  (b)   "a person authorised to seek access" means—

    (i)   in the case of an application by a local authority, an officer of the local authority or a person authorised by the authority to act on their behalf in connection with the enquiries; or

    (ii)   in the case of an application by an authorised person, that person.

  (3) Any person—

    (a)   seeking access to a child in connection with enquiries of a kind mentioned in subsection (1); and

    (b)   purporting to be a person authorised to do so,

shall, on being asked to do so, produce some duly authenticated document as evidence that he is such a person.

  (4) While an order under this section ("an emergency protection order") is in force it—

    (a)   operates as a direction to any person who is in a position to do so to comply with any request to produce the child to the applicant;

    (b)   authorises—

      (i)   the removal of the child at any time to accommodation provided by or on behalf of the applicant and his being kept there; or

      (ii)   the prevention of the child's removal from any hospital, or other place, in which he was being accommodated immediately before the making of the order; and

    (c)   gives the applicant parental responsibility for the child.

  (5) Where an emergency protection order is in force with respect to a child, the applicant—

    (a)   shall only exercise the power given by virtue of subsection (4)(b) in order to safeguard the welfare of the child;

    (b)   shall take, and shall only take, such action in meeting his parental responsibility for the child as is reasonably required to safeguard or promote the welfare of the child (having regard in particular to the duration of the order); and

    (c)   shall comply with the requirements of any regulations made by the Secretary of State for the purposes of this subsection.

  (6) Where the court makes an emergency protection order, it may give such directions (if any) as it considers appropriate with respect to—

    (a)   the contact which is, or is not, to be allowed between the child and any named person;

    (b)   the medical or psychiatric examination or other assessment of the child.

  (7) Where any direction is given under subsection (6)(b), the child may, if he is of sufficient understanding to make an informed decision, refuse to submit to the examination or other assessment.

  (8) A direction under subsection (6)(a) may impose conditions and one under subsection (6)(b) may be to the effect that there is to be—

    (a)   no such examination or assessment; or

    (b)   no such examination or assessment unless the court directs otherwise.

  (9) A direction under subsection (6) may be—

    (a)   given when the emergency protection order is made or at any time while it is in force; and

    (b)   varied at any time on the application of any person falling within any class of person prescribed by rules of court for the puposes of this subsection.

  (10) Where an emergency protection order is in force with respect to a child and—

    (a)   the applicant has exercised the power given by subsection (4)(b)(i) but it appears to him that it is safe for the child to be returned; or

    (b)   the applicant has exercised the power given by subsection (4)(b)(ii) but it appears to him that it is safe for the child to be allowed to be removed from the place in question,

he shall return the child or (as the case may be) allow him to be removed.

(11)   Where he is required by subsection (10) to return the child the applicant shall—

   (a)   return him to the care of the person from whose care he was removed; or
   (b)   if that is not reasonably practicable, return him to the care of—
      (i)   a parent of his;
      (ii)   any person who is not a parent of his but who has parental responsibility for him; or
      (iii)   such other person as the applicant (with the agreement of the court) considers appropriate.

(12)   Where the applicant has been required by subsection (10) to return the child, or to allow him to be removed, he may again exercise his powers with respect to the child (at any time while the emergency protection order remains in force) if it appears to him that a change in the circumstances of the case makes it necessary for him to do so.

(13)   Where an emergency protection order has been made with respect to a child, the applicant shall, subject to any direction given under subsection (6), allow the child reasonable contact with—

   (a)   his parents;
   (b)   any person who is not a parent of his but who has parental responsibility for him;
   (c)   any person with whom he was living immediately before the making of the order;
   (d)   any person in whose favour a contact order is in force with respect to him;
   (e)   any person who is allowed to have contact with the child by virtue of an order under section 34; and
   (f)   any person acting on behalf of any of those persons.

(14)   Wherever it is reasonably practicable to do so, an emergency protection order shall name the child; and where it does not name him it shall describe him as clearly as possible.

(15)   A person shall be guilty of an offence if he intentionally obstructs any person exercising the power under subsection (4)(b) to remove, or prevent the removal of, a child.

(16)   A person guilty of an offence under subsection (15) shall be liable on summary conviction to a fine not exceeding level 3 on the standard scale.

100.   Restrictions on use of wardship jurisdiction

(1)   Section 7 of the Family Law Reform Act 1969 (which gives the High Court power to place a ward of court in the care, or under the supervision, of a local authority) shall cease to have effect.

(2)   No court shall exercise the High Court's inherent jurisdiction with respect to children—

   (a)   so as to require a child to be placed in the care, or put under the supervision, of a local authority;
   (b)   so as to require a child to be accommodated by or on behalf of a local authority;
   (c)   so as to make a child who is the subject of a care order a ward of court; or
   (d)   for the purpose of conferring on any local authority power to determine any question which has arisen, or which may arise, in connection with any aspect of parental responsibility for a child.

(3)   No application for any exercise of the court's inherent jurisdiction with respect to children may be made by a local authority unless the authority have obtained the leave of the court.

(4)   The court may only grant leave if it is satisfied that—

   (a)   the result which the authority wish to achieve could not be achieved through the making of any order of a kind to which subsection (5) applies; and

(b)   there is reasonable cause to believe that if the court's inherent jurisdiction is not exercised with respect to the child he is likely to suffer significant harm.

(5)   This subsection applies to any order—

(a)   made otherwise than in the exercise of the court's inherent jurisdiction; and

(b)   which the local authority is entitled to apply for (assuming, in the case of any application which may only be made with leave, that leave is granted).

SCHEDULE 3

SUPERVISION ORDERS

Meaning of "responsible person"

1.   In this Schedule, "the responsible person", in relation to a supervised child, means—

(a)   any person who has parental responsibility for the child; and

(b)   any other person with whom the child is living.

Power of supervisor to give directions to supervised child

2.—(1)   A supervision order may require the supervised child to comply with any directions given from time to time by the supervisor which require him to do all or any of the following things—

(a)   to live at a place or places specified in the directions for a period or periods so specified;

(b)   to present himself to a person or persons specified in the directions at a place or places and on a day or days so specified;

(c)   to participate in activities specified in the directions on a day or days so specified.

(2)   It shall be for the supervisor to decide whether, and to what extent, he exercises his power to give directions and to decide the form of any directions which he gives.

(3)   Sub-paragraph (1) does not confer on a supervisor power to give directions in respect of any medical or psychiatric examination or treatment (which are matters dealt with in paragraphs 4 and 5).

Imposition of obligations on responsible person

3.—(1)   With the consent of any responsible person, a supervision order may include a requirement—

(a)   that he take all reasonable steps to ensure that the supervised child complies with any direction given by the supervisor under paragraph 2;

(b)   that he take all reasonable steps to ensure that the supervised child complies with any requirement included in the order under paragraph 4 or 5;

(c)   that he comply with any directions given by the supervisor requiring him to attend at a place specified in the directions for the purpose of taking part in activities so specified.

(2)   A direction given under sub-paragraph (1)(c) may specify the time at which the responsible person is to attend and whether or not the supervised child is required to attend with him.

(3)   A supervision order may require any person who is a responsible person in relation to the supervised child to keep the supervisor informed of his address, if it differs from the child's.

Psychiatric and medical examinations

4.—(1)   A supervision order may require the supervised child—

(a)   to submit to a medical or psychiatric examination; or

(b) to submit to any such examination from time to time as directed by the supervisor.

(2) Any such examination shall be required to be conducted—

(a) by, or under the direction of, such registered medical practitioner as may be specified in the order;

(b) at a place specified in the order and at which the supervised child is to attend as a non-resident patient; or

(c) at—

(i) a health service hospital; or

(ii) in the case of a psychiatric examination, a hospital or mental nursing home, at which the supervised child is, or is to attend as, a resident patient.

(3) A requirement of a kind mentioned in sub-paragraph (2)(c) shall not be included unless the court is satisfied, on the evidence of a registered medical practitioner, that—

(a) the child may be suffering from a physical or mental condition that requires, and may be susceptible to, treatment; and

(b) a period as a resident patient is necessary if the examination is to be carried out properly.

(4) No court shall include a requirement under this paragraph in a supervision order unless it is satisfied that—

(a) where the child has sufficient understanding to make an informed decision, he consents to its inclusion; and

(b) satisfactory arrangements have been, or can be, made for the examination.

Psychiatric and medical treatment

5.—(1) Where a court which proposes to make or vary a supervision order is satisfied, on the evidence of a registered medical practitioner approved for the purposes of section 12 of the Mental Health Act 1983, that the mental condition of the supervised child—

(a) is such as requires, and may be susceptible to, treatment; but

(b) is not such as to warrant his detention in pursuance of a hospital order under Part III of that Act,

the court may include in the order a requirement that the supervised child shall, for a period specified in the order, submit to such treatment as is so specified.

(2) The treatment specified in accordance with sub-paragraph (1) must be—

(a) by, or under the direction of, such registered medical practitioner as may be specified in the order;

(b) as a non-resident patient at such a place as may be so specified; or

(c) as a resident patient in a hospital or mental nursing home.

(3) Where a court which proposes to make or vary a supervision order is satisfied, on the evidence of a registered medical practitioner, that the physical condition of the supervised child is such as requires, and may be susceptible to, treatment, the court may include in the order a requirement that the supervised child shall, for a period specified in the order, submit to such treatment as is so specified.

(4) The treatment specified in accordance with sub-paragraph (3) must be—

(a) by, or under the direction of, such registered medical practitioner as may be specified in the order;

(b) as a non-resident patient at such place as may be so specified; or

(c) as a resident patient in a health service hospital.

(5) No court shall include a requirement under this paragraph in a supervision order unless it is satisfied—

(a) where the child has sufficient understanding to make an informed decision, that he consents to its inclusion; and

(b)   that satisfactory arrangements have been, or can be, made for the treatment.

(6)   If a medical practitioner by whom or under whose direction a supervised person is being treated in pursuance of a requirement included in a supervision order by virtue of this paragraph is unwilling to continue to treat or direct the treatment of the supervised child or is of the opinion that—

(a)   the treatment should be continued beyond the period specified in the order;

(b)   the supervised child needs different treatment;

(c)   he is not susceptible to treatment; or

(d)   he does not require further treatment,

the practitioner shall make a report in writing to that effect to the supervisor.

ACCESS TO HEALTH RECORDS ACT 1990
(1990, c. 23)

Preliminary

1.   "Health record" and related expressions

(1)   In this Act "health record" means a record which—

(a)   consists of information relating to the physical or mental health of an individual who can be identified from that information, or from that and other information in the possession of the holder of the record; and

(b)   has been made by or on behalf of a health professional in connection with the care of that individual;

but does not include any record which consists of information of which the individual is, or but for any exemption would be, entitled to be supplied with a copy under section 21 of the Data Protection Act 1984 (right of access to personal data).

(2)   In this Act "holder", in relation to a health record, means—

(a)   in the case of a record made by, or by a health professional employed by, a general practitioner—

(i)   the patient's general practitioner, that is to say, the general practitioner on whose list the patient is included; or

(ii)   where the patient has no general practitioner, the Family Practitioner Committee or Health Board on whose medical list the patient's most recent general practitioner was included;

(b)   in the case of a record made by a health professional for purposes connected with the provision of health services by a health service body, the health service body by which or on whose behalf the record is held;

(c)   in any other case, the health professional by whom or on whose behalf the record is held;

(3)   In this Act "patient", in relation to a health record, means the individual in connection with whose care the record has been made.

2.   Health professionals

(1)   In this Act "health professional" means any of the following, namely—

(a)   a registered medical practitioner;

(b)   a registered dentist;

(c)   a registered optician;

(d)   a registered pharmaceutical chemist;

(e)   a registered nurse, midwife or health visitor;

(f)   a registered chiropodist, dietician, occupational therapist, orthoptist or physiotherapist;

(g)   a clinical psychologist, child psychotherapist or speech therapist;

(h)   an art or music therapist employed by a health service body; and

(i)   a scientist employed by such a body as head of a department.

(2)   Subsection (1)(a) above shall be deemed to include any person who is provisionally registered under section 15 or 21 of the Medical Act 1983 and is engaged in such employment as is mentioned in subsection (3) of that section.

(3)   If, after the passing of this Act, an order is made under section 10 of the Professions Supplementary to Medicine Act 1960, the Secretary of State may by order make such consequential amendments of subsection (1)(f) above as may appear to him to be necessary or expedient.

(4)   The provisions of this Act shall apply in relation to health professionals in the public service of the Crown as they apply in relation to other health professionals.

Main provisions

3.   Right of access to health records

(1)   An application for access to a health record, or to any part of a health record, may be made to the holder of the record by any of the following, namely—

(a)   the patient;

(b)   a person authorised in writing to make the application on the patient's behalf;

(c)   where the record is held in England and Wales and the patient is a child, a person having parental responsibility for the patient;

(d)   where the record is held in Scotland and the patient is a pupil, a parent or guardian of the patient;

(e)   where the patient is incapable of managing his own affairs, any person appointed by a court to manage those affairs; and

(f)   where the patient has died, the patient's personal representative and any person who may have a claim arising out of the patient's death.

(2)   Subject to section 4 below, where an application is made under subsection (1) above the holder shall, within the requisite period, give access to the record, or the part of a record, to which the application relates—

(a)   in the case of a record, by allowing the applicant to inspect the record or, where section 5 below applies, an extract setting out so much of the record as is not excluded by that section;

(b)   in the case of a part of a record, by allowing the applicant to inspect an extract setting out that part or, where that section applies, so much of that part as is not so excluded; or

(c)   in either case, if the applicant so requires, by supplying him with a copy of the record or extract.

(3)   Where any information contained in a record or extract which is so allowed to be inspected, or a copy of which is so supplied, is expressed in terms which are not intelligible without explanation, an explanation of those terms shall be provided with the record or extract, or supplied with the copy.

(4)   No fee shall be required for giving access under subsection (2) above other than the following, namely—

(a)   where access is given to a record, or part of a record, none of which was made after the beginning of the period of 40 days immediately preceding the date of the application, a fee not exceeding the maximum prescribed under section 21 of the Data Protection Act 1984; and

(b)   where a copy of a record or extract is supplied to the applicant, a fee not exceeding the cost of making the copy and (where applicable) the cost of posting it to him.

(5)   For the purposes of subsection (2) above the requisite period is—

(a)   where the application relates to a record, or part of a record, none of which was made before the beginning of the period of 40 days immediately preceding the date of the application, the period of 21 days beginning with that date;

(b)   in any other case, the period of 40 days beginning with that date.

(6)   Where—
(a)   an application under subsection (1) above does not contain sufficient information to enable the holder of the record to identify the patient or, in the case of an application made otherwise than by the patient, to satisfy himself that the applicant is entitled to make the application; and
(b)   within the period of 14 days beginning with the date of the application, the holder of the record requests the applicant to furnish him with such further information as he may reasonably require for that purpose,
subsection (5) above shall have effect as if for any reference to that date there were substituted a reference to the date on which that further information is so furnished.

4.   Cases where right of access may be wholly excluded

(1)   Where an application is made under subsection (1)(a) or (b) of section 3 above and—
(a)   in the case of a record held in England and Wales, the patient is a child; or
(b)   in the case of a record held in Scotland, the patient is a pupil,
access shall not be given under subsection (2) of that section unless the holder of the record is satisfied that the patient is capable of understanding the nature of the application.
(2)   Where an application is made under subsection (1)(c) or (d) of section 3 above, access shall not be given under subsection (2) of that section unless the holder of the record is satisfied either—
(a)   that the patient has consented to the making of the application; or
(b)   that the patient is incapable of understanding the nature of the application and the giving of access would be in his best interests.
(3)   Where an application is made under subsection (1)(f) of section 3 above, access shall not be given under subsection (2) of that section if the record includes a note, made at the patient's request, that he did not wish access to be given on such an application.

5.   Cases where right of access may be partially excluded

(1)   Access shall not be given under section 3(2) above to any part of a health record—
(a)   which, in the opinion of the holder of the record, would disclose—
(i)   information likely to cause serious harm to the physical or mental health of the patient or of any other individual; or
(ii)   information relating to or provided by an individual, other than the patient, who could be identified from that information; or
(b)   which was made before the commencement of this Act.
(2)   Subsection (1)(a)(ii) above shall not apply—
(a)   where the individual concerned has consented to the application; or
(b)   where that individual is a health professional who has been involved in the care of the patient;
and subsection (1)(b) above shall not apply where and to the extent that, in the opinion of the holder of the record, the giving of access is necessary in order to make intelligible any part of the record to which access is required to be given under section 3(2) above.
(3)   Where an application is made under subsection (1)(c), (d), (e) or (f) of section 3 above, access shall not be given under subsection (2) of that section to any part of the record which, in the opinion of the holder of the record, would disclose—
(a)   information provided by the patient in the expectation that it would not be disclosed to the applicant; or
(b)   information obtained as a result of any examination or investigation to which the patient consented in the expectation that the information would not be so disclosed.
(4)   Where an application is made under subsection (1)(f) of section 3 above, access shall not be given under subsection (2) of that section to any part of the record which,

in the opinion of the holder of the record, would disclose information which is not relevant to any claim which may arise out of the patient's death.

(5) The Secretary of State may by regulations provide that, in such circumstances as may be prescribed by the regulations, access shall not be given under section 3(2) above to any part of a health record which satisfies such conditions as may be so prescribed.

6. Correction of inaccurate health records

(1) Where a person considers that any information contained in a health record, or any part of a health record, to which he has been given access under section 3(2) above is inaccurate, he may apply to the holder of the record for the necessary correction to be made.

(2) On an application under subsection (1) above, the holder of the record shall—

(a) if he is satisfied that the information is inaccurate, make the necessary correction;

(b) if he is not so satisfied, make in the part of the record in which the information is contained a note of the matters in respect of which the information is considered by the applicant to be inaccurate; and

(c) in either case, without requiring any fee, supply the applicant with a copy of the correction or note.

(3) In this section "inaccurate" means incorrect, misleading or incomplete.

7. Duty of health service bodies etc. to take advice

(1) A health service body or Family Practitioner Committee shall take advice from the appropriate health professional before they decide whether they are satisfied as to any matter for the purposes of this Act, or form an opinion as to any matter for those purposes.

(2) In this section "the appropriate health professional", in relation to a health service body (other than a Health Board which is the holder of the record by virtue of section 1(2)(a) above), means—

(a) where, for purposes connected with the provision of health services by the body, one or more medical or dental practitioners are currently responsible for the clinical care of the patient, that practitioner or, as the case may be, such one of those practitioners as is the most suitable to advise the body on the matter in question;

(b) where paragraph (a) above does not apply but one or more medical or dental practitioners are available who, for purposes connected with the provision of such services by the body, have been responsible for the clinical care of the patient, that practitioner or, as the case may be, such one of those practitioners as was most recently so responsible; and

(c) where neither paragraph (a) nor paragraph (b) above applies, a health professional who has the necessary experience and qualifications to advise the body on the matter in question.

(3) In this section "the appropriate health professional", in relation to a Family Practitioner Committee or a Health Board which is the holder of the record by virtue of section 1(2)(a) above, means—

(a) where the patient's most recent general practitioner is available, that practitioner; and

(b) where that practitioner is not available, a registered medical practitioner who has the necessary experience and qualifications to advise the Committee or Board on the matter in question.

Supplemental

8. Applications to the court

(1) Subject to subsection (2) below, where the court is satisfied, on an application made by the person concerned within such period as may be prescribed by rules of

court, that the holder of a health record has failed to comply with any requirement of this Act, the court may order the holder to comply with that requirement.

(2)   The court shall not entertain an application under subsection (1) above unless it is satisfied that the applicant has taken all such steps to secure compliance with the requirement as may be prescribed by regulations made by the Secretary of State.

(3)   For the purposes of subsection (2) above, the Secretary of State may by regulations require the holders of health records to make such arrangements for dealing with complaints that they have failed to comply with any requirements of this Act as may be prescribed by the regulations.

(4)   For the purpose of determining any question whether an applicant is entitled to be given access under section 3(2) above to any health record, or any part of a health record, the court—

(a)   may require the record or part to be made available for its own inspection; but

(b)   shall not, pending determination of that question in the applicant's favour, require the record or part to be disclosed to him or his representatives whether by discovery (or, in Scotland, recovery) or otherwise.

(5)   The jurisdiction conferred by this section shall be exercisable by the High Court or a county court or, in Scotland, by the Court of Session or the sheriff.

9.   Avoidance of certain contractual terms
Any term or condition of a contract shall be void in so far as it purports to require an individual to supply any other person with a copy of a health record, or of an extract from a health record, to which he has been given access under section 3(2) above.

10.   Regulations and orders
(1)   Regulations under this Act may make different provision for different cases or classes of cases including, in particular, different provision for different health records or classes of health records.

11.   Interpretation
In this Act—
"application" means an application in writing and "apply" shall be construed accordingly;
"care" includes examination, investigation, diagnosis and treatment;
"child" means an individual who has not attained the age of 16 years;
"general practitioner" means a medical practitioner who is providing general medical services in accordance with arrangements made under section 29 of the National Health Service Act 1977 or section 19 of the National Health Service (Scotland) Act 1978;
"Health Board" has the same meaning as in the National Health Service (Scotland) Act 1978;
"health service body" means—
(a)   a health authority within the meaning of the National Health Service Act 1977;
(b)   a Health Board;
(c)   a State Hospital Management Committee constituted under section 91 of the Mental Health (Scotland) Act 1984; or
(d)   a National Health Service trust first established under section 5 of the National Health Service and Community Care Act 1990 or section 12A of the National Health Service (Scotland) Act 1978;
"information", in relation to a health record, includes any expression of opinion about the patient;
"make", in relation to such a record, includes compile;
"parental responsibility" has the same meaning as in the Children Act 1989.

12. Short title, commencement, and extent

(2) This Act shall come into force on 1st November 1991.

NATIONAL HEALTH SERVICE AND COMMUNITY CARE ACT 1990
(1990, c. 19)

[Note: "Principal Act" means the National Health Service Act 1977]

Local Management

2. Family Health Services Authorities

(1) On and after the day appointed for the coming into force of this subsection —

(a) each existing Family Practitioner Committee shall be known as a Family Health Services Authority; and

(b) any reference in any enactment to a Family Practitioner Committee shall be construed as a reference to a Family Health Services Authority;

and the generality of this subsection is not affected by any express amendment made by this Act.

(2) In subsection (1) above "enactment" means —

(a) an enactment passed before the day appointed for the coming into force of subsection (1) above; and

(b) an enactment comprised in subordinate legislation made before that day.

(6) Nothing in this section shall cause a Family Health Services Authority to be included in the expression "health authority", as defined in the principal Act.

3. Primary and other functions of health authorities etc. and exercise of functions

(1) Any reference in this Act to the primary functions of a Regional, District or Special Health Authority is a reference to those functions for the time being exercisable by the authority by virtue of directions under section 11, section 13 or section 14 of the principal Act; and any reference in this Act to the primary functions of a Family Health Services Authority is a reference to the functions for the time being exercisable by the authority by virtue of this Act or section 15 of the principal Act.

(2) In addition to carrying out its primary functions, a Regional, District or Special Health Authority or a Family Health Services Authority may, as the provider, enter into an NHS contract (as defined in section 4 below) under which the goods or services to be provided are of the same description as goods or services which the authority already provides or could provide for the purposes of carrying out its primary functions.

(5) Nothing in this section or in the principal Act affects the power of a Regional, District or Special Health Authority at any time to provide goods or services under the principal Act for the benefit of an individual where —

(a) the provision of those goods or services is neither within the primary functions of the authority nor carried out pursuant to an NHS contract; but

(b) the condition of the individual is such that he needs those goods or services and, having regard to his condition, it is not practicable before providing them to enter into an NHS contract for their provision.

(6) In any case where —

(a) a Regional, District or Special Health Authority provides goods or services for the benefit of an individual as mentioned in subsection (5) above, and

(b) the provision of those goods or services is within the primary functions of another health authority or is a function of a health board,

the authority providing the goods or services shall be remunerated in respect of that provision by that other health authority or health board.

(7)   The rate of any remuneration payable by virtue of subsection (6) above shall be calculated in such manner or on such basis as may be determined by the Secretary of State.

(8)   In any case where —

(a)   a Regional, District or Special Health Authority provides goods or services for the benefit of an individual, and

(b)   the provision of those goods or services is not pursuant to an NHS contract, and

(c)   the individual is resident outside the United Kingdom and is of a description (being a description associating the individual with another country) specified for the purposes of this subsection by a direction made by the Secretary of State,

the authority shall be remunerated by the Secretary of State in respect of the provision of the goods or services in question at such rate or rates as he considers appropriate.

4.   NHS contracts

(1)   In this Act the expression "NHS contract" means an arrangement under which one health service body ("the acquirer") arranges for the provision to it by another health service body ("the provider") of goods or services which it reasonably requires for the purposes of its functions.

(2)   In this section "health service body" means any of the following, namely, —

(a)   a health authority;

(b)   a health board;

(c)   the Common Services Agency for the Scottish Health Service;

(d)   a Family Health Services Authority;

(e)   an NHS trust;

(f)   a recognised fund-holding practice;

(g)   the Dental Practice Board or the Scottish Dental Practice Board;

(h)   the Public Health Laboratory Service Board; and

(i)   the Secretary of State.

(3)   Whether or not an arrangement which constitutes an NHS contract would, apart from this subsection, be a contract in law, it shall not be regarded for any purpose as giving rise to contractual rights or liabilities, but if any dispute arises with respect to such an arrangement, either party may refer the matter to the Secretary of State for determination under the following provisions of this section.

(4)   If, in the course of negotiations intending to lead to an arrangement which will be an NHS contract, it appears to a health service body —

(a)   that the terms proposed by another health service body are unfair by reason that the other is seeking to take advantage of its position as the only, or the only practicable, provider of the goods or services concerned or by reason of any other unequal bargaining position as between the prospective parties to the proposed arrangement, or

(b)   that for any other reason arising out of the relative bargaining position of the prospective parties any of the terms of the proposed arrangement cannot be agreed, that health service body may refer the terms of the proposed arrangement to the Secretary of State for determination under the following provisions of this section.

(5)   Where a reference is made to the Secretary of State under subsection (3) or subsection (4) above, the Secretary of State may determine the matter himself or, if he considers it appropriate, appoint a person to consider and determine it in accordance with regulations.

(6)   By his determination of a reference under subsection (4) above, the Secretary of State or, as the case may be, the person appointed under subsection (5) above may specify terms to be included in the proposed arrangement and may direct that it be proceeded with; and it shall be the duty of the prospective parties to the proposed arrangement to comply with any such directions.

(7) A determination of a reference under subsection (3) above may contain such directions (including directions as to payment) as the Secretary of State or, as the case may be, the person appointed under subsection (5) above considers appropriate to resolve the matter in dispute; and it shall be the duty of the parties to the NHS contract in question to comply with any such directions.

(8) Without prejudice to the generality of his powers on a reference under subsection (3) above, the Secretary of State or, as the case may be, the person appointed under subsection (5) above may by his determination in relation to an arrangement constituting an NHS contract vary the terms of the arrangement or bring it to an end; and where an arrangement is so varied or brought to an end —

(a) subject to paragraph (b) below, the variation or termination shall be treated as being effected by agreement between the parties; and

(b) the directions included in the determination by virtue of subsection (7) above may contain such provisions as the Secretary of State or, as the case may be, the person appointed under subsection (5) above considers appropriate in order satisfactorily to give effect to the variation or to bring the arrangement to an end.

(9) In subsection (2) above "NHS trust" includes —

(a) such a trust established under the National Health Service (Scotland) Act 1978; and

(b) a body established in Northern Ireland and specified by an order made by statutory instrument by the Secretary of State as equivalent to an NHS trust established under this Part of this Act.

National Health Service trusts

5. NHS trusts

(1) Subject to subsection (2) or, as the case may be, subsection (3) below the Secretary of State may by order establish bodies, to be known as National Health Service trusts (in this Act referred to as NHS trusts), —

(a) to assume responsibility, in accordance with this Act, for the ownership and management of hospitals or other establishments or facilities which were previously managed or provided by Regional, District or Special Health Authorities; or

(b) to provide and manage hospitals or other establishments or facilities.

(2) In any case where the Secretary of State is considering whether to make an order under subsection (1) above establishing an NHS trust and the hospital, establishment or facility concerned is or is to be situated in England, he shall direct the relevant Regional Health Authority to consult, with respect to the proposal to establish the trust, —

(a) the relevant Community Health Council and such other persons or bodies as may be specified in the direction; and

(b) such other persons or bodies as the Authority considers appropriate; and, within such period (if any) as the Secretary of State may determine, the relevant Regional Health Authority shall report the results of those consultations to the Secretary of State.

(3) In any case where the Secretary of State is considering whether to make an order under subsection (1) above establishing an NHS trust and the hospital, establishment or facility concerned is or is to be situated in Wales, he shall consult the relevant Community Health Council and such other persons and bodies as he considers appropriate.

(4) In subsections (2) and (3) above —

(a) any reference to the relevant Regional Health Authority is a reference to that Authority in whose region the hospital, establishment or other facility concerned is, or is to be, situated; and

(b)   any reference to the relevant Community Health Council is a reference to the Council for the district, or part of the district, in which that hospital, establishment or other facility is, or is to be, situated.

(5)   Every NHS trust —

(a)   shall be a body corporate having a board of directors consisting of a chairman appointed by the Secretary of State and, subject to paragraph 5(2) of Schedule 2 to this Act, executive and non-executive directors (that is to say, directors who, subject to subsection (7) below, respectively are and are not employees of the trust); and

(b)   shall have the functions conferred on it by an order under subsection (1) above and by Schedule 2 to this Act.

(6)   The functions specified in an order under subsection (1) above shall include such functions as the Secretary of State considers appropriate in relation to the provision of services by the trust for one or more health authorities.

(7)   The Secretary of State may by regulations make general provision with respect to —

(a)   the qualifications for and the tenure of office of the chairman and directors of an NHS trust (including the circumstances in which they shall cease to hold, or may be removed from, office or may be suspended from performing the functions of the office);

(b)   the persons by whom the directors and any of the officers are to be appointed and the manner of their appointment;

(c)   the maximum and minimum numbers of the directors;

(d)   the circumstances in which a person who is not an employee of the trust is nevertheless, on appointment as a director, to be regarded as an executive rather than a non-executive director;

(e)   the proceedings of the trust (including the validation of proceedings in the event of a vacancy or defect in appointment); and

(f)   the appointment, constitution and exercise of functions by committees and sub-committees of the trust (whether or not consisting of or including any members of the board) and, without prejudice to the generality of the power, any such regulations, may make provision to deal with cases where the post of any officer of an NHS trust is held jointly by two or more persons or where the functions of such an officer are in any other way performed by more than one person.

(8)   Part I of Schedule 2 to this Act shall have effect with respect to orders under subsection (1) above; Part II of that Schedule shall have effect, subject to subsection (9) below, with respect to the general duties and the powers and status of NHS trusts; the supplementary provisions of Part III of that Schedule shall have effect; and Part IV of that Schedule shall have effect with respect to the dissolution of NHS trusts.

(9)   The specific powers conferred by paragraphs 14 and 15 in Part II of Schedule 2 to this Act may be exercised only to the extent that —

(a)   the exercise will not interfere with the duties of the trust to comply with directions under paragraph 6 of that Schedule; and

(b)   the exercise will not to any significant extent interfere with the performance by the trust of its obligations under any NHS contract or any obligations imposed by an order under subsection (1) above.

(10)   The Secretary of State may by order made by statutory instrument confer on NHS trusts specific powers additional to those contained in paragraphs 10 to 15 of Schedule 2 to this Act.

6.   Transfer of staff to NHS trusts

(1)   Subject to subsection (5) below, this section applies to any person who, immediately before an NHS trust's operational date —

(a)   is employed by a health authority to work solely at, or for the purposes of, a hospital or other establishment or facility which is to become the responsibility of the trust; or

(b)   is employed by a health authority to work at, or for the purposes of, such a hospital, establishment or facility and is designated for the purposes of this section by a scheme made by the health authority specified as mentioned in paragraph 3(1)(f) of Schedule 2 to this Act.

(2)   A scheme under this section shall not have effect unless approved by the Secretary of State.

(3)   Subject to section 7 below, the contract of employment between a person to whom this section applies and the health authority by whom he is employed shall have effect from the operational date as if originally made between him and the NHS trust.

(4)   Without prejudice to subsection (3) above —

(a)   all the health authority's rights, powers, duties and liabilities under or in connection with a contract to which that subsection applies shall by virtue of this section be transferred to the NHS trust on its operational date; and

(b)   anything done before that date by or in relation to the health authority in respect of that contract or the employee shall be deemed from that date to have been done by or in relation to the NHS trust.

(5)   In any case where —

(a)   an order under section 5(1) above provides for the establishment of an NHS trust with effect from a date earlier than the operational date of the trust, and

(b)   on or after that earlier date but before its operational date the NHS trust makes an offer of employment by the trust to a person who at that time is employed by a health authority to work (whether solely or otherwise) at, or for the purposes of, the hospital or other establishment or facility which is to become the responsibility of the trust, and

(c)   as a result of the acceptance of the offer, the person to whom it was made becomes an employee of the NHS trust,

subsections (3) and (4) above shall have effect in relation to that person's contract of employment as if he were a person to whom this section applies and any reference in those subsections to the operational date of the trust were a reference in those subsections to the operational date of the trust were a reference to the date on which he takes up employment with the trust.

(6)   Subsections (3) and (4) above are without prejudice to any right of an employee to terminate his contract of employment if a substantial change is made to his detriment in his working conditions; but no such right shall arise by reason only of the change in employer effected by this section.

(7)   A scheme under this section may designate a person either individually or as a member of a class or description of employees.

10.   Financial obligations of NHS trusts

(1)   Every NHS trust shall ensure that its revenue is not less than sufficient, taking one financial year with another, to meet outgoings properly chargeable to revenue account.

(2)   It shall be the duty of every NHS trust to achieve such financial objectives as may from time to time be set by the Secretary of State with the consent of the Treasury and as are applicable to it; and any such objectives may be made applicable to NHS trusts generally, or to a particular NHS trust or to NHS trusts of a particular description.

11.   Trust funds and trustees for NHS trusts

(1)   The Secretary of State may by order made by statutory instrument provide for the appointment of trustees for an NHS trust and any trustees so appointed shall have power to accept, hold and administer any property on trust for the general or any

specific purposes of the NHS trust (including the purposes of any specific hospital or other establishment or facility which is owned and managed by the trust) or for all or any purposes relating to the health service.

Fund-holding practices

14. Recognition of fund-holding practices of doctors

(1) Any one or more medical practitioners who are providing general medical services in accordance with arrangements under section 29 of the principal Act may apply to the relevant Regional Health Authority for recognition as a fund-holding practice.

(2) The relevant Regional Health Authority shall not grant recognition as a fund-holding practice unless the medical practitioner or, as the case may be, each of the medical practitioners concerned fulfils such conditions as may be prescribed.

(3) Subject to subsection (4) below, in relation to a medical practitioner, any reference in this Part of this Act to the relevant Regional Health Authority is a reference to that Authority which, in relation to the practitioner's relevant Family Health Services Authority, is the relevant Regional Health Authority.

(4) Where two or more medical practitioners wish to make an application under subsection (1) above and, apart from this subsection, the relevant Family Health Services Authority in respect of one or more of them would be different from that in respect of the other or others, then, for the purposes of this section and any other provisions relating to fund-holding practices, the relevant Family Health Services Authority for each of them shall be determined as if they were all practising in a single partnership.

(5) In the application of this section to any medical practitioner whose relevant Family Health Services Authority has a locality in Wales, for any reference to the relevant Regional Health Authority there shall be substituted a reference to the Secretary of State.

(6) Regulations may make provision with respect to —

    (a) the making of applications under subsection (1) above;

    (b) the granting and refusal of recognition as a fund-holding practice;

    (c) the conditions to be fulfilled for obtaining and continuing to be entitled to such recognition;

    (d) appeals against any refusal of such recognition by a Regional Health Authority;

    (e) withdrawing from, or becoming a member of, an existing recognised fund-holding practice;

    (f) the continuity or otherwise of a recognised fund-holding practice in the event of the death or withdrawal of a member or the addition of a new member; and

    (g) the operation of this section in a case where one or more of the medical practitioners wishing to make an application under subsection (1) above is also on the medical list of a health board;

and regulations making the provision referred to in paragraph (g) above may make such modifications of the preceding provisions of this section as the Secretary of State considers appropriate.

15. Payments to recognised fund-holding practices

(1) In respect of each financial year, every Family Health Services Authority shall be liable to pay to the members of each recognised fund-holding practice in relation to which it is the relevant Family Health Services Authority a sum determined by the relevant Regional Health Authority in such manner and by reference to such factors as the Secretary of State may direct (in this section referred to as an "allotted sum").

(2)   In respect of each financial year, every Family Health Services Authority which has a locality in Wales shall be liable to pay to the members of each recognised fund-holding practice in respect of whom it is the relevant Family Health Services Authority a sum determined by the Secretary of State in such manner and by reference to such factors as he may direct (in this section referred to as an "allotted sum").

(3)   The liability to pay an allotted sum under subsection (1) or subsection (2) above may be discharged, in whole or in part, in either of the following ways —

(a)   by making payments on account of the allotted sum at such times and in such manner as the Secretary of State may direct; and

(b)   by discharging liabilities of the members of the practice to any other person (including, in particular, liabilities under NHS contracts);

and any reference in the following provisions of this Part of this Act to payment of or of a part of an allotted sum includes a reference to the discharge, in accordance with this subsection, of the whole or part of the liability to pay that sum.

(4)   In any case where —

(a)   a Family Health Services Authority which has a locality in England makes a payment of or of any part of an allotted sum to the members of a recognised fund-holding practice, and

(b)   some of the individuals on the list of patients of any of the members of the practice reside in the region of a Regional Health Authority, which is not the relevant Regional Health Authority in respect of the members of the practice, or in Wales, or in the area of a Health Board,

the Authority making the payment shall be entitled to recover from that Regional Health Authority or, as the case may be, from the Secretary of State or that Health Board an amount equal to such portion of the payment as may be determined in accordance with directions given by the Secretary of State.

(5)   In any case where —

(a)   A Family Health Services Authority which has a locality in Wales makes a payment of or of any part of an allotted sum to the members of a recognised fund-holding practice, and

(b)   some of the individuals on the list of patients of any of the members of the practice reside in the region of a Regional Health Authority,

the Authority making the payment shall be entitled to recover from that Regional Health Authority an amount equal to such portion of the payment as may be determined in accordance with directions given by the Secretary of State.

(6)   The members of a recognised fund-holding practice may apply an allotted sum only for purposes specified in regulations under subsection (7) below.

(7)   Regulations shall make provision with respect to the purposes for which allotted sums are to be or may be applied and may make provision generally with respect to the operation of recognised fund-holding practices in relation to allotted sums; and the regulations may, in particular, —

(a)   require the members of a practice to pay to the relevant Regional Health Authority out of allotted sums paid to them an amount determined in accordance with the regulations as the basic cost of the drugs, medicines and listed appliances supplied pursuant to orders given by or on behalf of members of the practice;

(b)   provide that the goods and services, other than general medical services, which may be purchased by or on behalf of the members of a practice out of allotted sums for the individuals on the lists of patients of the members of the practice shall be such as may be specified in a list approved for the purpose under the regulations; and

(c)   impose a limit on the amount which may be spent out of an allotted sum on the provision of goods and services for any one individual, being a limit above which the cost of any goods and services for that individual in the financial year in question will fall to be met by the District Health Authority whose primary functions include the provision of goods and services (not necessarily the goods and services in question) to the individual concerned.

(8)   In the application of subsection (7) above to the members of a practice whose relevant Family Health Services Authority has a locality in Wales, for the reference in paragraph (a) of that subsection to the relevant Regional Health Authority there shall be substituted a reference to the Secretary of State.

(9)   In accordance with directions under section 17 of the principal Act, the relevant Family Health Services Authority shall monitor the expenditure of the members of a recognised fund-holding practice and may institute an audit and review in any case where the Authority consider it necessary to do so.

16.   Renunciation and removal of recognition as a fund-holding practice and withholding of funds

(1)   Regulations may make provision as to the circumstances in which the members of a recognised fund-holding practice may renounce that status and such regulations may, in particular, make provision as to —

(a)   the notice to be given and the number of members of the practice by whom it is to be given;

(b)   the procedure to be followed; and

(c)   the consequences of such a renunciation.

(2)   Regulations may make provision as to the circumstances in which and the grounds on which the relevant Regional Health Authority or, as the case may be, the Secretary of State may remove recognition from the members of a fund-holding practice, —

(a)   with immediate effect; or

(b)   with effect from the end of a particular financial year; or

(c)   with effect from such other date as may be specified by the Regional Health Authority or, as the case may be, the Secretary of State.

(3)   Where provision is made as mentioned in subsection (2) above, regulations shall make provision with respect to —

(a)   the procedure for the removal of recognition;

(b)   appeals against the removal of recognition by a Regional Health Authority; and

(c)   the consequences of the removal of recognition.

(4)   Without prejudice to the generality of the powers conferred by subsection (3) above, regulations making provision as mentioned in paragraph (c) of that subsection—

(a)   may provide for the transfer of rights and obligations from the members of the fund-holding practice to one or more District Health Authorities determined in accordance with the regulations;

(b)   may provide for the recovery of sums from the members of the practice; and

(c)   may require the members of the practice to furnish such information as may reasonably be required by the Regional Health Authority or, as the case may be, the Secretary of State.

(5)   The bringing of an appeal against the removal of recognition by a Regional Health Authority shall not be regarded as preserving the recognised status of the members of the fund-holding practice and, accordingly, subject to the outcome of the appeal, the relevant Regional Health Authority shall not be required, after the removal takes effect, to make any (or, as the case may be, any further) payment to the members of the practice of any part of the allotted sum for the financial year in question or, as the case may be, to determine and pay any allotted sum for a future financial year.

(6)   Where any part of an allotted sum has been applied by the members of a recognised fund-holding practice (or any one or more of them) for purposes other than those specified in regulations under section 15(7) above, regulations may make

provision for and in connection with the recovery by the relevant Regional Health Authority or, as the case may be, the Secretary of State of an amount equal to that part.

(7) Where provision is made as mentioned in subsection (6) above, regulations shall make provision with respect to appeals against the recovery of any amount by a Regional Health Authority.

17. Transfer of functions relating to recognised fund-holding practices

(1) If the Secretary of State by regulations so provides, such of the functions of a Regional Health Authority or, in Wales, the Secretary of State under sections 14 to 16 above as are specified in, or determined in accordance with, the regulations shall become functions of a Family Health Services Authority with effect from such date as may be prescribed.

(2) Regulations under this section shall make provision for determining the Family Health Services Authority which is to exercise any of the functions concerned in relation to the members of any existing recognised fund-holding practice and in relation to any medical practitioners wishing to apply for recognition.

(3) Without prejudice to the generality of section 126(4) of the principal Act, regulations under this section may make such incidental and consequential modifications of the principal Act and of sections 14 to 16 above as appear to the Secretary of State to be necessary or expedient in consequence of the transfer of functions effected by the regulations.

Indicative amounts

18. Indicative amounts for doctors' practices

(1) Subject to subsection (2) below, for each financial year, every Family Health Services Authority shall, by notice in writing given to each practice in relation to the members of which it is the relevant Family Health Services Authority, specify an amount of money (in this Act referred to as an "indicative amount") representing the basic price of the drugs, medicines and listed appliances which, in the opinion of the Authority, it is reasonable to expect will be supplied in that year pursuant to orders given by or on behalf of the members of that practice.

(2) Subsection (1) above does not apply with respect to a practice which is or forms part of a fund-holding practice recognised under section 14 above or with respect to a practice where —

(a) at least one member of the practice is on the medical list of a Health Board as well as on that of a Family Health Services Authority, and

(b) more patients on the lists of the members of the practice reside in Scotland than in England.

(3) For the purposes of this section, a "practice" means —

(a) a single medical practitioner who practises otherwise than in partnership; or

(b) any two or more medical practitioners who practise in partnership;

and any reference to the members of a practice shall be construed accordingly.

(4) The members of a practice shall seek to secure that, except with the consent of the relevant Family Health Services Authority or for good cause, the orders for drugs, medicines and listed appliances given by them or on their behalf are such that the basic price of the items supplied pursuant to those orders in any financial year does not exceed the indicative amount notified to the practice for that year under subsection (1) above.

(5) For the purpose of measuring the extent to which a practice is operating within the indicative amount notified to it under subsection (1) above for any financial year, a Family Health Services Authority shall set against that indicative amount an amount equal to the basic price of the drugs, medicines and listed appliances supplied in that year pursuant to orders given by or on behalf of members of the practice.

(6)   For the purposes of this section, regulations may make provision as to the specification of, or means of calculating, the basic price of any drugs, medicines or listed appliances.

21.   Schemes for meeting losses and liabilities etc. of certain health service bodies

(1)   The Secretary of State may by regulations made with the consent of the Treasury establish a scheme whereby any of the bodies specified in subsection (2) below may make provision to meet —

(a)   expenses arising from any loss of or damage to their property; and

(b)   liabilities to third parties for loss, damage or injury arising out of the carrying out of the functions of the bodies concerned.

(2)   The bodies referred to in subsection (1) above are —

(a)   health authorities;

(b)   NHS trusts; and

(c)   the Public Health Laboratory Service Board;

but a scheme under this section may limit the class or description of bodies which are eligible to participate in it.

(3)   Without prejudice to the generality of the power conferred by subsection (1) above, a scheme under this section may —

(a)   provide for the scheme to be administered by the Secretary of State or by a health authority or NHS trust specified in the scheme;

(b)   require any body which participates in the scheme to make payments in accordance with the scheme; and

(c)   provide for the making of payments for the purposes of the scheme by the Secretary of State.

(4)   Without prejudice to any other power of direction conferred on the Secretary of State, —

(a)   if the Secretary of State so directs, a body which is eligible to participate in a scheme shall do so; and

(b)   where a scheme provides for it to be administered by the Secretary of State, a health authority or NHS trust shall carry out such functions in connection with the administration of the scheme by the Secretary of State as he may direct.

(5)   Neither the Secretary of State nor any health authority or NHS trust administering a scheme under this section shall, by virtue of their activities under the scheme, be regarded as carrying on insurance business for the purposes of the Insurance Companies Act 1982.

60.   Removal of Crown immunities

(1)   Subject to the following provisions of this section, on and after the day appointed for the coming into force of this subsection, no health service body shall be regarded as the servant or agent of the Crown or as enjoying any status, immunity or privilege of the Crown; and so far as concerns land in which the Secretary of State has an interest, at any time when —

(a)   by virtue of directions under any provision of the National Health Service Act 1977, the Mental Health (Scotland) Act 1984 or the Health and Medicines Act 1988 or by virtue of orders under section 2 or section 10 of the National Health Service (Scotland) Act 1978, powers of disposal or management with respect to the land are conferred on a health service body, or

(b)   the land is otherwise held, used or occupied by a health service body,

the interest of the Secretary of State shall be treated for the purposes of any enactment or rule of law relating to Crown land or interests as if it were an interest held otherwise than by the Secretary of State (or any other emanation of the Crown).

(7)   In this section "health service body" means —

(a)   a health authority, within the meaning of the National Health Service Act 1977;

(b)   a Health Board or Special Health Board constituted under section 2 of the National Health Service (Scotland) Act 1978;

(c)   a State Hospital Management Committee constituted under section 91 of the Mental Health (Scotland) Act 1984;

(d)   a Family Health Services Authority;

(e)   the Common Services Agency for the Scottish Health Service;

(f)   the Dental Practice Board;

(g)   the Scottish Dental Practice Board; and

(h)   the Public Health Laboratory Service Board.

62.   Clinical Standards Advisory Group

(1)   There shall be established in accordance with this section a Clinical Standards Advisory Group (in this section referred to as "the Advisory Group") which shall have the following functions —

(a)   in accordance with a request made by the Health Ministers or any one of them, to provide advice on the standards of clinical care for, and the access to and availability of services to, national health service patients and, in this connection, to carry out such investigations into such matters (if any) and to make such reports in relation thereto as the Health Ministers may require;

(b)   in accordance with a request made by one or more health service bodies, to provide advice on, to carry out investigations into and to report on the standards of clinical care for, and the access to and availability of services to, national health service patients for whom services are or are to be provided by or on behalf of the body or bodies concerned; and

(c)   such other functions as may be prescribed by regulations.

(7)   In this section —

"clinical care" means any action which is taken in connection with the diagnosis of illness or the care or treatment of a patient, and which is taken solely in consequence of the exercise of clinical judgment;

SCHEDULE

SCHEDULE 2

PART II
DUTIES, POWERS AND STATUS

Specific duties

6.—(1)   An NHS trust shall carry out effectively, efficiently and economically the functions for the time being conferred on it by an order under section 5(1) of this Act and by the provisions of this Schedule and, with respect to the exercise of the powers conferred by section 5(10) of this Act and paragraphs 10 to 15 below, shall comply with any directions given to it by the Secretary of State, whether of a general or a particular nature.

(2)   An NHS trust shall comply with any directions given to it by the Secretary of State with respect to all or any of the following matters —

(a)   the qualifications of persons who may be employed as officers of the trust;

(b)   the employment, for the purpose of performing functions specified in the direction, of officers having qualifications or experience of a description so specified;

(c)   the manner in which officers of the trust are to be appointed;

(d)   prohibiting or restricting the disposal of, or of any interest in, any asset which, at the time the direction is given, the Secretary of State reasonably considers to have a value in excess of such sum as may be specified in an order under section 5(1) of this Act and in respect of which the Secretary of State considers that the interests of the National Health Service require that the asset should not be disposed of;

    (e)   compliance with guidance or directions given (by circular or otherwise) to health authorities, or particular descriptions of health authorities; and

    (f)   the implementation of awards relating to the distinction or merit of medical practitioners or dental practitioners or any class or classes of such practitioners.

7.—(1) For each accounting year an NHS trust shall prepare and send to the Secretary of State an annual report in such form as may be determined by the Secretary of State.

(2) At such time or times as may be prescribed, an NHS trust shall hold a public meeting at which its audited accounts and annual report and any report on the accounts made pursuant to subsection (3) of section 15 of the Local Government Finance Act 1982 shall be presented.

(3) In such circumstances and at such time or times as may be prescribed, an NHS trust shall hold a public meeting at which such document as may be prescribed shall be presented.

8. An NHS trust shall furnish to the Secretary of State such reports, returns and other information, including information as to its forward planning, as, and in such form as, he may require.

Specific powers

10. In addition to carrying out its other functions, an NHS trust may, as the provider, enter into NHS contracts.

11. An NHS trust may undertake and commission research and make available staff and provide facilities for research by other persons.

12. An NHS trust may —

    (a)   provide training for persons employed or likely to be employed by the trust or otherwise in the provision of services under the principal Act; and

    (b)   make facilities and staff available in connection with training by a university or any other body providing training in connection with the health service.

13. An NHS trust may enter into arrangements for the carrying out, on such terms as seem to the trust to be appropriate, of any of its functions jointly with any Regional, District or Special Health Authority, with another NHS trust or with any other body or individual.

14. According to the nature of its functions, an NHS trust may make accommodation or services or both available for patients who give undertakings (or for whom undertakings are given) to pay, in respect of the accommodation or services (or both) such charges as the trust may determine.

15. For the purpose of making additional income available in order better to perform its functions, an NHS trust shall have the powers specified in section 7(2) of the Health and Medicines Act 1988 (extension of powers of Secretary of State for financing the Health Service).

General powers

16.—(1) Subject to Schedule 3 to this Act, an NHS trust shall have power to do anything which appears to it to be necessary or expedient for the purpose of or in connection with the discharge of its functions, including in particular power —

    (a)   to acquire and dispose of land and other property;

    (b)   to enter into such contracts as seem to the trust to be appropriate;

    (c)   to accept gifts of money, land or other property, including money, land or other property to be held on trust, either for the general or any specific purposes of the NHS trust or for all or any purposes relating to the health service; and

(d)   to employ staff on such terms as the trust thinks fit.

(2)   The reference in sub-paragraph (1)(c) above to specific purposes of the NHS trust includes a reference to the purposes of a specific hospital or other establishment or facility which is owned and managed by the trust.

Status

18.   An NHS trust shall not be regarded as the servant or agent of the Crown or, except as provided by this Act, as enjoying any status, immunity or privilege of the Crown; and an NHS trust's property shall not be regarded as property of, or property held on behalf of, the Crown.

HUMAN FERTILISATION AND EMBRYOLOGY ACT 1990
(1990, c. 37)

Principal terms used

1.   Meaning of "embryo", "gamete" and associated expressions
(1)   In this Act, except where otherwise stated—
(a)   embryo means a live human embryo where fertilisation is complete, and
(b)   references to an embryo include an egg in the process of fertilisation,
and, for this purpose, fertilisation is not complete until the appearance of a two cell zygote.

(2)   This Act, so far as it governs bringing about the creation of an embryo, applies only to bringing about the creation of an embryo outside the human body; and in this Act—
(a)   references to embryos the creation of which was brought about *in vitro* (in their application to those where fertilisation is complete) are to those where fertilisation began outside the human body whether or not it was completed there, and
(b)   references to embryos taken from a woman do not include embryos whose creation was brought about *in vitro*.

(3)   This Act, so far as it governs the keeping or use of an embryo, applies only to keeping or using an embryo outside the human body.

(4)   References in this Act to gametes, eggs or sperm, except where otherwise stated, are to live human gametes, eggs or sperm but references below in this Act to gametes or eggs do not include eggs in the process of fertilisation.

2.   Other terms
(1)   In this Act—
"the Authority" means the Human Fertilisation and Embryology Authority established under section 5 of this Act,
"directions" means directions under section 23 of this Act,
"licence" means a licence under Schedule 2 to this Act and, in relation to a licence, "the person responsible" has the meaning given by section 17 of this Act, and
"treatment services" means medical, surgical or obstetric services provided to the public or a section of the public for the purpose of assisting women to carry children.

(2)   References in this Act to keeping, in relation to embryos or gametes, include keeping while preserved, whether preserved by cryopreservation or in any other way; and embryos or gametes so kept are referred to in this Act as "stored" (and "store" and "storage" are to be interpreted accordingly).

(3)   For the purposes of this Act, a woman is not to be treated as carrying a child until the embryo has become implanted.

Activities governed by the Act

3. Prohibitions in connection with embryos

(1) No person shall—
    (a) bring about the creation of an embryo, or
    (b) keep or use an embryo,
except in pursuance of a licence.

(2) No person shall place in a woman—
    (a) a live embryo other than a human embryo, or
    (b) any live gametes other than human gametes.

(3) A licence cannot authorise—
    (a) keeping or using an embryo after the appearance of the primitive streak,
    (b) placing an embryo in any animal,
    (c) keeping or using an embryo in any circumstances in which regulations prohibit its keeping or use, or
    (d) replacing a nucleus of a cell of an embryo with a nucleus taken from a cell of any person, embryo or subsequent development of an embryo.

(4) For the purposes of subsection (3)(a) above, the primitive streak is to be taken to have appeared in an embryo not later than the end of the period of 14 days beginning with the day when the gametes are mixed, not counting any time during which the embryo is stored.

4. Prohibitions in connection with gametes

(1) No person shall—
    (a) store any gametes, or
    (b) in the course of providing treatment services for any woman, use the sperm of any man unless the services are being provided for the woman and the man together or use the eggs of any other woman, or
    (c) mix gametes with the live gametes of any animal,
except in pursuance of a licence.

(2) A licence cannot authorise storing or using gametes in any circumstances in which regulations prohibit their storage or use.

(3) No person shall place sperm and eggs in a woman in any circumstances specified in regulations except in pursuance of a licence.

(4) Regulations made by virtue of subsection (3) above may provide that, in relation to licences only to place sperm and eggs in a woman in such circumstances, sections 12 to 22 of this Act shall have effect with such modifications as may be specified in the regulations.

(5) Activities regulated by this section or section 3 of this Act are referred to in this Act as "activities governed by this Act".

The Human Fertilisation and Embryology Authority, its functions and procedure

5. The Human Fertilisation and Embryology Authority

(1) There shall be a body corporate called the Human Fertilisation and Embryology Authority.

(2) The Authority shall consist of—
    (a) a chairman and deputy chairman, and
    (b) such number of other members as the Secretary of State appoints.

(3) Schedule 1 to this Act (which deals with the membership of the Authority, etc.) shall have effect.

6. Accounts and audit

(1) The Authority shall keep proper accounts and proper records in relation to the accounts and shall prepare for each accounting year a statement of accounts.

(2)   The annual statement of accounts shall comply with any direction given by the Secretary of State, with the approval of the Treasury, as to the information to be contained in the statement, the way in which the information is to be presented or the methods and principles according to which the statement is to be prepared.

(3)   Not later than five months after the end of an accounting year, the Authority shall send a copy of the statement of accounts for that year to the Secretary of State and to the Comptroller and Auditor General.

(4)   The Comptroller and Auditor General shall examine, certify and report on every statement of accounts received by him under subsection (3) above and shall lay a copy of the statement and of his report before each House of Parliament.

(5)   The Secretary of State and the Comptroller and Auditor General may inspect any records relating to the accounts.

(6)   In this section "accounting year" means the period beginning with the day when the Authority is established and ending with the following 31st March, or any later period of twelve months ending with the 31st March.

7.   Reports to Secretary of State

(1)   The Authority shall prepare a report for the first twelve months of its existence, and a report for each succeeding period of twelve months, and shall send each report to the Secretary of State as soon as practicable after the end of the period for which it is prepared.

(2)   A report prepared under this section for any period shall deal with the activities of the Authority in the period and the activities the Authority proposes to undertake in the succeeding period of twelve months.

(3)   The Secretary of State shall lay before each House of Parliament a copy of every report received by him under this section.

8.   General functions of the Authority

The Authority shall—

(a)   keep under review information about embryos and any subsequent development of embryos and about the provision of treatment services and activities governed by this Act, and advise the Secretary of State, if he asks it to do so, about those matters,

(b)   publicise the services provided to the public by the Authority or provided in pursuance of licences,

(c)   provide, to such extent as it considers appropriate, advice and information for persons to whom licences apply or who are receiving treatment services or providing gametes or embryos for use for the purposes of activities governed by this Act, or may wish to do so, and

(d)   perform such other functions as may be specified in regulations.

9.   Licence committees and other committees

(1)   The Authority shall maintain one or more committees to discharge the Authority's functions relating to the grant, variation, suspension and revocation of licences, and a committee discharging those functions is referred to in this Act as a "licence committee".

(2)   The Authority may provide for the discharge of any of its other functions by committees or by members or employees of the Authority.

(3)   A committee (other than a licence committee) may appoint sub-committees.

(4)   Persons, committees or sub-committees discharging functions of the Authority shall do so in accordance with any general directions of the Authority.

(5)   A licence committee shall consist of such number of persons as may be specified in or determined in accordance with regulations, all being members of the Authority, and shall include at least one person who is not authorised to carry on or participate in

any activity under the authority of a licence and would not be so authorised if outstanding applications were granted.

(6) A committee (other than a licence committee) or a sub-committee may include a minority of persons who are not members of the Authority.

(7) Subject to subsection (10) below, a licence committee, before considering an application for authority—

    (a) for a person to carry on an activity governed by this Act which he is not then authorised to carry on, or

    (b) for a person to carry on any such activity on premises where he is not then authorised to carry it on,

shall arrange for the premises where the activity is to be carried on to be inspected on its behalf, and for a report on the inspection to be made to it.

(8) Subject to subsection (9) below, a licence committee shall arrange for any premises to which a licence relates to be inspected on its behalf once in each calendar year, and for a report on the inspection to be made to it.

(9) Any particular premises need not be inspected in any particular year if the licence committee considers an inspection in that year unnecessary.

(10) A licence committee need not comply with subsection (7) above where the premises in question have been inspected in pursuance of that subsection or subsection (8) above at some time during the period of one year ending with the date of the application, and the licence committee considers that a further inspection is not necessary.

(11) An inspection in pursuance of subsection (7) or (8) above may be carried out by a person who is not a member of a licence committee.

10. Licensing procedure

(1) Regulations may make such provision as appears to the Secretary of State to be necessary or desirable about the proceedings of licence committees and of the Authority on any appeal from such a committee.

(2) The regulations may in particular include provision—

    (a) for requiring persons to give evidence or to produce documents, and

    (b) about the admissibility of evidence.

Scope of licences

11. Licences for treatment, storage and research

(1) The Authority may grant the following and no other licences—

    (a) licences under paragraph 1 of Schedule 2 to this Act authorising activities in the course of providing treatment services,

    (b) licences under that Schedule authorising the storage of gametes and embryos, and

    (c) licences under paragraph 3 of that Schedule authorising activities for the purpose of a project of research.

(2) Paragraph 4 of that Schedule has effect in the case of all licences.

Licence conditions

12. General conditions

The following shall be conditions of every licence granted under this Act—

    (a) that the activities authorised by the licence shall be carried on only on the premises to which the licence relates and under the supervision of the person responsible,

    (b) that any member or employee of the Authority, on production, if so required, of a document identifying the person as such, shall at all reasonable times be permitted to enter those premises and inspect them (which includes inspecting any equipment or records and observing any activity),

(c)   that the provisions of Schedule 3 to this Act shall be complied with,

(d)   that proper records shall be maintained in such form as the Authority may specify in directions,

(e)   that no money or other benefit shall be given or received in respect of any supply of gametes or embryos unless authorised by directions,

(f)   that, where gametes or embryos are supplied to a person to whom another licence applies, that person shall also be provided with such information as the Authority may specify in directions, and

(g)   that the Authority shall be provided, in such form and at such intervals as it may specify in directions, with such copies of or extracts from the records, or such other information, as the directions may specify.

13.   Conditions of licences for treatment

(1)   The following shall be conditions of every licence under paragraph 1 of Schedule 2 to this Act.

(2)   Such information shall be recorded as the Authority may specify in directions about the following—

(a)   the persons for whom services are provided in pursuance of the licence,

(b)   the services provided for them,

(c)   the persons whose gametes are kept or used for the purposes of services provided in pursuance of the licence or whose gametes have been used in bringing about the creation of embryos so kept or used,

(d)   any child appearing to the person responsible to have been born as a result of treatment in pursuance of the licence,

(e)   any mixing of egg and sperm and any taking of an embryo from a woman or other acquisition of an embryo, and

(f)   such other matters as the Authority may specify in directions.

(3)   The records maintained in pursuance of the licence shall include any information recorded in pursuance of subsection (2) above and any consent of a person whose consent is required under Schedule 3 to this Act.

(4)   No information shall be removed from any records maintained in pursuance of the licence before the expiry of such period as may be specified in directions for records of the class in question.

(5)   A woman shall not be provided with treatment services unless account has been taken of the welfare of any child who may be born as a result of the treatment (including the need of that child for a father), and of any other child who may be affected by the birth.

(6)   A woman shall not be provided with any treatment services involving—

(a)   the use of any gametes of any person, if that person's consent is required under paragraph 5 of Schedule 3 to this Act for the use in question,

(b)   the use of any embryo the creation of which was brought about *in vitro*, or

(c)   the use of any embryo taken from a woman, if the consent of the woman from whom it was taken is required under paragraph 7 of that Schedule for the use in question,

unless the woman being treated and, where she is being treated together with a man, the man have been given a suitable opportunity to receive proper counselling about the implications of taking the proposed steps, and have been provided with such relevant information as is proper.

(7)   Suitable procedures shall be maintained—

(a)   for determining the persons providing gametes or from whom embryos are taken for use in pursuance of the licence, and

(b)   for the purpose of securing that consideration is given to the use of practices not requiring the authority of a licence as well as those requiring such authority.

14.   Conditions of storage licences

(1)   The following shall be conditions of every licence authorising the storage of gametes or embryos—

(a)   that gametes of a person or an embryo taken from a woman shall be placed in storage only if received from that person or woman or acquired from a person to whom a licence applies and that an embryo the creation of which has been brought about *in vitro* otherwise than in pursuance of that licence shall be placed in storage only if acquired from a person to whom a licence applies,

(b)   that gametes or embryos which are or have been stored shall not be supplied to a person otherwise than in the course of providing treatment services unless that person is a person to whom a licence applies,

(c)   that no gametes or embryos shall be kept in storage for longer than the statutory storage period and, if stored at the end of the period, shall be allowed to perish, and

(d)   that such information as the Authority may specify in directions as to the persons whose consent is required under Schedule 3 to this Act, the terms of their consent and the circumstances of the storage and as to such other matters as the Authority may specify in directions shall be included in the records maintained in pursuance of the licence.

(2)   No information shall be removed from any record maintained in pursuance of such a licence before the expiry of such period as may be specified in directions for records of the class in question.

(3)   The statutory storage period in respect of gametes is such period not exceeding ten years as the licence may specify.

(4)   The statutory storage period in respect of embryos is such period not exceeding five years as the licence may specify.

(5)   Regulations may provide that subsection (3) or (4) above shall have effect as if for ten years or, as the case may be, five years there were substituted—

(a)   such shorter period, or

(b)   in such circumstances as may be specified in the regulations, such longer period,

as may be specified in the regulations.

15.   Conditions of research licences

(1)   The following shall be conditions of every licence under paragraph 3 of Schedule 2 to this Act.

(2)   The records maintained in pursuance of the licence shall include such information as the Authority may specify in directions about such matters as the Authority may so specify.

(3)   No information shall be removed from any records maintained in pursuance of the licence before the expiry of such period as may be specified in directions for records of the class in question.

(4)   No embryo appropriated for the purposes of any project of research shall be kept or used otherwise than for the purposes of such a project.

Grant, revocation and suspension of licences

16.   Grant of licence

(1)   Where application is made to the Authority in a form approved for the purpose by it accompanied by the initial fee, a licence may be granted to any person by a licence committee if the requirements of subsection (2) below are met and any additional fee is paid.

(2)   The requirements mentioned in subsection (1) above are—

(a)   that the application is for a licence designating an individual as the person under whose supervision the activities to be authorised by the licence are to be carried on,

(b)   that either that individual is the applicant or—

(i)   the application is made with the consent of that individual, and

(ii)   the licence committee is satisfied that the applicant is a suitable person to hold a licence,

(c)   that the licence committee is satisfied that the character, qualifications and experience of that individual are such as are required for the supervision of the activities and that the individual will discharge the duty under section 17 of this Act,

(d)   that the licence committee is satisfied that the premises in respect of which the licence is to be granted are suitable for the activities, and

(e)   that all the other requirements of this Act in relation to the granting of the licence are satisfied.

(3)   The grant of a licence to any person may be by way of renewal of a licence granted to that person, whether on the same or different terms.

(4)   Where the licence committee is of the opinion that the information provided in the application is insufficient to enable it to determine the application, it need not consider the application until the applicant has provided it with such further information as it may require him to provide.

(5)   The licence committee shall not grant a licence unless a copy of the conditions to be imposed by the licence has been shown to, and acknowledged in writing by, the applicant and (where different) the person under whose supervision the activities are to be carried on.

(6)   In subsection (1) above "initial fee" and "additional fee" mean a fee of such amount as may be fixed from time to time by the Authority with the approval of the Secretary of State and the Treasury, and in determining any such amount, the Authority may have regard to the costs of performing all its functions.

(7)   Different fees may be fixed for different circumstances and fees paid under this section are not repayable.

17.   The person responsible

(1)   It shall be the duty of the individual under whose supervision the activities authorised by a licence are carried on (referred to in this Act as the "person responsible") to secure—

(a)   that the other persons to whom the licence applies are of such character, and are so qualified by training and experience, as to be suitable persons to participate in the activities authorised by the licence,

(b)   that proper equipment is used,

(c)   that proper arrangements are made for the keeping of gametes and embryos and for the disposal of gametes or embryos that have been allowed to perish,

(d)   that suitable practices are used in the course of the activities, and

(e)   that the conditions of the licence are complied with.

(2)   References in this Act to the persons to whom a licence applies are to—

(a)   the person responsible,

(b)   any person designated in the licence, or in a notice given to the Authority by the person who holds the licence or the person responsible, as a person to whom the licence applies, and

(c)   any person acting under the direction of the person responsible or of any person so designated.

(3)   References below in this Act to the nominal licensee are to a person who holds a licence under which a different person is the person responsible.

18. Revocation and variation of licence

(1) A licence committee may revoke a licence if it is satisfied—

(a) that any information given for the purposes of the application for the grant of the licence was in any material respect false or misleading,

(b) that the premises to which the licence relates are no longer suitable for the activities authorised by the licence,

(c) that the person responsible has failed to discharge, or is unable because of incapacity to discharge, the duty under section 17 of this Act or has failed to comply with directions given in connection with any licence, or

(d) that there has been any other material change of circumstances since the licence was granted.

(2) A licence committee may also revoke a licence if—

(a) it ceases to be satisfied that the character of the person responsible is such as is required for the supervision of those activities or that the nominal licensee is a suitable person to hold a licence, or

(b) the person responsible dies or is convicted of an offence under this Act.

(3) Where a licence committee has power to revoke a licence under subsection (1) above it may instead vary any terms of the licence.

(4) A licence committee may, on an application by the person responsible or the nominal licensee, vary or revoke a licence.

(5) A licence committee may, on an application by the nominal licensee, vary the licence so as to designate another individual in place of the person responsible if—

(a) the committee is satisfied that the character, qualifications and experience of the other individual are such as are required for the supervision of the activities authorised by the licence and that the individual will discharge the duty under section 17 of this Act, and

(b) the application is made with the consent of the other individual.

(6) Except on an application under subsection (5) above, a licence can only be varied under this section—

(a) so far as it relates to the activities authorised by the licence, the manner in which they are conducted or the conditions of the licence, or

(b) so as to extend or restrict the premises to which the licence relates.

19. Procedure for refusal, variation or revocation of licence

(1) Where a licence committee proposes to refuse a licence or to refuse to vary a licence so as to designate another individual in place of the person responsible, the committee shall give notice of the proposal, the reasons for it and the effect of subsection (3) below to the applicant.

(2) Where a licence committee proposes to vary or revoke a licence, the committee shall give notice of the proposal, the reasons for it and the effect of subsection (3) below to the person responsible and the nominal licensee (but not to any person who has applied for the variation or revocation).

(3) If, within the period of twenty-eight days beginning with the day on which notice of the proposal is given, any person to whom notice was given under subsection (1) or (2) above gives notice to the committee of a wish to make to the committee representations about the proposal in any way mentioned in subsection (4) below, the committee shall, before making its determination, give the person an opportunity to make representations in that way.

(4) The representations may be—

(a) oral representations made by the person, or another acting on behalf of the person, at a meeting of the committee, and

(b) written representations made by the person.

(5) A licence committee shall—

(a) in the case of a determination to grant a licence, give notice of the determination to the person responsible and the nominal licensee,

(b) in the case of a determination to refuse a licence, or to refuse to vary a licence so as to designate another individual in place of the person responsible, give such notice to the applicant, and

(c) in the case of a determination to vary or revoke a licence, give such notice to the person responsible and the nominal licensee.

(6) A licence committee giving notice of a determination to refuse a licence or to refuse to vary a licence so as to designate another individual in place of the person responsible, or of a determination to vary or revoke a licence otherwise than on an application by the person responsible or the nominal licensee, shall give in the notice the reasons for its decision.

20. Appeal to Authority against determinations of licence committee

(1) Where a licence committee determines to refuse a licence or to refuse to vary a licence so as to designate another individual in place of the person responsible, the applicant may appeal to the Authority if notice has been given to the committee and to the Authority before the end of the period of twenty-eight days beginning with the date on which notice of the committee's determination was served on the applicant.

(2) Where a licence committee determines to vary or revoke a licence, any person on whom notice of the determination was served (other than a person who applied for the variation or revocation) may appeal to the Authority if notice has been given to the committee and to the Authority before the end of the period of twenty-eight days beginning with the date on which notice of the committee's determination was served.

(3) An appeal under this section shall be by way of rehearing by the Authority and no member of the Authority who took any part in the proceedings resulting in the determination appealed against shall take any part in the proceedings on appeal.

(4) On the appeal—

(a) the appellant shall be entitled to appear or be represented,

(b) the members of the licence committee shall be entitled to appear, or the committee shall be entitled to be represented, and

(c) the Authority shall consider any written representations received from the appellant or any member of the committee and may take into account any matter that could be taken into account by a licence committee,

and the Authority may make such determination on the appeal as it thinks fit.

(5) The Authority shall give notice of its determination to the appellant and, if it is a determination to refuse a licence or to refuse to vary a licence so as to designate another individual in place of the person responsible or a determination to vary or revoke a licence, shall include in the notice the reasons for the decision.

(6) The functions of the Authority on an appeal under this section cannot be discharged by any committee, member or employee of the Authority and, for the purposes of the appeal, the quorum shall not be less than five.

21. Appeals to High Court or Court of Session

Where the Authority determines under section 20 of this Act—

(a) to refuse a licence or to refuse to vary a licence so as to designate another individual in place of the person responsible, or

(b) to vary or revoke a licence,

any person on whom notice of the determination was served may appeal to the High Court or, in Scotland, the Court of Session on a point of law.

22. Temporary suspension of licence

(1) Where a licence committee—

(a) has reasonable grounds to suspect that there are grounds for revoking the licence under section 18 of this Act, and

(b) is of the opinion that the licence should immediately be suspended,

it may by notice suspend the licence for such period not exceeding three months as may be specified in the notice.

(2) Notice under subsection (1) above shall be given to the person responsible or, where the person responsible has died or appears to the licence committee to be unable because of incapacity to discharge the duty under section 17 of this Act, to some other person to whom the licence applies or the nominal licensee and a licence committee may, by a further notice to that person, renew or further renew the notice under subsection (1) above for such further period not exceeding three months as may be specified in the renewal notice.

(3) While suspended under this section a licence shall be of no effect, but application may be made under section 18(5) of this Act by the nominal licensee to designate another individual as the person responsible.

Directions and guidance

23. Directions: general

(1) The Authority may from time to time give directions for any purpose for which directions may be given under this Act or directions varying or revoking such directions.

(2) A person to whom any requirement contained in directions is applicable shall comply with the requirement.

(3) Anything done by a person in pursuance of directions is to be treated for the purposes of this Act as done in pursuance of a licence.

(4) Where directions are to be given to a particular person, they shall be given by serving notice of the directions on the person.

(5) In any other case, directions may be given—

(a) in respect of any licence (including a licence which has ceased to have effect), by serving notice of the directions on the person who is or was the person responsible or the nominal licensee, or

(b) if the directions appear to the Authority to be general directions or it appears to the Authority that it is not practicable to give notice in pursuance of paragraph (a) above, by publishing the directions in such way as, in the opinion of the Authority, is likely to bring the directions to the attention of the persons to whom they are applicable.

(6) This section does not apply to directions under section 9(4) of this Act.

24. Directions as to particular matters

(1) If, in the case of any information about persons for whom treatment services were provided, the person responsible does not know that any child was born following the treatment, the period specified in directions by virtue of section 13(4) of this Act shall not expire less than 50 years after the information was first recorded.

(2) In the case of every licence under paragraph 1 of Schedule 2 to this Act, directions shall require information to be recorded and given to the Authority about each of the matters referred to in section 13(2)(a) to (e) of this Act.

(3) Directions may authorise, in such circumstances and subject to such conditions as may be specified in the directions, the keeping, by or on behalf of a person to whom a licence applies, of gametes or embryos in the course of their carriage to or from any premises.

(4) Directions may authorise any person to whom a licence applies to receive gametes or embryos from outside the United Kingdom or to send gametes or embryos outside the United Kingdom in such circumstances and subject to such conditions as

may be specified in the directions, and directions made by virtue of this subsection may provide for sections 12 to 14 of this Act to have effect with such modifications as may be specified in the directions.

(5) A licence committee may from time to time give such directions as are mentioned in subsection (7) below where a licence has been varied or has ceased to have effect (whether by expiry, suspension, revocation or otherwise).

(6) A licence committee proposing to suspend, revoke or vary a licence may give such directions as are mentioned in subsection (7) below.

(7) The directions referred to in subsections (5) and (6) above are directions given for the purpose of securing the continued discharge of the duties of the person responsible under the licence concerned ("the old licence"), and such directions may, in particular—

(a) require anything kept or information held in pursuance of the old licence to be transferred to the Authority or any other person, or

(b) provide for the discharge of the duties in question by any individual, being an individual whose character, qualifications and experience are, in the opinion of the committee, such as are required for the supervision of the activities authorised by the old licence, and authorise those activities to be carried on under the supervision of that individual,

but cannot require any individual to discharge any of those duties unless the individual has consented in writing to do so.

(8) Directions for the purpose referred to in subsection (7)(a) above shall be given to the person responsible under the old licence or, where that person has died or appears to the licence committee to have become unable because of incapacity to discharge the duties in question, to some other person to whom the old licence applies or applied or to the nominal licensee.

(9) Directions for the purpose referred to in subsection (7)(b) above shall be given to the individual who under the directions is to discharge the duty.

(10) Where a person who holds a licence dies, anything done subsequently by an individual which that individual would have been authorised to do if the licence had continued in force shall, until directions are given by virtue of this section, be treated as authorised by a licence.

(11) Where the Authority proposes to give directions specifying any animal for the purposes of paragraph 1(1)(f) or 3(5) of Schedule 2 to this Act, it shall report the proposal to the Secretary of State; and the directions shall not be given until the Secretary of State has laid a copy of the report before each House of Parliament.

25. Code of practice

(1) The Authority shall maintain a code of practice giving guidance about the proper conduct of activities carried on in pursuance of a licence under this Act and the proper discharge of the functions of the person responsible and other persons to whom the licence applies.

(2) The guidance given by the code shall include guidance for those providing treatment services about the account to be taken of the welfare of children who may be born as a result of treatment services (including a child's need for a father), and of other children who may be affected by such births.

(3) The code may also give guidance about the use of any technique involving the placing of sperm and eggs in a woman.

(4) The Authority may from time to time revise the whole or any part of the code.

(5) The Authority shall publish the code as for the time being in force.

(6) A failure on the part of any person to observe any provision of the code shall not of itself render the person liable to any proceedings, but—

(a) a licence committee shall, in considering whether there has been any failure to comply with any conditions of a licence and, in particular, conditions requiring anything to be "proper" or "suitable", take account of any relevant provision of the code, and

(b) a licence committee may, in considering, where it has power to do so, whether or not to vary or revoke a licence, take into account any observance of or failure to observe the provisions of the code.

26. Procedure for approval of code

(1) The Authority shall send a draft of the proposed first code of practice under section 25 of this Act to the Secretary of State within twelve months of the commencement of section 5 of this Act.

(2) If the Authority proposes to revise the code or, if the Secretary of State does not approve a draft of the proposed first code, to submit a further draft, the Authority shall send a draft of the revised code or, as the case may be, a further draft of the proposed first code to the Secretary of State.

(3) Before preparing any draft, the Authority shall consult such persons as the Secretary of State may require it to consult and such other persons (if any) as it considers appropriate.

(4) If the Secretary of State approves a draft, he shall lay it before Parliament and, if he does not approve it, he shall give reasons to the Authority.

(5) A draft approved by the Secretary of State shall come into force in accordance with directions.

Status

27. Meaning of "mother"

(1) The woman who is carrying or has carried a child as a result of the placing in her of an embryo or of sperm and eggs, and no other woman, is to be treated as the mother of the child.

(2) Subsection (1) above does not apply to any child to the extent that the child is treated by virtue of adoption as not being the child of any person other than the adopter or adopters.

(3) Subsection (1) above applies whether the woman was in the United Kingdom or elsewhere at the time of the placing in her of the embryo or the sperm and eggs.

28. Meaning of "father"

(1) This section applies in the case of a child who is being or has been carried by a woman as the result of the placing in her of an embryo or of sperm and eggs or her artificial insemination.

(2) If—

(a) at the time of the placing in her of the embryo or the sperm and eggs or of her insemination, the woman was a party to a marriage, and

(b) the creation of the embryo carried by her was not brought about with the sperm of the other party to the marriage,

then, subject to subsection (5) below, the other party to the marriage shall be treated as the father of the child unless it is shown that he did not consent to the placing in her of the embryo or the sperm and eggs or to her insemination (as the case may be).

(3) If no man is treated, by virtue of subsection (2) above, as the father of the child but—

(a) the embryo or the sperm and eggs were placed in the woman, or she was artificially inseminated, in the course of treatment services provided for her and a man together by a person to whom a licence applies, and

(b) the creation of the embryo carried by her was not brought about with the sperm of that man,

then, subject to subsection (5) below, that man shall be treated as the father of the child.

(4) Where a person is treated as the father of the child by virtue of subsection (2) or (3) above, no other person is to be treated as the father of the child.

(5)   Subsections (2) and (3) above do not apply—

(a)   in relation to England and Wales and Northern Ireland, to any child who, by virtue of the rules of common law, is treated as the legitimate child of the parties to a marriage,

(b)   in relation to Scotland, to any child who, by virtue of any enactment or other rule of law, is treated as the child of the parties to a marriage, or

(c)   to any child to the extent that the child is treated by virtue of adoption as not being the child of any person other than the adopter or adopters.

(6)   Where—

(a)   the sperm of a man who had given such consent as is required by paragraph 5 of Schedule 3 to this Act was used for a purpose for which such consent was required, or

(b)   the sperm of a man, or any embryo the creation of which was brought about with his sperm, was used after his death,

he is not to be treated as the father of the child.

(7)   The references in subsection (2) above to the parties to a marriage at the time there referred to—

(a)   are to the parties to a marriage subsisting at that time, unless a judicial separation was then in force, but

(b)   include the parties to a void marriage if either or both of them reasonably believed at that time that the marriage was valid; and for the purposes of this subsection it shall be presumed, unless the contrary is shown, that one of them reasonably believed at the time that the marriage was valid.

(8)   This section applies whether the woman was in the United Kingdom or elsewhere at the time of the placing in her of the embryo or the sperm and eggs or her artificial insemination.

(9)   In subsection (7)(a) above, "judicial separation" includes a legal separation obtained in a country outside the British Islands and recognised in the United Kingdom.

29.   Effect of sections 27 and 28

(1)   Where by virtue of section 27 or 28 of this Act a person is to be treated as the mother or father of a child, that person is to be treated in law as the mother or, as the case may be, father of the child for all purposes.

(2)   Where by virtue of section 27 or 28 of this Act a person is not be be treated as the mother or father of a child, that person is to be treated in law as not being the mother or, as the case may be, father of the child for any purpose.

(3)   Where subsection (1) or (2) above has effect, references to any relationship between two people in any enactment, deed or other instrument or document (whenever passed or made) are to be read accordingly.

(4)   In relation to England and Wales and Northern Ireland, nothing in the provisions of section 27(1) or 28(2) to (4), read with this section, affects—

(a)   the succession to any dignity or title of honour or renders any person capable of succeeding to or transmitting a right to succeed to any such dignity or title, or

(b)   the devolution of any property limited (expressly or not) to devolve (as nearly as the law permits) along with any dignity or title of honour.

(5)   In relation to Scotland—

(a)   those provisions do not apply to any title, coat of arms, honour or dignity transmissible on the death of the holder thereof or affect the succession thereto or the devolution thereof, and

(b)   where the terms of any deed provide that any property or interest in property shall devolve along with a title, coat of arms, honour or dignity, nothing in those provisions shall prevent that property or interest from so devolving.

30.   Parental orders in favour of gamete donors

(1)   The court may make an order providing for a child to be treated in law as the child of the parties to a marriage (referred to in this section as "the husband" and "the wife") if—

    (a)   the child has been carried by a woman other than the wife as the result of the placing in her of an embryo or sperm and eggs or her artificial insemination,

    (b)   the gametes of the husband or the wife, or both, were used to bring about the creation of the embryo, and

    (c)   the conditions in subsections (2) to (7) below are satisfied.

(2)   The husband and the wife must apply for the order within six months of the birth of the child or, in the case of a child born before the coming into force of this Act, within six months of such coming into force.

(3)   At the time of the application and of the making of the order—

    (a)   the child's home must be with the husband and the wife, and

    (b)   the husband or the wife, or both of them, must be domiciled in a part of the United Kingdom or in the Channel Islands or the Isle of Man.

(4)   At the time of the making of the order both the husband and the wife must have attained the age of eighteen.

(5)   The court must be satisfied that both the father of the child (including a person who is the father by virtue of section 28 of this Act), where he is not the husband, and the woman who carried the child have freely, and with full understanding of what is involved, agreed unconditionally to the making of the order.

(6)   Subsection (5) above does not require the agreement of a person who cannot be found or is incapable of giving agreement and the agreement of the woman who carried the child is ineffective for the purposes of that subsection if given by her less than six weeks after the child's birth.

(7)   The court must be satisfied that no money or other benefit (other than for expenses reasonably incurred) has been given or received by the husband or the wife for or in consideration of—

    (a)   the making of the order,

    (b)   any agreement required by subsection (5) above,

    (c)   the handing over of the child to the husband and the wife, or

    (d)   the making of any arrangements with a view to the making of the order,

unless authorised by the court.

(8)   For the purposes of an application under this section—

    (a)   in relation to England and Wales, section 92(7) to (10) of, and Part I of Schedule 11 to, the Children Act 1989 (jurisdiction of courts) shall apply for the purposes of this section to determine the meaning of "the court" as they apply for the purposes of that Act and proceedings on the application shall be "family proceedings" for the purposes of that Act,

    (b)   in relation to Scotland, "the court" means the Court of Session or the sheriff court of the sheriffdom within which the child is, and

    (c)   in relation to Northern Ireland, "the court" means the High Court or any county court within whose division the child is.

(9)   Regulations may provide—

    (a)   for any provision of the enactments about adoption to have effect, with such modifications (if any) as may be specified in the regulations, in relation to orders under this section, and applications for such orders, as it has effect in relation to adoption, and applications for adoption orders, and

    (b)   for references in any enactment to adoption, an adopted child or an adoptive relationship to be read (respectively) as references to the effect of an order under this section, a child to whom such an order applies and a relationship arising by virtue of the enactments about adoption, as applied by the regulations, and for similar expressions in connection with adoption to be read accordingly, and the regulations may include such incidental or supplemental provision as appears to the Secretary of State necessary or desirable in consequence of any provision made by virtue of paragraph (a) or (b) above.

(10) In this section "the enactments about adoption" means the Adoption Act 1976, the Adoption (Scotland) Act 1978 and the Adoption (Northern Ireland) Order 1987.

(11) Subsection (1)(a) above applies whether the woman was in the United Kingdom or elsewhere at the time of the placing in her of the embryo or the sperm and eggs or her artificial insemination.

Information

31. The Authority's register of information

(1) The Authority shall keep a register which shall contain any information obtained by the Authority which falls within subsection (2) below.

(2) Information falls within this subsection if it relates to—
    (a) the provision of treatment services for any identifiable individual, or
    (b) the keeping or use of the gametes of any identifiable individual or of an embryo taken from any identifiable woman,
or if it shows that any identifiable individual was, or may have been, born in consequence of treatment services.

(3) A person who has attained the age of eighteen ("the applicant") may by notice to the Authority require the Authority to comply with a request under subsection (4) below, and the Authority shall do so if—
    (a) the information contained in the register shows that the applicant was, or may have been, born in consequence of treatment services, and
    (b) the applicant has been given a suitable opportunity to receive proper counselling about the implications of compliance with the request.

(4) The applicant may request the Authority to give the applicant notice stating whether or not the information contained in the register shows that a person other than a parent of the applicant would or might, but for sections 27 to 29 of this Act, be a parent of the applicant and, if it does show that—
    (a) giving the applicant so much of that information as relates to the person concerned as the Authority is required by regulations to give (but no other information), or
    (b) stating whether or not that information shows that, but for sections 27 to 29 of this Act, the applicant, and a person specified in the request as a person whom the applicant proposes to marry, would or might be related.

(5) Regulations cannot require the Authority to give any information as to the identity of a person whose gametes have been used or from whom an embryo has been taken if a person to whom a licence applied was provided with the information at a time when the Authority could not have been required to give information of the kind in question.

(6) A person who has not attained the age of eighteen ("the minor") may by notice to the Authority specifying another person ("the intended spouse") as a person whom the minor proposes to marry require the Authority to comply with a request under subsection (7) below, and the Authority shall do so if—
    (a) the information contained in the register shows that the minor was, or may have been, born in consequence of treatment services, and
    (b) the minor has been given a suitable opportunity to receive proper counselling about the implications of compliance with the request.

(7) The minor may request the Authority to give the minor notice stating whether or not the information contained in the register shows that, but for sections 27 to 29 of this Act, the minor and the intended spouse would or might be related.

32. Information to be provided to Registrar General
    (1)   This section applies where a claim is made before the Registrar General that a man is or is not the father of a child and it is necessary or desirable for the purpose of any function of the Registrar General to determine whether the claim is or may be well-founded.
    (2)   The Authority shall comply with any request made by the Registrar General by notice to the Authority to disclose whether any information on the register kept in pursuance of section 31 of this Act tends to show that the man may be the father of the child by virtue of section 28 of this Act and, if it does, disclose that information.
    (3)   In this section and section 33 of this Act, "the Registrar General" means the Registrar General for England and Wales, the Registrar General of Births, Deaths and Marriages for Scotland or the Registrar General for Northern Ireland, as the case may be.

33. Restrictions on disclosure of information
    (1)   No person who is or has been a member or employee of the Authority shall disclose any information mentioned in subsection (2) below which he holds or has held as such a member or employee.
    (2)   The information referred to in subsection (1) above is—
    (a)   any information contained or required to be contained in the register kept in pursuance of section 31 of this Act, and
    (b)   any other information obtained by any member or employee of the Authority on terms or in circumstances requiring it to be held in confidence.
    (3)   Subsection (1) above does not apply to any disclosure of information mentioned in subsection (2)(a) above made—
    (a)   to a person as a member or employee of the Authority,
    (b)   to a person to whom a licence applies for the purposes of his functions as such,
    (c)   so that no individual to whom the information relates can be identified,
    (d)   in pursuance of an order of a court under section 34 or 35 of this Act,
    (e)   to the Registrar General in pursuance of a request under section 32 of this Act, or
    (f)   in accordance with section 31 of this Act.
    (4)   Subsection (1) above does not apply to any disclosure of information mentioned in subsection (2)(b) above—
    (a)   made to a person as a member or employee of the Authority,
    (b)   made with the consent of the person or persons whose confidence would otherwise be protected, or
    (c)   which has been lawfully made available to the public before the disclosure is made.
    (5)   No person who is or has been a person to whom a licence applies and no person to whom directions have been given shall disclose any information falling within section 31(2) of this Act which he holds or has held as such a person.
    (6)   Subsection (5) above does not apply to any disclosure of information made—
    (a)   to a person as a member or employee of the Authority,
    (b)   to a person to whom a licence applies for the purposes of his functions as such,
    (c)   so far as it identifies a person who, but for sections 27 to 29 of this Act, would or might be a parent of a person who instituted proceedings under section 1A of the Congenital Disabilities (Civil Liability) Act 1976, but only for the purpose of defending such proceedings, or instituting connected proceedings for compensation against that parent,
    (d)   so that no individual to whom the information relates can be identified, or

(e)   in pursuance of directions given by virtue of section 24(5) or (6) of this Act.

(7)   This section does not apply to the disclosure to any individual of information which—

(a)   falls within section 31(2) of this Act by virtue of paragraph (a) or (b) of that subsection, and

(b)   relates only to that individual or, in the case of an individual treated together with another, only to that individual and that other.

34.   Disclosure in interests of justice

(1)   Where in any proceedings before a court the question whether a person is or is not the parent of a child by virtue of sections 27 to 29 of this Act falls to be determined, the court may on the application of any party to the proceedings make an order requiring the Authority—

(a)   to disclose whether or not any information relevant to that question is contained in the register kept in pursuance of section 31 of this Act, and

(b)   if it is, to disclose so much of it as is specified in the order,

but such an order may not require the Authority to disclose any information falling within section 31(2)(b) of this Act.

(2)   The court must not make an order under subsection (1) above unless it is satisfied that the interests of justice require it to do so, taking into account—

(a)   any representations made by any individual who may be affected by the disclosure, and

(b)   the welfare of the child, if under 18 years old, and of any other person under that age who may be affected by the disclosure.

(3)   If the proceedings before the court are civil proceedings, it—

(a)   may direct that the whole or any part of the proceedings on the application for an order under subsection (2) above shall be heard in camera, and

(b)   if it makes such an order, may then or later direct that the whole or any part of any later stage of the proceedings shall be heard in camera.

(4)   An application for a direction under subsection (3) above shall be heard in camera unless the court otherwise directs.

35.   Disclosure in interests of justice: congenital disabilities, etc.

(1)   Where for the purpose of instituting proceedings under section 1 of the Congenital Disabilities (Civil Liability) Act 1976 (civil liability to child born disabled) it is necessary to identify a person who would or might be the parent of a child but for sections 27 to 29 of this Act, the court may, on the application of the child, make an order requiring the Authority to disclose any information contained in the register kept in pursuance of section 31 of this Act identifying that person.

(2)   Where, for the purposes of any action for damages in Scotland (including any such action which is likely to be brought) in which the damages claimed consist of or include damages or solatium in respect of personal injury (including any disease and any impairment of physical or mental condition), it is necessary to identify a person who would or might be the parent of a child but for sections 27 to 29 of this Act, the court may, on the application of any party to the action or, if the proceedings have not been commenced, the prospective pursuer, make an order requiring the Authority to disclose any information contained in the register kept in pursuance of section 31 of this Act identifying that person.

(3)   Subsections (2) to (4) of section 34 of this Act apply for the purposes of this section as they apply for the purposes of that.

Conscientious objection

38.   Conscientious objection

(1)   No person who has a conscientious objection to participating in any activity governed by this Act shall be under any duty, however arising, to do so.

(2)   In any legal proceedings the burden of proof of conscientious objection shall rest on the person claiming to rely on it.

(3)   In any proceedings before a court in Scotland, a statement on oath by any person to the effect that he has a conscientious objection to participating in a particular activity governed by this Act shall be sufficient evidence of that fact for the purpose of discharging the burden of proof imposed by subsection (2) above.

Enforcement

39.   Powers of members and employees of Authority

(1)   Any member or employee of the Authority entering and inspecting premises to which a licence relates may—

(a)   take possession of anything which he has reasonable grounds to believe may be required—

(i)   for the purpose of the functions of the Authority relating to the grant, variation, suspension and revocation of licences, or

(ii)   for the purpose of being used in evidence in any proceedings for an offence under this Act,

and retain it for so long as it may be required for the purpose in question, and

(b)   for the purpose in question, take such steps as appear to be necessary for preserving any such thing or preventing interference with it, including requiring any person having the power to do so to give such assistance as may reasonably be required.

(2)   In subsection (1) above—

(a)   the references to things include information recorded in any form, and

(b)   the reference to taking possession of anything includes, in the case of information recorded otherwise than in legible form, requiring any person having the power to do so to produce a copy of the information in legible form and taking possession of the copy.

(3)   Nothing in this Act makes it unlawful for a member or employee of the Authority to keep any embryo or gametes in pursuance of that person's functions as such.

40.   Power to enter premises

(1)   A justice of the peace (including, in Scotland, a sheriff) may issue a warrant under this section if satisfied by the evidence on oath of a member or employee of the Authority that there are reasonable grounds for suspecting that an offence under this Act is being, or has been, committed on any premises.

(2)   A warrant under this section shall authorise any named member or employee of the Authority (who must, if so required, produce a document identifying himself), together with any constables—

(a)   to enter the premises specified in the warrant, using such force as is reasonably necessary for the purpose, and

(b)   to search the premises and—

(i)   take possession of anything which he has reasonable grounds to believe may be required to be used in evidence in any proceedings for an offence under this Act, or

(ii)   take such steps as appear to be necessary for preserving any such thing or preventing interference with it, including requiring any person having the power to do so to give such assistance as may reasonably be required.

(3)   A warrant under this section shall continue in force until the end of the period of one month beginning with the day on which it is issued.

(4)   Anything of which possession is taken under this section may be retained—

(a)   for a period of six months, or

(b)   if within that period proceedings to which the thing is relevant are commenced against any person for an offence under this Act, until the conclusion of those proceedings.

(5) In this section—

    (a) the references to things include information recorded in any form, and

    (b) the reference in subsection (2)(b)(i) above to taking possession of anything includes, in the case of information recorded otherwise than in legible form, requiring any person having the power to do so to produce a copy of the information in legible form and taking possession of the copy.

Offences

41. Offences

(1) A person who—

    (a) contravenes section 3(2) or 4(1)(c) of this Act, or

    (b) does anything which, by virtue of section 3(3) of this Act, cannot be authorised by a licence,

is guilty of an offence and liable on conviction on indictment to imprisonment for a term not exceeding ten years or a fine or both.

(2) A person who—

    (a) contravenes section 3(1) of this Act, otherwise than by doing something which, by virtue of section 3(3) of this Act, cannot be authorised by a licence,

    (b) keeps or uses any gametes in contravention of section 4(1)(a) or (b) of this Act,

    (c) contravenes section 4(3) of this Act, or

    (d) fails to comply with any directions given by virtue of section 24(7)(a) of this Act,

is guilty of an offence.

(3) If a person—

    (a) provides any information for the purposes of the grant of a licence, being information which is false or misleading in a material particular, and

    (b) either he knows the information to be false or misleading in a material particular or he provides the information recklessly,

he is guilty of an offence.

(4) A person guilty of an offence under subsection (2) or (3) above is liable—

    (a) on conviction on indictment, to imprisonment for a term not exceeding two years or a fine or both, and

    (b) on summary conviction, to imprisonment for a term not exceeding six months or a fine not exceeding the statutory maximum or both.

(5) A person who discloses any information in contravention of section 33 of this Act is guilty of an offence and liable—

    (a) on conviction on indictment, to imprisonment for a term not exceeding two years or a fine or both, and

    (b) on summary conviction, to imprisonment for a term not exceeding six months or a fine not exceeding the statutory maximum or both.

(6) A person who—

    (a) fails to comply with a requirement made by virtue of section 39(1)(b) or (2)(b) or 40(2)(b)(ii) or (5)(b) of this Act, or

    (b) intentionally obstructs the exercise of any rights conferred by a warrant issued under section 40 of this Act,

is guilty of an offence.

(7) A person who without reasonable excuse fails to comply with a requirement imposed by regulations made by virtue of section 10(2)(a) of this Act is guilty of an offence.

(8) Where a person to whom a licence applies or the nominal licensee gives or receives any money or other benefit, not authorised by directions, in respect of any supply of gametes or embryos, he is guilty of an offence.

(9)   A person guilty of an offence under subsection (6), (7) or (8) above is liable on summary conviction to imprisonment for a term not exceeding six months or a fine not exceeding level five on the standard scale or both.

(10)   It is a defence for a person ("the defendant") charged with an offence of doing anything which, under section 3(1) or 4(1) of this Act, cannot be done except in pursuance of a licence to prove—

(a)   that the defendant was acting under the direction of another, and

(b)   that the defendant believed on reasonable grounds—

(i)   that the other person was at the material time the person responsible under a licence, a person designated by virtue of section 17(2)(b) of this Act as a person to whom a licence applied, or a person to whom directions had been given by virtue of section 24(9) of this Act, and

(ii)   that the defendant was authorised by virtue of the licence or directions to do the thing in question.

(11)   It is a defence for a person charged with an offence under this Act to prove—

(a)   that at the material time he was a person to whom a licence applied or to whom directions had been given, and

(b)   that he took all such steps as were reasonable and exercised all due diligence to avoid committing the offence.

42.   Consent to prosecution

No proceedings for an offence under this Act shall be instituted—

(a)   in England and Wales, except by or with the consent of the Director of Public Prosecutions, and

(b)   in Northern Ireland, except by or with the consent of the Director of Public Prosecutions for Northern Ireland.

Miscellaneous and General

43.   Keeping and examining gametes and embryos in connection with crime, etc.

(1)   Regulations may provide—

(a)   for the keeping and examination of gametes or embryos, in such manner and on such conditions (if any) as may be specified in regulations, in connection with the investigation of, or proceedings for, an offence (wherever committed), or

(b)   for the storage of gametes, in such manner and on such conditions (if any) as may be specified in regulations, where they are to be used only for such purposes, other than treatment services, as may be specified in regulations.

(2)   Nothing in this Act makes unlawful the keeping or examination of any gametes or embryos in pursuance of regulations made by virtue of this section.

(3)   In this section "examination" includes use for the purposes of any test.

45.   Regulations

(1)   The Secretary of State may make regulations for any purpose for which regulations may be made under this Act.

(2)   The power to make regulations shall be exercisable by statutory instrument.

(3)   Regulations may make different provision for different cases.

(4)   The Secretary of State shall not make regulations by virtue of section 3(3)(c), 4(2) or (3), 30, 31(4)(a), or 43 of this Act or paragraph 1(1)(g) or 3 of Schedule 2 to this Act unless a draft has been laid before and approved by resolution of each House of Parliament.

(5)   A statutory instrument containing regulations shall, if made without a draft having been approved by resolution of each House of Parliament, be subject to annulment in pursuance of a resolution of either House of Parliament.

(6)   In this Act "regulations" means regulations under this section.

47. Index

The expressions listed in the left-hand column below are respectively defined or (as the case may be) are to be interpreted in accordance with the provisions of this Act listed in the right-hand column in relation to those expressions.

Expression	*Relevant provision*
Activities governed by this Act	Section 4(5)
Authority	Section 2(1)
Carry, in relation to a child	Section 2(3)
Directions	Section 2(1)
Embryo	Section 1
Gametes, eggs or sperm	Section 1
Keeping, in relation to embryos or gametes	Section 2(2)
Licence	Section 2(1)
Licence committee	Section 9(1)
Nominal licensee	Section 17(3)
Person responsible	Section 17(1)
Person to whom a licence applies	Section 17(2)
Statutory storage period	Section 14(3) to (5)
Store, and similar expressions, in relation to embryos or gametes	Section 2(2)
Treatment services	Section 2(1)

49.   Short title, commencement, etc.

(3)   Section 27 to 29 of this Act shall have effect only in relation to children carried by women as a result of the placing in them of embryos or of sperm and eggs, or of their artificial insemination (as the case may be), after the commencement of those sections.

(4)   Section 27 of the Family Law Reform Act 1987 (artificial insemination) does not have effect in relation to children carried by women as the result of their artificial insemination after the commencement of sections 27 to 29 of this Act.

SCHEDULES

SCHEDULE 1
THE AUTHORITY: SUPPLEMENTARY PROVISIONS

Status and capacity

1.   The Authority shall not be regarded as the servant or agent of the Crown, or as enjoying any status, privilege or immunity of the Crown; and its property shall not be regarded as property of, or property held on behalf of, the Crown.

2.   The Authority shall have power to do anything which is calculated to facilitate the discharge of its functions, or is incidental or conducive to their discharge, except the power to borrow money.

Expenses

3.   The Secretary of State may, with the consent of the Treasury, pay the Authority out of money provided by Parliament such sums as he thinks fit towards its expenses.

Appointment of members

4.—(1)   All the members of the Authority (including the chairman and deputy chairman who shall be appointed as such) shall be appointed by the Secretary of State.

(2)   In making appointments the Secretary of State shall have regard to the desirability of ensuring that the proceedings of the Authority, and the discharge of its functions, are informed by the views of both men and women.

(3)   The following persons are disqualified from being appointed as chairman or deputy chairman of the Authority—

(a)   any person who is, or has been, a medical practitioner registered under the Medical Act 1983 (whether fully, provisionally or with limited registration), or under any repealed enactment from which a provision of that Act is derived,

(b)   any person who is, or has been, concerned with keeping or using gametes or embryos outside the body, and

(c)   any person who is, or has been, directly concerned with commissioning or funding any research involving such keeping or use, or who has actively participated in any decision to do so.

(4)   The Secretary of State shall secure that at least one-third but fewer than half of the other members of the Authority fall within sub-paragraph (3)(a), (b) or (c) above, and that at least one member falls within each of paragraphs (a) and (b).

Tenure of office

5.—(1)   Subject to the following provisions of this paragraph, a person shall hold and vacate office as a member of the Authority in accordance with the terms of his appointment.

(2)   A person shall not be appointed as a member of the Authority for more than three years at a time.

(3)   A member may at any time resign his office by giving notice to the Secretary of State.

(4)   A person who ceases to be a member of the Authority shall be eligible for re-appointment (whether or not in the same capacity).

(5)   If the Secretary of State is satisfied that a member of the Authority—

(a)   has been absent from meetings of the Authority for six consecutive months or longer without the permission of the Authority, or

(b)   has become bankrupt or made an arrangement with his creditors, or, in Scotland, has had his estate sequestrated or has granted a trust deed for or entered into an arrangement with his creditors, or

(c)   is unable or unfit to discharge the functions of a member,
the Secretary of State may declare his office as a member of the Authority vacant, and notify the declaration in such manner as he thinks fit; and thereupon the office shall become vacant.

Proceedings

9.—(1)   The Authority may regulate its own proceedings, and make such arrangements as it thinks appropriate for the discharge of its functions.

(2)   The Authority may pay to the members of any committee or sub-committee such fees and allowances as the Secretary of State may, with the consent of the Treasury, determine.

10.—(1)   A member of the Authority who is in any way directly or indirectly interested in a licence granted or proposed to be granted by the Authority shall, as soon as possible after the relevant circumstances have come to his knowledge, disclose the nature of his interest to the Authority.

(2)   Any disclosure under sub-paragraph (1) above shall be recorded by the Authority.

(3)   Except in such circumstances (if any) as may be determined by the Authority under paragraph 9(1) above, the member shall not participate after the disclosure in any

deliberation or decision of the Authority or any licence committee with respect to the licence, and if he does so the deliberation or decision shall be of no effect.

11. The validity of any proceedings of the Authority, or of any committee or sub-committee, shall not be affected by any vacancy among the members or by any defect in the appointment of a member.

Investigation by Parliamentary Commissioner

14. The Authority shall be subject to investigation by the Parliamentary Commissioner and accordingly, in Schedule 2 to the Parliamentary Commissioner Act 1967 (which lists the authorities subject to investigation under that Act), the following entry shall be inserted at the appropriate place in alphabetical order—
"Human Fertilisation and Embryology Authority".

SCHEDULE 2
ACTIVITIES FOR WHICH LICENCES MAY BE GRANTED

Licences for treatment

1.—(1) A licence under this paragraph may authorise any of the following in the course of providing treatment services—
(a) bringing about the creation of embryos *in vitro*,
(b) keeping embryos,
(c) using gametes,
(d) practices designed to secure that embryos are in a suitable condition to be placed in a woman or to determine whether embryos are suitable for that purpose,
(e) placing any embryo in a woman,
(f) mixing sperm with the egg of a hamster, or other animal specified in directions, for the purpose of testing the fertility or normality of the sperm, but only where anything which forms is destroyed when the test is complete and, in any event, not later than the two cell stage, and
(g) such other practices as may be specified in, or determined in accordance with, regulations.
(2) Subject to the provisions of this Act, a licence under this paragraph may be granted subject to such conditions as may be specified in the licence and may authorise the performance of any of the activities referred to in sub-paragraph (1) above in such manner as may be so specified.
(3) A licence under this paragraph cannot authorise any activity unless it appears to the Authority to be necessary or desirable for the purpose of providing treatment services.
(4) A licence under this paragraph cannot authorise altering the genetic structure of any cell while it forms part of an embryo.
(5) A licence under this paragraph shall be granted for such period not exceeding five years as may be specified in the licence.

Licences for storage

2.—(1) A licence under this paragraph or paragraph 1 or 3 of this Schedule may authorise the storage of gametes or embryos or both.
(2) Subject to the provisions of this Act, a licence authorising such storage may be granted subject to such conditions as may be specified in the licence and may authorise storage in such manner as may be so specified.
(3) A licence under this paragraph shall be granted for such period not exceeding five years as may be specified in the licence.

Licences for research

3.—(1)   A licence under this paragraph may authorise any of the following—
  (a)   bringing about the creation of embryos *in vitro,* and
  (b)   keeping or using embryos,
for the purposes of a project of research specified in the licence.

(2)   A licence under this paragraph cannot authorise any activity unless it appears to the Authority to be necessary or desirable for the purpose of—
  (a)   promoting advances in the treatment of infertility,
  (b)   increasing knowledge about the causes of congenital disease,
  (c)   increasing knowledge about the causes of miscarriages,
  (d)   developing more effective techniques of contraception, or
  (e)   developing methods for detecting the presence of gene or chromosome abnormalities in embryos before implantation,
or for such other purposes as may be specified in regulations.

(3)   Purposes may only be so specified with a view to the authorisation of projects of research which increase knowledge about the creation and development of embryos, or about disease, or enable such knowledge to be applied.

(4)   A licence under this paragraph cannot authorise altering the genetic structure of any cell while it forms part of an embryo, except in such circumstances (if any) as may be specified in or determined in pursuance of regulations.

(5)   A licence under this paragraph may authorise mixing sperm with the egg of a hamster, or other animal specified in directions, for the purpose of developing more effective techniques for determining the fertility or normality of sperm, but only where anything which forms is destroyed when the research is complete and, in any event, not later than the two cell stage.

(6)   No licence under this paragraph shall be granted unless the Authority is satisfied that any proposed use of embryos is necessary for the purposes of the research.

(7)   Subject to the provisions of this Act, a licence under this paragraph may be granted subject to such conditions as may be specified in the licence.

(8)   A licence under this paragraph may authorise the performance of any of the activities referred to in sub-paragraph (1) or (5) above in such manner as may be so specified.

(9)   A licence under this paragraph shall be granted for such period not exceeding three years as may be specified in the licence.

General

4.—(1)   A licence under this Schedule can only authorise activities to be carried on on premises specified in the licence and under the supervision of an individual designated in the licence.

(2)   A licence cannot—
  (a)   authorise activities falling within both paragraph 1 and paragraph 3 above,
  (b)   apply to more than one project of research,
  (c)   authorise activities to be carried on under the supervision of more than one individual, or
  (d)   apply to premises in different places.

SCHEDULE 3
CONSENTS TO USE OF GAMETES OR EMBRYOS

Consent

1.   A consent under this Schedule must be given in writing and, in this Schedule, "effective consent" means a consent under this Schedule which has not been withdrawn.

2.—(1) A consent to the use of any embryo must specify one or more of the following purposes—

(a) use in providing treatment services to the person giving consent, or that person and another specified person together,

(b) use in providing treatment services to persons not including the person giving consent, or

(c) use for the purposes of any project of research,

and may specify conditions subject to which the embryo may be so used.

(2) A consent to the storage of any gametes or any embryo must—

(a) specify the maximum period of storage (if less than the statutory storage period), and

(b) state what is to be done with the gametes or embryo if the person who gave the consent dies or is unable because of incapacity to vary the terms of the consent or to revoke it,

and may specify conditions subject to which the gametes or embryo may remain in storage.

(3) A consent under this Schedule must provide for such other matters as the Authority may specify in directions.

(4) A consent under this Schedule may apply—

(a) to the use or storage of a particular embryo, or

(b) in the case of a person providing gametes, to the use or storage of any embryo whose creation may be brought about using those gametes,

and in the paragraph (b) case the terms of the consent may be varied, or the consent may be withdrawn, in accordance with this Schedule either generally or in relation to a particular embryo or particular embryos.

Procedure for giving consent

3.—(1) Before a person gives consent under this Schedule—

(a) he must be given a suitable opportunity to receive proper counselling about the implications of taking the proposed steps, and

(b) he must be provided with such relevant information as is proper.

(2) Before a person gives consent under this Schedule he must be informed of the effect of paragraph 4 below.

Variation and withdrawal of consent

4.—(1) The terms of any consent under this Schedule may from time to time be varied, and the consent may be withdrawn, by notice given by the person who gave the consent to the person keeping the gametes or embryo to which the consent is relevant.

(2) The terms of any consent to the use of any embryo cannot be varied, and such consent cannot be withdrawn, once the embryo has been used—

(a) in providing treatment services, or

(b) for the purposes of any project of research.

Use of gametes for treatment of others

5.—(1) A person's gametes must not be used for the purposes of treatment services unless there is an effective consent by that person to their being so used and they are used in accordance with the terms of the consent.

(2) A person's gametes must not be received for use for those purposes unless there is an effective consent by that person to their being so used.

(3) This paragraph does not apply to the use of a person's gametes for the purpose of that person, or that person and another together, receiving treatment services.

In vitro fertilisation and subsequent use of embryo

6.—(1) A person's gametes must not be used to bring about the creation of any embryo in vitro unless there is an effective consent by that person to any embryo the creation of which may be brought about with the use of those gametes being used for one or more of the purposes mentioned in paragraph 2(1) above.

(2)   An embryo the creation of which was brought about *in vitro* must not be received by any person unless there is an effective consent by each person whose gametes were used to bring about the creation of the embryo to the use for one or more of the purposes mentioned in paragraph 2(1) above of the embryo.

(3)   An embryo the creation of which was brought about *in vitro* must not be used for any purpose unless there is an effective consent by each person whose gametes were used to bring about the creation of the embryo to the use for that purpose of the embryo and the embryo is used in accordance with those consents.

(4)   Any consent required by this paragraph is in addition to any consent that may be required by paragraph 5 above.

Embryos obtained by lavage, etc.

7.—(1)   An embryo taken from a woman must not be used for any purpose unless there is an effective consent by her to the use of the embryo for that purpose and it is used in accordance with the consent.

(2)   An embryo taken from a woman must not be received by any person for use for any purpose unless there is an effective consent by her to the use of the embryo for that purpose.

(3)   This paragraph does not apply to the use, for the purpose of providing a woman with treatment services, of an embryo taken from her.

Storage of gametes and embryos

8.—(1)   A person's gametes must not be kept in storage unless there is an effective consent by that person to their storage and they are stored in accordance with the consent.

(2)   An embryo the creation of which was brought about *in vitro* must not be kept in storage unless there is an effective consent, by each person whose gametes were used to bring about the creation of the embryo, to the storage of the embryo and the embryo is stored in accordance with those consents.

(3)   An embryo taken from a woman must not be kept in storage unless there is an effective consent by her to its storage and it is stored in accordance with the consent.

SCHEDULE 4
MINOR AND CONSEQUENTIAL AMENDMENTS

Human Organ Transplants Act 1989 (c. 31.)

8.   Sections 27 to 29 of this Act do not apply for the purposes of section 2 of the Human Organ Transplants Act 1989 (restrictions on transplants between persons not genetically related).

MEDICINAL PRODUCTS: PRESCRIPTION BY NURSES ETC. ACT 1992
(1992, c. 28)

1.   Prescription only drugs etc.: authorisation of registered nurses, midwives and health visitors

(1)   In section 58 of the Medicines Act 1968 (medicinal products on prescription only) in subsection (1) (which specifies who are to be appropriate practitioners in relation to specified descriptions or classes of medicinal products) at the end of paragraph (c) there shall be inserted "and

(d)   registered nurses, midwives and health visitors who are of such a description and comply with such conditions as may be specified in the order".

(2)   In subsection (4) of that section (orders providing for exemptions etc.) at the end of paragraph (a) there shall be inserted the words "or, where the appropriate practitioner is a registered nurse, midwife or health visitor, such modifications as may be so specified".

6.   Short title, commencement and extent

(1)   This Act may be cited as the Medicinal Products: Prescription by Nurses etc. Act 1992.

(2)   Sections 1 to 3 above shall come into force on such day as the Secretary of State may by order made by statutory instrument appoint, and different days may be so appointed for different provisions or for different purposes.

STATUTORY INSTRUMENTS

THE NATIONAL HEALTH SERVICE (VENEREAL DISEASES) REGULATIONS 1974 (SI 1974, No. 29)

Confidentiality of information
2. Every Regional Health Authority and every District Health Authority shall take all necessary steps to secure that any information capable of identifying an individual obtained by officers of the Authority with respect to persons examined or treated for any sexually transmited disease shall not be disclosed except—

(a) for the purpose of communicating that information to a medical practitioner, or to a person employed under the direction of a medical practitioner in connection with the treatment of persons suffering from such disease or the prevention of the spread thereof, and

(b) for the purpose of such treatment or prevention.

NATIONAL HEALTH SERVICE (GENERAL MEDICAL AND PHARMACEUTICAL SERVICES) REGULATIONS 1974 (SI 1974, No. 160)

PART I
GENERAL

Interpretation
2.—(1) In these regulations, unless the context otherwise requires—
"the Act" means the National Health Service Act 1977;
"the Amendment Regulations" means the National Health Service (General Medical and Pharmaceutical Services) Amendment (No. 3) Regulations 1990;
"assistant" means a doctor who is acting as an assistant to a doctor on the medical list;
"chemist" means a registered pharmaceutical chemist who provides pharmaceutical services or an authorised seller of poisons within the meaning of the Pharmacy and Poisons Act 1933 who provides such services;
"child" means a person who has not attained the age of 16 years;
"child health surveillance list" shall be construed in accordance with regulation 3A(1);
"child health surveillance services" means the personal medical services described in paragraph 9B of the terms of service and Schedule 1A to these Regulations;
"Committee" means Family Practitioner Committee;
"doctor" means a fully registered medical practitioner;
"domiciliary visit" means a visit to either the place where the patient resides or the place, other than the doctor's practice premises, where the doctor is obliged, pursuant to paragraph 13A of the terms of service, to render personal medical services to the patient;
"drugs" includes medicines and chemical reagents;

"enactment" includes an enactment in a statutory instrument;

"Family Health Services Authority" means a body of that name established by the Secretary of State under section 10(1) of the National Health Service Act 1977;

"group practice" means an association of not less than two doctors both or all of whom—

(a) have their names included in the Committee's medical list;

(b) coordinate, in the course of regular contact between them, their respective obligations under the terms of service for doctors to provide personal medical services to their patients; and

(c) conduct and manage their practices from at least one common set of practice premises;

"Local Directory" means the Local Directory of Family Doctors maintained by a Committee pursuant to regulation 5A;

"locality", except in the expression controlled locality, means the locality for which a Committee is established;

"Local Obstetric Committee" means a committee recognised by the Secretary of State for a locality for the purpose of approving, in accordance with such conditions as the Secretary of State may determine after consultation with such organisations as he may recognise as representing doctors, the obstetric experience of a doctor;

"maternity medical services" means personal medical services in respect of pregnancy, confinement and the post-natal period provided by a doctor in accordance with such arrangements and subject to such conditions as may be determined by the Secretary of State after consultation with such organisations as he may recognise as representing doctors;

"medical card" means a card, in a form approved by the Secretary of State, issued to a person for the purpose of enabling him to obtain or establishing his title to receive general medical services other than contraceptive services and maternity medical services from a doctor and includes any similar card provided for the purpose of enabling a person to obtain medical benefit under the National Health Insurance (Medical Benefit) Regulations 1936;

"medical list" has the meaning assigned to it in regulation 4(1);

"medical officer" means a doctor in the service of the Department of Health and Social Security, or of the Welsh Office, as the case may be;

"medical records" means, in relation to any patient, the records maintained in respect of that patient pursuant to paragraph 30 of the terms of service;

"minor surgery list" shall be construed in accordance with regulation 3B(1);

"minor surgery services" means the personal medical services described in paragraph 9C of the terms of service and Schedule 1B to these Regulations;

"obstetric list" means a list of doctors whose experience in obstetrics is for the time being approved by the Local Obstetric Committee or the Secretary of State;

"parent" includes any adult person who, in the opinion of the doctor, is for the time being fulfilling the obligations normally attaching to a parent in respect of his child;

"practice area" means the area in which a doctor is under an obligation to visit patients, either by virtue of his application for inclusion on the medical list or any variation therein pursuant to the regulations or the terms of service;

"practice premises" means, in relation to any doctor, the premises at which he is obliged under the terms of service to attend at specified times in order to be consulted by, or to provide treatment or services for, his patients;

"restricted list principal" means a doctor who has undertaken to provide general medical services only to a restricted category of patients identified by reference to their connection with a particular establishment or organisation;

"restricted services principal" means a doctor who has undertaken to the Committee to provide general medical services limited to—
  (a) child health surveillance services;
  (b) contraceptive services;
  (c) maternity medical services; or
  (d) minor surgery services,
or to any combination of the above;
"terms of service" means, in relation to doctors, the terms of service contained or referred to in Part I of Schedule 1 to these regulations, . . .
"trainee general practitioner" means a doctor who is being trained in general practice under an arrangement approved by the Secretary of State:
"treatment" means medical attendance and treatment, but does not include child health surveillance services, contraceptive services, maternity medical services or minor surgery services unless the doctor has undertaken to provide such services to the person concerned in accordance with these regulations.
"the Tribunal" means the Tribunal constituted under section 46 of the National HealthService Act 1977;
  (2) These regulations shall apply to a person, firm or body corporate (other than a chemist, doctor or a dental practitioner) providing pharmaceutical services as they apply to a chemist.

PART II
DOCTORS

[Note: Family Practitioner Committee to be construed as a reference to a Family Health Services Authority by virtue of the National Health Service and Community Care Act 1990, s. 2(1)(2).]

Scope of services
  3.—(1) The services, arrangements for the provision of which, pursuant to sections 29 and 41 to 43 of the National Health Service Act 1977, it is, by virtue of section 15 of that Act, the duty of the Committee to administer, shall include—
  (a) all necessary and appropriate personal medical services of the type usually provided by general medical practitioners; and
  (b) giving advice to women on contraception, the medical examination of women seeking such advice, the treatment of such women and provision for the supply to such women of contraceptive substances and appliances (which services are hereinafter referred to as "contraceptive services");
  (bb) the provision by doctors of child health surveillance services and minor surgery services;
  (2) The arrangements to which paragraph (1) refers shall incorporate the terms of service, and Schedules 1C, 1D and 1E to these Regulations shall have effect for the purposes of paragraphs 25, 38B and 43A respectively of the terms of service.

Child health surveillance list
  3A.—(1) The Committee shall, on and after 1st April 1990, maintain a list (in these Regulations referred to as "a child health surveillance list") of the names of those doctors who have satisfied the Committee or, on appeal, the Secretary of State, in accordance with the following provisions of this regulation, that they have such medical experience and training as are necessary to enable them properly to provide child health surveillance services.
  (2) A doctor may apply, in accordance with paragraph (3), to a Committee for the inclusion of his name in the child health surveillance list required to be maintained by that Committee.

(3) An application for the purpose of paragraph (2) shall be made in writing and shall include the information specified in Part IV of Schedule 1 to these Regulations.

(4) Unless the doctor otherwise agrees, the Committee shall determine an application made in accordance with paragraph (3) within 2 months of receiving it.

(5) The Committee may, if it thinks fit, hold an oral hearing of any application and shall not refuse an application without giving the doctor an opportunity of an oral hearing.

(6) When determining an application the Committee shall have regard in particular to—

(a) any training undertaken by the doctor; and

(b) any medical experience gained by him,

during the period of five years immediately preceding the date of the application, which is relevant to the provision of child health surveillance services, and shall seek and take into account any medical advice it considers necessary to enable it to determine the application.

(7) The Committee shall determine an application by either—

(a) granting the application; or

(b) refusing the application.

(8) The Committee shall give notice in writing to the doctor of its determination and shall—

(a) where it refuses the application, inform him of the reasons for the determination and of his right of appeal under paragraph (9);

(b) where it grants the application, include the doctor's name in its child health surveillance list.

(9) If an application is refused the doctor may appeal in writing to the Secretary of State within 90 days of receiving notice in writing of the Committee's determination.

(10) On any appeal pursuant to paragraph (9), the Secretary of State—

(a) may, if he thinks fit, hold an oral hearing of the appeal;

(b) in determining the appeal, shall either confirm or reverse the determination of the Committee;

(c) where he reverses the determination of the Committee, shall direct that the Committee include the doctor's name in its child health surveillance list.

(11) Subject to paragraphs (12) to (16), a doctor's name may be removed by the Committee from the child health surveillance list only if—

(a) it has been removed from the medical list of any Committee pursuant to regulation 5(1) or 5B;

(b) the Committee has determined that the doctor has not provided child health surveillance services at any time during the past 5 years;

(c) the Committee has determined that the doctor has, in relation to any patient in respect of whom he has undertaken to provide child health surveillance services, failed, in a material respect, to comply with any requirement of paragraph 9B of the terms of service or Schedule 1A to these Regulations; or

(d) the Committee has determined that the doctor is no longer able to provide child health surveillance services.

(12) Before making any determination under sub-paragraph (b), (c) or (d) of paragraph (11) the Committee shall—

(a) give the doctor 28 days' written notice of its intention to do so, and

(b) afford the doctor an opportunity of making representations in writing or, if he so desires, orally to the Committee.

(13) Where the Committee makes a determination under sub-paragraph (b), (c) or (d) of paragraph (11), it shall send to the doctor a notice which shall include a statement—

(a)   to the effect that, subject to any appeal under paragraph (14), the doctor's name will, after 28 days from the date of notice, be removed from the child health surveillance list maintained by the Committee;

(b)   of the Committee's reasons for its determination; and

(c) of the doctor's right of appeal under paragraph (14).

(14)   A doctor who has received a notice sent in accordance with paragraph (13) may, within 21 days of receiving it, appeal to the Secretary of State against the determination of the Committee, and pending the determination of the appeal the Committee shall not remove his name from the child health surveillance list.

(15)   An appeal to the Secretary of State shall be made in writing and shall include a statement of the facts and contentions on which the doctor intends to rely; and on any such appeal the Secretary of State shall, if he allows the appeal, direct that the Committee shall not remove the doctor's name from the child health surveillance list.

(16)   The Committee shall comply with any direction given to it under this regulation.

Minor surgery list

3B.—(1)   The Committee shall, on and after 1st April 1990 maintain a list (in these Regulations referred to as "the minor surgery list") of the names of those doctors who have satisfied the Committee or, on appeal, the Secretary of State in accordance with the following provisions of this regulation that they have such medical experience, training and facilities as are necessary to enable them properly to provide all of the procedures listed in Schedule 1B to these Regulations.

(2)   A doctor may apply, in accordance with paragraph (3), to a Committee for the inclusion of his name in the minor surgery list required to be maintained by that Committee.

(3)   An application for the purpose of paragraph (2) shall be made in writing and shall include the information specified in Part V of Schedule 1 to these Regulations.

(4)   Unless the doctor otherwise agrees, the Committee shall determine an application made in accordance with paragraph (3) within 2 months of receiving it.

(5)   The Committee may, if it thinks fit, hold an oral hearing of any application and shall not refuse an application without giving the doctor an opportunity of an oral hearing.

(6)   When determining an application the Committee shall have regard in particular—

(a)   for the purpose of assessing the doctor's medical experience, to any—

(i)   postgraduate qualification held by him,

(ii)   training undertaken by him; and

(iii)   medical experience gained by him,

during the period of five years immediately preceding the date of the application, which is relevant to the provision of minor surgery services;

(b)   for the purpose of assessing the doctor's facilities, to the premises and the equipment to be used by the doctor in the provision of minor surgery services, and shall seek and take into account any medical advice it considers necessary to enable it to determine the application.

(7)   The Committee shall determine an application by either—

(a)   granting the application; or

(b)   refusing the application.

(8)   The Committee shall inform the doctor in writing of its determination and shall—

(a)   where it refuses the application, give notice in writing to him of the reasons for the determination and of his right of appeal under paragraph (9);

(b)   where it grants the application, include the doctor's name in its minor surgery list.

(9)   If an application is refused the doctor may appeal in writing to the Secretary of State within 90 days of receiving notice in writing of the Committee's determination.

(10)   On any appeal pursuant to paragraph (9), the Secretary of State—

(a)   may, if he thinks fit, hold an oral hearing of the appeal;

(b)   in determining the appeal, shall either confirm or reverse the determination of the Committee;

(c)   where he reverses the determination of the Committee, shall direct that the Committee include the doctor's name in its minor surgery list.

(11)   Subject to paragraphs (12) to (16), a doctor's name may be removed from the minor surgery list only if—

(a)   it has been removed from the medical list of any Committee pursuant to regulation 5(1) or 5B;

(b)   the Committee has determined that the doctor has not provided minor surgery services at any time during the past 5 years;

(c)   the Committee has determined that the doctor has, in relation to any patient in respect of whom he has undertaken to provide minor surgery services, failed, in a material respect, to comply with any requirement of paragraph 9C of the terms of service or Schedule 1B to these Regulations; or

(d)   the Committee has determined that the doctor is no longer able to provide minor surgery services.

(12)   Before making any determination under sub-paragraph (b), (c) or (d) of paragraph (11) the Committee shall—

(a)   give the doctor 28 days' written notice of its intention to do so; and

(b)   afford the doctor an opportunity of making representations in writing or, if he so desires, orally to the Committee.

(13)   Where the Committee makes a determination under sub-paragraph (b), (c) or (d) of paragraph (11), it shall send to the doctor a notice which shall include a statement—

(a)   to the effect that, subject to any appeal under paragraph (14), the doctor's name will, after 28 days from the date of the notice, be removed from the minor surgery list maintained by the Committee;

(b)   of the Committee's reasons for its determination; and

(c)   of the doctor's right of appeal under paragraph (14).

(14)   A doctor who has received a notice sent in accordance with paragraph (13) may, within 21 days of receiving it, appeal to the Secretary of State against the determination, and pending the determination of the appeal the Committee shall not remove his name from the minor surgery list.

(15)   An appeal to the Secretary of State shall be made in writing and shall include a statement of the facts and contentions on which the doctor intends to rely; and on any such appeal the Secretary of State shall, if he allows the appeal, direct that the Committee shall not remove the doctor's name from the minor surgery list.

(16)   The Committee shall comply with any direction given to it under this regulation.

Medical list

4.—(1)   The Committee shall prepare a list, to be called the medical list, of doctors—

(a)   entitled to be included on the list pursuant to regulation 7 and Part III of these regulations;

(b)   for the time being appointed under regulation 19.

(1A)   The medical list shall be divided into five Parts as follows:—

(a)   Part I shall contain the names of doctors who are full-time doctors;

(b)   Part II shall contain the names of doctors who are three-quarter-time doctors;

    (c)   Part III shall contain the names of doctors who are half-time doctors;

    (d)   Part IV shall contain the names of doctors who are job-sharing doctors;

    (e)   Part V shall contain the names of doctors who are restricted doctors.

(1B)   A Family Health Services Authority shall—

    (a)   as respects the name of any doctor included in its medical list on 1st January 1991; or

    (b)   when including the name of any doctor in its medical list after that date, assign the name to the Part of the list which is, by virtue of paragraph (1A), appropriate in the case of that doctor, having regard to the nature of any condition imposed in relation to him by the Medical Practices Committee under regulation 11A or treated as so imposed under regulation 12(3) of the Amendment Regulations.

    (2)   The medical list shall, in respect of any doctor whose name is included on it, indicate—

    (a)   if he is on the obstetric list and if he has undertaken to provide either general medical services including maternity medical services or general medical services limited to maternity medical services;

    (aa)   whether his name is included in either or both of the child health surveillance list and the minor surgery list;

    (b)   except in the case of a doctor who has requested otherwise, if he has undertaken to provide contraceptive services, and shall distinguish between a doctor who has so undertaken in respect only of patients for whom he or his partners have also undertaken other personal medical services and a doctor who has so undertaken without such restriction;

    (c)   if he has been relieved of the responsibility of providing services during certain periods under paragraph 15(2) of the terms of service as in force immediately prior to 1st April 1990 and the name of the doctor with whom the Committee has made arrangements for the provision of services during such periods;

    (d)   if he is included on the medical list by virtue of his appointment under regulation 19;

    (e)   if he is a restricted list principal or a restricted services principal.

    (3)   The medical list shall also indicate which doctors have been relieved of the responsibility to provide services during certain periods under paragraph 15(2) of the terms of service and shall indicate against those doctors' names the doctors with whom the Committee has made arrangements for the provision of services during such periods.

    (4)   The medical list shall contain in addition to the name of a doctor

    (a)   the address of the practice premises where he agrees to attend for the purpose of treating persons and the telephone number or numbers at which he is prepared to receive messages;

    (b)   particulars of the days and hours at which he agrees to be in attendance at such premises;

    (c)   particulars of the days and hours during which an appointments system is in operation;

    (d)   where he practises in partnership, the name of each partner;

    (dd)   where he participates in a group practice, the name of each other doctor in that group practice;

    (e)   an indication of the geographical boundary of his practice area by reference to a sketch, diagram or plan of a scale approved by the Committee, and any conditions as to his practice area attached to the granting of an application by the Medical Practices Committee or, on appeal, by the Secretary of State;

    (f)   provided that the doctor consents to its inclusion, his date of birth, or, if he does not so consent, the date of his first full registration as a medical practitioner (whether pursuant to the Medical Act 1983 or otherwise); and may, if the Committee thinks fit, be so arranged as to show the part of the area in which each doctor will provide treatment.

Removal from the Medical list

5.—(1) Where a Committee has determined that a doctor whose name has been included on the medical list—

(a) has died, or

(b) has ceased from being a registered medical practitioner, or

(c) is the subject of a direction given by the Professional Conduct Committee of the General Medical Council under section 36 of the Medical Act 1983 that his name be erased from the register or that his registration in the register be suspended or of an order made by that Committee under section 38(1) of that Act (immediate suspension), or

(d) is the subject of a direction by the Tribunal requiring the removal of his name from the medical list of the Committee,

the Committee shall with effect from the date of such determination or the date on which such direction or such order takes effect, whichever is the later, remove the doctor's name from the medical list.

(2) Where a Committee has determined in accordance with the succeeding provisions of this regulation that a doctor whose name has been included for the preceding six months on the medical list has not during that period provided any general medical services personally, the Committee may remove the doctor's name from the medical list.

(2A) For the purpose of calculating the period of six months referred to in paragraph (2) in relation to a doctor there shall be disregarded any period during which he provided no general medical services by reason only that his registration in the register of medical practitioners was suspended as mentioned in section 29(8) of the National Health Service Act 1977 (suspension by Health Committee or by interim order of Preliminary Proceedings Committee).

(3) Before making any determination under paragraph (2) the Committee shall—

(a) give the doctor 28 days' notice of its intention to do so,

(b) afford the doctor an opportunity of making representations to the Committee in writing or, if he so desires, orally to a sub-committee appointed by the Committee for the purpose, of which sub-committee at least a third of the members shall be doctors from a panel nominated by the Local Medical Committee, and

(c) consult the Local Medical Committee.

(4) Nothing in this regulation shall affect a doctor who is performing a period of relevant service and no determination under this regulation shall be made in respect of any such doctor until 6 months after he has completed that service.

(5) A doctor on whom a notice has been served under paragraph (2) may, within 21 days of receipt of the notice, appeal to the Secretary of State against a decision of the Committee to remove him from its medical list and pending the determination of the appeal the Committee shall not remove the doctor from the medical list.

The notice of appeal shall be in writing and shall set out the facts and contentions on which the doctor intends to rely; and on any such appeal the Secretary of State shall, if he allows the appeal, direct that the Committee shall not remove the doctor from the medical list.

Local Directory of Family Doctors

5A—(1) Subject to the requirements of this regulation and regulation 6A, the Committee shall, by 1st April 1990, prepare, and thereafter maintain, in addition to a medical list, a list to be known as the Local Directory of Family Doctors (in these Regulations called a "Local Directory") comprising, in respect of each doctor whose name is included in its medical list, the following information—

(a)   all the information included in respect of the doctor in the medical list of the Committee, other than—

   (i)   information included pursuant to regulation 4(2)(c); and

   (ii)   his date of birth, unless the doctor has agreed to its inclusion in the Local Directory;

(b)   where the doctor's date of birth is included in the medical list but he has not agreed to its inclusion in the Local Directory, the date of his first full registration as a medical practitioner (whether pursuant to the Medical Act 1983 or otherwise);

(c)   the sex of the doctor;

(d)   details of any medical qualification held by the doctor which he is entitled to have registered pursuant to section 16 of the Medical Act 1983 (registration of qualifications), including the date on which the qualification was awarded;

(e)   the nature of any clinic provided by the doctor for his patients and the frequency with which it is held;

(f)   the numbers of assistants and trainee general practitioners employed by him;

(g)   details of—

   (i)   the number of other persons employed or available at his practice premises to assist him in the discharge of his obligations under the terms of service,

   (ii)   the nature of the services provided by each such person, and

   (iii)   the average number of hours normally worked by each such person during each week;

(h)   the terms of any consent granted to the doctor by the Committee or, on appeal, by the Secretary of State, pursuant to paragraph 19 of the terms of service, concerning the use of a deputising service; and

(j)   where, and to the extent that, the doctor so requests—

   (i)   details of any languages, other than English, spoken by the doctor or by any person referred to in sub-paragraph (f) or (g),

   (ii)   details of any particular clinical interests of the doctor.

(2)   Paragraph (1) shall apply in the case of a restricted list principal or a restricted services principal only to the extent that the Committee sees fit.

(3)   The Committee may, to the extent that it sees fit, also include in the Local Directory other details or material relating to general medical services, general dental services, general ophthalmic services and pharmaceutical services in its locality under Part II of the National Health Service Act 1977.

(4)   A doctor shall, in respect of each Local Directory in which information about him is to be recorded, furnish the Committee by 1st January 1990 with so much of the information specified in sub-paragraphs (b) to (h) of paragraph (1) as may be requested by the Committee before 1st December 1989.

(5)   The Local Directory shall include the name of each doctor in alphabetical order.

(6)   Where a doctor practises in partnership or in a group practice with other doctors, the information regarding his practice which falls to be included in the Local Directory pursuant to paragraph (1)(e), (f), (g) and (j)(i) may, provided each doctor in the partnership or, as the case may be, the group practice agrees, be included in the entry relating to only one of those doctors.

(7)   Notwithstanding the provisions of regulation 31, the Committee may compile extracts from the information in the Local Directory by reference to geographical areas of the Committee's locality, and may make any such extract available to persons to whom, in the opinion of the Committee, it is likely to be of interest.

Removal from medical list on grounds of age

5B—(1)   A Committee shall, on 1st April 1991, remove from the medical list the name of any doctor who has, on or before that date, attained the age of 70 years.

NHS (General Medical etc.) Regulations 1974

(2) Where, on any day after 1st April 1991, a doctor whose name is included in the medical list attains the age of 70 years, the Committee shall thereupon remove his name from the list.

(3) A Committee shall give to any doctor whose name is to be removed from the medical list in accordance with paragraph (1) or (2)—

(a) notice in writing to that effect not less than 12 months nor more than 13 months before the date on which his name is to be removed;

(b) a further such notice not less than 3 months nor more than 4 months before that date,

but the failure to give notice to any doctor as required by sub-paragraph (a) or (b) shall not prevent the removal of that doctor's name from the medical list in accordance with paragraph (1) or (2).

(4) A doctor shall, for the purposes of this regulation, supply to the Committee by 1st February 1990 such evidence of his date of birth as the Committee may, by 1st January 1990, have in writing required from him.

Amendment of or withdrawal from the medical list

6.—(1) A doctor shall, unless it is impractical for him to do so, notify the Committee within 28 days of any occurrence requiring a change in the information recorded about him in the medical list.

(2) A doctor shall, unless it is impractical for him to do so, notify the Committee in writing at least 3 months in advance of any date on which he intends either—

(a) to withdraw his name from any of the medical list, the child health surveillance list, the obstetric list or the minor surgery list; or

(b) to cease to provide any of the following services, namely child health surveillance services, contraceptive services, maternity medical services, or minor surgery services.

(2A) The Committee shall—

(a) on being notified by any doctor pursuant to paragraph (1), amend the medical list in relation to that doctor;

(b) in the case of a notification pursuant to paragraph (2), so amend the medical list either—

(i) on the date which falls 3 months after the date of the notification; or

(ii) the date from which the Committee has agreed that the withdrawal or cessation shall take effect, whichever is the earlier.

(2B) A Family Health Services Authority shall, on being notified by the Medical Practices Committee that it has, in relation to any doctor whose name is included in the medical list, varied under regulation 11B any condition mentioned in paragraph (1)(a)(ii) or (c) of that regulation, amend the medical list by transferring the name of that doctor to the Part of the list which, having regard to the nature of the condition as varied, is appropriate in his case by virtue of regulation 4(1A).

(3) Any such notice may not be withdrawn except with the consent of the Committee.

(4) If representations are made to the Tribunal constituted under section 46 of the Act, that the continued inclusion of a doctor on the medical list would be prejudicial to the efficiency of the general medical services, he shall not, except with the consent of the Secretary of State and subject to such conditions as the Secretary of State may impose, be entitled to have his name removed from the medical list until the proceedings on such representations have been determined.

Amendment of the Local Directory

6A—(1) A doctor shall, unless it is impractical for him to do so, notify the Committee within 28 days of any occurrence requiring a change in the information recorded about him in the Local Directory.

(2)   The Committee shall, in the event of a notification pursuant to paragraph (1), make any necessary amendment to the Local Directory.

PART IV

Application for acceptance by doctors
14.—(1)   Subject to regulation 18, application to a doctor for inclusion on his list shall be made by delivering to the doctor a medical card or a form of application signed (in either case) by the applicant or a person authorised on his behalf.

(2)   (a)   A woman may apply to a doctor who has undertaken to provide contraceptive services (whether or not she is included in the list of a doctor for the provision of other personal medical services) to be accepted by him for the provision to her of contraceptive services;

(b)   such application shall be for the provision of such services for a term of 12 months from the date of acceptance; so however that either the woman or the doctor may terminate the provision to her by him of such services at any time during the term of 12 months;

(c)   on any such termination or at the end of the term of 12 months whichever first occurs the woman may apply or re-apply to a doctor to be accepted by him for the provision to her of such services and sub-paragraph (b) above shall apply to such further application.

(3)   A parent may, in relation to a child of his who is under the age of 5 years, apply to a doctor—

(a)   who is—

(i)   the doctor on whose list the child is included (in this paragraph referred to as "the child's doctor"),

(ii)   a doctor with whom the child's doctor is in partnership, or

(iii)   a doctor with whom the child's doctor is associated in a group practice; and

(b)   whose name is included in any medical list and in the child health surveillance list of the Committee,

for the provision of child health surveillance services in respect of that child for a period ending on the date on which that child attains the age of 5 years.

(4)   A person may apply to a doctor—

(a)   who is—

(i)   the doctor on whose list he is included (in this paragraph referred to as "his own doctor"),

(ii)   a doctor with whom his own doctor is in partnership, or

(iii)   a doctor with whom his own doctor is associated in a group practice; and

(b)   whose name is included in any medical list and the minor surgery list of the Committee,

for the provision of a procedure specified in Schedule 1B to these Regulations.

Assignment of persons to doctors
16.—(1)   If a person who is not on the list of any doctor has been refused acceptance by a doctor for inclusion on his list, or if a person who has been refused acceptance by a doctor as a temporary resident, applies to the Committee for assignment to a doctor, the Family Health Services Authority shall assign him to and notify accordingly such a doctor as they think fit, having regard to—

(a)   the distance between the person's residence and the practice premises of the doctors in the area;

(b)   whether within the previous 6 months the person has been removed from the list of any doctor in the area at the request of the doctor; and

(c)   such other circumstances, including those concerning the doctors in the area and their practices, as the Family Health Services Authority think relevant:
Provided that—
(i)   a doctor shall not be required to provide contraceptive services for a patient assigned to him under this paragraph, unless pursuant to the provisions of regulation 14(2), he accepts her for the provision of such services;
(ia)   a doctor shall not be required to provide either child health surveillance services or minor surgery services for a patient assigned to him under this paragraph unless, following an application pursuant to regulation 14(3) or (4) respectively, he has accepted that patient for the provision of such services;
(ii)   a person shall not, without the consent of the Secretary of State, be assigned under this paragraph to a doctor whose list exceeds the maximum permitted by these regulations.

(3)   The Family Health Services Authority may exempt from the liability to have persons assigned to him under this regulation any doctor who applies to the Committee for that purpose and in considering such an application shall have regard to the doctor's age and state of health and the number of persons on his list.

(4)   The Family Health Services Authority may grant to any doctor of a class mentioned in paragraph 5 of the terms of service the relief specified in that paragraph.

(5)   A doctor in respect of whom a Family Health Services Authority has made a determination ("the initial determination") under paragraph (1), (3) or (4) may, within 7 days of receiving notice of it, make representations in writing to that Authority against that determination.

(6)   Where a doctor makes representations under paragraph (5) the Family Health Services Authority shall give that doctor the opportunity to address it in the course of an oral hearing in support of those representations.

(7)   A doctor who has made representations against a determination under paragraph (1) shall remain responsible for the treatment of the person concerned until the expiry of 7 days after the next meeting of the Family Health Services Authority—
(a)   where there is an oral hearing under paragraph (6), following that hearing;
(b)   in any other case, following the making of representations under paragraph (5).

(8)   Where representations are made under paragraph (5) the Family Health Services Authority shall, subject to paragraph (9), review its initial determination and shall either confirm or revise it.

(9)   No person who participated in the making of an initial determination under this regulation shall participate in a review of that determination under paragraph (8).

(10)   The Family Health Services Authority shall, within 7 days of making a determination under paragraph (8), notify the doctor thereof, and, where an initial determination made under paragraph (1) has been revised, shall notify also the patient and the other doctor to whom the patient is assigned under the revised determination.

Limitation of number of persons on doctors' lists
17.—(1)   Except as provided in this regulation, the maximum number of persons a doctor may have on his lists in all areas in which he provides general medical services (in addition to any persons for whom he has accepted responsibility during certain periods only, under paragraph 15 of the terms of service and in addition to any persons whom he has accepted for the provision of contraceptive services only) shall be—
(a)   3,500 for a doctor carrying on practice otherwise than as an assistant or in a partnership;
(b)   4,500 for a doctor carrying on practice in partnership, subject to an average of 3,500 for each of the partners in the practice;
and so long as he employs an assistant or assistants (other than a trainee general practitioner) such further number not exceeding 2,000 for each assistant as the

Committee, or on appeal the Secretary of State, may decide in the light of the circumstances of the practice and the amount of time given to it by the assistant. The number of persons on the list of an assistant who is a principal with a list of his own shall be regarded for the purpose of this regulation as being on the list of a doctor or partners by whom he is employed.

(1A) For the purpose of determining under paragraph (1) the number of persons a doctor may have on his list, a doctor who is in partnership shall be treated as an assistant, and not a partner, unless the Committee or, on appeal, the Secretary of State is satisfied that he—

(a)   discharges the duties and exercises the powers of a principal in connection with the practice of the partnership; and,

(b)   either—

(i)   in the case of a full-time doctor, he is entitled to a share of the profits which is not less than one third of the share of the partner with the greatest share, or

(ii)   in the case of a three-quarter-time doctor but not less than 19 hours per week he is entitled to a share of the profits which is not less than one quarter of the share of the partner with the greatest share; or

(iii)   in the case of a half-time doctor but not less than 13 hours per week he is entitled to a share of the profits which is not less than one fifth of the share of the partner with the greatest share or

(iv)   in the case of a job-sharing doctor who practises in partnership with another job-sharing doctor and at least one further doctor, he is entitled to a share of the profits which, when added to the share of the other job-sharing doctor with whose hours his hours are being aggregated for the purposes of regulation 11A(d), is not less than one third of the share of the member of the partnership with the greatest share.

(2)(a)   Where an excess number is due to—

(i)   the creation of a partnership of which the doctor is a member, or

(ii)   the death or retirement of a partner or the cessation of employment of an assistant, and the doctor is actively seeking a new partner or assistant,

the Committee, on the doctor's undertaking not to accept further patients other than the children of existing patients, may permit him to retain, for such period not exceeding nine months as it may determine from the date of the event which gave rise to the excess number, in addition to such children, not more than the number of patients on his list (and in a case within (ii) above, on the list, if any, of his former partner) at that date.

(b)   The Committee with the consent of the Secretary of State may extend any period mentioned in the preceding sub-paragraph.

(c)   The Committee may in special circumstances with the consent of the Secretary of State, and subject, if the Secretary of State so determines, to his or their undertaking not to accept further patients other than children of existing patients, permit a doctor or partnership to have on his or their list or lists such greater number of persons than authorised under paragraph (1) as may be determined.

(3)   The Committee shall notify each doctor of the number of patients on his list as at the first day of each period of three months ending 31st March, 30th June, 30th September or 31st December and of the number of any excess. If there is an excess the doctor shall, within two months from the date on which an excess was notified to him, take steps to reduce his list to the maximum number permitted by this regulation by—

(a)   taking a partner, or

(b)   engaging an assistant, or

(c)   informing the Committee of the names of the necessary number of patients on his list whom he wishes to have removed from his list under paragraph 10 of the terms of service. If at the end of that time such measures have not been completely effective the Committee shall remove from his list the necessary number of patients and the selection of such patients shall be at the discretion of the Family Health Services Authority.

(4) If a doctor gives notice under paragraph (3)(c), the Committee shall send a notice to each person so named to inform him that he should apply to another doctor for acceptance:

Provided that if the Committee, after consulting the Local Medical Committee, accepts an application for the notices to name another doctor who is willing to accept the person on his list and who has given his written consent, so however that such acceptance will not result in an excess number of patients on that other doctor's list or if that other doctor is in partnership, on the average of the partnership lists, then the notices shall be issued accordingly and the name of any such person shall be included on the list of the doctor named in the notice until such time as the person has chosen another doctor or has informed the Committee in writing that he wishes not to be so included.

(5) Paragraph (4) shall also apply, with any necessary modification, where a doctor whose name is included on the medical list in respect of more than one address and who ceases to practise at one of them informs the Committee of his wish to have removed from his list the persons who would have attended for treatment at the address at which he will no longer practise.

(6) In carrying out its functions under this regulation, the Family Health Services Authority shall consult as necessary with any other such Authority of an adjoining locality whose medical list includes a doctor concerned.

(7) Nothing in this regulation shall restrict a doctor from accepting persons who apply to him as temporary residents, or exempt him from any liability under the terms of service to give treatment immediately required to any person who applies for acceptance or to give emergency treatment.

Change of doctor

18.—(1) Subject to the requirements of paragraph (2), a person who is on a doctor's list of patients may apply to any other doctor providing general medical services for acceptance on that other doctor's list of patients.

(2) An application pursuant to paragraph (1) shall be made in accordance with regulation 14(1).

(3) A person who has applied pursuant to paragraph (1) to, and been refused acceptance by, any doctor may apply to the Committee in whose locality he resides for assignment to a doctor whose name is included in the Committee's medical list.

(4) Subject as hereinafter provided, the Committee shall, on the death or on the removal or withdrawal from the medical list of a doctor, notify the persons on the list of that doctor of the death, removal or withdrawal.

(5) A Committee shall inform a doctor as soon as practicable of the removal of a patient from his list on transfer to the list of another doctor.

(6) Where a successor is, or successors are, appointed to a practice the Committee shall by notice in writing inform the persons on the list of the doctor who last carried on that practice of the names and addresses of the successor or successors and of any partners.

(6A) The notice mentioned in paragraph (6) shall state that the person to whom it is given is deemed, from the date specified in the notice, to be on the list of a named successor, unless that person within 14 days of that date gives notice in writing to the Committee that he does not wish to be included in the list of that successor.

(7) Where no successor is to be appointed to a practice, the Committee shall notify the persons on the list of the doctor who last carried on that practice of their right to apply to another doctor on the medical list for acceptance.

(8) A doctor who has performed a period of relevant service recognised by the Secretary of State for the purpose of these regulations and has returned to his practice

at the end of such service shall within one month of his return notify the Committee in writing that he has personally resumed practice. Where the Committee has been so notified it shall within 7 days send a notice to every person who was on the doctor's list at the beginning of such service, who is still residing at the address at which he was then residing and who has been transferred to the list of another doctor, stating that the first doctor has resumed practice and that the person will be restored to his list unless, not later than 14 days after the date of the notice, that person gives notice in writing to the Committee that he wishes to remain on the list of that other doctor. After the said period of 14 days has elapsed, the Committee shall inform each of the other doctors concerned of the persons who are transferred from his list to the list of the first doctor and shall also inform each other doctor of the persons who have elected to remain on his list.

(9)   When a doctor is relieved of the obligation to provide services at certain periods under paragraph 15 of the terms of service the Committee shall notify the persons on his list of the fact. If the doctor subsequently resumes responsibility for providing services at all times the Committee shall notify the persons on his list of the fact.

(10)   Nothing in this regulation shall require the Committee to give any notice of or concerning the making or termination of arrangements under regulation 19.

Temporary provision of general medical services

19.—(1)   The provisions of this regulation shall apply in relation to the making of arrangements for the temporary provision of general medical services.

(2)   Where a doctor ceases to be included on the medical list or his registration in the register is suspended as mentioned in section 29(8) of the National Health Service Act 1977, the Committee, after consultation with the Local Medical Committee, may—

(a)   make arrangements for the temporary provision of general medical services for that doctor's patients, which arrangements may consist of or include the appointment of one or more doctors to undertake the treatment of such persons;

(b)   where a doctor included on a medical list by virtue of regulation 4(1)(a) ceases by reason of death to be so included and within 7 days of the date of death any person applies to the Committee in writing on behalf of the estate of that doctor for the appointment of one or more named doctors, appoint one or more of the named doctors to undertake the treatment of the deceased doctor's patients.

(3)   The Committee may make such arrangements as it thinks fit for the accommodation and other needs of any doctor appointed under paragraph (2) and, in the case of any doctor appointed under paragraph (2)(b), shall where practicable first consult any person who applied to it for the appointment of that doctor.

(4)   Subject to paragraph (10), arrangements under paragraph (2) shall subsist for such period as the Committee may determine, but not beyond the date on which the vacancy is filled or the suspension referred to in paragraph (2) ceases to have effect.

(5)   Where it appears to a Committee, after consultation with the Local Medical Committee, that a doctor is incapable of carrying out adequately his obligations under the terms of service because of his physical or mental condition, it may require him to be medically examined.

(6)   Where a Committee is satisfied—

(a)   after receiving from the Local Medical Committee a report under paragraph (9) that because of his physical or mental condition; or

(b)   that because of continued absence, a doctor's obligations under the terms of service are not being carried out adequately, it may, after consultation with the Local Medical Committee and with the consent of the Secretary of State, make arrangements for the temporary provision of general medical services for that doctor's patients, which arrangements may consist of or include the appointment of one or more doctors to undertake the treatment of such persons.

(7)   Subject to paragraph (10), arrangements under paragraph (6) shall subsist for such period as the Committee may determine, but not, in a case to which paragraph (6)(a) applies, beyond the date on which the Committee is satisfied, after consulting the Local Medical Committee, that the doctor is fit to resume his practice.

(8)   A Committee may, before varying or terminating any arrangements made under paragraph (6) but after consulting the Local Medical Committee, require the doctor to be medically examined.

(9)   A doctor required under this regulation to be medically examined shall submit himself for medical examination by a doctor appointed by the Local Medical Committee, which having considered the report of the examining doctor shall make a report in writing to the Committee as to the doctor's fitness to carry out his obligations under the terms of service.

(10)   Where a Committee proposes that the arrangements under paragraph (2) or (6) shall continue for longer than one year or such shorter period as the Secretary of State may specify in any particular case, or beyond any further such period, it shall so notify the Secretary of State in writing not less than one month, or as soon as is practicable, before the expiry of that period or further period, and shall in each case obtain the consent of the Secretary of State to the continuance of the arrangements.

(11)   The Committee shall give reasonable notice in writing of the termination of arrangements under paragraph (2) or (6) to the doctor with whom they were made and shall, as soon as it is practicable, notify the Secretary of State in writing that such termination has taken place.

(12)   A Committee shall, where practicable, notify in writing, any doctor for the treatment of whose patients arrangements are made under this regulation of such arrangements and of their variation or termination.

(13)   Each doctor appointed under this regulation shall agree in writing to be bound throughout his appointment by the terms of service which were applicable to the doctor the treatment of whose patients he is appointed with or without other doctors to undertake, save that nothing in these paragraphs shall require him to provide child health surveillance services, contraceptive services, maternity medical services or minor surgery services which he has not undertaken to provide.

(14)   Any person on the list of the doctor for the treatment of whose patients arrangements are made under this regulation shall be deemed to remain on that list while those arrangements subsist, unless that person is transferred to the list of another doctor, and any person who applies to the doctor appointed under this regulation for acceptance shall, if accepted, be recorded by the Committee as being—

(a)   where that doctor is included on the medical list by virtue of regulation 4(1)(a), on his list;

(b)   in any other case, on the list of the doctor for the treatment of whose patients arrangements are made under this regulation.

(15)   The Committee may deduct from the remuneration of a doctor for the treatment of whose patients arrangements are made under paragraph (6) or consequent upon the suspension of whose registration arrangements are made under paragraph (2)(a) the cost, in part or in whole, of any such arrangements, and in the case of a doctor performing relevant service in an emergency recognised by the Secretary of State for the purpose of these regulations, the Committee shall deduct from his remuneration the cost of any such arrangements.

(16)   In the National Health Service Act 1977—

(a)   in its application to the temporary provision of general medical services section 29(4) (which prohibits, with exceptions, payments of a fixed salary) shall have effect as if the words "otherwise than the temporarily" were inserted after the words "general medical services" in that subsection;

(b)   section 30(1A) (which contains requirements as to knowledge of English) shall apply to a doctor appointed under regulation 19, and in respect of any such doctor section 30(1A) shall have effect as if for the words from "shall be entitled" to "referred to the Medical Practices Committee" in that subsection there were substituted the words "shall be appointed to provide general medical services temporarily".

Removal of person from doctor's list

20.—(1)   A person who no longer wishes to avail himself of general medical services may at any time give notice to the Committee that he wishes to be removed from a doctor's list and the Committee shall forthwith inform him and the doctor that on a specified date, being 14 days after the date of the receipt of the notice by the Committee, his name will be removed from the doctor's list.

(2)   Subject to the provisions of paragraph (4) where the Committee, on being informed by the doctor or after due enquiry, is satisfied that a person on the list of a doctor providing general medical services in its locality no longer resides at a place where that doctor is under an obligation under these regulations to visit and treat him, the Committee shall inform that person and the doctor that because of the person's change of address the doctor is no longer obliged to visit and treat the person if his condition so requires. The Committee shall advise the person either to obtain the doctor's agreement under paragraph 13 of the terms of service to visit him if his condition so requires, or to seek acceptance by another doctor, and shall inform him that if after the expiration of one month from the date of the letter of advice he has not acted in accordance with the advice, the Committee will remove him from his doctor's list. If at the expiration of a month, the Committee has not been notified of the action taken, it shall remove him from the doctor's list and inform the patient and doctor accordingly.

(3)   Where a person on the list of a doctor providing general medical services has moved to an address outside the Committee's locality or the address of that person is no longer known to the Committee, the Committee shall give to that doctor notice in writing that it intends, at the end of the period specified therein (being a period of six months commencing with the date of the notice, or such shorter period as in a particular case the Secretary of State may determine after consultation with such organisations as he may recognise as representing doctors), to remove the person from the doctor's list, and at the end of the said period the Committee shall remove the person from the doctor's list, unless within that period the doctor satisfies the Committee that he is still responsible for providing general medical services for that person, including visiting and treating him when necessary.

(4)   (a)   The Committee shall, on receiving particulars of persons who are pupils at, or staff or residents of, a school or residential institution where the doctor provides general medical services, forthwith remove from the doctor's list any person appearing on his list as pupils at, or staff or residents of, such a school or institution who are not shown in the said particulars.

(b)   Where the Committee has made a request to a school or institution to provide such particulars and has not received them it may, after consulting the doctor, remove from the doctor's list, if it thinks fit, any persons appearing thereon as pupils at, or staff or residents of, such school or institution.

Arrangements for temporary residents

21.—(1)   A person requiring treatment who—

(a)   is not on the list of a doctor providing general medical services in the locality where he is temporarily residing;

(b)   normally resides in a school or similar institution in the locality but is temporarily residing at home in that locality;

(c)   normally resides at home in the locality but is temporarily residing in any institution in that locality; or

(d)   is moving from place to place and is not for the time being resident in any place,
may apply to any doctor providing services in the locality in which he is temporarily residing to be accepted by him as a temporary resident and, subject to paragraph (2), if he is so accepted and is a person mentioned in sub-paragraph (a), (b) or (c) of this paragraph, he shall not be removed from the list of any doctor on which he is already included.

(2)   For the purposes of this regulation, a person shall be regarded as temporarily resident in a place, if when he arrives in that place, he intends to stay there for more than 24 hours but not more than 3 months; and if the Committee for the locality in which he is included on any doctor's list is satisfied, after due enquiry, that his stay in the locality of temporary residence has exceeded three months and that he has not returned to that Committee's locality, that Committee shall thereupon remove him from that doctor's list and, if practicable, inform him of that fact and of his entitlement to seek acceptance by any doctor, including the doctor by whom he has been treated as a temporary resident, in the locality in which he is living, and of the name and address of the Committee for that locality.

(3)   (a)   A woman to whom paragraphs (1) and (2) would apply if she required treatment, may apply to a doctor who has undertaken to provide contraceptive services in a locality in which she is temporarily resident, to be accepted by him for the provision to her as a temporary resident of contraceptive services.

(b)   Where a woman has been accepted by a doctor for the provision to her of contraceptive services under regulation 14(2), the provisions of paragraph (2) shall apply to terminate that provision as they apply to the removal of a patient from a doctor's list.

Doctors' lists

22.—(1)(a)   The Committee shall prepare and keep revised up to date for each doctor on its medical list, a list of the patients in its locality accepted by or assigned to the doctor under or by virtue of this Part of these regulations, otherwise than as a temporary resident, and any persons for whom he has under paragraph 15 of the terms of service accepted responsibility during certain periods only.

(b)   The Committee shall from time to time furnish the doctor with information in such form as the Secretary of State may determine with regard to persons included on or removed from those lists.

(2)   Subject to the provisions of regulation 18(7), a person accepted by a doctor for inclusion on his list shall be included on the list from the date on which notification of acceptance is received by the Committee.

(3)   Where a person for whose treatment a doctor is responsible dies, or is absent from the United Kingdom for a period of 3 months, he shall be removed from the doctor's list from the date on which the Committee first receives notification of the death or absence for 3 months.

(4)   Where such a person leaves the United Kingdom with the intention of being away for a period of 3 months or is in Her Majesty's Forces or is serving a prison sentence of more than 2 years or sentences totalling in the aggregate more than that period, he shall be removed from the doctor's list from the date on which the Committee first receives notification of such departure, enlistment or imprisonment.

(5)   Any removal from a doctor's list caused by the transfer of a person to the list of another doctor, otherwise than in pursuance of a notice given under regulation 18(7), shall take effect from the date on which the Committee receives notification of the acceptance of the person by the last-named doctor, or, subject to consent of the Committee, on such date, being not earlier than the date of such consent, as may be agreed between the doctors.

(6) Any other removal from a doctor's list shall take effect from the date on which notice of removal is sent by the Committee to the doctor or from such other date, not being earlier than that date, as may be specified in the notice.

PART V

Application for services

23.—(1) A woman who, after a doctor has diagnosed that she is pregnant, requires the provision of maternity medical services may arrange for the provision of such services with either—

(a) any doctor on the obstetric list, or

(b) the doctor on whose list she is included, or

(c) any doctor who has under regulation 21(1) accepted her as a temporary resident.

(2) A woman who has arranged with a doctor (in this regulation referred to as "the original doctor") for the provision of maternity medical services may terminate the arrangement—

(a) by so informing the Committee in writing;

(b) by so informing in writing the original doctor who shall within 7 days notify the Committee in writing, or

(c) by making a new arrangement with another doctor who shall within 7 days notify the Committee in writing of the new arrangement.

(3) Where a Committee receives notification in accordance with paragraph (2)(a) or (c) it shall within 7 days notify the original doctor in writing that the woman's arrangement with him has been terminated.

SCHEDULE 1

PART I

TERMS OF SERVICE FOR DOCTORS

Interpretation

1. In these terms of service, unless the context otherwise requires,—

(a) "assistant" includes a trainee general practitioner;

(b) "deputising service" means any person or body carrying on a business which consists of, or includes, providing a deputy or deputies for doctors for periods which normally do not exceed 48 consecutive hours;

(bb) "prescription form" means a form provided by the Committee or, where the doctor is on the medical list of more than one Committee, by the Committee which is responsible for the supply of that form and issued by a doctor to enable a person to obtain pharmaceutical services as defined by section 41 of the National Health Service Act 1977;

(c) "the regulations" means the National Health Service (General Medical and Pharmaceutical Services) Regulations 1974.

General

3. Where a decision whether any, and if so what, action is to be taken under these terms of service requires the exercise of professional judgment, a doctor shall not, in reaching that decision, be expected to exercise a higher degree of skill, knowledge and care than—

(a) in the case of a doctor providing child health surveillance services under paragraph 9B or minor surgery services under paragraph 9C, that which any general practitioner included in the child health surveillance list or, as the case may be, the minor surgery list may reasonably be expected to exercise; and

(b) in any other case, that which general practitioners as a class may reasonably be expected to exercise.

A doctor's patients

4.—(1)   Subject to paragraphs 10 to 12, a doctor's patients are—

(a)   persons who are recorded by the Committee as being on his list;

(b)   persons whom he has accepted or agreed to accept on his list, and who have not been notified to him by the Committee as having ceased to be on his list;

(c)   for the limited period specified in sub-paragraph (3), persons whom he has refused to accept;

(d)   persons who have been assigned to him under regulation 16;

(e)   for the limited period mentioned in sub-paragraph (4), persons in respect of whom he has been notified that an application has been made for assignment to him under the proviso to regulation 16(1);

(f)   persons whom he has accepted as temporary residents under paragraph 7 and regulation 21;

(g)   in respect of services under paragraph 8, 9B or 9C, persons to whom he has agreed to provide those services;

(h)   persons to whom he may be requested to give treatment which is immediately required owing to an accident or other emergency at any place in his practice area if—

(i)   he is not a doctor to whom paragraph 5 applies, and

(ii)   he is not, at the time of the request, relieved under paragraph 16(2) of his obligation to give treatment personally, and

(iii)   he is available to provide such treatment,

or any persons to whom he may be requested, and he agrees, to give treatment which is immediately required owing to an accident or other emergency at any place in the locality of any Committee on whose medical list he is included, provided, in either case, that there is no doctor who, at the time of the request, is under an obligation otherwise than under this sub-paragraph to give treatment to that person, or there is such a doctor but, after being requested to attend, he is unable to attend and give treatment immediately required;

(i)   persons in relation to whom he is acting as deputy to another doctor under these terms of service;

(j)   during the period of an appointment under regulation 19, persons whom he has been appointed to treat temporarily;

(k)   in respect of contraceptive services and maternity medical services, women for whom he has undertaken to provide either or both of such services; and

(l)   during the hours arranged with the Committee, any person whose own doctor has been relieved of responsibility during those hours under paragraph 15 and for whom he has accepted responsibility under that paragraph;

but no person shall, except in a case to which sub-paragraphs (h)(i) or (j) applies, be a patient for the purposes of this sub-paragraph if the doctor has been notified by the Committee that he is no longer responsible for the treatment of that person.

(2)   If a person applies to a doctor for treatment and claims to be on that doctor's list, but fails to produce his medical card on request and the doctor has reasonable doubts about that person's claim, the doctor shall give any necessary treatment and shall be entitled to demand and accept a fee under paragraph 32(f), subject to the provision for repayment contained in paragraph 33.

(3)   If a doctor refuses to accept for inclusion on his list a person who lives in his practice area and who is not on the list of another doctor practising in that area, or refuses to accept as a temporary resident a person to whom regulation 21 applies, he shall on request give that person any immediately necessary treatment for one period not exceeding 14 days from the date when that person was refused acceptance or until that person has been accepted by or assigned to another doctor, whichever period is the less.

(4)   Where the Committee has notified a doctor that it is applying for the Secretary of State's consent under the proviso to regulation 16(1), the doctor shall give the person

proposed for assignment any immediately necessary treatment until the Committee has notified him that—

(a) the Secretary of State has determined that the person shall not be assigned to that doctor, and

(b) either the person has been accepted by, or assigned to, another doctor or another doctor has been notified that an application has been made under the proviso to regulation 16(1) to assign that person to him;

but where the Secretary of State has determined that a person shall not be assigned to a doctor, and the Committee is satisfied, after due enquiry, that the person still wishes to be assigned to a doctor, the Committee shall as soon as practicable assign that person to another doctor or, as the case may be, seek the Secretary of State's consent to assignment to another doctor under the proviso to regulation 16(1).

5.   A doctor, who is elderly or infirm or who has been exempted by the Family Health Services Authority under regulation 16(3) from the liability to have persons assigned to him, may be relieved by the Family Health Services Authority of any liability for emergency calls arising between 7 p.m. on weekdays and 8 a.m. on the following morning and between 1 p.m. on Saturday and 8 a.m. on the following Monday to persons who—

(a) are not on his list, or

(b) are not temporary residents for whom he is responsible, or

(c) have not been accepted by him for the provision of maternity medical services.

Acceptance of patients

6.—(1) Subject to sub-paragraph (2), a doctor may agree to accept a person on his list if the person is eligible to be accepted by him.

(2) While a doctor is responsible for treating the patients of another doctor who has given notice of retirement to the Committee or has died, he may not consent to the transfer of any of those patients under regulation 18 to his own list or that of his partner or principal.

(3) When a doctor has agreed to accept a person on his list, he shall within 14 days of receiving it, or as soon thereafter as is practicable, send to the Committee the medical card or form of application, signed by or on behalf of both the person and the doctor. Where any person is authorised by the doctor to sign the card or form on behalf of that doctor, he shall, in addition to his own signature, add the doctor's name.

7.   A doctor may accept a person requiring treatment as a temporary resident in accordance with regulation 21 and the provisions of regulation 17 concerning the maximum number of persons he may have on his list shall not restrict him from accepting such a person as a temporary resident.

8.   A doctor may—

(a) take a cervical smear from a woman who would be eligible for acceptance by him as a temporary resident or for whom he has undertaken to provide maternity medical services; or

(b) vaccinate or immunise a person who would be eligible for acceptance by him as a temporary resident.

9.   A doctor may undertake to provide maternity medical services required by a woman on his list or by a woman whom he has accepted as a temporary resident, or, if he is a doctor on the obstetric list, by any woman.

Provision of child health surveillance services and minor surgery services

9A.   A doctor whose name is included in the medical list may, in respect of any person on his list or on the list of a doctor with whom he is in partnership or with whom he is associated in a group practice, undertake to provide—

(a) child health surveillance services, provided that—

    (i)   his name is also included in the child health surveillance list, and

    (ii)   the person in question is a child who is under the age of 5 years;

  (b) minor surgery services, provided that his name is included in the minor surgery list.

9B. A doctor who has undertaken, pursuant to paragraph 9A(a), to provide child health surveillance services to any child shall, in respect of that child—

  (a) provide all the services described in paragraph 1 of Schedule 1A to these Regulations, other than any examination so described which the parent refuses to allow the child to undergo, until the date upon which the child attains the age of 5 years;

  (b) maintain such records as are specified in paragraph 2 of that Schedule; and

  (c) furnish the relevant health authority with such information as is specified in paragraph 3 of that Schedule in accordance with the requirements of that paragraph.

9C.—(1) A doctor who has undertaken, pursuant to paragraph 9A(b), to provide minor surgery services in respect of any patient shall offer to provide any of the procedures described in Schedule 1B to these Regulations which it is, in his opinion, appropriate for him to provide in the case of that patient.

(2) Where a doctor provides minor surgery services in respect of a patient who is not included on his list, he shall inform in writing the doctor on whose list the patient is included of the outcome of the procedure.

(3) Nothing in paragraph 9A(b) or in this paragraph shall prevent any doctor personally performing, in the course of providing general medical services (otherwise than by way of minor surgery services) to a patient, a procedure described in Schedule 1B to these Regulations.

Termination of responsibility for patients

10. A doctor may have any person removed from his list by requiring the Committee so to do and the removal shall take effect on the date of acceptance by, or assignment to, another doctor or on the eighth day after the Committee is so required whichever first occurs, but, if the doctor is at the date when removal would take effect, treating the person otherwise than at intervals of more than 7 days, the doctor shall inform the Committee of the fact and removal shall take effect on the eighth day after the Committee receives notification from him that the patient no longer needs such treatment or upon acceptance by another doctor, whichever first occurs.

11. A doctor desiring to terminate his responsibility for a temporary resident may so inform the Committee; and the date on which his responsibility ceases shall be decided under paragraph 10, as if the temporary resident were a person on his list.

12. A doctor may cease to provide maternity medical services to a woman by agreement with her. In default of agreement the doctor may apply to the Committee for permission to terminate the arrangement and the Committee may terminate the arrangement after considering the representations, if any, made by either party and after consulting the Local Medical Committee. Where a doctor ceases to provide any maternity medical services, he shall inform any woman for whom he has arranged to provide such services that he is ceasing to provide them and that she may make fresh arrangements to receive those services from another doctor.

12A.—(1) An undertaking referred to in paragraph 9A(a) shall cease forthwith to be effective if—

  (a) either—

    (i)   the parent informs the doctor, or

    (ii)   the doctor informs the parent,

that he wishes the undertaking to have no further effect;

  (b) the child has been removed from the doctor's list, from that of his partner or from that of a doctor with whom he is associated in a group practice, as the case may be, and has not been transferred to any other of those lists;

(c)   the parent—
(i)   has been invited to arrange for the child to attend for an examination referred to in paragraph 1(b) of Schedule 1A to these Regulations, and
(ii)   fails within 42 days to respond to that invitation; or
(d)   any examination referred to in paragraph 1(b) of that Schedule is undertaken in respect of the child otherwise than by the doctor or a person acting on his behalf.

(2)   Where, in accordance with sub-paragraph (1), an undertaking referred to in paragraph 9A(a) has ceased to be effective, the doctor shall forthwith—
(a)   in a case to which any of heads (a), (c) or (d) of that sub-paragraph applies, so inform the Committee in writing; and
(b)   in a case to which either head (c) or (d) of that sub-paragraph applies, also so inform the parent in writing.

Nature of service to patients
13.—(1)   Subject to paragraphs 3, 13A and 36A, a doctor shall render to his patients all necessary and appropriate personal medical services of the type usually provided by general medical practitioners.
(2)   The services which a doctor is required by sub-paragraph (1) to render shall include the following: —
(a)   giving advice, where appropriate, to a patient in connection with the patient's general health, and in particular about the significance of diet, exercise, the use of tobacco, the consumption of alcohol and the misuse of drugs and solvents;
(b)   offering to patients consultations and, where appropriate, physical examinations for the purpose of identifying, or reducing the risk of, disease or injury;
(c)   offering to patients, where appropriate, vaccination or immunisation against Measles, Mumps, Rubella, Pertussis, Poliomyelitis, Diphtheria and Tetanus;
(d)   arranging for the referral of patients, as appropriate, for the provision of any other services under the National Health Service Act 1977;
(e)   giving advice, as appropriate, to enable patients to avail themselves of services provided by a local social services authority.
(3)   A doctor is not required by sub-paragraph (1) or (2)—
(a)   to provide to any person contraceptive services, child health surveillance services, minor surgery services nor, except in an emergency, maternity medical services, unless he has previously undertaken to the Committee to provide such services to that person; or
(b)   where he is a restricted services principal, to provide any category of general medical services which he has not undertaken to provide.

Provision of service to patients
13A—(1)   The services referred to in paragraph 13 shall be rendered by a doctor—
(a)   at his practice premises; or
(b)   if the condition of the patient so requires—
(i)   at the place where the patient was residing when he was accepted by the doctor pursuant to paragraph 6 or, as the case may be, when he was assigned to the doctor pursuant to regulation 16, or, in the case of a patient who was previously on the list of a doctor in a practice declared vacant, when the doctor succeeded to the vacancy, or
(ii)   at such other place as the doctor has informed the patient and the Committee is the place where he has agreed to visit and treat the patient if the patient's condition so requires; or
(iii)   in any other case, at some other place in the doctor's practice area.
(2)   Without prejudice to the generality of sub-paragraph (1) a doctor shall in particular make himself available for consultations at such places and at such times as have been approved by the Committee in his case, pursuant to paragraph 25.

Newly registered patients

13B—(1)   Subject to sub-paragraph (4) to (9), where a patient has been accepted on a doctor's list under paragraph 6 or assigned to a doctor's list under regulation 16, the doctor shall, in addition to and without prejudice to his other obligations in respect of that patient under these terms of service, within 28 days of the date of such acceptance or assignment invite the patient to participate in a consultation either at his practice premises or, if the condition of the patient so warrants, at such other place as the doctor is obliged, under paragraph 13A(1)(b), to render personal medical services to that patient.

(2)   Where a patient (or, in the case of a patient who is a child, his parent) agrees to participate in a consultation mentioned in sub-paragraph (1), the doctor shall, in the course of that consultation—

(a)   seek details from the patient as to his medical history and, so far as may be relevant to the patient's medical history, as to that of his consanguineous family, in respect of—

(i)   illnesses, immunisations, allergies, hereditary conditions, medication and tests carried out for breast or cervical cancer,

(ii)   social factors (including employment, housing and family circumstances) which may affect his health,

(iii)   factors of his lifestyle (including diet, exercise, use of tobacco, consumption of alcohol, and misuse of drugs or solvents) which may affect his health, and

(iv)   the current state of his health;

(b)   offer to undertake a physical examination of the patient, comprising—

(i)   the measurement of his height, weight and blood pressure, and

(ii)   the taking of a urine sample and its analysis to identify the presence of albumin and glucose;

(c)   record, in the patient's medical records, his findings arising out of the details supplied by, and any examination of, the patient under this sub-paragraph;

(d)   assess whether and, if so, in what manner and to what extent he should render personal medical services to the patient; and

(e)   in so far as it would not, in the opinion of the doctor, be likely to cause serious damage to the physical or mental health of the patient to do so, offer to discuss with the patient (or, where the patient is a child, the parent) the conclusions the doctor has drawn as a result of the consultation as to the state of the patient's health.

(3)   On each occasion where a doctor invites a patient or parent to participate in a consultation pursuant to sub-paragraph (1) he shall—

(a)   make the invitation in writing or, if the invitation is initially made orally, confirm it in writing, by a letter either handed to the patient or his representative or sent to the patient or parent at the address recorded in his medical records as being his last home address;

(b)   record in the patient's medical records the date of each such invitation and whether or not it was accepted;

(c)   where, as a result of making the invitation, the doctor becomes aware that the patient is no longer residing at the address shown in his medical records, advise the Committee accordingly.

(4)   A doctor shall not be obliged to offer a consultation pursuant to sub-paragraph (1)—

(a)   if he is a restricted services principal;

(b)   in respect of a child under the age of 5 years;

(c)   to any patient who, immediately before joining the list of the doctor, was a patient of a partner of the doctor and who, during the 12 months immediately preceding the date of his acceptance or assignment to the doctor's list, had participated in a consultation pursuant to sub-paragraph (1); or

(d)   to the extent allowed by the Committee, to any patient within a class of patients in respect of which the Committee or, on appeal, the Secretary of State has, pursuant to sub-paragraphs (5) to (8), deferred the doctor's obligation under sub-paragraph (1).

(5)   Where a doctor assumes responsibility for a list of patients on his succession to a practice declared vacant or otherwise becomes responsible for a significant number of new patients within a short period, he may apply, in accordance with sub-paragraph (6), to the Committee for the deferment of his obligation under sub-paragraph (1) for a period not exceeding 2 years from the date of the application.

(6)   An application pursuant to sub-paragraph (5) shall be made in writing and shall be accompanied by a statement of the doctor's proposals, by reference to particular classes of patient, with a view to securing that all eligible patients are invited to participate in a consultation pursuant to sub-paragraph (1) by the end of the period of the deferment.

(7)   Within 2 months of receiving an application the Committee shall determine it—
   (a)   by approving the application;
   (b)   by approving the application subject to conditions; or
   (c)   by refusing the application.

(8)   A doctor may appeal in writing to the Secretary of State against any refusal of an application, or against any condition subject to which an application is approved by a Committee pursuant to sub-paragraph (7)(b) and on determining such an appeal the Secretary of State shall either confirm the Committee's determination or substitute his own determination for that of the Committee.

(9)   The Secretary of State shall notify the doctor in writing of his determination and shall include with the notice a statement of his reasons for the determination.

Patients not seen within 3 years
13C.—(1)   Subject to sub-paragraph (2), a doctor shall, in addition to and without prejudice to any other obligation under these terms of service, invite each patient on his list who appears to him—
   (a)   to have attained the age of 16 years but who has not attained the age of 75 years; and
   (b)   to have neither—
      (i)   within the preceding 3 years attended either a consultation with, or a clinic provided by, any doctor in the course of his provision of general medical services , nor
      (ii)   within the preceding 12 months been offered a consultation pursuant to this sub-paragraph by any doctor, to participate in a consultation at his practice premises for the purpose of assessing whether he needs to render personal medical services to that patient.

(2)   Sub-paragraph (1) shall not apply in the case of a doctor who is a restricted services principal.

(3)   In the case of any patient who is included on the doctor's list on 1st April 1990, the first invitation to participate in a consultation pursuant to sub-paragraph (1) shall be made no later than 1st April 1991.

(4)   When inviting a patient to participate in a consultation pursuant to sub-paragraph (1) a doctor shall comply with the requirements of paragraph 13B(3).

(5)   Where a patient agrees to participate in a consultation mentioned in sub-paragraph (1), the doctor shall, in the course of that consultation—
   (a)   where appropriate, seek details from the patient as to his medical history and, so far as may be relevant to the patient's medical history, as to that of his consanguineous family, in respect of—
      (i)   illnesses, immunisations, allergies, hereditary diseases, medication and tests carried out for breast or cervical cancer,

(ii)   social factors (including employment, housing and family circumstances) which may affect his health,

(iii)   factors of his lifestyle (including diet, exercise, use of tobacco, consumption of alcohol, and misuse of drugs or solvents) which may affect his health, and

(iv)   the current state of his health;

(b)   offer to undertake a physical examination of the patient, comprising—

(i)   the measurement of his blood pressure, and

(ii)   the taking of a urine sample and its analysis to identify the presence of albumin and glucose;

(iii)   the measurement necessary to detect any changes in his body mass;

(c)   record, in the patient's medical records, his findings arising out of the details supplied by, and any examination of, the patient under this sub-paragraph;

(d)   assess whether and, if so, in what manner and to what extent he should render personal medical services to the patient; and

(e)   in so far as it would not, in the opinion of the doctor, be likely to cause serious damage to the physical or mental health of the patient to do so, offer to discuss with the patient the conclusions the doctor has drawn as a result of the consultation as to the state of the patient's health.

(6)   In this paragraph "body mass" means the figure produced by dividing the number of kilograms in the patient's weight by the square of the number of metres in his height.

Patients aged 75 years and over

13D.—(1)   Subject to sub-paragraph (2), a doctor shall, in addition to and without prejudice to any other obligations under these terms of service, in each period of 12 months beginning on 1st April in each year—

(a)   invite each patient on his list who has attained the age of 75 years to participate in a consultation; and

(b)   offer to make a domiciliary visit to each such patient, for the purpose of assessing whether he needs to render personal medical services to that patient.

(2)   Sub-paragraph (1) shall not apply in the case of any doctor who is a restricted services principal.

(3)   Any consultation pursuant to sub-paragraph (1) may take place in the course of a domiciliary visit pursuant to that sub-paragraph.

(4)   An invitation and an offer pursuant to sub-paragraph (1) shall be made by a doctor—

(a)   in the case of a patient who is over the age of 75 years and is on the doctor's list on 31st March 1990, by no later than 1st April 1991;

(b)   in the case of a patient who attains the age of 75 years on or after 1st April 1990, within 12 months of his 75th birthday;

(c)   in the case of a patient who—

(i)   is accepted by the doctor pursuant to paragraph 6, or assigned to him pursuant to regulation 16, after 1st April 1990, and

(ii)   who has attained the age of 75 years when he is so accepted or assigned, within 12 months of the date of his acceptance or assignment.

(5)   A doctor shall, when making an assessment following a consultation under sub-paragraph (1), record in the patient's medical records the observations made of any matter which appears to him to be affecting the patient's general health, including where appropriate the patient's—

(a)   sensory functions;

(b)   mobility;

(c)   mental condition;

(d)   physical condition including continence;

(e)   social environment;

(f)   use of medicines.

(6)   A doctor shall keep with the patient's medical records a report of any observations made in the course of a domiciliary visit made pursuant to sub-paragraph (1) which are relevant to the patient's general health.

(7)   When inviting a patient to participate in a consultation, or offering him a domiciliary visit, pursuant to sub-paragraph (1), a doctor shall comply with the requirements of paragraph 13B(3) as if that sub-paragraph referred to an offer as well as an invitation.

(8)   Where a patient has participated in a consultation pursuant to sub-paragraph (1), the doctor shall offer to discuss with him the conclusions he has drawn, as a result of the consultation, as to the state of the patient's health, unless to do so would, in the opinion of the doctor, be likely to cause serious harm to the physical or mental health of the patient.

14.   A doctor shall, unless prevented by an emergency, attend and treat any patient who attends for the purpose at the places and during the hours for the time being approved by the Committee under paragraph 25 other than a patient who attends when an appointment system is in operation and who has not previously made, and is not given an appointment to see the doctor then. In such a case the doctor may decline to attend and treat the patient during that surgery period, if the patient's health would not thereby be jeopardised and the patient is offered an appointment to attend within a reasonable time having regard to all the circumstances. The doctor shall take all reasonable steps to ensure that a consultation is not so deferred without his knowledge.

Duration of doctor's responsibility

15.—(1)   Subject to paragraph (2), a doctor is responsible for ensuring the provision to his patients of the services referred to in paragraph 13 throughout each day during which his name is included in the Committee's medical list.

(2) A doctor who was, pursuant to the provisions of this sub-paragraph as in force immediately prior to 1st April 1990, relieved by the Committee of such responsibility in respect of his patients during times approved by the Committee may continue to enjoy such relief for so long as his name is included in the medical list.

16.—(1)   Subject to sub-paragraphs (2), (3), (4) and (5) a doctor shall give treatment personally.

(2)   In the case of general medical services other than maternity medical services, child health surveillance services or minor surgery services, a doctor shall be under no obligation to give treatment personally to a patient if such reasonable steps as are appropriate are taken to ensure continuity of treatment, and treatment may be given—

(a)   by another doctor acting as deputy, whether or not he is a partner or assistant, or

(b)   if it is treatment which it is clinically reasonable in the circumstances to delegate, by a person whom the doctor has authorised and who is competent to carry out such treatment.

(3)   In the case of maternity medical services, a doctor on the obstetric list shall not without the consent of the Committee employ for the purposes of providing such services a deputy or assistant who is not, or is not qualified by experience to be, a doctor on the obstetric list, but this sub-paragraph shall not apply where there has been a summons to an obstetric emergency. In this sub-paragraph, a summons to an obstetric emergency means a summons by a midwife or on behalf of the patient to attend when medical attention is required urgently, in cases of illness of the patient or infant or in the case of any abnormality becoming apparent in the patient or infant during pregnancy, labour or the lying-in period.

(4)   In the case of child health surveillance services, a doctor who has, pursuant to paragraph 9A(a), undertaken to provide such services may employ for the purposes of

providing such services a deputy or an assistant whose name is included in a child health surveillance list or, with the consent of the Committee, some other deputy or assistant.

(5)   In the case of minor surgery services, a doctor who has, pursuant to paragraph 9A(b), undertaken to provide such services may employ a deputy or an assistant whose name is included in a minor surgery list to conduct a procedure described in Schedule 1B to these Regulations.

17.—(1)   In relation to his obligations under these terms of service, a doctor is responsible for all acts and omissions of any doctor acting as his deputy, whether or not he is a partner or assistant, or of any person employed by him or acting on his behalf: Provided that a doctor shall not be responsible for any act or omission for which a deputy is responsible under sub-paragraph (2).

(2)   A doctor who is included on the medical list, when acting as deputy to another doctor who is also included on that list, shall be responsible for his own acts and omissions in relation to the obligations under these terms of service of the doctor for whom he acts as deputy and for the acts and omissions of any person employed by him.

18.   A doctor shall inform the Committee of any standing deputising arrangements unless the deputy is an assistant of the doctor or is a doctor included on the medical list of a Committee, and the deputy will carry out these arrangements at the premises at which the doctor practises. When a doctor proposes to be absent from his practice for more than a week, he shall inform the Committee of the name of the doctor or doctors responsible for his practice during his absence.

19.—(1)   Before entering into arrangements with a deputising service for the provision of a deputy or deputies, a doctor shall obtain the consent of the Committee. In giving such consent, the Committee may also impose such conditions as it considers necessary or expedient to ensure the adequacy of such arrangements. Before refusing consent or imposing conditions, the Committee shall consult the Local Medical Committee.

(2)   The Committee may at any time, and shall periodically, review in consultation with the Local Medical Committee any such consent given or conditions imposed and may withdraw such consent or vary such conditions.

(3)   A doctor may appeal to the Secretary of State against refusal of consent or the imposition of a condition under sub-paragraph (1) or against withdrawal of consent or variation of conditions under sub-paragraph (2). In determining such an appeal the Secretary of State may substitute for the Committee's decision such decision and conditions as he thinks fit.

20.   A doctor shall take reasonable steps to satisfy himself that a doctor whom he proposes to employ as a deputy or assistant is not disqualified under section 46 of the Act for inclusion on the medical list of the Committee or has not given an undertaking that he will not apply for inclusion on a Committee's medical list; and he shall not without the consent of the Secretary of State knowingly employ a doctor who is so disqualified or has given such an undertaking.

21.—(1)   A doctor shall inform the Committee of the name of any assistant he employs and of the termination of such employment, and shall not employ any one or more assistants for a total period of more than three months in any period of 12 months without the consent of the Committee. The Committee shall periodically review and may withdraw any consent given, but, before refusing or withdrawing consent, the Committee shall consult the Local Medical Committee. The doctor may appeal to the Medical Practices Committee against refusal or withdrawal of consent.

(2)   Any withdrawal of consent under the foregoing sub-paragraph shall not have effect until the expiration of a period of one month after the date of notification of withdrawal: Provided that if a doctor appeals to the Medical Practices Committee against the withdrawal, and the Medical Practices Committee dismisses the appeal, the withdrawal

shall not take effect until after such date as that committee determines being not less than one month after the date of such dismissal.

22.   A doctor acting as a deputy may treat patients at places and at times other than those arranged by the doctor for whom he is acting, but due regard shall be had to the convenience of the patients.

23.   When issuing a document under these terms of service a deputy or assistant (other than a partner or assistant whose name is included on the medical list) shall enter on it the name of the doctor for whom he is acting, if it does not already appear, as well as signing the document himself.

Arrangements at practice premises

24.   A doctor shall provide proper and sufficient accommodation at his practice premises having regard to the circumstances of his practice, and shall, on receipt of a written request from the Committee, allow inspection of those premises at a reasonable time by a member or officer of the Committee or Local Medical Committee or both, authorised by the Committee for the purpose.

Employees

24A.—(1)   A doctor shall, before employing any person to assist him in the provision of general medical services, take reasonable care to satisfy himself that the person in question is both suitably qualified and competent to discharge the duties for which he is to be employed.

(2)   When considering the competence and suitability of any person for the purpose of sub-paragraph (1), a doctor shall have regard, in particular, to—

   (a)   that person's academic and vocational qualifications;

   (b)   that person's training and his experience in employment; and

   (c)   any guidance issued by the Committee pursuant to regulation 33B.

(3)   A doctor shall afford to each employee reasonable opportunities to undertake appropriate training with a view to maintaining that employee's competence.

Doctors' availability to patients

25.—(1)   Any doctor whose name is included in a medical list shall, after 31st March 1990—

   (a)   normally be available at such times and places as shall have been approved by the Committee or, on appeal, by the Secretary of State in his case, in accordance with the requirements of the following provisions of this paragraph, following an application by the doctor; and

   (b)   inform his patients about his availability in such manner as the Committee may require in accordance with sub-paragraph (14).

(2)   Subject to sub-paragraphs (2A), (2B), (3) and (4), a Family Health Services Authority shall not approve any application submitted by a doctor in relation to the times at which he is to be available unless it is satisfied that—

   (a)   the times proposed are such that the doctor will normally be available—

      (i)   in 42 weeks in any period of 12 months,

      (ii)   for no less than the number of hours in any such week which are specified in the condition imposed in relation to him under regulation 11A, and

      (iii)   on 5 days in any such week; and

   (b)   the hours for which the doctor will normally be available in any week are to be allocated between the days on which he will normally be available in that week in such a manner as is likely to be convenient to his patients;

   (c)   where the doctor is a three-quarter-time doctor or a half-time doctor, he is practising in partnership with—

      (i)   another doctor whose name is included in the medical list and who is himself a full-time doctor, or

     (ii)   two job-sharing doctors whose names are included in the medical list and whose hours are aggregated for the purposes of head (d) of this sub-paragraph;

    (d)   where the doctor is a job-sharing doctor—

     (i)   he is practising in partnership with another doctor whose name is included in the medical list, and

     (ii)   the hours for which both doctors will normally be available will in aggregate be not less than 26 hours in any week referred to in head (a)(i) of this sub-paragraph.

   (2A)   On any application made pursuant to sub-paragraph (1) by a three-quarter-time doctor or a half-time doctor—

    (a)   head (a)(iii) of sub-paragraph (2) shall not apply; and

    (b)   any approval of the application shall be subject to the condition that the approval shall lapse after the expiry of a period of 6 months from the date on which that doctor ceases to satisfy head (c) of sub-paragraph (2).

   (2B)   On any application made pursuant to sub-paragraph (1) by a job-sharing doctor—

    (a)   head (a)(iii) of sub-paragraph (2) shall apply so as to require either the job-sharing doctor or the other doctor referred to in sub-paragraph (2)(d) to be normally available on each of the days mentioned in that head;

    (b)   any approval of the application shall be subject to the condition that the approval shall lapse after the expiry of a period of 6 months from the date on which the doctor ceases to satisfy sub-paragraph (2)(d).

   (3)   On any application made pursuant to sub-paragraph (1) by a doctor who is a restricted list principal or a restricted services principal, sub-paragraph (2)(a)(i) and (iii), (c) and (d) shall not apply.

   (4)   The Family Health Services Authority may, in relation to the application of any full-time doctor who seeks normally to be available on only 4 days in any week referred to in sub-paragraph (2)(a)(i), excuse the doctor from the requirement of head (a)(iii) of that sub-paragraph and approve the application to the extent allowed by paragraph 25A.

   (5)   In this paragraph and in paragraph 25A, "available" means, in relation to a doctor, available to provide general medical services to his patients, and for the purposes of calculating the times at which a doctor is to be regarded as available—

    (a)   account may be taken of any period when the doctor is attending at his practice premises at any clinic provided by him for his own patients, and of any time spent making a domiciliary visit; but

    (b)   no account shall be taken of time spent by the doctor holding himself in readiness to make a domiciliary visit if required by any patient;

and "availability" shall be construed accordingly.

   (6)   An application by a doctor in relation to any place at which he is to be available shall not be approved by the Committee unless it is satisfied that—

    (a)   the place at which the doctor proposes to be available is likely to be convenient to his patients;

    (b)   the location of that place is in accordance with any condition imposed in his case pursuant to section 33 of the National Health Service Act 1977 (distribution of general medical services).

   (7)   An application for approval pursuant to sub-paragraph (1) shall be made in writing to the Committee and shall—

    (a)   include the information specified in Part I of Schedule 1C to these Regulations; and

    (b)   where appropriate, also include—

     (i)   in the case of a doctor to whom sub-paragraph (3) applies, the additional information specified in Part II of that Schedule,

(ii)   in the case of a doctor to whom sub-paragraph (4)(a) applies, the additional information specified in Part III of that Schedule,

(iii)   in the case of a doctor to whom sub-paragraph (4)(b) applies, the additional information specified in Part IV of that Schedule,

(8)   The Committee shall determine an application within 28 days of receiving it.

(9)   In determining any application, the Committee shall either—

(a)   grant approval;

(b)   grant approval subject to such conditions as the Committee sees fit to impose for the purpose of securing that the doctor is available at such times and places as are convenient to his patients; or

(c)   refuse approval.

(10)   The Committee shall notify the doctor in writing of its determination, and, where it refuses an application or grants an application subject to conditions, it shall send the doctor a statement in writing of the reasons for its determination and of the doctor's right of appeal under sub-paragraph (11).

(11)   A doctor may within 28 days of receiving a notification pursuant to sub-paragraph (10) appeal in writing to the Secretary of State against any refusal of approval or against any condition imposed pursuant to sub-paragraph (9).

(12)   The Secretary of State may when determining an appeal either confirm the determination of the Committee or substitute his own determination for that of the Committee.

(13)   The Secretary of State shall notify the doctor in writing of his determination and shall in every case include with the notification a written statement of the reasons for the determination.

(14)   The Committee may, as it considers appropriate, require a doctor to inform his patients, by displaying a notice at his practice premises or sending notices to them, about the times and places at which he is available.

(15)   A doctor may apply to a Family Health Services Authority for a variation of the times and places at which, in accordance with a determination under this paragraph ("the earlier determination"), he is required to be normally available, and sub-paragraphs (2) to (13) shall apply to the making and determination ("the subsequent determination") of an application under this sub-paragraph as if it were the first application by that doctor for the purposes of this paragraph.

(16)   Where an application made under sub-paragraph (15) is approved or is approved subject to conditions, for the purposes of sub-paragraphs (1) and (14) the earlier determination mentioned in sub-paragraph (15) shall cease to have effect and the subsequent determination mentioned in that sub-paragraph shall have effect instead—

(a)   where the subsequent determination is made by a Family Health Services Authority and no appeal is made, from the day falling 8 weeks after the date on which the doctor receives notification of that Authority's determination;

(b)   where the subsequent determination is made on appeal, from the day falling 8 weeks after the date on which the doctor receives notification of the Secretary of State's determination.

(17)   Where it appears to a Family Health Services Authority that a doctor's hours of availability are allocated for the purposes of sub-paragraph (2)(b) in a manner which may no longer be convenient to his patients, it may, subject to sub-paragraph (24), review the terms of—

(a)   any approval granted under sub-paragraph (9)(a) or (b); or

(b)   any direction given under sub-paragraph (19)(a);

by the Authority or the Secretary of State as to such allocation.

(18)   On any review under sub-paragraph (17) the Family Health Services Authority shall—

(a) give notice to the doctor of its proposed re-allocation of his hours of availability; and

(b) allow him 28 days within which to make representations to that Authority about its proposals.

(19) After considering any representations made in accordance with sub-paragraph (18)(b), the Family Health Services Authority shall either

(a) direct the doctor to revise the allocation of his hours of availability in the manner specified in the direction; or

(b) confirm that the existing allocation of the doctor's hours of availability continues to be convenient to his patients.

(20) A Family Health Services Authority shall notify the doctor in writing of its determination under sub-paragraph (19), and where it gives a direction statement in writing of the reasons for its determination and of the doctor's right of appeal under sub-paragraph (21).

(21) A doctor may, within 28 days of receiving notification under sub-paragraph (20), appeal in writing to the Secretary of State against a direction under sub-paragraph (19)(a).

(22) Sub-paragraphs (12) and (13) shall apply to any appeal made under sub-paragraph (21).

(23) A doctor in respect of whom a direction is given under sub-paragraph (19) shall revise the allocation of his hours of availability so as to give effect to the direction—

(a) where the direction is given by a Family Health Services Authority and no appeal is made, not later than 8 weeks after the date on which he receives notification under sub-paragraph (20);

(b) where the direction is given or confirmed on appeal, not later than 8 weeks after the date on which he receives notification of the Secretary of State's decision; and the allocation of hours as so revised shall be regarded as having been approved for the purposes of sub-paragraphs (1) and (14).

(24) No Family Health Services Authority shall undertake a review under sub-paragraph (17) on more than one occasion in any period of 2 years.

Records

30. A doctor shall—

(a) keep adequate records of the illnesses and treatment of his patients on forms supplied to him for the purpose by the Committee, and

(b) forward such records to the Committee on request as soon as possible, and

(c) within 14 days of being informed by the Committee of the death of a person on his list and in any case not later than one month of otherwise learning of such a death, forward the records relating to that person to the Committee.

Acceptance of fees

32. A doctor shall not, otherwise than under or by virtue of the provisions of the regulations, demand or accept a fee or other remuneration for any treatment, including maternity medical services, whether under these terms of service or not, which he gives to the person for whose treatment he is responsible under paragraph 4, except—

(a) from any statutory body for services rendered for the purpose of that body's statutory functions;

(b) from any body, employer or school for a routine medical examination of persons for whose welfare the body, employer or school is responsible, or an examination of such persons for the purpose of advising the body, employer or school of any administrative action they might take;

(c) for treatment which is not of a type usually provided by general practitioners and which is given—

(i)   pursuant to the provisions of sections 1 and 2 of the Health Services and Public Health Act 1968, or

(ii)   in a registered nursing home which is not providing services under the Health Service Acts,

if (in either case) the doctor is serving on the staff of a hospital providing services under the Health Service Acts as a specialist providing treatment of the kind the patient requires and if within 7 days from giving the treatment the doctor supplies the Committee, on a form provided by it for the purpose, with such information about the treatment as it may require;

(d)   under section 155 of the Road Traffic Act 1972;

(e)   from a dentist in respect of the provision at his request of an anaesthetic for a person for whom the dentist is providing general dental services;

(f)   when a doctor treats a patient under paragraph 4(2), in which case the doctor shall be entitled to demand and accept a reasonable fee (recoverable under paragraph 33) for any treatment given and for any drugs and appliances supplied, if he gives the patient a receipt on a form supplied by the Committee;

(h)   for attending and examining (but not otherwise treating) a patient at his request at a police station in connection with proceedings which the police are minded to bring against him;

(i)   for treatment consisting of an immunisation for which no remuneration is payable by the Committee in pursuance of the Statement made under regulation 24 and which is requested in connection with travel abroad;

(j)   for circumcising a patient for whom such an operation is requested on religious grounds and is not needed on any medical ground;

(k)   for prescribing or supplying medicine for a patient who requires to have it in his possession solely in anticipation of the onset of an ailment while he is outside the United Kingdom but for which he is not requiring treatment when the medicine is prescribed or supplied;

(l)   for a medical examination to enable a decision to be made whether or not it is inadvisable on medical grounds for a person to wear a seat belt;

33A.   Subject to paragraphs 32(f) and (k) and 38 and to the National Health Service (Charges for Drugs and Appliances) Regulations 1980, a doctor shall not demand or accept a fee or other remuneration from a patient of his for any prescription for or any supply of any drug or chemical reagent or appliance.

33B.   A doctor shall not without reasonable excuse demand or accept from Committee any fee or other remuneration to which he is not entitled under the provisions of the regulations, the Statement published under regulation 24 or the Drug Tariff.

Prescribing and dispensing

35.   A doctor shall supply drugs or appliances needed for immediate treatment of a patient before a supply can be obtained otherwise.

36.—(1)   Subject to paragraphs 36A and 38, a doctor shall order any drugs and chemical reagents or appliances which are needed for the treatment of any patient to whom he is providing treatment under these terms of service by issuing to that patient a prescription form, and such a form shall not be used in any other circumstances.

(2)   In issuing any such prescription form the doctor shall himself sign the form in ink with his initials, or forenames, and surname in his own handwriting and not by means of a stamp, and shall so sign only after particulars of the order have been inserted in the form, and—

(a)   the prescription shall not refer to any previous prescription;

(b)   a separate prescription form shall be used for each patient except where a doctor is prescribing in bulk for a school or institution under paragraph 37.

Practice leaflet

38B.—(1)   Subject to sub-paragraph (2), a doctor whose name is included in the medical list shall from 1st April 1990 compile in relation to his practice a document (in this paragraph called a "practice leaflet") which shall include the information specified in Schedule 1D to these Regulations.

(2)   Sub-paragraph (1) shall, in relation to a doctor referred to in regulation 4(2)(e), apply only to the extent that the Committee sees fit.

(3)   A doctor shall review his practice leaflet at least once in every period of 12 months, and shall make any amendments necessary to maintain its accuracy.

(4)   A doctor shall from 1st April 1990, or from such later date (being not later than 1st July 1990) as the Committee may allow, make available a copy of the most recent edition of his practice leaflet to the Committee, to each patient on his list and to any other person who, in the doctor's opinion, reasonably requires one.

(5)   A doctor who practises in partnership with other doctors whose names are included in the medical list shall satisfy the requirements of this paragraph if he makes available a practice leaflet, compiled and, where appropriate, revised in accordance with sub-paragraphs (1) and (3) which relates to the partnership as a whole; and in such a case a doctor may, if he so wishes, also produce a practice leaflet relating to his own activities.

Reports to the medical officer etc.

39.   A doctor shall—

(a)   supply in writing to a medical officer within such reasonable period as that officer may specify any relevant clinical information which he requests about a patient to whom the doctor under these terms of service has issued or has refused to issue a medical certificate, and

(b)   answer any inquiries by a medical officer about a prescription or medical certificate issued by the doctor under these terms of service or about any statement which the doctor has made in a report under these terms of service.

Inquiries about prescriptions and referrals

39A.—(1)   A doctor whose name is included in the medical list shall, subject to sub-paragraphs (2) and (3) below, sufficiently answer any inquiries, whether oral or in writing, from the Committee concerning—

(a)   any prescription form issued by the doctor under these terms of service;

(b)   the considerations by reference to which the doctor issues such forms under these terms of service;

(c)   the referral by the doctor under these terms of service of any patient to any other services provided under the National Health Service Act 1977; and

(d)   the considerations by reference to which the doctor refers patients to any such services.

(2)   An inquiry referred to in sub-paragraph (1) may be made only for the purpose either of obtaining information to assist the Committee to discharge its functions or of assisting the doctor in the discharge of his obligations under these terms of service.

(3)   A doctor shall not be obliged to answer any inquiry referred to in sub-paragraph (1) unless it is made by a doctor appointed under regulation 33A who produces on request written evidence that he is authorized by the Committee to make such an inquiry on behalf of the Committee.

Continued absence or disability of doctor

40.   Where it appears to the Committee after consultation with the Local Medical Committee, that a doctor is incapable of adequately carrying out his obligations under the terms of service because of physical or mental disability, he may be required by the Committee to supply to the Local Medical Committee for action under regulation 34 a

medical report by a suitably qualified doctor as to such aspects of his health as the Local Medical Committee may specify.

41. Where a Committee is satisfied—

(a) after receiving a report under paragraph 40 from the Local Medical Committee that because of physical or mental disability, or

(b) after consulting the Local Medical Committee, that because of continued absence, a doctor's obligations under the terms of service are not being adequately carried out, it may after consulting the Local Medical Committee and with the consent of the Secretary of State—

(i) make arrangements for securing the treatment of persons on the list of that doctor; or

(ii) give notice to the persons on his list that the doctor is for the time being in its opinion unable to carry out his obligations under the terms of service.

42. To enable the Committee to decide whether any arrangements made under paragraph 41(i) should be terminated, or where notice has been given under paragraph 41 (ii) whether a further notice should be given to the persons on the doctor's list that he is now, in the Committee's opinion, able to carry out his obligations under the terms of service, a doctor may be required by the Committee, after consultation with the Local Medical Committee, to supply to the Local Medical Committee for action under regulation 34 a medical report by a suitably qualified doctor as to such aspects of his health as the Local Medical Committee may specify.

43. The Committee may deduct from the doctor's remuneration in part or in whole the cost of any arrangements made under paragraph 41 and, if the doctor is performing relevant service in an emergency recognised by the Secretary of State for the purpose of the regulations, the Committee shall deduct from his remuneration the cost of arranging for any deputy.

Annual reports

43A.—(1) A doctor whose name is included in the medical list, shall provide annually to the Committee a report, in accordance with this paragraph, relating to the provision by him of personal medical services (in this paragraph called an "annual report").

(7) A Committee shall not disclose any annual report to any person, unless otherwise lawfully empowered to do so.

Incorporation of provisions of regulations etc.

44. Any provisions of the following affecting the rights and obligations of doctors shall be deemed to form part of the terms of service—

(a) the regulations;

(b) any statement published under regulation 24; and

(c) so much of Part 11 of the National Health Service (Service Committees and Tribunal) Regulations 1956 as amended as relates to—

(i) the investigation of questions arising between doctors and their patients and other investigations to be made by the medical service committee and the joint services committee and the action which may be taken by the Committee as a result of such investigations;

(ii) appeals to the Secretary of State from decisions of the Committee;

(iii) the investigation of cases of alleged excessive prescribing;

(iv) the investigation of certification;

(v) the investigation of record keeping;

(vi) decisions as to treatment for which fees may be charged;

(vii) the determination of the question whether a substance is a drug.

SCHEDULE 1A

CHILD HEALTH SURVEILLANCE SERVICES

1. The services referred to in paragraph 9B(a) of Schedule 1 shall comprise—
    (a) the monitoring—
      (i) by the consideration of information concerning the child received by or on behalf of the doctor, and
      (ii) on any occasion when the child is examined or observed by or on behalf of the doctor (whether pursuant to sub-paragraph (b) or otherwise),
of the health, well-being and physical, mental and social development (all of which characteristics are referred to in this Schedule as "development") of the child while under the age of 5 years with a view to detecting any deviations from normal development;
    (b) the examination of the child by or on behalf of the doctor on so many occasions and at such intervals as shall have been agreed between the Committee and the health authority in whose district the child resides (in this Schedule called "the relevant health authority") for the purposes of the provision of child health surveillance services generally in that district.
2. The records mentioned in paragraph 9B(b) of Schedule 1 shall comprise an accurate record of—
    (a) the development of the child while under the age of 5 years, complied as soon as is reasonably practicable following the first examination mentioned in paragraph 1(a) of this Schedule and, where appropriate, amended following each subsequent examination mentioned in that sub-paragraph; and
    (b) the responses (if any) to offers made to the child's parent for the child to undergo any examination referred to in paragraph 1(b) of this Schedule.
3. The information mentioned in paragraph 9B(c) of Schedule 1 shall comprise—
    (a) a statement, to be prepared and dispatched to the relevant health authority referred to in paragraph 1(b) of this Schedule as soon as is reasonably practicable following any examination referred to in paragraph 1(a) of this Schedule, of the procedures undertaken in the course of that examination and of the doctor's findings in relation to each such procedure;
    (b) such further information regarding the development of the child while under the age of 5 years as the relevant health authority may request.

SCHEDULE 1B

MINOR SURGERY PROCEDURES

Injections	intra articular
	peri articular
	varicose veins
	haemorrhoid
Aspirations	joints
	cysts
	bursae
	hydrocele
Incisions	abcesses
	cysts
	thrombosed piles
Excisions	sebaceous cysts
	lipoma
	skin lesions for histology

intradermal naevi, papilloma, dermatofibroma and similar
   conditions
warts
removal of toe nails (partial and complete)

Currette cautery   warts and verrucae

and cryocautery   other skin lesions (eg molluscum contagiosum)

Other   removal of foreign bodies
nasal cautery

SCHEDULE 1C

PART I

Information to be included with any application under paragraph 25 of Schedule 1

1.   The address of the proposed practice premises.

2.   The days in each week during which the doctor will normally be in attendance at the practice premises and available for consultation by his patients.

3.   The hours of each such attendance by the doctor.

4.   The hours of any attendance by the doctor on those occasions when he is not usually available to provide the full range of services specified in paragraph 13 of the terms of service (for example, for providing emergency treatment only).

5.   The frequency, duration and purpose of any clinic provided by the doctor.

6.   The estimated total time to be spent each week making any domiciliary visits.

7.   The doctor's proposals for notifying patients of the times and places approved by the Committee.

8.   The terms of any condition imposed by the Medical Practices Committee or the Secretary of State under section 33 of the National Health Service Act 1977.

9.   In the case of a doctor to whom paragraph 15(2) of the terms of service does not apply, his proposals for discharging his continuous responsibility for his patients.

SCHEDULE 1D

Information to be included in Practice leaflets

Personal and Professional Details of the Doctor

1.   Full name.

2.   Sex.

3.   Medical qualifications registered by the General Medical Council.

4.   Date and place of first registration as medical practitioner.

Practice Information

5.   The times approved by the Committee during which the doctor is personally available for consultation by his patients at his practice premises.

6.   Whether an appointments system is operated by the doctor for consultations at his practice premises.

7.   If there is an appointments system, the method of obtaining a non-urgent appointment and the method of obtaining an urgent appointment.

8.   The method of obtaining a non-urgent domiciliary visit and the method of obtaining an urgent domiciliary visit.

9.   The doctor's arrangements for providing personal medical services when he is not personally available.

10.   The method by which patients are to obtain repeat prescriptions from the doctor.

11.   If the doctor's practice is a dispensing practice, the arrangements for dispensing prescriptions.

12.   If the doctor provides clinics for his patients, their frequency, duration and purpose.

13.   The numbers of staff, other than doctors, assisting the doctor in his practice, and a description of their roles.

14.   Whether the doctor provides (1) maternity medical services (2) contraceptive services (3) child health surveillance services (4) minor surgery services.

15.   Whether the doctor works single-handed, in partnership, part-time or on a job share basis, or within a group practice.

16.   The nature of any arrangements whereby the doctor or his staff receive patients' comments on his provision of general medical services.

17.   The geographical boundary of his practice area by reference to a sketch, diagram or plan of a scale approved by the Committee.

18.   Whether the doctor's practice premises have suitable access for all disabled patients and, if not, the reasons why they are unsuitable for particular types of disability.

19.   If an assistant is employed, details for him as specified in paragraphs 1-4 of this Schedule.

20.   If the practice either is a general practitioner training practice for the purposes of the National Health Service (Vocational Training) Regulations 1979 or undertakes the teaching of undergraduate medical students, the nature of arrangements for drawing this to the attention of patients.

SCHEDULE 1E

Information to be provided in Annual reports

1.   The number of staff, other than doctors, assisting the doctor in his practice by reference to—

(i)   the total number but not by reference to their names;

(ii)   the principal duties of each employee and the hours each week the employee assists the doctor;

(iii)   the qualifications of each employee;

(iv)   the relevant training undertaken by each employee during the preceding 5 years.

2.   The following information as respects the practice premises:—

(i)   any variations in relation to floor space, design or quality since the last Annual Report.

(ii)   any such variations anticipated in the course of the forthcoming period of 12 months.

3.   The following information as respects the referral of patients to other services under the National Health Service Act 1977 during the period of the Report:—

(a)   as respects those by the doctor to a specialist—

(i)   the total number of patients referred as in-patients;

(ii)   the total number of patients referred as out-patients;

by reference in each case to whichever of the following clinical specialities applies and specifying in each case the name of the hospital concerned:

— General Surgical
— General Medical
— Orthopaedic
— Rheumatology (Physical Medicine)
— Ear, Nose and Throat
— Gynaecology
— Obstetrics
— Paediatrics
— Opthalmology
— Psychiatry
— Geriatrics

— Dermatology
— Neurology
— Genito-urinary
— X-ray
— Pathology
— Others (including plastic surgery, accident and emergency, endocrinology);
    (b) the total number of cases of which the doctor is aware (by reference to the categories listed in sub-paragraph (a)) in which a patient referred himself to services under the National Health Service Act 1977.
    4. The doctor's other commitments as a medical practitioner with reference to—
      (i) a description of any posts held; and
      (ii) a description of all work undertaken,
including, in each case, the annual hourly commitment.
    5. The nature of any arrangements whereby the doctor or his staff receive patients' comments on his provision of general medical services.
    6. The following information as respects orders for drugs and appliances:—
    (a) whether the doctor's practice has its own formulary;
    (b) whether the doctor uses a separate formulary;
    (c) the doctor's arrangements for the issue of repeat prescriptions to patients.

NATIONAL HEALTH SERVICE (SERVICE COMMITTEES AND TRIBUNAL) REGULATIONS 1974 (SI 1974, No. 455)

PART I
GENERAL

Interpretation
    2. (1) In these regulations, unless the context otherwise requires, the following expressions have the respective meanings hereby assigned to them:—
    "the Act" means the National Health Service Act 1977;
    "chemist" means a registered pharmaceutical chemist who provides pharmaceutical services, or an authorised seller of poisons within the meaning of the Pharmacy and Poisons Act 1933 who provides such services;
    "Committee" means the Family Practitioner Committee established for any locality;
    "conciliation" means the process of conciliation established and maintained by the Committee, pursuant to a direction under section 17 of the National Health Service Act 1977, with a view to resolving a matter giving rise to a complaint without recourse to an investigation under these Regulations;
    "dental officer" means—
      (a) for the purposes of regulation 18 (investigation of record keeping), a dentist in the service of the Dental Practice Board, or of the Welsh Office, as the case may be, and
      (b) for all other purposes, a dentist in the service of the Department of Health, or of the Welsh Office, as the case may be;
    "dentist" means a registered dental practitioner;
    "doctor" means a fully registered medical practitioner;
    "drugs" includes medicines and such chemical reagents as are for the time being listed for the purposes of section 38 of the Act;
    "General Manager" means the officer appointed by a Committee to act as its chief officer, or some other officer of the Committee duly authorised to act on his behalf;
    "General Service Regulations" means the National Health Service (General Medical and Pharmaceutical Services) Regulations 1974;

"Local Dental Committee", "Local Medical Committee", "Local Optical Committee" and "Local Pharmaceutical Committee" mean the committees of those names which are recognised by the Secretary of State in relation to a locality in pursuance of section 44 of the National Health Service Act 1977;
"locality" means the locality for which a Committee is established;
"medical officer" means a doctor in the service of the Department of Health and Social Security, or the Welsh Office, as the case may be;
"ophthalmic medical practitioner" means a doctor having the qualifications prescribed by regulation 3 of the Ophthalmic Services Regulations;
"optician" means
    (a) in the context of regulation 3(2)(d) and (e) and (6)(c)(iv), a registered ophthalmic optician within the meaning of the Opticians Act 1989;
    (b) in any other context, a registered ophthalmic optician within the meaning of that Act, or a body corporate enrolled in the list mentioned in section 9(1)(a) of that Act;
"pharmacist" means a registered pharmacist;
"practitioner" means a doctor, dentist or ophthalmic medical practitioner as the context may require;
"service committee" means a medical, pharmaceutical, dental or ophthalmic service committee or a joint services committee, as the context may require;
"the terms of service" means the terms of service for doctors contained in Part I of Schedule 1 to the General Service Regulations;
"treatment" in relation to general medical services has the same meaning as in the General Service Regulations;
"the Tribunal" means the Tribunal constituted under Section 46 of the Act.
  (2) These regulations shall apply to a person, firm or body corporate (other than a chemist or a practitioner) providing pharmaceutical services, as they apply to a chemist.

Constitution of service committees
  3. (1) Every Committee shall establish a medical service committee, a pharmaceutical service committee, a dental service committee, an ophthalmic service committee and a joint services committee, and may, where it sees fit, establish two or more medical service committees, pharmaceutical service committees, dental service committees and ophthalmic service committees.
  (2)(a) The medical service committee shall consist of a chairman and six other persons of whom three shall be lay persons appointed by the Family Health Services Authority and three shall be doctors appointed by the Local Medical Committee.
  (e) The joint services committee shall consist of a chairman and ten other persons of whom two shall be lay persons appointed by the Committee, two shall be appointed by the medical service committee from their members or deputies who are doctors, two shall be appointed by the dental service committee from their members or deputies who are dentists, two shall be appointed by the pharmaceutical service committee from their members or deputies who are chemists and two shall be appointed by the ophthalmic service committee from their members or deputies who are ophthalmic medical practitioners or opticians.

Time limits for complaining and notice of complaint
  4. (1) Subject to the provisions of regulation 5, the person desiring to make a complaint under this Part of these regulations against a doctor or an ophthalmic medical practitioner, a chemist or an optician, shall within thirteen weeks after the event which gave rise to the complaint give notice stating the substance of the matter which it is desired to have investigated.

Late complaints
5. (1) Where notice of a complaint is given after the expiry of the period specified in regulation 4(1) or (2) in relation to that notice, the service committee shall not investigate the matter giving rise to the complaint unless—

(a) they are satisfied that the failure to give such notice immediately before the expiry of that period and on any subsequent day falling before the date on which such notice was in fact given was occasioned by illness or by some other reasonable cause; and

(b) they have obtained—

(i) the consent of the practitioner, chemist, or as the case may be, optician, or

(ii) if such consent is refused, the consent of the Secretary of State.

(2) If an application for the Secretary of State's consent to an investigation is made, the General Manager shall furnish the Secretary of State and the practitioner, chemist or optician, with a copy of the said notice, a statement of the reasons for the failure to give notice in time and any further information which the Secretary of State may require, and the practitioner, chemist or optician shall be entitled within fourteen days after the receipt by him of such statement or further information to forward to the Secretary of State a statement of the grounds on which he contends that the investigation should not take place.

(3) If a service committee decides not to seek the consent of the practitioner, chemist or optician or of the Secretary of State to the investigation of a complaint, they shall give reasons for their decision. The General Manager shall notify the complainant of the decision of the service committee, and the reasons therefor, and also of his right of appeal to the Secretary of State.

(4) A complainant may appeal to the Secretary of State against a decision of a service committee not to seek the consent of the practitioner, chemist or optician or of the Secretary of State to the investigation of a complaint. Such an appeal shall be made in writing within fourteen days after the complainant is notified that consent to the investigation is not to be sought, and shall state the grounds of appeal.

(5) On receipt of such an appeal the Secretary of State shall notify the practitioner, chemist or optician of the grounds of the appeal and the practitioner, chemist or optician shall be entitled within fourteen days after the receipt by him of such statement of grounds to submit to the Secretary of State a statement of the grounds on which he contends that the investigation should not take place.

(6) The Secretary of State shall decide such an application or appeal giving reasons for his decision and may direct the service committee to investigate the matter which gave rise to the complaint notwithstanding the failure of the complainant to give notice within the periods specified in regulation 4.

Investigations by service committees
6. (1) Subject to the provisions of these regulations, any complaint made against a doctor in respect of an alleged failure to comply with the terms of service shall be investigated by the medical service committee, any complaint made against a chemist in respect of an alleged failure to comply with the terms of service shall be investigated by the pharmaceutical service committee, any complaint made against a dentist in respect of an alleged failure to comply with the terms of service shall be investigated by the dental service committee, and any complaint made against an ophthalmic medical practitioner or optician in respect of an alleged failure to comply with the terms of service shall be investigated by the ophthalmic service committee.

(2) Any complaint which under paragraph (1) is required to be investigated by more than one service committee may, in lieu of being so investigated, be investigated by a joint services committee.

(3) A complaint shall be investigated under this regulation if it is made by the Dental Practice Board or if, in the opinion of the chairman of the appropriate service

committee, the complaint relates to an alleged failure by the practitioner, chemist or optician concerned to comply with the terms of service in respect of any person who was, or who claimed to be, entitled to the provision of general medical, general dental, pharmaceutical or general ophthalmic services and—

(a)   the complaint is made by or with the authority of that person; or

(b)   the complaint is made on behalf of that person and he is incapable by reason of old age, sickness or other infirmity, of making a complaint, or is under the age of sixteen; or

(c)   that person is deceased:

Provided that where at the beginning of the hearing of a complaint before a service committee, or at any time thereafter, it appears that the complaint was not made as aforesaid it shall be deemed to have been properly referred to the service committee for investigation under the provisions of paragraph (6).

(3A)   Where, at any time after notice of a complaint has been given but before the Committee make a decision under regulation 10 of these Regulations in relation to that complaint, the practitioner, chemist or, as the case may be, optician to whom the complaint relates dies, no further action shall be taken under these Regulations in relation to that complaint.

(3B)   A complainant may withdraw his complaint—

(a)   at any time in the course of, or immediately following, conciliation, by giving written notice to the Committee of its withdrawal;

(b)   at any other time before the service committee present their report to the Committee—

(i)   by giving written notice to the Committee of his intention to withdraw it, and

(ii)   with the consent of the service committee.

(3C)   Where the name of the practitioner, chemist or, as the case may be, optician against whom a complaint is made was, at the time of the event, treatment or matter which gave rise to the complaint, included in a list maintained by the Committee under section 29, 36, 39 and 42 of the National Health Service Act 1977, the service committee shall, subject to the provisions of these Regulations, investigate the complaint, notwithstanding that the name of the practitioner, chemist or optician in question has since had his name removed, or has since withdrawn his name, from the list in question.

(4)   Where a complaint is made against a doctor in respect of the acts or omissions of a deputy whose name is also included in the medical list at the time of the event, treatment or matter which gives rise to the complaint, the complaint shall be deemed to have been made against both doctors.

(5)   Where a complaint is made against a doctor whose name is included in the medical list at the time of the event, treatment or matter which gives rise to the complaint, in respect of his acts or omissions whilst acting as deputy to a doctor whose name is also included in the list at that time, the complaint shall be deemed to have been made against both doctors.

(6)   (a)   Subject to the provisions of these regulations, the medical service committee in relation to doctors, the pharmaceutical service committee in relation to chemists, the dental service committee in relation to dentists and the ophthalmic service committee in relation to ophthalmic medical practitioners and opticians, shall investigate any matters referred to them by the Committee, by any duly authorised sub-committee thereof, or by the Dental Practice Board, which relate to the administration of general medical, pharmaceutical, general dental or general ophthalmic services, whether or not any such matter has been raised on complaint under the foregoing provisions of this regulation:

Provided that no question which involves an allegation against a practitioner, chemist or optician of a breach of the terms of service shall, without the consent of the Secretary of State, or of the practitioner, chemist or optician concerned, be referred for investigation under this paragraph except, in the case of a doctor or an ophthalmic medical practitioner, chemist or optician, within thirteen weeks after the event which gave rise to the allegation, or in the case of a dentist within six months after completion of the treatment or within thirteen weeks after the matter which gave rise to the allegation came to the notice of the referring body, whichever is the sooner; and such consent shall also be required where the Committee desire to refer a matter which came to the notice of the Dental Practice Board earlier than thirteen weeks from the date on which they informed the Committee of it. The provisions of paragraph (2) of regulation 5 with reference to the procedure to be adopted on application for the Secretary of State's consent shall apply to any application for his consent under this paragraph with such modification as the circumstances may require.

(b) Where the Committee, prior to a possible reference of any matter under the preceding sub-paragraph to the appropriate service committee, request the General Manager to seek the comments of the practitioner, chemist or optician concerned, the General Manager shall inform him of any alleged breach of the terms of service or of the reason for requesting the comments and, unless the Committee decide to the contrary, of the source of the information before them concerning the matter.

(8) If in the opinion of a service committee any matter referred to that service committee involves a question which under the provisions of paragraph (1) of regulation 6 is required to be investigated by another service committee the service committee shall in lieu of dealing with the matter themselves refer it to the joint services committee.

(10) Any matter which would otherwise be referred by the Committee or any duly authorised sub-committee thereof to the medical service committee, the pharmaceutical service committee, the dental service committee or the ophthalmic service committee for investigation may, if the Committee or sub-committee are satisfied that it is appropriate to the joint services committee, be referred by them to that committee.

(11) Where—

(a) the complainant or the practitioner, chemist or, as the case may be, optician against whom a complaint is made is a member of either the Committee or one of their service committees, or

(b) sub-paragraph (20) of paragraph 1 of Schedule 1 cannot be complied with by reason of the operation of sub-paragraph (13) of that paragraph; or

(c) the matter to be investigated is one which would, but for the operation of this paragraph, fall to be referred to the service committee, either by the Committee themselves or by any duly authorised sub-committee thereof, pursuant to regulation 6(6)(a), the Committee shall arrange with another Family Practitioner Committee for the complaint or the matter to be investigated and determined under these Regulations by that other Committee pursuant to regulation 11 of the National Health Service Functions (Directions and Authorities and Administration Arrangements) Regulations 1989.

Representation at hearing

7. The service committee shall, in the event of a hearing, permit a party to an investigation to be assisted in the presentation of his case by some other person:

Provided that no person who is a barrister or solicitor shall be entitled to conduct the case for any party by addressing the service committee or examining or cross-examining witnesses.

Hearings in private

8. Subject to the provisions of regulation 54, the proceedings at the hearing before the service committee shall be private and no person shall be admitted to those proceedings except—

(a)   the parties to the investigation and the persons, if any, permitted to appear for the purpose of assisting them;

(b)   the secretary or other duly authorised officer or member of the Local Medical, Pharmaceutical, Dental or Optical Committee, whichever is concerned;

(c)   persons whose attendance is required for the purpose of giving evidence and who shall, unless the service committee otherwise direct, be excluded from the hearing except when they are actually giving evidence; and

(d)   such officers of the Committee as they may appoint for the purpose.

Procedure of service committees

9.   Subject to the provisions of these regulations, Schedule 1 shall apply with respect to the investigation of complaints and the procedure of service committees.

Decision of Committee

10.   (1)   The Committee, after due consideration of the report presented to them by the service committee pursuant to paragraph 1(19) of Schedule 1, shall—

(a)   accept as conclusive the findings of fact made by the service committee;

(b)   draw such inferences from those findings of fact as they see fit, having regard to the service committee's report as it relates to the inferences which may properly be drawn from those findings;

(c)   determine whether the practitioner, chemist or, as the case may be, optician to whom the report relates has failed to comply with any one or more of his terms of service identified to him by the Chairman of the service committee pursuant to these Regulations; and

(d)   determine—

(i)   in accordance with any one or more of paragraphs (3), (5) and (8), but subject to paragraph (7), the action to be taken in relation to the practitioner, chemist or, as the case may be, optician, having regard to any recommendation made by the service committee pursuant to paragraph 1(19) of Schedule 1, or

(ii)   that no further action should be taken in relation to the report.

(2)   If the Committee decide either not to adopt the recommendation of the service committee or to take any action not recommended by the service committee, they shall record in writing their reasons for that decision.

(3)   Where, in the case of any doctor to whom a report of a service committee relates, the Committee are satisfied, after consultation with the Local Medical Committee, that, because of the number of persons included in his list, the doctor is unable to give adequate treatment to all of those persons, they may impose a special limit on the number of persons for whom the doctor may undertake to provide treatment.

(4)   Where, pursuant to paragraph (3), the Committee impose a special limit on the number of patients for whom a doctor may undertake to provide treatment, paragraphs (3) to (6) of regulation 17 of the National Health Service (General Medical and Pharmaceutical Services) Regulations 1974 (limitation of number of persons on doctors' lists) shall have effect in his case with suitable modifications and, in particular, as if references in those paragraphs—

(a)   to a maximum number were references to the special limit imposed under paragraph (3) of this regulation; and

(b)   to an excess were references to the extent to which the number of patients in the doctor's list exceeds that special limit.

(5)   Where it has been determined that a practitioner, chemist or, as the case may be, optician to whom the report of the service committee relates has failed to comply with any of his terms of service, the Committee may—

(a)   subject to paragraph (6) but without prejudice to sub-paragraph (b) of this paragraph, determine that there should be recovered from him, whether by way of a deduction from his remuneration or otherwise, any expenses (other than expenses incurred in connection with the investigation by the service committee) which, by reason of such failure, have been reasonably and necessarily incurred or, where the report relates to a dentist, are likely to be so incurred, by any person in obtaining further treatment, and that any such sums so recovered shall be paid to that person;

    (b)   determine that an amount not exceeding £500 shall be recovered from the practitioner, chemist or, as the case may be, optician, whether by way of withholding from his remuneration or otherwise;

    (c)   recommend to the Secretary of State that an amount in excess of £500 should be recovered from the practitioner, chemist or, as the case may be, optician, whether by way of withholding from his remuneration or otherwise;

    (d)   where the practitioner is a dentist, recommend to the Secretary of State that he should be required to submit to the Dental Practice Board for prior approval estimates in respect of any description of treatment specified in the recommendation;

    (e)   determine that the practitioner, chemist or, as the case may be, optician should be warned to comply more closely with his terms of service in future.

(7)   Where the Committee determine to make a recommendation under either or both of sub-paragraphs (c) or (d) of paragraphs (5), they shall not determine that action should be taken under any other provision of that paragraph.

(8)   Where the Committee are of the opinion that the continued inclusion of the name of a practitioner, chemist or, as the case may be, optician in a list maintained by the Committee pursuant to any of sections 29, 36, 39 and 42 of the National Health Service Act 1977 would be prejudicial to the efficiency of the services referred to in the section in question, they may make representations to that effect to the Tribunal.

(9)   As soon as may be practicable after the Committee have made their decision on the report of a service committee, the General Manager shall send to the parties to the investigation, to the Secretary of State and, where reasonably requested to do so by either party, to any member of either House of Parliament a copy of that report and of the Committee's decision thereon, and shall—

    (a)   where appropriate, inform the parties in writing of their right of appeal to the Secretary of State and of his power to award costs; and

    (b)   where they have made a recommendation under paragraph (5)(c) or (d), inform the practitioner, chemist or, as the case may be, optician of his right to make representations to the Secretary of State under the provisions of regulation 11(3).

(10)   Subject to paragraph (10A), where a Committee determine under this regulation that action should be taken in accordance with any of the provisions of paragraphs (3) and (5)(a), (b) and (e), that action shall be taken—

    (a)   by the Committee in whose list the name of the practitioner, chemist or, as the case may be, optician was included at the time of the event which gave rise to the complaint or reference; but this sub-paragraph shall not apply where, at the time when such action falls to be taken, his name is no longer included in that Committee's list but is included in the list of some other Committee; or

    (b)   where sub-paragraph (a) does not apply, by a Committee in whose list the name of the practitioner, chemist or, as the case may be, optician is included at the time when such action falls to be taken.

(11)   Any amount determined under paragraph (5)(a) or (b) as being recoverable shall be a debt owing by the practitioner, chemist or, as the case may be, optician to the Committee by which it is recoverable.

(12)   Where the Committee make a determination under the provisions of sub-paragraph (a), (b) or (e) of paragraph (5) of this regulation, no action shall be taken on that determination before —

    (a)   if no appeal is brought, the end of the period for bringing an appeal specified in regulation 11(2); or

(b)   if an appeal is brought, they have received the notice of the Secretary of State's decision of the appeal.

Appeal to Secretary of State from decision of Committee

11.   (1)   An appeal may be made to the Secretary of State—

(a)   by any party to an investigation, against a determination of the Committee under regulation 10(1)(c) which is adverse to him;

(b)   by a practitioner, chemist or, as the case may be, optician, against any determination by a Committee under regulation 10(1)(d) to take action in accordance with any one or more of paragraphs (3) or (5)(a) or (b);

(c)   by a practitioner, chemist or, as the case may be, optician, against any determination by a Committee that an overpayment has been made in respect of his remuneration; or

(d)   by a complainant who has asserted to the Committee that, by reason of the respondent's failure to comply with his terms of service, he has incurred or is likely to incur expenses in circumstances mentioned in regulation 10(5)(a), against a determination by the Committee under regulation 10(1)(d) which is adverse to him in that respect.

(1A)   Subject to paragraph (4), on an appeal to which paragraph (1) (a) or (c) applies, the Secretary of State shall inquire into the whole of the complaint or reference, on the basis of such evidence as was available to the service committee and of such further evidence as shall have been adduced on the appeal, and shall—

(a)   make such findings of fact as he sees fit; and

(b)   draw such inferences from those findings as he sees fit; and

(c)   in the case of an appeal to which paragraph (1) (a) above applies—

(i)   determine whether or not the practitioner, chemist or, as the case may be, optician is in breach of any one or more of his terms of service, and

(ii)   determine in accordance with any one or more of regulations 10(3), (4), (5)(a) and (e) and (6) (as modified in accordance with paragraph (1C) of this regulation), 14 and 15 whether any, and if so, what action should be taken in relation to that practitioner, chemist or, as the case may be, optician; or

(d)   in the case of an appeal to which paragraph (1)(c) above applies, determine whether there has been an overpayment and, if so, of what amount.

(1B)   On an appeal to which paragraph (1)(b) or (d) above applies, the Secretary of State shall—

(a)   accept as conclusive—

(i)   the findings of fact made by the service committee necessary for the purpose of the Committee's determination under regulation 10(1)(c),

(ii)   the inferences drawn by the Committee under regulation 10(1)(b), and

(iii)   any determination made by the Committee under regulation 10(1)(c) in relation to a failure to comply with the terms of service; and

(b)   determine—

(i)   in the case of an appeal to which paragraph (1)(b) above applies, in accordance with any one or more of regulations 10(3), (4), (5)(a) and (e) and (6) (as modified in accordance with paragraph (1C) of this regulation), 14 and 15, the action to be taken in relation to the practitioner, chemist or, as the case may be, optician to whom the report of the service committee relates,

(ii)   in the case of an appeal to which paragraph (1)(d) above applies, whether an amount should be recovered and paid as mentioned in regulation 10(5)(a), and if so, what amount, or

(iii)   in either case, that no further action should be taken in relation to that report.

(1C)   For the purposes of paragraphs (1A) (c)(ii) and (1B)(b)(i) of this regulation, paragraphs (3), (4), (5)(a) and (e) and (6) of regulation 10 shall have effect as if for any reference to "the Committee" there were substituted a reference to "the Secretary of State".

(2)   A notice of an appeal under this regulation shall be sent in writing to the Secretary of State within one month beginning on the date on which notification of the Committee's decision was sent to the appellant and shall contain a concise statement of facts and the grounds of appeal upon which the appellant intends to rely.

(3)   A practitioner, chemist, or optician may, in lieu of exercising his right of appeal, within one month from the date on which notification of the decision of the Committee was sent to him, make representations to the Secretary of State against a recommendation of the Committee under paragraph 5(c) or (d) of regulation 10.

(4)   Where, pursuant to regulation 10(8), a Committee have made representations to the Tribunal following their consideration of a report of a service committee, the Secretary of State may, for the purpose of any appeal under regulation 11(1)(a) against a decision of that Committee following their consideration of that report, treat as conclusive any relevant finding of fact of the Tribunal.

Procedure on appeal
12.   (1)   If the Secretary of State, after considering the notice of appeal and any further particulars furnished by the appellant, is of the opinion that the said notice and particulars disclose no reasonable grounds of appeal or that the appeal is otherwise vexatious or frivolous, he may determine the appeal by dismissing it forthwith:
Provided that an appeal by a practitioner, chemist or optician under regulation 11(1)(a) against a decision in which the Committee have determined to take action under paragraphs (3) or (5)(a), (b), (c) or (d) of regulation 10 shall not be dismissed without an oral hearing unless the appellant does not desire such a hearing.

(6)(a)   A party to an appeal when an oral hearing takes place shall be entitled to appear and be heard in person, or by counsel or solicitor, or by any officer or member of any organisation of which he is a member, or by any member of his family, or by any friend.

(b)   A Committee or other body being a party to any appeal shall be entitled to appear by a member or by the General Manager or other officer duly appointed for the purpose or by counsel or solicitor.

(7)   A party to an appeal shall not, except with the consent of the Secretary of State or, in the case of an oral hearing, of the person or persons holding the inquiry, be entitled to rely upon any facts or contentions which do not appear to the Secretary of State or to the person or persons holding the inquiry to have been raised before the service committee in the course of the proceedings in respect of which the appeal is brought:
Provided that this paragraph shall not apply in the case of a hearing if at least seven days before the hearing notice is given in writing to the Secretary of State or to the person or persons holding the inquiry of any new facts or contentions upon which the party intends to rely.

(8)   The person or persons holding the inquiry shall draw up a report and present it to the Secretary of State who shall take it into consideration and determine the appeal.

(9)   Where the Secretary of State determines an appeal under the provisions of paragraphs (1), (3) or (8), he shall notify the parties of his decision and the reasons therefor, and his decision shall be final and conclusive.

(10)   The Committee may, with the consent of the Secretary of State, make such contribution as they think fit, and if directed by the Secretary of State shall make such contribution as he may determine towards the costs of the appeal incurred by the complainant or by the practitioner, chemist or optician.

Procedure on withholding money

14. (1)   If the Secretary of State is satisfied—

(a)   after considering—

(i)   (whether in the course of an appeal to him under regulation 11(1)(b) or in the course of representations made to him under regulation 11(3) or otherwise) any report made by a service committee and the decision of the Committee thereon to the effect that there has been a breach of the terms of service,

(ii)   the report of the person or persons holding an inquiry under paragraph (5) of regulation 12, or

(iii)   any report of the Tribunal after an inquiry under Part III of these Regulations,

that such practitioner, chemist or optician has failed to comply with the terms of service applicable to him; or

(b)   after considering the report of a Local Medical Committee to whom a matter has been referred for consideration under regulation 18 or of any person or persons determining any matter under that regulation to the effect that a doctor has failed or neglected to comply with paragraph 30 of the terms of service applicable to him, that such doctor has failed or neglected to comply with the said paragraph,

he may, subject as hereinafter provided, direct the Committee to recover such amount as he thinks fit either by deduction from the remuneration of the practitioner, chemist or optician or otherwise, and such sum shall be a debt owing by the practitioner, chemist or optician to the Committee.

(2)   (a)   Before directing the recovery of any such amount, the Secretary of State shall afford the practitioner, chemist or optician an opportunity of making representations to him on the matter within one month of notice having been sent to him as to the nature of the direction which the Secretary of State is minded to make, except in cases in which the facts have already been the subject of an oral hearing in the course of an appeal to the Secretary of State, or in cases in which the practitioner, chemist or optician had the right to make representations under regulation 11(3) and the Secretary of State does not propose to direct the recovery of a larger amount than that specified by the Committee.

(b)   Where the practitioner, chemist or optician desires to make representations orally, whether under sub-paragraph (a) of this paragraph or under regulation 11(3), the Secretary of State shall appoint a person or persons to hear the representations. The Committee and the Local Medical, Pharmaceutical, Dental or Optical Committee, as the case may be, shall be entitled to be represented at such hearing and to take such part in the proceedings as the persons appointed to hear the representations may think proper. The persons appointed to hear the representations of a doctor or a dentist shall include a practitioner selected for the purpose by the Secretary of State from the panel of doctors or dentists, as the case may be, hereinafter referred to in this regulation. The persons appointed to hear the representations of a chemist, an ophthalmic medical practitioner or an optician shall include a person belonging to the same branch of the service as the person making the representations.

(3)   (a)   An advisory committee (hereinafter referred to as "the medical advisory committee") shall be constituted for the purpose of assisting the Secretary of State in the discharge of his duties under this regulation in relation to doctors. Before directing the Committee to withhold money in respect of a breach of the terms of service applicable to doctors the Secretary of State shall, where such breach is of a kind specified in the following sub-paragraph, and in any other case may, refer the case to the medical advisory committee and consider any report which they may make to him thereon.

(b)   Breaches of the terms of service to which the last preceding sub-paragraph of this regulation relates are failure to exercise reasonable skill and care in the treatment of a patient, failure to visit or treat a patient whose condition so requires, failure to order or supply any necessary drugs or appliances for the use of a patient or failure to discharge the obligations imposed on a doctor to give a patient the requisite assistance to enable him to obtain any treatment which is not within the scope of the doctor's obligations under the terms of service.

(4)   The medical advisory committee shall consist of the Chief Medical Officer or a Deputy Chief Medical Officer of the Department of Health and Social Security and of two other medical officers, and of three doctors appointed by the Secretary of State so far as may be in rotation from a panel of doctors who are, or have been, doctors engaged in the provision of general medical services nominated by a body which is, in the Secretary of State's opinion, representative of doctors engaged in the provision of general medical services. The Chief Medical Officer, or a Deputy Chief Medical Officer, shall act as chairman, and the chairman together with one medical officer and two doctors appointed from the said panel shall form a quorum.

Investigation of excessive prescribing by doctors

16.   (1)   (a)   Where it appears to the Secretary of State after an investigation of the orders for drugs and appliances given by one or more doctors (including any assistant of any such doctor) to persons provided with general medical services and of the accounts furnished by any such doctor for drugs and appliances supplied to such persons that there is a prima facie case for considering that by reason of the character or quantity of the drugs or appliances so ordered or supplied the cost is in excess of what was reasonably necessary for the proper treatment of these persons, the Secretary of State may refer the matter to the Local Medical Committee (hereinafter in this regulation referred to as "the Local Committee") for their consideration.

(b)   Where any doctor is on more than one medical list the Secretary of State may refer the matter to the Local Committee for the locality of the Committee which is the responsible Committee for the purposes of the Statement published pursuant to regulation 24 of the General Service Regulations and that Local Committee shall consider the matter in relation to all the lists concerned.

(2)   (a)   Where any reference has been made to a Local Committee under the preceding paragraph, the Local Committee shall furnish any doctor concerned with a statement indicating the matters on which an explanation is required and shall afford him reasonable opportunity of appearing before and being heard by them, or, if he thinks fit, of submitting to them any statement in writing; and a representative or representatives of the Secretary of State shall be entitled, in the event of a hearing, to attend and be heard by the Local Committee.

(b)   Where any reference is made in relation to orders or accounts given or furnished by a doctor as a deputy for another doctor, the Local Committee may, to such extent as they consider material, require information concerning the orders or accounts given or furnished in respect of the persons concerned by the doctor for whom he was deputising.

(c)   Where references are made in relation to two or more doctors the Local Committee may if the doctors so agree consider them during the same proceedings.

(3)   After considering the case the Local Committee shall decide whether by reason of the character or quantity of the drugs or appliances ordered or supplied as aforesaid by the doctor or doctors concerned any cost has been incurred in excess of what was reasonably necessary and, if so, what sum is, in the opinion of the Local Committee, a reasonable estimate of the excess cost incurred by each doctor.

(4)   Where the Local Committee have decided that excess cost has been so incurred by reason of the drugs or appliances ordered or supplied by any doctor, they shall inform the Committee, the doctor or doctors concerned and the Secretary of State of their decision and may add a statement of any considerations to which in their opinion

the Committee and the Secretary of State should have regard in making any recommendation or decision with reference to the withholding of money from the doctor or doctors concerned. The Local Committee shall also notify the doctor or doctors concerned in writing of their right of appeal to the Secretary of State.

(5) Any aggrieved doctor shall be entitled to appeal against the decision of the Local Committee by sending to the Secretary of State notice of appeal within one month from the date on which notice of the Local Committee's decision was received. The Secretary of State shall appoint as referee or referees a person or persons (not exceeding three in number and not being an officer or officers of the Department of Health and Social Security or the Welsh Office) of whom at least one shall be a doctor, who shall hear and determine the appeal. They shall have power to determine the appeal by a majority.

(6) If the Secretary of State is dissatisfied with the decision of the Local Committee in any case referred to them under paragraph (1) he may appoint as referee or referees a person or persons to hear and determine the matter in the manner provided in the last preceding paragraph, and the provisions of that paragraph including those relating to the person or persons to be appointed shall apply accordingly.

(7) After consideration of the decision of the local Committee or, if an appeal has been made or the matter has been referred for hearing and determination under the last foregoing paragraph, after consideration of the decision of the person or persons determining the appeal or matter, the Committee shall, if such decision is that excessive cost has been incurred, make a recommendation to the Secretary of State with regard to the withholding of money from any doctor concerned, and the Secretary of State may direct the Committee to withhold such sum as he thinks fit, and the provisions of regulation 14, including the right of the doctor to make representations to the Secretary of State, shall apply accordingly.

(8) Where under the provisions of paragraph (1) a matter has been referred to the Local Committee for the locality of the responsible Committee, paragraphs (4) and (7) shall have effect as if the reference to "the Committee" was a reference to the Committee of each of the localities in which the doctor is on the medical list.

Investigation of certification

17. (1) Where it appears to the Secretary of State, after an investigation of the medical certificates issued under and for the purposes of the National Insurance Act 1965 and of the National Insurance (Industrial Injuries) Act 1965 by a doctor to persons for whose treatment he is responsible under the terms of service applicable to him, that there is a prima facie case for considering that the doctor has failed to exercise reasonable care in the issue of such certificates, the Secretary of State may refer the matter for consideration to the Local Medical Committee (hereinafter in this regulation referred to as "the Local Committee"), or to a joint committee of two or more Local Committees constituted in such manner as he may approve and any reference in this regulation to the Local Committee shall be construed as including any such joint committee.

(2) Any reference to the Local Committee under the last preceding paragraph shall be accompanied by a statement indicating the matters on which it appears to the Secretary of State that an explanation is required.

(3) (a) The Local Committee shall furnish the doctor concerned with a copy of the said statement and shall afford him reasonable opportunity of submitting to them a statement in writing and of appearing before and being heard by them.

(b) A copy of any such statement by the doctor shall be forwarded to the Secretary of State by the Local Committee for his observations and a representative or representatives of the Secretary of State shall be entitled, in the event of a hearing, to attend and be heard by the Local Committee.

(4) (a) After considering the case the Local Committee shall draw up a report of their findings on the question whether there has been a failure on the part of the doctor to exercise reasonable care in certification, and, if so, what is the extent and gravity of the failure, together with a recommendation as to the action, if any, which should be taken by the Secretary of State.

(b) The Local Committee shall forward the report to the Secretary of State and shall furnish the doctor with a copy of the report. The Local Committee shall also notify the doctor in writing of his right of appeal to the Secretary of State.

(5) (a) The doctor shall be entitled to appeal against any findings of the Local Committee contained in the report by sending to the Secretary of State notice of appeal within one month from the date on which a copy of the report was received by him and the provisions of paragraph (5) of regulation 16 relating to the determination of appeals shall apply accordingly.

(b) If the Secretary of State is dissatisfied with any findings of the Local Committee he may appoint a person or persons to hear and determine the matter in the manner provided in paragraph (5) of regulation 16 and the provisions of that paragraph including those relating to the person or persons to be appointed shall apply accordingly.

(6) After consideration of the findings and recommendation of the Local Committee or, if an appeal has been made or the matter has been referred for hearing and determination under the last preceding paragraph, after consideration of the findings of the person or persons determining the appeal or matter, the Secretary of State may, if he is satisfied that there has been a failure on the part of the doctor to exercise reasonable care in certification, direct the Committee to withhold such amount as he thinks fit from the remuneration of the doctor, and the provisions of regulation 14, including the doctor's right to make representations to the Secretary of State, shall apply accordingly.

Investigation of record keeping
18. (1) Where it appears to the Secretary of State, after an examination by the medical officer or the dental officer of any record cards held by a doctor, or a dentist other than a salaried dentist, that there is a prima facie case for considering that the doctor has failed to carry out his obligations under paragraph 30 of the terms of service, so far as such obligations involve the recording of clinical data regarding his patients, or that the dentist has failed to carry out his obligations under paragraph 23 of the terms of service, the Secretary of State may refer the matter for consideration to the Local Medical or Dental Committee, whichever is appropriate, hereinafter in this regulation referred to as "the Local Committee".

(2) Any such reference to the Local Committee shall be accompanied by a statement of the grounds for considering that such obligations have not been fulfilled.

(3) (a) The Local Committee shall furnish the practitioner concerned with a copy of the said statement and shall afford him reasonable opportunity of submitting to them a statement in writing and of appearing before and being heard by them.

(b) A copy of any such statement by the practitioner shall be forwarded to the Secretary of State by the Local Committee for his observations and a representative or representatives of the Secretary of State shall be entitled, in the event of a hearing, to attend and be heard by the Local Committee.

(4) If so required by notice in writing signed by the chairman of the Local Committee, the practitioner shall—
(a) produce at the hearing all record cards held by him or such of the record cards as may be specified in the notice;
(b) give in the case of a doctor to any members of the Local Committee specified in the notice, or in the case of a dentist to the dental officer, access at all reasonable times

to the practitioner's surgery or other place where the record cards are kept, for the purpose of inspection of such record cards and furnish such persons with any such record cards and with any necessary information with regard thereto as they may require.

(5) After considering the case the Local Committee shall report to the Secretary of State whether there has been a failure on the part of the practitioner to carry out his said obligations and, if so, the extent and gravity of such failure and shall make a recommendation as to the action, if any, which should be taken by the Secretary of State. A copy of such report shall be forwarded by the Local Committee to the practitioner. The Local Committee shall also notify the practitioner in writing of his right of appeal to the Secretary of State.

(6) (a) The practitioner shall be entitled to appeal against any findings of the Local Committee contained in the report by sending to the Secretary of State notice of appeal within one month from the date on which a copy of the report was received by him and the provisions of paragraph (5) of regulation 16 relating to the determination of appeals shall apply accordingly.

(b) If the Secretary of State is dissatisfied with the findings of the Local Committee he may appoint a person or persons to hear and determine the matter in the manner provided in paragraph (5) of regulation 16 as modified by the preceding sub-paragraph, and those provisions, including those relating to the person or persons to be appointed, shall apply accordingly.

(7) In this regulation "record cards" means—

(a) in the case of a doctor, the cards on which he is required to keep records of the illnesses of his patients and of his treatment of them under paragraph 30 of the terms of service.

Power of Local Medical, Pharmaceutical, Dental and Optical Committees to consider complaints

24. (1) The Local Medical committee shall have power to consider any complaint made to them by any doctor against a doctor practising in the locality for which the Local Medical committee is constituted involving any question of the efficiency of the general medical services.

Interpretation and forms

25. (1) In this part of these regulations, unless the context otherwise requires, the following expressions have the respective meanings hereby assigned to them:—

"inquiry" means an inquiry held in accordance with the provisions of this part of these regulations;

"representation" means a representation made to the Tribunal that the continued inclusion of a doctor in any medical list, or a chemist in any pharmaceutical list, or a dentist in any dental list, or an ophthalmic medical practitioner or optician in any ophthalmic list, would be prejudicial to the efficiency of the general medical, pharmaceutical, general dental or general ophthalmic services as the case may be;

"application" means an application made to the Tribunal or the Secretary of State by a practitioner, chemist, or optician for a direction that he should no longer be disqualified for inclusion in any list or lists to which a still effective direction by the Tribunal or the Secretary of State relates, and "applicant" shall be construed accordingly;

"complainant" means any person or body making a representation to the Tribunal;

"respondent" means in the case of a representation any practitioner, chemist, or optician against whom a representation is made, and, in the case of an application, any person or body upon whose representation the direction to which the application relates was made.

Representation and preliminary statement
28. (1) A representation shall—
  (a) be made in writing;
  (b) be signed by the complainant or on his behalf by some person authorised by him;
  (c) include a preliminary statement of the alleged facts and the grounds upon which he intends to rely,
and shall be sent to the clerk of the Tribunal.
  (2) The Tribunal may if they think fit—
  (a) direct the complainant to furnish such further particulars of those facts or grounds as they may reasonably require; and
  (b) where a fact does not appear to them to be within the personal knowledge of the complainant, require details of the source of his information about that fact and of the grounds for the complainant's belief that the information is true; and
  (c) require any preliminary statement under this regulation to be verified by statutory declaration.

Power to refuse inquiry
29. If it appears to the Tribunal, after due consideration of any representation or of any preliminary statement furnished to them by the complainant, not being a Committee, that no good cause has been shown why an inquiry should be held, they may refuse to hold an inquiry and shall inform the complainant accordingly.

Proceedings in camera
38. Subject to the provisions of regulation 54, the proceedings shall be held in camera unless the respondent has applied for the inquiry to be held in public.

Procedure at inquiry
39. Subject to the provisions of these regulations, the procedure at the inquiry shall be within the discretion of the Tribunal.

Appearance by representative
40. (1) Any Committee or other body (whether corporate or unincorporate) entitled to appear at the inquiry may appear by a member or by the General Manager or other officer duly appointed for the purpose or by counsel or solicitor.
  (2) The complainant and the respondent shall be entitled to appear and be heard at the inquiry in person or by counsel or solicitor, or by any officer or member of any organisation of which he is a member, or by any member of his family, or by any friend.

Evidence
41. The complainant and the respondent or their representatives shall be entitled at the inquiry to produce evidence, including evidence not produced prior to the inquiry, and to call witnesses to whom questions may be put by or on behalf of any party.

Power to dispense with oral inquiry
45. Notwithstanding anything in this part of these regulations, where the grounds on which any representation is based consist solely of an allegation that the respondent has been convicted of a criminal offence and he admits the truth of such allegation, the Tribunal may, with the consent of the respondent, dispense with an oral inquiry and determine the case upon such documentary evidence as may be submitted to them.

Report by Tribunal
46. (1) At the conclusion of the inquiry the Tribunal shall, as soon as may be, issue a statement under the hand of the chairman containing their findings of fact, the conclusions which they have reached and such directions as they may give under

sub-section (2) of section 46 of the Act, and any order they may decide to make with respect to the costs of the parties.

(2)   A copy of such statement shall be forwarded by the Tribunal to the Secretary of State, the respondent, and the complainant or the applicant, as the case may be, and the Secretary of State shall send a copy of the statement to such Committees as appear to him to be concerned.

(3)   The Tribunal shall give notice to the respondent in writing of his right of appeal to the Secretary of State against any direction given by them for the removal of his name from any list.

Appeal to Secretary of State
47.   (1)   The respondent may appeal to the Secretary of State against any direction given by the Tribunal for the removal of his name from any list by submitting to the Secretary of State a notice of appeal within one month from the date on which notice of his right to make such appeal has been forwarded to him.

(2)   The notice of appeal shall contain a concise statement of the facts and contentions upon which the appellant intends to rely.

Procedure on appeal from Tribunal
48.   (1)   The Secretary of State shall appoint a person to hear the appeal and report thereon to him. He shall also appoint for the purpose of assisting the person hearing the appeal—
     (a)   where the appellant is a doctor, a doctor from the panel of doctors referred to in regulation 14;
The Secretary of State shall consider the report made by the person hearing the appeal and in the case of a doctor or dentist any recommendation made by the medical or dental advisory committee constituted under regulation 14 to whom he shall refer such report, and shall thereafter give his decision and shall send a notice thereof to the appellant, the Tribunal, the complainant and such Committees as may appear to him to be concerned.

(2)   Regulations 31, 34, 35, 38, 39, 40 and 41 shall, with the necessary modifications, apply to the hearing of appeals under this regulation in like manner as to an inquiry.

(2A)   Where an appellant to whom notice of a hearing has been given in accordance with regulation 34(1) (as modified pursuant to paragraph (2) of this regulation) fails to appear at the hearing, the person hearing the appeal may, after having regard to all the circumstances including any explanation offered for the absence, proceed to hear the appeal notwithstanding the absence.

(3)   The appellant may, at any time before the day appointed for the hearing, withdraw the appeal by giving notice of such withdrawal in writing to the Secretary of State, and when an appeal has been withdrawn the Secretary of State shall forthwith confirm the direction of the Tribunal.

Power to extend time limits
53.   (1)   The Secretary of State may, on the application of any person desiring either—
     (a)   to appeal under the provisions of regulation 5(4), 11(1), 13, 16 to 18, 20 or 23;
or
     (b)   to make representations under the provisions of regulation 11(3), 14(2)(a) or 15(1)(a) or (b),
extend the time for giving notice of appeal or, as the case may be, making representations, and may do so although such application is not made until after the expiration of the time prescribed for giving notice of appeal or making representations.

(2)   An application under paragraph (1) shall be in writing to the Secretary of State stating the grounds for the application.

Referral of matters to professional bodies

53A.   (1)   Where, in relation to any complaint or reference made under Part II of these Regulations—

(a)   a Family Health Services Authority makes a determination under regulation 10(1); and

(b)   having regard to the facts found by the service committee in relation to that matter, that Authority considers that the matter should be brought to the attention of the relevant professional body,

it may refer to that body any documents in its possession connected with that complaint or reference.

(2)   Where, in relation to any complaint or reference under that Part—

(a)   the Secretary of State—

(i)   receives, pursuant to regulation 10(9), a copy of the report of a service committee and the decision of a Family Health Services Authority thereon, or

(ii)   makes a determination following a recommendation by a Family Health Services Authority under regulation 10(5)(c) or (d) or an appeal under regulation 11; and

(b)   that matter has not been the subject of a reference by the Family Health Services Authority under paragraph (1); and

(c)   the Secretary of State considers that the matter should be brought to the attention of the relevant professional body, he may refer to that body any documents in his possession connected with that complaint or reference.

(3)   In this regulation, "the relevant professional body" means—

(a)   in relation to a doctor, the General Medical Council.

THE MENTAL HEALTH (HOSPITAL, GUARDIANSHIP AND CONSENT TO TREATMENT) REGULATIONS 1983
(SI 1983, No. 893)

PART I

Interpretation

2.   (1)   In these regulations, unless the context otherwise requires

"the Act" means the Mental Health Act 1983

"appropriate medical officer" has the same meaning as in section 16(5) of the Act;

"the Commission" means the Mental Health Act Commission;

"document" means any application, recommendation, record, report, order, notice or other document;

"private guardian", in relation to a patient, means a person, other than a local social services authority, who acts as guardian under the Act;

"served", in relation to a document, includes addressed, delivered, given, forwarded, furnished or sent.

(2)   Except insofar as the context otherwise requires, any reference in these regulations to—

(a)   a numbered section is to the section of the Act bearing that number;

(b)   a numbered regulation or Schedule is to the regulation in or Schedule to these regulations bearing that number and any reference in a regulation to a numbered paragraph is a reference to the paragraph of that regulation bearing that number;

(c)   a numbered form is a reference to the form in Schedule 1 bearing that number.

PART III
FUNCTIONS OF GUARDIANS AND NEAREST RELATIVES

Duties of private guardians

12. It shall be the duty of a private guardian—

(a) to appoint a registered medical practitioner to act as the nominated medical attendant of the patient;

(b) to notify the responsible local social services authority of the name and address of the nominated medical attendant;

(c) in exercising the powers and duties conferred or imposed upon him by the Act and these regulations, to comply with such directions as that authority may give;

(d) to furnish that authority with all such reports or other information with regard to the patient as the authority may from time to time require;

(e) to notify the authority

(i) on the reception of the patient into guardianship of his address and the address of the patient,

(ii) except in a case to which paragraph (f) applies, of any permanent change of either address, before or not later than 7 days after the change takes place;

(f) where on any permanent change of his address, the new address is in the area of a different local social services authority, to notify that authority

(i) of his address and that of the patient,

(ii) of the particulars mentioned in paragraph (b),

and to send a copy of the notification to the authority which was formerly responsible; and

(g) in the event of the death of the patient, or the termination of the guardianship by discharge, transfer or otherwise, to notify the responsible local social services authority as soon as reasonably practicable.

Visits to patients subject to guardianship

13. The responsible local social services authority shall arrange for every patient received into guardianship under Part II of the Act to be visited at such intervals as the authority may decide, but in any case at intervals of not more than 3 months, and at least one such visit in any year shall be made by a practitioner approved by the Secretary of State for the purposes of section 12 (general provisions as to medical recommendations).

Performance of functions of nearest relative

14.—(1) Subject to the conditions of paragraph (2), the nearest relative of a patient may authorise in writing any person other than the patient or a person mentioned in section 26(5) (persons deemed not to be nearest relative) to perform in respect of the patient the functions conferred upon the nearest relative by or under Part II of the Act or these regulations and may revoke such authority.

(2) The conditions mentioned in paragraph (1) are that, on making or revoking such authority, the nearest relative shall forthwith give the authority, or give notice in writing of the revocation of such authority, to

(a) the person authorised;

(b) in the case of a patient liable to be detained in a hospital, the managers of that hospital;

(c) in the case of a patient subject to guardianship, the responsible local social services authority and to the private guardian, if any.

(3) Any such authority shall take effect upon receipt of the authority by the person authorised, and any revocation of such authority shall take effect upon the receipt of the notice by the person authorised.

(4) A person for the time being authorised in accordance with the preceding paragraphs shall exercise the functions mentioned in paragraph (1) on behalf of the nearest relative.

Discharge by nearest relative
15.—(1) Any order made by the nearest relative of the patient under section 23 for the discharge of a patient who is liable to be detained under Part II of the Act shall be served upon the managers of the hospital where the patient is liable to be detained and may be in the form set out in Form 34.

(2) Any order made by the nearest relative of the patient under section 23 for discharge of a patient subject to guardianship under the Act shall be served upon the responsible local social services authority and may be in the form set out in Form 35.

(3) Any report given by the responsible medical officer for the purposes of section 25 (restrictions on discharge by nearest relative) shall be in the form set out in Part I of Form 36 and the receipt of that report by the managers of the hospital in which the patient is liable to be detained shall be in the form set out in Part II of Form 36.

PART IV
CONSENT TO TREATMENT

Consent to treatment
16.—(1) For the purposes of section 57 (treatment requiring consent and a second opinion)—
(a) the form of treatment to which that section shall apply, in addition to the treatment mentioned in subsection (1)(a) of that section (any surgical operation for destroying brain tissue or for destroying the functioning of brain tissue), shall be the surgical implantation of hormones for the purpose of reducing male sexual drive;
(b) the certificates required for the purposes of subsection (2)(a) and (b) of that section shall be in the form set out in Form 37.

(2) For the purposes of section 58 (treatment requiring consent or a second opinion)—
(a) the form of treatment to which that section shall apply, in addition to the administration of medicine mentioned in subsection (1)(b) of that section, shall be electro-convulsive therapy; and
(b) the certificates required for the purposes of subsection (3)(a) and (b) of that section shall be in the form set out in Forms 38 and 39 respectively.

PART V
CORRESPONDENCE OF PATIENTS

Inspection and opening of postal packets
17.—(1) Where under section 134(4) (inspection and opening of postal packets addressed to or by patients in hospital) any postal packet is inspected and opened, but neither the packet nor anything contained in it is withheld under section 134(1) or (2), the person who so inspected and opened it, being a person appointed under section 134(7) to perform the functions of the managers of the hospital under that section ("the person appointed"), shall record in writing—
(a) that the packet had been so inspected and opened;
(b) that nothing in the packet has been withheld; and
(c) his name and the name of the hospital,
and shall, before resealing the packet, place the record in that packet.

(2) Where under section 134(1) or (2) any postal packet or anything contained in it is withheld by the person appointed
(a) he shall record in a register kept for the purpose
(i) that the packet or anything contained in it has been withheld,

(ii)   the date on which it was so withheld,

(iii) the grounds on which it was so withheld,

(iv)   a description of the contents of the packet withheld or of any item withheld, and

(v)   his name; and

(b) if anything contained in the packet is withheld, he shall record in writing

(i)   that the packet has been inspected and opened,

(ii)   that an item or items contained in the packet have been withheld,

(iii) a description of any such item,

(iv)   his name and the name of the hospital, and

(v)   in any case to which section 134(1)(b) or (2) applies, the further particulars required for the purposes of section 134(6),

and shall, before resealing the packet, place the record in that packet.

(3)   In a case to which section 134(1)(b) or (2) applies

(a)   the notice required for the purposes of section 134(6) shall include

(i)   a statement of the grounds on which the packet in question or anything contained in it was withheld, and

(ii)   the name of the person appointed who so decided to withhold that packet or anything contained in it and the name of the hospital; and

(b)   where anything contained in a packet is withheld the record required by paragraph (2)(b) above shall, if the provisions of section 134(6) are otherwise satisfied, be sufficient notice to the person to whom the packet is addressed for the purposes of section 134(6).

Review of decisions to withhold postal packets

18.—(1) Every application for review by the Commission under section 121(7) (review of any decision to withhold a postal packet, or anything contained in it, under section 134)—

(a)   shall be made in such manner as the Commission may accept as sufficient in the circumstances of any particular case or class of case and may be made otherwise than in writing; and

(b)   shall be made, delivered or sent to an office of the Commission.

(2)   Any person making such an application shall furnish to the Commission the notice of the withholding of the postal packet or anything contained in it, given under section 134(6), or a copy of that notice.

(3)   For the purpose of determining any such application the Commission may direct the production of such documents, information and evidence as it may reasonably require.

THE MENTAL HEALTH REVIEW TRIBUNAL RULES 1983
(SI 1983, No. 942)

PART I
INTRODUCTION

Interpretation

2.—(1) In these Rules, unless the context otherwise requires—

"the Act" means the Mental Health Act 1983;

"admission papers" means the application for admission under section 2 of the Act and the written recommendations of the two registered medical practitioners on which it is founded;

"assessment application" means an application by a patient who is detained for assessment and entitled to apply under section 66(1)(a) of the Act or who, being so entitled, has applied;

"the authority's statement" means the statement provided by the responsible authority pursuant to rule 6(1);

"chairman" means the legal member appointed by the Lord Chancellor as chairman of the Mental Health Review Tribunal under paragraph 3 of Schedule 2 to the Act or another member of the tribunal appointed to act on his behalf in accordance with paragraph 4 of that Schedule or section 78(6) of the Act as the case may be;

"decision with recommendations" means a decision with recommendations in accordance with section 72(3)(a) of the Act;

"health authority" has the same meaning as in the National Health Service Act 1977;

"nearest relative" means a person who has for the time being the functions under the Act of the nearest relative of a patient who is not a restricted patient;

"party" means the applicant, the patient, the responsible authority, any other person to whom a notice under rule 7 or rule 31(c) is sent or who is added as a party by direction of the tribunal;

"president" means the president of the tribunal as defined in paragraph 6 of Schedule 2 to the Act;

"private guardian" in relation to a patient means a person, other than a local social services authority, who acts as guardian under the Act;

"proceedings" includes any proceedings of a tribunal following an application or reference in relation to a patient;

"provisional decision" includes a deferred direction for conditional charge in accordance with section 73(7) of the Act and a notification to the Secretary of State in accordance with section 74(1) of the Act;

"reference" means a reference under section 67(1), 68(1) or (2), 71(1), (2) or (5) or 75(1) of the Act;

"registration authority" means the authority exercising the functions of the Secretary of State under the Nursing Homes Act 1975;

"responsible authority" means—

    (a) in relation to a patient liable to be detained under the Act in a hospital or mental nursing home, the managers of the hospital or home as defined in section 145(1) of the Act; and

    (b) in relation to a patient subject to guardianship, the responsible local social services authority as defined in section 34(3) of the Act;

"the Secretary of State's statement" means a statement provided by the Secretary of State pursuant to rule 6(2) or (3);

"tribunal" in relation to an application or a reference means the Mental Health Review Tribunal constituted under section 65 of the Act which has jurisdiction in the area in which the patient, at the time the application or reference is made, is detained or is liable to be detained or is subject to guardianship, or the tribunal to which the proceedings are transferred in accordance with rule 17(2), or, in the case of a conditionally discharged patient, the tribunal for the area in which the patient resides.

PART II
PRELIMINARY MATTERS

Making an application

3.—(1) An application shall be made to the tribunal in writing, signed by the applicant or any person authorised by him to do so on his behalf.

(2) The application shall wherever possible include the following information—

    (a) the name of the patient;

    (b) the patient's address, which shall include—

(i)   the address of the hospital or mental nursing home where the patient is detained; or

(ii)   the name and address of the patient's private guardian; or

(iii)   in the case of a conditionally discharged patient or a patient to whom leave of absence from hospital has been granted, the address of the hospital or mental nursing home where the patient was last detained or is liable to be detained; together with the patient's current address;

(c)   where the application is made by the patient's nearest relative, the name and address of the applicant and his relationship to the patient;

(d)   the section of the Act under which the patient is detained or is liable to be detained;

(e)   the name and address of any representative authorised in accordance with rule 10 or, if none has yet been authorised, whether the applicant intends to authorise a representative or wishes to conduct his own case.

(3)   If any of the information specified in paragraph (2) is not included in the application, it shall in so far as is practicable be provided by the responsible authority or, in the case of a restricted patient, the Secretary of State, at the request of the tribunal.

Notice of application

4.—(1)   On receipt of an application, the tribunal shall send notice of the application to—

(a)   the responsible authority;

(b)   the patient (where he is not the applicant); and

(c)   if the patient is a restricted patient, the Secretary of State.

(2)   Paragraph (1) shall apply whether or not the power to postpone consideration of the application under rule 9 is exercised.

Preliminary and incidental matters

5.   As regards matters preliminary or incidental to an application, the chairman may, at any time up to the hearing of an application by the tribunal, exercise the powers of the tribunal under rules 6, 7, 9, 10, 12, 13, 14(1), 15, 17, 19, 20, 26 and 28.

Statements by the responsible authority and the Secretary of State

6.—(1)   The responsible authority shall send a statement to the tribunal and, in the case of a restricted patient, the Secretary of State, as soon as practicable and in any case within 3 weeks of its receipt of the notice of application; and such statement shall contain—

(a)   the information specified in Part A of Schedule 1 to these Rules, in so far as it is within the knowledge of the responsible authority; and

(b)   the report specified in paragraph 1 of Part B of that Schedule; and

(c)   the other reports specified in Part B of that Schedule, in so far as it is reasonably practicable to provide them.

(2)   Where the patient is a restricted patient, the Secretary of State shall send to the tribunal, as soon as practicable and in any case within 3 weeks of receipt by him of the authority's statement, a statement of such further information relevant to the application as may be available to him.

(3)   Where the patient is a conditionally discharged patient, paragraphs (1) and (2) shall not apply and the Secretary of State shall send to the tribunal as soon as practicable, and in any case within 6 weeks of receipt by him of the notice of application, a statement which shall contain—

(a)   the information specified in Part C of Schedule 1 to these Rules, in so far as it is within the knowledge of the Secretary of State; and

(b)   the reports specified in Part D of that Schedule, in so far as it is reasonably practicable to provide them.

(4)   Any part of the authority's statement or the Secretary of State's statement which, in the opinion of—

    (a)   (in the case of the authority's statement) the responsible authority; or

    (b)   (in the case of the Secretary of State's statement) the Secretary of State,

should be withheld from the applicant or (where he is not the applicant) the patient on the ground that its disclosure would adversely affect the health or welfare of the patient or others, shall be made in a separate document in which shall be set out the reasons for believing that its disclosure would have that effect.

(5)   On receipt of any statement provided in accordance with paragraph (1), (2) or (3), the tribunal shall send a copy to the applicant and (where he is not the applicant) the patient, excluding any part of any statement which is contained in a separate document in accordance with paragraph (4).

Notice to other persons interested

7.   On receipt of the authority's statement or, in the case of a restricted patient, the Secretary of State's statement, the tribunal shall give notice of the proceedings—

    (a)   where the patient is liable to be detained in a mental nursing home, to the registration authority of that home;

    (b)   where the patient is subject to the guardianship of a private guardian, to the guardian;

    (c)   where the patient's financial affairs are under the control of the Court of Protection, to the Court of Protection;

    (d)   where any person other than the applicant is named in the authority's statement as exercising the functions of the nearest relative, to that person;

    (e)   where a health authority has a right to discharge the patient under the provisions of section 23(3) of the Act, to that authority;

    (f)   to any other person who, in the opinion of the tribunal, should have an opportunity of being heard.

Appointment of the tribunal

8.—(1)   Unless the application belongs to a class or group of proceedings for which members have already been appointed, the members of the tribunal who are to hear the application shall be appointed by the chairman.

(2)   A person shall not be qualified to serve as a member of a tribunal for the purpose of any proceedings where—

    (a)   he is a member or officer of the responsible authority or of the registration authority concerned in the proceedings; or

    (b)   he is a member or officer of a health authority which has the right to discharge the patient under section 23(3) of the Act; or

    (c)   he has a personal connection with the patient or has recently treated the patient in a professional medical capacity.

(3)   The persons qualified to serve as president of the tribunal for the consideration of an application or reference relating to a restricted patient shall be restricted to those legal members who have been approved for that purpose by the Lord Chancellor.

Powers to postpone consideration of an application

9.—(1)   Where an application or reference by or in respect of a patient has been considered and determined by a tribunal for the same or any other area, the tribunal may, subject to the provisions of this rule, postpone the consideration of a further application by or in respect of that patient until such date as it may direct, not being later than—

    (a)   the expiration of the period of six months from the date on which the previous application was determined; or

    (b)   the expiration of the current period of detention, whichever shall be the earlier.

(2)   The power of postponement shall not be exercised unless the tribunal is satisfied, after making appropriate inquiries of the applicant and (where he is not the applicant) the patient, that postponement would be in the interests of the patient.

(3)   The power of postponement shall not apply to—

(a)   an application under section 66(1)(d) of the Act;

(b)   an application under section 66(1)(f) of the Act in respect of a renewal of authority for detention of the patient for a period of six months, unless the previous application or reference was made to the tribunal more than three months after the patient's admission to hospital or reception into guardianship.

(c)   an application under section 66(1)(g) of the Act;

(d)   any application where the previous application or reference was determined before a break or change in the authority for the patient's detention or guardianship as defined in paragraph (7).

(4)   Where the consideration of an application is postponed, the tribunal shall state in writing the reasons for postponement and the period for which the application is postponed and shall send a copy of the statement to all the parties and, in the case of a restricted patient, the Secretary of State.

(5)   Where the consideration of an application is posponed, the tribunal shall send a further notice of the application in accordance with rule 4 not less than 7 days before the end of the period of postponement and consideration of the application shall proceed thereafter, unless before the end of the period of postponement the application has been withdrawn or is deemed to be withdrawn in accordance with the provisions of rule 19 or has been determined in accordance with the next following paragraph.

(6)   Where a new application which is not postponed under this rule or a reference is made in respect of a patient, the tribunal may direct that any postponed application in respect of the same patient shall be considered and determined at the same time as the new application or reference.

(7)   For the purpose of paragraph (3)(d) a break or change in the authority for the detention or guardianship of a patient shall be deemed to have ocurred only—

(a)   on his admission to hospital in pursuance of an application for treatment or in pursuance of a hospital order without an order restricting his discharge; or

(b)   on his reception into guardianship in pursuance of a guardianship application or a guardianship order; or

(c)   on the application to him of the provisions of Part II or Part III of the Act as if he had been so admitted or received following—

(i)   the making of a transfer direction, or

(ii)   the ceasing of effect of a transfer direction or an order or direction restricting his discharge; or

(d)   on his transfer from guardianship to hospital in pursuance of regulations made under section 19 of the Act.

PART III
GENERAL PROVISIONS

Representation, etc.

10.—(1)   Any party may be represented by any person whom he has authorised for that purpose not being a person liable to be detained or subject to guardianship under the Act or a person receiving treatment for mental disorder at the same hospital or mental nursing home as the patient.

(2)   Any representative authorised in accordance with paragraph (1) shall notify the tribunal of his authorisation and postal address.

(3)   As regards the representation of any patient who does not desire to conduct his own case and does not authorise a representative in accordance with paragraph (1) the tribunal may appoint some person to act for him as his authorised representative.

(4) Without prejudice to rule 12(3), the tribunal shall send to an authorised representative copies of all notices and documents which are by these Rules required or authorised to be sent to the person whom he represents and such representative may take all such steps and do all such things relating to the proceedings as the person whom he represents is by these Rules required or authorised to take or do.

(5) Any document required or authorised by these Rules to be sent or given to any person shall, if sent or given to the authorised representative of that person, be deemed to have been sent or given to that person.

(6) Unless the tribunal otherwise directs, a patient or any other party appearing before the tribunal may be accompanied by such other person or persons as he wishes, in addition to any representative he may have authorised.

Medical examination

11. At any time before the hearing of the application, the medical member or, where the tribunal includes more than one, at least one of them shall examine the patient and take such other steps as he considers necessary to form an opinion of the patient's mental condition; and for this purpose the patient may be seen in private and all his medical records may be examined by the medical member, who may take such notes and copies of them as he may require, for use in connection with the application.

Disclosure of documents

12.—(1) Subject to paragraph (2), the tribunal shall, as soon as practicable, send a copy of every document it receives which is relevant to the application to the applicant, and (where he is not the applicant) the patient, the responsible authority and, in the case of a restricted patient, the Secretary of State and any of those persons may submit comments thereon in writing to the tribunal.

(2) As regards any documents which have been received by the tribunal but which have not been copied to the applicant or the patient, including documents withheld in accordance with rule 6, the tribunal shall consider whether disclosure of such documents would adversely affect the health or welfare of the patient or others and, if satisfied that it would, shall record in writing its decision not to disclose such documents.

(3) Where the tribunal is minded not to disclose any document to which paragraph (1) applies to an applicant or a patient who has an authorised representative it shall nevertheless disclose it as soon as practicable to that representative if he is—

(a) a barrister or solicitor,

(b) a registered medical practitioner;

(c) in the opinion of the tribunal, a suitable person by virtue of his experience or professional qualification;

provided that no information disclosed in accordance with this paragraph shall be disclosed either directly or indirectly to the applicant or (whether he is not the applicant) to the patient or to any other person without the authority of the tribunal or used otherwise than in connection with the application.

Directions

13. Subject to the provisions of these Rules, the tribunal may give such directions as it thinks fit to ensure the speedy and just determination of the application.

Evidence

14.—(1) For the purpose of obtaining information, the tribunal may take evidence on oath and subpoena any witness to appear before it or to produce documents, and the president of the tribunal shall have the powers of an arbitrator under section 12(3) of the Arbitration Act 1950 and the powers of a party to a reference under an arbitration agreement under subsection (4) of that section, but no person shall be compelled to give any evidence or produce any document which he could not be compelled to give or produce on the trial of an action.

(2)   The tribunal may receive in evidence any document or information notwithstanding that such document or information would be inadmissible in a court of law.

Further information
15.—(1). Before or during any hearing the tribunal may call for such further information or reports as it may think desirable, and may give directions as to the manner in which and the persons by whom such material is to be furnished.

(2)   Rule 12 shall apply to any further information or reports obtained by the tribunal.

Adjournment
16.—(1)   The tribunal may at any time adjourn a hearing for the purpose of obtaining further information or for such other purposes as it may think appropriate.

(2)   Before adjourning any hearing, the tribunal may give such directions as it thinks fit for ensuring the prompt consideration of the application at an adjourned hearing.

(3)   Where the applicant or the patient (where he is not the applicant) or the responsible authority requests that a hearing adjourned in accordance with this rule be resumed, the hearing shall be resumed provided that the tribunal is satisfied that resumption would be in the interests of the patient.

(4)   Before the tribunal resumes any hearing which has been adjourned without a further hearing date being fixed it shall give to all parties and, in the case of a restricted patient, the Secretary of State, not less than 14 days' notice (or such shorter notice as all parties may consent to) of the date, time and place of the resumed hearing.

Transfer of proceedings
17.—(1)   Where any proceedings in relation to a patient have not been disposed of by the members of the tribunal appointed for the purpose, and the chairman is of the opinion that it is not practicable or not possible without undue delay for the consideration of those proceedings to be completed by those members, he shall make arrangements for them to be heard by other members of the tribunal.

(2)   Where a patient in respect of whom proceedings are pending moves within the jurisdiction of another tribunal, the proceedings shall, if the chairman of the tribunal originally having jurisdiction over those proceedings so directs, be transferred to the tribunal within the jurisdiction of which the patient has moved and notice of the transfer of proceedings shall be given to the parties and, in the case of a restricted patient, the Secretary of State.

Two or more pending applications
18.—(1)   The tribunal may consider more than one application in respect of a patient at the same time and may for this purpose adjourn the proceedings relating to any application.

(2)   Where the tribunal considers more than one application in respect of the patient at the same time, each applicant (if more than one) shall have the same rights under these Rules as he would have if he were the only applicant.

Withdrawal of application
19.—(1)   An application may be withdrawn at any time at the request of the applicant provided that the request is made in writing and the tribunal agrees.

(2)   If a patient ceases to be liable to be detained or subject to guardianship in England and Wales, any application relating to that patient shall be deemed to be withdrawn.

(3)   Where an application is withdrawn or deemed to be withdrawn, the tribunal shall so inform the parties and, in the case of a restricted patient, the Secretary of State.

PART IV
THE HEARING

Notice of hearing

20. The tribunal shall give at least 14 days' notice of the date, time and place fixed for the hearing (or such shorter notice as all parties may consent to) to all the parties and, in the case of a restricted patient, the Secretary of State.

Privacy of proceedings

21.—(1) The tribunal shall sit in private unless the patient requests a hearing in public and the tribunal is satisfied that a hearing in public would not be contrary to the interests of the patient.

(2) Where the tribunal refuses a request for a public hearing or directs that a hearing which has begun in public shall continue in private the tribunal shall record its reasons in writing and shall inform the patient of those reasons.

(3) When the tribunal sits in private it may admit to the hearing such persons on such terms and conditions as it considers appropriate.

(4) The tribunal may exclude from any hearing or part of a hearing any person or class of persons, other than a representative of the applicant or of the patient to whom documents would be disclosed in accordance with rule 12(3), and in any case where the tribunal decides to exclude the applicant or the patient or their representative or a representative of the responsible authority, it shall inform the person excluded of its reasons and record those reasons in writing.

(5) Except in so far as the tribunal may direct, information about proceedings before the tribunal and the names of any persons concerned in the proceedings shall not be made public.

(6) Nothing in this rule shall prevent a member of the Council on Tribunals from attending the proceedings of a tribunal in his capacity as such provided that he takes no part in those proceedings or in the deliberations of the tribunal.

Hearing procedure

22.—(1) The tribunal may conduct the hearing in such manner as it considers most suitable bearing in mind the health and interests of the patient and it shall, so far as appears to it appropriate, seek to avoid formality in its proceedings.

(2) At any time before the application is determined, the tribunal or any one or more of its members may interview the patient, and shall interview him if he so requests, and the interview may, and shall if the patient so requests, take place in the absence of any other person.

(3) At the beginning of the hearing the president shall explain the manner of proceeding which the tribunal proposes to adopt.

(4) Subject to rule 21(4), any part and, with the permission of the tribunal, any other person, may appear at the hearing and take such part in the proceedings as the tribunal thinks proper; and the tribunal shall in particular hear and take evidence from the applicant, the patient (where he is not the applicant) and the responsible authority who may hear each other's evidence, put questions to each other, call witnesses and put questions to any witness or other person appearing before the tribunal.

(5) After all the evidence has been given, the applicant and (where he is not the applicant) the patient shall be given a further opportunity to address the tribunal.

PART V
DECISIONS, FURTHER CONSIDERATION AND MISCELLANEOUS PROVISIONS

Decisions

23.—(1) Any decision of the majority of the members of a tribunal shall be the decision of the tribunal and, in the event of an equality of votes, the president of the tribunal shall have a second or casting vote.

(2) The decision by which the tribunal determines an application shall be recorded in writing; the record shall be signed by the president and shall give the reasons for the decision and, in particular, where the tribunal relies upon any of the matters set out in section 72(1) or (4) or section 73(1) or (2) of the Act, shall state its reasons for being satisfied as to those matters.

(3) Paragraphs (1) and (2) shall apply to provisional decisions and decisions with recommendations as they apply to decisions by which applications are determined.

Communication of decisions

24.—(1) The decision by which the tribunal determines an application may, at the discretion of the tribunal, be announced by the president immediately after the hearing of the case and, subject to paragraph (2), the written decision of the tribunal, including the reasons, shall be communicated in writing within 7 days of the hearing to all the parties and, in the case of a restricted patient, the Secretary of State.

(2) Where the tribunal considers that the full disclosure of the recorded reasons for its decision to the patient in accordance with paragraph (1) would adversely affect the health or welfare of the patient or others, the tribunal may instead communicate its decision to him in such manner as it thinks appropriate and may communicate its decision to the other parties subject to any conditions it may think appropriate as to the disclosure thereof to the patient; provided that, where the applicant or the patient was represented at the hearing by a person to whom documents would be disclosed in accordance with rule 12(3), the tribunal shall disclose the full recorded grounds of its decision to such a person, subject to any conditions it may think appropriate as to disclosure thereof to the patient.

(3) Paragraphs (1) and (2) shall apply to provisional decisions and decisions with recommendations as they apply to decisions by which applications are determined.

(4) Where the tribunal makes a decision with recommendations, the decision shall specify the period at the expiration of which the tribunal will consider the case further in the event of those recommendations not being complied with.

Further consideration

25.—(1) Where the tribunal has made a provisional decision, any further decision in the proceedings may be made without a further hearing.

(2) Where the tribunal has made a decision with recommendations and, at the end of the period referred to in rule 24(4), it appears to the tribunal after making appropriate inquiries of the responsible authority that any such recommendation has not been complied with, the tribunal may reconvene the proceedings after giving to all parties and, in the case of a restricted patient, the Secretary of State not less than 14 days' notice (or such shorter notice as all parties may consent to) of the date, time and place fixed for the hearing.

PART VI
REFERENCES AND APPLICATIONS BY PATIENTS DETAINED
FOR ASSESSMENT

References

29. The tribunal shall consider a reference as if there had been an application by the patient and the provisions of these Rules shall apply with the following modifications—

    (a) rules 3, 4, 9 and 19 shall not apply;

    (b) the tribunal shall, on receipt of the reference, send notice thereof to the patient and the responsible authority; provided that where the reference has been made by the responsible authority, instead of the notice of reference there shall be sent to the responsible authority a request for the authority's statement;

    (c) rules 5, 6 and 7 shall apply as if rule 6(1) referred to the notice of reference, or the request for the authority's statement, as the case may be, instead of the notice of application;

(d)   a reference made by the Secretary of State in circumstances in which he is not by the terms of the Act obliged to make a reference may be withdrawn by him at any time before it is considered by the tribunal and, where a reference is so withdrawn, the tribunal shall inform the patient and the other parties that the reference has been withdrawn.

Making an assessment application
   30.—(1)   An assessment application shall be made to the tribunal in writing signed by the patient or any person authorised by him to do so on his behalf.
   (2)   An assessment application shall indicate that it is made by or on behalf of a patient detained for assessment and shall wherever possible include the following information—
      (a)   the name of the patient;
      (b)   the address of the hospital or mental nursing home where the patient is detained;
      (c)   the name and address of the patient's nearest relative and his relationship to the patient;
      (d)   the name and address of any representative authorised by the patient in accordance with rule 10 or, if none has yet been authorised, whether the patient intends to authorise a representative or wishes to conduct his own case.
   (3)   If any of the information specified in paragraph (2) is not included in the assessment application, it shall in so far as is practicable be provided by the responsible authority at the request of the tribunal.

Appointment of a tribunal and hearing date
   31.   On receipt of an assessment application the tribunal shall—
      (a)   fix a date for the hearing, being not later than 7 days from the date on which the application was received, and the time and place for the hearing;
      (b)   give notice of the date, time and place fixed for the hearing to the patient;
      (c)   give notice of the application and of the date, time and place fixed for the hearing to the responsible authority, the nearest relative (where practicable) and any other person who, in the opinion of the tribunal, should have an opportunity of being heard;
and the chairman shall appoint the members of the tribunal to deal with the case in accordance with rule 8.

Provision of admission papers, etc.
   32.—(1)   On receipt of the notice of an assessment application, or a request from the tribunal, whichever may be the earlier, the responsible authority shall provide for the tribunal copies of the admission papers, together with such of the information specified in Part A of Schedule 1 to these Rules as is within the knowledge of the responsible authority and can reasonably be provided in the time available and such of the reports specified in Part B of that Schedule as can reasonably be provided in the time available.
   (2)   The responsible authority shall indicate if any part of the admission papers or other documents supplied in accordance with paragraph (1) should, in their opinion, be withheld from the patient on the ground that its disclosure would adversely affect the health or welfare of the patient or others and shall state their reasons for believing that its disclosure would have that effect.
   (3)   The tribunal shall make available to the patient copies of the admission papers and any other documents supplied in accordance with paragraph (1), excluding any part indicated by the responsible authority in accordance with paragraph (2).

General procedure, hearing procedure and decisions
   33.   Rule 5, rule 8 and Parts III, IV and V of these Rules shall apply to assessment applications as they apply to applications in so far as the circumstances of the case permit and subject to the following modifications—

(a)   rule 12 shall apply as if any reference to a document being withheld in accordance with rule 6 was a reference to part of the admission papers or other documents supplied in accordance with rule 32 being withheld;

(b)   rule 16 shall apply with the substitution, for the reference to 14 days' notice, of a reference to such notice as is reasonably practicable;

(c)   rule 20 shall not apply;

(d)   rule 24 shall apply as if the period of time specified therein was 3 days instead of 7 days.

SCHEDULE 1

STATEMENTS BY THE RESPONSIBLE AUTHORITY AND THE SECRETARY OF STATE

PART A
INFORMATION RELATING TO PATIENTS (OTHER THAN CONDITIONALLY DISCHARGED PATIENTS)

1.   The full name of the patient.

2.   The age of the patient.

3.   The date of admission of the patient to the hospital or mental nursing home in which the patient is currently detained or liable to be detained, or of the reception of the patient into guardianship.

4.   Where the patient is being treated in a mental nursing home under contractual arrangements with a health authority, the name of that authority.

5.   Details of the original authority for the detention or guardianship of the patient, including the Act of Parliament and the section of that Act by reference to which detention was authorised and details of any subsequent renewal of or change in the authority for detention.

6.   The form of mental disorder from which the patient is recorded as suffering in the authority for detention (including amendments, if any, under section 16 or 72(5) of the Act, but excluding cases within section 5 of the Criminal Procedure (Insanity) Act 1964).

7.   The name of the responsible medical officer and the period which the patient has spent under the care of that officer.

8.   Where another registered medical practitioner is or has recently been largely concerned in the treatment of the patient, the name of that practitioner and the period which the patient has spent under his care.

9.   The dates of all previous tribunal hearings in relation to the patient, the decisions reached at such hearings and the reasons given. (In restricted patient cases this requirement does not relate to decisions before 30th September 1983.

10.   Details of any proceedings in the Court of Protection and of any receivership order made in respect of the patient.

11.   The name and address of the patient's nearest relative or of any other person who is exercising that function.

12.   The name and address of any other person who takes a close interest in the patient.

13.   Details of any leave of absence granted to the patient during the previous 2 years, including the duration of such leave and particulars of the arrangements made for the patient's residence while on leave.

PART B
REPORTS RELATING TO PATIENTS (OTHER THAN CONDITIONALLY DISCHARGED PATIENTS)

1.   An up-to-date medical report, prepared for the tribunal, including the relevant medical history and a full report on the patient's mental condition.

2.   An up-to-date social circumstances report prepared for the tribunal including reports on the following—
   (a)   the patient's home and family circumstances, including the attitude of the patient's nearest relative or the person so acting;
   (b)   the opportunities for employment or occupation and the housing facilities which would be available to the patient if discharged;
   (c)   the availability of community support and relevant medical facilities;
   (d)   the financial circumstances of the patient.
3.   The views of the authority on the suitability of the patient for discharge.
4.   Any other information or observations on the application which the authority wishes to make.

PART C
INFORMATION RELATING TO CONDITIONALLY DISCHARGED PATIENTS

1.   The full name of the patient.
2.   The age of the patient.
3.   The history of the patient's present liability to detention including details of offence(s), and the dates of the original order or direction and of the conditional discharge.
4.   The form of mental disorder from which the patient is recorded as suffering in the authority for detention. (Not applicable to cases within section 5 of the Criminal Procedure (Insanity) Act 1964.)
5.   The name and address of any medical practitioner responsible for the care and supervision of the patient in the community and the period which the patient has spent under the care of that practitioner.
6.   The name and address of any social worker or probation officer responsible for the care and supervision of the patient in the community and the period which the patient has spent under the care of that person.

PART D
REPORTS RELATING TO CONDITIONALLY DISCHARGED PATIENTS

1.   Where there is a medical practitioner responsible for the care and supervision of the patient in the community, an up-to-date medical report prepared for the tribunal including the relevant medical history and a full report on the patient's mental condition.
2.   Where there is a social worker or probation officer responsible for the patient's care and supervision in the community, an up-to-date report prepared for the tribunal on the patient's progress in the community since discharge from hospital.
3.   A report on the patient's home circumstances.
4.   The views of the Secretary of State on the suitability of the patient for absolute discharge.
5.   Any other observations on the application which the Secretary of State wishes to make.

THE DATA PROTECTION (SUBJECT ACCESS MODIFICATION) (HEALTH) ORDER 1987 (SI 1987, No. 1903)

2.   In this Order—
   "the Act" means the Data Protection Act 1984;
   "care" includes examination, investigation and diagnosis;
   "dental practitioner" and "medical practitioner" mean, respectively, a person registered under the Dentists Act 1984 and the Medical Act 1983;

"health authority" has the same meaning as in section 128(1) of the National Health Service Act 1977;

"Health Board" has the same meaning as in section 108(1) of the National Health Service (Scotland) Act 1978;

"Health and Social Services Board" has the same meaning as in Article 16 of the Health and Personal Social Services (Northern Ireland) Order 1972;

"health professional" means any person listed in the Schedule to this Order; and

"the subject access provisions" has the meaning which it has for the purposes of Part IV of the Act.

3.—(1) This Order applies to personal data consisting of information as to the physical or mental health of the data subject if—

(a) the data are held by a health professional; or

(b) the data are held by a person other than a health professional but the information constituting the data was first recorded by or on behalf of a health professional.

(2) This Order is without prejudice to any exemption from the subject access provisions contained in any provision of the Act or of any Order made under the Act.

4.—(1) The subject access provisions shall not have effect in relation to any personal data to which this Order applies in any case where either of the requirements specified in paragraph (2) below is satisfied with respect to the information constituting the data and the obligations contained in paragraph (5) below are complied with by the data user.

(2) The requirements referred to in paragraph (1) above are that the application of the subject access provisions—

(a) would be likely to cause serious harm to the physical or mental health of the data subject; or

(b) would be likely to disclose to the data subject the identity of another individual (who has not consented to the disclosure of the information) either as a person to whom the information or part of it relates or as the source of the information or enable that identity to be deduced by the data subject either from the information itself or from a combination of that information and other information which the data subject has or is likely to have.

(3) Paragraph (2) above shall not be construed as excusing a data user—

(a) from supplying the information sought by the request for subject access where the only individual whose identity is likely to be disclosed or deduced as mentioned in sub-paragraph (b) thereof is a health professional who has been involved in the care of the data subject and the information relates to him or he supplied the information in his capacity as a health professional; or

(b) from supplying so much of the information sought by the request as can be supplied without causing serious harm as mentioned in sub-paragraph (a) thereof or enabling the identity of another individual to be disclosed or deduced as mentioned in sub-paragraph (b) thereof, whether by the omission of names or other particulars or otherwise.

(4) In relation to data to which this Order applies, section 21 of the Act shall have effect as if subsections (4)(b) and (5) were omitted and as if the reference in subsection (6) to the consent referred to in the said section 21(4)(b) were a reference to the consent referred to in paragraph (2)(b) above.

(5) A data user who is not a health professional shall not supply information constituting data to which this Order applies in response to a request under section 21 and shall not withhold any such information on the ground that one of the requirements specified in paragraph (2) above is satisfied with respect to the information unless the data user has first consulted the person who appears to the data user to be the appropriate health professional on the question whether either or both of those requirements is or are so satisfied.

(6)   In paragraph (5) above "the appropriate health professional" means—

(a)   the medical practitioner or dental practitioner who is currently or was most recently responsible for the clinical care of the data subject in connection with the matters to which the information which is the subject of the request relates; or

(b)   where there is more than one such practitioner, the practitioner who is the most suitable to advise on the matters to which the information which is the subject of the request relates; or

(c)   where there is no practitioner available falling within sub-paragraph (a) or (b) above, a health professional who has the necessary experience and qualifications to advise on the matters to which the information which is the subject of the request relates.

(7)   Section 21(8) of the Act shall have effect, in relation to data to which this Order applies, as if the reference therein to a contravention of the foregoing provisions of that section included a reference to a contravention of the provisions contained in this Article.

SCHEDULE

HEALTH PROFESSIONALS

DESCRIPTION	STATUTORY DERIVATION *(where applicable)*
Registered medical practitioner	Medical Act 1983, section 55.
Registered dentist	Dentists' Act 1984, section 53(1).
Registered optician	Opticians Act 1958, section 30(1).
Registered pharmaceutical chemist or druggist	Pharmacy Act 1954, section 24(1). Pharmacy (Northern Ireland) Order 1976, Article 6(1).
Registered nurse, midwife or health visitor	Nurses, Midwives and Health Visitors Act 1979, section 10.
Registered chiropodist, dietician, occupational therapist, orthoptist or physiotherapist (subject to the Note below.)	Professions Supplementary to Medicine Act 1960, section 1(2).
Clinical psychologist, child psychotherapist or speech therapist	
Art therapist or music therapist employed by a health authority, Health Board or Health and Social Services Board	
Scientist employed by such an authority or Board as a head of department	

**THE PUBLIC HEALTH (INFECTIOUS DISEASES) REGULATIONS 1988
(SI 1988, No. 1546)**

Interpretation

2.—(1)   In these Regulations, unless the context otherwise requires—

"the Act" means the Public Health (Control of Disease) Act 1984;

"appropriate District Health Authority" means the District Health Authority within which a district of a local authority or a port health district is wholly or partly situated;

"appropriate medical officer" means—

(a) in a case where the District Health Authority has appointed a Director of Public Health, the Director of Public Health, and

(b) in any other case, the registered medical practitioner designated by the District Health Authority for the purposes of these Regulations;

"District Health Authority" means a District Health Authority established under section 8(1) of the National Health Service Act 1977;

"certificate" means a certificate required by section 11 of the Act to be sent by a registered medical practitioner to a proper officer;

"International Health Regulations" means the International Health Regulations (1969) as adopted by the World Health Assembly on 25th July 1969 and as amended by the 26th World Health Assembly in 1973 and by the 34th World Health Assembly in 1981;

"port health authority" means a port health authority constituted by an order made, or having effect as if made, by the Secretary of State under section 2 of the Act, and includes the port health authority for the Port of London as constituted under section 7 of the Act;

"port health district" means the district of a port health authority;

Public health enactments applied to certain diseases
3. There shall apply to the diseases listed in column (1) of Schedule 1 the enactments in the Act listed in column (2) of that Schedule with the modifications specified in column (2).

Modification of section 35 of the Act as it is applied to certain diseases
4. Where in Schedule 1 reference is made to section 35 of the Act as modified by this regulation, that section shall apply to the disease specified with the modification that in subsection (1)(a) the words "or

(ii) though not suffering from such a disease, is carrying an organism that is capable of causing it,"
shall be omitted.

Modification of section 38 of the Act as it is applied to acquired immune deficiency syndrome
5. In its application to acquired immune deficiency syndrome section 38(1) of the Act shall apply so that a justice of the peace (acting if he deems it necessary ex parte) may on the application of any local authority make an order for the detention in hospital of an inmate of that hospital suffering from acquired immune deficiency syndrome, in addition to the circumstances specified in that section, if the justice is satisfied that on his leaving the hospital proper precautions to prevent the spread of that disease would not be taken by him—

(a) in his lodging or accommodation, or

(b) in other places to which he may be expected to go if not detained in the hosptal.

Cases of infectious disease to be specially reported
6.—(1) In this regulation "a disease subject to the International Health Regulations" means cholera, including cholera due to the *eltor* vibrio, plague, smallpox, including variola minor (alastrim), and yellow fever.

(2) Without prejudice to paragraph (3), a proper officer shall, if his district or port health district is in England immediately inform the Chief Medical Officer for England, or, if his district or port health district is in Wales immediately inform the Chief Medical Officer for Wales of—

(a) any case or suspected case of a disease subject to the International Health Regulations and

(b) any serious outbreak of any disease (including food poisoning) which to his knowledge has occurred in his district or port health district, and he shall similarly inform the appropriate medical officer of the appropriate District Health Authority.

(3)   A proper officer who receives a certificate in respect of any case of—
  (a)   a disease subject to the International Health Regulations,
  (b)   leprosy,
  (c)   malaria or rabies contracted in Great Britain, or
  (d)   a viral haemorrhagic fever

shall immediately send a copy to the Chief Medical Officer for England if the address of the patient in the certificate is in England or to the Chief Medical Officer for Wales if such address is in Wales.

Immunisation and vaccination

10.   Where a case of any notifiable disease or of any disease mentioned in Schedule 1 (other than tuberculosis) occurs in a district or port health district, the proper officer of that district or port health district and of any adjacent district or port health district may, if he considers it in the public interest, arrange for the vaccination or immunisation, without charge, of any person in his district or port health district who has come or may have come or may come in contact with the infection and is willing to be vaccinated or immunised.

Confidentiality of documents

12.   Any certificate, or copy, and any accompanying or related document, shall be sent in such a manner that its contents cannot be read during transmission; and the information contained therein shall not be divulged to any person except—
  (a)   so far as is necessary for compliance with the requirements of any enactment (including these Regulations), or
  (b)   for the purposes of such action as any proper officer considers reasonably necessary for preventing the spread of disease.

Enforcement and publication

13.—(1)   These Regulations shall be enforced and executed—
  (a)   in the district of a local authority, by the local authority thereof; and
  (b)   in a port health district, by the port health authority thereof, so far as these Regulations are in terms applicable thereto.

(2)   Every local authority shall send to any registered medical practitioner who after due enquiry is ascertained to be practising in their district—
  (a)   a copy of these Regulations and
  (b)   a copy of sections 10 and 11 of the Act.

SCHEDULE 1
THE ENACTMENTS IN THE ACT APPLIED TO PARTICULAR DISEASES

(1) *Diseases*	(2) *Enactments applied*
Acquired immune deficiency syndrome	Sections 35, 37, 38 (as modified by regulation 5), 43 and 44.
Acute encephalitis Acute poliomyelitis Meningitis Meningococcal septicaemia (without meningitis)	Sections 11, 12, 17 to 24, 26, 28 to 30, 33 to 35 (as modified by regulation 4), 37, 38, 44 and 45.

(1) *Diseases*	(2) *Enactments applied*
Anthrax	Sections 11, 12, 17 to 22, 24, 26, 28 to 30, 33 to 35 (as modified by regulation 4), 37, 38 and 43 to 45.
Diphtheria Dysentery (amoebic or bacillary) Paratyphoid fever Typhoid fever Viral hepatitis	Sections 11, 12, 17 to 24, 26, 28 to 30, 33 to 38, 44 and 45.
Leprosy	Sections 11, 12, 17, 19 to 21, 28 to 30, 35 (as modified by regulation 4) 37, 38 and 44.
Leptospirosis Measles Mumps Rubella Whooping cough	Sections 11, 12, 17 to 22, 24, 26, 28 to 30, 33 to 35 (as modified by regulation 4), 37, 38, 44 and 45.
Malaria Tetanus Yellow fever	Sections 11, 12, 18 and 35 (as modified by regulation 4).
Ophthalmia neonatorum	Sections 11, 12, 17, 24 and 26.
Rabies	Sections 11, 12, 17 to 26, 28 to 30 and 32 to 38.
Scarlet fever	Sections 11, 12, 17 to 22, 24, 26, 28 to 30, 33 to 38, 44 and 45.
Tuberculosis	Sections 12, 17 to 24, 26, 28 to 30, 35 (as modified by regulation 4), 44 and 45; in addition— (a) section 11 shall apply where the opinion of the registered medical practitioner that a person is suffering from tuberculosis is formed from evidence not derived solely from tuberculin tests, and (b) sections 25, 37 and 38 shall apply to tuberculosis of the respiratory tract in an infectious state.
Viral haemorrhagic fever	Sections 11, 12, 17 to 38, 43 to 45 and 48.

THE GENERAL MEDICAL COUNCIL PRELIMINARY PROCEEDINGS COMMITTEE AND PROFESSIONAL CONDUCT COMMITTEE (PROCEDURE) RULES ORDER OF COUNCIL 1988
(SI 1988, No. 2255)

Interpretation
    2.—(1) In these Rules, unless the context otherwise requires:
      "the Act" means the Medical Act 1983;
      "case relating to conviction" means a case where it is alleged that a practitioner has been convicted, whether while registered or not, in the British Islands of a criminal offence;
      "case relating to conduct" means a case where a question arises whether conduct of a practitioner constituted serious professional misconduct;

"the Committee" means, in Part III of the rules, the Preliminary Proceedings Committee and, in Parts IV to VII of the rules, the Professional Conduct Committee;

"complainant" means a body or person by whom a complaint has been made to the Council;

"the Council" means the General Medical Council or a Committee of the Council acting under delegated power;

"the Health Committee (Procedure) Rules" means Rules made by the Council in the exercise of the powers conferred on them by paragraph 1 of Schedule 4 to the Act and references to those Rules are to the Rules currently in force and, unless the contrary intention appears, to such Rules as amended;

"lay member of the Council" means a member who is nominated in accordance with paragraph 4 of Schedule 1 to the Act, and who is neither fully registered nor the holder of any qualification registrable under the Act;

"the legal assessor" means an assessor appointed by the Council under paragraph 7 of Schedule 4 to the Act;

"medical member of the Council" means a member who is elected or appointed to the Council in accordance with paragraphs 1–3 of Schedule 1 to the Act, and who is fully registered, provisionally registered, or registered with limited registration;

"party" has the meaning given in paragraph 13 of Schedule 4 to the Act;

"person acting in a public capacity" means an officer of a Health Authority, Health Board, Common Services Agency or Board of Governors of a hospital, or of a Local or Area Medical Committee or Family Practitioner Committee, or of a Hospital Medical Staff Committee or body exercising similar functions, or of a Licensing Body (that is, a University or other body granting primary United Kingdom qualifications), acting as such, or of a Government Department or local or public authority, or any person holding judicial office, or any officer attached to a Court, or the Solicitor to the Council;

"practitioner" means a person registered (in any way) under the Act and includes a person who has previously been registered and whose registration is currently suspended under section 36 or section 42 of the Act; and references to the practitioner, in relation to any complaint, information or proceedings, are references to the practitioner who is alleged to have been convicted, or whose fitness to practise or conduct is or has been called into question, as the case may be;

"the President" means the President of the Council and includes any other member appointed under rule 4, or under rule 5(2) to (4) of the Health Committee (Procedure) Rules, to undertake functions of the President in initial consideration of cases under rules 5 to 8, 10, and 14 and, if the other member has been appointed to be Chairman of the Preliminary Proceedings Committee, functions of the President under rules 13, 18, 19, 22, 27, 46 and 52(2);

"the Register", in relation to fully or provisionally registered persons, means the Register of Medical Practitioners, and in relation to persons with limited registration means the Register of Medical Practitioners with limited Registration;

"the Registrar" means the Registrar of the Council;

"the Solicitor" means any Solicitor, or any firm of Solicitors, appointed by the Council, or any partner of such a firm.

PART II
INITIAL CONSIDERATION OF CASES

Appointment of member to conduct initial consideration of cases

4.—(1) No case shall be considered by the Preliminary Proceedings Committee unless it has first been considered

    (a) by a medical member of the Council appointed under this rule, or

(b)   by a medical member of the Council appointed under rule 5(2) or (3) of the Health Committee (Procedure) Rules, or exercising the President's powers or functions under rule 5(4) of those Rules,
and referred by such member to the Committee.

(2)   Subject to paragraph (3), the Council shall appoint the President under this rule.

(3)   If the President proposes to sit either on the Professional Conduct Committee or on the Health Committee, or if for any other reason the President does not wish to undertake the initial consideration of cases under these Rules, the President shall then nominate some other medical member of the Council whom the Council shall appoint under this rule, and reference in these Rules to the President shall be construed as including references to such member.

(4)   The President may nominate medical members of the Council whom the Council shall appoint to undertake the initial consideration of cases under these Rules in relation to which the member nominated and appointed under paragraph (3) is for any reason unable to act.

(5)   The President shall also nominate a lay member of the Council, whom the Council shall appoint, to assist him, or any medical members of the Council appointed under this rule, in the initial consideration of complaints.

(6)   Without prejudice to the generality of the foregoing, if at any time the President is absent or unable to act, anything authorised or required by these Rules to be done by the President may be done by any other medical member of the Council authorised in that behalf by the President or (if the President be unable to give authority) authorised by the Council or by the Preliminary Proceedings Committee on behalf of the Council.

Allegations as to conviction

5.—(1)   Where information in writing is received by the Registrar from which it appears to him that a practitioner has been convicted in the British Islands of a criminal offence, and the conviction is not of a description excepted from the operation of this rule by or under a direction of the Preliminary Proceedings Committee, the Registrar shall write to the practitioner:—

(a)   notifying him of the receipt of the information;

(b)   informing the practitioner of the date of the next meeting of the Preliminary Proceedings Committee; and

(c)   inviting the practitioner to submit any observations which he may wish to offer.

(2)   The Registrar shall submit to the President every case in which information of a conviction is received together with any observations received from the practitioner.

Allegations as to professional misconduct

6.—(1)   Where a complaint in writing or information in writing is received by the Registrar and it appears to him that a question arises whether conduct of a practitioner constitutes serious professional misconduct the Registrar shall submit the matter to the President.

(2)   Unless the complaint or information has been received from a person acting in a public capacity the matter shall not proceed further unless and until there has been furnished to the satisfaction of the President one or more statutory declarations or affidavits in support thereof; and every such statutory declaration or affidavit shall state the address and description of the deponent and the grounds for his belief in the truth of any fact therein which is not within his personal knowledge.

(3)   Subject to rule 6(4) unless it appears to the President that the matter need not proceed further he shall direct the Registrar to write to the practitioner

(a)   notifying him of the receipt of a complaint or information and stating the matters which appear to raise a question whether the practitioner has committed serious professional misconduct;

(b)   forwarding a copy of any statutory declaration or affidavit furnished under paragraph (2);

(c)   informing the practitioner of the date of the next meeting of the Preliminary Proceedings Committee to which the case may be referred; and

(d)   inviting the practitioner to submit any explanation which he may have to offer.

(4)   Where it appears to the President that a complaint need not proceed further (whether or not a statutory declaration or affidavit has been received in support thereof), he shall direct that the complainant be so informed, provided that no such direction shall be made except with the concurrence of the lay member appointed under rule 4(5).

Furnishing evidence of fitness to practice

7.   If in a case (whether relating to conviction or conduct) it appears to the President that the fitness to practise of the practitioner may be seriously impaired by reason of a physical or mental condition the President shall also direct the Registrar to inform the practitioner accordingly and to invite him to furnish medical evidence of his fitness to practise for consideration by the Preliminary Proceedings Committee:

Provided that nothing in these Rules shall prevent the President in such a case from remitting it to the person appointed under rule 5 of the Health Committee (Procedure) Rules for action under those Rules, or, if he is himself that person, from initiating action under those Rules, as an alternative to referring the case to the Preliminary Proceedings Committee.

Invitation to practitioner to appear before the Preliminary Proceedings Committee in certain circumstances

8.   If in any case (whether relating to conviction or conduct) it appears to the President that the circumstances are such that the Preliminary Proceedings Committee may wish to make an order for interim suspension or for interim conditional registration under section 42(3) of the Act, the President shall direct the Registrar to notify the practitioner accordingly and to inquire whether he wishes to appear before the Preliminary Proceedings Committee and be heard on the question whether such an order should be made in his case, and to inform the practitioner that for this purpose he may be represented before the Committee as provided in rule 53(2).

Duty to supply rules

9.   The Registrar shall send a copy of these rules with any letter sent for the purpose of rule 5(1), 6(3), or 8.

Reference to Preliminary Proceedings Committee

10.—(1)   Subject to the foregoing rules every case relating to conviction which is not of a description excepted from the operation of this rule by or under a direction of the Preliminary Proceedings Committee shall be referred to that Committee, together with any observations or evidence furnished by the practitioner under rule 5 or 7.

(2)   Subject to the foregoing rules and to paragraph (4) the President may direct the Registrar to refer any case relating to conduct to the Preliminary Proceedings Committee together with any statutory declaration or affidavit, information, explanation or other evidence furnished under rule 6 or 7:

Provided that the President shall not decide not to refer a complaint to the Preliminary Proceedings Committee except with the concurrence of the lay member appointed under rule 4(5).

(3)   No case relating to conduct shall be so referred for consideration at any meeting of the Preliminary Proceedings Committee without the consent of the practitioner unless the letter required by rule 6(3) was despatched at least 28 days before the date of that meeting.

(4)   If in any case relating to conduct the President decides not to refer the case to the Preliminary Proceedings Committee under paragraph (2), a complainant, informant or practitioner shall be notified of that decision but

(a)   shall have no right of access to any document relating to the case submitted to the Council by any other person; and

(b)   if the President so directs, shall not be entitled to a statement of the reasons for the President's decision.

PART III
PROCEDURE OF THE PRELIMINARY PROCEEDINGS COMMITTEE

Determination by Preliminary Proceedings Committee

11.—(1)   The Committee shall consider any case referred to them under rule 10 or under the provisions of the Health Committee (Procedure) Rules and, subject to those rules, determine:

(a)   that the case shall be referred to the Professional Conduct Committee for inquiry, or

(b)   that the case shall be referred to the Health Committee for inquiry, or

(c)   that the case shall not be referred to either Committee.

(2)   When referring a case to the Professional Conduct Committee the Preliminary Proceedings Committee shall indicate the convictions, or the matters which in their opinion appear to raise a question whether the practitioner has committed serious professional misconduct, to be so referred and to form the basis of the charge or charges:

Provided that where the Committee refer any case relating to conduct to the Professional Conduct Committee and the Solicitor (or the complainant) later adduces grounds for further allegations of serious professional misconduct of a similar kind, such further allegations may be included in the charge or charges in the case, or the evidence of such grounds for further allegations may be introduced at the inquiry in support of that charge or those charges, notwithstanding that such allegations have not been referred to the Committee or formed part of the subject of a determination by the Committee.

(3)   Before referring a case to the Health Committee the Committee may direct the Registrar to invite the practitioner to submit to examination by one or more medical examiners, to be chosen by the President from among those nominated under Schedule 2 to the Health Committee (Procedure) Rules, and, if the practitioner so elects, by another medical practitioner nominated by him, and to agree that such examiners should furnish to the Council reports on the practitioner's fitness to practise, either generally or on a limited basis, with recommendations for the management of his case. If the Committee consider that the information before them is sufficient to justify reference to the Health Committee, but that the Health Committee would be assisted by such reports, they may refer the case forthwith but invite the practitioner to submit to examination as aforesaid before the case is considered by the Health Committee.

(4)   When referring a case to the Health Commitee the Committee shall indicate the nature of the alleged condition by reason of which it appears to them that the fitness to practise of the practitioner may be seriously impaired.

(5)   If the Committee decide not to refer a case to the Professional Conduct Committee or to the Health Committee, the Registrar shall inform the practitioner and the complainant (if any) of the decision in such terms as the Committee may direct.

Order for interim suspension or interim conditional registration

12.—(1)   If the Committee decide that a case ought to be referred for inquiry either to the Professional Conduct Committee or to the Health Committee they may, in accordance with section 42(3) to (6) of the Act, proceed as provided in the following paragraphs of this rule.

(2)(a)   If the Committee are satisfied that to do so is necessary for the protection of members of the public, they may make an order that the practitioner's registration be suspended for such period not exceeding two months as they may specify in the order.

(b)   If the Committee are satisfied that to do so is necessary for the protection of members of the public or is in the interests of the practitioner, they may order that the registration of the practitioner shall be conditional on his compliance with such requirements and during such period, not exceeding two months, as they may specify in the order.

(3)   No order may be made under this rule unless the practitioner has been afforded an opportunity of appearing before the Preliminary Proceedings Committee and being heard on the question whether such an order should be made in his case; and for this purpose the practitioner may be represented before the Committee as provided in rule 53(2) and may also be accompanied by his medical adviser:
Provided that, if the practitioner does not appear and the Registrar satisfies the Committee that the requirements of rule 54 have been met, the Committee may make an order under this rule if they think fit, notwithstanding the practitioner's failure to appear.

(4)   Any decision by the Committee that a case should be referred for inquiry by the Professional Conduct Committee or by the Health Committee and any order by the Committee for a suspension or for conditional registration shall be notified to the practitioner by the Registrar in accordance with the requirements of rule 54.

Further investigations and provisional determination
   13.—(1)   Before coming to a determination under rule 11(1) the Committee may if they think fit cause to be made such further investigations, or obtain such advice or assistance from the Solicitor, as they may consider requisite.

(2)   Where the Committee are of opinion that further investigations are desirable or where at the time when the Committee are considering a case no explanation or observations have yet been received from the practitioner, they may if they think fit make a provisional determination that the case shall be referred to the Professional Conduct Committee or to the Health Committee and where they make such a determination—

(a)   the President may, after consulting the Committee, and if the Committee so agree, direct either that no reference shall be made or that the Committee's determination shall become absolute;

(b)   if the President directs that no reference shall be made, the Registrar shall notify the members of the Preliminary Proceedings Committee and shall inform the practitioner and the complainant (if any) in such terms respectively as the President may direct.

Fresh allegation as to conviction or conduct
   14.   Notwithstanding anything in the foregoing rules, where
(a)   in any case relating to conviction the Committee determine that no inquiry shall be held; or
(b)   in any case relating to conduct
   (i)   the President decides that no reference to the Committee need be made; or
   (ii)   the Committee determine that no reference for inquiry shall be made,
and the Registrar, in a case falling under (a) above, at any time subsequently receives information that the practitioner has again been convicted or, in a case falling under (b) above, within two years of the decision or determination receives information or a complaint as to the conduct of the practitioner, the President may direct that the original conviction, information or complaint be referred, or referred again, to the

Committee, together with the subsequent conviction, information or complaint, as the case may be, and the original decision or determination referred to in (a) or (b) above shall be disregarded.

Preliminary Proceedings Committee to meet in private
15. The Committee shall meet in private.

Non-disclosure of documents or reasons in cases not referred for inquiry
16. Where the Committee have decided not to refer a case for inquiry no complainant, informant or practitioner shall have any right of access to any documents relating to the case submitted to the Council by any other person, nor shall the Committee be required by a complainant, informant, or practitioner to state reasons for their decision.

PART IV
INTERMEDIATE PROCEDURES WHERE A CASE IS REFERRED TO THE PROFESSIONAL CONDUCT COMMITTEE

Notice of Inquiry
17.—(1) As soon as may be after a case has been referred to the Committee for inquiry, the Solicitor shall send to the practitioner in compliance with rule 54 a notice, in these rules called a "Notice of Inquiry", which shall:
(a) specify, in the form of a charge or charges, the matters into which the inquiry is to be held, and
(b) state the day, time and place at which the inquiry is proposed to be held.
(2) In a case relating to conduct, the charge shall include a statement which identifies the alleged facts upon which the charge is based.
(3) Except with the agreement of the practitioner, the inquiry shall not be fixed for any date earlier than twenty-eight days after the date of posting the Notice of Inquiry.
(4) A Notice of Inquiry shall be in the form set out in Schedule 2, with such variations as circumstances may require.
(5) In any case where there is a complainant, a copy of the Notice of Inquiry shall be sent to him.

Postponement of inquiry
18.—(1) The President may if he thinks fit postpone the holding of an inquiry to such later date or such later meeting of the Committee as he may determine.
(2) The Solicitor shall, as soon as may be, give to all parties to whom a Notice of Inquiry has been sent notification of any decision to postpone an inquiry, and shall inform them at that time or subsequently of the date fixed for the hearing of the postponed inquiry.

Cancellation of inquiry
19.—(1) Where, after a complaint or information has been referred to the Committee for inquiry, it appears to the President that the inquiry should not be held, he may after consulting the Preliminary Proceedings Committee, and if that Committee so agree, direct that the inquiry shall not be held; and if at the time the President so directs no Notice of Inquiry has been sent, rule 17 shall not have effect:
Provided that in any case where there is a complainant the President shall, before he consults the Preliminary Proceedings Committee as aforesaid, communicate or endeavour to communicate with the complainant with a view to obtaining the observations of the complainant as to whether the inquiry should be held.
(2) For the purpose of consultation under paragraph (1) the Preliminary Proceedings Committee shall not be required to meet.
(3) As soon as may be after the giving of any such direction the Solicitor shall give notice thereof to the practitioner and to the complainant (if any).

Access to documents

20. Without prejudice to rule 16 the Solicitor (or the complainant as the case may be) shall on the request of any party to an inquiry and on payment of the proper charges send to him copies of any statutory declaration, affidavit, explanation, answer, admission or other statement or communication sent to the Council by a party to the inquiry or any statement in writing in the possession of the Solicitor or the complainant made by a person who may be called by the Solicitor or the complainant to give evidence at the inquiry, other than medical evidence of fitness to practise furnished in response to an invitation under rule 7 or a confidential communication sent to the Council in response to applications under rules 38(1)(a)(iii) or rule 49(1):

Provided that nothing in this rule shall compel the Solicitor to produce copies of any written advice or other document or communication sent by himself to the Council.

Notice to produce documents

21. Any party to any inquiry may at any time give to any other party notice to produce any document relevant to the inquiry alleged to be in the possession of that party.

Amendment of charge before the opening of an inquiry

22.—(1) Where before a hearing by the Committee it appears to the President that a charge should be amended, including such amendment as contemplated under the proviso to rule 11(2), the President shall give such directions for the amendment of the charge as he may think necessary to meet the circumstances of the case unless, having regard to the merits of the case, the required amendments cannot be made without injustice.

(2) Where in the opinion of the President it is expedient, in consequence of the exercise by him of the powers conferred by paragraph (1), that the inquiry should be postponed, the President shall give such directions in that behalf as appear necessary.

(3) The Solicitor shall as soon as may be give notice in writing to the practitioner and to the complainant (if any) of any exercise by the President of his powers under either paragraph (1) or (2).

PART V
PROCEDURE OF THE PROFESSIONAL CONDUCT COMMITTEE AT THE ORIGINAL HEARING OF ANY CASE

Procedure where the practitioner does not appear

23.—(1) Where the practitioner does not appear and is not represented, the Committee may nevertheless proceed with the inquiry if the Solicitor satisfies them that all reasonable efforts have been made in compliance with rule 54 to serve the Notice of Inquiry on the Practitioner.

(2) If the Committee are so satisfied they may, if they think fit, proceed and the following provisions of these Rules shall not apply:

    rule 24(2) and (3);
    rule 25(1)(c), (d), (e), (f) and (g);
    rule 26(2);
    rule 27(1)(a), (e), (f), (g), (h), (i) and (j); and
    rule 28(2).

Opening of inquiry — Reading of charge, submissions of objections and amendment of charge

24.—(1) The inquiry shall open by the reading of the charge or charges to the Committee.

(2) After the reading of the charge or charges the practitioner may submit any objection on grounds of law to any charge or part of a charge and any other party may reply to such an objection.

(3)   If any objection raised under paragraph (2) is upheld no further proceedings shall be taken with regard to the charge or part of a charge to which that objection relates.

(4)   Where at any stage of an inquiry it appears to the Committee that a charge should be amended, the Committee may, after hearing the parties and consulting the legal assessor, if they are satisfied that no injustice would be caused, make such amendments to the charge as appear necessary or desirable.

Cases relating to conviction

25.—(1)   In cases relating to conviction, the following order of proceedings shall be observed as respects proof of convictions alleged in the charge or charges:-

(a)   The Solicitor shall adduce evidence of the convictions.

(b)   If, as respects any conviction, no evidence is so adduced, the Chairman of the Committee shall announce that the conviction has not been proved.

(c)   The Chairman shall ask the practitioner whether he admits each conviction of which evidence is so adduced and, in respect of any conviction so admitted by the practitioner, the Chairman shall announce that the conviction has been proved.

(d)   The practitioner may then, in respect of the convictions not admitted, address the Committee and may adduce evidence, oral or documentary, including his own, in his defence.

(e)   At the close of the evidence for the practitioner, the Solicitor may, with the leave of the Committee, adduce evidence to rebut any evidence adduced by the practitioner.

(f)   The Solicitor may then address the Committee.

(g)   The practitioner may then address the Committee.

(2)   On the conclusion of the proceedings under paragraph (1), the Committee shall consider every conviction alleged in the charge or charges, other than any conviction admitted by the practitioner or which the Chairman has announced has not been proved, and shall determine whether it has been proved; and the Chairman of the Committee shall announce their determinaton.

Circumstances, character, history and pleas in mitigation in case relating to conviction

26.—(1)   Where the Committee have found that a conviction has been proved the Chairman shall invite the Solicitor to address the Committee, and to adduce evidence, as to the circumstances leading up to the conviction and as to the character and previous history of the practitioner.

(2)   The Chairman shall then invite the practitioner to address the Committee by way of mitigation and to adduce evidence as aforesaid.

(3)   The Committee shall then proceed in accordance with rules 30 and 31.

Cases relating to conduct

27.—(1)   In cases relating to conduct, the following order of proceedings shall be observed as respects proof of the facts alleged in the charge or charges:-

(a)   The Chairman shall ask the practitioner whether he admits any or all of the facts alleged in the charge or charges and, in respect of any facts so admitted by the practitioner, the Committee shall record a finding that such facts have been proved and the Chairman shall so announce. Where all the facts are admitted the remainder of this rule other than sub-paragraphs (e) and (f) of this paragraph, shall not apply.

(b)   Where none, or some only, of the facts are admitted the Solicitor, or the complainant if any, shall open the case against the practitioner and present the facts alleged on which the charge or charges is or are based.

(c)   The Solicitor, or the complainant, as the case may be, may adduce evidence of the facts alleged which have not been admitted by the practitioner.

(d)   If as respects any charge no evidence is so adduced, the Committee shall record and the Chairman shall announce a finding that the practitioner is not guilty of serious professional misconduct in respect of the matter to which that charge relates.

(e)   At the close of the case against him the practitioner may make either or both of the following submissions, namely:-

(i)   in respect of any or all of the facts alleged and not admitted in the charge or charges, that no sufficient evidence has been adduced upon which the Committee could find those facts proved;

(ii)   in respect of any charge, that the facts of which evidence has been adduced or which have been admitted are insufficient to support a finding of serious professional misconduct;

and where any such submission is made, the Solicitor or the complainant, as the case may be, may answer the submission and the practitioner may reply thereto.

(f)   If a submission is made under the last foregoing paragraph, the Committee shall consider and determine whether the submission should be upheld; and if the Committee determine to uphold such a submission as respects any charge, they shall record, and the Chairman shall announce, a finding that the practitioner is not guilty of serious professional misconduct in respect of the matters to which the charge relates.

(g)   The practitioner may then address the Committee concerning any charge which remains outstanding and may adduce evidence, oral or documentary including his own, in his defence.

(h)   At the close of the evidence for the practitioner, the Solicitor or the complainant, as the case may be, may, with the leave of the Committee, adduce evidence to rebut any evidence adduced by the practitioner.

(i)   The Solicitor, or the complainant, as the case may be, may then address the Committee.

(j)   The practitioner may then address the Committee.

(2)   On the conclusion of proceedings under paragraph (1) the Committee shall consider and determine:

(i)   which, if any, of the remaining facts alleged in the charge and not admitted by the practitioner have been proved to their satisfaction, and

(ii)   whether such facts have been so found proved or admitted would be insufficient to support a finding of serious professional misconduct, and shall record their finding.

(3)   The Chairman shall announce that finding and, if as respects any charge the Committee have found that none of the facts alleged in the charge have been proved to their satisfaction, or that such facts as have been so proved would be insufficient to support a finding of serious professional misconduct, the Committee shall record and the Chairman shall announce a finding that the practitioner is not guilty of serious professional misconduct in respect of the matters to which that charge relates.

Circumstances, character, history and pleas in mitigation in cases relating to conduct

28.—(1)   Where, in proceedings under rule 27, the Committee have recorded a finding, whether on the admission of the practitioner or because the evidence adduced has satisfied them to that effect, that the facts, or some of the facts, alleged in any charge have been proved, the Chairman shall invite the Solicitor or the complainant, as the case may be, to address the Committee as to the circumstances leading to those facts, the extent to which such facts are indicative of serious professional misconduct on the part of the practitioner, and as to the character and previous history of the practitioner. The Solicitor or the complainant may adduce oral or documentary evidence to support an address under this rule.

(2)   The Chairman shall then invite the practitioner to address the Committee by way of mitigation and to adduce evidence as aforesaid.

Finding of serious professional misconduct

29.—(1) The Committee shall then consider and determine whether, in relation to the facts proved in proceedings under rule 27, and having regard to any evidence adduced and arguments or pleas addressed to them under rule 28, they find the practitioner to have been guilty of serious professional misconduct. They shall record, and the Chairman shall announce, their finding.

(2) If the Committee determine that the practitioner has not been guilty of such misconduct, they shall record, and the Chairman shall announce, a finding to that effect.

Determination whether to make a direction

30.—(1) Where in any case the Committee have found a conviction proved or have judged that a practitioner has been guilty of serious professional misconduct they may, if they think fit, postpone their determination whether to make a direction until such future date or meeting of the committee as they may specify, in order to obtain and consider further evidence of the conduct of the practitioner. If they so decide, the Chairman shall announce that decision.

(2) If the Committee decide that no such postponement is necessary, they shall consider and determine whether it shall be sufficient to make no direction and conclude the case and, if they so determine, the Chairman shall, subject to the provisions of rule 34, announce that determination.

Directions of the Committee

31.—(1) If the Committee determine neither to postpone their determination under rule 30(1) nor that it shall be sufficient to conclude the case under rule 30(2), they shall proceed to make a direction in accordance with the following provisions of this rule.

(2)(a) The Committee shall first consider and determine whether it shall be sufficient to direct that the registration of the practitioner shall be conditional on his compliance, during such period not exceeding three years as the Committee may specify, with such requirements as the Committee may think fit to impose for the protection of members of the public or in his interests.

(b) If the Committee so determine they shall then consider and decide the nature and duration of the conditions to be imposed, and shall so direct.

(3) If the Committee determine that it will not be sufficient to impose conditions on the practitioner's registration they shall next consider and determine whether it shall be sufficient to direct that the practitioner's registration shall be suspended; and, if they so decide, they shall direct that such suspension should be for such period, not exceeding twelve months, as they may specify in the direction.

(4) If the Committee determine that it will not be sufficient to direct suspension in accordance with paragraph (3), they shall thereupon direct that the name of the practitioner shall be erased from the Register.

(5) In any case where the Committee have determined that the registration of any practitioner shall be suspended or be subject to conditions for a specified period, they may, when announcing the direction to give effect to such determination, intimate that they will, at a meeting to be held before the end of such period, resume consideration of the case with a view to determining whether or not they should then direct that the period of suspension or of conditional registration should be extended or the conditions varied or that the name of the practitioner should be erased from the Register.

Order for immediate suspension of registration

32. If in any case the Committee determine to suspend the registration of a practitioner or to erase his name from the Register, the Committee shall then also consider and determine whether it is necessary for the protection of members of the public or would be in the best interests of the practitioner to order that his registration shall be suspended forthwith.

Revocation of order for interim suspension or interim conditional registration
33. If in any case an order has been made by the Preliminary Proceedings Committee under rule 12 for interim suspension or for interim conditional registration the Professional Conduct Committee may, if they think fit, revoke such order.

Announcement of findings, direction, etc. of Committee
34. The Chairman shall announce any finding, determination, direction, or revocation of the Committee under these rules in such terms as the Committee may approve and, where the announcement is one that a conviction has been proved or that the practitioner has been judged guilty of serious professional misconduct but the Committee do not propose to make any direction, may, without prejudice to the terms in which any other announcement may be made, include any expression of the Committee's admonition in respect of the practitioner's behaviour giving rise to the charge or charges in question.

Cases relating both to conviction and to conduct
35. Where in the case of any inquiry it is alleged against the practitioner both that he has been convicted and that he has been guilty of serious professional misconduct, the following shall be the procedure:-
    (a) The Committee shall first proceed with every charge that the practitioner has been convicted until they have completed the proceedings required by rule 25.
    (b) The Committee shall then proceed with every charge that the practitioner has been guilty of such conduct as aforesaid until they have completed the proceedings required by rule 27.
    (c) The Committee shall then take any proceedings required by any of rules 26 and 28 to 33.

Inquiries into charges against two or more practitioners
36. Nothing in these rules shall be construed as preventing one inquiry being held into charges against two or more practitioners; and where such an inquiry is held the foregoing rules shall apply with the necessary adaptations and subject to any directions given by the Committee as to the order in which proceedings shall be taken under any of those rules in relation to the several practitioners.

PART VI
RESUMED HEARINGS BY THE PROFESSIONAL
CONDUCT COMMITTEE

Direction for resumed hearing
37.—(1) In any case where the Committee have determined that the registration of a practitioner shall be suspended or be subject to conditions for a specified period, and have given no intimation, under rule 31(5), and, as a consequence of the receipt during the said specified period of information as to the conduct or a conviction of the practitioner since the date of the direction to give effect to the determination, it appears to the President that the Committee should consider whether or not the period of suspension or conditional registration should be extended or the conditions varied or revoked or the name of the practitioner erased from the Register, he shall direct the Solicitor to notify the practitioner that the Committee will resume consideration of the case at such meeting as the President shall specify.
    (2) Where, in any case, the Committee have—
    (a) decided to postpone their determination under rule 30 for a specified period or to a specified meeting, or

(b)   directed that the practitioner's registration should be subject to conditions and intimated that they will resume consideration of the case at a specified meeting or date, or

(c)   suspended the practitioner's registration and intimated that they will resume consideration of the case at a specified meeting or date,

and it subsequently appears to the President, in consequence of the receipt of information to the credit or discredit of the practitioner in relation to his conduct since the original hearing, or for some other reason, that the Committee should resume consideration of the case at an earlier meeting or date than that originally specified, the President may direct the Solicitor to notify the practitioner that the Committee will resume consideration of the case at such meeting or date as the President shall specify.

(3)   Without prejudice to the generality of paragraphs (1) and (2), wherein any case the Committee have imposed conditions upon a practitioner's registration, and it appears to the President from information subsequently received that the practitioner is not complying with such conditions, then, whether or not the conditions imposed by the Committee required the practitioner to reappear before them at a future date or meeting, the President may direct the Solicitor to notify the practitioner that the Committee will resume consideration of the case at such meeting as the President shall specify.

(4)   In any case in which the President has given a direction under paragraphs (1) to (3) the Committee shall then resume consideration of the case on the date or at the meeting specified in the direction notwithstanding their earlier decision.

Notice of resumed hearing

38.—(1)   Where the Committee are to resume a previous hearing in circumstances specified in paragraph (2)—

(a)   the Solicitor shall, not later than six weeks before the day fixed for the resumption of the proceedings, send to the practitioner in compliance with rule 54 a Notice which shall—

(i)   specify the day, time and place at which the proceedings are to be resumed and invite him to appear thereat;

(ii)   in any case where the President has exercised his powers under rule 37(1) to (3) state the nature of the information in consequence of which he has exercised his powers;

(iii)   if the Committe have so directed, invite the practitioner to furnish the Registrar with the names and addresses of professional colleagues and other persons of standing to whom the Council will be able to apply for confidential information as to their knowledge of his conduct since the time of the original inquiry;

(b)   in any case where there is a complainant a copy of the Notice shall be sent to him.

(2)   The circumstances to which paragraph (1) applies shall be:

(i)   where under any of the foregoing provisions of these Rules the determination of the Committee in any case stands postponed; or

(ii)   where the Committee have directed that the registration of a practitioner shall be conditional or shall be suspended, and have intimated that before the end of the period of conditional registration or suspension they will resume consideration of the case; or

(iii)   where the President has so directed under rule 37(1) to (3); or

(iv)   where, following reference of a case to the Health Committee, the Health Committee certify to the Committee under rule 51(3), their opinion that the fitness to practise of the practitioner is not seriously impaired by reason of his condition.

New charge at resumed hearing

39.—(1)   If, since the original hearing, a new charge or charges against the practitioner have been referred to the Committee, the Committee shall first proceed with such new charge or charges in accordance with the provisions of rule 24 and rule 25 or 27, as the case may be.

(2)   The Committee shall take any proceedings required by rule 26 or rules 28 and 29, as the case may be, in relation to such new charge or charges, concurrently with the proceedings prescribed in rule 40 and shall have regard to their findings in relation to such charge or charges in making any direction in accordance with rules 41 to 43.

Procedure at resumed hearing

40.—(1)   Subject to the provisions of rule 39, at the meeting at which the proceedings are resumed, the Chairman of the Committee shall first invite the Solicitor to recall, for the information of the Committee, the position in which the case stands.

(2)   If in any case the President has exercised his powers under rule 37, the Solicitor shall adduce evidence of the conduct or conviction of the practitioner which led to the exercise of those powers.

(3)   The Committee may—
  (a)   hear any other party to the proceedings,
  (b)   receive such further oral or documentary evidence in relation to the case, or as to the conduct of the practitioner since the previous hearing, as they think fit; and nothing herein contained shall be construed as preventing the receipt by the Committee of evidence as to any conviction, not being a conviction which is the subject of a charge before the Committee.

(4)   The Committee shall then proceed in accordance with the following rules, as the circumstances of the case may so require.

Procedure following postponement under rule 30

41.—(1)   If at the previous hearing the Committee, under rule 30, postponed their determination whether to make a direction to enable further evidence to be considered, they shall next consider and decide whether they should further postpone their determination; if they so decide, they may direct such further postponement until such future date or meeting of the Committee as they may specify.

(2)   If the Committee decide that they should not further postpone their determination they shall proceed to consider and determine whether it shall be sufficient to make no direction and conclude the case.

(3)   If the Committee determine that it shall not be sufficient to conclude the case, they shall proceed to make a direction in accordance with the provisions of paragraphs (2) to (4) of rule 31.

Procedure where conditional registration had been imposed

42.—(1)   If at the previous hearing the Committee had directed that the registration of the practitioner should be subject to conditions, the Committee shall first judge whether the practitioner has failed to comply with any of the requirements imposed on him as conditions of his registration.

(2)(a)   If the Committee judge that the practitioner has not so failed to comply they shall then consider and determine whether:
    (i)   to revoke the direction made at the previous hearing, that the registration of the practitioner be subject to conditions (in which case they shall so direct); or
    (ii)   to vary the conditions imposed under the direction made at the previous hearing (in which case they shall so direct); or
    (iii)   to make no further direction, and allow the case to conclude on the expiry of the period for which the direction made at the previous hearing applies.
  (b)   If the Committee determine not to revoke the direction or vary the condition or conditions imposed at the previous hearing, or to allow the case to conclude as aforesaid, they shall proceed to impose a further period of conditional registration and

shall consider and decide the nature of the conditions and the further period, not exceeding twelve months, for which they shall apply, and shall so direct.

(3)(a)If the Committee judge that the practitioner has so failed to comply, they shall next consider and determine whether it shall be sufficient:

    (i)   to vary the conditions imposed under the direction made at the previous hearing; or, if not,

    (ii)   to direct that the current period of conditional registration shall be extended for such further period not exceeding twelve months as they may specify, with or without variation of the conditions imposed under the direction made at the previous hearing; or, if not,

    (iii)   to direct that the registration of the practitioner shall be suspended for such period not exceeding twelve months as they may specify and, if they determine that one of the foregoing courses of action shall be sufficient, they shall so direct.

(b) If the Committee determine that none of the courses of action under sub-paragraph (a) shall be sufficient, they shall thereupon direct that the name of the practitioner shall be erased from the Register.

Procedure where registration has been suspended

43.—(1) Where at a previous hearing the Committee directed that the practitioner's registration should be suspended, the Committee shall consider and determine whether it shall be sufficient:

    (a)   to make no further direction; or, if not,

    (b)   to direct that the registration of the practitioner shall be conditional on his compliance during such period not exceeding three years as the Committee may specify, with such requirements as the Committee may think fit to impose for the protection of members of the public or in his interests (in which case the Committee shall then consider and decide the nature and duration of the conditions to be imposed); or, if not,

    (c)   to direct that the current period of suspension shall be extended for such further period, not exceeding twelve months, from the time when it would otherwise expire as they may specify.

(2) If the Committee determine that it shall not be sufficient to adopt a course under paragraph (1)(a), (b) or (c) they shall direct that the name of the practitioner shall be erased from the Register.

(3) If the Committee determine to pursue a course under paragraph (1)(b), or (c) or paragraph (2) they shall make a direction to that effect.

Announcement of determination at resumed hearing

44. The Chairman shall announce the determination or determinations of the Committee under the foregoing rules in such terms as the Committee may approve.

Subsequent application of rules where case is continued

45. The provisions of rules 37 and 39 to 44 shall also apply in any case where the determination of the Committee has been further postponed at a resumed hearing or in which the Committee have previously directed at a resumed hearing that a period of suspension or conditional registration should be extended or further extended.

PART VII
APPLICATIONS FOR RESTORATION AFTER ERASURE

Procedure for consideration of applications for restoration

46. Where a person applies for the restoration of his name to the Register under section 41 of the Act, the following provisions shall have effect:-

    (a)   Subject to any direction given by the President in special circumstances, an application shall not be considered by the Committee at any meeting unless, not less than twenty-one days before the first day of that meeting, there has been delivered to the Registrar a statutory declaration made by the applicant as nearly as possible in the form set out in Schedule 3.

(b) At the hearing of the application, the Chairman shall first invite the Solicitor to recall the circumstances in which the applicant's name was erased from the Register and, if he so desires, to address the Committee and to adduce evidence as to the conduct of the applicant since that time.

(c) The Chairman shall next invite the applicant to address the Committee and, if he so desires, to adduce evidence as to his conduct since his name was erased from the Register.

(d) The Committee may, if they think fit, receive oral or written observations on the application from any body or person on whose complaint the applicant's name was erased from the Register.

(e) The Committee may, if they think fit, adjourn consideration of any application to such future meeting as they may specify, and may require the applicant to submit evidence of his conduct since his name was erased from the Register.

(f) Subject to the foregoing provisions of this rule the procedure of the Committee in connection with such applications shall be such as they may determine.

PART VIII
GENERAL

Adjournment of proceedings

47. The Preliminary Proceedings Committee and the Professional Conduct Committee may adjourn any of their proceedings or meetings from time to time as they think fit.

Exclusion of public from hearings in certain cases

48.—(1) Subject to the provisions of rule 50(5), and to the following paragraphs of this rule, all proceedings before the Professional Conduct Committee shall take place in the presence of all parties thereto who appear therein and shall be held in public.

(2)(a) If any party to any proceedings or any witness therein makes an application to the Committee for the public to be excluded from any proceedings or part thereof, then if it appears to the Committee that any person would suffer undue prejudice from a public hearing or that for any other reason the circumstances and nature of the case make a public hearing unnecessary or undesirable, the Committee may direct that the public shall be so excluded.

(b) Where no such application has been made the Committee may of their own initiative direct that the public shall be excluded from any proceedings or part thereof if it appears to the Committee, after hearing the views of the parties thereon, that to do so would be in the interests of justice or desirable having regard to the nature either of the case or of the evidence to be given.

(c) A direction under this paragraph shall not apply to the announcement in pursuance of any of these rules of a determination of the Committee.

(3) Subject to the provisions of paragraph 7 of Schedule 4 to the Act and of any rules made thereunder the Committee may deliberate in camera (with or without the legal assessor) at any time and for any purpose during or after the hearing of any proceedings.

Consideration of confidential reports at resumed hearings

49.—(1) Where, under rule 30 or rule 41, the Professional Conduct Committee postpone or further postpone their determination whether to make a direction or, under rule 31, rule 42 or rule 43, impose conditions upon a practitioner's registration or suspend the registration of a practitioner and give an intimation under rule 31(5), or the

President determines under rule 37(1) to (3) that they will resume consideration of the case, or where the Committee adjourn consideration of an application under rule 46(e), the Committee may require the practitioner to furnish the Registrar with the names and addresses of professional colleagues and other persons of standing to whom the Council will be able to apply for information, to be given confidentially, as to their knowledge of his conduct since the time of the original or of any previous hearing.

(2)   Where any practitioner or applicant has supplied to the Committee or to the Registrar on his behalf the name of any person to whom reference may be made confidentially as to his conduct, the Committee may consider any information received from such person in consequence of such reference without disclosing the same to the practitioner.

Evidence
50.—(1)   The Professional Conduct Committee may receive oral, documentary or other evidence of any fact or matter which appears to them relevant to the inquiry into the case before them:
Provided that, where any fact or matter is tendered as evidence which would not be admissible as such if the proceedings were criminal proceedings in England, the Committee shall not receive it unless, after consultation with the legal assessor, they are satisfied that their duty of making due inquiry into the case before them makes its reception desirable.

(2)   Without prejudice to the generality of the last preceding paragraph the Committee may, if satisfied that the interests of justice will not thereby be prejudiced, admit in evidence without strict proof copies of documents which are themselves admissible, maps, plans, photographs, certificates of conviction and sentence, certificates of registration of birth or marriage or death, the records (including the registers) of the Council, the notes of proceedings before the Committee and before other tribunals and the records of such tribunals, and the Committee may take note without strict proof of the professional qualifications, the registration, the address and the identity of the practitioner and of any other person.

(3)   The Committee may accept admissions made by any party and may in such case dispense with proof of the matters admitted.

(4)   The Committee may cause any person to be called as a witness in any proceedings before them, whether or not the parties consent thereto. Questions may be put to any witness by the Committee or by the legal assessor with the leave of the Chairman.

(5)   Without leave of the Committee no person (other than a party to the proceedings) shall be called as a witness by either party in proceedings before the Professional Conduct Committee unless he has been excluded from the proceedings until he is called to give evidence:
Provided that this rule shall not prevent the Committee from receiving evidence relating to the posting, receipt or service of documents, the production of documents, and evidence in rebuttal of evidence given by or on behalf of the practitioner or as part of the case against him.

Reference and transfer of cases to the Health Committee
51.—(1)   Notwithstanding any other provisions in these rules, where in the course of an inquiry, at either the original or a resumed hearing, it appears to the Professional Conduct Committee that a practitioner's fitness to practise may be seriously impaired by reason of his physical or mental condition, the Committee may refer that question to the Health Committee for determination, and any such referral may be made whether or not the Professional Conduct Committee order in accordance with powers conferred by the Act that the practitioner's registration shall be conditional on his compliance with specified requirements.

(2)   When referring a case under this rule to the Health Committee the Professional Conduct Committee may also direct that, before the case is considered by the Health Committee, the practitioner shall be invited to submit to examination by one or more medical practitioners to be chosen by the President from among those nominated under Schedule 2 to the Health Committee (Procedure) Rules, and, if the practitioner so elects, by another medical practitioner nominated by him, and to agree that such examiners should furnish to the Council reports on the practitioner's fitness to practise, either generally or on a limited basis, with recommendations for the management of his case.

(3)   If, following a reference under this rule, the Health Committee subsequently certify to the Professional Conduct Committee their opinion that the fitness of the practitioner to practise is not seriously impaired by reason of his physical or mental condition, rule 38 shall apply, and the Professional Conduct Committee shall resume their inquiry in the case and dispose of it.

(4)   If, following a reference under this rule, the Health Committee certify to the Professional Conduct Committee their opinion that the fitness of the practitioner to practise is seriously impaired by reason of his physical or mental condition, the Professional Conduct Committee shall cease to exercise their functions in relation to the case.

Voting

52.—(1)   The following provisions shall have effect as to the taking of the votes of the Preliminary Proceedings Committee and the Professional Conduct Committee on any question to be determined by them:-

(a)   The Chairman of the Committee shall call upon the members present to signify their votes by raising their hands, signify his own vote, and declare the way in which the question appears to him to have been determined.

(b)   If the result so declared by the Chairman is challenged by any member, the Chairman shall—

(i)   call upon each member severally to declare his vote,

(ii)   announce his own vote, and

(iii)   announce the number of members of the Committee who have voted each way and the result of the vote.

(2)   In proceedings of the Preliminary Proceedings Committee, or in consideration of cases by that Committee under rule 13 or rule 19, if the votes are equal, the President shall have an additional casting vote.

(3)   In proceedings of the Professional Conduct Committee, if the votes are equal the question shall be deemed to have been resolved in favour of the practitioner. For the purpose of this paragraph a determination by the Professional Conduct Committee to postpone their determination whether to make a direction shall be taken to be in favour of a practitioner unless he has indicated to the Committee that he is opposed to such postponement.

Representation

53.—(1)   Any party being a body corporate or an unincorporated body of persons may appear by their clerk or other officer duly appointed for the purpose or by counsel or solicitor.

(2)   Any party being an individual may appear either in person or by counsel or solicitor, or by any officer or member of any professional organisation of which he is a member, or by any member of his family, and any reference to a practitioner, complainant or other party shall be construed as including a reference to any person by whom he is represented.

THE GENERAL MEDICAL COUNCIL PROFESSIONAL CONDUCT COMMITTEE (EC PRACTITIONERS) (PROCEDURE) RULES ORDER OF COUNCIL 1989 (SI 1989, No. 1837)

PART I
PRELIMINARY

Interpretation
2.—(1) In these rules, unless the context otherwise requires,
"the principal rules" means the General Medical Council Preliminary Proceedings Committee and Professional Conduct Committee (Procedure) Rules 1988;
"the Act", "the Council", "the President", "the Registrar", "the legal assessor", "the Solicitor", "complainant", "party" and "person acting in a public capacity" have the meanings assigned to them in rule 2 of the principal rules, and those meanings shall also apply for the purpose of those of the principal rules which are applied by rules 6 and 14;
"practitioner" means a registered EC practitioner or a visiting EC practitioner who is the subject of an inquiry under these rules;
"case relating to disqualification" means a case where it is alleged that an EC practitioner has been registered as a fully registered medical practitioner when a disqualifying decision was in force in respect of him;
"case relating to conviction or conduct" means a case where it is alleged that a visiting EC practitioner has been convicted of a criminal offence in any member State of the Communities where he was practising medicine or has been guilty of serious professional misconduct;
"disqualifying decision" has the meaning assigned to it by section 44(2) of the Act;
"registered EC practitioner" means a person who has been registered as a fully registered medical practitioner by virtue of section 3(b) of the Act;
"visiting EC practitioner" means a national of a member State of the Communities who holds medical qualifications entitling him to registration under section 3(b) of the Act but is not so registered and who renders medical services while visiting the United Kingdom by virtue of section 18(1) of the Act.

PART II
INITIAL CONSIDERATION OF CASES

Cases relating to disqualification
3. Where information in writing from a person acting in a public capacity or a complaint supported by a statutory declaration or affidavit is received by the Registrar, from which it appears to him that a disqualifying decision was in force in respect of a registered EC practitioner at the time when he was registered by virtue of section 3(b) of the Act, and that that practitioner has been so registered for a period of not less than one month throughout which period the said decision has had effect but is no longer in force, the Registrar shall write to the practitioner.
(i)   informing him of the particulars of the information or complaint received;
(ii)   inviting him to submit within 28 days of the date of despatch of the letter any observations which he may wish to offer;
(iii)   enclosing copies of these rules and of the principal rules and, where a complaint has been received, of the statutory declaration or affidavit furnished in support thereof; and
(iv)   advising him that an inquiry may be held into the matter by the Professional Conduct Committee.

Cases relating to conviction or conduct
4. Where information in writing from a person acting in a public capacity or a complaint supported by one or more statutory declarations or affidavits is received by the Registrar, from which it appears to him that a visiting EC practitioner has been convicted of a criminal offence in any member State where he was practising medicine or may have been guilty of serious professional misconduct, the Registrar shall write to the practitioner,

    (i)   informing him of the particulars of the information or complaint received;

    (ii)   inviting him to submit within 28 days of the date of despatch of the letter any observations which he may wish to offer;

    (iii)   enclosing copies of these rules and of the principal rules and, where a complaint has been received, of the statutory declarations or affidavit furnished in support thereof; and

    (iv)   advising him that an inquiry may be held into the matter by the Professional Conduct Committee.

Reference to Professional Conduct Committee
5. Subject to the foregoing rules the President shall, on the expiry of the period specified in rule 3(ii) or 4(ii), unless it appears to him in the light of any observations submitted by the practitioner or for any other reason that the matter need proceed no further, direct the Registrar to refer the case (whether it be a case relating to disqualification or a case relating to conviction or conduct) to the Professional Conduct Committee for inquiry.

PART III
PROCEDURE OF PROFESSIONAL CONDUCT COMMITTEE

Intermediate procedure
6. Where a case has been referred under these rules to the Professional Conduct Committee, rules 17, 18, 19, 20, 21, 22 and 24 of the principal rules shall apply as if:-

    (1)   the word "practitioner" in those rules had the meaning assigned to it in rule 2;

    (2)   in rule 17(4) of the principal rules a reference to the Schedule to these rules were substituted for reference to Schedule 2 to the principal rules;

    (3)   in rule 19 of the principal rules the reference to the Preliminary Proceedings Committee were omitted and a reference to rule 7 were substituted for the reference to rule 17 of the principal rules;

    (4)   in rule 20 of the principal rules the words "without prejudice to rule 16" were omitted, and

    (5)   in rule 22(1) of the principal rules the words "including such amendment as contemplated under the proviso to rule 11(2)" were omitted.

Conduct of hearing
7. When the charge, or charges, have been read, subject to rule 8:-

    (1)   in respect of any charge, or charges, to which no objection has been upheld:

    (a)   the Solicitor, or the complainant, if any, may address the Committee and shall adduce evidence of the facts on which the charge or charges are based;

    (b)   the practitioner may then address the Committee and adduce evidence in respect of any facts which he does not admit;

    (c)   at the close of the evidence for the practitioner, the Solicitor, or the complainant, if any, may, with the leave of the Committee, adduce evidence to rebut any evidence adduced by the practitioner;

    (d)   the Solicitor, or the complainant, if any, may then address the Committee;

    (e)   the practitioner may then address the Committee.

    (2)   On the conclusion of the proceedings under paragraph (1) the Committee shall consider the facts alleged in the charge or charges, other than any facts which have been

admitted by the practitioner, and shall find whether the facts or any of the facts have been proved.

(3)   Where the facts admitted by the practitioner or found proved by the Committee comprise those on which any charge or part of any charge is based the Chairman shall announce that the charge or part of the charge has been proved: Provided that this paragraph shall not apply to any charge alleging that the practitioner has been guilty of serious professional misconduct.

(4)   If in any case relating to conviction or conduct any charge alleges that the practitioner has been guilty of serious professional misconduct and the Committee find that the facts or some of the facts in the charge or part thereof have not been proved, the Committee shall record a finding that the practitioner is not guilty of serious professional misconduct in respect of the facts which have not been proved and the Chairman shall announce that finding.

Procedure where the practitioner does not appear
8.   Where the practitioner does not appear and is not represented, but the Committee have decided to proceed with the inquiry, paragraphs (1)(b), (c), (d) and (e) of rule 7 shall not apply.

Circumstances, character, history and pleas in mitigation
9.—(1)   Where the Committee have found that some or all of the facts alleged in the charge or charges have been proved, the Chairman shall invite the Solicitor to address the Committee, and to adduce evidence as to the circumstances leading up to the facts found proved, as to the character and previous history of the practitioner and, if the charge against the practitioner is one of serious professional misconduct, as to the extent to which those facts are indicative of serious professional misconduct on the part of the practitioner.

(2)   The Chairman shall then invite the practitioner to address the Committee by way of mitigation and to adduce evidence as aforesaid.

Finding of serious professional misconduct
10.   If, in any case relating to conviction or conduct, any charge alleges that the practitioner has been guilty of serious professional misconduct and the facts or some of the facts on which that charge is based have been proved, whether by admission or otherwise, the Committee shall consider whether the facts proved support a finding of such misconduct and shall find whether or not such charge is proved, and the Chairman shall announce the Committee's finding.

Determination whether to make a direction
11.—(1)   Where any charge brought against a practitioner under these rules has been found proved, the Committee may, if they think fit, postpone their determination whether to make a direction until such future date or meeting of the Committee as they may specify, in order to obtain and consider further evidence of the conduct of the practitioner. If they so decide, the Chairman shall announce that decision.

(2)   If the Committee decide that no such postponement is necessary, they shall consider and determine whether it shall be sufficient, subject to the provisions of rule 7(4), to make no direction or to impose no prohibition in this respect.

Determinations of the Committee
12.   If the Committee decide that it will not be sufficient to make no direction or impose no prohibition then,
     (a)   if the case is one relating to disqualification, the Committee shall direct that the practitioner's registration shall be suspended for a period not exceeding the period first mentioned in section 44(5) of the Act in relation to the facts found proved;
     (b)   if the case is one relating to conviction or conduct, the Committee shall prohibit him for rendering medical services in the United Kingdom in the future either:

    (i)   for such period as the Committee may specify; or

    (ii) indefinitely.

Announcement of finding or determination

13. The Chairman shall announce the finding or findings or determination of the Committee under these rules in such terms as the Committee may approve and, when the finding is one that the charge or charges have been proved but the Committee do not propose to make any further direction or impose any prohibition, may, without prejudice to the terms in which other findings may be announced, include any expression of the Committee's admonition in respect of the practitioner's behaviour giving rise to the charge or charges.

PART IV
GENERAL

14. Rules 36, 47, 48, 50, 52, 53, 54 and 55 of the principal rules shall apply to proceedings under these rules as if any references in any of those rules to "practitioner" had the meaning assigned to that word in rule 2 and as if the references to the Preliminary Proceedings Committee in rules 47 and 52 of the principal rules had been omitted.

THE HUMAN ORGAN TRANSPLANTS (UNRELATED PERSONS) REGULATIONS 1989 (SI 1989, No. 2480)

Citation, commencement and interpretation

1.—(3)   In these Regulations:-

"the Act" means the Human Organ Transplants Act 1989;

"the Authority" means the authority constituted by regulation 2 of these Regulations;

"donor" means a living person from whom it is proposed to remove an organ;

"recipient" means a person into whom it is proposed to transplant an organ.

Constitution of the Unrelated Live Transplant Regulatory Authority

2.—(1)   There is hereby constituted for the purposes of section 2(3) of the Act an authority called the Unrelated Live Transplant Regulatory Authority.

(2)   The Authority shall consist of a chairman appointed by the Secretary of State and of such number of other members appointed by him, not being less than 7 or more than 11, as he thinks fit.

(3)   The chairman and at least 3 other members of the Authority shall be registered medical practitioners and at least 4 members of the Authority shall be persons who are not, and have not at any time been, registered medical practitioners.

(4)   The tenure of office of the chairman and any other member of the Authority shall be on such terms and for such period as the Secretary of State shall specify on appointing him.

(5)   The procedure of the Authority shall be such as the Authority may determine.

Transplants between persons who are not genetically related

3.—(1)   The prohibition in section 2(1) of the Act (restriction on transplants between persons not genetically related) shall not apply in cases where a registered medical practitioner has caused the matter to be referred to the Authority and where the Authority is satisfied:-

    (a)   that no payment has been, or is to be, made in contravention of section 1 of the Act;

    (b)   that the registered medical practitioner who has caused the matter to be referred to the Authority has clinical responsibility for the donor; and

(c)   except in a case where the primary purpose of removal of an organ from a donor is the medical treatment of that donor, that the conditions specified in paragraph (2) of this regulation are satisfied.

(2)   The conditions referred to in paragraph (1)(c) of this regulation are:-

(a)   that a registered medical practitioner has given the donor an explanation of the nature of the medical procedure for, and the risk involved in, the removal of the organ in question;

(b)   that the donor understands the nature of the medical procedure and the risks, as explained by the registered medical practitioner, and consents to the removal of the organ in question;

(c)   that the donor's consent to the removal of the organ in question was not obtained by coercion or the offer of an inducement;

(d)   that the donor understands that he is entitled to withdraw his consent if he wishes, but has not done so;

(e)   that the donor and the recipient have both been interviewed by a person who appears to the Authority to have been suitably qualified to conduct such interviews and who has reported to the Authority on the conditions contained in sub-paragraphs (a) to (d) above and has included in his report an account of any difficulties of communication with the donor or the recipient and an explanation of how those difficulties were overcome.

UNITED KINGDOM TRANSPLANT SUPPORT SERVICE AUTHORITY REGULATIONS 1991 (SI 1991, No. 408)

Citation, commencement and interpretation

1(1)   These Regulations may be cited as the United Kingdom Transplant Support Service Authority Regulations 1991 and shall come into force on 1st April 1991.

(2)   In these Regulations, unless the context otherwise requires —

"the Act" means the National Health Service Act 1977;

"the Authority" means the United Kingdom transplant Support Service Authority established by the United Kingdom Transplant Support Service Authority (Establishment and Constitution) Order 1991;

"donor" means a person who provides or offers to provide any of his organs with a view to the organ being transplanted into another person, and includes a dead person from whom an organ is retrieved;

"member" in relation to the Authority does not include its chairman;

"NHS trust" means an NHS trust established in pursuance of section 5(1) of the National Health Service and Community Care Act 1990;

"non-officer member" and "officer member" mean respectively a member who is not, or who is, an officer of the Authority;

"organ" means any part of a human body or any product derived from the human body;

"recipient" means a person who undergoes or is to undergo a surgical operation for the implantation of one or more organs removed from a living or dead person;

"transplant centre" means a hospital or other institution, or department of it, which undertakes surgical operations for the transplantation of human organs.

Functions of the Authority

2(1)   Subject to paragraphs (3) and (4) of this regulation and in accordance with such directions as the Secretary of State may give under the Act, the Authority shall exercise on his behalf the Secretary of State's functions under the enactments specified in column 1 of the Schedule to these Regulations (the subject matter of the relevant function being indicated in column 2 of that Schedule) so far as they relate to assisting in, and facilitating or promoting, the provision of a service for the transplantation of organs.

(2)   Without prejudice to the generality of paragraph (1) of this regulation, the functions mentioned in that paragraph include the functions of—

(a)   acquiring, recording, updating, keeping and making available information about donors and recipients and organs which are or may be available for transplantation and other related matters;

(b)   identifying persons who are potentially suitable recipients for organs, and notifying transplant centres of the availability or potential availability of organs;

(c)   giving advice about, or making arrangements for, the transport of organs for transplantation;

(d)   generally facilitating the standardisation of practices in respect of storage, transport and transplantation of organs;

(e)   providing an organ matching and tissue-typing service;

(f)   supplying standardised reagents and sera to transplant centres and laboratories;

(g)   providing education and training for persons involved or to be involved with the transplantation of organs, including identifying the need for such education or training.

(3)   The powers of the Secretary of State under section 2 of the Act shall be exercisable by the Authority only to such extent as may be necessary for the proper exercise of one or more other functions which the Secretary of State has directed the Authority to exercise on his behalf.

(4)   Nothing in these Regulations is to be taken as giving directions for the exercise of any functions conferred on or vested in the Secretary of State with respect to the making of any order or Regulations.

(5)   In exercising the functions of the Secretary of State under section 25 of the Act, such changes shall be made with respect to the supplies of human blood as are determined by the Secretary of State.

SCHEDULE

Enactments Conferring Functions Exercisable by the Authority (reg 2)

Column (1)	Column (2)
Enactment	*Subject matter*
The Health Services and Public Health Act 1968 section 63(1),(3), (5) and (6)	Providing instruction, and providing materials and premises necessary for or in connection with providing any such instruction, for persons involved or to be involved with the transplantation of organs.
The Act Section 2	Providing services considered appropriate for discharging duties imposed on the Secretary of State and doing other things calculated to facilitate the discharge of any such duty.
Section 3(1)(f)	Providing services required for the diagnosis and treatment of illness.
Section 5(2)(d)	Conducting research into matters relating to the causation, prevention, diagnosis or treatment of illness and into any such other matters connected with any service provided under the Act as the Authority considers to be appropriate.
Section 23(1)	Arranging with any person or body (including voluntary organisations) for that person or body to assist in providing any service under the Act.
Section 23(2)	Making available to certain persons or bodies (including voluntary organisations) facilities and services of persons employed in connection with such facilities.

Section 23(3)   Agreeing terms and making payments in respect
                                   of facilities or services provided under section 23
                                   of the Act.
Section 25   Making available supplies of human blood or any
                                   part of a human body or supplies of any other
                                   substances or preparations not readily obtainable
                                   to any person on such terms, including terms as to
                                   charges as the Authority considers to be
                                   appropriate, subject to section 62 of the Act.
Section 121   Determining charges for prescribed services
                                   provided in respect of prescribed non-residents.

THE ABORTION REGULATIONS 1991 (SI 1991, No. 499)

Interpretation
   2. In these Regulations "the Act" means the Abortion Act 1967 and "practitioner"
means a registered medical practitioner.

Certificate of opinion
   3.—(1)   Any opinion to which section 1 of the Act refers shall be certified—
   (a)   in the case of a pregnancy terminated in accordance with section 1(1) of the
Act, in the form set out in Part I of Schedule 1 to these Regulations, and
   (b)   in the case of a pregnancy terminated in accordance with section 1(4) of the
Act, in the form set out in Part II of that Schedule.
   (2)   Any certificate of an opinion referred to in section 1(1) of the Act shall be given
before the commencement of the treatment for the termination of the pregnancy to
which it relates.
   (3)   Any certificate of an opinion referred to in section 1(4) of the Act shall be given
before the commencement of the treatment for the termination of the pregnancy to
which it relates or, if that is not reasonably practicable, not later than 24 hours after
such termination.
   (4)   Any such certificate as is referred to in paragraphs (2) and (3) of this regulation
shall be preserved by the practitioner who terminated the pregnancy to which it relates
for a period of not less than three years beginning with the date of the termination.
   (5)   A certificate which is no longer to be preserved shall be destroyed by the person
in whose custody it then is.

Notice of termination of pregnancy and information relating to the termination
   4.—(1)   Any practitioner who terminates a pregnancy in England or Wales shall give
to the appropriate Chief Medical Officer—
   (a)   notice of the termination, and
   (b)   such other information relating to the termination as is specified in the form
set out in Schedule 2 to these Regulations,
and shall do so by sending them to him in a sealed envelope within 7 days of the
termination.
   (2)   The appropriate Chief Medical Officer is—
   (a)   where the pregnancy was terminated in England, the Chief Medical Officer of
the Department of Health, Richmond House, Whitehall, London, SW1A 2NS; or
   (b)   where the pregnancy was terminated in Wales, the Chief Medical Officer of
the Welsh Office, Cathays Park, Cardiff, CF1 3NQ.

Restriction on disclosure of information
   5.   A notice given or any information furnished to a Chief Medical Officer in pursuance
of these Regulations shall not be disclosed except that disclosure may be made—

    (a) for the purposes of carrying out their duties—
      (i) to an officer of the Department of Health authorised by the Chief Medical Officer of that Department, or to an officer of the Welsh Office authorised by the Chief Medical Officer of that Office, as the case may be, or
      (ii) to the Registrar General or a member of his staff authorised by him; or
    (b) for the purposes of carrying out his duties in relation to offences under the Act or the law relating to abortion, to the Director of Public Prosecutions or a member of his staff authorised by him; or
    (c) for the purposes of investigating whether an offence has been committed under the Act or the law relating to abortion, to a police officer not below the rank of superintendent or a person authorised by him; or
    (d) pursuant to a court order, for the purposes of proceedings which have begun; or
    (e) for the purposes of bona fide scientific research; or
    (f) to the practitioner who terminated the pregnancy; or
    (g) to a practitioner, with the consent in writing of the woman whose pregnancy was terminated; or
    (h) when requested by the President of the General Medical Council for the purpose of investigating whether there has been serious professional misconduct by a practitioner, to the President of the General Medical Council or a member of its staff authorised by him.

SCHEDULE 1   Regulation 3(1)

PART I

ABORTION ACT 1967   CERTIFICATE A

Not to be destroyed within three years of the date of operation

**Certificate to be completed before an abortion is
performed under Section 1(1) of the Act**

I, ...
(Name and qualifications of practitioner in block capitals)

of ....

....
(Full address of practitioner)

Have/have not* seen/and examined* the pregnant woman to whom this certificate relates at

....

....
(full address of place at which patient was seen or examined)

on ....

and I ....
(Name and qualifications of practitioner in block capitals)

of ....

....
(Full address of practitioner)

Have/have not* seen/and examined* the pregnant woman to whom this certificate relates at

....

....
(Full address of place at which patient was seen or examined)

on ....

We hereby certify that we are of the opinion, formed in good faith, that in the case

of ....
(Full name of pregnant woman in block capitals)

of ....

....
(Usual place of residence of pregnant woman in block capitals)

(Ring appropriate letter(s))	A	the continuance of the pregnancy would involve risk to the life of the pregnant woman greater than if the pregnancy were terminated;
	B	the termination is necessary to prevent grave permanent injury to the physical or mental health of the pregnant woman;
	C	the pregnancy has NOT exceeded its 24th week and that the continuance of the pregnancy would involve risk, greater than if the pregnancy were terminated, of injury to the physical or mental health of the pregnant woman;
	D	the pregnancy has NOT exceeded its 24th week and that the continuance of the pregnancy would involve risk, greater than if the pregnancy were terminated, of injury to the physical or mental health of any existing child(ren) of the family of the pregnant woman;
	E	there is a substantial risk that if the child were born it would suffer from such physical or mental abnormalities as to be seriously handicapped.

This certificate of opinion is given before the commencement of the treatment for the termination of pregnancy to which it refers and relates to the circumstances of the pregnant woman's individual case.

Signed ....   **Date** ....

Signed ....   **Date** ....

* Delete as appropriate   Form HSA1 (revised 1991)

206512   B*

PART II

SCHEDULE 1

IN CONFIDENCE   Certificate B

Not to be destroyed within three years of the date of operation

ABORTION ACT 1967

CERTIFICATE TO BE COMPLETED IN RELATION TO ABORTION PERFORMED

IN EMERGENCY UNDER SECTION 1(4) OF THE ACT

I,..

(Name and qualifications of practitioner in block capitals)

of ....

....

(Full address of practitioner)

hereby certify that I *am/was of the opinion formed in good faith that it *is/was necessary immediately to terminate the pregnancy of

....

(Full name of pregnant woman in block capitals)

of ....

....

(Usual place of residence of pregnant woman in block capitals)

(Ring
appropriate
number)

in order 1.   to save the life of the pregnant woman; or

2.   to prevent grave permanent injury to the physical or mental health of the pregnant woman.

This certificate of opinion is given—

A. before the commencement of the treatment for the termination of the pregnancy to which it relates; or,

(Ring
appropriate
letter)

if that is not reasonably practicable, then

B. not later than 24 hours after such termination.

Signed ....

Date..

*Delete as appropriate

206512 B*2

SCHEDULE 2

Regulation 4

IN CONFIDENCE   **ABORTION NOTIFICATION**

ABORTION ACT 1967
FORM OF NOTIFICATION (England and Wales)

This form is to be COMPLETED BY THE PRACTITIONER TERMINATING THE PREGNANCY and sent in a sealed envelope within SEVEN DAYS of the termination to:-

The Chief Medical Officer		The Chief Medical Officer
Department of Health		Welsh Office
Richmond House		Cathays Park
79 Whitehall	OR	CARDIFF
LONDON		CF1 3NQ
SW1A 2NS		

in respect of the termination of the pregnancy in Wales

PLEASE USE BLOCK CAPITALS AND NUMERALS FOR DATES THROUGHOUT

1.   PRACTITIONER TERMINATING THE PREGNANCY

NAME   I, ...

PERMANENT   of ....
ADDRESS

hereby give notice that I terminated the pregnancy of the woman named overleaf, and to the best of my knowledge the particulars on this form are correct. **I further certify that I joined/did not join† in giving Certificate A having seen/not seen† and examined/not examined †her before doing so.**

Signature .... Date ....

2.   CERTIFICATION   In all non-emergency cases state particulars of practitioners who joined in giving Certificate A.

1. To be completed in **all** cases.   2. Do **not** complete if the operating practitioner joined in giving Certificate A.

NAME   ....

PERMANENT   ....
ADDRESS   ....

(tick appropriate box)

Did the practitioner named at 1 certify that he saw/and examined the pregnant woman before giving the certificate?   ☐ YES ☐ NO

Did the practitioner named at 2 certify that he saw/and examined the pregnant woman before giving the certificate?   ☐ YES ☐ NO

DO NOT COMPLETE IF SECTION 20 BELOW APPLIES   Please leave these boxes blank

**3.   NAME AND   ....
ADDRESS OF PLACE
OF TERMINATION   ....**   ☐☐☐☐☐

(tick appropriate box)

Was the patient a NHS case terminated in an approved place under an agency agreement?   ☐ YES ☐ NO   ☐

†delete as appropriate

Form HSA4 (Revised 1991)

4. WOMAN'S FULL NAME AND PERMANENT ADDRESS (INCLUDING COUNTRY IF RESIDENT OUTSIDE ENGLAND AND WALES)

Surname

Forename(s)

Address

....

....

.... Postcode ☐☐☐☐■☐☐☐

Please leave these boxes blank

☐

PRESENT ADDRESS IN ENGLAND AND WALES

....

....

.... Postcode ☐☐☐☐■☐☐☐

☐☐☐☐■☐☐☐

☐

5. DATE OF BIRTH ....DAY ....MONTH ....YEAR ☐☐☐☐☐☐

(tick appropriate box)

6. MARITAL STATUS

1 ☐ Single   3 ☐ Widowed   5 ☐ Separated

2 ☐ Married   4 ☐ Divorced   NK ☐ Not Known

☐

7. PARITY

Number of woman's previous:- a. (i) Livebirths .... ☐

(Enter number - If NIL enter 0)

(ii) Stillbirths .... ☐

(iii) Spontaneous miscarriages .... ☐

b. Legal terminations .... ☐

8*. ADMISSION

Date of admission to place of termination   ....DAY ....MONTH ....YEAR ☐☐☐☐☐☐

9*. TERMINATION

Date of termination   ....DAY ....MONTH ....YEAR ☐☐☐☐☐☐

10*. DISCHARGE

Date of discharge from place of termination   ....DAY ....MONTH ....YEAR ☐☐☐☐☐☐

11*. DAY CASE

(tick appropriate box)

Was this a planned day case?   ☐ YES   ☐ NO   ☐

* If the method of treatment used to terminate the pregnancy was <u>Antiprogesterone with Prostaglandin without any supplementary surgical termination</u> do not complete sections 8-11 but INSTEAD complete section 20

12. GESTATION 1.   Specify number of weeks by completing a <u>or</u> b as appropriate

a. Pregnancy has NOT exceeded its 24th week

Gestation estimated at..............weeks

b. Pregnancy HAS exceeded its 24th week (ensure that section 14 is also completed)

Gestation estimated at ....weeks

☐☐

2.   Methods of estimation **(tick appropriate box(es))**

☐ LMP   ☐ Ultrasound   ☐ Other - specify:- ....

☐

13. GROUNDS   The certified ground(s) for terminating the pregnancy stated on CERTIFICATE A were:-

(tick appropriate box(es))

☐ **A** that the continuance of the pregnancy would involve risk to the life of the pregnant woman greater than if the pregnancy were terminated.

A State main medical condition(s):-

☐ **B** that the termination is necessary to prevent grave permanent injury to the physical or mental health of the pregnant woman.

B State main medical condition(s):-

☐ **C** that the pregnancy has NOT exceeded its 24th week and that the continuance of the pregnancy would involve risk, greater than if the pregnancy were terminated, of injury to the physical or mental health of the pregnant woman.

C State main medical condition(s):-

☐ **D** that the pregnancy has NOT exceeded its 24th week and that the continuance of the pregnancy would involve risk, greater than if the pregnancy were terminated, of injury to the physical or mental health of any existing child(ren) of the family of the pregnant woman.

D State number of children:-

☐

☐ **E** that there is a substantial risk that if the child were born it would suffer from such physical or mental abnormalities as to be seriously handicapped:- STATE

EITHER   (i) (a) Diagnosis...

(b) Method(s) of diagnosis (tick appropriate box(es))

☐ Amniocentesis   ☐ Ultrasound   ☐ Chorionic Villus Sampling   ☐ Other - specify ....

☐☐☐☐

OR   (ii) Condition in pregnant woman causing suspected condition in fetus. Complete 1 <u>and</u> 2

1. Condition in woman - specify:-...

2. Suspected condition in fetus - specify:-...

EMERGENCY ONLY Termination was immediately necessary, as stated on CERTIFICATE B:-

☐ **F** to save the life of the pregnant woman

F or G - state main medical condition(s):-

OR

☐ **G** to prevent grave permanent injury to the physical or mental health of the pregnant woman

14. OVER 24 WEEKS GESTATION   If the pregnancy was terminated after it had exceeded its 24th week please give below a full statement of the medical condition of the pregnant woman/fetus.

(tick appropriate box)   **Please leave these boxes blank**

15. SELECTIVE TERMINATION Was this a selective termination?   ☐ YES   ☐ NO

    State:- (i) original number of fetuses ....

    (ii) number of fetuses reduced to ....

    All other relevant sections of the form should also be completed

---

(tick appropriate boxes)

16. METHOD   Cervical preparation?   ☐ YES   ☐ NO

....

Surgical termination:-   *Medical termination:-

☐ Vacuum aspiration   ☐ Prostaglandin only

☐ Dilatation and Evacuation   ☐ Prostaglandins with:- **(tick appropriate boxes)**

☐ Hysterotomy   ☐ Oxytocin

☐ Hysterectomy   ☐ Antiprogesterone (if used see also section 20 below)

☐ Other surgical - specify:-   ☐ Other medical agents-specify:-

....

* Do not enter an evacuation of retained products of conception as a further method of termination.

---

17. COMPLICATIONS*   **(tick appropriate box(es))**

☐ None   ☐ Haemorrhage   ☐ Uterine Perforation   ☐ Sepsis

☐ Other - specify:- ....

*Do not enter an evacuation of retained products of conception as a complication.

---

18. STERILISATION   **(tick appropriate box)**

Was a sterilisation operation performed?   ☐ YES   ☐ NO

---

19. DEATH OF WOMAN   In the case of death, specify:-

(i) Date ....DAY ....MONTH ....YEAR

(ii) Cause ....

---

20. ANTIPROGESTERONE WITH PROSTAGLANDIN   Do not complete this section <u>unless</u> the method used was Antiprogesterone with Prostaglandin

(i) Date of treatment with <u>Antiprogesterone</u> ....DAY ....MONTH ....YEAR

Name ....

Address of place of treatment ....

(ii) Date of treatment with <u>Prostaglandin</u> ....DAY ....MONTH ....YEAR

Name ....

Address of place of treatment ....

(iii) Date termination confirmed ....DAY ....MONTH ....YEAR

(tick appropriate box)

(iv) Was the patient a NHS case treated under an agency agreement?   ☐ YES   ☐ NO

HEALTH CIRCULARS

HEALTH CIRCULAR HC(82)16

DEPARTMENT OF HEALTH AND SOCIAL SECURITY

To: Regional Health Authorities   )
District Health Authorities   )
Special Health Authorities for   ) for action
   London Postgraduate Teaching Hospitals)
Boards of Governors   )

Family Practitioner Committees   )
Community Health Councils   ) for information   September 1982

SUPPLY OF INFORMATION ABOUT HOSPITAL PATIENTS IN THE CONTEXT OF CIVIL LEGAL PROCEEDINGS

Summary

This Circular draws attention to recent legislation concerning the powers of the High Court to order disclosure of documents before and in proceedings for personal injury or death and sets it in the context of existing guidance on voluntary disclosure of information about hospital patients contemplating or engaged in civil legal proceedings.

Existing Guidance and Practice

1.   Guidance on the voluntary release of information about patients contemplating or engaged in civil legal proceedings is contained in HM(59)88. Paragraphs 3 and 4 (the texts of which are reproduced at Annex A) advise on the action to be taken by health authorities when a request for case notes[1] or information from them is received from the patient concerned or his representative. This advice remains applicable, in particular that authorities should not stand on their strict rights in these circumstances and that the doctor concerned must always be consulted where medical matters are in any way involved.

2.   It has since become a widely accepted practice for disclosure in these circumstances to be made to the applicant's medical adviser. This practice is commended as a means of ensuring that case notes are correctly interpreted for the applicant's benefit.

Powers of High Court to Order Disclosure in Advance of Proceedings

3.   In addition to the inherent power to order disclosure between parties to proceedings which have been commenced the High Court has for some years had powers to order disclosure of relevant documents where the applicant and the person ordered to make disclosure are both likely to be parties to proceedings in cases of personal injury or death (and to order disclosure to a party to such proceedings which have commenced from someone who is not a party to them). Such powers were first

conferred in the Administration of Justice Act 1970. A decision of the House of Lords in 1978 in a Northern Ireland case (McIvor v Southern Health and Social Services Board) established that under that Act, if the court did make an order, the documents would have to be made available to the applicant and that there was no power to restrict disclosure, as had earlier been the practice, to a medical or other adviser of the applicant. HN(78)95, which is cancelled by this Circular, drew the attention of authorities to this decision.

4. Since then, there have been further changes in the law and the relevant powers of the High Court, as amended, are now contained in Sections 33(2) and 34(1) and (2) of the Supreme Court Act 1981. The text of these sections is reproduced in Annex B, together with that of Section 35 which contains supplementary provisions. Under the new law, which came into operation on 1 January 1982, the court has power to order production to the applicant or, on such conditions as may be specified in the order, to

(a) the applicant's legal advisers, or

(b) the applicant's legal advisers and any medical or other professional adviser of the applicant, or

(c) if the applicant has no legal adviser, to any medical or other professional adviser of the applicant.

Requests for Information from Patients

5. In considering requests from patients or their authorised representatives for disclosure of case notes or information from them in connection with actual or possible litigation, authorities should continue to observe the spirit of HM(59)88. In cases of doubt account should be taken of the powers of the High Court to order disclosure in advance of proceedings. It would not be appropriate for health authorities to adopt a more stringent test than would be likely to be applied by the court when considering an application under Section 33(2) or 34(2) of that Act since this could have the effect of forcing the applicant to resort to court action when there was no real doubt as to the outcome. Authorities are reminded that for the purpose of an order under Section 33(2) of the Act the applicant would not need to convince the court of the merits of his claim against the authority, but he would, under the Rules of the Supreme Court, be required to state the grounds on which he was likely to be a party to subsequent proceedings.

Requests from Third Parties for Information about Patients

6. Where a request (as opposed to a subpoena or court order) for information is received not from the patient himself or his authorised representative but from some other party engaged in or contemplating legal proceedings with him, the information requested should not be supplied without the written consent of the patient concerned and of the doctor concerned where medical matters are in any way involved. This replaces the advice in Paragraph 5 of HM(59)88 which is withdrawn.

Action on Receiving an Order or Subpoena

7. Any health authority officer (for example, a hospital medical records officer) who is served with a court order or subpoena for the production of case notes or the giving of evidence based on them should immediately notify the District Administrator. The District Administrator should notify the doctor concerned (normally the consultant in charge of the case, or his successor) and should consider whether the authority's legal advisers and any other members of staff concerned should be informed. While there should be no delay in acting on the order, in cases of doubt the authority's and the doctor's legal advisers may need to advise on whether an appeal should be entered against it. In complying with an order for the production of documents care should be taken to ensure that the documents are made available only to the person or persons to whom the court has ordered the production, and that any conditions specified in the order are observed.

Action

10. Health authorities are asked to bring the contents of this Circular to the attention of all staff who may be involved with orders or requests for disclosure of information about patients.

ANNEX A
SUPPLY OF INFORMATION ABOUT HOSPITAL PATIENTS ENGAGED IN LEGAL PROCEEDINGS (EXTRACT FROM HM(59)88)

3. Where a request for records or reports is made on what are manifestly insubstantial grounds, the hospital cannot be expected to grant it, but where information is being sought in pursuance of a claim of prima facie substance against the Board or Committee or a member of their staff or both, the decision is more difficult and each request must be examined on its own merits, in the light of legal advice, and of course in consultation with any member of their medical or dental staff directly concerned in the outcome of the claim (in this connection see HM(54)32). The production of case notes and similar documents is not obligatory before the stage of discovery in the actual proceedings is reached,[2] but the Minister does not feel that boards and committees, especially as they are public authorities, would either wish or be well advised to maintain their strict rights in this connection except for some good reason bearing on the defence to the particular claim or on the ground that the request is made without substantial justification.

4. Where the information is required in a matter which has nothing to do with the hospital or any member of its staff, for example in litigation between the patient and a third party, hospital authorities should be prepared to help by providing, as far as possible, the information asked for subject always to the consent of the patient.[3] Sometimes the information sought may be entirely unrelated to medical matters — for example the date of the patient's admission or discharge; whether he was a private patient and signed the appropriate form of undertaking; and if so, the amount paid by way of hospital charges. Such information may properly be given by the Secretary of the Board or Committee, without reference to the medical staff. But in all cases — and they will undoubtedly be the majority — where medical matters are in any way involved (for example where information is wanted about the diagnosis made on admission, details of treatment, conditions on discharge, or prognosis) the doctor or dentist who was in charge of the patient's treatment at the hospital, or his successor, should be consulted. It is self-evident that this must be done when a medical or dental report is being asked for. But the principle is equally important when the request is only for extracts from the case notes, since it is necessary for the doctor or dentist to ensure that any extracts which are made are not misleading, and also that their disclosure to the patient cannot in any way be harmful medically to him — it would no doubt often be undesirable to let the patient himself have so detailed a report or such full extracts from the medical records as it would be proper to give to his general practitioner. This decision is one which can be made only by a professionally qualified person. At the same time it is imperative that no material information which can in any way be relevant to the matter should be withheld in such a way as to convey a wrong picture.

---

[1] This Circular is concerned primarily with hospital patients' case notes, including records and information contained therein which have been compiled by non-medical staff, because most requests and orders for disclosure will be for such records. The advice, adapted as necessary to fit the particular circumstances of each case, is also applicable to records held outside hospitals (other than those held by family practitioners or Family Practitioner Committees), for example by clinical medical officers in the community health services, by district nurses, health visitors, midwives or community psychiatric nurses.

[2] There is now an exception to this, namely where a court order is made under the Supreme Court Act 1981 (see Paragraph 4 of the main body of this Circular).

[3] Where the request for information is not from the patient himself or his authorised representative see Paragraph 6 of the main body of the Circular.

HEALTH CIRCULAR HC(88)37, HN (FP)(88)18
DEPARTMENT OF HEALTH AND SOCIAL SECURITY

To: Regional Health Authorities   )
     District Health Authorities   ) for action
     Special Health Authorities   )

     Community Health Councils   ) for information
     Family Practitioner Committees)   June 1988

HOSPITAL COMPLAINTS PROCEDURE ACT 1985

Unless otherwise notified, this Circular but not the directions to which it refers will cease to be valid on 31 May 1993.

Summary
1.   This Circular encloses at Annex A a copy of the directions required by S.1 of the Hospital Complaints Procedure Act 1985 and advises on the procedure to be operated in respect of complaints by hospital patients.

Background
2.   The Hospital Complaints Procedure Act received the Royal Assent in July 1985. The Act requires the Secretary of State to issue directions on the complaints procedure to be operated in respect of hospital patients and the steps to publicise the procedure.
3.   Health Authorities were invited in 1986 to comment on proposals for handling complaints. The consultation exercise offered the opportunity to re-examine existing complaints procedures. Many authorities confirmed either that their local practices corresponded already to the proposed procedures or that arrangements were being made to align their procedures accordingly.
4.   The directions enclosed at Annex A confirm the arrangements which health authorities are obliged to make for dealing with complaints and for publicising these. The remainder of this circular advises how authorities may interpret the requirements of the directions.

The Need for a Complaints Procedure
5.   Patients are entitled to bring to the attention of health authorities aspects of their care and treatment about which they are unhappy. The Department recognises that suggestions, constructive criticism and complaints can be valuable aids to management in maintaining and developing better standards of health care. It is important that no one (staff or patients) should be inhibited from making valid complaints and that there is full confidence that these will be given full, proper and speedy consideration. Many matters that trouble patients can be dealt with as they arise. Staff should be encouraged to be aware of and to deal with these in a way which reassures the patient and to bring the complaint to the attention of management when this is appropriate.

Procedural Requirements
6.   The basis of any complaints procedure is good communication. Problems of communication between patients and staff can generate misunderstandings which can result in complaints. Good communications may help defuse awkward situations. However, not all complaints can be dealt with on the spot and in this informal way. Some complaints will be of such concern to the patient that they warrant consideration and a formal response by a senior officer of the authority or it may be that the complaint is comparatively trivial but the patient feels unwilling or unable to discuss the matter with the staff who are directly involved. Again, good communications will be necessary to ensure that the complainant can give full expression to his concerns and that the full facts about the complaint are obtained.

7.   The directions outline the mandatory requirements which health authorities must adopt in establishing complaints procedures. They involve

(i)   *A designated officer.* Each Health Authority must designate a senior officer for each hospital or group of hospitals for which it is responsible. The designated officer should be located in the hospital for which he is responsible and his whereabouts made known to facilitate contact by patients or those acting on a patient's behalf. The Unit General Manager might be the appropriate person for this task. The designated officer will be the recipient of formal complaints made by or on behalf of patients and will be accountable for the investigation of complaints other than those involving clinical judgment, serious untoward incidents, disciplinary proceedings, physical abuse of patients or criminal offences. Where the designated officer is also the Unit General Manager he may well be directly involved in these particular complaints. But investigation of these may also involve other senior officers, e.g. the Regional Medical Officer (RMO) or the equivalent or the District General Manager (DGM), or members of the Authority (see sub-paragraph (iv) below). The designated officer should not be denied access to relevant records which are essential for the investigation of a complaint. The designated officer should normally be available to assist in cases of minor grievances which the patient feels unable to discuss with e.g. ward staff.

(ii)   *Who may complain.* Any person who is or has been a patient at the hospital (either as an in-patient or out-patient) is eligible to make a complaint. If the person concerned has died or is otherwise unable to act for himself the complaint should be accepted from a close relative, or friend, or a body or individual suitable to represent him. The designated officer must be satisfied that where the patient is capable, the complaint is being made with his knowledge and consent.

(iii)   *Investigating the complaint.* In investigating the complaint, the designated officer must ensure that he has a full picture from the complainant of the events complained about. This may involve a preliminary interview to clarify the nature of the complaint or to obtain further information. It may be possible at this stage to resolve the issue to the complainant's satisfaction without taking the matter further. Care must be taken not to prejudice the outcome of any further investigation.

The designated officer, in liaison with other appropriate senior officers, should circulate details of the complaint to the staff concerned for their comments and seek to agree a reply. General complaints about, for example, the hotel services would be sent to the Head of the Department concerned for advice on a reply. Care must be taken not to introduce delays into the system by allowing excessive periods for comment. The aim should be to process the complaint speedily and thoroughly at all stages. The complainant must be kept informed of progress and where appropriate interim replies or holding letters must be sent.

Where the designated officer considers that a complaint carries a threat of litigation he should seek legal advice on whether and in what form an investigation might proceed to minimise the risk of prejudicing any civil proceedings. The possibility of legal proceedings should not prevent the officer undertaking the investigations necessary to uncover faults in procedures and/or prevent a recurrence.

(iv)   *Further action to certain complaints.* Where the complaint concerns:

(a)   the exercise of *Clinical Judgment* which cannot be resolved by discussion with the consultant concerned;

(b)   what the authority is satisfied constitutes *a serious untoward incident* involving harm to a patient;

(c)   the conduct of hospital medical or dental staff which the Authority considers ought to be the subject of *disciplinary proceedings*;

(d)   the alleged *physical abuse of patients*;

(e)   a possible *criminal offence*;

the designated officer should bring the matter to his senior officers' attention (or if appropriate the RMO) without delay so that appropriate action can be taken to ensure that the complaint is dealt with promptly in accordance with the Department's guidelines and local procedures.

(v) *Conclusion of an investigation.* When an investigation into a complaint has been completed the designated officer must complete a report and send a letter detailing the results of the investigation to the person who made the complaint, to any person who is involved in the complaint and where appropriate to the manager of any Department or service concerned. The letter should be informative both as to the reasons for any failure in service and any steps taken to prevent a recurrence and should contain an apology where appropriate. If the complainant remains dissatisfied he should be advised to refer the matter to the Health Service Commissioner unless the complaint is clearly outside the Health Service Commissioner's jurisdiction or the complainant proposes to take further action through the courts.

(vi) *Monitoring complaints.* Health Authorities must monitor the arrangements. The purpose of this requirement is to ensure that health authorities monitor trends in complaints and can direct that appropriate action is taken. The designated officer should therefore provide summaries of complaints for the health authority. These summaries should be anonymised to preserve confidentiality of patients. The monitoring role must be undertaken by the authority itself, a committee of the authority or specified authority members. Progress in dealing with complaints should be kept under review by the District General Manager who should report to the Authority at quarterly intervals about any cases outstanding.

(vii) *Publicity.* Publicity must be given to the procedure. This is an essential part of improving the public perception of the complaints procedure. Health authorities should consider giving publicity to the procedures using:

(a) *Admission booklets.* Information about making a complaint should be given in the hospital booklet issued to patients on or prior to admission to hospital and available in hospital outpatient departments. It is essential for the location of the designated officer to be included.

(b) *Leaflets.* A leaflet explaining the complaints procedure and including a reference to the Health Service Commissioner's role in investigating complaints should be available for all patients. In addition to explaining the procedure in straightforward terms, the leaflet should give the location of the designated officer. Authorities should consider the need to make leaflets available in ethnic minority languages.

(c) *Notices.* These should be displayed in health authority premises including reception areas. Notices should give the location of the designated officer to whom appropriate comments, suggestions and complaints should be addressed.

(d) *CHCs.* Publicity material should be available to CHCs for information and issue to the public.

(e) *Staff Training.* All staff will need to be made aware of the complaints procedure and to know the name and location of the designated officer to enable them to refer patients. Training will be needed to ensure that staff attitudes are positive and do not deter legitimate complaints.

Additional Procedures

8.   In considering their procedures health authorities are asked to take the following elements, which are not requirements under the directions, into account.

(i) *Form of complaint.* It is not a requirement that a complaint should be in writing. But it is important that a note be made in cases where the complaint is not readily settled and where a dispute as to the precise nature of the complaint might arise. This is particularly so when a formal investigation is likely. Where the complainant is unable to put the formal complaint in writing the designated officer should ensure that a record of the complaint is made and ask the complainant to sign it. A refusal to sign by the complainant should not delay investigation of the complaint.

(ii) *Time limits.* Complaints should be made and dealt with as quickly as possible. The longer the delay the more memories fade and less fruitful the investigation of the complaint. It is reasonable to expect that complaints should be made within three months of the incident giving rise to the complaint and publicity should encourage this. However there may be circumstances in which this recommended time limit may not be appropriate and the directions provide the designated officer with the discretion to extend the period if it is considered that the complainant has good reason for delay.

(iii) *Complaints about the Community Health Services.* Complaints about the Community Health Services do not come within the scope of the procedures to be laid down in the directions under the Hospital Complaints Procedure Act 1985. Health Authorities are asked to consider that the procedure directed for the handling of general complaints about hospital services should also be adopted in respect of the community health services.

Investigation by statutory authorities

The Health Service Commissioner

9. Section 1(2) of the Hospital Complaints Procedure Act provides that nothing in the procedure promulgated in the directions shall preclude investigation by the Health Service Commissioner. The Health Service Commissioner may therefore investigate a complaint about health authority services or maladministration if a complainant is not satisfied with the conduct or outcome of the health authority's own investigations. The Health Service Commissioner cannot investigate complaints relating to actions taken solely in consequence of the exercise of clinical judgment. Whether the action is taken solely in consequence of the exercise of clinical judgment will be determined by the Health Service Commissioner.

The Mental Health Act Commission

10. Section 120(1) of the Mental Health Act empowers the Mental Health Act Commission to investigate any complaint which a detained patient thinks has not been dealt with satisfactorily by the hospital managers. Nothing in the directions preclude such investigation by the Mental Health Act Commission.

The Police

11. The District General Manager must be consulted where it appears that a criminal offence may have been committed. Where the allegation is serious and substantial the police must be notified immediately.

Complaints about Clinical Judgment

12. The current procedures for dealing with complaints relating to the exercise of clinical judgment by hospital medical and dental staff are subject to an agreement with the medical profession. The procedures were outlined in circular HC(81)5 Annex Part III (A copy is attached as Annex B).

13. The procedures provide for the complainant to be accompanied by a relative or personal friend. It is for the complainant to decide who the friend is. Such a person is there to help and support the complainant and not to act as an advocate nor in a way which detracts from the clinical nature of the consultation. The friend may sometimes help a less articulate complainant explain their concerns but this should not be allowed to create an adversarial situation.

Cancellation of Circulars

14. The guidance contained in HN(78)39, HC(81)5, HN(82)16, HN(83)31 and DA(86)14 is hereby withdrawn and those circulars should be regarded as cancelled.

ANNEX A
DIRECTIONS ON HOSPITAL COMPLAINTS PROCEDURES

The Secretary of State for Social Services, in exercise of the powers conferred on him by Section 17 of the National Health Service Act 1977, hereby directs:-
    (i)   each district health authority in England or Wales;
and each of the following special health authorities:–
    Each of the Authorities for the London Postgraduate Teaching Hospitals;
    The Board of Governors of the Eastman Dental Hospital;
    Broadmoor Hospital Board;
    Moss Side and Park Lane Hospitals Board;
    Rampton Hospital Board;
to make arrangements, as specified or described in the following paragraphs of these directions, for dealing with complaints made by, or on behalf of, persons who are or have been patients at any hospital for the management of which that authority is responsible and for monitoring the effectiveness of, and for publicising, the arrangements made for dealing with such complaints; and
    (ii)   that such arrangements should be made and brought into force not later than 29 July 1988.
    1.   In these Directions:-
    "authority" means any district health authority or special health authority to whom these directions are given;
    "complainant" means a person who is or who has been a patient at a hospital or the person acting on behalf of any such patient in making a complaint in relation to such hospital;
    "designated officer" means a person who has been designated by a health authority as having responsibility for dealing with complaints made in relation to that hospital or group of hospitals.
    2.   (1)   For each hospital or group of hospitals for which an authority has responsibility, there must be an officer designated by the authority as having responsibility for dealing with complaints made in relation to that hospital or group of hospitals.
    (2)   The duties of a designated officer must include responsibility for receiving, and seeing that action is taken upon, any formal complaint made at the hospital or hospitals for which he is given responsibility and, where the complainant had indicated a wish for him so to do, assisting in dealing with a complaint that is likely to be able to be dealt with informally.
    (3)   Except to the extent that the subject matter of a complaint falls within any of the categories specified in the next sub-paragraph of these directions the duties of the designated officer must include responsibility for investigating and reporting on the investigation of any formal complaint to the complainant, to any person involved in the complaint, and to such other persons as the authority may require.
    (4)   To the extent that the subject matter of any complaint made at a hospital or group of hospitals for which a designated officer is responsible:-
    (a)   concerns the exercise of clinical judgment by a hospital doctor or dentist and cannot be resolved by discussion with the consultant concerned; or
    (b)   relates to what the authority is satisfied constitutes a serious untoward incident involving harm to a patient; or
    (c)   relates to the conduct of hospital medical or dental staff which the authority considers ought to be the subject of disciplinary proceedings; or
    (d)   gives reasonable grounds for inviting a police investigation as to whether a criminal offence may have been committed;
the duties of the designated officer in accordance with arrangements made pursuant to these directions shall not involve responsibility for investigating the complaint but the

designated officer shall be required to bring the matter to the attention of his authority who shall, in the case of a matter specified in (a), (b) or (c) of this sub-paragraph, secure that the matter is promptly dealt with in accordance with the appropriate procedure laid down in guidance issued to authorities by the Department of Health and Social Security in respect of England and by the Welsh Office in respect of Wales.

(5)   Arrangements made may include provision for a designated officer to have the assistance of other officers of the authority in carrying out his duties under those arrangements and, with the agreement of the designated officer, such other officers may act on his behalf in the performance of those duties.

3.   Each authority shall secure that arrangements are made for staff at any hospital for which that authority is responsible to seek to deal informally to the satisfaction of the complainant with any complaint made at that hospital and to advise any complainant, whose complaint cannot be so dealt with to his satisfaction, to make a formal complaint to the designated officer for that hospital.

4.   Arrangements for making formal complaints should secure that such complaints are made or recorded in writing. Such complaints should normally be made within three months of the matter complained of arising although the designated officer ought to have a discretion to allow a longer period if satisfied that the complainant had good cause for not having made the complaint earlier. Arrangements made should secure that formal complaints are investigated promptly and that both the complainant and any hospital staff involved are afforded an opportunity to bring to the attention of the designated officer any information or comments they wish to make that are relevant to his investigation of the complaint.

5.   Each authority must monitor arrangements made for dealing with complaints at hospitals for which it is responsible. Arrangements must be made for reports to be prepared at quarterly intervals for use by the authority in monitoring progress on the procedure for dealing with complaints, for considering trends in complaints and for taking remedial action on complaints as appropriate.

6.   Each authority shall take such steps as are necessary to ensure that any patients at, or visitors to, any hospital for which the authority is responsible, as well as the staff working at the hospital, and any Community Health Council covering an area served by that hospital, are fully informed of the arrangements for dealing with complaints made at the hospital and are informed of the identity and location of the designated officer for such hospital.

ANNEX B
MEMORANDUM OF AN AGREEMENT FOR DEALING WITH COMPLAINTS RELATING TO THE EXERCISE OF CLINICAL JUDGMENT BY HOSPITAL MEDICAL AND DENTAL STAFF
(FIRST ISSUED AS PART OF CIRCULAR HC(81)5)

First Stage

18.   As explained in Paragraph 5 of Part I, a complaint may initially be made, and dealt with, orally or in writing. Complaints concerning clinical matters may be made direct to the consultant concerned, or to a health authority or one of its officers. In either case it is the responsibility of the consultant in charge of the patient to look into the clinical aspects of the complaint. This must be the first step in handling the complaint at the first stage.

19.   If another member of the medical[1] staff is involved, the consultant should discuss the complaint with the doctor concerned at the outset and at all later stages in this procedure. It may be helpful to discuss the complaint with the patient's general practitioner. The consultant should try to resolve the complaint within a few days preferably by offering to see the complainant[2] to discuss the matter and seek to resolve

his anxieties. If there is any delay, he should get in touch with the complainant and explain the reason. When the consultant sees the complainant, he should make a brief, strictly factual, record in the hospital notes.

20. Where a complaint is made which involves hospital medical staff other than consultants, the consultant in charge of the patient and the doctor concerned should both be involved in the handling of the complaint at all stages.

21. If the consultant feels the risk of legal action is significant, he should at once bring the matter to the notice of the district general manager. Where there are non-clinical aspects to a complaint made direct to a consultant, the consultant should inform the district general manager, who will arrange for these aspects of the complaint to be considered by an appropriate member of staff.

22. Where a complaint which has a clinical element is made to the authority or one of its officers, the district general manager should show the complaint to the consultant concerned and refer the clinical aspects to him.

23. The normal practice will be for the district general manager to send a written reply to the complainant on behalf of the authority. Any reference to clinical matters in the reply, whether interim or final, should be agreed by the consultant concerned. Sometimes it may be appropriate to confine this to mentioning that the clinical aspects had been discussed between the consultant and the complainant. On occasion, the consultant may wish to send the complainant a written reply direct covering the clinical aspects.

Second Stage

24. Where a complainant is dissatisfied with the reply he has received at the first stage, he may renew his complaint either to the authority, one of its general managers or to the consultant. In any case, if he has not so far put his complaint in writing, he should now be asked to do so before his complaint is considered further. The next step, in this second stage, is for the Regional Medical Officer (RMO) to be at once informed; this should be done by the consultant, informing the district general manager that he has done so. The RMO will discuss the matter with the consultant.

25. At this point, the consultant may indicate to the RMO that he also wishes to discuss the matter with his professional colleagues. After these discussions, he may consider that a further talk with the complainant might resolve the complaint. If this fails, or if the consultant feels that such a meeting would serve no useful purpose, the RMO should discuss with the consultant the value of offering to the complainant the procedure outlined more fully below — whereby the RMO would arrange for two independent consultants to see the complainant jointly to discuss the problem. If in the light of his discussion with the consultant and — where necessary — the complainant, the RMO considers it appropriate, the procedure of the third stage should be set in motion.

Third Stage — Independent Professional Review

26. The procedure at the third stage is intended to deal with complaints which are of a substantial nature, but which are not prima facie (and in the light of legal advice where appropriate) likely to be the subject to more formal action either by the health authority or through the courts. The procedure is intended for use in suitable instances as an alternative to the inquiry procedures provided in HM(66)15, though these will remain available for use when necessary. It would not be appropriate if legal powers such as subpoena seem likely to be required. Nor it is intended that the new procedure should be invoked for complaints of a trivial nature.

27. Arrangements should be made by the RMO for all aspects of the case to be considered by two independent consultants in active practice in the appropriate speciality or specialties. They should be nominated by the Joint Consultants Committee. At least one should be a doctor working in a comparable hospital in another Region.

These "second opinions" should have the opportunity to read all the clinical records. They should discuss the case with the consultant concerned and any other member of the medical staff involved as well as with the complainant. The meeting between the two independent consultants and the complainant should be in the nature of a medical consultation. The consultant who had been in charge of the patient at the time of the event giving rise to the complaint should not be present at the meeting, but should be available if required. The complainant should, if he wishes, be accompanied by a relative or personal friend and might wish to ask the general practitioner to be present.

28.   "Second opinions" should discuss the clinical aspects of the problem fully with the complainant. In cases in which it is their view that the clinical judgment of the medical staff concerned has been exercised responsibly, they should endeavour to resolve the complainant's anxieties. The view they have reached and the outcome of the discussion with the complainant should be reported to the RMO on a confidential basis.

29.   In other cases the "second opinions" might feel that discussion with the medical staff concerned would avoid similar problems arising in the future. When they had held such a discussion they would inform the complainant and would explain to him, as far as appropriate, how it was hoped to overcome the problems which had been identified. They should not provide a detailed report for the complainant but they should report the action they had taken to the RMO. The "second opinions" would also consider whether there were any other circumstances which had contributed to the problems in the case and on which they could usefully make recommendations, which they would include in their report to the RMO. These might include matters requiring action by the health authority, for example the workload carried by the medical or nursing staff.

30.   In exceptional cases it may appear to the "second opinions", at any stage of an investigation, that the particular case is not appropriate to the second opinions procedure and that the complaint would be best pursued by alternative means. In this event they should report to the RMO accordingly.

Concluding Action by the Health Authority

31.   The district general manager will, on completion of the review by the "second opinions", write formally to the complainant on behalf of the authority, with a copy to the consultant. The district general manager will, where appropriate, explain any action the authority has taken as a result of the complaint but, where clinical matters are concerned, he will follow the RMO's advice regarding the comment which would be appropriate. So far as the authority is concerned the matter will remain confidential unless previous or subsequent publicity makes it essential for the authority to reply publicly, in which case comment on clinical matters will be confined to the terms of the district general manager's letter.

The Health Service Commissioner

32.   Complaints relating to clinical judgment remain outside the responsibility of the Health Service Commission. However, it will be possible for him to advise complainants whose complaints contain elements of clinical judgment of the availability of the procedure described in this part of the Memorandum.

---

[1]   In this Memorandum the terms "medical" and "doctor" include "dentist" in appropriate cases.

[2]   The doctor's first responsibility is to the patient, hence this memorandum is concerned with complaints made by patients. It applies also to complaints made by parents or guardians of minors, and relatives of those patients with physical or mental disability limiting their competence to deal with the matter themselves, and of deceased patients. The term "complainant" is used to cover all such cases.

HEALTH CIRCULAR HC(89)34, HC(FP)(89)22

To:
Regional Health Authorities
District Health Authorities
Special Health Authorities

Family Practitioner Committees   ) for
Community Health Councils   ) information   December 1989

CLAIMS OF MEDICAL NEGLIGENCE AGAINST NHS HOSPITAL AND COMMUNITY DOCTORS AND DENTISTS

This circular will be cancelled and deleted from the current communications index on 1 December 1993 unless notified separately.

Summary
This circular describes the arrangements to apply from 1 January 1990 to the handling of claims of negligence against medical and dental staff employed in the hospital and community health services. General practitioners are not directly affected by these new arrangements, unless they have a contract of employment (for example, as a hospital practitioner) with a health authority.

Action Required
Health authorities are asked, with effect from 1 January 1990, to:

(i)   assume responsibility for new and existing claims of medical negligence;

(ii)   ensure a named officer has sufficient authority to make decisions on the conduct of cases on the Authority's behalf;

(iii) cease to require their medical and dental staff to subscribe to a recognised professional defence organisation and cease to reimburse two-thirds of medical defence subscriptions;

(iv)   encourage their medical and dental staff to ensure they have adequate defence cover as appropriate;

(v)   distribute urgently to all their medical and dental staff, including those with honorary NHS contracts, copies of a leaflet explaining the new arrangements (which will be sent separately).

Handling Claims of Medical Negligence
Claims lodged on or after 1 January 1990

1.   Health authorities, as corporate bodies, are legally liable for the negligent acts of their employees in the course of their NHS employment. From 1 January 1990 health authorities will also be formally responsible for the handling and financing of claims of negligence against their medical and dental staff. With regard to claims lodged on or after 1 January 1990, it is for each health authority to determine how it wishes claims against its medical or dental staff to be handled. Health authorities may wish to make use of the services of the medical defence organisations (at rates to be agreed), but they may also put the work out to other advisers or deal with it in-house, provided they have the necessary expertise.

Claims notified to an MDO before 1 January 1990

2.   Subject to final agreement with the medical defence organisations (MDOs) on the detailed financial arrangements, health authorities will take over financial responsibility for cases outstanding at 1 January 1990. The medical defence organisations have been asked to inform health authorities of the cases in which they may have a substantial liability.

3. Health authorities are entitled to take over the management of any cases outstanding, since they will become liable for the costs and damages arising. However, they are strongly advised to employ the MDOs to continue to handle such claims, in consultation with them and on their behalf, until completion. This is essential not only because of the amount of work in progress, but mainly because the re-insurance cover of the MDOs for claims initiated before 1990 would remain valid only if the MDO currently handling the case continued to do so. If required, health authorities should cooperate with an MDO's re-insurers in the conduct of a claim. Since some of the cover is on an aggregate basis the advice in this paragraph applies to both large and small claims. Health authorities are asked to give prior notice to the Department (finance contact point at paragraph 17) where they wish to adopt a different approach in the handling of claims notified before 1 January 1990.

General handling principles

4. Health authorities should take the essential decisions on the handling of claims of medical negligence against their staff, using MDOs or other bodies as their agents and advisers. Authorities should particularly ensure that authority is appropriately delegated to enable decisions to be made promptly, especially where representatives are negotiating a settlement, and are asked to give such authority to a named officer.

5. In deciding how a case should be handled, and in particular whether to resist a claim or seek an out-of-court settlement, health authorities and those advising them should pay particular attention to any view expressed by the practitioner(s) concerned and to any potentially damaging effect on the professional reputation of the practitioner(s) concerned. They should also have clear regard to:

  (i) any point of principle or of wider application raised by the case; and
  (ii) the costs involved.

6. Where a case involves both a health authority and a general medical practitioner (or any other medical or dental practitioner in relation to work for which a health authority is not responsible), the health authority should consult with the practitioner(s) cited or their representative to seek agreement on how the claim should be handled. Where a health authority (or its employees) alone is cited, but there is reason to believe that the action or inaction of a practitioner outside the health authority's responsibility was a material factor in the negligence concerned, the health authority should similarly consult with a view to obtaining a contribution to the eventual costs and damages. Conversely, in cases where such a practitioner alone is cited, there may be circumstances in which an MDO asks the health authority to make a similar contribution, as if it were a defendant. In any such circumstances, health authorities should cooperate fully in the formulation of the defence and should seek to reach agreement out of court on the proportion in which any costs and damages awarded to the plaintiff should be borne.

7. It is open to the practitioner concerned to employ at his or her expense an expert adviser, but the practitioner can be represented separately in court only with the agreement of the Court. The plaintiff and the health authority may agree to separate representation for the practitioner, but under normal circumstances the health authority should not do so if it considers that this would lead to additional costs or damages falling on the health authority.

Coverage of the Scheme and Practical Arrangements

8. The Health Departments' views on some of the questions that have arisen about the coverage and practical operation of the new arrangements are at Annex A. The indemnity scheme applies to all staff in the course of their HCHS employment, including those engaged through private agencies. The Annex is to be reproduced as a leaflet, which the Health Departments will shortly be making available to health authorities who should distribute them to all their medical and dental staff, including those with honorary NHS contracts.

9.   Since authorities will be taking financial responsibility in cases of medical negligence it will no longer be necessary for them to require employed staff to subscribe to a recognised professional defence organisation, for example, as in the recommended form of consultant contract at Annex D of PM(79)11. Authorities should inform their medical and dental staff that the provision no longer applies, but they should encourage such staff to ensure that they have adequate defence cover as appropriate.

Financial Arrangements
Pooling arrangements for major settlements

10.   Where they have not already done so RHAs are strongly recommended to introduce arrangements (for both medical and non-medical negligence) so as to share with Districts the legal costs and damages of individual large settlements or awards, whose incidence can be quite random. The Department will be making arrangements for Authorities without an RHA, for example the London SHAs, to limit the financial effects on them of substantial settlements.

Funding of claims

11.   Subject to final agreement with the MDOs, the public sector will have access to a share of the MDOs' reserves in respect of the hospital and community health services. It is expected that the MDOs will each establish a fund to be drawn on according to criteria set by the Health Departments. The Health Departments will be introducing a transitional scheme under which these reserves will be made available to assist health authorities to meet the costs of particularly large settlements. These will usually, but not necessarily, be cases which arose from incidents before 1 January 1990. The Departments propose to set a threshold, initially £300,000 in England and Wales; 80 per cent of the costs of a settlement above this threshold, including the legal costs, would be met from this source, until the identified funds are exhausted. Detailed information on the means of access to the funds will be given in the December 1989 edition of "Financial Matters".

NHS Trusts

12.   NHS Trusts will be responsible for claims of negligence against their medical and dental staff. The Departments are considering what arrangements will apply to NHS Trusts and further guidance will be issued in due course.

Monitoring Resource Consequences

13.   To enable the Department of Health to assess the resource consequences of these changes, health authorities will be required to submit a return (in the form set out at Annex B) shortly after the end of each financial year, starting with the period 1 January – 31 March 1990 in order to obtain an early indication of the costs of the scheme.

Review

14.   The Health Departments plan to review the operation of these arrangements in 1992, including the effects on individual practitioners.

ANNEX A
MEDICAL NEGLIGENCE: NEW NHS ARRANGEMENTS

Introduction

1.   New arrangements for dealing with medical negligence claims in the hospital and community health services are being introduced from 1 January 1990. Subject to final agreement with the medical defence organisations on the financial arrangements, health authorities will take direct financial responsibility for cases initiated before that date, as well as for new claims. In future, medical and dental staff employed by health

authorities (health boards in Scotland and Northern Ireland) will no longer be required under the terms of their contracts to subscribe to a medical defence organisation. However, the health authority indemnity will cover only health authority responsibilities. The Health Departments advise practitioners to maintain their defence body membership in order to ensure they are covered for any work which does not fall within the scope of the indemnity scheme.

Set out below are the Health Departments' replies to some of the questions most commonly asked about the operation of the new arrangements.

2. *Why is this change necessary?*
Medical defence subscriptions rose rapidly in the 1980s, because of growth both in the number of medical negligence cases and in the size of the awards made by the courts. Subscriptions tripled between 1986 and 1988, and the Doctors' and Dentists' Review Body concluded that to take account of the increase in subscriptions through practitioners' pay would lead to distortions in pay and pensions. The pressure to relate subscription rates to the practitioner's specialty underlined the difficulty of maintaining the system. The Health Departments issued in March 1989 a proposal for a health authority indemnity. The new arrangements follow discussions with the medical defence organisations, the medical profession, health authority management and other interested bodies.

Coverage
3. *Who is covered by the health authority indemnity scheme?*
Health authorities as employers are liable at law for the negligence (acts or omissions) of their staff in the course of their NHS employment. The legal position is the same for medical and dental staff as for other NHS employees, but for many years doctors and dentists have themselves taken out medical defence cover through the three medical defence organisations (MDOs). Under the indemnity scheme, health authorities will take direct responsibility for costs and damages arising from medical negligence where they (as employers) are vicariously liable for the acts and omissions of their medical and dental staff.

4. *Does this include clinical academics and research workers?*
Health authorities are vicariously liable for the work done by university medical staff and other research workers under their honorary contracts in the course of their NHS duties, but not for pre-clinical or other work in the university.

5. *Is private work in NHS hospitals covered by the indemnity scheme?*
Health authorities will not be responsible for a consultant's private practice, even in an NHS hospital. However, where junior medical staff are involved in the care of private patients in NHS hospitals, they would normally be doing so as part of their contract with the health authority. It remains advisable that any junior doctor who might be involved in any work outside the scope of his or her employment should have medical defence (or insurance) cover.

6. *Is Category 2 work covered?*
Category 2 work (e.g. reports for insurance companies) is by definition not undertaken for the employing health authority, and will therefore not be covered by the indemnity scheme; medical defence cover would be appropriate.

7. *Are GMC disciplinary proceedings covered?*
Health authorities should not be financially responsible for the defence of medical staff involved in GMC disciplinary proceedings. It is the responsibility of the practitioner concerned to take out medical defence cover against such an eventuality.

8. *Is a hospital doctor doing a GP locum covered?*
This would not be the responsibility of the health authority, since it would be general practice. The hospital doctor and the general practitioners concerned should ensure that there is appropriate medical defence cover.

9. *Is a GP seeing his own patient in hospital covered?*
A GP providing medical care to patients in hospital under a contractual arrangement, e.g. where the GP was employed as a clinical assistant, will be covered by the health authority indemnity. On the other hand, if the health authority is essentially providing only hotel services and the patient(s) remain in the care of the GP, the GP would be responsible and medical defence cover would be appropriate.

10. *Are GP trainees working in general practice covered?*
In general practice the responsibility for training and for paying the salary of a GP trainee rests with the trainer (with funds from the FPC). Where the trainee's medical defence subscription is higher than the subscription of an SHO in the hospital service, he or she may apply through the trainer for the difference in subscription to be reimbursed. While the trainee is receiving a salary in general practice it is advisable that both the trainee and the trainer, and indeed other members of the practice, should have medical defence cover.

11. *Are clinical trials covered?*
The new arrangements do not alter the current legal position. If the health authority was responsible for a clinical trial authorised under the Medicines Act 1968 or its subordinate legislation and that trial was carried out by or on behalf of a doctor involving NHS patients of his, such a doctor would be covered by the indemnity scheme. Similarly, for a trial not involving medicines, the health authority would take financial responsibility unless the trial were covered by such other indemnity as may have been agreed between the health authority and those responsible for the trial. In any case, health authorities should take steps to make sure that they are informed of clinical trials in which their staff are taking part in their NHS employment and that these trials have the required Research Ethics Committee approval.

12. *Would a doctor be covered if he was working other than in accordance with the duties of his post?*
Such a doctor would be covered by the health authority indemnity for actions in the course of NHS employment, and this should be interpreted liberally. For work not covered in this way the doctor may have a civil, or even in extreme circumstances criminal, liability for his actions.

13. *Are doctors attending accident victims ("Good Samaritan" acts) covered?*
By definition, "Good Samaritan" acts are not part of the doctor's work for the employing authority. Medical defence organisations are willing to provide low-cost cover against the (unusual) event of a doctor performing such an act being sued for negligence.

14. *Are doctors in public health medicine or in community health services doing work for local authorities covered? Are occupational physicians covered?*
Doctors in public health medicine, or clinical medical officers, carrying out local authority functions under their health authority contract would be acting in the course of their NHS employment. They will therefore be covered by the health authority indemnity. The same principle applies to occupational physicians employed by health authorities.

15. *Will NHS hospital doctors working for other agencies, e.g. the Prison Service, be covered?*
In general, health authorities will not be financially responsible for the acts of NHS staff when they are working on a contractual basis for other agencies. (Conversely, they will be responsible where, for example, a Ministry of Defence doctor works in an NHS hospital.) Either the agency commissioning the work would be responsible, or the doctor should have medical defence cover. However, health authorities' indemnity should cover work for which they pay a fee, such as domiciliary visits and family planning services.

16. *Are retired doctors covered?*
The health authority indemnity will apply to acts or omissions in the course of NHS employment, regardless of when the claim was notified. Health authorities will thus cover doctors who have subsequently left the Service, but they may seek their cooperation in statements in the defence of a case.

17. *Are doctors offering services to voluntary bodies such as the Red Cross or hospices covered?*
The health authority would be responsible for the doctor's actions only if the health authority were responsible for the medical staffing of the voluntary body. If not, the doctors concerned may wish to ensure that they have medical defence cover, as they do at present.

18. *Will a health authority provide cover for a locum hospital doctor?*
A health authority will take financial responsibility for the acts and omissions of a locum doctor, whether "internal" or provided by an external agency.

19. *Are private sector rotations for hospital staff covered?*
The medical staff of independent hospitals are responsible for their own medical defence cover, subject to the requirements of the hospital managers. If NHS staff in the training grades work in independent hospitals as part of their NHS training, they would be covered by the health authority indemnity, provided that such work was covered by an NHS contract.

20. *Will academic General Practice be covered?*
The Health Departments have no plans to extend the health authority indemnity to academic departments of general practice. In respect of general medical services FPCs will be making payments by fees and allowances which include an element for expenses, of which medical defence subscriptions are a part.

Practical Arrangements

21. *On what basis will medical defence organisations handle claims for health authorities?*
MDOs, in advising on claims for health authorities, will act as their agents; the charging arrangements for such services are for agreement between the MDO and the Authority concerned.

22. *Will doctors be reimbursed by MDOs for the "unexpired" portion of their subscriptions?*
This is a matter between each MDO and its members.

23. *Will membership of a medical defence organisation continue to be a contractual obligation?*
On an individual basis doctors and dentists may wish to continue their membership in order to receive the cover referred to in paragraphs 5–20 above, as well as the other legal and advisory services provided by the MDOs. The Health Departments are advising

health authorities that they should no longer require their medical and dental staff to subscribe to an MDO, but a health authority could require a doctor to be a member of an MDO if the doctor were to be carrying out private work on NHS premises. The two-thirds reimbursement of subscriptions will cease at the end of 1989.

24.   *Will medical defence subscriptions be tax-allowable in future?*
The Health Departments understand that medical defence subscriptions will continue to be allowable under income tax rules.

25.   *What hapens if a doctor wishes to contest a claim which the health authority would prefer to settle out of court, e.g. where a point of principle or a doctor's reputation is at stake?*
While the final decision in a case rests with the health authority since it will bear the financial consequences, it should take careful note of the practitioner's view. Health authorities may seek the advice of the relevant MDO on whether a case should be contested, and they should not settle cases without good cause.

26.   *If a doctor wishes to have separate representation in a case, what would be the extent of his liability?*
Since it is the health authority which is sued for the medical negligence of its staff and which will in future be solely financially liable, then it must have the ultimate right to decide how the defence of a case is to be handled. Subject to this, a health authority may welcome a practitioner being separately advised in a case without cost to the health authority. However, if a practitioner claims that his interests in any case are distinct from those of the health authority and wishes to be separately represented in the proceedings, he will need the agreement of the plaintiff, the health authority and the court. If liability is established, he could have to pay not only his own legal expenses but also any further costs incurred as a result of his being separately represented. The health authority would remain liable for the full award of damages to the plaintiff.

27.   *Will health authorities put restrictions on the clinical autonomy of doctors?*
Health authorities have a responsibility to organise services in a manner which is in the best interests of patients. In the past, medical defence organisations have advised doctors and dentists on patterns of practice carrying unacceptable dangers to patients. However, there is no question of health authorities barring certain services which carry risks but are a high priority for patients.

28.   *Will health authorities be able to secure statements from doctors for the defence of a case of medical negligence?*
Health authorities will need cooperation from medical and dental staff if they are to defend cases. As part of this, practitioners should supply such statements or documents as the health authority or its solicitors may reasonably require in investigating or defending any claim. A doctor's refusal without good reason to provide a statement could result in the health authority being unable to defend itself properly and so incurring additional costs.

29.   *Will health authorities be able to trace doctors who formerly worked for them?*
It is accepted that health authorities may have difficulty in tracing the doctors responsible, especially if they were junior medical staff at the time, and in securing statements from them; they may find the MDOs helpful in this respect. Often, however, good medical records kept at the time will be of more value than statements made some years after the event.

30.   *Will the new arrangements apply to NHS Trust hospitals (self-governing units)?*
As employers, NHS Trusts will be vicariously liable for the acts of their employed medical and dental staff, and will take the financial responsibility for negligence. Further guidance will be issued in due course.

Financial Effects

31. *How can District Health Authorities meet damages which could be as much as £1m for a single case?*

RHAs have been asked to make arrangements under which they will provide an element of cost-sharing with Districts for medical negligence costs above a certain level, as most RHAs do for non-medical negligence actions at present. And for a transitional period health authorities will have access (under certain criteria) to some of the reserves of the MDOs.

32. *The incidence of medical negligence damages may be uneven as between Regions; how will that be met?*

It is quite likely that some Regions will have to pay out more under the new arrangements than they would in reimbursing two-thirds of medical defence subscriptions. The funds from the MDOs will be of some help in the short term, but in the longer run the incidence of medical negligence costs and damages will fall on the Regions where they arise.

ANNEX B

INFORMATION TO BE RETURNED ANNUALLY, NO LATER THAN 31 MAY (STARTING 31/5/90)

1. The following information should be supplied for the previous financial year:

    i. The number of claims of medical negligence against the health authority and/or its employees, including the number of cases brought forward from an earlier period;

    ii. The number of such cases settled during the period with the health authority's costs, including damages payable, in the following cost bands:

	Number of cases	£	£
(a)		0 – 100,000	
(b)		100,000 – 200,000	
(c)		200,000 – 300,000	
(d)		over £300,000	

    iii. The total cost of the settlements reached or awards made; distinguishing

    (a) the Authority's costs from the payment of the plaintiff's costs and damages; and

    (b) an estimate of costs and damages attributable to medical negligence, as distinct from negligence of other staff.

2. Returns to be sent to: FPS1A2, Room 426 Portland Court, 158–176 Great Portland Street, London W1N 5TB.

HEALTH CIRCULAR HC(90)22
A GUIDE TO CONSENT
FOR EXAMINATION OR TREATMENT

CHAPTER 1
A PATIENT'S RIGHTS IN ACCEPTING TREATMENT

1. A patient has the right under common law to give or withhold consent prior to examination or treatment (except in special circumstances which are described in Chapter 2, paragraphs 10–15, and Chapter 4). This is one of the basic principles of health care. Subject to certain exceptions the doctor or health professional and/or health authority may face an action for damages if a patient is examined or treated without consent.

2. Patients are entitled to receive sufficient information in a way that they can understand about the proposed treatments, the possible alternatives and any substantial risks, so that they can make a balanced judgment. Patients must be allowed to decide whether they will agree to the treatment, and they may refuse treatment or withdraw consent to treatment at any time.

3. Care should be taken to respect the patient's wishes. This is particularly important when patients may be involved in the training of professionals in various disciplines and students. An explanation should be given of the need for practical experience and agreement obtained before proceeding. It should be made clear that a patient may refuse to agree without this adversely affecting his or her care.

4. When patients give information to health professionals they are entitled to assume that the information will be kept confidential and will not be disclosed to anyone without their consent other than for the provision of their health care. The only exceptions to this general rule are where disclosure is ordered by a Court; required by statute; or considered to be in the public interest e.g. for some forms of research. Further information will be issued shortly in health circulars on "Confidentiality, Use and Disclosure of NHS Information" and "Guidance on Local Research Ethics Committees." Where disclosure is made in the public interest appropriate safeguards must be applied.

CHAPTER 2
HEALTH PROFESSIONAL'S ROLE IN ADVISING THE PATIENT AND OBTAINING CONSENT TO TREATMENT

Advising the patient

1. Where a choice of treatment might reasonably be offered the health professional may always advise the patient of his/her recommendations together with reasons for selecting a particular course of action. Enough information must normally be given to ensure that they understand the nature, consequences and any substantial risks of the treatment proposed so that they are able to take a decision based on that information. Though it should be assumed that most patients will wish to be well informed, account should be taken of those who may find this distressing.

2. The patient's ability to appreciate the significance of the information should be assessed. For example with patients who:
  i.   may be shocked, distressed or in pain;
  ii. have difficulty in understanding English;
  iii. have impaired sight, or hearing or speech;
  iv. are suffering from mental disability but who nevertheless have the capacity to give consent to the proposed procedure *(see also Chapter 5 — Consent by patients suffering from mental disorder)*.

3. Occasionally and subject to the agreement of the patient, and where circumstances permit, it may help if a close family member or a friend can be present at the discussion when consent is sought. If this is not possible another member of the staff may be able to assist the patient in understanding. Where there are language problems, it is important an interpreter be sought whenever possible.

4. A doctor will have to exercise his or her professional skill and judgment in deciding what risks the patient should be warned of and the terms in which the warning should be given. However, a doctor has a duty to warn patients of substantial or unusual risk inherent in any proposed treatment. This is especially so with surgery but may apply to other procedures including drug therapy and radiation treatment. Guidance on the amount of information and warnings or risk to be given to patients can be found in the judgment of the House of Lords in the case of Sidaway v Gov of Bethlem Royal Hospital [1985] AC 871 *(See also Chapter 6)*.

Obtaining consent

5. Consent to treatment may be implied or express. In many cases patients do not explicitly give express consent but their agreement may be implied by compliant actions, e.g. by offering an arm for the taking of a blood sample. Express consent is given when patients confirm their agreement to a procedure or treatment in clear and explicit terms, whether orally or in writing.

6. Oral consent may be sufficient for the vast majority of contacts with patients by doctors and nurses and other health professionals. Written consent should be obtained for any procedure or treatment carrying any substantial risk or substantial side effect. If the patient is capable, written consent should always by obtained for general anaesthesia, surgery, certain forms of drug therapy, e.g. cytotoxic therapy and therapy involving the use of ionising radiation. Oral or written consent should be recorded in the patient's notes with relevant details of the health professional's explanation. Where written consent is obtained it should be incorporated into the notes.

7. *Standard consent form.* The main purpose of written consent is to provide documentary evidence that an explanation of the proposed procedure or treatment was given and that consent was sought and obtained. The model consent forms *(see Appendices)* set out the requirements for obtaining valid consent to treatment in terms which will be readily understood by the patient. In the majority of cases these forms will be used by registered medical or dental staff but there may be occasions when other health professionals will wish to record formally that consent has been obtained for a particular procedure. A separate form is available for their use.

8. It should be noted that the purpose of obtaining a signature on the consent form is not an end in itself. The most important element of a consent procedure is the duty to ensure that patients understand the nature and purpose of the proposed treatment. Where a patient has not been given appropriate information then consent may not always have been obtained despite the signature on the form.

9. Consent given for one procedure or episode or treatment does not give any automatic right to undertake any other procedure. A doctor may, however, undertake further treatment if the circumstances are such that a patient's consent cannot reasonably be requested and provided the treatment is immediately necessary and the patient has not previously indicated that the further treatment would be unacceptable.

SPECIAL CIRCUMSTANCES

Treatment of Children and Young people

10. *Children under the age of 16 years.* Where a child under the age of 16 achieves a sufficient understanding of what is proposed, that child may consent to a doctor or other health professional making an examination and giving treatment. The doctor or health professional must be satisfied that any such child has sufficient understanding of what is involved in the treatment which is proposed. A full note should be made of the factors taken into account by the doctor in making his or her assessment of the child's capacity to give a valid consent. In the majority of cases children will be accompanied by their parents during consultations. Where, exceptionally, a child is seen alone, efforts should be made to persuade the child that his or her parents should be informed except in circumstances where it is clearly not in the child's best interests to do so. Parental consent should be obtained where a child does not have sufficient understanding and is under age 16 save in an emergency where there is not time to obtain it.

11. *Young people over the age of 16 years.* The effect of Section 8 of the Family Law Reform Act 1969 *(see Chapter 3)* is that the consent of a young person who has attained 16 years to any surgical, medical or dental treatment is sufficient in itself and it is not necessary to obtain a separate consent from the parent or guardian. In cases

where a child is over age 16 but is not competent to give a valid consent, then the consent of a parent or guardian must be sought. However, such power only extends until that child is 18.

12. *Refusal of parental consent to urgent or life-saving treatment.* Where time permits, court action may be taken so that consent may be obtained from a judge. Otherwise hospital authorities should rely on the clinical judgment of the doctors, normally the consultants, concerned after a full discussion between the doctor and the parents. In such a case the doctor should obtain a written supporting opinion from a medical colleague that the patient's life is in danger if the treatment is withheld and should discuss the need to treat with the parents or guardian in the presence of a witness. The doctor should record the discussion in the clinical notes and ask the witness to countersign the record. In these circumstances and where practicable the doctor may wish to consult his or her defence organisation. If he/she has followed the procedure set out above and has then acted in the best interests of the patient and with due professional competence and according to their own professional conscience, they are unlikely to be criticised by a court or by their professional body.

Adult or competent young person refusing treatment
13.   Some adult patients will wish to refuse some parts of their treatment. This will include those whose religious beliefs prevent them accepting a blood transfusion. Whatever the reason for the refusal such patients should receive a detailed explanation of the nature of their illness and the need for the treatment or transfusion proposed. They should also be warned in clear terms that the doctor may properly decline to modify the procedure and of the possible consequences if the procedure is not carried out. If the patient then refuses to agree, and he or she is competent, the refusal must be respected. The doctor should record this in the clinical notes and where possible have it witnessed.

Teaching on patients
14.   Detailed guidance about medical students in hospitals is the subject of a separate circular to be issued shortly. It should not be assumed, especially in a teaching hospital, that a patient is available for teaching purposes or for practical experience by clinical medical or dental or other staff under training.

Examination or Treatment without the patient's consent
15.   The following are examples of occasions when examination or treatment may proceed without obtaining the patient's consent:
     i.   For life-saving procedures where the patient is unconscious and cannot indicate his or her wishes.
     ii.   Where there is a statutory power requiring the examination of a patient, for example, under the Public Health (Control of Disease) Act 1984. However an explanation should be offered and the patient's cooperation should nevertheless be sought.
     iii.   In certain cases where a minor is a ward of court and the court decides that a specific treatment is in the child's best interests.
     iv.   Treatment for mental disorder of a patient liable to be detained in hospital under the Mental Health Act 1983 *(see Chapter 5)*.
     v.   Treatment for physical disorder where the patient is incapable of giving consent by reason of mental disorder, and the treatment is in the patient's best interest *(see Chapter 5)*.

CHAPTER 4
EXAMPLES OF TREATMENTS WHICH HAVE RAISED CONCERN

Maternity Services
1. Principles of consent are the same in maternity services as in other areas of medicine. It is important that the proposed care is discussed with the woman, preferably in the early antenatal period, when any special wishes she expresses should be recorded in the notes, but of course the patient may change her mind about these issues at any stage, including during labour.

2. Decisions may have to be taken swiftly at a time when the woman's ability to give consent is impaired, e.g. as a result of medication, including analgesics. If the safety of the woman or child is at stake the obstetrician or midwife should take any reasonable action that is necessary. If, in the judgment of the relevant health professional, the woman is temporarily unable to make a decision, it may be advisable for the position to be explained to her husband or partner if available, but his consent (or withholding of consent) cannot legally over-ride the clinical judgment of the health professional, as guided by the previously expressed wishes of the patient herself.

Breast Cancer
3. The usual principles of explaining proposed treatment and obtaining the patient's consent should be followed in treating cases of breast cancer. Breast cancer does not normally require emergency treatment. The patient needs reassurance that a mastectomy will not be performed without her consent, and that unless she has indicated otherwise the need for any further surgery will be fully discussed with her in the light of biopsy and other results. This is a particular case of the principle, set out in para 9 of Chapter 2, that consent to an initial treatment or investigation does not imply consent to further treatment.

Tissue and Organ Donation: Risk of Transmitted Infection
4. Where tissues or organs are to be transplanted, the recipient should be informed at the time when consent to operation is obtained of the small, but unavoidable risk of the transplant being infected. Further guidance is available in a CMO letter, "HIV Infection, tissue banks and organ donation" (PL/CMO/92).

CHAPTER 5
CONSENT BY PATIENTS SUFFERING FROM MENTAL DISORDER

1. Consent to treatment must be given freely and without coercion and be based on information about the nature, purpose and likely effects of treatment presented in a way that is understandable by the patient. The capacity of the person to understand the information given will depend on their intellectual state, the nature of their mental disorder, and any variability over time of their mental state. The ability of mentally disordered people to make and communicate decisions may similarly vary from time to time.

2. The presence of mental disorder does not by itself imply incapacity, nor does detention under the Mental Health Act. Each patient's capability for giving consent, has to be judged individually in the light of the nature of the decision required and the mental state of the patient at the time.

Mental Health Legislation — treatment for mental disorders
3. The Mental Health Act 1983 took a major step forward in providing for mentally disordered people, detained in hospital under the powers of the Act, to be given treatment for **mental disorder,** without their consent where they are incapable of

giving consent. Certain procedures and safeguards are laid down in relation to specific groups of treatment, including the need for mutidisciplinary discussion and the agreement of doctors appointed to give a second opinion.

Mental Incapacity and treatment for physical conditions

4.   The Mental Health Act 1983 does not contain provisions to enable treatment of **physical disorders** without consent either for detained patients or those people who may be suffering from mental disorder but who are not detained under the Mental Health Act.

The administration of treatment for physical conditions to people incapable of giving consent and making their own treatment decisions is a matter of concern to all involved in the care of such people, whether they are detained in hospital or in hospital but non-detained, in residential care or in the community.

The House of Lords' decision In Re F [1989] 2 WLR 1025; [1989] 2 All ER 545

5.   This decision helped to clarify the common law in relation to general medical and surgical treatment of people who lack the capacity to give consent. No-one may give consent on behalf of an adult but the substantive law is that a proposed operation or treatment is lawful if it is in the best interests of the patient and unlawful if it is not. Guidance given in that case is set out below.

i.   In considering the lawfulness of medical and surgical treatment given to a patient who for any reason, temporary or permanent, lacks the capacity to give or to communicate consent to treatment, it was stated to be axiomatic that treatment which is necessary to preserve the life, health or well-being of the patient may lawfully be given without consent.

ii.   The standard of care required of the doctor concerned in all cases is laid down in Bolam v Friern Hospital Management Committee [1957] 1 WLR 582, namely, that he or she must act in accordance with a responsible body of relevant professional opinion.

iii.   In many cases, it will not only be lawful for doctors, on the ground of necessity to operate or give other medical treatment to adult patients disabled from giving their consent, it will also be their common law duty to do so.

iv.   In the case of the mentally disordered, when the state is permanent or semi-permanent, action properly taken may well transcend such matters as surgical operation or substantial medical treatment and may extend to include such (humdrum) matters as routine medical and dental treatment and even simple care such as dressing and undressing and putting to bed.

v.   In practice, a decision may involve others besides the doctor. It must surely be good practice to consult relatives and others who are concerned with the care of the patient. Sometimes, of course, consultation with a specialist or specialists will be required; and in others, especially where the decision involves more than a purely medical opinion, an inter-disciplinary team will in practice participate in the decision.

Documentation

6.   Proposals for treatment should as a matter of good practice, be discussed with the multidisciplinary team and where necessary other doctors and, with the consent of the patient where this is possible, with their nearest relative or friend. The decisions taken should be documented in the clinical case notes. In cases involving anaesthesia, and surgery, or where the treatment carries substantial or unusual risk it would also be advisable for documentation to record that the patient is incapable of given consent to treatment and that the doctor in charge of the patient's treatment is of the opinion that the treatment proposed should be given and that it is in the patient's best interests. A model form is suggested to register medical opinion — where a patient is incapable of giving consent (Appendix B).

Sterilisation

7.   In **Re F** it was said that special features applied in the case of an operation for sterilisation. Having regard to those matters, it was stated to be highly desirable as a matter of good practice to involve the court in the decision to operate. In practice an application should be made to a court whenever it is proposed to perform such an operation. The procedure to be used is to apply for a declaration that the proposed operation for sterilisation is lawful, and the following guidance was given as to the form to be followed in such proceedings:

   i.   applications for a declaration that a proposed operation on or medical treatment for a patient can lawfully be carried out despite the inability of such patient to consent thereto should be by way of originating summons issuing out of the Family Division of the High Court;

   ii.   the applicant should normally be those responsible for the care of the patient or those intending to carry out the proposed operation or other treatment, if it is declared to be lawful;

   iii.   the patient must always be a party and should normally be a respondent. In cases in which the patient is a respondent the patient's guardian *ad litem* should normally be the Official Solicitor. In any cases in which the Official Solicitor is not either the next friend or the guardian *ad litem* of the patient or an applicant he shall be a respondent;

   iv.   with a view to protecting the patient's privacy, but subject always to the judge's discretion, the hearing will be in chambers, but the decision and the reasons for that decision will be given in open court.

CHAPTER 6
THE SIDAWAY CASE

The question of how much information and warning of risk which should be given to a patient was considered by the House of Lords in the case of Sidaway v Gov of Bethlem Royal Hospital [1985] AC 871. Lord Bridge indicated that a decision on what degree of disclosure of risks is best calculated to assist a particular patient to make a rational choice as to whether or not to undergo a particular treatment must primarily be a matter of clinical judgment. He was of the further opinion that a judge might in certain circumstances come to the conclusion that the disclosure of a particular risk was so obviously necessary to an informed choice that no reasonably prudent medical man would fail to make it. The kind of case which Lord Bridge had in mind would be an operation involving a substantial risk of grave adverse consequences. Lord Templeman stated that there was no doubt that a doctor ought to draw the attention of a patient to a danger which may be special in kind or magnitude or special to the patient. He further stated that it was the obligation of the doctor to have regard to the best interests of the patient but at the same time to make available to the patient sufficient information to enable the patient to reach a balanced judgment if he chooses to do so.

CONSENT FORM

For medical or dental investigation, treatment or operation

Health Authority . . . .   Patient's Surname . . . .

Hospital . . . .   Other Names . . . .

Unit Number. . . . .   Date of Birth . . . .

Sex: *(please tick)*   Male ☐   Female ☐

DOCTORS OR DENTISTS *(This part to be completed by doctor or dentist. See notes on the reverse)*

TYPE OF OPERATION INVESTIGATION OR TREATMENT

I confirm that I have explained the operation investigation or treatment, and such appropriate options as are available and the type of anaesthetic, if any (general/regional/sedation) proposed, to the patient in terms which in my judgement are suited to the understanding of the patient and/or to one of the parents or guardians of the patient

Signature. . . . .   Date . . . /. . . /. . . . .

Name of doctor or dentist . . . .

PATIENT/PARENT/GUARDIAN

1. Please read this form and the notes overleaf very carefully.

2. If there is anything that you don't understand about the explanation, or if you want more information, you should ask the doctor or dentist.

3. Please check that all the information on the form is correct. If it is, and you understand the explanation, then sign the form.

I am the patient/parent/guardian *(delete as necessary)*

I agree	■ to what is proposed which has been explained to me by the doctor/dentist named on this form.
	■ to the use of the type of anaesthetic that I have been told about.
I understand	■ that the procedure may not be done by the doctor/dentist who has been treating me so far.
	■ that any procedure in addition to the investigation or treatment described on this form will only be carried out if it is necessary and in my best interests and can be justified for medical reasons.
I have told	■ the doctor or dentist about any additional procedures I would <u>not</u> wish to be carried out straightaway without my having the opportunity to consider them first.

Signature   . . . .

Name   . . . .

Address   . . . .

(if not the patient)   . . . .

. . . .

NHS *Management Executive*

NOTES TO:

Doctors, Dentists

A patient has a legal right to grant or withhold consent prior to examination or treatment. Patients should be given sufficient information, in a way they can understand, about the proposed treatment and the possible alternatives. Patients must be allowed to decide whether they will agree to the treatment and they may refuse or withdraw consent to treatment at any time. The patient's consent to treatment should be recorded on this form (further guidance is given in HC(90)22 *(A Guide to Consent for Examination or Treatment.)*

Patients

■ The doctor or dentist is here to help you. He or she will explain the proposed treatment and what the alternatives are. You can ask any questions and seek further information. You can refuse the treatment.

■ You may ask for a relative, or friend, or a nurse to be present.

■ Training health professionals is essential to the continuation of the health service and improving the quality of care. Your treatment may provide an important opportunity for such training, where necessary under the careful supervision of a senior doctor or dentist. You may refuse any involvement in a formal training programme without this adversely affecting your care and treatment.

CONSENT FORM

For sterilisation or vasectomy

Health Authority	Patient's Surname . . . .
Hospital	Other Names . . . .
Unit Number.	Date of Birth . . . .
	Sex: *(please tick)* Male ☐ Female ☐

DOCTORS *(This part to be completed by doctor. See notes on the reverse)*

TYPE OF OPERATION: STERILISATION OR VASECTOMY

Complete this part of the form

I confirm that I have explained the procedure and any anaesthetic (general/regional) required, to the patient in terms which in my judgement are suited to his/her understanding.

Signature. . . . .   Date. . . . /. . . /. . . . .

Name of doctor . . . .

PATIENT

1. Please read this form very carefully.

2. If there is anything that you don't understand about the explanation, or if you want more information, you should ask the doctor.

3. Please check that all the information on the form is correct. If it is, and you understand the explanation, then sign the form.

I am the patient

I agree	■ to have this operation, which has been explained to me by the doctor named on this form.
	■ to have the type of anaesthetic that I have been told about.
I understand	■ that the operation may not be done by the doctor who has been treating me so far.
	■ that the aim of the operation is to stop me having any children and it might not be possible to reverse the effects of the operation.
	■ that sterilisation/vasectomy can sometimes fail, and that there is a very small chance that I may become fertile again after some time.
	■ that any procedure in addition to the investigation or treatment described on this form will only be carried out if it is necessary and in my best interests and can be justified for medical reasons.
I have told	■ the doctor about any additional procedures I would <u>not</u> wish to be carried out straightaway without my having the opportunity to consider them first.
For vasectomy I understand	■ that I may remain fertile or become fertile again after some time.
	■ that I will have to use some other contraceptive method until 2 tests in a row show that I am not producing sperm, if I do not want to father any children.

Signature   . . . .

NHS Management Executive

NOTES TO:

Doctors

A patient has a legal right to grant or withhold consent prior to examination or treatment. Patients should be given sufficient information, in a way they can understand, about the proposed treatment and the possible alternatives. Patients must be allowed to decide whether they will agree to the treatment and they may refuse or withdraw consent to treatment at any time. The patient's consent to treatment should be recorded on this form (further guidance is given in HC(90)22 *(A Guide to Consent for Examination or Treatment.)*

Patients

- The doctor is here to help you. He or she will explain the proposed procedure, which you are entitled to refuse. You can ask any questions and seek further information.

- You may ask for a relative, or friend, or a nurse to be present.

- Training health professionals is essential to the continuation of the health service and improving the quality of care. Your treatment may provide an important opportunity for such training, where necessary under the careful supervision of a senior doctor. You may refuse any involvement in a formal training programme without this adversely affecting your care and treatment.

CONSENT FORM

For treatment by a health professional other than doctors or dentists

Health Authority	Patient's Surname . . . .
Hospital	Other Names . . . .
Unit Number	Date of Birth . . . .
	Sex: *(please tick)* Male ☐ Female ☐

HEALTH PROFESSIONAL *(This part to be completed by health professional. See notes on the reverse)*

TYPE OF TREATMENT PROPOSED

Complete this part of the form

I confirm that I have explained the treatment proposed and such appropriate options as are available to the patient in terms which in my judgement are suited to the understanding of the patient and/or to one of the parents or guardians of the patient.

Signature. . . . .   Date . . . . / . . . / . . . . .

Name of health professional . . . .

Job title of health professional . . . .

PATIENT/PARENT/GUARDIAN

1. Please read this form and the notes overleaf very carefully.

2. If there is anything that you don't understand about the explanation, or if you want more information, you should ask the health professional who has explained the treatment proposed.

3. Please check that all the information on the form is correct. If it is, and you understand the treatment proposed, then sign the form.

I am the patient/parent/guardian *(delete as necessary)*

I agree   ■ to what is proposed which has been explained to me by the health professional named on this form.

Signature   . . . .

Name   . . . .

Address   . . . .

(if not the patient)   . . . .

. . . .

NHS *Management Executive*

NOTES TO:

Health Professionals, other than doctors or dentists

A patient has a legal right to grant or withhold consent prior to examination or treatment. Patients should be given sufficient information, in a way they can understand, about the proposed treatment and the possible alternatives. Patients must be allowed to decide whether they will agree to the treatment and they may refuse or withdraw consent to treatment at any time. The patient's consent to treatment should be recorded on this form (further guidance is given in HC(90)22 *(A Guide to Consent for Examination or Treatment.)*

Patients

■ The health professional named on this form is here to help you. He or she will explain the proposed treatment and what the alternatives are. You can ask any questions and seek further information. You can refuse the treatment.

■ You may ask for a relative, or friend, or another member of staff to be present.

■ Training health professionals is essential to the continuation of the health service and improving the quality of care. Your treatment may provide an important opportunity for such training, where necessary under the careful supervision of a fully qualified health professional. You may refuse any involvement in a formal training programme without this adversely affecting your care and treatment.

Medical or dental treatment of a patient who is unable to consent because of mental disorder

Health Authority . . . .

Hospital . . . .

Unit Number . . . .

Patient's Surname . . . .

Other Names . . . .

Date of Birth . . . .

Sex: *(please tick)*   Male ☐   Female ☐

NOTE

If there is any doubt about the ability of a mentally disordered patient to give consent to treatment, the Registered Medical Practictioner in charge of the patient should be asked to interview the patient. If, in his or her opinion, the patient is able to give valid consent to medical, dental or surgical treatment, he or she should be asked to do so and no-one further need be involved.

If the patient is considered unable to give valid consent it is considered good practice to discuss any proposed treatment with the next of kin.

For surgical or dental operations the form should also be signed by the Registered Medical or Dental Practitioner who carries out the treatment.

DOCTORS/DENTISTS

Describe investigation, operation or treatment proposed.

(Complete this part of the form)

In my opinion . . . . is not capable of giving consent to treatment. In my opinion the treatment proposed is in his/her best interests and should be given.

The patient's next of kin have/have not been so informed. *(delete as necessary)*

Date: . . . .

Signature

. . . .

Name of Registered Medical Practitioner
in charge of the patient:

. . . .

Signature

. . . .

Name of Second Registered Medical/Dental
Practitioner who is providing treatment:

. . . .

NHS *Management Executive*

GENERAL MEDICAL COUNCIL

PROFESSIONAL CONDUCT AND DISCIPLINE: FITNESS TO PRACTISE
(February 1991)

The first part of this pamphlet describes the statutory basis and machinery of the Council's jurisdiction in cases of professional misconduct and criminal offences. The second part deals with various forms of misconduct which have led or may lead to proceedings by the former Disciplinary Committee or by the present Professional Conduct Committee which has superseded it. The third part contains more specific and positive advice in certain areas of professional conduct. The final part describes the statutory basis and machinery of the Council's jurisdiction in relation to practitioners whose fitness to practise is seriously impaired by their physical or mental condition.

PART I
THE DISCIPLINARY PROCESSES OF THE COUNCIL

Statutory provisions

1. Disciplinary powers were first conferred on the Council by the Medical Act 1858, which established the Council and the Register. The Council's jurisdiction in relation to professional misconduct and criminal offences is now regulated by sections 36 and 38–45 of and Schedule 4 to the Medical Act 1983. The Act provides that if any registered practitioner:

   (a) is found by the Professional Conduct Committee to have been convicted in the British Islands of a criminal offence, or

   (b) is judged by the Professional Conduct Committee to have been guilty of serious professional misconduct,

the Committee may if it thinks fit direct that his name shall be erased from the Register, or that his registration shall be suspended for a period not exceeding 12 months, or that his registration shall be conditional on his compliance, during a period not exceeding three years, with such requirements as the Committee thinks fit to impose for the protection of members of the public or in his interests.

2. These powers apply to practitioners holding full, provisional or limited registration.

Convictions

3. The term "conviction", used in this pamphlet, is restricted to a determination by a criminal court in the British Islands. A conviction in itself gives the Professional Conduct Committee jurisdiction even if the criminal offence did not involve professional misconduct. The Committee is however particularly concerned with convictions for offences which affect a doctor's fitness to practise.

4. In considering convictions the Council is bound to accept the determination of a court as conclusive evidence that the doctor was guilty of the offence of which he was convicted. Doctors who face a criminal charge should remember this if they are advised to plead guilty, or not to appeal against a conviction, in order to avoid publicity or a

severe sentence. It is not open to a doctor who has been convicted of an offence to argue before the Professional Conduct Committee that he was in fact innocent. *It is therefore unwise for a doctor to plead guilty in a court of law to a charge to which he believes that he has a defence.*

5. A finding or a decision of a Medical Service Committee or other authority under the National Health Service does not amount to a conviction for these purposes. A charge of serious professional misconduct may however, if the facts warrant, be made in respect of conduct which has previously been the subject of proceedings within the National Health Service or before an overseas court or medical council; or in respect of conduct of which a doctor has been found guilty by a British criminal court but placed on probation or discharged conditionally or absolutely.

The meaning of "serious professional misconduct"

6. The expression "serious professional misconduct" was substituted by the Medical Act 1969 for the phrase "infamous conduct in a professional respect" which was used in the Medical Act 1858. The phrase "infamous conduct in a professional respect" was defined in 1894 by Lord Justice Lopes as follows:

"If a medical man in the pursuit of his profession has done something with regard to it which will be reasonably regarded as disgraceful or dishonourable by his professional brethren of good repute and competency, then it is open to the General Medical Council, if that be shown, to say that he has been guilty of infamous conduct in a professional respect."

7. In another judgment delivered in 1930 Lord Justice Scrutton stated that:

"Infamous conduct in a professional respect means no more than serious misconduct judged according to the rules, written or unwritten, governing the profession."

8. In proposing the substitution of the expression "serious professional misconduct" for the phrase "infamous conduct in a professional respect" the Council intended that the phrases should have the same significance.

The Professional Conduct Committee and the Preliminary Proceedings Committee

9. The Professional Conduct Committee is elected annually by the Council and consists of 32 members, of whom only 11 sit on any case. Of the 32 members, 18 are elected members of the Council and six are lay members. The Committee normally sits in public and its procedure is closely akin to that of a court of law. Witnesses may be subpoenaed and evidence is given on oath. Doctors who appear before the Committee may be, and usually are, legally represented.

10. The Preliminary Proceedings Committee consists of 11 members, and is also elected annually. It sits in private and on the basis of written evidence and submissions determines which cases should be referred for inquiry by the Professional Conduct Committee. It may also refer cases to the Health Committee (see Part IV of this pamphlet).

11. The Professional Conduct and Preliminary Proceedings Committees are advised on questions of law by a Legal Assessor, who is usually a Queen's Counsel and must be a barrister, advocate or solicitor of not less than ten years' standing.

Rules of procedure

12. The proceedings of the Professional Conduct and Preliminary Proceedings Committees are governed by rules of procedure made by the Council after consultation with representative medical organisations, and approved by the Privy Council. The current rules were made in 1988 and are printed by H.M. Stationery Office as Statutory Instrument 1988 No. 2255. Other rules govern the functions of the Legal Assessor and the procedure for appeals to the Judicial Committee of the Privy Council.

Proceedings: the preliminary stages

13.   Cases giving rise to proceedings by the Preliminary Proceedings Committee or the Professional Conduct Committee are of two kinds — those arising from a conviction of a doctor in the courts and those where a doctor is alleged to have done something which amounts to serious professional misconduct. In either kind of case the Council acts only when relevant matters have been brought to its notice.

14.   Convictions of doctors are normally reported to the Council by the police. Unless the conviction is of a minor motoring or other trivial offence it is normally referred to the Preliminary Proceedings Committee.

15.   Information or complaints concerning behaviour which may be regarded as serious professional misconduct reach the Council from a number of sources. Frequently they concern matters which have already been investigated through some other procedure — for example a Medical Service Committee, or a Committee of Inquiry in the hospital service. Information or complaints received from individual doctors or members of the public, as distinct from public authorities, must be supported by evidence of the facts alleged in the form of one or more affidavits or statutory declarations made in a prescribed form before a Commissioner for Oaths or a Justice of the Peace.

16.   Every complaint or item of information received is scrutinised meticulously. Only a very small proportion are found both to relate to matters which could be regarded as raising a question of serious professional misconduct and to be supported, or capable of being supported, by adequate evidence. Where it appears from the allegations made that a question of serious professional misconduct may arise, but the evidence initially received is insufficient or does not comply with the Rules, the Council's Solicitor may be asked to make inquiries to establish the facts. A decision whether to proceed with an allegation of serious professional misconduct is then taken by the President or by another medical member of the Council appointed for the purpose. A decision not to proceed, for example, because the matter does not raise a question of serious professional misconduct, is taken only after consultation between the President (or the medical member of the Council) and a lay member appointed to assist in the screening of cases. In a case where it is decided to proceed the doctor is informed of the allegations and is invited to submit a written explanation, which may include evidence in answer to the allegations. Any such explanation is placed before the Preliminary Proceedings Committee when it considers the case.

Powers of the Preliminary Proceedings Committee: warning letters and letters of advice

17.   After considering a case of conviction or of alleged serious professional misconduct the Preliminary Proceedings Committee may decide either:
   (a)   to refer the case to the Professional Conduct Committee for inquiry; or
   (b)   to send the doctor a letter; or
   (c)   to take no further action.

18.   Many cases considered by the Preliminary Proceedings Committee are disposed of by a warning letter or a letter of advice — for example cases where a doctor has been convicted for the first time of driving a motor car when under the influence of drink, or of shoplifting, or cases where a doctor's professional conduct appears to have fallen below the proper standard but not to have been so serious as to necessitate a public inquiry.

19.   If on considering a conviction, or allegations of serious professional misconduct, it appears to the Preliminary Proceedings Committee that the doctor may be suffering from a physical or mental condition which seriously impairs his fitness to practise, the Committee may refer the case to the Health Committee instead of the Professional Conduct Committee.

20.   If the Preliminary Proceedings Committee decides to refer a case either to the Professional Conduct Committee or to the Health Committee, it may make an order for the interim suspension of the doctor's registration or for interim conditional registration if it is satisfied that this is necessary for the protection of members of the public or is in the doctor's own interests. Such orders may be made for a period not exceeding two months and are intended to be effective only until the case has been considered by the Professional Conduct Committee or by the Health Committee. No such order can be made unless the doctor has been offered an opportunity of appearing before the Preliminary Proceedings Committee and being heard on the question whether such an order should be made. For this purpose the doctor may be legally represented.

Inquiries before the Professional Conduct Committee

21.   As already mentioned, the Professional Conduct Committee is bound to accept the fact that a doctor has been convicted as conclusive evidence that he was guilty of the offence of which he was convicted. Provided therefore that a doctor admits a conviction, proceedings in cases of conviction are concerned only to establish the gravity of the offence and to take due account of any mitigating circumstances. In cases of conduct however the allegations, unless admitted by the doctor, must be *strictly proved by evidence*, and the doctor is free to dispute and rebut the evidence called. If facts alleged in a conduct charge are found by the Committee to have been proved, the Committee must subsequently determine whether, in relation to those facts, the doctor has been guilty of serious professional misconduct. Before taking a final decision the Committee invites the doctor or his legal representative to call attention to any mitigating circumstances and to produce testimonials or other evidence as to character. The Committee takes account of the previous history of the doctor.

22.   The primary concerns of the Professional Conduct Committee are to protect the public and to uphold the reputation of the medical profession. Subject to these overriding considerations, the Committee will consider what is in the best interests of the doctor himself. If in the course of an inquiry it appears to the Committee that a doctor's fitness to practise may be seriously impaired by reason of his physical or mental condition, the Committee may refer that question to the Health Committee for determination. If the Health Committee finds that it is so impaired, the Professional Conduct Committee will then take no further action in the case.

Powers of the Professional Conduct Committee at the conclusion of an inquiry

23.   At the conclusion of an inquiry in which a doctor has been proved to have been convicted of a criminal offence, or judged to have been guilty of serious professional misconduct, the Professional Conduct Committee must decide on one of the following courses:

(a)   to conclude the case;

(b)   to postpone its determination;

(c)   to direct that the doctor's registration be conditional on his compliance, for a period not exceeding three years, with such requirements as the Committee may think fit to impose for the protection of members of the public or in his interests;

(d)   to direct that the doctor's registration shall be suspended for a period not exceeding 12 months; or

(e)   to direct the erasure of the doctor's name from the Register.

Postponement of determination

24.   In any case where the Committee's determination is postponed, the doctor's name remains on the Register during the period of postponement. When postponing its determination to a later meeting the Committee normally intimates that the doctor will be expected before his next appearance to furnish the names of professional colleagues

and other persons of standing to whom the Council may apply for information, to be given in confidence, concerning his conduct since the previous hearing. The replies received from these referees, together with any other evidence as to the doctor's conduct, are then taken into account when the Committee resumes consideration of the case. If the information is satisfactory, the case will then normally be concluded. If however the evidence is not satisfactory, the determination may be postponed for a further period, or the Committee may direct suspension or erasure or may impose conditions on the doctor's registration.

Conditional registration

25.   Examples of conditions which may be imposed are that the doctor should not engage in specified branches of medical practice, or that he should practise only in a particular appointment or under supervision. Another is that he should not prescribe or possess controlled drugs. Another is that he should take specified steps to remedy evident deficiencies in his knowledge, clinical skills, professional attitudes and/or abilities to manage or communicate.

26.   When a doctor's registration has for a period been subject to conditions the Committee may, on resuming consideration of his case, revoke the direction for conditional registration, or revoke or vary any of the conditions, or it may extend the original period of conditional registration. If a doctor is judged by the Professional Conduct Committee to have failed to comply with any of the conditions of his registration, the Committee may direct either suspension of his registration or erasure.

Suspension of registration

27.   If a doctor's registration is suspended, the doctor ceases to be entitled to practise as a registered medical practitioner during that period. When a doctor's registration has been suspended the Committee may, after notifying the doctor, resume consideration of his case before the end of the period of suspension. At that time, if the Committeee thinks fit, it may extend the original period of suspension or order erasure or impose conditional registration. Before resuming consideration of the case in such circumstances the Committee may, as when postponing its determination, ask the doctor to give the names of referees from whom information may be sought as to his conduct in the interval. This information will be taken into account when the Committee resumes consideration of the case.

Erasure

28.   Whereas suspension can be ordered only for a specified period, a direction to erase remains effective unless and until the doctor makes a successful application for the restoration of his name to the Register. Such an application cannot be made until at least ten months have elapsed since the original order took effect.

Appeal procedure and immediate suspension

29.   When the Committee has directed that a doctor's name shall be erased or that his registration shall be suspended or that his registration shall be subject to conditions, the doctor has 28 days in which to give notice of appeal against the direction to the Judicial Committee of the Privy Council. During that period and, if he gives notice of appeal, until the appeal is heard, his registration is not affected unless the Professional Conduct Committee has made a separate order that the doctor's registration shall be suspended forthwith. The Committee may make such an order if it is satisfied that to do so is necessary for the protection of members of the public or would be in the best interests of the doctor. There is a right of appeal against an order for immediate suspension to the High Court (in Scotland, the Court of Session), but such an appeal, whether successful or not, does not affect the right of appeal to the Judicial Committee of the Privy Council referred to above.

Restoration to the Register after disciplinary erasure
30. Applications for restoration may legally be made at any time after ten months from the date of erasure. If such an application is unsuccessful, a further period of at least ten months must elapse before a further application may be made. The names of many doctors which have been erased have subsequently been restored to the Register, after an interval. An applicant may, and normally does, appear in person before the Professional Conduct Committee. He may be legally represented. The Committee determines every application on its merits, having regard among other considerations to the nature and gravity of the original offence, the length of time since erasure, and the conduct of the applicant in the interval.

PART II
CONVICTIONS AND FORMS OF PROFESSIONAL MISCONDUCT WHICH MAY LEAD TO DISCIPLINARY PROCEEDINGS

31. This part of the pamphlet mentions certain kinds of criminal offences and of professional misconduct which have in the past led to disciplinary proceedings. It does not pretend to be a complete code of professional ethics, or to specify all criminal offences or forms of professional misconduct which may lead to disciplinary action. To do this would be impossible, because from time to time with changing circumstances the Council's attention is drawn to new forms of professional misconduct.

32. Any abuse by a doctor of any privileges and opportunities afforded to him or any grave dereliction of professional duty or serious breach of medical ethics may give rise to a charge of serious professional misconduct. In discharging their respective duties the Preliminary Proceedings Committee and Professional Conduct Committee must proceed as judicial bodies. Only after considering the evidence in each case can these Committees determine the gravity of a conviction or decide whether a doctor's behaviour amounts to serious professional misconduct. Doctors who seek detailed advice on professional conduct in particular circumstances should consult a medical defence society or professional association. The Council can rarely give such advice because of its judicial function.

33. In the following paragraphs areas of professional conduct and personal behaviour which need to be considered have been grouped under five main headings:
— Neglect or disregard by doctors of their professional responsibilities to patients for their care and treatment
— Abuse of professional privileges or skills
— Personal behaviour: conduct derogatory to the reputation of the medical profession
— The advertising of doctors' services
— Disparagement of professional colleagues.

34. These headings have been adopted for convenience, but such classifications can only be approximate. In most cases the nature of the offence or misconduct will be readily apparent. In some cases, such as those involving personal relationships between doctors and patients or questions of advertising, doctors may experience difficulty in recognising the proper principles to apply in various circumstances. In relation to these matters Part III of this pamphlet gives further advice.

Neglect or disregard of personal responsibilities to patients for their care and treatment

Responsibility for standards of medical care
35. In pursuance of its primary duty to protect the public the Council may institute disciplinary proceedings when a doctor appears *seriously* to have disregarded or neglected his professional duties, for example by failing to visit or to provide or arrange treatment for a patient when necessary. Many cases of this kind which have been investigated by a Medical Service Committee or other complaints procedure under the

National Health Service machinery (see Part I above) are reported to the Council, but cases which have arisen in other ways may also be considered.

36.   The public are entitled to expect that a registered medical practitioner will afford and maintain a good standard of medical care. This includes:

(a)   conscientious assessment of the history, symptoms and signs of a patient's condition;

(b)   sufficiently thorough professional attention, examination and, where necessary, diagnostic investigation;

(c)   competent and considerate professional management;

(d)   appropriate and prompt action upon evidence suggesting the existence of a condition requiring urgent medical intervention; and

(e)   readiness, where the circumstances so warrant, to consult appropriate professional colleagues.

37.   A comparable standard of practice is to be expected from medical practitioners whose contribution to a patient's care is indirect, for example those in laboratory and radiological specialities.

38.   The Council is concerned with errors in diagnosis or treatment, and with the kind of matters which give rise to action in the civil courts for negligence, only when the doctor's conduct in the case has involved such a disregard of his professional responsibility to patients or such a neglect of his professional duties as to raise a question of serious professional misconduct. A question of serious professional misconduct may also arise from a complaint or information about the conduct of a doctor which suggests that he has endangered the welfare of patients by persisting in unsupervised practice of a branch of medicine in which he does not have the appropriate knowledge and skill and has not acquired the experience which is necessary.

39.   Apart from a doctor's personal responsibility to patients, doctors who undertake to manage, to direct, or to perform clinical work for organisations offering private medical services should satisfy themselves that those organisations provide adequate clinical and therapeutic facilities for the services offered.

Delegation of medical duties to professional colleagues

40.   The Council recognises that in many branches of professional practice a doctor cannot himself at all times attend to all his patients' needs. It is therefore both necessary and desirable that arrangements should be made whereby the professional responsibilities of a doctor may be undertaken, during his absence from duty, by a suitably qualified professional colleague. A general practitioner who makes use of deputising services has a duty to satisfy himself that the deputies who may attend his patient are registered medical practitioners who have the appropriate experience, knowledge and skill to discharge the duties for which they will be responsible. Similarly, doctors under contract of service, such as consultants in hospital practice, and doctors engaged in private practice on either a part-time or a whole-time basis, should seek to ensure that proper arrangements are put in hand to cover their own duties, or those of their junior colleagues, during any period of absence, by doctors with appropriate qualifications and experience. Consultants and other senior hospital staff should delegate to junior colleagues only those duties which are within their capabilities.

41.   Any deputising arrangements should make provision for prompt and proper communication between the deputy and the doctor who has primary responsibility for the patients' care. However, so far as the Council is concerned, the deputy is himself responsible for any neglect or disregard of his professional responsibilities towards patients of the doctor for whom he is deputising.

Delegation of medical duties to nurses and others

42.   The Council recognises and welcomes the growing contribution made to health care by nurses and other persons who have been trained to perform specialised

functions, and it has no desire either to restrain the delegation to such persons of treatment or procedures falling within the proper scope of their skills or to hamper the training of medical and other health students. But a doctor who delegates treatment or other procedures must be satisfied that the person to whom they are delegated is competent to carry them out. It is also important that the doctor should retain ultimate responsibility for the management of his patients because only the doctor has received the necessary training to undertake this responsibility.

43.   For these reasons a doctor who improperly delegates to a person who is not a registered medical practitioner functions requiring the knowledge and skill of a medical practitioner is liable to disciplinary proceedings. Accordingly the Council has in the past proceeded against those doctors who employed assistants who were not medically qualified to conduct their practices. It has also proceeded against doctors who by signing certificates or prescriptions or in other ways have enabled persons who were not registered medical practitioners to treat patients as though they were so registered.

Abuse of professional privileges or skills

Abuse of privileges conferred by law: Misuse of professional skills

Prescribing of drugs

44.   The prescription of controlled drugs is reserved to members of the medical profession and of certain other professions, and the prescribing of such drugs is subject to statutory restrictions. The Council has regarded as serious professional misconduct the prescription or supply of drugs of dependence otherwise than in the course of bona fide treatment. Disciplinary proceedings have also been taken against doctors convicted of offences against the laws which control drugs where such offences appear to have been committed in order to gratify the doctor's own addiction or the addiction of other persons.

Medical certificates

45.   A doctor's signature is required by statute on certificates for a variety of purposes on the presumption that the truth of any statement which a doctor may certify can be accepted without question. Doctors are accordingly expected to exercise care in issuing certificates and similar documents, and should not certify statements which they have not taken appropriate steps to verify. Any doctor who in his professional capacity signs any certificate or similar document containing statements which are untrue, misleading or otherwise improper renders himself liable to disciplinary proceedings.

Termination of pregnancy

46.   The termination of pregnancy is regulated by the law and doctors must observe the law in relation to such matters. A criminal conviction in the British Islands of termination of pregnancy in circumstances which contravene the law in itself affords grounds for a charge before the Professional Conduct Committee.

Abuse of privileges conferred by custom: Professional confidence; Undue influence; Personal relationships between doctors and patients

47.   Patients grant doctors privileged access to their homes and confidences, and some patients are liable to become emotionally dependent upon their doctors. Good medical practice depends upon the maintenance of trust between doctors and patients and their families, and the understanding by both that proper professional relationships will be strictly observed. In this situation doctors must exercise great care and discretion in order not to damage this crucial relationship. Any action by a doctor which breaches this trust may raise a question of serious professional misconduct.

48.   Three particular areas may be identified in which this trust may be breached:

(a)   A doctor may improperly disclose information which he obtained in confidence from or about a patient.

(b) A doctor may improperly exert influence upon a patient to lend him money or to alter the patient's will in his favour.

(c) A doctor may enter into an emotional or sexual relationship with a patient (or with a member of a patient's family) which disrupts that patient's family life or otherwise damages, or causes distress to, the patient or his or her family.

Further advice is given in Part III of this pamphlet in relation to the first and last of these matters.

Personal behaviour: conduct derogatory to the reputation of the profession

49. The public reputation of the medical profession requires that every member should observe proper standards of personal behaviour, not only in his professional activities but at all times. This is the reason why a doctor's conviction of a criminal offence may lead to disciplinary proceedings even if the offence is not directly connected with the doctor's profession. In particular, three areas of personal behaviour can be identified which may occasion disciplinary proceedings:

— Personal misuse or abuse of alcohol or other drugs
— Dishonest behaviour
— Indecent or violent behaviour.

Personal misuse or abuse of alcohol or other drugs

50. In the opinion of the Council, convictions for drunkenness or other offences arising from misuse of alcohol (such as driving a motor car when under the influence of drink) indicate habits which are discreditable to the profession and may be a source of danger to the doctor's patients. After a first conviction for drunkenness a doctor may expect to receive a warning letter. Further convictions may lead to an inquiry by the Professional Conduct Committee or the Health Committee.

51. A doctor who treats patients or performs other professional duties while he is under the influence of drink or drugs, or who is unable to perform his professional duties because he is under the influence of drink or drugs, is liable to disciplinary proceedings or to inquiry by the Council into his fitness to practise.

Dishonesty: improper financial transactions

52. Doctors are liable to disciplinary proceedings if they are convicted of criminal deception (obtaining money or goods by false pretences), forgery, fraud, theft or any other offence involving dishonesty.

53. The Council takes a particularly serious view of dishonest acts committed in the course of a doctor's professional practice (whether under the National Health Service or otherwise), or against patients or colleagues. Such acts, if reported to the Council, may result in disciplinary proceedings. Among the circumstances which may have this result are the improper demand or acceptance of fees from patients contrary to the statutory provisions which regulate the conduct of the National Health Service and, in particular:

(a) the charging of fees to in-patients or out-patients treated at National Health Service hospitals, when the proper steps have not been taken to ensure that such patients enjoy the status of resident or non-resident private patients, as required by statute;

(b) knowingly and improperly seeking to obtain from a Family Practitioner Committee or other health authority any payment to which the doctor is not entitled, including the improper issue of National Health Service prescriptions either to patients on the doctor's dispensing list or to patients whom the doctor, or another member of the practice, is treating under private contract.

54. Disciplinary proceedings may also result from other improper arrangements calculated to extend, or otherwise benefit, a doctor's practice, whether in relation to the provision of specialist services or in general practice. These include, for example,

pressure by a specialist to persuade a patient to accept private treatment by reliance upon representations about the comparative availability of treatment under the National Health Service and privately. Improper arrangements made for the transfer of patients to a general practitioner's National Health Service list without the knowledge and consent of the patient, or in a manner contrary to the National Health Service regulations, have also in the past led to disciplinary proceedings.

55.   The Council also takes a serious view of the prescribing or dispensing of drugs or appliances for improper motives. The motiviation of doctors may be regarded as improper if they have prescribed a drug or appliance in which they have a direct financial interest or if they have prescribed a product manufactured or marketed by an organisation from which they have accepted an improper inducement. Further guidance on this matter is contained in paragraphs 111–115 of this pamphlet.

56.   The Council has also regarded with concern arrangements for fee-splitting under which one doctor would receive part of a fee paid by a patient to another doctor and the association of a medical practitioner with any commercial enterprise engaged in the manufacture or sale of any substance which is claimed to be of value in the prevention or treatment of disease but is of undisclosed nature or composition.

57.   Doctors, like lay members or officers of any health authority, have a duty to declare an interest before participating in discussion which could lead to the purchase by a public authority of goods or services in which they, or a member of their immediate family, have a direct or indirect pecuniary interest. Non-disclosure of such information may, under certain circumstances, amount to serious professional misconduct.

Indecency and violence

58.   Indecent behaviour to or a violent assault on a patient would be regarded as serious professional misconduct. Any conviction for assault or indecency would render a doctor liable to disciplinary proceedings, and would be regarded with particular gravity if the offence were committed in the course of a doctor's professional duties or against his patients or colleagues.

The advertising of doctors' services

59.   The Council encourages doctors to provide factual information about their professional qualifications and services. The term "advertising" is used by the Council to mean the provision of information about doctors and their services, in any form, to the public or other members of the profession. There is a general requirement that any advertising in this country must be "legal, decent, honest and truthful", and that it should conform with the other requirements of the British Code of Advertising Practice. But the advertising of doctors' services must be subject to additional restriction in order to ensure that the public is not misled or put at risk in any way.

60.   It is the duty of all doctors to satisfy themselves that the content and presentation of any material published about their services, and the manner in which it is distributed, conform with the guidance given both in this section and in paragraphs 90–108. This applies whether a doctor personally arranges for such publication or permits or acquiesces in its publication by others. Failure to abide by the Council's guidance may call a doctor's professional conduct into question.

61.   In no circumstances should the distribution of advertising material be undertaken so frequently or in such a manner as to put recipients, including prospective patients, under pressure. Such a course of action is in the interest neither of patients nor of the medical profession.

Comment about professional colleagues

62.   Doctors are frequently called upon to express a view about a colleague's professional practice. This may, for example, happen in the course of a medical audit or peer review procedure, or when a doctor is asked to give a reference about a

colleague. It may also occur in a less direct and explicit way when a patient seeks a second opinion, specialist advice or an alternative form of treatment. Honest comment is entirely acceptable in such circumstances, provided that it is carefully considered and can be justified, that it is offered in good faith and that it is intended to promote the best interests of patients.

63.   Further, it is any doctor's duty, where the circumstances so warrant, to inform an appropriate person or body about a colleague whose professional conduct or fitness to practise may be called in question or whose professional performance appears to be in some way deficient. Arrangements exist to deal with such problems, and they must be used in order to ensure that high standards of medical practice are maintained.

64.   However, gratuitous and unsustainable comment which, whether directly or by implication, sets out to undermine trust in a professional colleague's knowledge or skills is unethical.

CONCLUSION

The nature of serious professional misconduct

65.   As stated in paragraph 32 of this pamphlet the question whether any particular course of conduct amounts to serious professional misconduct is a matter which falls to be determined by the Professional Conduct Committee after considering the evidence in each individual case. This applies equally to the categories of misconduct described in Part II and to the situations contemplated in Part III. Further, it must be emphasised that the categories of misconduct described in Part II cannot be regarded as exhaustive. Any abuse by a doctor of any of the privileges and the opportunities afforded to him, or any grave dereliction of professional duty or serious breach of medical ethics, may give rise to a charge of serious professional misconduct.

PART III
ADVICE ON STANDARDS OF PROFESSIONAL CONDUCT AND ON MEDICAL ETHICS

66.   Section 35 of the Medical Act 1983 provides that the powers of the Council shall include that of providing, in such manner as the Council thinks fit, advice for members of the medical profession on standards of professional conduct or on medical ethics. The Council has approved the following paragraphs giving general advice on personal relationships between doctors and patients, on professional confidence, on the reference of patients to and acceptance of patients by specialists, on circumstances in which difficulties in relation to self-promotion most commonly arise and on relationships between the medical profession and the pharmaceutical and allied industries.

67.   The Council will also respond to inquiries from individual doctors about questions of professional conduct, although many of these doctors are advised to consult their medical defence society or professional association. The Council will also provide advice to individual doctors concerning their own professional conduct if, after receiving a complaint against them and seeking the doctor's observations on the complaint, it appears that such advice is necessary.

Personal relationships between doctors and patients

68.   Paragraphs 47–48 of this pamphlet, dealing with the abuse by doctors of certain privileges conferred on them by custom, explain why doctors must exercise great care and discretion not to damage the crucial relationship between doctors and patients, and identify three areas in which experience shows that this trust is liable to be breached. The following paragraphs relate to one of these areas — personal relationships between a doctor and a patient (or a member of the patient's family) which disrupt the patient's family life or otherwise damage the maintenance of trust between doctors and patients.

69.   The Council has always taken a serious view of a doctor who uses his

professional position in order to pursue a personal relationship of an emotional or sexual nature with a patient or the close relative of a patient. Such abuse of a doctor's professional position may be aggravated in a number of ways. For example, a doctor may use the pretext of a professional visit to a patient's home to disguise his pursuit of the personal relationship with the patient (or, where the patient is a child, with the patient's parent). Or he may use his knowledge, obtained in professional confidence, of the patient's marital difficulties to take advantage of that situation. But these are merely examples of particular abuses.

70.   The question is sometimes raised whether the Council will be concerned with such relationships between a doctor and a person for whose care the doctor is contractually responsible but whom he has never actually treated, or between a doctor and a person whom the doctor has attended professionally in the distant past. In view of the great variety of circumstances which can arise in cases of this nature, the Council's judicial position has prevented it from offering specific advice on such matters. It can however be said that the Council is primarily concerned with behaviour which damages the crucial relationship between doctors and patients, and that this relationship normally implies actual consultation.

71.   The trust which should exist between doctors and patients can be severely damaged when, as a result of an emotional relationship between a doctor and a patient, the family life of that patient is disrupted. This may occur without sexual misconduct between the doctor and the patient.

72.   The foregoing paragraphs refer to personal relationships between doctors and patients or the close relatives of patients. The Council is not concerned with personal relationships between doctors and other persons.

73.   Cases have been reported to the Council where a doctor when attending a patient professionally has indecently assaulted her or exposed himself to her. As will be clear from paragraph 58 of this pamphlet, such behaviour may render the doctor liable to criminal proceedings; it may also in the absence of a criminal conviction be treated as serious professional misconduct.

74.   For convenience these paragraphs describe a situation where the doctor is a man and the patient a woman. Similar principles would apply if the doctor were a woman and the patient a man or to a homosexual relationship.

75.   Innocent doctors are sometimes caused anxiety by unsolicited declarations of affection by patients or threats that a complaint will be made on the grounds of a relationship which existed only in the patient's imagination. As indicated in paragraph 16 of this pamphlet, all complaints received by the Council are screened most carefully, and action is taken only when the evidence received is sufficient to require investigation.

Principles governing the reference of patients to, and their acceptance by, doctors providing specialist services

Reference of patients to specialists

86.   The medical profession in this country has always considered that it is in the best interests of patients for one doctor to be fully informed about and responsible for the comprehensive management of a patient's medical care, but increasing specialisation within medicine has led members of the public to an awareness of high standards of expertise and often to seek direct access to these. In this situation general practitioners have a double duty — to educate their patients to an understanding of the central position of their primary role, and also to consider carefully any request by a patient for a specialist opinion even if the general practitioner is not convinced that such consultation is essential. In order to continue to fulfil their central role, general practitioners must have information about the range of specialist expertise which other doctors are qualified and available to provide, especially in their locality.

Acceptance of patients by specialists

87.   Although an individual patient is free to seek to consult any doctor, the Council wishes to affirm its view that, in the interests of the generality of patients, a specialist should not usually accept a patient without reference from the patient's general practitioner. If a specialist does decide to accept a patient without such reference, the specialist has a duty immediately to inform the general practitioner of his findings and recommendations before embarking on treatment, except in emergency, unless the patient expressly withholds consent or has no general practitioner. In such cases the specialist must be responsible for the patient's subsequent care until another doctor has agreed to take over that responsibility.

88.   Doctors connected with organisations offering clinical, diagnostic or medical advisory services must therefore satisfy themselves that the organisation discourages patients from approaching it without first consulting their own general practitioners, and that the guidance set out in paragraphs 86 and 87 above is fully observed at all times.

89.   In expressing these views the Council recognises and accepts that in some areas of practice specialist and hospital clinics customarily accept patients referred by sources other than their general practitioners. In these circumstances the specialist still has the duty to keep the general practitioner informed.

The advertising of doctors' services

The need for good communication

90.   Good communication between doctors and patients, and between one doctor and another, is fundamental to the provision of good patient care, and those who need information about the services of doctors should have ready access to it. Patients need such information in order to make an informed choice of general practitioner and to make the best use of the services the general practitioner offers. Doctors, for their part, need information about the services of their professional colleagues. General practitioners in particular need information about specialist services so that they may advise patients and refer them, where appropriate, for further investigation or treatment.

91.   People seeking medical attention for themselves or their families can nevertheless be particularly vulnerable to persuasive influence, and patients are entitled to protection from misleading advertisements. The promotion of doctors' medical services as if the provision of medical care were no more than a commercial activity is likely both to undermine public trust in the medical profession and, over time, to diminish the standards of medical care which patients have a right to expect.

92.   This section offers guidance to doctors in various types of medical practice about the content and distribution of notices and other material providing information about their services. It discusses the following matters:
— the distinction between the advertising of general practitioner services and specialist services;
— information about general practitioner services;
— information about specialist services;
— information about organisations offering medical services;
— information to companies, firms and similar organisations;
— information about associations of doctors;
— other public references to doctors.

The distinction between the advertising of general practitioner services and specialist services

93.   The Council distinguishes between the advertising of general practitioner services — which in this context includes advertising by doctors offering the sight test — and the advertising of specialist services. Information about the services provided by

general practitioners should be made widely available to the public in the areas where those doctors practise. Specialists may provide information to professional colleagues but not to the public, except to the limited extent described in paragraph 98. This distinction reflects the 'referral system' upon which general and specialist practice in the United Kingdom are based and which exists to protect patients. Most individuals, when choosing a general practitioner, are in good health and able to make a rational choice on the basis of factual information. People requiring the attention of a specialist may, by contrast, be ill or in a vulnerable state and need the advice of a general practitioner before being referred for further investigation or treatment. Equally, the specialist to whom a patient is referred needs information of the patient's relevant medical history and of any treatment which may already be under way.

Information about general practitioner services

Lists of general practitioners

94. Patients are best able to make an informed choice of family doctor if they have ready access to comprehensive, up-to-date, well-presented and easily understood information about all the general practitioners practising in their area. Lists including factual information, presented in an objective and unbiased manner, about the doctors and their professional qualifications, the facilities available and the practice arrangements should be distributed widely to the public. Full use should be made of the places in each area where members of the public can expect to find local information. It is best if such material is published by a body with statutory responsibilities for primary care services, or by some other body which has no reason to favour individual doctors or practices. As far as is practicable, material published in this way should provide the same items of information about each doctor and practice.

Notices about individual general practitioners or practices

95. General practitioners should provide the public with practice leaflets giving factual information about their professional qualifications, services and practice arrangements and including, if they wish, a statement about their approach to medical practice. Up-to-date information of this kind should be available at doctors' surgeries. It should also be placed in libraries and other places where the public would normally expect to find information in their locality. General practitioners may, if they so decide, distribute such information on an unsolicited basis within the areas which they serve, provided that the distribution is not targeted in such a way as to put the recipients under pressure. General practitioners may also publish factual information of their services in the press, directories or other media. Doctors' services should not however be advertised by means of unsolicited visits or telephone calls, by doctors or by people acting on their behalf, with the aim of recruiting patients; such activities may render a doctor liable to disciplinary proceedings by the Council.

96. In addition to complying with the general requirements governing advertising in this country, which are referred to in paragraph 59 above, general practitioners publishing information about their services should not abuse the trust of patients or attempt to exploit their lack of medical knowledge. Especially, they must not offer guarantees to cure particular complaints. Advertising material should contain only factual information and must not include any statement which could reasonably be regarded as misleading or as disparaging the services provided by other doctors, whether directly or by implication. No claim of superiority should be made either for the services offered or for a particular doctor's personal qualities, professional qualifications, experience or skills.

97. Doctors are responsible for ensuring that any nameplates, noticeboards or other signs about their practices are sufficient to inform the public of the existence or location of the premises while not being used to draw public attention to the services of one

doctor or practice at the expense of others. In cases of doubt a professional association, a medical defence society or the Local Medical Committee should be consulted.

Information about specialist services

98. Specialists may keep their professional and managerial colleagues informed of the services they offer and of their practice arrangements. Material circulated in this way should not however disparage, directly or by implication, the services provided by other doctors, nor should it claim superiority for the specialist's personal qualities, qualifications, experience or skills. The name, professional qualifications, address and telephone number of a specialist may be included in national and local directories and similar publications, and doctors who are suitably qualified may, if they wish, include their names in more than one list within a single publication. Information about individual specialists should not otherwise be made available directly to the public, although the membership lists of associations of doctors may be released as indicated in paragraph 105.

99. Just as the public are assisted by comprehensive lists of local general practitioners, so doctors are best able to offer their patients informed advice if they themselves have up-to-date, factual information about all the specialist medical services which are available. Doctors may reasonably expect to be provided with such information by the local hospitals, clinics and other medical organisations, both in the National Health Service and in the private sector, where specialists practise.

Information about organisations offering medical services

100. Medical services are offered to the public not only by individual doctors but by a wide variety of organisations such as hospitals, screening centres, nursing homes, advisory bureaux or agencies, and counselling centres. Some of these, especially those within the private sector, advertise their services to the public and the principles set out in paragraph 96, concerning the advertising of general practitioner services, apply also to such advertising. In addition, the advertisements should not make invidious comparisons with other organisations, either within or outside the National Health Service, or with the services of particular doctors, nor should they claim superiority for the professional services offered or for any doctors connected with the organisation.

101. Doctors who have any kind of financial or professional relationship with such an organisation, or who use its facilities, are deemed by the Council to bear some responsibility for the organisation's advertising. This also applies to doctors who accept for examination or treatment patients referred by any such organisation. All such doctors must therefore make it their business to acquaint themselves with the nature and content of the organisation's advertising, and must exercise due diligence in an effort to ensure that it conforms with this guidance. Should any question be raised about a doctor's conduct in this respect, it will not be sufficient for any explanation to be based on the doctor's lack of awareness of the nature or content of the organisation's advertising, or lack of ability to exert any influence over it.

102. Such doctors should also avoid personal involvement in promoting the services of this kind of organisation, for example by public speaking, broadcasting, writing articles or signing circulars, and should not permit the organisation's promotional material to claim superiority for their professional qualifications and experience. Nor should they allow a personal address or telephone number to be used as an inquiry point on behalf of an organisation.

103. Further guidance on financial relationships between doctors and such organisations is given in paragraphs 109 and 110.

Information to companies, firms and similar organisations

104. Doctors who wish to offer medical services, such as medico-legal or occupational health services or medical examinations, to a company or firm, a school or club,

or a professional practitioner or association may send factual information about their qualifications and services to a suitable person, and may where appropriate place a factual advertisement in a relevant trade journal, provided that the same principles are observed as in the guidance given in paragraph 96 about the advertising of general practitioner services. Doctors must not however use the provision of such services as a means to put pressure upon individuals to become their patients and should observe the guidance in paragraphs 86–89 concerning communication with each individual's general practitioner.

Information about associations of doctors

105. Members of the public who are seeking medical advice or treatment occasionally approach an association of doctors for a list of its members. Such a list may be released in response to a direct request, but it is essential that no list should imply that those listed are the only doctors who are qualified to practice in a particular branch of medicine or that the inclusion of a doctor's name carries some form of recommendation. The lists which are released should include only those doctors who are eligible for registration by the Council as having completed higher specialist or vocational training. Any association of doctors which wishes to release lists of its members in response to requests by the public should therefore first consult the Council for guidance as to the form which the list should take.

Other public references to doctors

The use of professional directories
106. Factual information about a doctor who is appropriately qualified may be published in a professional directory of persons offering particular services, provided that it is open to all doctors practising in the relevant specialty to be included. Doctors should not however cause, sanction or acquiesce in the publication of their names or practice details in any professional directory or book which purports to make recommendations as to the quality of particular doctors or their services.

Publicity material about companies or other organisations
107. The name and qualifications of a doctor who is a director of a company may be shown on the company's notepaper. Doctors should however take steps to avoid the inclusion, in material published by any company or organisation with which they are associated, of references which draw attention to their attainments in ways likely to promote their professional advantage, whether or not the business of their company is connected with medical practice.

Articles, books and broadcasting by doctors
108. Books or articles written by doctors may include their names, qualifications, appointments and details of other publications. Similar information may be given where doctors participate in the broadcast presentation and discussion of medical and related topics. Difficulties in this area arise chiefly when material included in articles, books or broadcasts by doctors, or the manner in which it is referred to, is likely to imply that the doctor is especially recommended for patients to consult. Doctors should see to it that no such implication is given. Where a doctor in clinical practice writes articles or columns which offer advice to the public on medical conditions or problems, or offers telephone or other recorded advice on such subjects, or broadcasts about them, it should be explicitly stated that the doctor cannot offer individual advice or see individual patients as a result.

Financial relationships between doctors and independent organisations providing clinical, diagnostic or medical advisory services

109. A doctor who recommends that a patient should attend at, or be admitted to, any private hospital, nursing home or similar institution, whether for treatment by the

doctor himself or by another person, must do so only in such a way as will best serve, and will be seen best to serve, the medical interests of the patient. Doctors should therefore avoid accepting any financial or other inducement from such an institution which might compromise, or be regarded by others as likely to compromise, the independent exercise of their professional judgment. Where a doctor has a financial interest in an organisation to which he proposes to refer a patient for admission or treatment, whether by reason of a capital investment or a remunerative position, he should always disclose that he has such an interest before making the referral.

110.   The seeking or acceptance by a doctor from such an institution of any inducement for the referral of patients to the institution, such as free or subsidised consulting premises or secretarial assistance, may be regarded as improper. Similarly the offering of such inducements to colleagues by doctors who manage or direct such institutions may be regarded as improper.

Relationships between the medical profession and the pharmaceutical and allied industries

111.   The medical profession and the pharmaceutical industry have common interests in the research and development of new drugs of therapeutic value and in their production and distribution for clinical use. Medical practice owes much to the important advances achieved by the pharmaceutical industry over recent decades. In addition, much medical research and postgraduate medical education are facilitated by the financial support of pharmaceutical firms.

112.   Advertising and other forms of sales promotion by individual firms within the pharmaceutical and allied industries are necessary for their commercial viability and can provide information which is useful to the profession. Nevertheless, a prescribing doctor should not only choose but also be seen to be choosing the drug or appliance which, in his independent professional judgment and having due regard to economy, will best serve the medical interests of his patient. Doctors should therefore avoid accepting any pecuniary or material inducement which might compromise, or be regarded by others as likely to compromise, the independent exercise of their professional judgment in prescribing matters. *The seeking or acceptance by doctors of unreasonable sums of money or gifts from commercial firms which manufacture or market drugs or diagnostic or therapeutic agents or appliances may be regarded as improper.* Examples of inducements which the Council may regard as improper are set out below.

Clinical trials of drugs

113.   It may be improper for a doctor to accept per capita or other payments from a pharmaceutical firm in relation to a research project such as the clinical trial of a new drug, unless the payments have been specified in a protocol for the project which has been approved by the relevant national or local ethical committee. It may be improper for a doctor to accept per capita or other payments under arrangements for recording clinical assessments of a licensed medicinal product, whereby he is asked to report reactions which he has observed in patients for whom he has prescribed the drug, unless the payments have been specified in a protocol for the project which has been approved by the relevant national or local ethical committee. It is improper for a doctor to accept payment in money or kind which could influence his professional assessment of the therapeutic value of a new drug.

Gifts and loans

114.   It may be improper for an individual doctor to accept from a pharmaceutical firm monetary gifts or loans or expensive items of equipment for his personal use. No exception can, however, be taken to grants of money or equipment by firms to institutions such as hospitals, health care centres and university departments, when they are donated specifically for purposes of research.

Acceptance of hospitality
115.   It may be improper for individual doctors or groups of doctors to accept lavish hospitality or travel facilities under the terms of sponsorship of medical postgraduate meetings or conferences. However, no exception is likely to be taken to acceptance by an individual doctor of a grant which enables him to travel to an international conference or to acceptance, by a group of doctors who attend a sponsored postgraduate meeting or conference, of hospitality at an appropriate level, which the recipients might normally adopt when paying for themselves.

PART IV
FITNESS TO PRACTISE: PROCEDURES ASSOCIATED WITH
THE HEALTH COMMITTEE

116.   Provisions of the Medical Act 1978, now consolidated in the Medical Act 1983, gave the Council jurisdiction in cases where the fitness to practise of a doctor is seriously impaired by reason of his physical or mental condition. Those provisions require the Council to make rules to govern the consideration of such cases and to establish a Health Committee to which a proportion, but not all, of the cases may eventually be referred. The rules, which were first made in 1980 after consultation with professional bodies and are approved by the Privy Council, are the Health Committee (Procedure) Rules. The current rules were made in 1987 and are published as Statutory Instrument 1987 No. 2174.

117.   Before these rules came into force a significant proportion of the cases reaching the Council's previous disciplinary machinery arose from the mental condition of the doctor. For example, a doctor who had become addicted to alcohol might as a result fail to visit his patients or be convicted of driving a motor car with excess alcohol in his blood. A doctor who had become addicted to drugs might commit offences against the Misuse of Drugs Act or other laws in order to gratify his addiction. A doctor suffering from senile dementia might fail to visit and treat his patients. Such cases could in the past be dealt with only by holding a disciplinary hearing if the doctor had been convicted in the courts or behaved in a way amounting to serious professional misconduct. Moreover the Council was unable to deal with other cases where a doctor's fitness to practise was seriously impaired by reason of a physical or mental condition in such a way as to imperil his patients, embarrass his professional colleagues and indeed jeopardise his own health, career and professional position but the doctor had not been convicted of a criminal offence or behaved in a way amounting to serious professional misconduct.

118.   In devising procedures for the consideration of a doctor's fitness to practise, the Council was concerned to make it easier for a sick doctor's professional colleagues to exercise persuasion on the doctor to seek treatment for his condition and so wherever possible to avoid the need to refer a case to the Health Committee. Where the Council receives information suggesting that the fitness to practise of a doctor may be seriously impaired, the information is first considered by the President or other member of the Council appointed for the purpose. This member is known as the Preliminary Screener. If he is satisfied from the evidence that a question does arise whether the doctor's fitness to practise is seriously impaired, the doctor is then informed of this and invited to agree within 14 days to submit to examination by at least two medical examiners. These medical examiners are chosen by the Preliminary Screener from panels of examiners nominated by professional bodies. Examiners are nominated in all parts of the United Kingdom so that examinations may be arranged locally if this is considered appropriate. It is also open to the doctor at this stage both to nominate other medical practitioners to examine him and report to the Preliminary Screener on his fitness to practise and to submit observations or other evidence in regard to this.

119. Where a doctor agrees to submit to examination the medical examiners are asked to report on his fitness to engage in practice either generally or on a limited basis and on the management of his case which they recommend. When the Preliminary Screener has received their reports these are communicated to the doctor. He is then asked to state within 28 days whether he is prepared voluntarily to undertake to accept the recommendations of the medical examiners as to the management of his case, including any limitations on his practice which they recommend. If he does so, the Preliminary Screener will then normally request a medical supervisor, who may already be treating him, to monitor the doctor's progress. Provided that the Preliminary Screener is satisfied that the doctor is implementing his undertaking no further action is taken.

120. It is only when the doctor refuses to be medically examined, or to accept the recommendations of the medical examiners, or if having accepted them he subsequently fails to follow them, or his condition deteriorates significantly, that the Preliminary Screener, after consulting at least two other members of the Council appointed for the purpose, may refer the case to the Health Committee. Cases may occasionally be referred to the Health Committee by the Preliminary Proceedings Committee or Professional Conduct Committee where a doctor has been convicted or is alleged to have commited serious professional misconduct, but it appears to either Committee that the fitness to practise of the doctor may be seriously impaired by reason of a physical or mental condition.

121. The Health Committee is elected annually by the Council and comprises a Chairman, Deputy Chairman, nine other medical members of the Council and one lay member. It meets in private and in most cases the principal evidence before it consists of the reports of the medical examiners. Its proceedings are regulated by rules and are of a judicial nature. The Health Committee is assisted both by a legal assessor and by medical assessors. The medical assessors are chosen by the Preliminary Screener from panels nominated by professional bodies. One medical assessor is chosen having regard to the nature of the physical or mental condition which is alleged to impair the doctor's fitness to practise; the other is chosen from the same branch of medicine as that of the doctor whose case is being considered. The Health Committee may if it thinks fit either adjourn consideration of a case or proceed to determine whether the doctor's fitness to practise is seriously impaired. If it finds that the doctor's fitness to practise is seriously impaired, it may impose conditions on his registration for a period not exceeding three years or suspend his registration for a period not exceeding 12 months. Cases where conditions have been imposed or a doctor's registration has been suspended are reviewed by the Health Committee from time to time.

122. There is a right of appeal to the Judicial Committee of the Privy Council from a decision of the Health Commitee, but only on a question of law.

[NOTE: The following text replaces paragraphs 76 to 85 in the GMC's publication — Professional Conduct and Discipline: Fitness to Practise.]

PROFESSIONAL CONFIDENCE

Principles

1. Patients are entitled to expect that the information about themselves or others which a doctor learns during the course of a medical consultation, investigation or treatment, will remain confidential. Doctors therefore have a duty not to disclose to any third party information about an individual that they have learned in their professional capacity, directly from a patient or indirectly, except in the cases discussed in paragraphs 6–16 below.

2. Where a patient, or a person properly authorised to act on a patient's behalf, consents to disclosure, information to which the consent refers may be disclosed in

accordance with that consent. An explicit request by a patient that information should not be disclosed to particular people, or indeed to any third party, must be respected save in the most exceptional cases, for example where the health, safety or welfare of someone other than the patient would otherwise be at serious risk.

3. Doctors carry prime responsibility for the protection of information given to them by patients or obtained in confidence about patients. They must therefore take steps to ensure, as far as lies in their control, that the records, manual or computerised, which they keep or to which they have access, are protected by effective security systems with adequate procedures to prevent improper disclosure.

4. Most doctors in hospital and general practice are working in health care teams, some of whose members may need access to information, given or obtained in confidence about individuals, in order to perform their duties. It is for doctors who lead such teams to judge when it is appropriate for information to be disclosed for that purpose. They must leave those whom they authorise to receive such information in no doubt that it is given to them in professional confidence. The doctor also has a responsibility to ensure that arrangements exist to inform patients of the circumstances in which information about them is likely to be shared and the opportunity to state any objection to this.

5. A doctor who decides to disclose confidential information about an individual must be prepared to explain and justify that decision, whatever the circumstances of the disclosure.

Disclosures without the consent of the patient

6. Doctors who are faced with the difficult decision whether to disclose information without a patient's consent must weigh carefully the arguments for and against disclosure. If in doubt, they would be wise to discuss the matter with an experienced colleague or to seek advice from a medical defence society or professional association. The following paragraphs discuss circumstances of this kind.

Disclosure in relation to the clinical management of a patient

7. In exceptional circumstances a doctor may consider it undesirable, for medical reasons, to seek a patient's consent to the disclosure of confidential information. In such cases information may be disclosed to a relative or some other person but only when the doctor is satisfied that it is necessary in the patient's best medical interests to do so.

8. Deciding whether or not to disclose information is particularly difficult in cases where a patient cannot be judged capable of giving or withholding consent to disclosure. One such situation may arise where a doctor believes that a patient may be the victim of physical or sexual abuse. In such circumstances the patient's medical interests are paramount and may require the doctor to disclose information to an appropriate person or authority.

9. Difficulties may also arise when a doctor believes that a patient, by reason of immaturity does not have sufficient understanding to appreciate what the treatment or advice being sought may involve. Similar problems may arise where a patient lacks understanding because of illness or mental incapacity. In all such cases the doctor should attempt to persuade the patient to allow an appropriate person to be involved in the consultation. If the patient cannot understand or be persuaded, but the doctor is convinced that the disclosure of information would be essential to the patient's best medical interests, the doctor may disclose to an appropriate person or authority the fact of the consultation and the information learned in it. A doctor who decides to disclose information must be prepared to justify that decision and must inform the patient before any disclosure is made.

Disclosure required by statute

10. Information may be disclosed in order to satisfy a specific statutory requirement, such as notification of an infectious disease or of attendance upon a person known or suspected to be addicted to controlled drugs.

Disclosure in the public interest

11. Rarely, cases may arise in which disclosure in the public interest may be justified, for example a situation in which the failure to disclose appropriate information would expose the patient, or someone else, to a risk of death or serious harm.

Disclosure in connection with judicial proceedings

12. Where litigation is in prospect, unless the patient has consented to disclosure or a court order has been made, information should not be disclosed by a doctor merely in response to demands from other people such as a third party's solicitor or an official of the court. A doctor may disclose such information as may be ordered by a judge or presiding officer of the court, as may a doctor summoned to assist a Coroner, Procurator Fiscal or similar officer either at an inquest or when the need for an inquest is being considered. In such circumstances the doctor should first establish the precise extent of the information which needs to be disclosed, and should not hesitate to make known any objections to the proposed disclosure, particularly when the order would involve the disclosure of confidential information about third parties.

13. Information may also be disclosed at the direction of the Chairman of a Committee of the Council which is investigating a doctor's fitness to practise, when the Committee has determined that the interests of justice and/or the public require such disclosure, and provided that every reasonable effort has first been made to seek the consent of the patient or patients concerned.

Disclosure for the purposes of medical teaching, medical research and medical audit

14. Medical teaching, research and medical audit necessarily involve the disclosure of information about individuals, often in the form of medical records, for purposes other than their own health care. Where such information is used in a form which does not enable individuals to be identified, no question of breach of confidentiality will usually arise. Where the disclosure would enable one or more individuals to be identified, the patients concerned, or those who may properly give permission on their behalf, must wherever possible be made aware of that possibility and be advised that it is open to them, at any stage, to withhold their consent to disclosure.

Disclosure to employers and insurance companies

15. Special problems relating to confidentiality can arise where doctors have responsibilities not only to patients but also to third parties as, for example, where a doctor assesses a patient for an employer or an insurance company. In such circumstances, the doctor should ensure that at the outset patients understand the purpose of any consultation or examination, are aware of the doctor's obligation to the employer or insurance company and consent to be seen by the doctor on those terms. Doctors should undertake assessments for insurance, or of an employee's fitness to work, only where the patient has given written consent.

Disclosure after a patient's death

16. The fact of a patient's death does not of itself release a doctor from the obligation to maintain confidentiality. In cases where consent has not previously been given, the extent to which confidential information may properly be disclosed by a doctor after someone's death cannot be specified in absolute terms and will depend on the circumstances. These include the nature of the information disclosed, the extent to which it has already appeared in published material and the period which has elapsed since the person's death.

General Medical Council
44 Hallam Street
London W1N 6AE   November, 1991

INDEX

BLACKSTONE'S STATUTES

TITLES IN THE SERIES